DEVELOPMENTAL PSYCHOLOGY

Fifth Edition

DEVELOPMENTAL PSYCHOLOGY

Robert V. Kail

Purdue University

Rita Wicks-Nelson

West Virginia Institute of Technology

PRENTICE HALL
Englewood Cliffs, New Jersey 07632

Library of Congress Cataloging-in-Publication Data

KAIL, ROBERT V.
    Developmental psychology / Robert V. Kail, Rita Wicks-Nelson.—
5th ed.
      p. cm.
    Rev. ed. of: Developmental psychology / Robert M. Liebert, Rita
Wicks-Nelson, Robert V. Kail. 4th ed. c1986.
    Includes bibliographical references and index.
    ISBN 0-13-205162-1
    1. Developmental psychology. I. Wicks-Nelson, Rita (date)
II. Liebert, Robert M. (date) Developmental psychology.
III. Title.
BF713.L53   1993
155—dc20   92-31404
                                         CIP

Acquisitions Editor: Susan F. Brennan
Production Editor: Marianne Peters
Editor-in-Chief: Charlyce Jones Owen
Art Director: Florence Dara Silverman/Anne T. Bonanno
Interior Design: Meryl Poweski
Cover Design: Jerry Votta
Prepress Buyer: Kelly Behr
Manufacturing Buyer: Mary Ann Gloriande
Photo Editor: Lori Morris-Nantz
Photo Research: Elsa Peterson
Supplements Editor: Sharon Chambliss
Copy Editor: Stephen C. Hopkins
Editorial Assistant: Jenny Katsaros

 © 1993, 1986, 1981, 1977, 1974 by Prentice-Hall, Inc.
A Simon & Schuster Company
Englewood Cliffs, New Jersey 07632

Printed in the United States of America
10 9 8 7 6 5 4 3 2 1

ISBN 0-13-205162-1

Prentice-Hall International (UK) Limited, *London*
Prentice-Hall of Australia Pty. Limited, *Sydney*
Prentice-Hall Canada Inc., *Toronto*
Prentice-Hall Hispanoamericana, S.A., *Mexico*
Prentice-Hall of India Private Limited, *New Delhi*
Prentice-Hall of Japan, Inc., *Tokyo*
Simon & Schuster Asia Pte. Ltd., *Singapore*
Editora Prentice-Hall do Brasil, Ltda., *Rio de Janeiro*

Brief Contents

Contents

ix   *Contents*

Preface

My aim in preparing the fifth edition of *Developmental Psychology* was to create a book that would help students to appreciate both the splendor of human development and the strides that psychologists have made in understanding development. At the same time, I wanted to provide students with insights that would make their own interactions with children—as teachers, parents, or simply as citizens—more informed and more fulfilling. The result is a book that, like the previous editions, presents a broad but selective introduction to developmental psychology as a branch of science that is at once basic and applied.

To achieve these ends, I have followed a number of guidelines. Collectively, they form the general orientation of the book.

1. *Research, theory, and application are inseparable.* The best way to answer a question or solve a problem that involves real-live children is to have a theory that specifies effective solutions, and the best theories are the ones that have been documented with extensive research. Throughout this book, I illustrate the close links among theory, research, and practice.

2. *The beauty of human development can truly be appreciated only by examining its many different forms.* Some aspects of development reflect the biological heritage that is shared by all humans. However, projected on this common biological backdrop are unique trajectories of development that depend upon the cultural context in which the child develops. This variety in human development is emphasized throughout the book.

3. *There is a fundamental continuity among all developmental processes.* The text is organized topically, so that different aspects of development can be examined in detail. However, these different aspects are completely interwoven in the lives of real, growing children. Throughout

the text, these connections between biological, intellectual, and social components of development are highlighted.

ORGANIZATION OF THE BOOK

The book begins with Part 1, "Cornerstones of Development." Chapter 1 offers a brief overview of the history of developmental psychology as a science and includes an introduction to the theories and research methods that have guided its development. Chapter 2 begins with the genetic bases of development, then considers pregnancy and birth. Chapter 3 focuses on infancy; we will see that biology has given babies powerful mental and social skills that pave the way for later development. Chapter 4 brings us to the individual's physical, neural, and motor development, and includes consideration of the wide array of factors that influence and are influenced by physical growth and change.

Part 2 is entitled "Learning and Cognition." We begin, in Chapter 5, with language, which is presented as a cornerstone for mental and social development. Chapters 6 and 7 extend our discussion to theory and research in cognitive development, beginning with a broad discussion of both Piaget's theory and various neo-Piagetian work and then going on to newer information-processing approaches. Chapter 8 takes us to intelligence, including theories of intelligence, how intelligence is measured, and individuals with exceptional intelligence.

The next four chapters comprise Part 3, "Socialization and Social Skills." Chapter 9 begins with a discussion of processes and factors which influence socialization, emphasizing the family. Chapter 10 moves beyond the family and considers children's interactions with their peers. Chapter 11 examines how children learn to behave in ways that are valued by their cultures. Finally, Chapter 12 examines the acquisition of sex-roles: how boys and girls learn the behaviors that cultures believe are appropriate for males and females.

In Part 4, "Perspectives from Child Development," the knowledge of children that is presented in the first three parts of the book is used to understand two aspects of development. Chapter 13 deals with how development can go awry; it considers the full range of behavioral difficulties that can arise in childhood. Chapter 14 examines the transition from childhood to adulthood, and focuses on some of the unique challenges and problems that adolescents face.

CHANGES TO THE FIFTH EDITION

Readers familiar with previous editions of this book will recognize a number of changes in this edition. The entire book has been brought up to date; more than 600 new references have been added. Some other major changes include the following:

▶ Chapter 1 describes the contextual approach as a major theoretical perspective on development.

▶ Chapter 2 includes material on heredity, as well as the description of prenatal development that previously appeared in Chapter 3.

▶ Chapter 3 includes material on learning, perception, and attachment that previously appeared in Chapter 4; it also includes a new section on temperament.

▶ Chapter 4 features substantially expanded treatment of physical growth, as well as new material on the development of the nervous system and the development of motor skills.

▶ Chapter 5 now describes the constraints that children use to learn words.

▶ Chapter 6 presents Robbie Case's neo-Piagetian theory of development.

▶ Chapter 7 now describes research on attention and problem solving, as well as the mechanisms of growth that are associated with the information-processing perspective.

▶ Chapter 8 now begins with theories of intelligence and includes Robert Sternberg's triarchic theory.

▶ Chapter 9 includes new material on latchkey children, sibling relations, the Black extended family, and the changing family.

▶ Chapter 10 is new to this edition and is devoted to the rapidly expanding body of research that concern's children's social interaction. It begins with peer interaction, then considers friendship and the influence of groups, and ends with popularity and rejection.

▶ Chapter 11 includes material on self-control, moral reasoning, prosocial behavior, and aggression that appeared in Chapters 10 and 11 of the fourth edition.

▶ Chapter 12 describes new efforts, in the laboratory and in naturalistic settings, to move children beyond traditional sex-role stereotypes.

▶ Chapter 13 features a section on children with conduct disorders.

▶ Chapter 14 is limited to adolescence in this edition. Adolescence is viewed as the transition from childhood to adulthood, and the text focuses on some of the unique challenges of this transition, such as identity, work, and sexuality. ◀

PEDAGOGICAL FEATURES

In preparing this edition, my aim was to write a book that was both clear to students and engaging to them as well. I have made a concerted effort to present the intricacies of modern developmental psychology to students in straightforward terms. At the same time, this is a compassionate book, in the sense that its topic—growing children who delight us with their laughter and bewilder us with their problems—is not one that should be subjected solely to cold-blooded analysis.

Each chapter begins with an outline and vignettes that highlight the central topics. Key terms are introduced in **boldface**. They are defined in the margins when they first appear as well as in a glossary at the end of the book. One or more Close-Ups in each chapter allow the student to examine special topics in more depth. Each chapter concludes with a numbered summary of the key concepts that were introduced.

SUPPLEMENTARY MATERIALS

A complete package of supplementary materials is available for students and instructors:

ABC News/PH Video Library for Child Development contains eleven segments from ABC news programs (*20/20, Nightline, Prime Time Live,* and *This Week with David Brinkley*). Segments range in length from about five minutes to forty, and they deal with topics such as education, autism, day care, and the effects of television on children.

Student study guide contains, for each chapter, outlines and objectives, and practice exam questions.

Instructor's manual contains, for each chapter, outlines and objectives, plus suggestions for classroom activities, lectures, topics for papers, films, and transparencies.

Test bank includes approximately 1500 multiple-choice, true-false, and essay questions. The test bank is available in printed form and on computer disk (in IBM and Macintosh formats). In addition, instructors can obtain individually tailored exams by contacting Prentice Hall's testing service.

Transparencies. Two sets are available, each containing approximately 25 color transparencies.

ACKNOWLEDGMENTS

I owe a debt of thanks to many people. At Prentice Hall, Carol Wada and Susan Brennan were instrumental in helping to make this edition become a reality; Marianne Peters orchestrated the many activities that were involved in actually producing the book. At Purdue, Laura Curry and Linda Chapman helped in ways that are too numerous to mention. Finally, the developmental psychologists listed here reviewed the manuscript during its preparation; without their thoughtful comments, this book would be less complete, less accurate, and less interesting: Don Cousins, Rhode Island College; Jean E. Dumas, Purdue University; Lisa Friedenberg, University of North Carolina at Asheville; Venu G. Gupta, Kutztown University; Paul A. Miller, Arizona State University West; Barbara A. Morrongiello, University of Guelph; Margaret L. Signorella, Penn State; Lee A. Thompson, Case Western Reserve University; and Marek Wosinski, Arizona State University.

Robert Kail

DEVELOPMENTAL PSYCHOLOGY

Cornerstones of Development

In the 1980s a sperm bank in southern California captured national attention. This was no ordinary sperm bank. Instead, it stored the sperm of Nobel prize winners and other geniuses—sperm that was to be used to produce "super babies."

An assumption underlying this sperm bank is that "heredity is destiny." That is, the genes in the sperm of geniuses are thought to be sufficient to create another generation of brilliant individuals. If this assumption is true, what is the role of experience in the development of human beings? Does "heredity as destiny" mean that a pregnant woman's behavior, as is seen in this woman who is smoking, does not influence the baby-to-be? And does it mean that parents'

efforts to provide stimulation for an infant, such as can be seen in this infant's active and responsive environment, are all for naught?

The first unit of this book will provide answers to these questions by focusing on the impact of biology on development. We begin, in Chapter 2, by describing how development occurs during pregnancy, paving the way for birth. In Chapter 3, we will see that biology has endowed even very young babies with powerful skills that allow them to interpret their worlds. And, in Chapter 4, we will trace the impact of biology on development later in childhood and in adolescence.

C·H·A·P·T·E·R 1

What Is Developmental Psychology?

At conception we begin as a tiny cell, too small to be seen except with a microscope. Gradually each of us is transformed into a baby, a child, an adolescent, and finally a mature adult. This astonishing development proceeds along several parallel tracks. One is physical and involves the growth of bones, muscles, the nervous system, and bodily organs. At the same time, there is continuing mental growth, shown by an increasing ability to solve problems and deal with ideas. Social growth also occurs continuously as we become better able to deal with others and to adjust to the needs and demands of the world around us. Because physical, mental, and social development proceed side by side, we are able to recognize categories of development (infant, toddler, child, adolescent, adult). From toddlerhood through childhood, adolescence, and adulthood this remarkable pattern of growth and change continues.

Developmental psychology is the branch of psychology concerned with when and how we change over time. Developmental psychologists study people of all ages in an attempt to understand when and how physical, mental, and social functions change and interact throughout the entire life span. Simply put, it is a very broad field.

The aim of this first chapter is to give you a feel for the scope of developmental psychology. We begin, as we will in every chapter of this book, by describing the major themes of the chapter.

► Views of childhood and adolescence have changed throughout history. You may be surprised to learn that only recently have scholars recognized that we all develop continually. The idea of childhood as a separate and distinct period did not really emerge until the last century; recognition of adolescence and the preschool years as distinct phases of development is even more recent. We will look at these different views of childhood and explain why these views have changed.

► As scientists began to study these distinct phases of development, a common set of basic questions emerged. For example, psychologists studying the development of intelligence, personality, and abnormal behavior all confronted the issue of "nature" versus "nurture": Does a specific aspect of development depend primarily upon a person's heredity or a person's experiences? These and other central questions that guide research on development are explored later in this chapter.

► Efforts to answer major questions about development have led to the formation of theories of development. Theories function to organize established facts and to guide research into areas that might not otherwise attract interest. Like a prospector's map showing the way to a secret treasure, theories may lead us to expect substantial yields in areas that, on the surface, seem to have little promise. Several important theories of development will be examined in this chapter.

► Theories lead to predictions, and research is designed to test these predictions. Developmental psychologists have an extensive catalog of research tools that can be used to evaluate theoretical predictions and, thereby, help us to learn more about development. We shall describe these research tools and illustrate how they are used to construct research that will yield insights into the many facets of development. ◄

Developmental psychology The branch of psychology that studies how people change throughout the life span.

CHANGING PORTRAITS OF CHILDHOOD

In medieval times children were viewed as "ill formed adults at the edges of society" (Kessen, 1965), a notion reflected in the art of the time (see Figure 1-1). The seventeenth and eighteenth centuries saw flourish the idea of childhood as a special period in which youngsters had unique psychological, educational, and physical needs. But how to understand these needs and cope with them remained a controversial subject.

This debate is most clearly seen in the differing views of philosophers John Locke (1632–1704) and Jean Jacques Rousseau (1712–1778). Locke asserted that at birth the human infant is a tabula rasa, or "blank slate," and that experience, transmitted through the senses, molds each human into a unique individual. Locke burdened parents with the responsibility of teaching their children self-control and rationality, and of planning the environment and experiences of their offspring from the moment of birth. Rousseau, in contrast, saw the newborn human as a "noble savage," endowed with an innate sense of justice and morality. He believed all virtues are inborn and develop naturally. For Rousseau, human nobility was imperiled by an interfering society.

By the middle of the nineteenth century, progress in science and engineering had produced many changes in North America and Europe. Travel was more reliable and more comfortable with the advent of the railroad and the steamboat. Communication was more rapid with the invention of the telephone and telegraph. These advances led to a greater faith in science as the means of improving society. At the same time, issues concerning children became important (Sears, 1975). Children, it was believed, required a thorough education if society was to have an informed citizenry. Reformers rallied for improved care for abandoned children. Interest in science and in children merged to bring about a new approach to understanding childhood: Speculation about the child's

FIGURE 1-1
Portraits of childhood: (a) Sir Walter Raleigh and son, painted in the seventeenth century, shows that little distinction was made between childhood and adulthood, for the child is depicted simply as a miniature adult. (b) We see the mood of childhood as it has recently emerged in Mary Cassatt's *Mother and Child.*

"nature" was replaced by efforts to record and to study actual behavior and development. This was the dawn of contemporary developmental psychology.

The impetus for this new science came from many sources. Evolutionary biology and its founder, Charles Darwin (1809–1882), generated the nineteenth century's interest in all types of development. Darwin theorized that individuals are most likely to survive—and be able to produce their own offspring—if they are well adapted to the environments in which they live. Darwin initially emphasized the survival value of physical characteristics, but later he included behavioral characteristics, which drew attention to the importance of psychological development. It is not well known that Darwin traced his son's emotional development in a detailed diary, in what was among the first of the *baby biographies*. The observations included in the biographies were often subjective, and conclusions were sometimes reached on minimal evidence. Nevertheless, the systematic and extensive records in the biographies paved the way for objective, analytic research.

Prominent in the research that followed the baby biographies was G. Stanley Hall (1844–1924). He administered questionnaires to large groups of children of different ages to ascertain age trends in children's beliefs, knowledge, and feelings as they grew older. Hall also turned to children to study such topics as perception, memory, and learning. Hall is best remembered, however, for his many accomplishments in the organization of developmental psychology. He founded the first scientific journal in English devoted to developmental psychology; he founded a child study institute at Clark University; he wrote the first textbooks on adolescence and aging; and he was the first president of the American Psychological Association (White, 1992).

Meanwhile, in France Alfred Binet (1857–1911) had begun to distinguish between intellectually normal and subnormal children. At the same time, he began to study memory and perception in children and to develop the first mental tests (which we will discuss further in Chapter 8). In Vienna Sigmund Freud (1856–1939) had startled the world with his suggestion that the experiences of early childhood seemed to account for patterns of behavior in adulthood.

By the 1920s developmental psychology had become the source of solutions to practical problems. John B. Watson, the founder of behaviorism, had begun to write and lecture on child-rearing practices. Clinics were established for the purpose of assessing children and advising parents. This interest led to an enormous investment in child development research. Short-term studies were set up in numerous university-based nursery schools, and long-range (or longitudinal) projects were established at such places as Berkeley and Yale in the United States, as well as in several European cities.

Infancy, childhood, and adolescence were now seen as the psychological as well as the physical precursors to adulthood. Developmental psychologists investigated the complex processes by which individuals progress through these phases of development. Early in these efforts scientists realized that understanding virtually any aspect of development involves answering the same set of fundamental questions, which we discuss in the next section of this chapter.

RECURRING QUESTIONS IN DEVELOPMENTAL PSYCHOLOGY

In their search for underlying causes and explanations, modern developmental psychologists face three issues that seem to arise regardless of the aspect of development being studied: heredity versus environment, continuity versus discontinuity, and universal versus culturally specific paths of development.

Heredity versus Environment

We all know that people differ in striking and important ways. Some individuals are very outgoing, others are more reserved, and a few are quite timid. Likewise, some people are highly creative, whereas others are less imaginative and may prefer more conventional ways of thinking and acting. These examples of individual differences raise the question of whether each of us is born with our particular characteristics or whether we are a product of the environment in which we were brought up. The problem has been termed the *heredity-environment issue,* or the *nature-nurture controversy.* This has been an ongoing debate for developmental psychologists. How much of the individual's behavior is formed by his or her biological and genetic makeup? How much by social and environmental influences?

These questions overlook the fact that heredity and environment must interact in order to produce behavior (Anastasi, 1958). Because both make an absolutely necessary contribution to behavior, the idea that these factors merely differ in quantity or importance is not likely to get us very far. Instead, we must ultimately ask how biological and environmental influences combine to result in various kinds of behavior. Much of this book is devoted to explaining how these two forces interact.

Continuity versus Discontinuity

Two types of behavioral change are often identified in the study of human development: those that are gradual or continuous and those that are sudden or discontinuous.

To understand this distinction, consider the following example suggested by the work of Jean Piaget (whose theory of cognitive development is discussed in Chapter 6). An experimenter begins by showing a 4-year-old child two short, wide glass beakers, each containing the same quantity of milk. The youngster is asked whether both beakers have an equal amount of fluid, and he or she agrees that they do. Then, while the child watches, the experimenter pours the entire contents of one of these beakers into a third beaker—a tall, thin one. When the child is asked to compare the two beakers that now contain milk, he or she will often say that the tall,

FIGURE 1-2
In the conservation of liquid experiment devised by Jean Piaget, children are asked whether two equal amounts of water remain equal when poured into dissimilar containers. Preschoolers often believe that there is more water in the tall, slender beaker. The transition from this sort of thinking to understanding that the amount remains the same regardless of beaker shape might reflect a gradual quantitative change, or it could be an abrupt qualitative change.

thin beaker has more milk in it than the original short, wide one. But older children, like adults, will immediately point out that the two beakers must have the same amount of milk, since the volume of the two original beakers was equal at the beginning, and no liquid was lost or gained by pouring the contents of one of them into a container of a different shape.

How and why does this transition in thinking, in the handling of this problem, occur? Is there a qualitative change in thinking or discontinuity from one mode of thinking to another as the child grows older? Or would the change, if we were able to watch it more closely, appear to be a gradual, continuous process of growing sophistication? The former viewpoint leads to the suggestion that development proceeds in a series of relatively discrete *stages* that should be identified and described. As we shall see, this is the conclusion that, with some qualifications, Piaget reached in examining the child's intellectual development. Some stage theorists have also argued that many aspects of human emotional and social development proceed in the same discontinuous fashion.

Other theorists have emphasized the possibility that development may only seem discontinuous. They claim that observers who compare children of different ages may be unable to detect gradual changes as they occur and thus may take large or dramatic shifts as evidence of discontinuity. Even if the same children are observed over time, the frequency and nature of the observations can play an important role in determining whether developmental changes seem gradual or relatively abrupt.

Throughout this book we will encounter many instances of both types of developmental change.

Universal versus Culturally Specific Paths of Development

In the cities of Brazil it is common to see 10- to 12-year-old children who are street vendors, selling candy and fruit to bus passengers or pedestrians. These children lack formal education and often cannot even identify the numbers on paper money. Nevertheless, they know how to purchase their goods from wholesale stores, to make change for customers, and to keep track of their sales (Saxe, 1988). These youngsters have developed their own systems for representing numbers and for calculating. Their systems are apparently quite different from those taught to children in most Western schools, but they are perfectly adequate for the sellers' computing needs.

Although we have had only a brief glimpse of the life of child vendors in Brazil, we can see that their course of development seems quite unlike that of children growing up in the United States and Canada. However, even within North American countries a "typical" or "usual" path of development is a myth. These countries include many different ethnic groups, each with its own set of values concerning children and their upbringing. This cultural variety has increased in the 1980s and 1990s with the arrival of new groups of immigrants, such as Hispanics and Vietnamese. The challenge to developmental psychology, then, is to explain how growth can proceed along so many different routes and with so many different destinations.

One approach has been to argue that despite these apparent differences, the processes responsible for development are the same for all children. Piaget, for example, claimed that all individuals—regardless of experience, upbringing, or culture—proceed through four basic modes of thought. The outward manifestation of these modes depends upon the culture in which the child develops, but the basic modes of thought are universal. Theorists in this camp stress that different outcomes are simply variations on a basic developmental theme, just as different varieties of roses come from the same basic processes of growth.

Challenging this view are theorists who emphasize the enormous

FIGURE 1-3

Lives of child peddlers in Brazil seem very different from those of most children living in North America. Can one theory account for development of all children, or must theories be specific to particular cultures?

Culture The full set of specific knowledge, attitudes, behaviors, and products that characterize an identifiable group of people.

Theories A framework used to organize and condense known facts and to derive testable hypotheses.

role of culture in human development. This group insists that a child's development cannot be divorced from the cultural context in which it occurs. A child's **culture**—defined broadly as the knowledge, attitudes, behaviors, and products associated with a group of people—is not simply part of the canvas on which development is painted; rather, culture is the palette of colors used to paint development. Given the assortment of distinct cultures worldwide, each culture may require a unique explanation; thus, for example, unique principles may be needed to explain the development of child vendors in Brazil, African-American children in the United States, and Ukrainian children in the western provinces of Canada.

As we shall see, modern theories differ in their emphases on development as a universal versus a culturally specific process. In addition to theories that emphasize either of these extremes, we will encounter theories that strike a balance between the two.

THE ROLE OF THEORY

Even in our brief discussion thus far it has been impossible to avoid the word "theory." What functions do theories serve in developmental psychology? Let's see.

Theories provide a basis for organizing and condensing known facts. They should also enable us to predict future events. To do this, a theory must be testable and thus potentially capable of being proved wrong. It must lead to the derivation of specific hypotheses or predictions that can be confirmed or disconfirmed.

Modern developmental research has for the most part been guided by five broad formal theories, each of which merits a brief introduction here.

FIGURE 1-4
Arnold Gesell emphasized the role of maturational forces in development.

Maturational theory The view that most psychological changes reflect an inevitable unfolding over time.

Maturation The changes that take place more or less inevitably over time in all normal members of a species, as long as they are provided with an environment suitable to the species.

Psychoanalytic theory A theory proposed by Freud in which development is explained in terms of the interplay between components of personality.

Maturational Theory

Maturational theory has been one of the major theories in developmental psychology (Caldwell and Richmond, 1962). The idea behind this theory is that most of the changes that take place in children over time occur because of a specific and prearranged scheme within the body. **Maturation**, according to this view, reveals the natural unfolding of the plan, and patterns of growth charted over time are like the smoky trail of a skywriting plane, which shows us only that part of the mission that is already completed.

The view that all development, from infant nursing patterns to the emergence of moral values, is largely self-regulated by the unfolding of natural processes and biological plans was popularized by Arnold Gesell (1940, 1956). Gesell primarily studied children's physical and motor development. Most developmentalists agree that physical growth is heavily influenced by maturation. However, as we shall see in later chapters, much controversy has been generated by the claim that mental development and personality development proceed according to a biological plan.

Psychoanalytic Theory

Freud's **psychoanalytic theory** ranks among the most far-reaching and influential views in modern history. Freud, too, was convinced that people mature psychologically according to principles that apply universally. But he was also convinced that each individual personality is shaped by experience in a social context. Freud insisted that early experiences establish patterns that endure through the entire life span.

Freud's theory of development focuses on internal, or intrapsychic,

FIGURE 1-5
Sigmund Freud's theory emphasized the impact of early experiences on children's development.

events. Freud believed that personality consists of three components or structures: the **id**, the **ego**, and the **superego**. Present at birth, the id is characterized as a reservoir of primitive instincts and drives; it is the force that presses for immediate gratification of bodily needs and wants. The ego is the practical, rational component of personality. It begins to emerge during the first year of life in response to the fact that the infant cannot always have what it wants. An example of the emerging ego is seen in the child's learning of other strategies for coaxing adults into action when crying does not produce immediate results. Between the third and fourth years of life the superego, or "moral agent" of personality, develops as the child identifies with its same-sexed parent and begins to incorporate adult standards of right and wrong.

Freud also proposed that development occurs in universal stages that do not vary in sequence. These stages are largely determined by an innate tendency to reduce tension and to achieve a pleasurable experience. Each stage is given its unique character by the development of sensitivity in a particular part of the body called an erogenous zone—that is, an area particularly sensitive to erotic stimulation—at a particular time in the developmental sequence. Freud described these stages as "psychosexual" to indicate that development is the outcome of the successive focusing on and reducing of tensions in various erogenous zones that predominate at different times in life. Each stage is associated with a particular conflict that must be resolved before the individual can move psychologically to the next stage.

Freud's most important insight is that humans are not always conscious of their own motives. He attributed great strength, durability, and enormous motivational properties to unconscious impulses, and he warned that the rational and the rationalizing person are not easy to tell apart. The influence of Freud's views will be evident in several chapters of this book.

Social Learning Theory

John B. Watson was among the first psychologists to champion Locke's view that the infant's mind is a blank slate on which experience writes. Watson held that the child learns to be what he or she becomes, usually in a social context. He assumed that with the correct techniques anything could be learned by almost anyone. B. F. Skinner explained learning on the basis of external reward and punishment, as another learning-oriented psychologist, E. L. Thorndike, had begun to do years before.

Modern **social learning theory** was developed by Albert Bandura (1977, 1986). He accepted the idea that conditioning, reward, and punishment all contribute to social development, but he questioned whether all (or even most) of what actually goes on during childhood learning can be explained in these terms. Children learn by observation, he argued, and this type of learning can take place without any direct reward or punishment at all. This approach speaks directly to the issue of processes of social development. It has inspired a large body of research, as we will see.

Id An aspect of personality described by Freud that is a reservoir of primitive instincts and drives that press for the immediate gratification of bodily needs and wants.

Ego The practical, rational component of personality in Freud's theory.

Superego The moral component of personality, according to Freud.

Social learning theory A view of development that emphasizes the role of observation as well as conditioning, reward, and punishment.

FIGURE 1-6
Albert Bandura recognized that socialization involves learning from positive and negative consequences, but his social learning theory emphasizes the role of observation of others (social models).

Cognitive-Developmental Theory

Still another way to approach psychological development is to focus on thought processes and knowledge. As we have mentioned already, Jean Piaget took just such an approach in his **cognitive-developmental theory**. Piaget postulated four basic periods in cognitive development, each characterized by unique and more sophisticated type of reasoning.

Piaget was primarily interested in the interaction of biological maturation and environmental experience; he emphasized that these two forces work together to cause most developmental change. For example, a preschool boy who believes that the amount of milk in a short, wide beaker increases merely by pouring it into a tall, thin one will overcome his misconception only when he is sufficiently mature to appreciate the underlying principle of conservation and when he has had an opportunity to explore the effects of pouring for himself.

Another important aspect of Piaget's theory is that it is holistic. That is, in Piaget's theory cognitive and social development are assumed to be closely linked. For example, children cannot take another's point of view into account in social situations until they understand the basic principle that objects in the physical environment look different from different perspectives.

Because Piaget's theory attempts to tie together maturation and experience on the one hand and cognitive and social development on the other, it has inspired developmentalists with a wide variety of interests.

Cognitive-developmental theory A theory, proposed by Jean Piaget, in which development consists of four stages, each with a unique type of thinking.

FIGURE 1-7
Jean Piaget focused on
the development of
thought processes and
knowledge in his
approach to cognitive-
developmental theory.

Ecological Theory

Most developmental psychologists agree that the environment is an important force in many aspects of development. However, only ecological theorists have focused on the complexities of environments and their links to development. For **ecological theory**, which gets its name from the branch of biology dealing with the relation of living things to their environment and to one another, human development is inseparable from the environmental contexts in which a child develops.

The best-known proponent of this approach is Urie Bronfenbrenner (1979, 1989), who proposes that developmentalists must consider the immediate as well as broader contexts of development. Like many other theorists, Bronfenbrenner notes that development is strongly influenced by people and objects in the child's immediate environment. Parents, peers, siblings, and teachers, for example, are among the obvious individuals that influence a child's development. But unique to the ecological approach is recognition that the environment's impact on development extends beyond these factors in the immediate environment. To illustrate, let's examine how children acquire a positive attitude toward education. Most theorists, including Bronfenbrenner, would emphasize the importance of role models, such as parents and teachers, in teaching children to value education. However, the ecological approach would emphasize that role models cannot be considered in isolation; instead, the interplay of role models must be considered. For example, conflicts may arise when parents who prize academic excellence find their child placed with a teacher who devotes most of his attention to youngsters who are struggling academically. Other difficulties may ensue when the parents' values con-

Ecological theory An
approach that focuses on
the need to study
development in the
contexts or settings in
which it naturally occurs.

FIGURE 1-8
In Urie Bronfenbrenner's ecological theory, the focus is on the cultural context in which children develop.

flict with those of the child's friends, who may rather watch music videos than read or study.

The analysis of environmental context extends further. According to ecological theorists, we also need to consider the environments in which the role models behave. The teacher who spends relatively little time with talented youngsters may be doing so because the principal of the school has made it clear that attention to underachieving students is an important factor in teacher evaluations; therefore time spent by the teacher with students who excel will not be rewarded. The principal, in turn, may be responding to pressure from a school board, which may be establishing priorities based on its perception of the values in the community.

Thus, just as the movement of a billiard ball depends upon the direction and velocity of both adjacent and distant balls, development can be influenced by contexts that are immediate and by those that are more removed. Emphasis on these multiple, interactive contexts of development is a unique contribution of the ecological approach that will be illustrated in many chapters in this book.

At one time developmental psychologists believed that a single theory would prevail over the others, but it has become plain that agreement at this level is impossible. The five theories discussed here are so all-encompassing that today we think of them more as viewpoints than as scientific formulations. Psychologists do not usually follow one or another theory; instead, they often select aspects of various theories to form new combinations as they investigate specific topics. The theories, too, continuously interact, combine, and change.

RESEARCH IN DEVELOPMENTAL PSYCHOLOGY

All research in developmental psychology shares a commitment to the **scientific method**. This method distinguishes the studies we have drawn upon in this book from casual observation and other informal methods of studying people. At the general level the scientific method specifies appropriate ways of studying people, provides a language for thinking about and reporting evidence, and gives guidelines for evaluating the evidence that has been accumulated.

The central requirement of the scientific method is objectivity. This means that the evidence put forth in support of a hypothesis must be derived from procedures that can be repeated and from results that can be verified by others. Even when we are interested in theoretical ideas that have no specific concrete form, we must define them in terms of procedures and responses that can be observed. Intelligence, for example, is a theoretical construct often operationalized as scores on IQ tests. Similarly, mother-child attachment is often operationally defined by the child's clinging to the mother.

Often theories such as those just described provide the starting point for research. That is, a theory generates predictions that a developmental psychologist may want to test. For some phenomena, full-fledged theories of development do not exist. In these cases an investigator may examine the development of related phenomena or how the phenomena develop in other species. This information will be used to formulate **hypotheses**, propositions or predictions that are to be tested in research. Finally, sometimes research is conducted because we need answers to important questions about children and their upbringing. Is watching too much television harmful for children? Does day care detract from infants' feelings of affection for their parents? Does contact with children from other cultural and ethnic backgrounds cause children to be more accepting of others? Through research, answers to questions like these can be used to help formulate sound public policy and to provide guidelines for teachers and parents alike.

Observation and Description

Regardless of the reason for conducting the research, the steps involved are usually similar. All research begins by deciding how to measure the phenomenon of interest. For example, suppose a researcher wished to describe how adolescents make friends. It would first be necessary to decide how to measure "making friends" and to determine the number of adolescents who are to participate in the study. These decisions would be made partly on practical grounds and partly on the basis of the specific goals of the study, but there are some general principles to be followed.

REPRESENTATIVE SAMPLING. The question of whom to observe revolves around the problem of sampling. Rarely does an investigator's interest end with the particular individuals observed in a study. Rather, the actual subjects are chosen to represent some larger group. In studying

Scientific method An approach to understanding nature that emphasizes careful observation, the construction of hypotheses, and the evaluation of these according to the evidence.

Hypothesis A prediction derived from a theory.

adolescents' friendships, for example, 20 individuals might be studied. But the purpose of the investigation would not be merely to learn about these particular people but about friendships among adolescents in general. The 20 teenagers would be a **representative sample**, from which the investigator draws inferences about the friendships of some larger population (for example, adolescents in general). Researchers in such situations must satisfy their critics that the sample is really representative of the population of interest.

Studying representative samples of populations of interest is one technique; **case studies** are another. Case studies are studies of the behavior of individuals. For example, systematic biographies of individual children from birth or early childhood were the earliest source of data for developmental psychology and are still useful today for some purposes. Case studies are very flexible because simple observation can be done in various ways and in nearly any situation. This flexibility has a price, however. Because one or two children hardly make up a representative sample, we cannot be sure that what is true for them is also true for a larger group of children. Most contemporary developmental psychologists view case studies as, at best, a preliminary or adjunct research method that cannot replace or rival broader and more systematic studies with representative samples.

MEASUREMENT PROCEDURES. Our hypothetical investigator would also face the related questions of how and when to measure the adolescents' friendships. This would involve finding or creating a method for recording friendship formation in adolescents. One common approach would be to interview adolescents using a set of questions devised beforehand. The questions would probe aspects of friendship formation central to the investigator's hypothesis. For example, if one hypothesis was that teenagers are likely to become friends if they have interests in common, then research subjects might be told the following:

> Tom and Dave just met each other at school. Tom likes to read, plays clarinet in the school orchestra, and rarely watches school football games; Dave also likes to read, is a member of student council, and plays on the school football team. Do you think Tom and Dave will become good friends?

Subjects in the study would answer this question, perhaps by using a rating scale, indicating whether they believe it is very likely or very unlikely that the boys will become friends.

This approach is useful because it leads directly to information that bears on the hypothesis and is relatively convenient to collect (particularly if the questions can be prepared in written form and administered to groups of subjects). The chief drawback associated with interviews and questionnaires is accuracy. For a number of reasons, people often respond inaccurately. In the example of friendship, responses may reflect what adolescents *believe* to be important in the formation of friendships rather than factors that actually *are* important. Teenagers may be wrong simply because they are not careful observers of their own and others' behaviors.

Response bias is another problem: For many questions, some re-

Representative sample A group of individuals that accurately and proportionately displays the characteristics of some larger population of interest to a researcher.

Case study The systematic description of the behavior of a single individual.

FIGURE 1-9

Interviews allow an investigator to question subjects directly about a range of topics. However, the answers obtained may not always be accurate.

sponses are more socially acceptable than others, and most people are more likely to select socially acceptable answers than socially unacceptable ones. For many adolescents, for example, it would be socially unacceptable to admit that one is completely inexperienced sexually. This problem is compounded when people are asked questions about their past behavior: Memory of past events or situations (for example, how many friends a child had as a preschooler) tends to be positively distorted, so that the people, events, or situations one recalls are remembered in a favorable light.

These weaknesses do not undermine interviews and questionnaires entirely, but they do underscore the need for additional, confirming evidence, usually by *direct observation* of the phenomenon of interest. Let's return to the question of friendship formation in adolescents. Our hypothetical investigator might find a setting in which many youngsters are likely to form new friendships. A summer camp would be a possibility. Another would be a junior high school that draws students from several elementary schools. Both represent situations in which friendships are likely to develop between children who are initially strangers.

Having identified a setting in which friendships can be studied, the next step would be to create a method for observing friendship formations. This method would have to be one that could be applied consistently from one teenager to another and from one observer to another. In turn, this would mean that the relevant class of behaviors would have to be defined, a means of recording them would have to be selected, and appropriate times for making the records would have to be chosen and justified. In the camp setting an investigator might decide to observe a youngster's behavior at meals because mealtime involves all campers. The investigator might decide to record where children sit and with whom they talk during mealtime.

These procedures would then be taught to observers, and the investigator would have to demonstrate that the procedures are clear and precise enough to be *reliable*. To demonstrate reliability, two observers independently watching children should agree quite closely in their observations.

Determining Cause and Effect

In the examples mentioned so far, we have emphasized producing adequate descriptions of behavior and behavioral change. Many investigations in developmental psychology are designed to go beyond description to explain what has been observed. Suppose that in our earlier example of adolescent friendships some teenagers formed many friendships quickly, whereas other teens seemed to be more hesitant about making new friends. Such a result might raise the question of why adolescents differ in the ease with which they make new friends.

"Why" questions arise frequently in developmental research, and answering them is at the heart of what we usually mean by explanation. There are two broad ways of trying to answer questions about cause and effect. One is to propose hypotheses about what factors influence the behavior of interest and then to manipulate these factors and observe the effects. The other way is to examine factors associated with the behavior of interest and then to construct a useful causal model without manipulation. The first are usually referred to as experimental methods; the second are called nonexperimental, or correlational, methods.

EXPERIMENTAL METHODS. The classic "true experiment" in science is designed to lead to unambiguous inferences about cause and effect. In developmental psychology the true experiment requires the investigator to begin with one or more treatments, circumstances, or events (**independent variables**) hypothesized to produce some effect on behavior. Subjects are then assigned randomly to conditions that differ in the treatment they are given; then an appropriate measure (the **dependent variable**) is taken for all subjects. This then determines if different treatments had the expected effect. Because subjects are assigned so that each has an equal chance of being assigned to each treatment condition (the definition of **random assignment**), it can be assumed that in the long run the groups will not differ except in the treatment they have received. Any observed differences can be attributed to the differential treatment the subjects received in the experiment, rather than to other factors. There are, in fact, many different versions of the true experiment, but they all derive from the underlying logic just described.

Suppose, for example, that an investigator believed adolescents can learn more from a short story in a quiet room than in a room in which loud music is playing. A test of this hypothesis might be done in a high school. The investigator would first seek the cooperation of the appropriate school authorities and families. The research participants would be told about the general nature of the experiment and the role they would be expected to play (reading a short story and then taking a test on the material read), but they would not be told the specific hypothesis until

Independent variable A condition in an experimental situation created by the experimenter or a manipulation of the subject by the experimenter.

Dependent variable A measurable aspect of the subject's behavior that may change as the independent variable is altered.

Random assignment When subjects have an equal chance of being assigned to any of the conditions in an experiment.

they were "debriefed" at the end of the experiment. A suitable short story would be identified or written especially for the experiment, and subjects would be brought to the same location (perhaps an available room in the school) where they would read the story and then take the same test on its contents. Based on random assignment, individual subjects would read the story either while the room was quiet or while loud music was being played. The loud music would be the same music, played at the same volume, for all subjects in the loud-music condition. All subjects would read the identical story under circumstances held as constant as possible except for the presence or absence of the music. All would get the same amount of time to read the story, and all would be given the same test afterward. If scores on the test were, on the average, better in the quiet condition than in the loud-music condition (as determined by an appropriate statistical test), the investigator could say with confidence that the music had an unfavorable effect on reading and learning the story (the dependent variable). Causal inference is possible in this example because there would be a direct manipulation of the independent variable (presence or absence of music) under controlled conditions.

Developmental psychologists usually conduct experiments in laboratory-like settings because such settings allow full control over the variables that may influence the outcome of the research. A shortcoming of laboratory work is that the behavior of interest is not studied in its natural setting. Consequently, there is always the potential problem that the results may be artificial—that is, they may be specific to the laboratory setting and not representative of the behavior in the "real world."

One solution to this problem is the **field experiment**, which encompasses all the procedures that characterize a true experiment, but in a setting where the behaviors might occur naturally. In one well-known study of the effect of television on behavior (Friedrich and Stein, 1973), children attending a morning nursery school program were randomly assigned to classes in which they viewed (a) programs that frequently depicted aggression, such as *Batman* and *Superman* cartoons, (b) *Mister Rogers' Neighborhood*, which emphasizes prosocial behavior, such as the importance of cooperation and sharing, or (c) films that highlighted neither aggression nor prosocial behavior. The TV watching occupied about 30 minutes; the rest of the morning was devoted to traditional nursery school activities. Throughout the morning the children were watched by trained observers.

The results showed that children who watched aggressive programs were less likely to obey rules, whereas those who watched the prosocial programs were more likely to obey rules. This is a particularly convincing result because randomization of subjects to conditions meant that the differences in the dependent variable (degree of obedience to rules) could be linked directly to the independent variable (type of program). The pitfalls of extrapolating results from laboratory to a natural setting were avoided because the study was conducted in the natural setting.

NONEXPERIMENTAL (CORRELATIONAL) METHODS. Many investigators have attempted to draw causal inferences using what is called **passive correlation** rather than manipulation. Instead of creating different expe-

Field experiment An experiment that includes independent and dependent variables and that is conducted in the setting where the behavior occurs naturally.

Passive correlation A study in which investigators examine associations that exist naturally between variables.

FIGURE 1-10
Field experiments allow investigators to determine cause-and-effect relations about behavior as it occurs in its natural setting.

riences for subjects (as in the experimental method), researchers study differences in experience that have occurred naturally. For example, to determine the relation between viewing violent TV shows and demonstrating aggressive behavior, investigators have obtained reports of youngsters' TV-viewing preferences and related these to various measures of aggressive behavior, such as school records or teachers' reports.

In this approach, researchers typically compute a **correlation coefficient** to describe the relation between variables. Correlation coefficients indicate both the direction and the magnitude of the relation and may range from +1.00 to −1.00.

The direction of the relation is shown by the sign of the coefficient. A positive sign means that high scores on one variable, X, tend to be associated with high scores on another variable, Y, and low scores on X tend to go with low scores on Y. For example, a positive correlation is found between children's age and height; older children are likely to be taller. A negative sign means that high scores on X tend to be associated with low scores on Y, and low scores on X with high scores on Y. Age and quickness of reflexes are usually found to be negatively correlated in adults; as people grow older, their reflexes become slower.

The magnitude or strength of a correlation is indicated by the absolute value of the coefficient (disregarding the sign). Correlation coefficients of +0.60 and −0.60 are equivalent with respect to how strongly the variables under consideration are related. The strongest relation is indicated when the correlation is either +1.00 or −1.00; in both cases the two variables are perfectly correlated so that either can be determined from the other with perfect accuracy. As the coefficient decreases in absolute value, the magnitude of the relation becomes weaker, and the ability to estimate one variable from the other decreases. A coefficient of 0.00

Correlation coefficient A measure of the direction and magnitude of the relation between two variables.

21

indicates that the variables are unrelated: Knowledge of one does not tell us anything at all about the other.

A pattern of simple correlations allows the researcher to demonstrate the direction and magnitude of relations between variables. Unlike the true experiment, however, this often leaves the question of cause and effect unanswered. For example, TV viewing of violence and aggressive behavior are correlated positively: The more TV violence a youngster watches, the more aggressive he or she is likely to be. But this does not necessarily imply that viewing violence on TV causes aggressive behavior. There are two other plausible ways of interpreting the relation. One possibility, reflecting the directionality problem in nonexperimental research, is that a preoccupation with aggression may cause a youngster to watch more than the average amount of TV violence. That is, instead of TV-violence viewing causing aggressiveness, aggressiveness may cause TV-violence viewing. Another possibility is that the relation may be caused by some third variable. For example, youngsters who receive little supervision from their parents may be the ones most likely to watch violent shows and the ones most likely to be aggressive.

Both the third-variable and directionality problems can be avoided to some extent by using more complex nonexperimental designs, such as looking at patterns of correlation over time and showing that they fit one causal model far better than another. However, even these methods do not provide the certainty of a true experiment. Nevertheless, nonexperimental data often suggest certain causal relations, and many developmental psychologists draw on them, especially in situations where true experimentation is impossible because of practical or ethical problems.

FIGURE 1-11
In nonexperimental methods, the emphasis is on naturally occurring behavior. An example would be the amount of televised violence that children watch, as recorded by their parents.

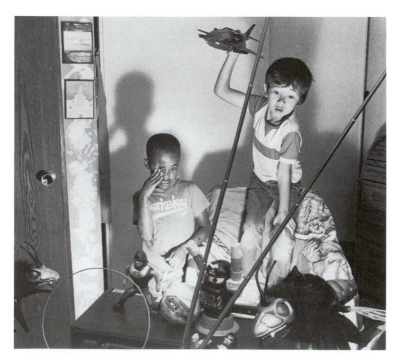

Longitudinal study The process of observing or testing an individual or individuals at different points in their lives, noting stability and change in their behavior and characteristics over time.

Cross-sectional study A study of groups of different individuals of various ages at a specific point in time in order to determine developmental changes.

THE IMPORTANCE OF CONVERGING EVIDENCE. Even from our relatively brief discussion it can be seen that each of the research methods used by developmentalists has both strengths and weaknesses. There is no one best method, and the selection of a specific method usually depends as much on practical considerations as on suitability. For these reasons, no single investigation can definitely settle a question. Developmental psychologists rarely rely on one study, or even one method, to reach conclusions. As illustrated in the Close-Up, they prefer to find converging evidence from as many sources as possible.

Demonstrating Developmental Trends

Many investigations in developmental psychology are aimed at identifying changes that occur with increasing age. There are two ways of approaching such questions: the longitudinal method and the cross-sectional method.

In a **longitudinal study** the same individuals are observed or tested repeatedly at different points in their lives, and stability or change in characteristics or behavior is noted over time. In a **cross-sectional study**, each individual is observed only once, but developmental changes are identified by including persons of different ages in the study. Development is charted not by observing the change in the same individuals over time but by noting the differences between individuals of different ages at the same point in calendar time.

FIGURE 1-12
In a longitudinal study, depicted in the left panel, the same subjects are tested repeatedly. In the example, subjects are tested at 4 years of age in 1980, at 8 years of age in 1984, and so on. In a cross-sectional study, depicted in the center panel, children of different ages are tested at the same time. In the example, 4-, 8-, 12-, 16-, and 20-year-olds are all tested in 1980. A cross-sequential study, depicted in the right panel, combines elements of both types of studies. As in a cross-sectional study, different age groups participate; as in a longitudinal study, subjects are tested on multiple occasions. In the example, 4-, 8-, 12-, and 16-year-olds are tested in 1980 and retested in 1984 when they are 8, 12, 16, and 20 years of age.

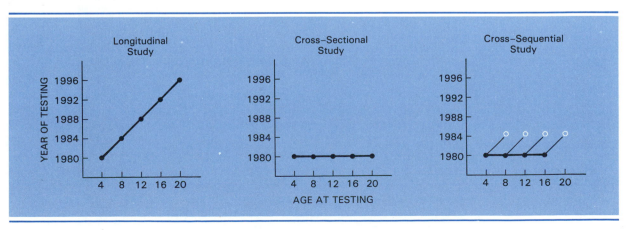

CLOSE-UP

Converging Evidence in the Study of Aggressive Juveniles

Although we often speak of today's youth as the leaders of tomorrow, it is equally appropriate to say that today's youth are the criminals of tomorrow: In the United States, more than 25 percent of all violent and property crime is committed by youth under the age of 18: In 1990 alone, more than 2,000 adolescents were arrested for murder and manslaughter (Uniform Crime Reports for the United States, 1990). This state of affairs has led developmental psychologists to study the characteristics of juvenile offenders, with the ultimate goal of devising effective treatment programs.

Research by Slaby and Guerra (1988, 1990) illustrates research of this sort and demonstrates the strength of conclusions that are based on converging results from both experimental and correlational work. In their first study, Slaby and Guerra (1988) used a correlational approach to examine links between aggressive behavior and the understanding of social situations. Subjects in the research were read stories like the following:

You're playing on your school's softball team and have a big game coming up. You've been trying to practice as much as you can after school. One day you go outside to practice with a friend but can't find any bats. You see a guy (girl) sitting on the bench just twirling a bat around. "Hey, let me borrow that for a while," you say. "No way," says the guy (girl).

After each story, subjects were asked questions that probed their interpretation of the stories. The subjects included adolescents who rarely used physical force to get their way, those who used physical force frequently, and those incarcerated in a correctional facility for committing a violent crime. The results indicated a consistent relation between responses to the stories and adolescents' aggressiveness. For example, violent and aggressive adolescents were likely to interpret the problem in hostile terms: "The guy won't let you have the bat, even though he's not using it." In contrast, the interpretation by unaggressive adolescents was nonhostile: "You don't have a bat and want to practice." When asked how they might solve the problem, aggressive and violent adolescents offered considerably fewer solutions and were less able to predict the consequences of their chosen

THE LOGIC OF LONGITUDINAL RESEARCH. As the name implies, the longitudinal approach involves a "lengthwise" account of development over a period of time, and it has long been recognized as the most obvious and direct way to "see" actual growth occurring. In one of the earliest longitudinal studies on record, Philibert Guéneau de Montbeillard measured the change in height of a single child over the 17 years between 1759 and 1776. Much later, changes in height as related to age were charted in a large sample of children who participated in the Harvard Growth Studies (1922–1934). The longitudinal method was applied next to the development of truly psychological characteristics—the emergence of emotional and social behavior, along with intellectual functioning. One such study, begun by Lewis Terman in 1921, focused on children with IQ test scores so high that many would consider them geniuses. Terman's aim solution. Overall, the correlation between aggressiveness and the number of responses on the total questionnaire was -0.84, indicating that greater aggression and violence among subjects was associated with less sophisticated responding to the problems represented in the stories.

One interpretation of this relation is that a less sophisticated understanding of social situations leads some individuals to respond aggressively. That is, some adolescents may always interpret conflict as reflecting another person's aggression, and they may habitually respond to conflicts with aggression because they do not understand that other solutions are possible. Of course, this explanation—that unsophisticated social reasoning leads to aggression—is not the only plausible explanation of the correlation between these variables. Another possibility is the third-variable problem mentioned on page 22: The correlation may simply reflect the fact that both variables are highly correlated with intelligence: Less intelligent adolescents are more prone to aggression and less likely to understand social situations.

A second study, an experiment, allowed Guerra and Slaby (1990) to distinguish between these interpretations. Adolescents who had been incarcerated for committing violent acts were assigned randomly to either training or control conditions. The training condition consisted of 12 one-hour sessions designed to increase adolescents' understanding of social situations. For example, they were taught to pay attention to nonhostile cues in a social situation, to think of alternative ways of responding to social problems, and to evaluate responses in terms of their consequences. Supervisors at the correctional facility judged that juveniles who had received the training were better adjusted after training than before. They were less aggressive, less impulsive, and more flexible in their solutions. In contrast, juveniles in the control condition were as aggressive, impulsive, and inflexible as before.

Thus, a correlational study followed by an experimental study involving direct manipulation of a key variable—the presence or absence of instruction designed to increase juveniles' social understanding—converge on the same conclusion. Juveniles act violently, at least in part, because they know no other ways to respond to situations. Well-conducted research of this sort offers the promise of both greater understanding and more effective treatment for violent adolescents.

was to follow the development of these gifted children to determine what kind of adults they would become and whether their lives would be extraordinary (we discuss some of Terman's findings in Chapter 8).

The longitudinal approach is well suited to studying almost any aspect of the course of development. More important, it is the only way to answer certain questions about the stability (or instability) of behavior: Will characteristics (such as aggression, dependency, or mistrust) observed in infancy or early childhood persist into adulthood? Will a traumatic event, such as being abandoned by one's parents, influence later social and intellectual development? How long will the beneficial effects of special academic training in the preschool years last? Such questions can be explored only by using the repeated measurement technique of the longitudinal approach.

The approach, however, has disadvantages that may frequently offset its strengths. An obvious one is cost: The expense of merely keeping up with a large sample of individuals can be staggering. A related problem is sample constancy over time. Experience has shown how difficult it is in a highly mobile society to maintain contact with people over several years (as long as 30 years in some longitudinal studies!). Even among those who do not move away, some participants lose interest and choose not to continue in the study. These "dropouts" are often significantly different from their more research-minded peers, and this may distort the outcome of the study. For example, a group of individuals may seem to show intellectual growth between the seventeenth and twenty-fifth years of life. What has actually happened, however, is that those who found earlier testing most difficult are the very ones who have quit the study, and thereby their absence from the study has inadvertently raised the group's average scores on the next round of tests. Fortunately, statistical techniques can partly correct these problems (Labouvie, Bartsch, Nesselroade, and Baltes, 1974).

Even if the sample remains constant, the fact that individuals are given the same test many times may make them "test-wise." Improvement over time may be attributed to development, when it actually stems from practice with a particular test. Changing the test from year to year would solve the test-wise problem, but such changes raise the question of how to compare responses to different tests.

THE LOGIC OF THE CROSS-SECTIONAL APPROACH. The cross-sectional approach, with its focus on the behavior of individuals of different ages at the same point in time, avoids almost all the problems associated with repeated testing; it avoids costly recordkeeping and sample attrition as well.

This approach, however, is not without problems of its own. The most serious logical tangle is the problem of cohort effects, meaning that differences between age groups or **cohorts** may result as easily from chance environmental events as from significant developmental processes. Suppose, for example, that a researcher devises a way to measure how imaginative children are and then tests a group of 5-year-olds and a group of 10-year-olds as a first step in studying the development of imagination. Let us say that the 5-year-olds were found to be more imaginative than the 10-year-olds. Can we then conclude that imagination declines within this period? Not without raising serious objections. If testing were carried out in, say, 1992, a critic might point out that our 10-year-olds were born in 1982 and our 5-year-olds in 1987, which means they differ in "generation" as well as age. Our society may have changed enough between 1982 and 1987 to make the experiences that influence the growth of imagination very different for the two different generations of children. A new curriculum adopted to nourish the imagination may have been too late for the children born in 1982, but it may have benefited the younger children. Alternatively, the country may have been recovering from an economic recession that more severely affected the lives of the older chil-

Cohort A group of people of the same age.

dren. Because social conditions change, they can be expected to affect distinct generations differently, making differences between age groups difficult to interpret.

THE CROSS-SEQUENTIAL APPROACH. Because the longitudinal and cross-sectional approaches have complementary strengths and weaknesses, some researchers have suggested combining the two approaches into **cross-sequential designs**. The basic idea is not only to study individuals of different ages simultaneously (as in the cross-sectional approach), but also to follow the individuals and retest them after some period of time has elapsed (as in the longitudinal approach). The advantage of this arrangement is that it provides direct information about the presence of cohort differences, while allowing a shorter and more economical study.

Suppose, for example, that a team of investigators was interested in determining how mathematical reasoning increases between the ages of 6 and 12. The investigators might give 6-, 8-, and 10-year-olds a test of mathematical reasoning and then retest each youngster two years later, when the cohorts were 8, 10, and 12 years of age. The design would provide information on mathematical reasoning at four different ages (6, 8, 10, and 12) using only three cross-sectional groups. At the same time, longitudinal changes could be estimated over a six-year period even though the investigation would take only two years to complete. Using appropriate, though somewhat complex, statistical procedures, the relative contributions of cohort differences and rate of change over time can also be estimated reasonably well.

Ethical Responsibilities

As investigators are selecting what subjects and methods will be used, they must pay careful attention to the welfare of the individuals who will be participating in the research. Until the end of World War II individual investigators were expected to establish ethical standards and safeguards for the subjects in their research. In the past several decades, however, professional organizations and government agencies have formulated formal codes of research conduct that specify the rights of human research subjects and the procedures to be used to protect human subjects. The following essential guidelines are included in all these codes:

1. *Minimize risks to research participants.* If alternative methods are available for answering the same question, then choose the method with the least potential for harm or stress for research participants. During the research, investigators are obligated to monitor the chosen method and to avoid any unforeseen stress or harm.

2. *Describe the research to potential subjects so they can determine if they wish to participate.* Ideally, prospective research subjects should be given all the details of the research so they can make an informed decision about whether to participate. But some potential subjects, such as infants or mentally retarded individuals, may be unable to make this

Cross-sequential design
A combination of cross-sectional and longitudinal studies in which several different age groups are followed longitudinally.

decision for themselves. In these cases consent must be obtained from parents or legal guardians.

3. *Avoid deception; if subjects must be deceived, provide a thorough explanation of the true nature of the experiment as soon as possible.* Some developmental research requires that subjects *not* be told about all aspects of a study until after they have participated. The need for such deception has often been claimed in studies of honesty, sharing, and aggression, to name a few. In these cases providing complete information about the study in advance might easily bias or distort subjects' responses. Here, investigators are obligated to determine if the importance of the study warrants deception and to determine the harm or stress likely to be caused by the deception. When investigators decide the deception is necessary and will cause minimal harm, then the research may be conducted. As soon as it is feasible—typically just after the experiment—any false information given to research subjects must be corrected, and a rationale for deception must also be provided.

4. *Results should be anonymous or confidential.* Ideally, when individuals have participated in research, their individual results should be anonymous, which means that data pertaining specifically to them absolutely cannot be linked to their name. On occasions where anonymity is not possible, research results should be confidential, which means that the identities of the individual subjects remain known only to the investigator conducting the study.

Planning developmental research, then, involves selecting methods and experimental designs that not only yield useful information about the topic but also preserve the rights of research participants. Concern for human subjects makes some research unethical. To illustrate, a true experiment on the impact of divorce on children's development would require that children be assigned randomly to conditions in which some marriages remain intact and some end in divorce. Obviously, such manipulation is ethically unthinkable. Throughout this book we will see how investigators have tried to balance their needs for evidence with the need to protect human subjects.

OVERVIEW OF THE BOOK

The rest of this book is a modern tale of human development as we understand it from the research methods and theories we have introduced in this chapter. The book includes four units. The first, called "Cornerstones of Development," is devoted to the genetic and biological bases of human development and to infancy. The second unit, "Learning and Cognition," is devoted to the intellect. We explore how children learn, think, reason, and solve problems. The third unit, "Socialization and Social Skills," concerns the processes by which children acquire the mores and customs of their society. In the final unit, "Perspectives from Child Development," our knowledge of development during infancy and childhood is used to understand abnormal development and to provide insights into the transition to adolescence and young adulthood.

Human development is a topic that touches all of us in some way. We hope that greater understanding of children and their development will lead to more fulfilling interactions with children and adolescents and to more informed decisions concerning children and adolescents, be they personal decisions concerning the upbringing of individual children or social policy decisions that affect children worldwide.

SUMMARY

1.   Developmental psychology studies all the changes in physical, mental, and social functioning that occur throughout the life span.

2.   Development refers to a process of growth and change in capability over time as a function of both maturation and interaction with the environment.

3.   The idea of a special period of development in human beings did not become scientifically important until the middle of the nineteenth century. Thereafter there was much interest in children's and adolescents' physical, cognitive, and social development.

4.   Three questions pervade theory and research in developmental psychology: the relative contributions of hereditary versus environmental factors to development; the degree to which development is continuous or discontinuous, and the degree to which development is a universal or culturally specific process.

5.   Five important theories have guided developmental psychology: maturational theory, psychoanalytic theory, social learning theory, cognitive-developmental theory, and ecological theory. Theories offer predictions that must be scientifically tested by research.

6.   All research in developmental psychology shares a commitment to the scientific method, which means that research procedures and results must be subject to verification by others. Data obtained from samples must be representative of the populations in which the researcher is interested. The measurement procedures used must be reliable; that is, they must be clear and consistent from one sample to another and from one observer to another.

7.   Two major classes of methods are used in developmental research to explain what has been observed and why. Experimental methods involve direct manipulation of treatments and subsequent measurement of their effects. They can lead to unambiguous inferences about cause and effect. Nonexperimental (correlational) methods attempt to determine causal relations from events that have occurred without interference, such as examining the naturally occurring relation between the viewing of violent TV programs and the demonstration of aggressive behavior. A correlation coefficient indicates the degree of relation between two sets of data by showing both the direction (positive or negative) and the magnitude (high or low) of the relation. The correlation may range from $+1.00$ (a perfect positive relation) to -1.00 (a perfect negative relation), with 0.00 indicating no relation. Nonexperimental methods are limited in their ability

to determine cause and effect by the directionality problem and the third-variable problem.

8.   Developmental studies aimed at identifying changes that occur with increasing age (developmental trends) may take either a longitudinal or a cross-sectional approach. In a longitudinal study the same individuals are observed and tested at different ages. In a cross-sectional study there is usually only one observation for each individual, and developmental trends are identified by studying individuals of different ages. The cross-sequential approach combines both longitudinal and cross-sectional techniques and overcomes some of the difficulties of each.

9.   Research is guided by ethical guidelines ensuring that the procedures involved minimize the risk for the subjects of the study, that subjects make an informed decision to participate, that deception is avoided, and that findings relating to individuals are confidential.

C·H·A·P·T·E·R   2

Biological Foundations of Development

Many scientists in the early 1800s believed that the reproductive cells contained a completely preformed human, who simply grew larger in the uterus (Simpson, Pittendrigh, and Tiffany, 1957). Such ideas are amusing and fantastic to us today, but the truth about heredity, prenatal development, and birth is just as amazing. In our look at the current understanding of these topics, we focus on what usually happens in these phases of development, and we also look at what can happen in unusual cases. Let's start with some glimpses of what is to come in this chapter.

▶   We are all alike—we have two arms, two legs, two eyes; we crawl and then walk; we speak; we express joy and anger, and elation; we form attachments to other humans. Yet we also differ—in hair color and body size; in artistic and intellectual abilities; in maturity; and in tendencies to be excitable or placid, outgoing or introverted, selfish or altruistic. How can this be? Answers to this question come, in part, from studying the basic structures of life—the chromosomes and genes that make up every body cell. In the first part of the chapter we shall examine the mechanisms by which genes direct much of our early development and continue to regulate change throughout life.

▶   Few experiences so readily evoke a sense of awe and wonder as the birth of a child. This event marks the end of months of excitement that are often accompanied by worries about the development of the baby-to-be. Is development progressing normally? What factors might pose risks for development? And what about birth itself? What complications can arise in this very last phase of pregnancy? We answer these questions in the second and third parts of this chapter.   ◀

FIGURE 2-1
This drawing illustrates a view, common as recently as the early 1800s, that sperm cells contain miniature versions of adult humans.

GENETIC BASES OF DEVELOPMENT

Chromosome A threadlike structure in the cell nucleus that contains the genetic code in the form of DNA.

Ova Egg cells produced in the ovaries that combine with sperm to produce the zygote.

Sperm The male reproductive cell produced in the testicles.

Autosomes All the chromosomes in human cells except the sex chromosomes.

Sex chromosomes The two chromosomes, X and Y, that determine an individual's sex.

Mitosis Typical cell

The Basic Stuff of Nature

We are becoming so sophisticated about nature that it is difficult to grasp how recent our knowledge is. An egg cell was not even discovered in the ovary of a mammal until 1831 (Grinder, 1967). And despite long speculation, it was only in this century that the fundamentals of heredity began to be well understood.

Today it is known that all the cells of the body—whether bone, muscle, or nerve cells—have a nucleus that contains **chromosomes**. The exact form and number of chromosomes is distinct for each species. All human cells except the reproductive cells (**ova** and **sperm**) contain 23 pairs of chromosomes. Twenty-two pairs of these, called the **autosomes**, are alike for both sexes; but one pair, the **sex chromosomes**, differs in females and males. Figure 2-2 shows the chromosome complement for both sexes. Note that the sex chromosomes in females are alike; they are both X chromosomes. Males, in contrast, have one X and one Y chromosome.

Ova and sperm differ from other cells in the number of chromosomes they contain. Most body cells multiply by **mitosis**, in which the chro-

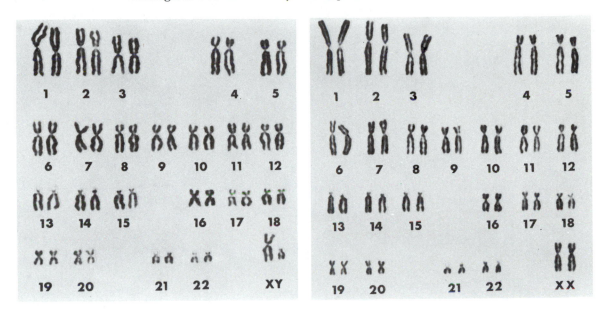

FIGURE 2-2
The chromosome complement in all human cells except the reproductive cells.
On the left is the male complement, with an X and Y chromosome; on the right
is the female complement, with two X chromosomes.

division in which
chromosomes in each
cell duplicate before the
cell itself divides into
two identical daughter
cells.

Meiosis The specialized
cell division of the
reproductive cells that
occurs during cell
maturation, resulting in
the ova and sperm
having half of the
number of chromosomes
as all the other cells in
the human body.

Gene The functional unit
of chromosomes that acts
as a blueprint for
development.

**DNA (deoxyribonucleic
acid)** Strands of
phosphate and sugar that
carry genetic information
in chromosomes from
generation to generation.

mosome set first doubles, the cell divides into two cells, and then each
new cell receives a complete chromosome set. In contrast, the reproductive
cells undergo **meiosis**, a specialized cell division during maturation that
results in their carrying only 23 single chromosomes, one from each of
the original 23 pairs. When the ovum and sperm unite sexually, each
provides half the chromosomes of the newly forming organism.

Segments of chromosomes that are functional units are called **genes**.
The basic genetic stuff of life resides in the genes in the form of **deoxyribonucleic acid (DNA)**. One of the most dramatic scientific breakthroughs
of this century was the description of the structure and function of DNA.
In 1962, Francis Crick, James Watson, and Maurice Wilkins received the
Nobel Prize for their work on a model of DNA. They proposed that the
DNA molecule consists of two strands of phosphate and sugar groups
connected by nitrogen-carrying bases. The bases always occur in specific
pairs: adenine with thymine, and guanine with cytosine. The molecule
is shaped like a double helix, resembling a spiral staircase, with the steps
being the paired bases, which can be arranged in any order along the
molecule (Figure 2-3).

As simple as it appears, this structure gives DNA remarkable characteristics. For one, DNA duplicates ingeniously. The DNA strands uncoil
themselves and the base pairs separate, leaving single strands with single
bases. These units then combine with other single DNA units produced
by the cell—with the bases being properly paired. The new DNA is thus
identical to the original.

DNA is also well suited to manage biochemical functioning in the
cells. Human beings have perhaps as many as 100,000 genes, each of which
consists of spirals of DNA that, on the average, are made up of many

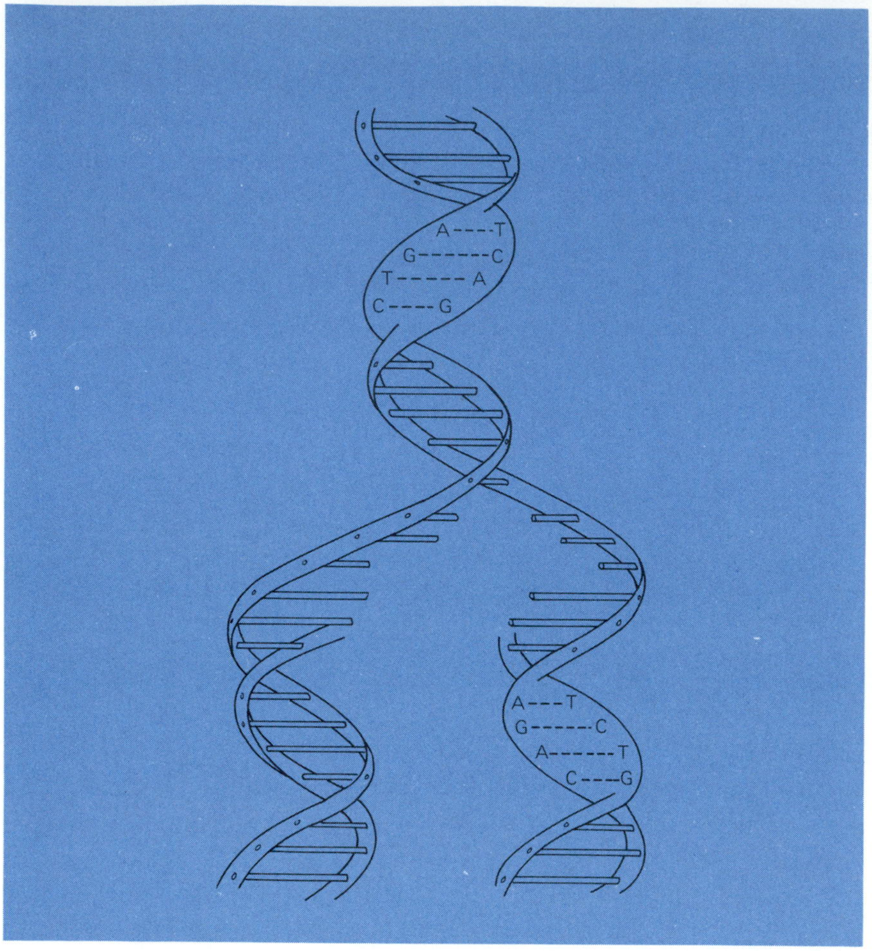

FIGURE 2-3
Diagram of the DNA molecule. When DNA replicates, the strands uncoil and the base pairs separate. The single units then combine with other single units, with the bases always pairing in specific ways. The molecules vary, however, because the base pairs can line up on the strands in various orders. Genetic information is carried by the ordering of the bases. The letters refer to the four bases: A—adenine, T—thymine, G—guanine, C—cytosine.

Enzymes Protein substances that play a critical role in the body's biochemistry.

Structural genes Genes that are involved in the production of proteins.

Regulator genes Genes that control the structural genes, turning them "on" or "off" as necessary to meet the body's needs.

hundreds of base pairs. The arrangement of the bases on the outer strands is critical. This arrangement is carried from the nucleus out into the cell, where the information is used to direct the production of proteins (Scarr and Kidd, 1983). Proteins are complex substances that make up many parts of the body, such as the fingernails and the hemoglobin in the blood. They also make up **enzymes**, the chemical catalysts critical in controlling the biochemical reactions necessary for life. Genes that are directly involved in protein production are sometimes called **structural genes**. Structural genes are turned on and off by other genes according to the needs of the organism. These "on-off" genes are known as **regulator genes**. This regulation of protein production is basic to developmental change throughout the life span (Scarr-Salapatek, 1975). Prenatal development and biological changes at puberty are perhaps the most dramatic examples of such genetic timing.

Thus, one's "inheritance" actually refers to the genes located on the 23 pairs of chromosomes that result from the union of the 23 chromosomes provided by the female's ovum and the 23 provided by the male's sperm. How can genes be responsible for similarities (two arms, two legs) as well as differences (height, temperament) among humans? The answer to this question, which was discovered more than 100 years ago in Austria, is described in the next section of the chapter.

Allele A single member of a gene pair.

Homozygous A term used to describe gene pairs whose alleles are the same.

Heterozygous A term used to describe gene pairs whose alleles are different.

Dominant gene A gene that will display its characteristic in an offspring when it is paired with an allele carrying a dissimilar form for the particular characteristic.

Recessive gene A gene that will display its characteristic only when it is paired with an allele carrying the same particular characteristic.

Genotype The entire genetic endowment of an individual.

Phenotype The outward manifestation of one's genetic makeup.

Genetic Mechanisms

Johann Gregor Mendel (1828–1884) was an Austrian monk who conducted his experiments in the garden of his monastery. Mendel first published his studies in 1865, but they initially received little attention. At the turn of the century, however, Mendel's work was rediscovered almost simultaneously by several other researchers.

Using common garden peas, Mendel carefully cross-fertilized true-breeding smooth-seeded and wrinkle-seeded plants to see what would happen in the next generation. All the offspring displayed smooth seeds. When these second-generation plants were allowed to self-fertilize, however, the third-generation plants had both smooth and wrinkled seeds, in the ratio of 3:1. A similar pattern was found for several other characteristics (see Table 2-1). Mendel wanted to explain why some characteristics disappeared in the second generation and then reappeared in one-fourth of the third generation.

Mendel assumed that the parent plants each contained two hereditary factors that were forms for the particular characteristic. These factors were later called genes, and each form of the gene pair, an **allele**. Mendel proposed that each parent passed on only one allele to the offspring. If the offspring received the same form of allele from each parent, it was **homozygous** for the characteristic. If it received different forms from each parent, it was **heterozygous**. Mendel also proposed that one form was **dominant** over the other, always displaying itself. The other allele, the **recessive** form, displayed itself only in the absence of the dominant form. A form not showing itself may still be present, to be passed on to future generations. Mendel therefore distinguished **genotype**, the genetic form of a trait or characteristic, from **phenotype**, the expressed form of a trait.

By applying these assumptions, Mendel was able to explain his curious findings. The first-generation parents each carried two genes for a particular characteristic; but one parent carried only genes for the dominant form (for example, smooth seeds), and the other parent carried only genes for the recessive form (for example, wrinkled seeds). The second-generation plants thus each inherited a gene for the dominant form and a gene for the recessive form, but they displayed the dominant form (for

---

TABLE 2-1
Mendel's Experiment with the Pea Plant

Parent Plants, First Generation	All Second-Generation Plants	Third-Generation Plants*
Smooth vs. wrinkled seeds	Smooth	2.96:1
Yellow vs. green seeds	Yellow	3.01:1
Violet vs. white flowers	Violet	3.15:1
Green vs. yellow pods	Green	2.82:1
Tall vs. dwarf stem length	Tall	2.84:1

*Ratio of dominant to recessive characteristic.
Source: The Royal Horticultural Society, London.

Polygene inheritance
Inheritance of a characteristic that is influenced by many genes.

example, smooth seeds). When these plants were self-fertilized, however, 25 percent of their offspring inherited two recessive alleles and thus displayed the recessive form (for example, wrinkled seeds).

Today we know that Mendel's assumptions, along with other suggestions he made, help account for particular patterns of inheritance found not only in plants but in other species as well. These Mendelian patterns of inheritance involve the transmission of characteristics that are influenced by only one or a few gene pairs. In some cases human studies support Mendel's ideas, and his assumptions account for the results. In other instances research findings have needed a variety of further explanations. For example, dominant and recessive genes do not always express themselves fully, for they depend on other genes and the environment. Also, several alleles exist for some genes. In addition, genes located on the sex chromosomes are expressed in unique patterns. Moreover, many characteristics appear to be influenced not only by a single gene pair but by many genes (**polygene inheritance**). Let's examine some of these variations.

SINGLE GENE PAIR, RECESSIVE INHERITANCE. Many human traits that are influenced by a single gene pair are displayed only when both parents transmit the recessive form, as in Mendel's original experiments. These include straight hair, the abnormalities of albinism, forms of cystic fibrosis, and the disease phenylketonuria (PKU).

Figure 2-4 shows the genetic mechanism involved in the transmission of PKU when the parents are heterozygous for the characteristic. Each

FIGURE 2-4

Inheritance of phenylketonuria occurs when both parents are heterozygous for the condition. On the average, 25 percent of the children will display the condition, even though their parents do not.

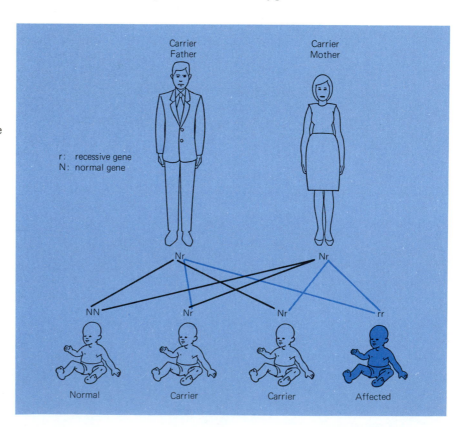

parent has an equal chance of passing on the recessive gene for the trait (r) and the normal dominant gene (N). The result is a 25 percent chance that any one of their offspring will inherit the recessive gene from both parents. The offspring who do inherit the recessive gene from both parents will have the disorder and transmit it to another generation. A 50 percent chance exists for an offspring to inherit one recessive and one dominant gene. In this case the child does not display PKU, but he or she carries the recessive as well as the dominant gene. A 25 percent chance exists that an offspring will inherit two dominant genes, not display the disorder, and transmit only the dominant gene to later generations.

This single gene pair, recessive inheritance pattern underlies many disorders in humans. It is one reason for prohibiting closely related individuals from having offspring. Because all families carry harmful recessive genes, marriage within families increases the chance that both parents will carry the same recessive genes, setting up the situation described in Figure 2-4.

SINGLE GENE, DOMINANT INHERITANCE. A characteristic carried by a dominant gene will always display itself when passed on to offspring. As you can see in Figure 2-5, one pattern occurs when the dominant gene is carried heterozygously by one parent and not at all by the other. In this case there is a 50 percent chance that the gene will be transmitted and displayed in the children. Examples of human characteristics inherited in this way include curly hair, the ability to curl the tongue back, and polydactyly (having extra fingers and toes).

FIGURE 2-5
Inheritance of Huntington's chorea occurs when one parent carries the dominant gene and the other does not. On the average, 50 percent of the children will display the disease and perhaps pass it to the next generation.

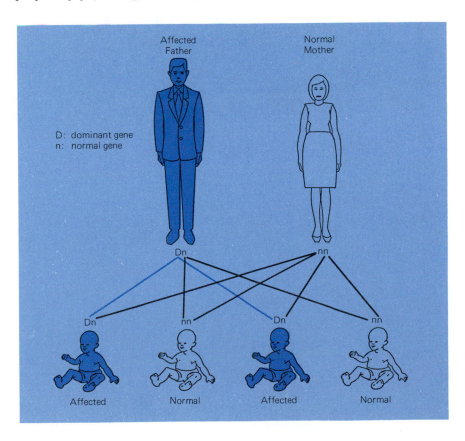

Another example is Huntington's chorea, a fatal disease characterized by progressive degeneration of the nervous system. Limb spasms, mental deterioration, and psychotic behavior develop, typically at 40 to 45 years of age (Stern, 1973). By this age most adults have already produced offspring, many of whom will later display the disease themselves.

SEX-LINKED INHERITANCE. Certain characteristics are said to be sex linked because they are influenced by genes on the sex chromosomes. The Y chromosome does not have many genes, whereas the X chromosome has more than 150 (McKusick, 1990). In some cases of sex-linked inheritance the relevant allele is recessive and located on the X chromosome. One example of this is hemophilia, a disease in which the blood does not clot normally; another is red-green color blindness. The frequency of the sex-linked characteristic is higher in males than in females; red-green color blindness, for example, is eight times more frequent in males (McClearn, 1970). Why is this so? Suppose a female receives from her mother the recessive gene that may produce color blindness. The daughter will probably *not* be color blind because the X chromosome she received from her father will most likely contain the dominant gene for normal color vision. When a son receives the recessive color blindness gene from his mother, its influence cannot be offset by a dominant normal-vision gene from his father because the Y chromosome he receives from his father has no gene for normal color vision (see Figure 2-6). The same reasoning can be used

FIGURE 2-6
Inheritance of red-green color blindness occurs when the father carries the gene for normal vision and the mother carries one gene for normal vision and one for color blindness. Daughters have a 50 percent chance of being carriers; sons have a 50 percent chance of being color blind and a 50 percent chance of having normal vision and of not carrying the color-blindness gene.

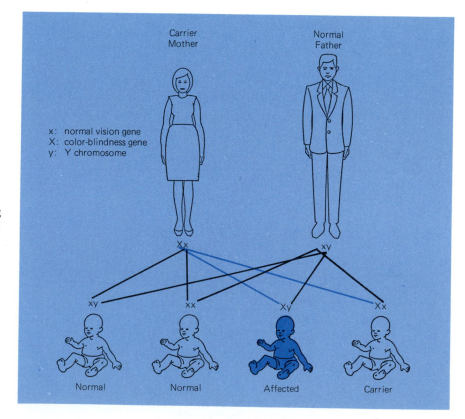

Consanguinity study A way to determine the genetic bases of a trait by examining people who differ in how closely they are related to one another.

to demonstrate that all color-blind women must have had fathers who were also color blind. Can you see why?*

POLYGENE INHERITANCE. So far we have discussed only relatively simple Mendelian patterns that involve one gene pair, often resulting in either one characteristic or another. Mendel's pea plants displayed seeds that were either smooth or wrinkled; in humans, albinism is present or absent. Over 2,000 such characteristics are known or suspected in humans (Plomin, DeFries, and McClearn, 1990), and well over 150 such characteristics produce the mental abnormalities associated with retardation.

Countless other characteristics are influenced by several genes. These traits do not present an either-or situation; rather, they are displayed along a continuum. In the case of intelligence, for example, individuals are not just extremely bright or very dull; instead, they fall into the entire range between those extremes. The same is true for height, weight, skin color, and temperament. Each of the many genes involved contributes only a small influence. As the number of genes increases, so does the number of phenotypes, until separate phenotypes cannot be distinguished (McClearn, Plomin, Gora-Maslak, and Crabbe, 1991). Figure 2-7 shows this relation.

In studying polygene inheritance, we cannot trace the effects of each gene. Instead, we examine the distributions of traits in populations with complex statistical methods. It is assumed that population traits are due to both genetic and environmental effects, so researchers try to separate these components by comparing groups of people who are either unrelated or related in certain ways.

One common approach, called the **consanguinity study**, is based on the fact that closely related people have more genes in common than people not as closely related. For example, a parent and a child share one-half of their genes, as do siblings, on the average. First cousins, however, share only one-eighth. If a trait is influenced by genes, parents and their children should be more alike than first cousins. Furthermore, cousins

---

*A color-blind woman must have received the recessive color-blind gene from both her mother and her father. If her father carried color blindness on his X chromosome, he must have been color blind because his Y chromosome does not have a color-vision gene.

FIGURE 2-7
As the number of genes increases, so does the number of resulting phenotypes. Involvement of many genes results in the characteristic's being displayed along a continuum.
(Adapted from I. H. Herskowitz, Genetics. Boston: Little, Brown & Co., 1965.)

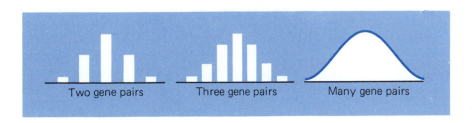

Two gene pairs   Three gene pairs   Many gene pairs

FIGURE 2-8
If a trait or characteristic is inherited, children should resemble their parents more than other relatives with whom they share fewer genes (for example, first cousins).

would be more alike than unrelated people. The consanguinity study is based on this reasoning: As the degree of relation among individuals increases, so should their similarity for an inherited characteristic.

The problem with this method is that close relatives might be similar because they share more similar environments as well as more genes. This *confound*, or confusion, always exists in consanguinity studies unless relatives have been reared in different homes. Thus the method can be a helpful first step in research, but the results must be interpreted cautiously and followed up with other kinds of research.

Another common way to study genetic factors is the **twin study**, which is based on the important difference between identical (*monozygotic*) and fraternal (*dizygotic*) twins. Identical twins develop from a single union of egg and sperm, so they have identical genotypes. Fraternal twins, in contrast, develop from two separate unions, and so like nontwin siblings they share, on the average, 50 percent of their genes. The degree to which identical twins are more alike on a characteristic than are fraternal twins suggests the influence of genetic endowment.

As it turns out, identical twins are more alike than fraternal twins in many physical and psychological characteristics, including height, weight, intelligence, and personality (Plomin, DeFries, and McClearn, 1990). These likenesses might easily lead to the conclusion that heredity certainly plays a role in the development of many traits. The issue is not settled so quickly, however. The twin method assumes the environments shared by identical twins are no more alike than the environments shared by fraternal twins.

Twin study A way to reveal genetic factors in which identical twins are compared with fraternal twins.

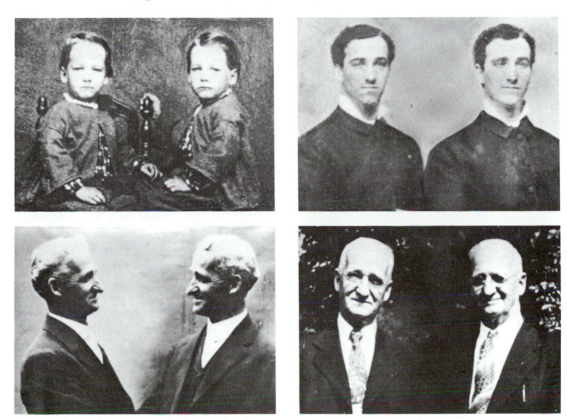

FIGURE 2-9
Photographs of a pair of identical twins taken at ages 5, 20, 55, and 86.

But identical twins share more activities, have more friends in common, dress more alike than fraternal twins, and, of course, they are always of the same sex (Loehlin and Nichols, 1976). Others may perceive identical twins as more alike and may treat them more alike than they do fraternal twins. Could greater similarity of environment underlie the greater similarity of identical twins? Perhaps. But there is evidence that neither physical nor environmental similarity is related to personality or intellectual similarity in twins (Matheny, Wilson, and Dolan, 1976). Nevertheless, findings from studies with twins are most convincing when they are complemented by results from yet another method, the **adoption study**.

When parents bring up their biological children, the source of any parent-child similarity observed later is uncertain. Parents transmit genes that may be responsible for similarities, but the social transmission of abilities, attitudes, and personality is also involved. In contrast, parents who bring up adopted children influence them only by social transmission. This reasoning is at the heart of adoption studies, which compare adopted children both with their biological families and with their adoptive families. Resemblances between adopted children and their biological families suggest genetic effects; resemblances between adopted children and their adoptive families suggest environmental influences.

The logic of these studies requires that the children cease to have

Adoption study An approach to reveal genetic factors in which relations are examined among adopted children, their biological parents, and their adoptive parents.

contact with their biological families soon after birth. Furthermore, they should be placed randomly in adoptive homes. However, adoption agencies often try to place youngsters in homes similar to those of their biological parents. This can bias the results of adoption studies. The biological and adoptive parents may be genetically similar—which means that the adoptive parents may be genetically similar to their adopted children. In this case similarities between children and adopted parents would reflect a genetic as well as an environmental component (Horn, 1983).

The simultaneous use of well-designed and well-controlled adoption and twin methods can tell us much about hereditary and environmental effects. Research of this sort suggests that heredity plays an important role in intelligence, personality, and abnormal behavior. We will explore these topics in detail later in this book (in Chapters 3, 8, and 13, particularly). Now, however, let us examine some genetic effects that are not inherited.

Chromosome Abnormalities

We have seen that many human behaviors and characteristics are transmitted through heredity from one generation to the next. But one type of genetic effect, chromosome abnormalities, is usually *not* inherited. Chromosome aberrations fall into two categories: abnormal number and abnormal structure. Abnormalities in number probably occur during meiosis, when ova and sperm are developing, although they may also occur early in the development of the fertilized egg. In either case, the chromosome pair does not separate as it should, causing either an extra chromosome or the loss of a chromosome in the cells. Abnormalities in structure involve chromosome breakage and reunion in various deviant arrangements. Radiation, chemicals, viruses, mutations, and the age of the parents are all implicated as possible causes of chromosome abnormalities.

In humans, chromosome aberrations account for about 50 percent of spontaneous abortions and for about 6 percent of deaths occurring at or shortly after birth. Nearly 1 percent of live newborns carry chromosome defects, although not all of these infants show deficits (Alberman, 1982; Hamerton, 1982; Jagiello, 1982).

In the following sections, we describe one disorder that is traced to an additional autosome; then we examine four disorders that involve abnormalities of the sex chromosomes.

Down syndrome A chromosomal aberration resulting in moderate to severe retardation caused by an extra twenty-first chromosome.

DOWN SYNDROME. Individuals with **Down syndrome** show from moderate to severe retardation and are strikingly alike in physical appearance. They frequently have small skulls, chins, and ears; short, broad necks, hands, and feet; flat nasal bridges; sparse hair, and a fissured tongue. Perhaps most recognizable is a fold over the eyelid, which appears oriental to Westerners and suggested the name *mongolism*, a name for the syndrome that is no longer used. There is substantial risk of heart defects, intestinal malfunction, and leukemia (Robinson and Robinson, 1976). Aside from the usual physical characteristics and poor muscle tone, Down syndrome babies may not at first appear mentally deficient. During the first two years, however, deficits begin to emerge. Development in many areas

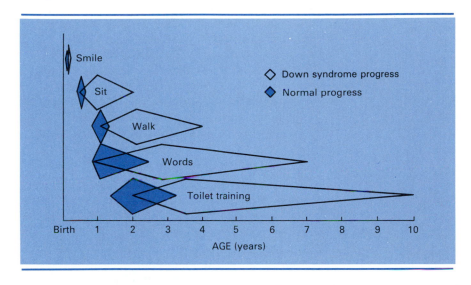

then lags behind that of the average child and continues over a much longer time period. (Figure 2-10).

For many years both genetic and environmental factors were suspected in Down syndrome. However, twin studies suggested a genetic basis: Identical twins are almost invariably both affected, but this outcome is much less common for fraternal twins (Plomin, 1990). In 1959 it was discovered that most cases of Down syndrome are caused by an extra twenty-first chromosome and that this condition is not inherited. The risk that a woman will bear a child with Down syndrome increases markedly with the mother's age. Modern methods of analyzing chromosomes indicate that the mother contributes the extra twenty-first chromosome in approximately 95 percent of the cases (Antonarakis et al., 1991).

KLINEFELTER'S SYNDROME. **Klinefelter's syndrome** is the most common sex-chromosome abnormality; it occurs in 1 out of 500 male newborns. Most individuals suffering from this defect have an additional X chromosome (XXY), though in some variations multiple X chromosomes are present, as in 49, XXXXY (Sheridan, Radlinski, and Kennedy, 1990). Mothers of Klinefelter's syndrome males tend to be older than those in the general population. About 25 percent of these males exhibit below-normal intelligence and suffer from atypical sexual development: They often have small genitals, a lack of sperm, low levels of male sex hormones, and female development of the breasts. They tend to be introverted, passive, timid, lacking in self-confidence, and impaired in sexual interest (Bancroft, Axworthy, and Ratcliffe, 1982). They are also very tall. Treatment with male sex hormones can be helpful to varying degrees; it can facilitate penis enlargement, hair growth, and deep-voice development.

TURNER'S SYNDROME. In this disorder, which occurs only in females, the individuals have only one X chromosome instead of two. **Turner's syndrome** females lack normal ovarian tissue and do not develop sexually. They are short in stature and thick in body build; they often have webbed

Klinefelter's syndrome A chromosomal aberration found exclusively in males that is associated with atypical sexual development and below normal intelligence.

Turner's syndrome A chromosome aberration, found in females who lack a second X chromosome, associated with mild mental retardation, failure to develop secondary sex characteristics, and short stature.

necks, prominent earlobes, and abnormalities of the elbows, knees, kidneys, and aortas. Mild levels of mental retardation may exist, but more typical are problems of memory and in perception of spatial relations (Downey et al., 1991). Some evidence indicates that they also are less able to infer emotions from facial expressions, which may be why they are more likely to experience social problems (McCauley, Kay, Ito, and Treder, 1987). Treatment with female sex hormones can bring about sexual development, and adjustment can be quite satisfactory.

XYY COMPLEMENT. This abnormality, which occurs in about 1 in 1,000 male births, attracted enormous attention when it was first revealed in a report associating it with both mental retardation and aggressive behavior (Jacobs, Brunton, and Melville, 1965). Males with XYY complement abnormality were unusually tall and appeared with high frequency among institutionalized criminals. Follow-up data disclosed that XYY males tended to show behavioral disorders at an early age and were less likely to have violent siblings than normal males in a control group (Price and Whatmore, 1967). Several case studies appeared to confirm the relation between the XYY configuration and mental deficiency and aggression. Forssman (1967), for example, described an atypically tall XYY male who had an IQ of 69 at age 16 and who had become extremely aggressive during adolescence.

The most intriguing aspect of this abnormality was the association of the Y chromosomes and violence. Later research cast doubt on this interpretation, however. A study by Witkin and his colleagues (1976) of over 4,000 men in Denmark substantiated the atypical height, the low intelligence, and the high frequency of XYY men in penal institutions. But the criminal XYY men had not been involved in violent acts; if anything, their crimes appeared rather mild. These investigators concluded that low intelligence, not extreme aggression, could underlie the quite mild criminal behavior and lead to their imprisonment. Other research with XYY boys, however, revealed no predisposition to violence and antisocial behavior but suggested instead a depressive reaction to stress (Ratcliffe and Field, 1982).

"FRAGILE" X. Relatively recently attention has been called to "fragile" X chromosomes, so called because the long arm of the X chromosome tends to break (Madison, Mosher, and George, 1986). Males with the condition frequently have large ears and, after puberty, oversized testicles and long faces. This abnormality appears to be the second most common cause of mental retardation. Although moderate retardation is common in males, retardation in females appears mild. Other behaviors associated with the syndrome include language deficits and hyperactivity (Ho, Glahn, and Ho, 1988).

The defect is transmitted in a sex-linked pattern. With two X chromosomes, females are protected, whereas males suffer the full consequence of a "fragile" X. Treatment for the fragile X syndrome with folic acid is promising: It reduces the chances of breakage and makes behavior problems less likely (Ho et al., 1988).

Our discussion of chromosome abnormalities makes it obvious that individual development can sometimes be dramatically affected by genetic programming. In these instances, the range of possibilities for full normal development falls below average for at least some areas. Nevertheless, development still varies with environmental factors such as medical care, educational opportunities, and diet playing an important role. If there is one critical lesson that has emerged from explorations of biological influences on human development, it is that genetic and environmental variables work hand in hand throughout the life cycle. Let's look at how "nature" and "nurture" work together.

Nature and Nurture

AN EXAMPLE OF NATURE-NURTURE INTERACTION: PKU. If you look at the fine print on the back of a can of diet soda, you'll see the warning:

Phenylketonurics: Contains phenylalanine

This message actually signals a clear example of how heredity interacts with the environment. In phenylketonuria—PKU for short—an important liver enzyme is absent or inactive. Ordinarily this enzyme converts phenylalanine—found in dairy products, bread, and fish—into tyrosine. Without this enzyme, phenylalanine accumulates and results in the production of substances that are injurious to the nervous system.

Phenylketonuria occurs in 1 case per 20,000 live babies. The defect occurs only when both parents pass on the defective gene. Infants born with this defect tend to have blue eyes, fair hair, and light-colored skin. Generally, they are irritable, hyperactive, and short tempered. Many have seizures and abnormal brainwaves, impaired communication, bizarre movements, and perceptual problems (Cytryn and Lourie, 1980).

It is possible to detect PKU within the first two weeks of life with urine or blood tests, and screening programs are prevalent throughout the United States. Early detection is extremely important because children placed on diets that limit the intake of phenylalanine within the first few weeks of life show only minimal impairment. But if diet is not corrected early, there will be substantial and permanent intellectual impairment. The pattern is shown in Figure 2-11.

The PKU syndrome is an interesting example of how heredity and the environment interact to determine behavior. Noticeable retardation does not appear in children who carry the genetic component if they are given a special diet early enough. In contrast, children with the defective genetic endowment and an uncontrolled diet are frequently retarded.

NATURE AND NURTURE IN DEVELOPMENT. Phenylketonuria is a specific example of gene-environment interaction. Now let's turn to the broader question of how genetic endowment and the environment are related over the life span.

At the beginning of this chapter we noted the many ways in which humans are similar physically and behaviorally. Many of these charac-

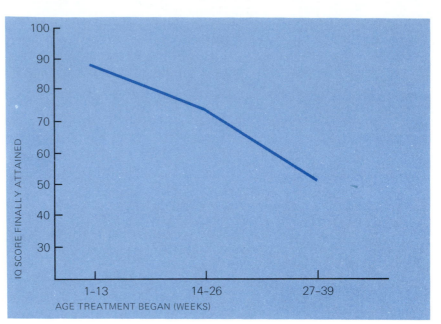

FIGURE 2-11
The effect of diet restriction on the intellectual development of children who inherit PKU. The later diet treatment begins, the less effective it is.
(Data from Baumeister. Copyright 1967, the American Association on Mental Deficiency.)

Canalization A genetic predisposition for the development of certain characteristics thought to be adaptive for a species.

Reaction range The broadest possible expression of a genotype.

Passive gene-environment relation A component of Scarr and McCartney's (1983) model of heredity and environment in which parents pass on genes to their offspring and provide an environment that reflects their own genotypes.

teristics that are common to all humans are controlled by genes. Development of these characteristics is very difficult to disrupt. Characteristics like these are said to be strongly **canalized** (Turkheimer and Gottesman, 1991; Wilson, 1978). Behaviors that are critical to survival may be the most strongly canalized—as if nature had decided not to be overly trusting of nurture. For example, most infants babble by the time they are 3 to 6 months old and walk by 15 months. Only drastic environmental events prevent these characteristics from developing. In these instances development has a well-defined destination, and detours that lead away from this destination are resisted.

For many characteristics, however, how genes are expressed depends greatly on interaction with the environment. Thus, for example, in individuals who have the genotype for "very tall" height, height may vary depending on individual diet. The broadest possible expression of a genotype is the **reaction range**. "Very tall" individuals might vary from 6 feet 5 inches to 6 feet 9 inches but not go outside this range. A set of genes does not fix a corresponding characteristic. Rather, genes contribute to determining a range of potential, and interactions with the environment determine the phenotype.

Innumerable environmental factors can interact with the gene complement. Social experiences—such as the opportunity for social attachment and how individuals are accepted or rejected, encouraged or discouraged, attended to or ignored—are likely to be important. So is the quality and amount of intellectual, perceptual, and motor stimulation. Physical characteristics of the environment, such as diet and exposure to chemicals and disease, must also be considered.

These factors need not affect all aspects of development in the same way. On the contrary, gene-environment interactions are probably specific

FIGURE 2-12

Active niche building is a powerful influence on the development of individual differences.

Evocative gene-environment relation A component of Scarr and McCartney's (1983) model of heredity and environment in which each genotype evokes a unique response from the environment.

Active gene-environment relation A component of Scarr and McCartney's (1983) model of heredity and environment in which people seek environments that fit their genotype.

to particular traits (Wachs, 1983). Furthermore, the nature of gene-environment interactions may well change with development.

In a provocative and influential analysis Sandra Scarr and Kathleen McCartney (1983) proposed that three general relations exist between heredity and environment. In a **passive gene-environment relation**, parents pass on genotypes to their children. In addition, they provide an early environment that results, in part, from their own genetic makeups. To illustrate, parents who excel intellectually may transmit genes that influence their children in this direction, and they are also likely to provide books, museum visits, and stimulating discussions that have similar influence. In an **evocative gene-environment relation**, different genotypes evoke different responses from the environment. Thus children with certain genotypes may pay attention to their teachers and ask relevant questions and, in turn, receive more positive attention in school than children who show little interest. In an **active gene-environment relation**, individuals actively seek environments related to their genetic makeup. In-

CLOSE-UP

Infertility and the New Reproductive Technology

On October 12, 1991, Arlette Schweitzer gave birth to fraternal twins, a girl and a boy. What makes these births unusual is that the babies are her grandchildren. Mrs. Schweitzer's daughter was born without a uterus and, thus, could not become pregnant. Mrs. Schweitzer's daughter's eggs were fertilized with her daughter's husband's sperm, and the resulting zygotes were implanted in Mrs. Schweitzer's uterus.

This is just one of the most recent events in a series of remarkable advances that began with the birth of Louise Brown, the world's first "test-tube" baby, in 1978. The impetus for these advances is the fact that about 15 percent of American couples are unable to conceive, despite having attempted conception with a year of regular, unprotected sexual intercourse. In many cases, infertility can be traced to one of three common problems: (1) stress, which may disrupt ovulation or make ejaculation difficult; (2) the timing of intercourse, which should be between the tenth and eighteenth day after the onset of the menstrual cycle, since this is the time that ovulation is most likely to occur; and (3) behaviors that interfere with conception, such as douching immediately after intercourse or keeping the testes too warm (by wearing tight underwear or by taking frequent hot baths), which reduces the production of sperm (Frey, Stenchever, and Warren, 1989).

If infertility cannot be linked to the these causes, a number of more complicated options are available (Stangell, 1988). If a woman ovulates irregularly, making it difficult to time intercourse, drugs can be used that usually trigger ovulation three to eight days after the drugs are administered. Another approach, **artificial insemination**, is used when there seems to be a low sperm count, when sperm are not very active, or when the woman's cervix seems to be hostile to sperm. Sperm are inserted directly into the uterus. This procedure, which can be done either with the prospective father's sperm or with sperm from a do-

---

tellectually able children may actively seek peers, adults, and activities that strengthen their intellectual development.

The three previous examples are positive relations in that the effects of heredity and environment complement one another; that is, genetic tendencies are encouraged and maintained by experience. But negative relations also occur. A negative passive relation exists, for example, when a child whose genetic disposition is to be quiet and withdrawn has socially outgoing parents who expose this child to group activities. Here, the environment set up by the parents works against the child's genetic disposition. An example of a negative evocative relation occurs when teachers and friends react to this quiet child by encouraging participation in group games.

Scarr and McCartney speculate that the importance of gene-environment relations changes with development. The influence of the passive kind of relation decreases from infancy to adolescence, and the importance of the active kind increases. As individuals grow older they increasingly select aspects of the environment to which they respond, aspects they learn about or they ignore. The selections are related to the motivational,

Artificial insemination A procedure used to attempt to fertilize an ovum in which sperm cells are inserted medically in the uterus.

nor, typically results in pregnancy in more than half of the attempts.

One of the newest procedures is **in vitro fertilization** (IVF). In the first step of this elaborate procedure, a drug is administered to stimulate development of ova. Growth of the ova is monitored with blood testing and an ultrasound scanning procedure. When several ova appear to be mature, ultrasound scanning is used to guide a long needle through the vaginal wall to the follicles of the ovary. Fluid is extracted containing the ova. A few hours later, the ova are mixed in a petri dish with sperm (either from the prospective father or another donor). About 24 hours later, the ova are checked for fertilization; usually several fertilized eggs will be transferred into the woman's uterus, using a plastic catheter. Success rates for IVF vary considerably; a success rate of 10–15 percent is probably a reasonable estimate.

Pregnancy is somewhat more likely in a variation of IVF known as GIFT, for *gamete intrafallopian transfer*. The primary difference here is that in a single procedure the ova are retrieved, mixed with sperm, and returned to the Fallopian tube.

For couples who have suffered years of frustration, guilt, and depression because of their inability to conceive, the new reproductive technologies—particularly IVF and GIFT—seem to offer the promise that they, too, can have children. All is not rosy, however. As noted already, most efforts at IVF and GIFT do not succeed; indeed, failures far outnumber successes. When successful, the odds are much greater than normal that a woman will carry twins or triplets (because multiple eggs are transferred to increase the odds that at least one ovum will implant in the uterine wall). In addition, the procedure is expensive: Each attempt costs approximately $10,000.

Clearly, then, the new reproductive technologies have increased the number of alternatives for infertile couples. But pregnancy on demand is still in the realm of science fiction. For many couples the old-fashioned alternative of adopting a child should be considered. For the cost of a single attempt at IVF, a couple could pursue a private adoption with a much greater chance of a happy ending.

In vitro fertilization A technique in which ova and sperm are mixed in a petri dish to create a zygote, which is then inserted into the woman's uterus.

personality, and intellectual aspects of their genotypes. According to Scarr and McCartney, this active niche building is the most powerful connection between people and their environments. It is the most direct expression of the genotype in experience.

Central to this theory is the argument that, although genetic and environmental influences are both necessary for development, the genotype comes first. It influences both the child's phenotype and the rearing environment. It plays a critical role in determining which environments are actually experienced by the child and what effects they have on the child. In short, the genotype guides and drives experience.

This theory suggests how heredity and the environment may interact to shape development over the life span. Will the theory stand the test of time? Scarr and McCartney suggest several ways in which it can be tested, and some of this research is underway (Scarr, 1992). Sorting out the links among nature, nurture, and development is one of the most complex tasks in all of developmental psychology. We can be sure, however, that these influences start with conception and prenatal development, which we examine next.

PRENATAL DEVELOPMENT

Conception takes place when an ovum is released by an ovary and joins with a sperm in the Fallopian tube leading from the ovary to the uterus (see Color Plates A and B following). When an ovum and sperm cell unite, the sex of the new organism is determined immediately. The ovum and sperm each carry 23 single chromosomes, including one sex chromosome. An X-chromosome sperm united with the X-chromosome ovum produces a female zygote. A Y-chromosome sperm united with the X-chromosome ovum produces a male zygote. Theoretically, there should be an equal chance of the zygote's being male or female, but in fact more males are conceived, for the ratio of male to female births is approximately 106:100.

Sometimes a zygote divides very early and develops into identical twins. In other cases two conceptions occur simultaneously, resulting in fraternal twins. Twin births occur in about 1 in every 83 deliveries in the United States, and two-thirds of these are fraternal pairs (Plomin et al., 1990). The rate of twinning increases with a woman's age until the late thirties. Black women have a greater chance of having twins than white women, who in turn have a greater chance than women of Asian heritage. There may also be some inherited tendency to produce twins. A woman who has a sister with twins or is a twin herself has a higher than average chance of bearing twin children (Scheinfeld, 1973).

Sequence of Development: Zygote, Embryo, Fetus

Development before birth takes place in three stages or periods: zygote, embryo, and fetus. Within a few days after conception, the fertilized ovum, called a **zygote**, journeys down the Fallopian tube toward the uterus (Figure 2-13). The zygote has already begun to multiply by mitosis, at first slowly and then more rapidly (see Color Plate C). A hollow ball of perhaps 100 cells burrows into the uterine wall. The inner part is destined to be a new individual, and the outer layer develops into the life-support sys-

Zygote The cell mass that is the result of the union of an ovum and a sperm.

FIGURE 2-13
Diagram of conception and early development. The ovum leaves the ovary and is fertilized by a sperm in the Fallopian tube. The resulting zygote immediately begins to develop and travels to the uterus within a few days.
(Adapted from K. L. Moore, Before We Are Born. *Philadelphia: W. B. Saunders, 1974, p. 25.)*

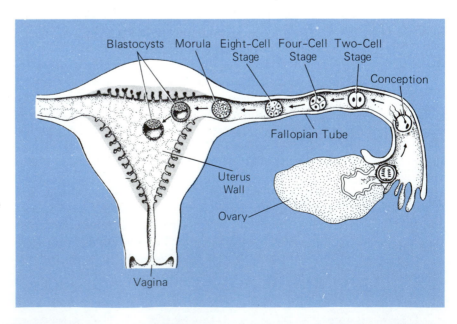

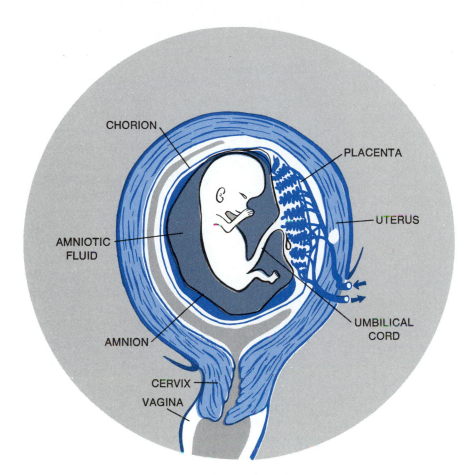

Labels in figure: CHORION, PLACENTA, UTERUS, AMNIOTIC FLUID, AMNION, UMBILICAL CORD, CERVIX, VAGINA

FIGURE 2-14

The developing child floats freely within the amnion except where it is attached to the placenta by the umbilical cord.

(From W. A. Kennedy, Child Psychology, 2nd ed. Englewood Cliffs, N.J.: Prentice-Hall, Inc., 1975, p. 49. Reprinted by permission of Prentice-Hall, Inc.)

Chorion The outer embryonic membrane that is associated with the formation of the placenta.

Amnion A thin membrane that forms a sac around the embryo; the sac is filled with amnionic fluid in which the embryo and fetus grows.

Umbilical cord The "lifeline" composed of arteries and veins that serves as a transport system between the developing child and his or her mother.

Placenta A structure that develops in the uterus following conception and through which nutrients and wastes are exchanged between mother and fetus.

Embryo In prenatal development, the name assigned to the developing organism from about the second to eighth week after conception.

tem: the **chorion** (outer sac), the **amnion** (inner sac), the **umbilical cord**, and the **placenta**. The umbilical cord (Figure 2-14) is a lifeline, its arteries and veins serving as a transport system between the developing child and the mother. The vessels in the umbilical cord make indirect contact with the adult's system at the placenta. Nutrients, oxygen, some vitamins, drugs, hormones, and some disease-producing organisms pass to the developing child; waste materials pass in the opposite direction through the mother for elimination.

The period of the **embryo** begins during the second week after implantation in the uterus and lasts until about the eighth week of gestation. It is a dramatic time of rapid growth in which cell and organ differentiation occur. By two months the embryo is slightly more than one inch long and roughly resembles a human being. The body appears top heavy and the head is bent over. The ears, eyes, mouth, and jaws are clearly recognizable. The limbs, beginning as broad buds, lengthen and begin to form fingers and toes. The spinal cord and other parts of the nervous system take shape.

Most organs exist at least in some rudimentary form. The heart, at first disproportionately large, begins to beat (see Color Plates D and E).

From about the eighth week until birth the developing organism is called a **fetus**. The rate of growth reaches its peak during the early fetal period and then declines. Development involves further growth of existing structures, changes in body proportion, and refinement in functions. Only a few parts make their first appearance at this time—the hair, nails, and external sex organs. Bones harden, and the lower body region grows so that the head is no longer quite so dominant (see Color Plates F–J).

The beginning of the fetal period occurs when the prospective mother becomes especially aware of the developing child (Rugh and Shettles, 1971). Spontaneous movement can be felt at about 16 weeks. Some fetuses are quiet, whereas others kick and squirm a great deal. The arms bend at the wrist and elbow, and the hands can form a fist. The fetus can frown, squint, and open its mouth. Reaction to stimulation is global at first but soon becomes specific. For example, if the eyelids are touched at the end of the third month, squinting occurs instead of a previous jerking of the entire body. Many **reflexes**, which are automatic and unlearned responses to specific stimuli, appear: The fetus begins swallowing, coughing, and sucking.

Changes during the last three months of pregnancy prepare the fetus for living independently. For example, respiratory movements are practiced even though oxygen is being provided through the placenta. Vital functions for swallowing, urinating, and moving the gastrointestinal tract become refined. Weight gain is noticeable. A fetus born after about 26 weeks stands a good chance of survival, although a full term of 38 weeks is normal and optimal (see Color Plate K).

General Risk Factors

Fetus In prenatal development, the name assigned to the developing organism from about the eighth week after conception until birth.

Reflex An unlearned and automatic response that is triggered by a specific stimulus.

Teratology The study of prenatal malformations and other deviations from normal prenatal development.

Critical period A very short span of time in the life of an organism during which it may be especially sensitive to specific influence.

Few of us believe today that an evil eye cast upon a pregnant woman brings a deformed child, or that the amount of reading a mother does during pregnancy influences intelligence. Nevertheless, the mother's body, through its interaction with the fetus by way of the placenta, provides the entire fetal environment. This fact has two implications for prenatal care. First, adequate diet, rest, exercise, and regular medical checkups are important. Second, efforts should be made to avoid agents or circumstances that could cause abnormal or less than optimal development for the child.

The study of malformations and other deviations from normal prenatal development is called **teratology**. A basic principle of prenatal growth is that structures emerge in a fixed order, and that rapid differentiation and growth occur during **critical periods**. The embryonic period and the beginning of the fetal period are critical for most body systems, and during these weeks exposure to teratogens, agents that can cause fetal malformation, can produce major structural damage. As Figure 2-15 shows, the critical time is somewhat different for the different body parts. Still, the amount of exposure affects the outcome, and individuals probably vary in susceptibility to certain teratogens.

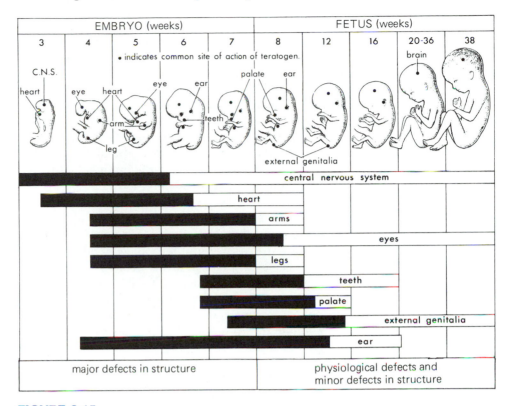

FIGURE 2-15

The early months of prenatal development are critical, although the period of maximal sensitivity varies somewhat for the different body parts. The black-shaded areas indicate maximal sensitivity; the white areas indicate less sensitivity.

(Adapted from K. L. Moore, Before We Are Born. *Philadelphia: W. B. Saunders, 1974, p. 96.)*

We now know about many possible influences on the developing child. Let's begin with some general factors.

MATERNAL AGE.   Women over 35 years of age are at greater risk for giving birth to infants with defects. Premature births and infant deaths are also greater among women in this age group (for example, Shaw, Croen, and Curry, 1991; *Vital and Health Statistics*, 1972). In older women, the ova, which have been present in an immature state from birth, may have been affected by aging or exposure to chemicals, drugs, and other harmful agents. Teenage women are also at risk, perhaps because the reproductive system may not be fully developed. Also, pregnant teenagers often have poor prenatal care (Culp et al., 1988).

MATERNAL NUTRITION.   Because the mother is the sole source of nutrition for the unborn child, a diet providing the proper balance of proteins, fats, carbohydrates, minerals, and vitamins is vital. Many correlational studies of humans indicate a relation between maternal diet deficiencies and prematurity, low birth weight, stillbirth, growth retardation, and poor mental functioning (Knobloch and Pasamanick, 1974; Susser, 1991). Diet deficiencies during the first trimester of pregnancy are especially harmful, but deficiencies during the last trimester may also be important because of the rapid growth during that time (Lester, 1975). For women who are pregnant with twins, adequate nutrition is particularly important to meet the increased energy needs (Dubois et al., 1991). Despite these findings, we still have much to learn about the effects of maternal nutrition. Poor nutrition may simply not meet the dietary needs of the fetus; it may also act indirectly by increasing the mother's vulnerability to pregnancy complications and disease.

MATERNAL STRESS.   The effects of maternal stress are even less understood than the effects of maternal nutrition. Much of the research on stress involves animals; in general, anxiety and stress in pregnant animals can alter offspring behavior, such as increasing emotionality (Thompson and Grusec, 1970). It seems reasonable that maternal emotions could influence the growing child. The emotions act through the autonomic nervous system that activates the endocrine glands, which, in turn, regulate the secretion of hormones such as adrenalin. Because hormones can pass through the placenta, they may affect the fetus. In one study, motor depression in newborns was associated with anxiety found in prospective mothers during the last month of pregnancy (Standley, Soule, and Copans, 1979). However, motor depression was also related to use of medication during childbirth, so there is no way to know if the infants were affected by anxiety, by medication, or by both. The most that can be said is that maternal stress may affect the fetus (Stechler and Halton, 1982). In general we do not expect serious effects from mild stress, but the risk of serious complications may increase with severe, prolonged stress.

RH INCOMPATIBILITY.   The **Rh factor**, named after the rhesus monkey in which it was first discovered, is an inherited protein found in the blood of 85 percent of the general population. Difficulty arises only when the father carries the factor (Rh positive), the mother does not (Rh negative), and the child develops as Rh positive. If the offspring's blood comes into contact with the mother's through the placenta, the mother's system may manufacture antibodies to ward off the foreign Rh protein. The antibodies destroy the child's oxygen-carrying red blood cells, a condition known as **erythroblastosis**, and death or mental retardation can occur.

These effects do not usually show up during the first pregnancy because the Rh factor cannot cross the placenta. However, the mother may receive the Rh factor when the placenta separates at birth, and she may then begin to manufacture antibodies. Should she become pregnant again, the antibodies, which can cross the placenta, are available to damage the fetus. This process can be prevented by administering a substance that deters antibody formation, rhoGAM, to the mother at the birth of her first child.

Rh factor An inherited protein found in the blood that can cause erythroblastosis when the father carries a positive Rh factor, the mother does not, and the child develops as Rh positive.

Erythroblastosis A disorder in which the offspring's red blood cells are destroyed by antibodies produced in the mother's system in reaction to the foreign protein (Rh factor) in the fetus's blood that is threatening her system.

Some Specific Risks

MATERNAL DISEASES. Table 2-2 lists some maternal diseases implicated in fetal defect and death. Rubella (German measles) and cytomegalovirus disease (CMV) are potentially the most dangerous of the infectious diseases.

In 1942 Australian physicians noted that women who contracted Rubella early in pregnancy had a high incidence of defective babies. If it crosses from the mother to the fetus through the placenta, the Rubella virus can result in miscarriage; stillbirth; premature birth; deafness; blindness; heart, liver, and pancreas defects; and mental retardation. Estimates of defect caused by Rubella during the first month of pregnancy are as high as 50 percent, but exposure during the last two trimesters is not considered harmful. Women can thus be most dangerously exposed to Rubella before they realize they are pregnant. During the 1964 worldwide epidemic of Rubella, an estimated 20,000 to 30,000 babies in the United States were born with defects (Chess, 1974). Fortunately, pregnant women who have already had Rubella or taken the vaccine are unlikely to contract the disease.

The strain of virus causing CMV is widespread in human adults, especially among those in the lower social classes (Jensen, Benson, and Bobak, 1981). Transmitted by way of the respiratory and reproductive systems, the virus rarely causes any symptoms in adults. However, it can result in miscarriages and stillbirths, as well as in undersized and damaged neonates (newborns). The infants commonly suffer from nervous system abnormalities such as **microcephaly** (an excessively small head), oversized livers and spleens, and anemia and other blood abnormalities. No prevention or treatment exists for CMV.

TABLE 2-2
Maternal Diseases That Can Cause Prenatal Damage

AIDS	Death; brain damage
Anemia (iron deficiency)	Death; brain impairment
Cytomegalovirus	Death; stillbirth; mental retardation; liver, spleen, and blood disorders; microcephaly
Diabetes mellitus	Death; stillbirth; respiratory difficulties; metabolic disturbances
Influenza A	Malformations
Mumps	Death; malformations; heart disease
Pneumonia	Early death
Rubella	Death; prematurity; deafness; blindness; heart, liver, pancreas defects; mental retardation
Scarlet fever	Early death
Syphilis	Death; blindness; deafness; mental retardation
Toxoplasmosis	Mental retardation; heart defects; brain defects; death
Tuberculosis	Death; lowered resistance to tuberculosis

Microcephaly An excessively small head, caused by many disorders such as CMV.

A noninfectious maternal disease that can be extremely hazardous is diabetes mellitus (Naeye, 1990). Along with the possibility of inheriting diabetes, the unborn child is subjected to a generally unhealthy uterine environment. If the mother is not treated, the probability of fetal death and stillbirth is 50 percent. In addition, many of the surviving babies do show some abnormalities: An enlarged pancreas, excessive weight, a puffy appearance, respiratory difficulty, and metabolic disorders such as low blood sugar are evident in babies born to diabetic mothers. With medical care, risk is greatly reduced (Moore, 1983).

Acquired immune deficiency syndrome, commonly known as AIDS, was first identified in 1981. In the early 1990s an estimated 20,000 children in the United States were infected with the human immunodeficiency virus (HIV), which causes AIDS (Caspe, 1991). Most infected children are born to mothers who became infected from intravenous drug use. In one study (Hutto et al., 1991), 30 percent of the babies born to infected mothers were themselves infected, most by age 6 months; 25 percent died before their first birthday. The virus attacks the brain, with the result that microcephaly is common, as are cognitive, language, and motor deficits (Schmitt et al., 1991). There is preliminary evidence that two drugs— zidovudine and deoxyinosine—may reduce some of the AIDS symptoms (Butler et al., 1991; Krasinski, 1991). These drugs do not, however, cure the disease, and many children cannot use them because of side effects. At this point the only way to avoid having an HIV-infected child is for a woman to be sure that she is not infected.

DRUGS. The best general policy for the prospective mother is to avoid all drugs unless they are professionally recommended and monitored. In a culture as drug dependent as ours, however, this is not always easy. Table 2-3 gives a general summary of the possible effects of some drugs and chemicals. We look here at some specific cases.

1. *Thalidomide.* One particularly tragic example of drug-caused birth defects involved the drug *thalidomide*, which was synthesized in 1953

TABLE 2-3
Possible Prenatal Effects of Some Drugs and Chemicals

Alcohol	Growth retardation; microcephaly; disfigurations; cardiac anomalies; behavioral and cognitive deficits
Antihistamines	Fetal death; malformations, especially of the limbs
Aspirin (in excess)	Bleeding in the newborn; possible circulatory anomalies
Barbituates	Depressed breathing; drowsiness during the first week of life
Heroin, morphine	Convulsions; tremors; death; withdrawal symptoms
Lead	Anemia; hemorrhage; miscarriage
Quinine	Deafness
Thalidomide	Malformations, especially of the limbs
Tobacco	Low birth weight; prematurity; high heart rate; convulsions

Fetal alcohol syndrome
The pattern of congenital malformation of the fetus due to the daily consumption of three or more drinks by the mother during pregnancy.

and at first appeared to be a harmless sleep-inducing agent. Late in 1959, however, reports describing the malformed infants of mothers who had taken thalidomide during pregnancy began to mount, especially in Germany (Jensen, Benson, and Bobak, 1981). The drug was primarily harmful when taken 1 to 2 months after the woman's last menstrual cycle. Furthermore, the type of damage was linked closely to the time the drug was taken. For example, women who took the drug 34–38 days postmenstrually were likely to have babies missing an outer ear; women who took the drug 38–42 days postmenstrually were likely to have babies with an outer ear that was deformed. Other malformations caused by the drug included the stunting or complete absence of arms, legs, and fingers. Abnormalities of the internal organs also occurred.

2. *Alcohol.* Drinking large quantities of alcohol is known to harm the developing embryo and fetus, for alcohol crosses the placenta and disrupts the development of the central nervous system (West, 1986). Maternal consumption of three or more alcoholic drinks per day during pregnancy is associated with a distinct pattern of malformation called **fetal alcohol syndrome**. Children with this syndrome show permanent growth retardation; microcephaly and brain-cell abnormalities; eye, ear, and other facial disfigurations; joint and limb abnormalities; heart defects; mental retardation; and attentional deficits (Figure 2-16). Even a small daily consumption of alcohol by pregnant women may result in offspring with reduced intelligence and poorer motor skill at 4 years of age (Barr, Streissguth, Darby, and Sampson, 1990; Streissguth et al., 1989).

3. *Narcotics.* Maternal use of narcotics is associated with prematurity, low birth weight, and fetal death. Many children of addicted mothers are addicted themselves, and most show withdrawal symptoms within

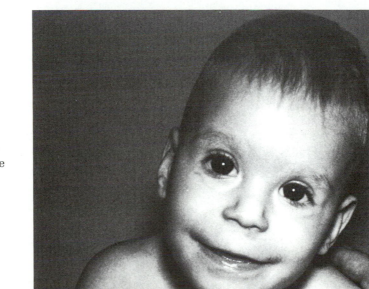

FIGURE 2-16
This child and her deceased mother were diagnosed as suffering from fetal alcohol syndrome. Several typical features are evident: narrow eye openings, a thin upper lip, and drooping of the upper eyelids.

4 to 24 hours after birth. They may display irritability, shrill crying, tremors, an inability to sleep, hyperactivity, respiratory problems, huge appetites, diarrhea, and vomiting. These disturbances may last for 1 to 8 weeks (Davis and Templer, 1988).

Long-term effects are not well established. In one study (Kaltenbach and Finnegan, 1987), infants born to drug-dependent mothers were compared to infants who had not been exposed to drugs during prenatal development. Although the infants born to drug-dependent mothers were smaller at birth, at age 6 months the two groups of infants did not differ in their rate of mental development nor in the outcome of a complete neurological exam. Other studies provide some evidence of poor attention span and poor motor coordination in the children of drug-dependent mothers (Hutchings and Fifer, 1986).

Yet another problem is that the behaviors associated with drug addiction withdrawal (for example, irritability and crying) place these infants at risk for poor parenting. That is, parents may find they are unable to console and comfort an infant undergoing withdrawal; this failure may interfere with the development of strong, secure attachment relationships between these infants and their mothers. Instead, the attachment relationship is more likely to be insecure or avoidant (Rodning, Beckwith, and Howard, 1989). These forms of attachment, which are discussed in detail in Chapter 3, place children at greater risk for later behavioral problems.

4. *Cigarette smoking.* The potential damage of cigarette smoking during pregnancy had been suspected for several years before a large-scale study by Simpson in 1957 found that smokers had a high risk of delivering prematurely (Ferreira, 1969). Many later studies confirmed that smoking is associated with prematurity and low birth weight, possibly due to the effects of nicotine and the byproducts of carbon monoxide. Whether these children suffer later growth and cognitive deficiencies is still debated. Some investigators report that smoking during pregnancy is associated with deficits in cognitive skills like verbal ability (Fried and Watkinson, 1990). Several other investigators, however, report no impact of prenatal exposure to smoking on later mental and behavioral development (Barr et al., 1990; Richardson et al., 1989).

5. *Marijuana.* When mothers smoke marijuana during pregnancy, their infants are more likely to have disrupted sleep than are infants born to mothers who do not smoke marijuana (Scher et al., 1988). In addition, in at least one study children who had been exposed to marijuana in utero were, as 4-year-olds, more likely to have language and memory deficits (Fried and Watkinson, 1990).

6. *Caffeine.* Most pregnant women consume some caffeine, either in the form of coffee, tea, colas, or chocolate. Caffeine is a stimulant that can cross the placenta. Depending upon the amount consumed, caffeine can affect motor activity and sleep. Pregnant women who consume large amounts of caffeine (for example, ten 6-ounce cups of coffee daily) are more likely to give birth to smaller babies and to babies with birth defects (Buelke-Sam, 1986). Consumed in smaller amounts during pregnancy, caffeine intake increases the odds that infants will have reduced muscle tone and will not be easily consoled (Hronsky and Emory, 1987).

The long-term effects of moderate caffeine consumption are still not clear. One team of investigators found that caffeine consumption during pregnancy was unrelated to intelligence at age 4; it *was* related to motor development but not consistently (Barr et al., 1990; Streissguth et al., 1989).

7. *Aspirin.* Many women take aspirin or acetaminophen (the active ingredient in Tylenol and other over-the-counter analgesics) during their pregnancies, typically for headache. Use of aspirin during pregnancy is associated with an increased risk of birth defects but use of acetaminophen is not (Streissguth et al., 1987). Taking even small amounts of aspirin (for example, 1 per day) late in pregnancy increases the possibility of intracranial hemorrhage (Stuart et al., 1982). Prenatal exposure to aspirin— but not acetaminophen—has long-term effects: When women took aspirin during pregnancy, their children were likely to have lowered intelligence and to have less-developed attention and motor skills (Barr et al., 1990; Streissguth et al., 1987).

ENVIRONMENTAL HAZARDS. One of the hazards of life in an industrialized world is that people are exposed to toxins in food, water, and air. Often the quantity is so slight that adults are not harmed unless the exposure persists over years. However, exposure that is innocuous to adults may be harmful to fetuses or infants. For example, expectant mothers in Japan who had eaten fish contaminated with methyl mercury from industrial wastes were more likely to give birth to babies with cerebral palsy (Miller, 1974). Similarly, in the United States women who consumed fish contaminated with polychlorinated biphenyl, or PCB, had children who, as 4-year-olds, tended to have below average verbal and memory abilities (Jacobson, Jacobson, and Humphrey, 1990).

Today x-rays are seldom taken during pregnancy except in emergencies. This is because radiation may lead to leukemia, microcephaly, cataracts, stunted growth, miscarriages, and stillbirths. Studies of exposure to microwave radiation have generally shown relatively few harmful effects. However, there are at present relatively few studies, and most are with animals, so it would be premature to call microwave radiation safe with regard to human development (Jensh, 1986).

Some occupations are potentially hazardous. Pregnant women who are involved in the manufacture of electrical and metal goods are more likely to give birth prematurely or to have infants of low birth weight (Sanjose, Roman, and Beral, 1991). Overwork can also place pregnant women at risk. In one study women who worked 40 hours or more per week had nearly 50 percent more low birth weight infants than did women who worked 1–20 hours (Peoples-Sheps et al., 1991).

PATERNAL INFLUENCES. Males who are exposed to toxic substances may run the risk of fathering children with birth defects. In studies with animals, administering narcotics, alcohol, and caffeine to males has produced offspring with birth defects. One study involved male operating-room personnel who were exposed to anesthetic gases. Wives of these men had significantly higher rates of miscarriages, and their offspring were more likely to be born with defects (Kolata, 1978).

How can these effects be explained? Sperm cells may be damaged by the toxins. Sperm can also carry some toxins, such as cocaine, directly to the egg, where they interfere with normal development (Yazigi, Odem, and Polakoski, 1991). Yet another possibility is that the detrimental substances might act through the semen. Some substances (for example, thalidomide and narcotics) are, in fact, excreted in the semen and enter the female circulation through the vaginal walls. During pregnancy they might contaminate the fetus through the placenta (Kolata, 1978).

For readers wanting to know if specific substances are "safe" during pregnancy, our discussion may seem short on firm answers. Often we have said that "long-term effects are not clear." Some of this inconclusiveness stems from the practicalities of doing research on this topic. Many infants are exposed to multiple teratogens. For example, pregnant women who drink alcohol are also likely to smoke and drink coffee (Barr et al., 1990). This makes it difficult to discriminate an effect that is unique to any particular substance. Another problem is that the extent of prenatal exposure can often only be estimated from a woman's responses to interviews or questionnaires. These replies may be incorrect, leading to inaccuracies in estimates of the harm associated with the substance.

The inconclusiveness also stems, to a substantial degree, from the fact that few substances are simply safe or dangerous. Instead, the harm associated with a substance depends upon the timing and amount of exposure. Some substances are particularly harmful early in pregnancy but less so later on, whereas others are most dangerous late in pregnancy. The harm associated with differing amounts of exposure is difficult to determine because the "dose-danger" relation can take many forms. Each additional exposure may simply increase the possibility of harm by the same amount. Alternatively, a substance may be safe until some critical amount of exposure is reached; beyond this "threshold" harm increases rapidly with each additional exposure. And the dose-danger relation may not be the same for all women, depending, for example, on their health or weight.

All these factors combine to make it difficult to offer guaranteed statements concerning the safety of particular substances. Probably the best policy is to avoid most drugs and related substances throughout pregnancy. In addition, thorough prenatal care will help to assure that pregnant women are healthy and perhaps better able to resist the impact of some teratogens. Such care will often involve tests that assess the progress of fetal development. We'll examine some of these in the next section.

Ultrasound A method of prenatal diagnosis in which sound waves are passed through a pregnant woman's abdomen and the reflected sound waves are then used to generate a video or photographic image of the fetus.

Prenatal Diagnosis and Treatment

Until recently fetal development could not be determined directly or precisely and obstetricians were able to estimate fetal size and position only by feel. This situation has changed dramatically in the past 20 years. New procedures now allow a more detailed assessment of prenatal development. The most common is **ultrasound**, in which sound waves are directed

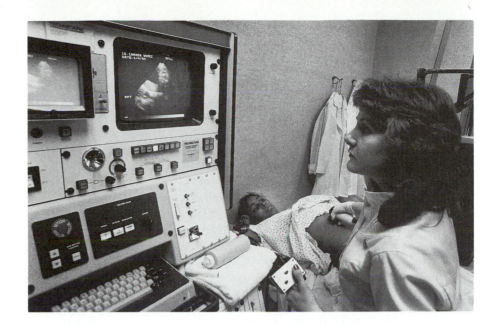

FIGURE 2-17
Ultrasound is used to assess the progress of fetal development.

at the fetus. The reflected waves are used to generate an image of the fetus that can be inspected to determine the position of the fetus, its due date and size, and if major body parts are developing normally (see Color Plate J).

A limitation of ultrasound is that many defects are not readily visible with this method alone (Pitkin, 1991). To check for unseen defects a useful procedure is **amniocentesis**. Guided by an ultrasound image, a physician inserts a needle into the sac that surrounds the developing child and a sample of amniotic fluid is drawn from the sac. The fluid and the cells floating in it can then be examined for biochemical and chromosomal abnormalities. For example, Down syndrome and sickle-cell anemia are inherited disorders that can be detected by analyzing fetal cells. In an even newer procedure, **chorionic villus sampling—CVS** for short—a tube is threaded into the uterus, where a sample of embryonic tissue is extracted. As with amniocentesis, the cells can be analyzed for defects. The advantage of CVS over amniocentesis is that testing can take place in the eighth week of pregnancy instead of waiting until the sixteenth week, as is necessary with amniocentesis.

Another procedure involves analyzing a pregnant woman's blood for alpha-fetoprotein. Excess alpha-fetoprotein many indicate either twins or a defect in the "neural tube" that becomes the spinal cord.

Ultrasound and the test for alpha-fetoprotein are rapidly becoming standard components of prenatal care for all pregnant women. Amniocentesis and CVS are particularly recommended when a genetic disorder is suspected in the family or when the prospective mother is over 35 years old, because these factors increase the risk of genetic problems. Not only are these procedures safe—performed correctly they do not increase the risk of miscarriage—but they are also very accurate. Analysis of amniotic fluid, for example, is correct virtually 100 percent of the time.

The advantages of prenatal diagnosis are obvious. Carriers of PKU, sickle-cell anemia, and countless other diseases can be identified. Down syndrome and other chromosome abnormalities can be diagnosed. Until recently, prospective parents who had received the bad news of birth

Amniocentesis A method of prenatal diagnosis in which a needle is injected into the amnionic sac to obtain a sample of fetal cells for testing.

Chorionic villus sampling (CVS) A method of prenatal diagnosis in which a tube is inserted into the uterus to obtain a sample of embryonic tissue for testing.

defects with prenatal diagnosis were put in the position of making the difficult decision of whether to continue a pregnancy or abort the pregnancy. The number of options is beginning to grow, however, with advances in the new field of fetal treatment and surgery (Harrison and Adzick, 1991). Some disorders have been treated successfully in utero. In one case (Davidson, Richards, Schatz, and Fisher, 1991) a fetus had developed a large goiter—a swelling in the neck due to an enlarged thyroid gland. This condition could complicate delivery and, after birth, might cause newborn asphyxia and death. A sample of blood taken from the vein in the umbilical cord indicated low thyroxine, one of the two major thyroid hormones. To remedy the deficit, thyroxine was injected into the amniotic fluid, and as a result the goiter became smaller. After birth, which was routine, the goiter was only slightly enlarged and thyroid functioning was normal.

Even more amazing are instances of fetal surgery. Here, the fetus is removed from the uterus, surgery is performed, and the fetus is returned to the uterus. Surgery of this sort is being used to treat *diaphragmatic hernia*. In this condition the diaphragm, which separates the lungs from the rest of the abdominal organs, develops improperly. As a consequence the abdominal organs compress the lungs. This is not a problem during prenatal development because the oxygen is not supplied by the fetal lungs. However, most babies with diaphragmatic hernia die at birth because they are unable to breathe. Surgery for this disorder involves cutting through the pregnant woman's abdominal wall and uterus to expose the fetus; then surgery is performed on the fetal abdomen to position the organs properly and to repair the hole in the diaphragm that is the source of the problem (Kolata, 1990).

Surgery like this is highly experimental and often fails. But as more experience is gained and new technology is developed, there is every reason to believe that more prenatal problems will be treated successfully by surgery.

Accompanying progress in prenatal diagnosis and treatment is concern about the implications of our new knowledge. One implication is seen in the practice of **eugenics**, the attempt to improve the human species through inheritance. As early as 1883, Sir Francis Galton suggested that the human species could be improved by encouraging talented people to mate (Karp, 1976). The idea was not new, but it became particularly popular in the United States during the 1920s. The results were laws restricting the immigration of supposedly "inferior" people into the United States and laws mandating compulsory sterilization for the mentally retarded, criminals, and other "socially inadequate" individuals. Even though sterilization laws are now unconstitutional and immigration laws are less stringent, our constantly expanding knowledge of prenatal development and ever more sophisticated technologies open up new and perhaps dangerous possibilities. We need to apply our knowledge and skills wisely if we are to protect individuals as well as society and our species as a whole.

Eugenics The attempt to improve the genetic characteristics of a species.

Lightening The beginning of the biological preparation for birth in which the head of the fetus turns downward toward the birth canal, relieving the pressure against the mother's diaphragm.

Labor The process by which the fetus is expelled from its mother's uterus, occurring within a few

BIRTH

hours to a few weeks after lightening.

Afterbirth The placental membranes, which are discharged after the fetus has emerged from the uterus.

Lamaze program A program in which women are taught techniques that help them to relax throughout labor and delivery so that use of drugs can be minimized.

Birth center A medical clinic in which doctors, nurses, and other staff members encourage natural childbirth.

Birthing room A room in a medical facility in which a pregnant woman will stay for labor and delivery; it is constructed to be homelike to help women feel more relaxed.

Biological preparation for birth begins with **lightening**. The head of the fetus turns down so that birth occurs with the head first. The fetus's movement into this position relieves ("lightens") the pressure against the mother's diaphragm so that she can breathe more freely. **Labor**, the process by which the fetus is expelled from its mother's uterus, occurs within a few hours to a few weeks after lightening. Labor is divided into three stages (Figure 2-18). In stage one, the cervix of the uterus dilates and frequently the amnion ruptures, allowing the escape of amnionic fluids. The first stage generally takes from 7 to 12 hours, but it varies greatly among individual women. The fetus emerges during the second stage, which usually lasts from one-half to two hours (see Color Plate L). Stage three involves the expulsion of the placental membranes, the **afterbirth**. The average length of labor in the United States is 14 hours for the first child, and less for subsequent births.

In the United States many couples now seek to make childbirth more "natural." They believe that parents should have greater control over the birth experience than traditionally run hospitals have permitted. They prefer greater participation by the father and other family members, avoidance of what they consider unnecessary medical procedures, and minimization of anesthesia. Many enroll in **Lamaze programs**, which emphasize relaxation and breathing techniques for the women during labor and encourage the men to help throughout labor and delivery (Lamaze, 1970). Also popular with these couples are **birth centers**, which are clinics staffed by medical personnel committed to natural childbirth, and **birthing rooms**, which are homelike hospital rooms where couples participate fully

FIGURE 2-18
The three stages of childbirth.

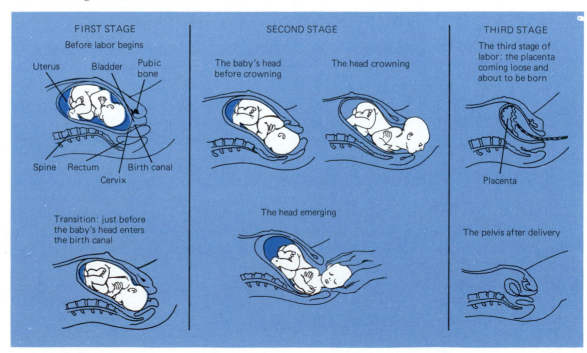

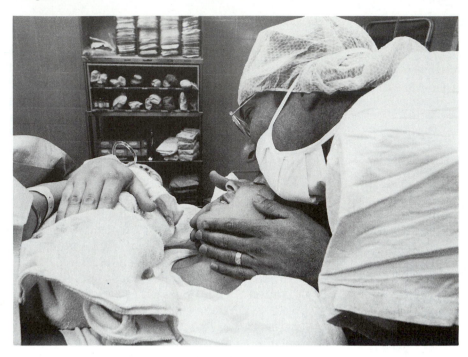

FIGURE 2-19
This baby is about 15 seconds old.

in decisions but receive some medical assistance. Home delivery has grown in popularity; this often involves a midwife or nurse practitioner who consults with a physician. Some professionals fear that inadequate medical service in these settings might endanger infants and mothers. Such settings can be dangerous when the mother has health problems and a history of birthing difficulties, particularly when full medical services cannot be easily reached in emergencies. Otherwise, alternative settings for childbirth appear safe and seem to provide great satisfaction to most couples who select them.

Birth Complications

Breech position An abnormal birth position for the fetus, in which the buttocks of the fetus emerge first instead of the head.

Caesarean section The surgical removal of the fetus through the uterine and abdominal walls.

Anoxia A lack of oxygen to the fetus at birth, caused when the umbilical cord fails to provide oxygen and when the newborn has not yet begun to use his or her lungs.

Birth is not usually a complicated business. In fact, it generally proceeds according to expectations, but sometimes there are problems. Among the difficulties that can arise is the abnormal positioning of the infant. The normal fetal position for birth is head first, face down. If the buttocks emerge first, the full **breech position**, or if the fetus is in a face-up position, delivery is more difficult and dangerous. In the past, surgical instruments were used to facilitate delivery of babies positioned abnormally. Today, however, such instruments are used more cautiously because they can cause brain damage when they are applied to the baby's head. For a variety of reasons (for example, the fetus is too large for the mother or the fetus must be delivered early to ward off the threat of disease) fetuses are sometimes delivered by **Caesarean section**, a surgical opening of the uterus and abdominal walls.

Another difficulty is **anoxia**, or a lack of oxygen, which may occur

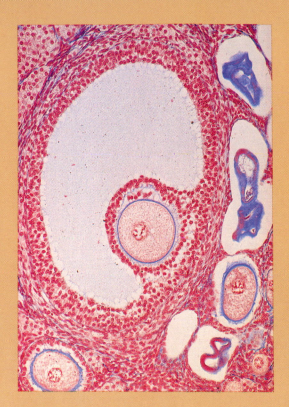

COLOR PLATE A. (*left*) This is an ovum—the human egg cell—just before maturation. It is about 1/200 of an inch in diameter.

COLOR PLATE B. (*below*) A human sperm cell is a small fraction of the size of the egg—about 1/90,000 as large—and yet both egg and sperm contribute half of the new individual's genes. As soon as one sperm cell has fertilized the egg, the remaining sperm (a few hundred million) are unable to penetrate its membrane.

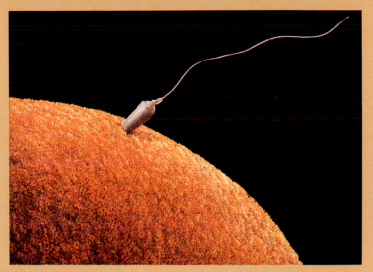

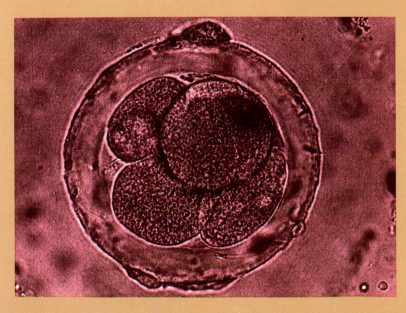

COLOR PLATE C. (*left*) By approximately 10 hours after conception, the fertilized egg—now called a zygote—has divided once, creating two cells, and has divided a second time, creating the four cells shown here.

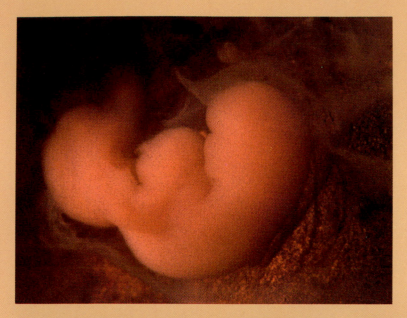

COLOR PLATE D. (*left*) By one month after conception, the fertilized egg is now known as a zygote and is securely implanted within the walls of the uterus. The heart has begun to beat, the neural tube that will form the spinal cord has begun to close, and "buds" that will become arms and legs begin to sprout.

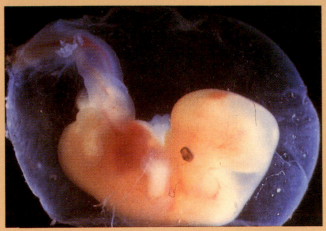

COLOR PLATE E. (*above*) The amniotic sac that surrounds this 6- to 8-week-old embryo can be seen clearly. The eyes, which make their appearance at about 5 weeks after conception, are also evident.

COLOR PLATE F. (*right*) By the tenth week, the developing organism is now called a fetus. The eyelids are formed and have sealed the eyes, protecting them. The toes and fingers can be seen easily in this photograph.

COLOR PLATE G. (*left*) This photograph depicts the fetus at 16 to 20 weeks after conception. During this period, the fetus grows rapidly, increasing substantially in length and weight. The ribs are clearly visible as are major blood vessels.

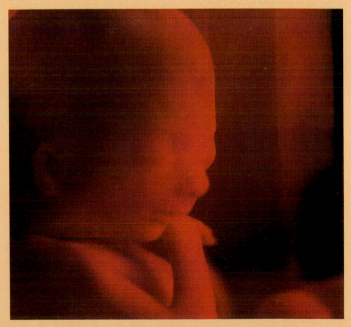

COLOR PLATES H (*left*) and I. (*above*) These photographs show a 20-week-old fetus. At this age, a typical fetus weighs about 4 ounces, and the mother can first feel its movements. She may recognize regular periods when the fetus is alert and when it is asleep.

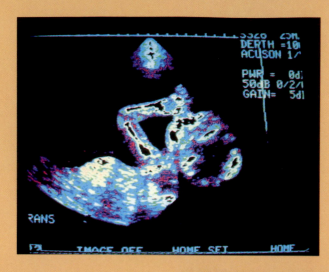

COLOR PLATE J. (*left*) A 25-week-old fetus is seen sucking in this ultrasound image. The original ultrasound was in black and white; the color was added by computer to help to distinguish different parts of the fetus.

COLOR PLATE K. (*below*) This photograph shows a fetus at 8 to 9 months after conception, just before birth. The fetus has acquired a protective layer of fat, which is why the skin is now opaque (in contrast to the transparent look of Color Plate G). The skin is covered by an oily substance called vernix that protects the skin during its long immersion in amniotic fluid.

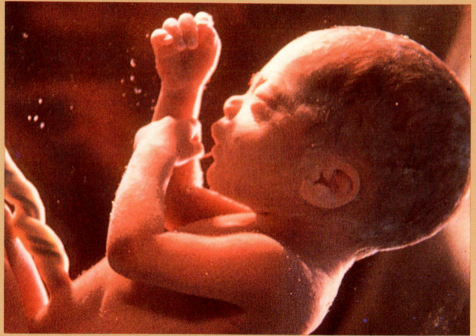

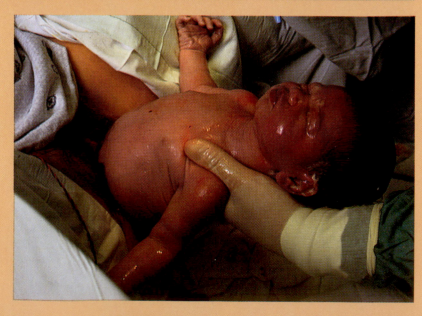

COLOR PLATE L. (*left*) A typical birth in which the head and shoulders are delivered first.

at birth if the umbilical cord fails to provide oxygen until the newborn begins to use its lungs. This may happen if the cord is damaged, knotted, squeezed shut, or detached too soon, or if the respiratory system does not react properly. The nervous system is especially sensitive to oxygen loss, and severe anoxia may result in mental retardation and cerebral palsy.

The purpose of medication during childbirth is to reduce the mother's pain and stress. Many of the drugs administered to the mother reach the child through the placenta. Short-term side effects from these drugs on the newborn have been shown on sucking, nursing, visual attentiveness, motor performance, and sleep (Adams, 1989; Brazelton, 1970; Sanders-Phillips, Strauss, and Gutberlet, 1988). The side effects vary with the specific drug, the dosage, and the point during delivery when it is administered.

The evidence for long-term side effects is not clear. Some investigators have reported harmful side effects that have persisted into the preschool years. However, it has not been possible to determine if these are the long-term effects of medication or the parents' response to the short-term effects. That is, delayed development in babies may reflect the medication's impact on the infant's nervous system. What might be happening, of course, is that parents respond differently to these babies based on their medication-influenced behavior in the first few months of life (Brazelton, Nugent, and Lester, 1987).

The Newborn

At birth the newborn child is approximately 20 inches long and weighs about 7½ pounds. It has smooth skin, a relatively large head, a flat nose, a high forehead, and receding jaws. These standard features soon develop into more individual characteristics.

It is often said that newborns are not very interesting; they seem to do little but eat, sleep, and cry. To some degree this is true. However, the more we are able to evaluate newborns, the more we appreciate how much is actually happening. What, in fact, can the neonate do? And how do we find out?

One of the most useful and popular measures of an infant's condition at birth is the Apgar instrument, devised by Virginia Apgar in 1953. The measure is simply a rating of heart rate, respiration, reflex irritability, muscle tone, and color, taken one minute after birth. It is sometimes repeated three, five, and ten minutes later. Each of the five dimensions is scored as 0, 1, or 2, with the larger numbers indicating the more superior condition. The Apgar rating is particularly helpful in alerting medical staff to life-threatening conditions at the time of birth.

A second measure used widely by clinicians and academicians is the Brazelton Neonatal Behavioral Assessment Scale (Brazelton, 1973). The 26 items on the scale measure motor skill, response to stimuli such as noise or a pin prick, general alertness, and cuddliness. This scale discriminates neonates from different cultures as well as those born prematurely, drug addicted, and developmentally disabled (Brazelton, Nugent, and Lester, 1987).

TABLE 2-4
Some Neonatal Reflexes

Babinski	Stroking the sole of the foot results in the spreading out of the toes and the upward extension of the big toe.
Babkin	Pressing the neonate's palm causes the mouth to open, the head to turn sideward, and the eyes to close.
Galant	Stroking the neonate's back along the spine results in the trunk's arching toward the side.
Moro	Withdrawing physical support (dropping, allowing the head to drop, changing position) or presenting a sharp noise results in the arms extending outward and returning to midline.
Palmar grasp	Touching the palm causes the fingers to grasp the object.
Placing	Stroking the top of the foot with an edge, such as a table edge, results in raising the foot and placing it on the edge.
Plantar grasp	Touching the balls of the foot results in inward flexion of the toes.
Rooting	Stroking the cheek or corner of the mouth causes the head to turn toward the object and to move in a way that looks as if the neonate is searching for something to suck.
Stepping	Holding the infant upright with the feet touching a surface results in stepping movements.
Sucking	Placing an object in the mouth results in sucking.

FIGURE 2-20
Four reflexes present at birth.

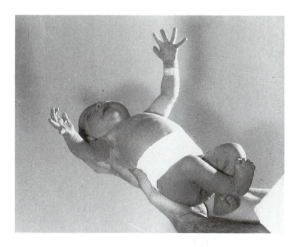

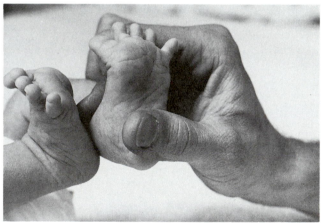

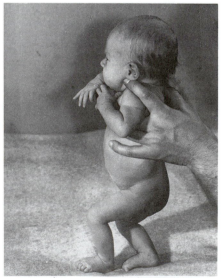

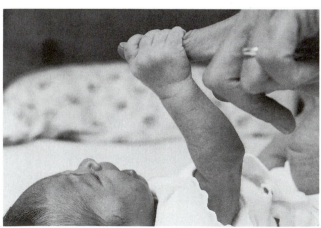

REFLEXIVE MOTOR BEHAVIOR. Newborns cannot support their heads, voluntarily grasp objects, or hold up their feet. However, neonatal behavior is rich in reflexes: Close to 100 reflexes have been described at one time or another (see Table 2-4 and Figure 2-20). Some are directly related to vital functions, such as breathing, blinking, sneezing, sucking, swallowing, and rooting. Postural reflexes help maintain the orientation of the body in space (Capute et al., 1978). Primitive reflexes, such as the Moro, Babinski, and grasp reflexes, seem to have little purpose, although researchers speculate that they may be left over from evolution.

A substantial number of the neonatal reflexes persist into adulthood, but many of the postural and primitive reflexes seem to disappear during the first year. Their appearance, strength, and disappearance at specific times are signs of the nervous system's functioning.

SENSORY AND LEARNING CAPACITY. In order to behave at all, the neonate must be able to sense the environment. It has been difficult to determine the quality of early sensory abilities because neonates obviously cannot tell us about their experiences. However, newer research methods confirm that all the basic senses are operating at some level at birth. The world outside the uterus is immediately seen, heard, smelled, tasted, and felt. And soon after birth infants show some capacity to learn—that is, to change because of experience. Within a few months their behavioral repertoire increases remarkably in size and complexity. (In Chapter 3 we look at these early sensory and learning processes in detail.)

STATES OF CONSCIOUSNESS. Neonatal behavior has been classified according to levels of consciousness; these levels include sleep states, drowsiness, alert activity, waking activity, and crying (Brazelton, 1973). Such states of consciousness, described in Table 2–5, depend heavily on biological variables such as hunger and the sleep-awake cycle. The amount of time spent in each state varies with individuals and changes with age.

One of the most obvious characteristics of newborns is that they sleep a great deal, but each sleep session is for a relatively short period of time. This, however, gradually changes. For example, newborns sleep for about 17 hours a day, but 3- to 5-year-olds sleep about 11 hours a day. As babies

---

TABLE 2-5
Levels of Consciousness in Infancy

Deep sleep	Eyes closed, no body movement except occasional startles; even breathing
Light sleep (REM)	Eyes closed but rapid eye movements evident, random body and facial movements, irregular breathing
Drowsiness	Eyes open or closed but when open they are glazed, variable activity, breathing irregular
Quiet alert	Eyes open and brightly fixating external stimuli, little movement, breathing somewhat variable
Active alert	Eyes open, very active motor movements with some fussiness, irregular breathing
Crying	Crying with eyes open or closed, motor activity, irregular breathing, little attention to external environment

Source: Adapted from Brazelton, 1973.

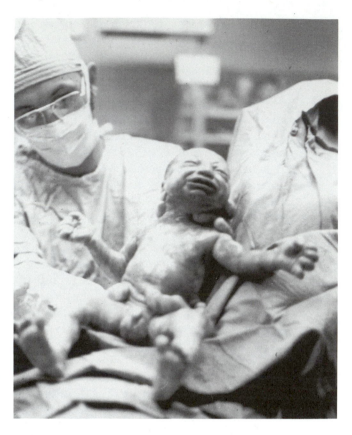

FIGURE 2-21
A newborn in the alert, inactive state. This infant appears to be focusing intently on a source of stimulation.

develop, they sleep less often but for longer periods, with the longest period at night, much to everyone's delight. From birth to about 3 to 5 years of age, the proportion of REM (rapid eye movement) sleep to nonREM sleep decreases from about 50 percent to 20 percent, which is the proportion found in adults (Anders, Carskadon, and Dement, 1980). During REM sleep in adults brainwaves register fast activity, heart and lung function increases, and dreaming occurs. Although the function of REM sleep is not well understood, lack of REM sleep has been associated with behavioral disturbances ranging from irritability to hallucinations.

As the amount of sleep decreases in young babies, alertness and wakefulness increase. The alert inactive state has been singled out as especially important in development. It is then that infants appear to inspect the environment deliberately, and thereby to learn more about the world (Figure 2-21). Alertness and activity increasingly become tied to the social environment. During this state, then, newborns start to travel the road that will lead them through the complexities of infant development, which we consider in depth in the next chapter.

Prematurity

The length of pregnancy is 40 weeks because gestation is calculated from the start of the last menstrual period, about 2 weeks prior to conception. Infants may be born before or after the usual term. When born before the thirty-eighth week, the neonate is preterm or premature; when born 42 or more weeks into gestation, it is postterm.

Premature babies have a higher risk of death than normal-term infants, and risk increases with the degree of prematurity. Premature babies do less well than full-term infants on measures of visual behavior, language development, and general development (Crnic, Ragozin, Greenberg, Robinson, and Basham, 1983; Rose, 1983). However, when premature and full-term infants are equated for *gestational age*—that is, time since conception rather than time since birth—they perform similarly on many measures of development (Allen and Alexander, 1990; Barrera, Rosenbaum, and Cunningham, 1987).

Low Birth Weight

Traditionally, the term *low birth weight* referred to babies who weighed 2500 grams (5.5 pounds) or less at birth. However, advances in prenatal and neonatal care have resulted in the survival of ever smaller babies. The terms *very low birth weight* and *extremely low birth weight* are now applied to babies weighing less than 1500 grams (3.3 pounds) and 1000 grams (2.2 pounds), respectively.

The prognosis for babies with extremely low birth weight is not good. Many do not survive, and those who do often suffer a major disability. In one study (Astbury, Orgill, Bajuk, and Yu, 1990) just 52 percent of the extremely low birth weight babies survived until discharge; of these survivors about one-third suffered major impairments that interfered with a regular lifestyle. Other investigators (Saigal et al., 1991) found that at age 8 years of age, a substantial percentage of extremely low birth weight children had deficits in cognitive, academic, and motor skills.

Much the same pattern is found for babies with very low birth weights. Survival rates are higher, but survivors often show deficits on tests of intelligence, scholastic achievement, and motor skill (Klein, Hack, and

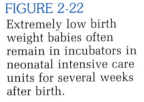

FIGURE 2-22
Extremely low birth weight babies often remain in incubators in neonatal intensive care units for several weeks after birth.

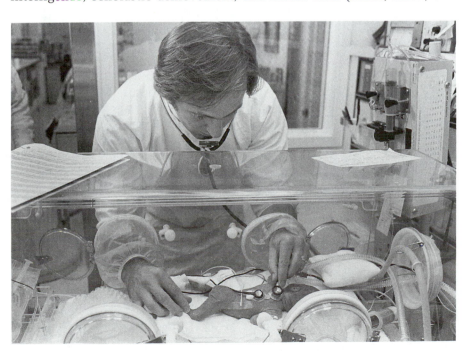

Breslau, 1989). For babies who weigh more than 1500 grams, the prospects are better. For them, and, to a lesser extent, for extremely low and very low birth weight infants, there is much variation in the developmental level eventually reached. Many will develop normally; only a small proportion of them differ from full-term children (Kopp and Krakow, 1983). So the important question is the following: For babies born prematurely and those with low birth weights, what determines the eventual outcome?

One factor is the extent of the birth and pregnancy complications. Nervous system damage, physical handicaps, and illness appear related to poor outcome (Holmes et al., 1982). The **continuum of reproductive casualty** refers to the fact that the risk of atypical development depends upon the number and severity of complications associated with pregnancy and birth (Knobloch and Pasamanick, 1974). For low birth weight infants with relatively few complications, the chances for normal development are much greater than for those with many complications (Landry, Chapieski, Fletcher, and Denson, 1988).

But there is more to the equation than just the number of pregnancy and birth complications. Children from poor socioeconomic environments have less chance to overcome these complications than those from middle-class environments. A striking example of the interplay of birth factors and environment emerged from a longitudinal investigation of 1,000 children living on the island of Kauai, Hawaii (Werner, 1980). These children were studied from the beginning of pregnancy to 18 years of age. Observations of 60 variables were recorded during pregnancy, birth, and the early period of life. Records were also kept of any problems the children displayed. In addition, information was obtained about the environments in which the children were reared, including economic status, parental intelligence, and family stability.

Birth complications were related to poor outcomes at ages 2, 10, and 18 years, but these outcomes were primarily because of the impact of poor environments. For example, at age 2, the children who were physically, intellectually, and socially the most retarded had experienced both the most severe birth complications and the poorest environments. In contrast, children growing up in middle-class homes who had suffered the most severe birth complications were almost comparable in intelligence to children with no birth complications who lived in low social class homes. Except for a small group of children with moderate or severe complications, the influence of social-class factors was stronger than the effects of birth complications (Werner, 1980).

Recognizing the strong impact of the environment, Sameroff and Chandler (1975) note that a **continuum of caretaking casualty** influences the eventual results of birth and pregnancy complications more than biological factors. This refers to the range of the quality of care infants and children receive, which is related to economic strain, medical attention, parenting skills, and social support systems. The continuum of reproductive casualty and the continuum of caretaking casualty both influence the outcome of development. Outcomes are most likely to be favorable for infants with few complications and excellent caretaking; the least favorable outcomes are associated with many complications and poor caretaking. The encouraging finding, however, is that excellent caretaking

Continuum of reproductive casualty The relation between the degree of pregnancy and birth complications and the degree of adverse developmental outcomes.

Continuum of caretaking casualty The relation between the quality of the caretaking environment and the quality of the child's development.

can often compensate for all but the most severe complications associated with pregnancy and birth.

SUMMARY

1. All human cells except the reproductive cells contain 23 pairs of chromosomes, whose functional units are called genes. Due to the specialized cell-division process of meiosis, the ova and sperm contain only 23 single chromosomes, one from each of the original pairs. At fertilization each parent thus contributes half the chromosome complement to the new organism, the fetus.

2. The basic genetic material resides in the genes in the form of deoxyribonucleic acid (DNA). DNA has the ability to replicate itself and to direct biochemical functioning and development.

3. Our understanding of genetic mechanisms began with Gregor Mendel's experiments with pea plants. Mendel suggested that each parent passes on one form (allele) of each gene, and that some forms are recessive and some dominant. When a characteristic is determined by one gene pair, the dominant form always displays itself. The recessive form displays itself only in the absence of the dominant form.

4. Some human characteristics are inherited from recessive, dominant, and sex-linked genes. Other characteristics, such as intelligence, are influenced by a combination of many genes (polygene inheritance). The major methods used to study these characteristics are family studies, twin studies, and adoption studies.

5. Genetic processes are implicated in many defects and diseases. Examples of hereditary diseases are PKU and Huntington's chorea. Some disorders caused by noninherited chromosome abnormalities are Down, Klinefelter's, Turner's, the XYY, and the "fragile" X syndromes.

6. Phenylketonuria (PKU) is an abnormal condition that is inherited when both parents transmit the defective gene. The mental retardation that commonly occurs is reduced or eliminated when children are put on special diets early in life.

7. The genes are in continuous interaction with the environment, so there is no one-to-one relationship between the gene complement (genotype) and the overt characteristics (phenotype) of the organism. Genetic effects are probably more powerful for some characteristics than for others. Characteristics strongly influenced by genes are said to be strongly canalized, and are those characteristics critical to survival. A genotype may be expressed in various environmental conditions; the broadest possible expression is called the range of reaction.

8. One theory of how genetic and environmental effects operate over the life span to shape development proposes three genotype-environment relations: passive, evocative, and active. As development progresses, evocative and active effects become more important than passive effects.

9. The joining of an ovum and a sperm cell results at conception in the formation of the zygote, which differentiates into all body parts during the prenatal period. When the sperm cell contains an X chromosome, a female organism results. When the sperm contains a Y chromosome, the new organism is male. On occasion, the zygote divides early and develops into identical twins. In other instances, two conceptions occur almost simultaneously, resulting in fraternal twins.

10.   For the 15 percent of couples who are infertile, pregnancy sometimes is achieved with drugs, artificial insemination, in vitro fertilization, or gamete intrafallopian transfer.

11.   Three periods of prenatal development are identified: zygote, embryo, and fetus. The period of the zygote begins at conception and ends during the second week of pregnancy, after implantation in the uterus. The second to eighth weeks constitute the period of the embryo; most body parts begin to develop during this time. The fetal period is from the eighth week to birth; it is characterized primarily by refinement and growth of existing structures.

12.   Influences on prenatal development include maternal age, diet, stress, the Rh factor, and specific teratogens, agents, or conditions that may result in abnormalities in the child. Among the major categories of teratogens are maternal disease, drugs, and environmental hazards.

13.   Prenatal diagnosis is helpful in identifying disorders in the developing fetus. Common procedures for all pregnant women are ultrasound and blood testing for alpha-fetoprotein; for women over 35 or those at risk for genetic disorders, amniocentesis and chorionic villus sampling are often used. Prospective parents use the results of prenatal diagnosis to decide whether to continue or to abort a pregnancy; in addition, treating a fetus afflicted with a disorder is still experimental, although becoming more common.

14.   Birth typically occurs at about 38 weeks after conception (40 weeks' gestation). Lightening, the movement of the fetus into the birth position, is soon followed by the three stages of labor. Birth is usually predictable and uncomplicated, but abnormal positioning of the fetus, anoxia, and the excessive use of anesthesia for the mother can cause complications.

15.   The medical condition and capacities of the neonate can be evaluated with the Apgar and Brazelton scales. Neonates display diverse reflexes, basic sensory and learning abilities, and various states of consciousness.

16.   Infants born prematurely or at low birth weights are at risk for a variety of problems. The greater the degree of birth and pregnancy complications, the more likely the eventual outcome will be poor. This relation between the developmental outcome and the degree of birth and pregnancy complications is referred to as the continuum of reproductive casualty. The quality of the child's rearing environment also influences developmental outcome; this is referred to as the continuum of caretaking casualty.

C·H·A·P·T·E·R 3

Infancy

Sensation Stimulation of the sensory receptors by physical energy from the internal and external environment.

Perception The selection, organization, and modification by the brain of specific input from the different sense organs.

The first year of life is the focus of an extraordinary amount of research. This may seem surprising: After all, most of us cannot recall our first year of life and have only vague memories of our first few years. But this is in fact the time when a great many later patterns are set. All major theories of development look at the early months and years of life as times of important psychological growth. Infants are surprisingly competent creatures, filled with skills that can be revealed with clever experimentation. Let's look at some of these skills that are the focus of this chapter.

▶   Perception is the infant's window on the world. What does the view look like? Is the infant's perceptual experience—through sight, sound, and touch, for example—organized like an adult's? Or are infants overwhelmed by a barrage of sensory information, and can they only make sense of bits and pieces of information? The first part of this chapter, devoted to the infant's perceptual processes, will provide answers to these questions.

▶   Parents talk to their babies, adorn their cribs with mobiles, and provide them with educational toys. A pregnant woman can even buy a belt with loudspeakers so that her fetus can listen to tapes (of speech, for example) in utero. Underlying these practices is a belief that these experiences influence development. That is, infants are thought to learn from these experiences—their behavior is changed due to these experiences. What kinds of learning occur in infancy? What factors aid infants' learning and what limit their learning? These questions are the focus of the second part of this chapter.

▶   Humans are "social animals," and the formation of the first social relationship is an exciting, emotional event. Between 6 and 9 months of age, infants form an intense relationship with their primary caretaker, usually the mother. What are the steps that lead to this relationship and what factors influence its nature? What are the consequences of an inadequate relationship? Research and theories that address these questions will be examined in the third part of this chapter.

▶   Even as infants, some children seem to gravitate naturally to people, whereas others prefer to play with objects. Some infants exhaust their parents because they have endless energy, attacking each day with limitless vigor; other babies are more subdued and spend their day in quieter activities. These differences in behavior can be so consistent that even young babies seem to have well-defined personalities. What are the dimensions of infant personality? How do they arise and how do they influence development during infancy? These questions will be examined in the fourth part of this chapter, which concerns the temperamental aspects of infancy.   ◀

PERCEPTUAL PROCESSES

Stimulation from the environment bombards us from the moment of birth. Two related processes, **sensation** and **perception**, enable us to receive stimulation and organize it. These terms are often confusing because they overlap in meaning. Sensation involves stimulation of the sensory receptors by physical energy from the internal and external environment. The retina of the eye, for example, reacts to light and translates this information into nerve impulses. The nerve impulses are transmitted to the brain, which reacts to the stimulation in various ways. It is at this point that perception is said to occur. The brain may select, organize, and modify sensory input. It integrates the impulses from the different sense organs and compares the impulses with previous input. In a way, then, sensation and perception are actually names for different points in a complex process of information gathering that ultimately leads to "knowing."

The study of perception in children and adults typically involves presenting the individuals with stimuli and asking them to respond in some way—for example, by pressing a button or answering questions. Because these methods obviously cannot be used with infants, researchers have had to devise other ways to collect data. Some of these methods rely on physiological responses such as heart rate and dilation of the pupils of the eyes. Other research methods rely on simple motor behaviors that infants can perform, such as head turning, sucking, and fixating the eyes on objects.

Researchers using techniques like these have discovered that infants' perceptual skills are quite remarkable. In virtually every sensory modality, infants are surprisingly capable of organizing and interpreting sensory information. Let's examine infants' perceptual processes in different sensory modes, beginning with the "chemical senses" of smell and taste.

Smell and Taste

The sense of smell, or **olfaction**, appears to be one of the most highly developed senses in the newborn (Rovee, Cohen, and Shlapack, 1975). In fact, premature babies as young as 28 weeks of age may be able to detect odors (Sarnat, 1978). Infant discrimination of odors was tested in a series of investigations in which the babies were placed in a special apparatus, a stabilimeter, which measures activity level and breathing (Figure 3-1). A cotton swab saturated with an odorant was then placed beneath their nostrils, and changes in activity and breathing were taken as measures of the ability to detect the odor of various substances. Neonates of about 1 to 3 days of age discriminated the four odors used. They also habituated— that is, they responded more weakly to repeated presentations (Engen, Lipsitt, and Kaye, 1963; Lipsitt, Engen, and Kaye, 1963). By about a week after birth, infants may be able to detect their mothers by the sense of smell (MacFarland, 1975). They also seem able to localize odors in space, because they turn away from aversive odors (Rieser, Yonas, and Wikner, 1976).

Displeasure and pleasure can be seen in another way—by facial expression (Steiner, 1979). Newborns were tested with food-related odors that had been rated as pleasant or unpleasant by adults. Although the infants had had no contact with food, they reacted to the odors rated as pleasant with a relaxed retraction of the lips, sucking, and licking. Their reactions to the unpleasant odors included depression of the corners of the mouth, arching of the lips, and spitting and salivation. Similarly,

Olfaction The sense of smell.

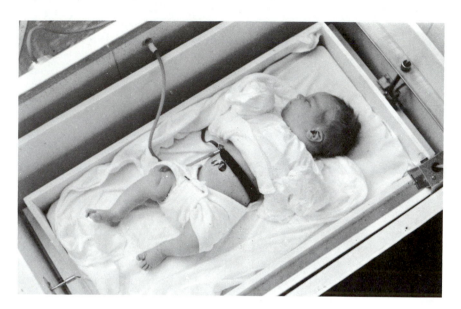

FIGURE 3-1
This neonate is being tested in a stabilimeter, which is sensitive to activity level. The apparatus around the abdomen is a pneumograph, which measures breathing.

infants orient in the direction of the breast odor of a nursing woman, but they turn away from the odor of that same woman's armpit and from the breast odor of another woman who is not nursing (Makin and Porter, 1989).

Smell perception undergoes some further development after infancy, but by 6 years of age sensitivity to odors is well developed and remains relatively stable for much of the life span (McCartney, 1968; Rovee, Cohen, and Shlapack, 1975).

Like the sense of smell, taste perception exists at birth or prior to birth. The receptors for taste, found primarily on the tongue but also in other parts of the mouth and in the throat, are present early in prenatal development. Quite possibly the fetus is sensitive to the taste of amniotic fluid, which is bitter and salty. There is no doubt that the infant is able to distinguish the basic four tastes of salty, sour, bitter, and sweet, and that the level of sensitivity is quite high (Crook, 1987). Furthermore, a distinct preference for sweet has been demonstrated. Even when presented with a substance that is more nutritious but less sweet, infants prefer the sweeter substance (Bower, 1977). They react to sweetness by eager sucking, licking the upper lip, and showing an expression that resembles a smile (Steiner, 1979). Newborns appear to perceive saltiness somewhat neutrally or with displeasure, and they display definite displeasure at bitter and sour substances (Rosenstein and Oster, 1988).

Taken together, the infant's preferences for odors and taste have obvious survival value. Infants prefer odors and tastes associated with feeding, which simplifies the transition to a new source of nutrients in the first days of life.

Touch and Pain

Humans respond to tactile stimulation early in life (Reisman, 1987). Premature infants respond to touch with fanning of the toes, slight motor responses, and waking from half-sleep. Touching various areas of the

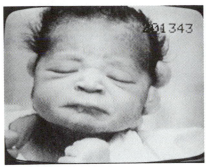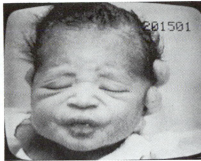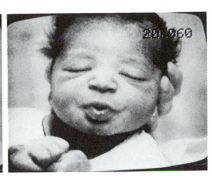

FIGURE 3-2
Infants respond distinctively to different tastes.

neonate's body produces many of the reflexes discussed in Chapter 2, including the Babinski, the grasp, and the rooting reflexes.

Perception of pain is probably not well developed at birth, but it rapidly improves. Fewer pinpricks and less electric shock are required to arouse a 5-day-old infant than a neonate (Lipsitt and Levy, 1959; Spears and Hohle, 1967). Babies only a few days old also appear to experience pain from circumcision. Their heart rates change and they cry in a manner indicating the physiological stress associated with pain: Compared with cries not associated with pain, the pain cry is higher pitched and much briefer (Porter, Porges, and Marshall, 1988).

Tactile stimulation is important early in life as a means of signaling contact with the mother. As young children develop sufficient motor ability to handle objects and move within their surroundings, they use tactile information to learn about the world, distinguishing hard floor from soft carpet and round balls from square blocks.

Hearing

Very young infants respond to sound with a variety of reactions—sudden startles, muscle changes, breathing disruptions, eye blinking, and changes in heart rate and activity level. These responses make it clear that infants can hear, but scientists have just begun to understand the specifics of infant hearing. Sensitivity to sound increases during infancy. Adults can hear some faint sounds that infants cannot, particularly if the sounds are low pitched (Trehub, Schneider, Thorpe, and Judge, 1991). Infants are able to discriminate different pitches, and by 6 months of age, their skill rivals that of adults (Spetner and Olsho, 1990). Infants can also discriminate sounds of different duration: Six-month-olds can detect a sound that is only 20 milliseconds (one-fiftieth of a second) briefer than a sound they have been hearing previously (Morrongiello and Trehub, 1987).

We can summarize all of these accomplishments by saying that hearing is effective at birth and becomes remarkably sensitive in the first few months after birth. This advanced skill should not be too surprising: As we'll see in Chapter 5, infants begin to understand speech by their first birthday, which requires a highly sophisticated hearing system.

Another important function of sound is to help us locate objects.

Infants will turn their eyes in the direction of a source of sound (Butterworth and Castillo, 1976), although they seem unable to locate the exact position (Bower, 1974). In several experiments, Morrongiello and her colleagues (Morrongiello, 1988; Morrongiello, Fenwick, and Chance, 1990) have shown that localization skill improves rapidly in the first 6 months after birth; thereafter skill continues to improve, but more slowly. In the experiments, infants were seated in a semicircle of loudspeakers that were not visible in the darkened room. Sounds were presented and the infants' responses were videotaped. With infants 8 weeks of age, the smallest change in sound location that would consistently cause infants to look in a new direction was 27 degrees; this dropped to 17 degrees at 24 weeks and 4 degrees at 18 months.

Infants also use sound to determine the distance of an object. Clifton, Perris, and Bullinger (1991) first showed an attractive rattle to 7-month-olds, then turned off the lights and shook the rattle. If the rattle was placed about 6 inches away, infants typically would reach toward the rattle; if it were placed about 2 feet away, infants would not reach. Infants apparently used sound to distinguish near objects, which they could reach, from far objects, which they could not. Thus, by the middle of the first year, infants are reasonably able to use sound to determine both an object's direction and distance.

Seeing the World

In many ways, vision may be considered our most important sense. Adults report that they value their eyesight more than any of their other senses. They relate vision to comprehension by saying "I see what you mean." Visual stimulation is an extremely important source of contact between infants and the environment. Indeed, whenever they are awake, infants seem to be preoccupied with looking at the broad environment or examining particular parts of it. No reinforcement is needed for this activity other than sufficiently interesting sights (Fantz, 1969). Perhaps for these reasons, more research has been devoted to vision than to any other perceptual process.

Until a few decades ago, newborns were believed to be incapable of processing visual information meaningfully. Today we know that the visual system is relatively well developed at birth and that the neonate demonstrates considerable visual ability. Every structure in the visual system undergoes some early postnatal change, however (Hickey and Peduzzi, 1987). Cells in the retina shift their location, the optic nerve completes myelination, and connections between neurons in the visual cortex grow dramatically in number. It would be surprising not to see parallel growth in visual capacities.

Seeing Patterns

Infants respond to brightness immediately after birth. The newborn is also sensitive to movement. A few days after birth babies are able to track some

Visual acuity The ability of individuals to detect both small stimuli and small details of large visual patterns.

Optokinetic nystagmus An involuntary sideways movement of the eye in response to moving stimuli.

moving objects, although this response is uneven and focus is easily lost. These responses tell us that infants can see, but they give no insights into the clarity of what they see. Perhaps infants see objects as undifferentiated "blobs." The degree of detail that infants see is their **visual acuity**.

An adult's acuity can be evaluated by asking the individual to identify letters or patterns on charts. An adult's acuity is the smallest pattern that can be identified consistently. One way that this technique has been adapted for infants takes advantage of the involuntary sideward movements of the eyes in response to moving stimuli, known as **optokinetic nystagmus**. When infants are presented with a striped pattern, for example, sideward movements of the eyes occur only when the babies detect the stripes. The width of the spaces between the stripes can then be taken as a measure of visual acuity: The more narrow the stripe that elicits optokinetic nystagmus, the better the acuity. Such measurements show that young infants see at 20 feet what adults normally see at 200 to 400 feet; between 6 months and 1 year of age, an infant's acuity approaches that of an adult with normal vision (Banks and Dannemiller, 1987).

Acuity indicates the resolving power of vision—how clearly objects can be seen. However, perceiving patterns also involves several higher-order properties. For example, people distinguish figure from background and we recognize a pattern based on the organization of elements (see Figure 3-3). Many of these higher-order properties emerge in the first few months after birth. Psychologists have discovered a regular developmental progression in the way that patterns are scanned. At first infants are captivated with particular individual features of objects or patterns. This has been revealed by studies in which simple geometric figures are displayed to the infant, while a camera records the scanning of the infant's eyes. Newborns and 1-month-olds tend to look at a single prominent feature (Bronson, 1991). This is often an edge of the figure, where contrast (that is, contour) is the highest. However, 2- and 4-month-olds begin to scan the interior of the pattern as well, and generally distribute their scanning more evenly over the entire object (Aslin, 1987).

Other investigators have traced the development of rules of perceptual grouping. When adults view the line segments shown in Figure 3-3, they "see" a square. Apparently, 3-month-olds do as well: If 3-month-olds are shown a pattern like the one in Figure 3-3, except that one segment has been moved so that it is no longer aligned, they are likely to gaze at the displaced line. This extra attention must reflect the perception by the infant that the misplaced line segment distorts the pattern, because the segment itself is identical to all the others in the pattern (van Giffen and Haith, 1984).

Even more impressive evidence that young infants organize their perception of patterns comes from a study by Ghim (1990). For six familiarization trials, infants were shown a square. Two test trials followed, using the stimuli shown in Figure 3-4. These figures are composed of the same elements, but only the stimulus labeled A gives rise to the subjective experience of seeing a square. When pattern A was paired with the other stimuli shown in Figure 3-4, 3-month-olds typically looked longer at stimuli B, C, and D. Apparently, they experienced the square created from the

FIGURE 3-3

Because of perceptual grouping, we perceive these disconnected line segments to be a square.

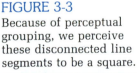
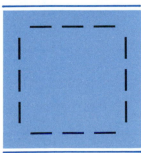

FIGURE 3-4

Although all the patterns are made up of the same elements, only pattern A gives rise to the experience of seeing a square.

(From H. Ghim, "Evidence for perceptual organization in infants: Perception of subjective contours by young infants," in Infant Behavior and Development, 13, 1990, 221–248, fig. 1. Reprinted by permission of Ablex Publishing Corporation.)

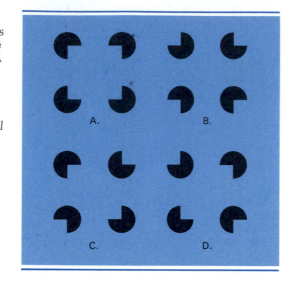

elements in pattern A, making this seem more familiar, which caused them to look more at the relatively unfamiliar patterns—B, C, and D.

The human face is one pattern that is particularly salient and important to infants. Today we know that perception of the face follows the general course of perceptual growth (Aslin, 1987). Newborns readily look at faces, presumably because they are attracted to stimuli that move (the eyes and mouth) and have dark and light contrast. At first infants scan the outer edges of the face and fixate the eyes and other points of contrast. By 2 months of age they focus more on the interior parts of the face while attending to the eyes as well (Figure 3-5). At about 3 months of age, infants begin to perceive the face as a unique grouping of elements: Dannemiller and Stephens (1988) found that when face and nonface stimuli were matched for a number of important variables (for example, the amount of black/white contrast or the size and number of elements), 1 1/2-month-olds

FIGURE 3-5

At first infants tend to scan the periphery of faces and points of contrast. They soon shift their interest more to the interior of the face.

(Adapted from P. Salapatek, "Pattern perception in early infancy," in L. B. Cohen and P. Salapatek (Eds.), Infant Perception: From Sensation to Cognition, Vol. 1. New York: Academic Press, 1975.)

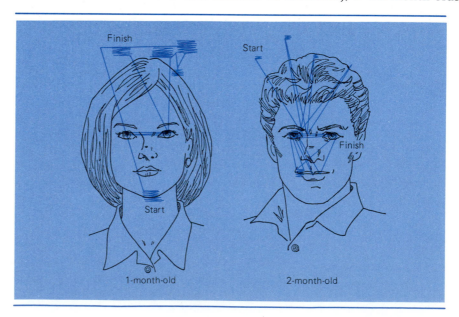

Infancy

looked at face and nonface stimuli equally; however, at 3 months, infants looked much longer at the faces, suggesting that infants recognized this configuration of elements as being facelike.

This sequence has broad implications. Because the face is a source of social and emotional information, it is important in the development of various interactions that infants have with adults. Later in this chapter, we will explore how infants' perceptions influence their social and emotional development.

Color

Color is one of the most interesting aspects of our visual experience. But color is more than simply aesthetically pleasing; color can aid our perception. Infants could use color of hair and eyes, for example, to help to determine if a face is familiar.

The basis of color perception is the wavelength of light. The retina consists of three types of color-sensitive receptors, called **cones**, each of which is sensitive to a specific range of wavelengths of light.

Color vision is limited in newborns, but it develops rapidly. Newborns apparently cannot distinguish grey from blue, but 1-month-olds can (Maurer and Adams, 1987). This result indicates the development of a functioning cone that is sensitive to short-wavelength light (blues). One-month-olds can also discriminate green from red, which implies that the medium- and long-wavelength cones are functioning; however, 1-month-olds do not discriminate yellow from green or yellow from red, which may indicate cones that are not yet fully functional or immaturities in the neural circuitry that links the cones together (Adams, 1989).

By 2 to 3 months of age, an infant's color perception is apparently quite similar to that of mature individuals (Teller and Bornstein, 1987). In particular, infants, like adults, tend to see categories of color. For example, if a yellow light's wavelength is gradually increased, it will suddenly be perceived as a shade of red rather than as a shade of yellow. Perception of color as categories has been demonstrated by showing infants lights of wavelengths that correspond to what adults see as blue, green, yellow, and red. Infants repeatedly presented with one wavelength will gradually stop looking at the light, as if bored with it. For instance, infants might be repeatedly shown a light with a wavelength of 600 nanometers (billionths of a meter), which adults judge to be yellow. A different light is then presented, one that adults judge to be from the same yellow color category as the initial light: a light with a wavelength of 580 nanometers, which adults also consider yellow. By 3 months of age, infants respond to such a light as if it were a familiar color—they look at it about the same amount as they look at the 600-nanometer light. If, instead, the wavelength of light is changed by the same amount but comes from a new adult color category—to 620 nanometers, which adults judge to be red—the infants' amount of looking increases significantly. These responses indicate that infants view the stimuli much as adults would, that is, they see categories of color (Teller and Bornstein, 1987).

Cones Receptors in the retina of the eye that are sensitive to color.

One implication of these findings is that human categorization of colors is not the result of language or naming systems. Instead, an innate tendency to perceive color categories gives rise to language categories for color.

Depth Perception

Humans experience the environment as having three dimensions despite the fact that the source of visual experience—the retina—is only two dimensional. This means that the third dimension, depth, must be constructed. Many years ago it was determined that perception of depth is almost as accurate in 4-year-olds as in adults (Updegraff, 1930). Are infants also able to extract information about depth from their visual experience?

To investigate the question, Eleanor Gibson and Richard Walk conducted some classic experiments using a special experimental setup, which they called the visual cliff. The "cliff," shown in Figure 3-6, was constructed from a heavy sheet of glass with a platform in the center that is raised slightly above the surface of the glass. The center platform, covered with a patterned material, was wide enough to hold the baby when it is creeping. The "shallow" side of the cliff was created by fastening the same patterned material directly beneath the glass on one side of the platform. The illusion of depth was created on the other, "deep" side of the platform by placing the material several feet below the glass. The infant's mother stood at either the deep or the shallow side and beckoned to the child to come to her (Gibson and Walk, 1960; Walk and Gibson, 1961).

Gibson and Walk began by testing 36 infants between $6\frac{1}{2}$ and 14 months of age. The results were quite clear: Twenty-seven of the infants were willing to crawl off the center onto the shallow side, but only three ventured into the deep area. A number of infants actually crawled away from their mothers when called from the deep side; others cried, presumably because it appeared to them that it was not possible to reach their mothers without crossing the brink. Clearly, infants old enough to crawl display perception of depth.

Are younger infants capable of perceiving depth? Campos, Langer, and Krowitz (1970) devised a measure that did not require locomotive abilities and thus could be used with younger infants. The investigators simply placed 44- to 115-day-old infants on either the shallow or the deep side of the visual-cliff apparatus and measured changes in heart rates. The study showed that infants as young as 2 months of age reacted differently to the sides of the cliff.

Although studies of infants with the visual cliff suggest that infants perceive depth, they provide little information about how infants go about it. More recent experimentation has revealed that by age 7 months, infants rely upon most of the same major types of cues to depth that adults use to infer depth. **Binocular cues** to depth are those associated with the fact that the two eyes receive slightly different images of the same object. The disparity is greatest for an object that is very close, and this disparity gets smaller as objects become more distant. By 4 months of age, many infants

Binocular cues Cues to depth perception that involve comparison of the visual images in both eyes.

Pictorial cues Cues to depth perception provided by stimuli.

Linear perspective A cue to depth perception in which distant objects take up less space in the visual field.

Texture gradient A cue to depth perception conveyed by the fact that texture is more dense for distant objects.

Kinetic cues Cues to depth perception that are derived from the movement of objects.

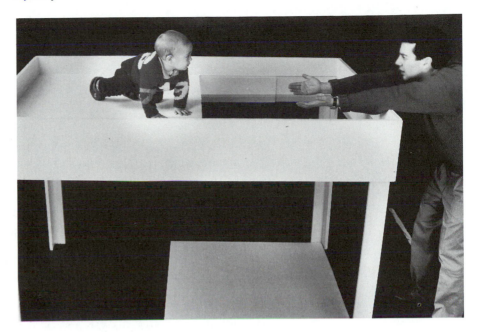

FIGURE 3-6

An infant on the visual cliff crawls to his parent across the "shallow" side but refuses to do so on the "deep" side, even though he has tactual evidence that the cliff is solid.

FIGURE 3-7

The toys in the photograph are actually the same distance from the infant, but the lower stimulus toy appears closer because linear perspective and texture gradient convey depth. By 7 months of age, infants reach for the toy that appears closer. This indicates their use of linear perspective and texture gradient to infer depth.

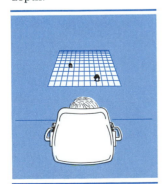

use binocular cues to determine depth; by 6 months, most do (Yonas and Owsley, 1987).

Pictorial cues have long been used by artists to convey depth. The familiar example of a picture of railroad tracks receding into the horizon provides two examples. **Linear perspective** is illustrated by the lines depicting the rails converging on a single point on the horizon. **Texture gradient** is illustrated by the horizontal lines depicting the ties under the rails, which are first spaced widely apart but gradually become closer together until they finally blur together as they near the horizon of the picture.

Yonas and his colleagues (Arterberry, Yonas, and Bensen, 1989) have shown that 7-month-olds use these cues to depth. In their procedure, which is shown in Figure 3-7, two toys appeared to be resting on a checkered surface that contained both linear perspective and texture gradient as cues to depth. In fact, the checkered surface was a flat photograph. Infants were tested with one eye covered so that binocular cues could not be used. Most 7-month-olds reached for the toy that appeared closer, suggesting that they used linear perspective and texture gradient to infer depth. In contrast, 5-month-olds reached for the two toys equally often.

Kinetic cues represent the third category of information about depth. The key to all kinetic cues is motion: When an object moves, the retinal images of it change, and these changing images can provide clues to depth. For example, if a mother moves toward her infant, the retinal images of the mother become larger; this change is interpreted to mean that the mother is getting closer. Similarly, when objects pass one another, one may momentarily obscure the other; the change is interpreted to mean that the obscured object is farther away. By 5 months of age, infants are able to use kinetic cues like these to infer depth (Craton and Yonas, 1988).

Interaction of the Perceptual Systems

So far we have discussed the perceptual systems as independent systems. But perception frequently involves the simultaneous use of more than one system. For example, eye-hand coordination requires the interaction of vision and touch; learning to read aloud requires the interaction of vision and hearing.

VISION AND TOUCH. These two perceptual systems appear to be integrated in young infants (Rose and Ruff, 1987). Vision-touch interaction has been investigated by having children explore objects with one perceptual system, and by then determining whether the information acquired can be transferred to the other perceptual system. For example, babies who are allowed to explore objects tactually later choose those objects when allowed visually to explore several objects without touching them. This kind of transfer occurs by at least 6 months of age, depending on the characteristics of the objects and the time permitted for exploration (Rose and Orlian, 1991).

Vision and touch are sometimes integrated in even younger infants. In one study (Gibson and Walker, 1984), 1-month-olds were allowed to explore either soft or hard plastic objects with their mouths, without seeing the objects. They were then shown objects that looked identical to the original ones; one of the objects could be squeezed (it thus "looked" soft), but the other could not be squeezed (thus "looking" hard). Infants looked longer at the object that they had not mouthed previously. Infants apparently could relate what they had mouthed (soft or hard) to what they saw.

Both visual and tactual exploration of objects becomes more systematic with age. Thus, it might be expected that as children age they take in more information, which in turn leads to better recognition and transfer. In fact, intersensory recognition does improve throughout the preschool years (Bryant, 1974).

VISION AND HEARING. Vision and hearing, too, seem to be integrated at birth; when infants hear sounds, they orient their eyes in the direction from which the sounds come. Aronson and Rosenbloom (1971) examined the reactions of 3-week-old babies to a situation in which their usual expectations for sound were not met. Mothers and their infants were positioned on opposite sides of a window, and the mothers spoke to the infants through microphones. Their voices were then displaced so that the sounds seemed to come from a few feet to the right or left of the mothers. The infants were definitely disturbed by the situation. Young infants oriented their eyes midway between the location of their mother's mouth and the source of the sounds, whereas older infants looked at their mothers but turned their heads to better pick up the sounds (Aronson and Dunkel, cited in Bower, 1974). The older babies appeared able to deal with the two perceptual systems as independent of each other.

Young babies can also link sound and vision according to synchrony. Spelke (1979) simultaneously showed 4-month-olds a film of a toy monkey and another film of a toy donkey. Each toy animal bounced up and down, but at a different rate. A sound track that matched the rhythm of one of

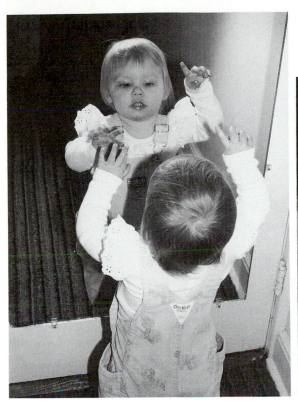
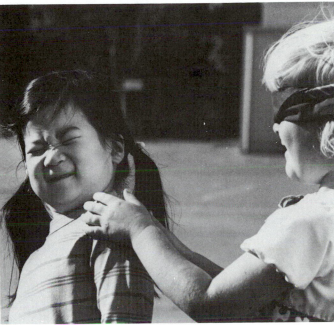

FIGURE 3-8
Intersensory perception involves translating information from one sense modality into another.

the animals was also played along with the films. The infants looked longer at the toy animals whose actions were synchronized with the sound track. They apparently were able to identify the way in which the visual information matched the auditory information. Several studies of this sort indicate that 4-month-olds are able to unite auditory and visual information under a number of different conditions (Bahrick, 1988; Spelke, 1987).

Integration of auditory and visual information at a more abstract level has been reported in one study (Wagner, Winner, Cicchetti, and Gardner, 1981). The infants in this research, most of whom were 9 to 13 months old, were presented with pairs of visual and auditory stimuli that matched each other along abstract dimensions. For example, a broken line/continuous line (the visual pair) was matched with a pulsing tone/continuous tone (the auditory pair). Or an arrow pointing up/arrow pointing down (the visual stimuli) was matched with an ascending tone/descending tone (the auditory pair). Using a complex experimental design, the researchers were able to determine whether the infants perceived similarity between the matching visual and auditory stimuli. For three of the eight stimuli sets, the infants did so. The ability is quite remarkable because infants typically do not experience the events to which they were experimentally exposed.

The work described in this section indicates that the perceptual abilities of young infants are geared for rapid and active interaction with the environment. We can see that infants are well equipped to interpret experiences. But what is the impact of the experiences that infants have? Answers to this question are found in the study of infant learning. We turn now to this aspect of infant functioning.

LEARNING: THE ABILITY TO BENEFIT FROM EXPERIENCE

Humans learn from experience from the very first week of life. This learning occurs in many forms, which we will examine in the next several pages. However, common to all forms is that the infant's behavior is changed as a result of exposure to stimuli.

Habituation

When presented a strong or interesting stimulus, an individual startles reflexively and orients to the stimulus. That is, he or she moves rapidly, fixates the eyes on the object, and shows physiological changes in heart rate and brain-wave patterns. After repeated presentation of the stimulus, these responses diminish and eventually disappear. This process of "getting used to" a stimulus is called **habituation**. It is considered a type of learning because responses are changed by experience with environmental stimulation.

Habituation Diminished responding that occurs after repeated presentation of the same stimulus.

Habituation has been shown in newborn infants. Researchers discovered, for example, that when a simple geometric figure such as a triangle or square was shown, 3-day-olds looked at it for about 20 seconds on the first presentation but for less than 10 seconds by the fourth presentation (Slater, Morison, and Rose, 1984). Similarly, in another study it was found that when speech was played through one of two loudspeakers

FIGURE 3-9
This infant has habituated to the sounds in the environment.

placed to an infant's left or right, most newborns would, on first hearing, turn their head toward the source of the speech; after several trials, they no longer turned their heads (Zelazo et al., 1989). In both studies, newborns first oriented to the novel stimulus, then gradually attended to it less.

Habituation is a simple form of learning, yet one that is very useful, particularly to infants. Responding to stimuli takes energy and effort, which is wasted if the stimuli are not biologically important. Habituation means that infants are less likely to waste energy on biologically nonsignificant stimuli (Rovee-Collier, 1987). This becomes clear if we consider the infant whose family lives near a busy highway. When the newborn first arrives home from the hospital, a passing truck or bus will probably cause the infant to startle and to cry, perhaps disrupting the infant's feeding. As time passes, the infant gets used to the loud noise of the vehicles and soon seems not to notice it; the infant's energy is no longer diverted from biologically important events like feeding.

Classical Conditioning

Classical conditioning A form of learning in which, through paired presentation with an unconditioned stimulus, a neutral stimulus elicits the response associated with that unconditioned stimulus.

Unconditioned response (UR) A reflexive response to a stimulus.

Conditioned response (CR) A response to a conditioned stimulus that is acquired through pairing of that stimulus with an unconditioned stimulus.

Conditioned stimulus (CS) A stimulus that, when paired with an unconditioned stimulus, comes to elicit a conditioned response.

Unconditioned stimulus (US) A stimulus that reflexively elicits an unconditioned response.

Contingency An expectation that, given presentation of a conditioned stimulus, the unconditioned stimulus will follow.

Like habituation, classical conditioning involves a change in the situations in which a particular reflexive or innate response will occur. The difference is that in habituation the individual stops responding to situations that had previously elicited the response; in **classical conditioning**, the individual begins to respond to situations that had not previously elicited the response. Thus, in a fundamental way, classical conditioning is a more active learning process than is habituation.

Classical conditioning was first revealed in Ivan Petrovich Pavlov's well-known experiments with dogs. He placed meat powder into the mouths of dogs and then measured the flow of the dog's digestive juices. During the course of this work, the dogs often appeared to anticipate the food, so that salivary flow began even before any meat powder had been introduced. Pavlov reasoned that since untrained dogs salivated when meat powder was placed on their tongues, salivation was a natural or **unconditioned response (UR)**. But salivation that came to be elicited by the *sight* of the food alone had to be acquired by some form of experience and was thus a learned or **conditioned response (CR)**.

This reasoning led Pavlov to investigate how conditioned responses are formed. He presented the dogs with the sound of a tone (**conditioned stimulus**, or **CS**), followed in a few seconds by food (**unconditioned stimulus**, or **US**). After a number of presentations, saliva was secreted before the meat powder was presented, apparently in response to the CS. This salivation was the CR.

Pavlov viewed classical conditioning as a mechanical process of forming associations between stimuli (CS and US) that occurred together in time. In modern theories (for example, Pearce and Hall, 1980), however, conditioning is a process in which subjects learn **contingencies** between the CS and US. That is, the CS serves as a cue or signal that the US will follow, and subjects form expectations that the US will appear based upon presentation of the CS.

The importance of classical conditioning in human development is that this form of learning operates over a wide variety of stimuli and responses. During infancy, it may have particular significance during feeding: Most of the infant behaviors that are involved in feeding, such as turning one's head to acquire food, sucking to consume food, or secreting saliva to aid digestion, can be classically conditioned in very young babies (Rovee-Collier, 1987).

Illustrative is research by Blass, Ganchrow, and Steiner (1984), who tested 1- to 2-day-olds. The US was a solution of sucrose, which, when squirted into a newborn's mouth, elicits a UR of sucking. The CS consisted of an experimenter lightly stroking the infant's forehead; this was chosen as a CS because although mothers in many species stroke their infants' faces while feeding, stroking does not spontaneously elicit sucking. For newborns in a conditioning group, the experimenter stroked the infant for 10 seconds, after which sucrose was squirted into the infant's mouth for 10 seconds. For newborns in a control group, stroking the forehead and sucrose were not paired systematically. The key finding was that in the 10 seconds of stroking, infants in the conditioning group sucked three times more often than infants in the control condition; presentation of the CS (stroking) led infants in the conditioning group to expect the US (sucrose).

This interpretation was supported by the infants' behavior during an **extinction** phase in which the CS was presented but the US did not follow: Almost all the newborns in the conditioning group cried, compared with no infants in the control group. Crying seemed to reflect the infants' displeasure that their expectations established by presentation of the CS had been violated.

More direct evidence that infants form expectations comes from work by Haith and his colleagues (for example, Canfield and Haith, 1991). Simple pictures were presented briefly in a predictable sequence: Two pictures were presented in succession on the left, followed by one picture to the right, followed by two more pictures to the left, and so on. In the 1 second between pictures, even 2-month-olds looked in the location where they expected the next picture to appear (for example, looking to the right after two pictures had appeared on the left).

Classical conditioning is not always obtained with infants. The state of the infant—that is, the infant's drowsiness or alertness—plays a role; so does the length of time between the presentation of the CS and the US, with younger infants requiring a longer time interval than older infants (Little, Lipsitt, and Rovee-Collier, 1984).

A growing body of research also suggests that certain stimuli and responses may be conditioned or associated more easily than others. For example, young babies can be conditioned readily when the conditioning task involves feeding. This ease of learning or **preparedness** to learn is considered a biologically determined species difference that is important to adaptation to the environment (Fitzgerald and Brackbill, 1976). So sucking and head turning in the human infant, both of which are likely to be adaptive, are relatively easily conditioned.

In contrast to rapid conditioning with feeding, the conditioning of

Extinction The gradual diminution of a conditioned response, resulting in the eventual elimination of the response.

Preparedness The idea that members of a species are genetically influenced to learn certain responses more readily than other responses.

aversive or noxious events has been extremely difficult to demonstrate in young infants. This difficulty may stem from the possibility that such learning is not terribly useful to young infants:

> In primitive hunter-gatherer societies, human infants are thought to have remained in continuous physical contact with an adult during their first year (Konner, 1977). Under these circumstances, there would have been no selection pressures for the very young to anticipate noxious events. . . . In effect, then, the classical aversive conditioning paradigm does not simulate a significant problem that very young infants in natural circumstances must solve. (Rovee-Collier, 1987, p. 115)

Responses to noxious stimuli, such as electric shock or loud noises, can be conditioned in older infants. In many species, the youngest age at which such conditioning can be readily demonstrated coincides with the age when infants begin to move independently—a time when awareness of aversive events assumes much greater survival value (Rovee-Collier, 1987).

Operant Conditioning

Operant conditioning (or instrumental learning) focuses on the consequences that follow behavior. The pioneer investigator in this area was E. L. Thorndike. In a typical experiment, Thorndike (1898) placed a cat in a slatted cage with food located outside; escape led to a food reward. The cat had to perform a particular response, such as pulling a cord or pressing a lever, to open the door. Sooner or later, it "accidentally" performed the act and succeeded in escaping. On subsequent trials the act that led to escape was more likely to occur than it had previously. From his observations, Thorndike formulated a general law, the law of effect, applicable to the behavior of all organisms: "Any act which in a given situation produces satisfaction becomes associated with that situation, so that when the situation recurs the act is more likely than before to recur also" (Thorndike, 1905, p. 203).

Later, B. F. Skinner and many others continued and extended the work Thorndike had begun. These theorists referred to the organism's behaviors as **operants**. A consequence that strengthens an operant is a **reinforcer**. A consequence that weakens an operant is a **punisher**.

Operant learning occurs in many species across a wide variety of circumstances. It has been responsible for pigeons learning to peck on keys, chimpanzees learning human sign language, and children acquiring academic, physical, and social skills. It would seem that such a prominent process would start early. Does it begin at birth? Until the 1960s it had been impossible to demonstrate operant conditioning in newborns or very young infants, primarily due to the infant's limited range of responses. Eventually this problem was overcome, by using responses that infants have mastered. In one example, sucking was used as the basis for conditioning (DeCasper and Sigafoos, 1983). When infants suck on a nipple, they usually will suck several times, then rest, then repeat with another set, or burst, of sucks. In this study, 2- to 3-day-olds sucked on a nipple connected to equipment that could measure when infants sucked. During

Operant Any behavior of an organism.

Reinforcer Any consequence to a behavior that strengthens the behavior.

Punisher Any consequence to a behavior that weakens the behavior.

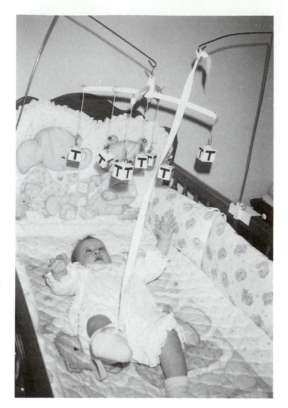

FIGURE 3-10

When this infant kicks, the ribbon connecting the leg to the mobile causes the mobile to move. Infants rapidly learn this relation and kick more. Here kicking is the response, and the mobile's movement is the reinforcer.

a baseline period, the investigators determined the average time between each burst of sucking. In the reinforcement phase that followed, some infants were reinforced if the time between bursts of sucking was longer than it had been during the baseline phase; other infants were reinforced if the time between bursts was shorter. For both groups, the reinforcer was a tape recording of the sound of a heart beating. To illustrate these procedures, if an infant had averaged 6 seconds between bursts of sucking during baseline, then a burst that followed the previous burst by 4 seconds or less would activate the tape recording of the heart beat. In fact, both groups of newborns modified their sucking when the reinforcement was introduced.

As was true for classical conditioning, operant conditioning involves the formation of expectations. In the case of operant conditioning, the infant forms the expectation that the operant will be followed by the reinforcer (or that the operant will be followed by a punisher). Infants' formation of these expectations was demonstrated by Lewis, Allesandri, and Sullivan (1990). The 2- to 8-month-olds in their study had learned that pulling a string that was attached to their wrist would be reinforced by presentation of a smiling face with musical accompaniment. Infants' facial expressions were videotaped during the extinction phase when the pulling motion was no longer reinforced. Compared with infants in the control condition, infants who had learned the contingency were more apt to appear surprised and to look at the wrist where the string was attached. In addition, these infants were more likely to become angry and to cry. Collectively, these results convey the strong impression that by 8 weeks of age, infants' expectations had been violated and they were upset and angered by this violation.

It is easy to imagine how operant conditioning plays an important role throughout development, particularly in infancy. The mother's milk is a potent reinforcer, as is attention from her and other people. Later in this chapter, we will see how reinforcement may explain the formation of strong emotional bonds between infants and their parents.

Observational Learning

Observational learning involves learning about the world from observing the actions of others. It plays a role in all aspects of development—from learning motor skills to accomplishing intellectual tasks to participating in social interactions (Bandura, 1977). In its most obvious form, observational learning involves imitating another's behavior. It is well established that imitation occurs within a few months after birth (Legerstee, 1991).

More controversial is the claim that imitation occurs from the first days of life. Some investigators have presented evidence that very young infants are able to imitate a variety of facial gestures and expressions. Meltzoff and Moore (1977, 1989) exposed 2- to 3-week-olds to a human model who made specific facial gestures, such as sticking out the tongue and opening and closing the mouth. They concluded that the infants did indeed imitate these gestures.

Subsequent studies have shown that imitation of tongue and mouth movements can be observed in infants who are not yet 1 hour old (Reissland, 1988) and that newborns can also imitate an adult's head movements (Meltzoff and Moore, 1989). Field and her colleagues (1982) presented evidence that newborns imitated three facial expressions. As Figure 3-11 shows, the expressions were happy, sad, and surprised. These demonstrations are important because they seem to indicate an unexpectedly high degree of competence in infancy.

These findings have been challenged, however. Some investigators have been unable to demonstrate imitation. In a study conducted by Abravanel and Sigafoos (1984), infants between 4 and 21 weeks of age were presented with three facial expressions and two bodily gestures (for example, hand opening, eye blinking, tongue protruding). Little evidence for imitation was found overall: Only in some instances did 4- to 6-week-olds partly protrude their tongues after observing the model engage in this behavior. Similarly, Kaitz and her colleagues (1988) found no evidence that newborns imitated happy, sad, and surprised facial expressions.

The conflicts in the research findings touch on a theoretical issue: Major theories of learning and cognitive development predict that imitating an act like tongue protrusion does not occur very early in life. Such imitation requires that infants match their own bodily movements with stimuli that they perceive only through vision. This kind of matching, it is widely thought, can occur only after greater experience and, perhaps, after biological maturation of the mental apparatus. If imitation does occur, how can it be explained? One view is that this form of imitation is simply an innate social reflex that can be elicited by specific stimuli. This explanation becomes less convincing, however, as the list of imitated be-

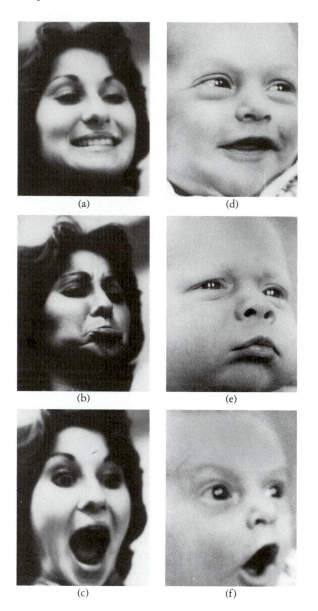

(a)

(b)

(c)

(d)

(e)

(f)

FIGURE 3-11
Photographs of a model's happy, sad, and surprised expressions and a newborn's corresponding expressions.

haviors grows. Instead, it becomes more plausible to conclude that within the constraints of their limited perceptual and motor skills infants can imitate what they see, and they may be more likely to do so if the modeled act is biologically significant (Meltzoff, Kuhl, and Moore, 1991).

A brief summary of this chapter so far would read something like this:

Soon or shortly after birth, infants perceive the world reasonably accurately and they readily learn from their experiences.

Undoubtedly, the most important experiences that infants have during their first year are with other humans, particularly their parents. The rapid development of perception and learning means that infants are well prepared to participate in interactions with other people. Let's examine how this important human function develops during infancy.

ATTACHMENT: THE FIRST SOCIAL RELATIONSHIP

The development of social and emotional behavior in early life rivals the dramatic rate of growth in perception and learning. Social relations do not appear suddenly, of course; they emerge gradually as a product of the interplay of the maturing child with its primary caregivers. **Attachment** is the term that refers to the enduring social-emotional relationship that develops between an infant and another person, usually a parent or primary caregiver. Almost all infants in all cultures form attachments, and only extreme departures in child-rearing practices prevent their formation (Ainsworth, 1977).

Theoretical Views

Sigmund Freud was perhaps the first theorist to propose that the mother (or the mother substitute) becomes the child's first object of attachment, this due to her role in satisfying the infant's need for nourishment and her association with the pleasurable sensations that accompany feeding. Research did not support Freud's belief of a connection between early feeding and weaning practices and later personality development (Caldwell, 1964). It did suggest, however, that the absence of the mother during infancy led to poor developmental outcomes (Campos et al., 1983). Emotional, physical, and intellectual problems are fairly common in children who experience extreme isolation and are deprived of interactions with others.

Freud's view was replaced by a view that originated in ethology. According to John Bowlby (1969), who was a pioneer in the application of the ethological view to human development, grasping, clinging, sucking, crying, smiling, and several other behaviors are biologically "wired-in" to elicit caregiving and protection from adults.

Consider, for example, crying, which is among the most noticeable of the infant's behaviors that serve to attract attention. Crying may be caused by hunger, sudden sounds, and visual stimulation (Wolff, 1969). It is unappealing to most adults; mothers in particular may react with quickened heart rates and annoyance. Thus, a desire to end the crying, as well as a desire to meet the child's needs, probably account for much early caregiving.

Smiling may serve much the same function. When parents observe their infant's smile, they appear amused and delighted. The smile is considered "cute" and perhaps is an intimate communication of happiness and contentment. Newborns may imitate a smiling adult, but smiling is more likely to occur when a child is sleeping lightly (Konner, 1982), and such smiles appear to be related to the internal state of the child. The true social smile does not occur until the second month of life, when the infant responds to external stimuli with satisfaction and pleasure. Soon smiling

Attachment The affectionate, reciprocal relationship that is formed between one individual and another, especially between a child and the primary caregivers.

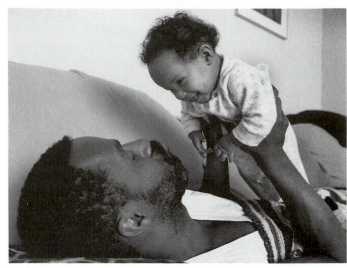

FIGURE 3-12
Smiling and crying elicit caregiving from adults.

occurs to a variety of environmental events—the presence of toys, a sleeping cat, a playful father. Most important, smiling rapidly becomes part of the communication between child and caretakers. Parents and infants reward each other with smiles for certain kinds of behavior, influencing each other in the process (Gewirtz, 1991).

Even the simple physical appearance of infants elicits adult caregiving (Alley, 1983). Adults seem disposed to protect and display affection to infants based on the children's sizes and their body proportions. Other infantile characteristics such as roundness, softness, skin smoothness, helplessness, and perhaps even a lack of coordination may also be especially appealing to adults.

These characteristics of infants and the responses they elicit from adults form a reciprocal system that is the basis for attachment. Bowlby argued that evolutionary pressures would favor children who become attached to caregivers by increasing their chances of survival in a potentially hostile environment.

Bowlby's ideas have been extremely influential and helpful in interpreting parent-child interaction. Babies do look at their mothers, touch them, cry for attention, smile, and move close to their mothers. During and following separation from their mothers, they cry and look in the direction where they last saw their mothers. Moreover, the process is a reciprocal one: A mother responds to her infant's smiling, looking, and crying. This pattern of attachment is reasonably similar in very different societies (Ainsworth, 1967) and may be a species-wide characteristic that is biologically programmed.

Learning theorists explain attachment differently. One learning approach analyzes attachment in terms of the principles of operant conditioning (Gewirtz, 1972, 1991). This view suggests that the interaction between infant and caregiver is mutually reinforcing, so that each comes to exert control over the other's behavior. The mother (or mother substitute) satisfies the basic needs of the child, providing positive reinforcement and removing aversive stimuli. In providing food, a primary reinforcer, the mother and her behavior become secondary reinforcers. The child responds positively by smiling, cooing, or ceasing to cry, which in turn reinforces the parent's behavior. This reciprocal interaction results in mutual attachment.

The learning view differs from the ethological view on some details, but both converge on the same general conclusion: Through continual mutual stimulation and continual responding, infants and caregivers become especially important to each other. Within a relatively short period of time, a relationship develops that is considered crucial to the child's growth. Let's examine the steps involved in the formation of this relationship.

Growth of Attachment

Although most infants form attachments to specific people at about 6 to 8 months of age (Figure 3-13), attachment is a gradual process that requires certain cognitive and social-emotional skills (Ainsworth, 1982).

To begin with, infants must establish boundaries between themselves and the external environment, and they must discriminate between people and objects. Maturation is probably involved in these processes, but so is learning. Infants learn, for example, that crying brings an adult into view.

FIGURE 3-13

For most infants attachment occurs between 6 to 8 months of age.
(Adapted from H. R. Schaffer and P. E. Emerson, "The development of social attachments in infancy," in Monographs of the Society for Research in Child Development, 29, no. 3 (1964). Copyright 1964 by the Society of Research in Child Development, Inc. Reproduced by permission.)

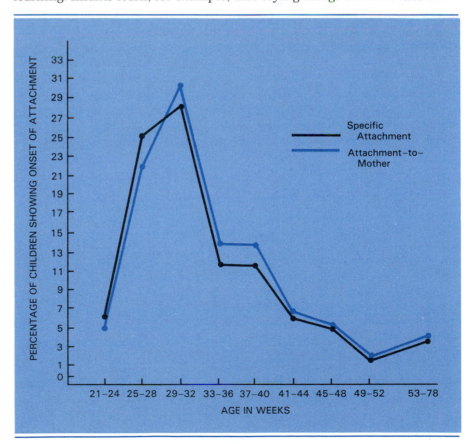

Success in operating on the environment helps the infant to distinguish himself or herself from the rest of the world. It also aids in the discrimination between people and objects. Most infants give sustained attention to another person by about 4 weeks of age and begin to show clearly differentiated responses to persons and objects shortly thereafter.

The next requirement is that the infant be able to discriminate familiar and unfamiliar people. Recognition of the mother may already have begun. The simplest way to assess this is to present the mother and a stranger (or their pictures) to the child. If the infant looks at the mother more than at the stranger, then at least passive discrimination must be taking place. We can also look for active discrimination—for example, if the baby smiles differently toward the mother or actively reaches out for her. Such behaviors are observed in most babies by the time they are 6 months old. Nevertheless, smiles, cries, looks, vocalizations, and approaches are directed toward an array of persons; infants typically go quite readily to most others.

At about 6 months of age, selective orientation to the mother occurs. Crying, smiling, clinging, looking, and approaching are now directed much more to the mother. In the mother's presence, the baby might explore the environment but also intermittently return to the mother or look in her direction, checking on her whereabouts. The attached child protests by crying or otherwise showing distress when the mother leaves the room. When the mother reappears, the child may cry intensely or stop crying; either behavior suggests that the baby expects attention.

These behaviors require certain abilities on the part of the young child: perceptual discrimination, rudimentary memory, understanding that objects exist even though they are out of sight, and some idea that people cause events to happen (Hodapp and Mueller, 1982). Attachment indicates that the child has established trust and confidence in the mother. This is shown by the child's greater willingness to explore the environment in her presence than in the presence of a stranger or when alone.

Soon after the attachment relation forms, infants use parents' emotional expressions to help them understand the world. This phenomenon, known as **social referencing**, entails infants using the emotional information that they garner from others to guide them in novel or ambiguous situations. Infants in an unfamiliar environment will look at their mother or father, as if searching for cues to help them interpret the situation. In a study by Hirshberg and Svejda (1990), 12-month-olds were shown novel toys that made sounds (for example, a stuffed alligator that hissed). For some toys, parents were instructed to look happy; for others, parents looked afraid. When parents looked afraid, their infants, too, appeared distressed. Also, infants looked at their parents more often and stayed further away from the toys. Thus, infants use their parents' emotions to regulate their own behavior. Social referencing provides infants with a powerful tool for making their way in an ambiguous environment.

Social referencing
Searching another's face or behavior for information about ambiguous environmental events.

VARIETIES OF ATTACHMENT. Not all attachment relationships are the same. In fact, three qualitatively different forms of attachment are common. These have been identified using a paradigm known as the Strange Situation, developed by Ainsworth and Wittig (1969). The Strange Situ-

Secure attachment A relation between infant and mother in which, after separation from the mother, the infant maintains proximity to the mother and seeks interactions with her.

Insecure attachment A relation between infant and mother in which, after separation from the mother, the infant does not respond positively to the mother.

Avoidant group A type of insecure attachment in which, after separation from the mother, the infant avoids the mother.

Resistant group A type of insecure attachment in which, after separation from the mother, an infant desires interactions with the mother but also appears angry with the mother.

ation is a brief procedure conducted in a room with toys. The procedure involves separating the child involuntarily from the mother in an unfamiliar environment that includes an unfamiliar adult. Over a series of eight episodes an infant is observed alone, with the mother, with the mother and a stranger, and with only the stranger. A variety of behaviors are recorded to assess attachment and exploration under this stressful situation. The results of several studies demonstrate individual differences that divide children into three major categories.

Infants classified as **securely attached** behave in a way predicted by Bowlby's ethological theory. After involuntary separation from their mothers, they attempt to reestablish interaction and proximity, and they act positively toward their parents. When in the presence of their mothers they actively explore the environment, using the mothers as a secure base. Other infants are classified as **insecurely attached**. Some of them, the **avoidant group**, actively avoid their returning mothers by looking away, turning away, or ignoring them. Other insecurely attached children, labeled the **resistant group**, act ambivalently: They seek interaction and contact but angrily, or they subtly reject it as well.

These classifications based on infants' behavior in the Strange Situation are related to the infants' behaviors at home. When securely and insecurely attached infants are observed in their routine activities at home, securely attached infants try to maintain interactions with the mother and are easily comforted by her. They expect her to be responsive, are oriented toward people rather than the objects, and are self-confident (Vaughn and Waters, 1990). These classifications seem to apply to children growing up in different cultures, too. In countries in North America, Western Europe, and Asia, most children form secure attachments to their mothers. In Western Europe and North America, avoidant attachments are more common than resistant attachments; in Israel and Japan, the reverse is true (van IJzendoorn and Kroonenberg, 1988).

Sensitive interaction between infants and caregivers is crucial in

FIGURE 3-14
Patterns of attachment between infants and caretakers are quite similar across societies.

determining the quality of attachment (Ainsworth, 1982). Sensitivity involves responding to the child in a predictable and appropriate way. Emotional intensity may come into play, as well as the mutual delight mother and child receive from their interactions (Ainsworth and Bell, 1974). Mothers of securely attached infants, for example, are likely to notice when their baby smiles or talks, and they typically interpret their baby's signals correctly; and interactions between mother and baby tend to be coordinated and satisfying. In contrast, mothers of insecurely attached infants often respond only to prolonged or intense signals from their baby, are irritated by the baby's demands, and seem awkward or uncomfortable when interacting with their infant (Pederson et al., 1990).

Although these findings are compatible with a view that maternal sensitivity fosters secure attachment, the results are not conclusive. More convincing are findings from longitudinal studies in which maternal behavior early in life is linked to the quality of attachment. Studies of this sort support the proposed link between maternal sensitivity and the quality of attachment. Isabella and Belsky (1991) studied interactions between mothers and infants at 3 and 9 months, and they then assessed the attachment of these infants to their mothers when they were 12 months old. For infants who were securely attached at 12 months, their mothers had interacted sensitively with them at 3 and 9 months; that is, the mothers had responded consistently and appropriately to the infant's behavior. Mothers of avoidant infants were intrusive and tended to overstimulate their infants at 3 and 9 months; mothers of resistant infants were inconsistent in their interactions, but often they were uninvolved with their infants.

We can summarize these and other similar findings (for example, Lewis and Feiring, 1989) in the following way: Secure attachment stems from predictable relationships in which infants' needs are met and in which both infant and mother participate. The avoidant relationship may develop as the infant's only defense against an intrusive mother; the ambivalent relationship may reflect the infant's frustration at being unable to establish consistent and predictable involvement from its mother.

Attachment to Others

Although the infant's first attachment is often to the mother, attachments to others occur quite early. Schaffer and Emerson (1964) were among the first to investigate the formation of attachments to other family members. As a measure of attachment, they used reports of infant crying or protesting following brief everyday separations from specific individuals. Schaffer and Emerson found that a very high percentage of babies did indeed form first attachments to their mothers. But shortly afterward, or sometimes simultaneously, attachments were formed with familiar persons, such as fathers, grandparents, and siblings. By 6 months of age, over 50 percent of the infants were attached to their fathers as well as to their mothers, and by 18 months of age, over 70 percent were attached to both parents.

Subsequent research confirmed these basic results. Infants almost invariably become attached to both parents (Kotelchuck, Zelazo, Kagan,

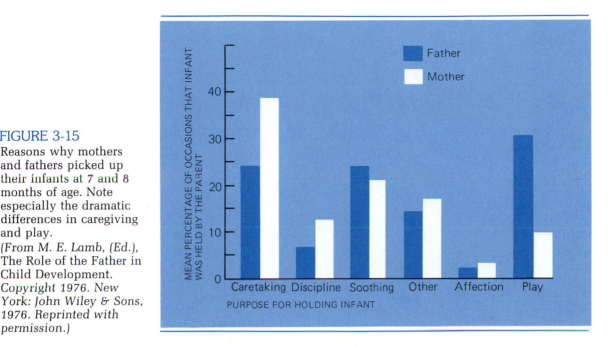

FIGURE 3-15

Reasons why mothers and fathers picked up their infants at 7 and 8 months of age. Note especially the dramatic differences in caregiving and play.

(From M. E. Lamb, (Ed.), The Role of the Father in Child Development. Copyright 1976. New York: John Wiley & Sons, 1976. Reprinted with permission.)

and Spelke, 1975). Moreover, the quality of attachment is usually the same for mothers and fathers: In an analysis of data from ten separate studies, Fox, Kimmerly, and Schafer (1991) found that nearly half of the infants were securely attached to both mother and father, while about 15 percent were insecurely attached to both parents. About 40 percent were securely attached to one parent only. Interestingly, although sex-role stereotypes might lead us to expect that most infants in this group would be securely attached to the mother but insecurely attached to the father, this was *not* the case: In infants who were securely attached to only one parent, that parent was just as likely to be the father as the mother.

However, the basis for attachments with mothers and fathers may be different because mothers and fathers interact differently with their offspring (Figure 3-15). Fathers most frequently pick up their infants for the purposes of play, while mothers are far more likely to pick up infants for caregiving or to move them away from undesirable activities. Also, mothers and fathers differ in the way that they play with infants. Fathers' play tends to be physical and emotionally arousing; mothers' play is more likely to be verbal and less arousing, and to involve toys or games such as pat-a-cake (Bridges, Connell, and Belsky, 1988).

These differences have led some theorists to propose that infant-mother and infant-father relationships serve different purposes. The mother, as the primary attachment figure, is the source of comfort and reassurance when infants are distressed. The father's function, in contrast, may be to teach infants how to get along with others. Physical play, for example, provides opportunities for older infants to learn how to respond to affective cues from an adult and to see how their own affect influences others (Parke, MacDonald, Beitel, and Bhavnagri, 1988).

Infants' initial attachments are usually to their parents, but they

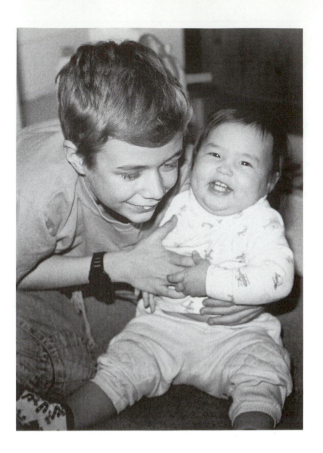

develop emotional bonds with others as well. Infants become attached to older brothers and sisters, particularly when these siblings are themselves securely attached (Teti and Ablard, 1989). Also, infants who attend day care become attached to their professional caregivers (Goosens and van IJzendoorn, 1990). As with parents, these attachments are most likely to be secure when the caregivers are sensitive in their interactions with the infant. However, do these attachments come at the expense of secure attachments to parents? This question is important because of the large number of children who receive alternative care because their mothers and fathers are employed outside the home. Considerable research has been generated to answer this question, and we will examine the results in the Close-Up on pages 102–3.

Consequences of Attachment

Attachment is the first social relationship, and many theorists believe it is the prototype for most subsequent social relationships. According to this view, secure attachment—which involves trust in the caregiver—should be related to later confidence and skill in dealing with peers and in performing other tasks of the preschool period (Sroufe and Fleeson, 1986).

Several investigations support this prediction: Compared with young children who were insecurely attached as infants, children who were securely attached typically interact more skillfully with their peers and seem to enjoy those interactions more. Park and Waters (1989), for example, observed pairs of 3- and 4-year-olds playing together. All pairs consisted of children who were best friends. However, in some pairs, both children were securely attached; in others, one child was securely attached but the other was insecurely attached. Observations of the children's play revealed a number of differences. In pairs in which both children were securely attached, the children were more likely to follow one another's suggestions, to agree with one another's preferences, to share secrets, and to settle disagreements peacefully and fairly. In contrast, in pairs that included insecurely attached children, the children were more likely to grab possessions, more likely to be aggressive verbally, and more likely to reject one another (for example, "I don't want to play with you").

The overall impression from the Park and Waters (1989) study is that secure pairs interacted with one another more skillfully and seemed happier in their interactions. This pattern, which is common to many studies (for example, Sroufe, Fox, and Pancake, 1983), does not lead to the conclusion that children who were insecurely attached as infants are destined for a lifetime of unhappy, unsatisfying social relationships. Although their play may involve more discord and more effort to assert control, the play of insecurely attached children generally falls within the broad boundaries of typical children's play and is not "abnormal." In fact, efforts to link the quality of attachment to behavior disorders have not been very successful: Insecurely attached children generally are no more likely to have behavioral problems than are children who are securely attached (Fagot and Kavanagh, 1990). As Lewis and his colleagues (1984) put it, "Infants are neither made invulnerable by secure attachments nor are they doomed by insecure attachments to later psychopathology" (p. 123).

We should also note that a direct link between secure attachment and later behavior cannot be assumed from these findings. The circumstances and the particular caregivers that foster secure attachment in infancy may continue to support the child in a desirable way. Parents who sensitively meet the needs of their infants may continue the same sensitive interactions as their children grow older.

TEMPERAMENT

If you have the opportunity to observe several young babies simultaneously—at an infant-care center, for example—you will be struck by the variety of their behaviors. Some infants are quiet most of the time, whereas others cry often and impatiently; some infants have endless energy, others seem almost listless; some infants respond warmly to strangers, others are much more tentative. These differences resemble what we think of as "personality"—a consistent style or pattern to an infant's behavior. In work with infants and young children, this aspect of psychological functioning is known as **temperament**.

Temperament
Personality-like characteristics of infants, such as emotionality and activity level.

Temperamental aspects of human development have been studied intensely in recent years. A good deal of emphasis has been placed on identifying the dimensions of temperament. The pioneers in this area were Thomas, Chess, and Birch (1970). They followed the development of 141 children for over a decade by interviewing the parents periodically—

CLOSE-UP

Working Mothers and Attachment

In 1995, nearly two-thirds of all mothers of preschool children in the United States will work outside the home (McBride, 1990). Many of these children will be cared for by nonrelatives—some in private homes and some in day-care or nursery school programs. Millions of young children are thus experiencing maternal separation and multiple caregivers in the normal course of events.

Some studies indicate that care by someone other than the mother is not harmful to children who begin such care after their first birthday (Clarke-Stewart and Fein, 1983). To the contrary, these studies suggest that youngsters in day care advance more rapidly intellectually. In addition, children who attend early childhood programs are more socially competent and mature. They are more self-confident, assertive, outgoing, self-sufficient, and knowledgeable about the world.

Some aspects of children's social behavior are negative: The children may be less agreeable, less polite, and less compliant. But because these kinds of negative behaviors typically increase during the preschool period, they may actually reflect maturation.

Aside from some possible advantages of day care, there is great concern over the impact of day care on infants because of the possibility that daily separation from the mother will disrupt the attachment process. According to this "separation from mother" view, diagrammed in Figure 3-17a, infants may believe that they are being rejected by a mother who leaves them daily. Or they may believe that the mother will not be available in times of distress. If infants interpret maternal separation in these ways, insecure attachment may result (Jaeger and Weinraub, 1990).

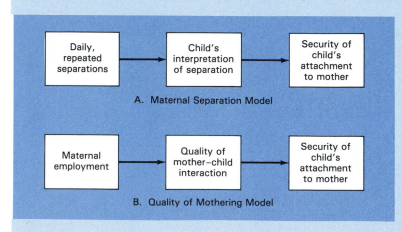

FIGURE 3-17

Two models of the relations between maternal employment and attachment. The top diagram depicts the "separation from mother" model. The bottom diagram depicts the "quality of mothering" model. *(From E. Jaeger, and M. Weinraub, "Early nonmaternal care and infant attachment: In search of process," in K. McCartney (Ed.),* Child Care and Maternal Employment: A Social Ecology Approach. New Directions for Child Development, *no. 49. (San Francisco: Jossey-Bass, 1990), p. 74. Copyright © 1990 by Jossey-Bass Inc., Publishers.)*

every 3 months during the first year, every 6 months during years 1 to 5, and annually after age 5. The interviews were structured so that parental statements such as "my baby couldn't stand a new food" had to be restated by the parent as a specific description. In addition, some home observations were conducted by individuals unfamiliar with the child's behavioral history. The researchers concluded that children show distinct in-

In fact, infants are more likely to form insecure attachments when mothers work full time outside the home. The effect is not large: In an analysis of 17 studies including over 1,200 infants, 36 percent of the babies of working mothers were insecurely attached, compared to 29 percent of the babies of mothers who were not employed outside the house or who worked only part time (Clarke-Stewart, 1989). Thus, although most mothers who work full time will form secure attachments with their infants, the risk of insecure attachment does increase when mothers work full time.

What factors seem to increase the likelihood of insecure attachment? The amount of time that infants spend in alternative care is one. Infants who spend only a few hours a week in alternative care are not at risk; the risk level increases rapidly for infants who spend 20 or more hours weekly in alternative care (Belsky and Rovine, 1990). First-born children are more likely to be affected (Barglow, Vaughn, and Molitor, 1987), and sons are more likely to be affected than daughters (Chase-Lansdale and Owen, 1987). The type and quality of care may play a role, but the nature of this influence has been difficult to discern because child care comes in so many forms, each of which can vary from poor to excellent (Vandell and Corasanti, 1990).

This constellation of results cannot be readily accommodated by the "separation from mother" view. A more complex alternative, termed the "quality of mothering" view, is shown in Figure 3-17b. Here, separation from mother per se is not central. Instead, a mother's full-time employment interacts with a host of factors—her attitude toward work, the involvement of other family members in caregiving and household chores, the characteristics of the child, and the quality of child care, to name a few—to affect the overall quality of mother-infant interaction. If the collective impact of these factors is to reduce the quality of mother-infant interaction, then insecure attachment may be more likely (Jaeger and Weinraub, 1990).

To illustrate this argument, let's consider two hypothetical working women. One works because she enjoys her work, she receives much help with the infant and around the house from other family members, and she takes her temperamentally easy infant to a day-care center with well-trained caregivers and a favorable ratio of caregivers to infants. A second woman would rather not work but does so to bolster the family income; she receives minimal help at home from other family members and takes her temperamentally difficult baby to a center with poorly trained and outnumbered caregivers. Obviously, these women represent two extreme cases. In the first, everything is in favor of the mother and infant developing a high-quality relationship that will lead to secure attachment; in the second case, everything is stacked against the mother and infant, making the development of an insecure attachment likely.

Most real working women, their infants, and their families fall somewhere between these two extremes. The likelihood of a secure attachment becomes greater if the experiences of women, their infants, and their families are closer to the first case than the second. Consequently, the concern of working women who are prospective mothers should not be work per se or day care per se. Instead, the factors in Figure 3-17b need to be considered collectively, with the aim of assessing the overall quality of mother-infant interactions that result when a mother returns to work outside the home.

dividuality in temperament during the first weeks of life. Many of the children could be classified as "easy," "difficult," or "slow-to-warm-up" based on general mood, intensity of reactions, and adaptability to new situations (Chess and Thomas, 1986).

The Thomas and Chess work launched the modern study of infant temperament. Their ideas remain influential today, but there are now other theories as well. One prominent theory of temperament has been proposed by Buss and Plomin (1975, 1984). For these theorists, temperament refers to inherited characteristics that are relatively stable throughout childhood. They propose three dimensions of temperament:

1. *Emotionality*. This dimension refers to the strength of the infant's emotional response to a situation, the ease with which that response is triggered, and the ease with which the infant can be returned to a nonemotional state. Some infants have strong emotional responses to situations. Their distress, fear, or anger is palpable, seems to have a relatively low threshold, and is not easily mollified. Other infants have emotional responses that seem subdued, are relatively difficult to elicit, and are soothed readily.

2. *Activity*. This dimension refers to the tempo and vigor of a child's activity. Active infants are always busy exploring their environment and enjoying vigorous play. Inactive infants have a more controlled behavioral tempo and usually prefer quieter forms of play.

3. *Sociability*. This dimension refers to a preference for being with other people. Some infants relish contact with and attention from other people and prefer play that involves others; some infants enjoy solitude and are quite content to play alone with toys.

Other theories of temperament have been proposed (for example, Rothbart, 1989), and it is too early to indicate which is most consistent with the evidence. What we should note are the commonalities in these views of temperament. Specifically, there is agreement that temperament consists of a relatively small number of dimensions that are biologically based. The number of dimensions and their precise natures are still being debated, but most major theories include dimensions like emotionality, activity, and sociability.

Let's begin our study of temperament by looking at two aspects that are central to all of the theories—that temperament is biologically based and that it is relatively stable.

Biological Bases of Temperament

Peripheral nervous system The part of the nervous system that runs toward and away from the brain and spinal cord.

Somatic nervous system A division of the peripheral nervous system consisting of neurons that are linked to skeletal muscles.

Autonomic nervous system A division of the peripheral nervous system consisting of neurons that are linked to smooth muscles, such as those in the stomach and intestines.

Most theorists believe that temperament is biologically based. Consistent with this claim is the fact that monozygotic twins often resemble one another temperamentally more than do dizygotic twins. For example, monozygotic twins are more similar than dizygotic twins in activity, sociability, and emotionality (Braungart, Plomin, DeFries, and Fulker, 1992). Results like these indicate that the emotionality and activity dimensions of temperament are largely inherited.

Twin studies are useful for determining if a temperamental dimension has a biological basis. However, these studies provide no insights into the specific biological underpinnings of each temperamental dimension. To understand this issue, let's examine emotionality, which may have its biological roots in the autonomic nervous system. You may recall that the nerves outside the brain and spinal cord form the **peripheral nervous system**, which is further divided into the **somatic** and **autonomic nervous systems**. Nerves in the somatic nervous system are connected to

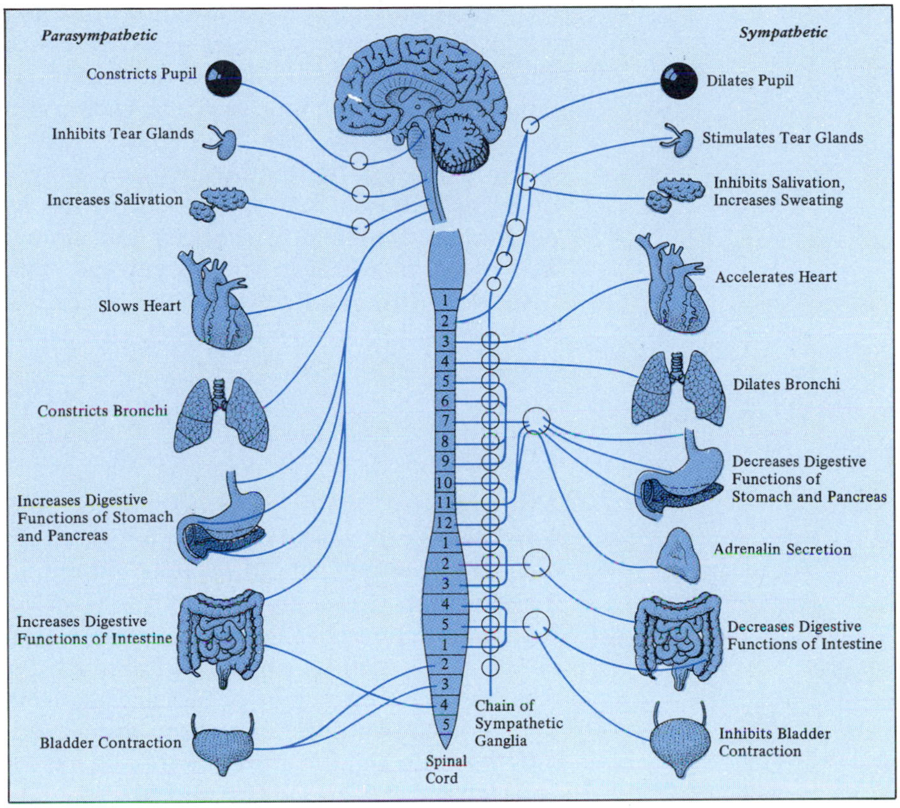

FIGURE 3-18
The sympathetic and parasympathetic components of the autonomic nervous system. The sympathetic component arouses the body in response to distress; the parasympathetic component controls routine functioning. *(From J. M. Darley, S. Glucksberg, and R. A. Kinchla, Psychology, 5th ed., © 1990, p. 59. Reprinted by permission of Prentice Hall, Englewood Cliffs, New Jersey.*

Sympathetic component The component of the autonomic nervous system that functions during stressful situations.

Parasympathetic component The component of the autonomic nervous system that controls ordinary body functions.

skeletal muscles, such as the muscles used to move fingers and arms. Nerves in the autonomic nervous system are linked to *smooth* muscles. Examples would include the muscles in the stomach and intestines that are used to digest food, the muscles in the walls of blood vessels, and the muscles in the bladder.

Typically, each smooth muscle is connected by pairs of nerves. One nerve belongs to the **sympathetic component** of the autonomic nervous system. Figure 3-18 shows that the sympathetic nervous system arouses the body in times of distress or emergencies. When you are frightened or angry, nerves in the sympathetic system increase the flow of blood, dilate your pupils, slow down digestion, and relax the bladder. When the crisis is past, the **parasympathetic component** of the autonomic nervous system takes over: Digestion proceeds, muscles in the bladder contract, and blood flow is reduced. Thus the basic rule is that the parasympathetic system controls the ordinary functions of the body; the sympathetic system takes over during stressful times.

The link between the autonomic nervous system and emotionality is that one of its component systems may dominate the other, causing differences in temperament (Buss and Plomin, 1984). The idea is that in emotional individuals, the sympathetic component may dominate; in individuals who are less emotional, the parasympathetic component may dominate.

Work linking emotionality to physiological indices has just begun. An example is research measuring **cortisol**, a hormone produced by the adrenocortical system, which is activated along with the sympathetic component of the autonomic nervous system during times of stress. Gunnar and her colleagues (1989) found that when infants are exposed to stress— separation from the mother in the Strange Situation experiment—the increase in the amount of cortisol in the infant's saliva was related to emotionality. Infants who responded more negatively to the separation had greater increases in salivary cortisol. Although the exact mechanisms involved in the cortisol-emotionality link are still being debated, this research is clearly an exciting step toward identifying specific biological bases of temperament.

Stability

A dimension of temperament is stable if an infant responds in a reasonably consistent fashion over an extended period of time. Emotional 2-month-olds, for example, should become emotional 12-month-olds. Studies of main temperamental dimensions reveal reasonable stability: Worobey and Blajda (1989) assessed infants' temperaments at 2 and 12 months of age. For each age, mothers completed the Infant Behavior Questionnaire, which measures six dimensions of temperament, including activity level, smiling, and soothability. Correlations computed between scores at 2 and 12 months were significant for five of the six categories. To illustrate, the correlation between the mothers' assessments of activity level at 2 and 12 months was 0.40. Correlations for fear and soothability were 0.33 and 0.50, respectively.

This outcome, which is fairly typical of longitudinal studies of infant temperament (Bates, 1987), is consistent with the view that temperamental dimensions are moderately consistent throughout infancy. A shortcoming to this sort of evidence is that mothers provided the data on both occasions. Their responses are moderately stable, but this does not necessarily indicate that the infants are unchanging. The stability may stem from the fact that a mother's initial impression of her infant's temperament may color her later perceptions of her infant and bias her ratings toward stability. For this reason, longitudinal studies of objective measures of temperament are invaluable.

Let's examine two studies, both of which indicate temperamental stability with behavioral measures. Worobey and Lewis (1989) videotaped newborns while a sample of blood was drawn to test for PKU (see Chapter 2). These same babies were videotaped again at 2 months when they received their first inoculation. The intensity of the child's response to these two stressful experiences was correlated, with $r = 0.37$. Newborns who had reacted emotionally to the blood sampling by crying and grimacing tended to respond emotionally, at 2 months of age, to the inoculation.

Similarly, Stifter and Fox (1990) studied responses in two situations known to be moderately stressful to infants: In the first situation, newborns were given a pacifier and allowed to suck for 60 seconds; then the pacifier

Cortisol A hormone secreted during times of stress.

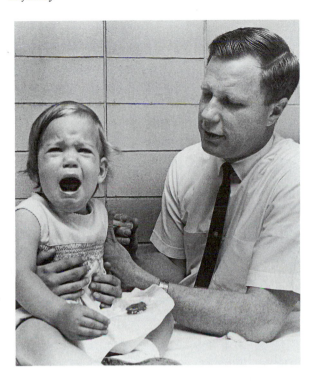

FIGURE 3-19
Infants with emotional temperaments cry readily in response to a stressful event, such as an inoculation, and they are more difficult to soothe.

was removed. In the second situation, when infants were 5 months old, mothers gently restrained their arms, prohibiting all movement. Of the newborns who cried when the pacifier was removed, 53 percent cried when their hands were restrained; of the newborns who did not cry, 72 percent did not cry when their hands were restrained. In other words, emotional reactivity, as indicated by crying, was consistent from birth to 5 months of age.

These studies are typical of research showing that emotionality is fairly consistent throughout infancy. Similar evidence demonstrates stability through infancy of other major temperamental dimensions (Bates, 1987). However, the stability is far from absolute. In the Stifter and Fox (1990) study, for example, about one-third of the infants cried on one occasion but not on the other. Apparently, temperament can change with development. One view is that

> temperaments may be expected to display both continuity and change over the course of development. . . . The events of childhood are likely to modify the personality tendencies that have been built in, and therefore temperaments must undergo change. Like other strong dispositions, however, temperaments resist change and therefore manifest at least some stability over time. (Buss and Plomin, 1984, p. 15)

In the course of infant development, for example, the stability of emotionality might depend upon the characteristics of parents. In fact, emotional 3-month-olds are likely to be less emotional at age 9 months if their mothers have high self-esteem, are positive about their marriages, and interact easily with them (Belsky, Fish, and Isabella, 1991).

This example illustrates how temperament may influence the outcome of development: Depending upon their temperament, infants may elicit different experiences and may respond differently to the same experiences. In the next few pages, we consider some of the ways in which temperament is linked to infant development.

Links to Infant Development

ATTACHMENT. The relation of temperament to attachment is complex. When the infant is separated from the mother in the Strange Situation experiment, difficult babies cry more, as do active babies (Vaughn, Lefever, Seifer, and Barglow, 1989). However, recall that quality of attachment is based primarily upon the infant's response to the mother's return following separation. Here, temperamental dimensions are unrelated to crying and are also unrelated to the infant's efforts to maintain contact with the mother (Vaughn et al., 1989). The net result is that there is no relation between temperament and quality of attachment. Secure attachment is just as likely in "difficult" babies as in "easy babies," and it is just as likely in "active" babies as in "inactive" ones.

The picture may change if the infant's temperament is considered jointly with the mother's personality. Some evidence indicates that particular combinations of infant temperament and maternal personality may not be conducive to the formation of secure attachments. Mangelsdorf and her colleagues (1990) found that for emotional infants, insecure attachment was more likely when the mother's personality was characterized as rigid and traditional. For infants low on the emotionality scale, the mother's personality had no impact on attachment.

This result, and others that suggest links among attachment, infant temperament, and maternal personality (for example, Belsky, Fish, and Isabella, 1991), can be accommodated through the "quality of mothering" model described in Figure 3-17. When a mother's personality conflicts with her infant's temperament, this may reduce the quality of care that the mother provides, thereby making it more likely that insecure attachment will result.

INFLUENCES OF EXPERIENCE. As we noted at the beginning of this chapter, psychologists have long believed that experiences during infancy have a special impact on directing the course of development. Because of the importance of early experience, psychologists have tried to identify those experiences that are particularly likely to benefit development as well as those that may be particularly harmful. Implicit in much of this work is the assumption that experiences are either harmful or beneficial for all children. As evidence has accumulated, however, many theorists have come to doubt that experiences have the same effect on all children. Instead, the same experience may be beneficial or harmful, depending on the child (Wachs and Gruen, 1982).

Temperament is one characteristic that has been shown to influence the impact of experience. For example, in a study by Wachs (1987), the impact of experience differed for active 12-month-olds and less active 12-month-olds. Among less active 12-month-olds, the frequency with which

FIGURE 3-20

Guidance from a parent is usually beneficial for less active babies but can interfere with an active baby's effort to explore.

parents named objects for children was positively related to infants' efforts to master toys (for example, when the infant attempted to understand how the toys worked). That is, infants whose parents named objects often were more likely to show mastery of toys. For active infants, the opposite was true: Mastery was less likely when parents named objects frequently. Gandour (1989) found an analogous relation with 15-month-olds. Among less active toddlers, the frequency with which mothers directed their child's attention was positively related to the child's exploration of novel toys. For active children, directing attention was negatively related to exploration.

Active infants apparently prefer to examine new objects by themselves. "Help" from an adult—in the form of naming objects or directing attention—is actually intrusive and interferes with the infant's mastery. However, less active infants are less inclined to undertake exploration spontaneously; for them, these experiences are not interfering but are facilitative instead.

Attachment and the influences of experiences are two key areas in which general statements concerning infant development can be seen to vary with an infant's particular temperament. The number of aspects of human development that are affected by temperament is certain to grow as we learn more about temperament. The result will be a broader picture of development that includes both general images of development as well as important variations of those images.

SUMMARY

1.   Sensation involves stimulation of the sensory receptors by physical energies from the internal and external environment. Perception is the selection, organization, and modification of sensory input.

2.   Neonates discriminate odors, find some more pleasant than others, and have the limited ability to localize odors in space. They distinguish sweet, bitter, salty, and sour tastes, and they prefer sweetness. Neonates respond to touch, sometimes with reflexes; in a short period of time they have a well-established sensitivity to pain. Auditory perception is remarkably sensitive in discriminating sounds and in localizing objects in space.

3.   Visual perception has been studied extensively in babies. Early in life infants respond to brightness and movement. Acuity, the ability to detect small stimuli and small details, approaches normal levels by the time the infant is 6 to 12 months of age. Babies perceive color and use binocular, pictorial, and kinetic cues to determine the dimension of depth.

4.   Different perceptual systems are coordinated. Infants can integrate information from vision and touch as well as information from vision and hearing.

5.   The very young infant is able to benefit from experience due to the ability to learn. Infants habituate to a stimulus presented repeatedly: When it is first presented, they orient to the stimulus; with repeated presentation, they are less likely to respond to the stimulus.

6.   Classical conditioning involves the formation of the expectancy that when the conditioned stimulus (CS) is presented, the unconditioned stimulus (US) will follow. Infants can be classically conditioned, particularly when the conditioning task involves feeding. Operant conditioning, too, can be demonstrated with infants; it involves formation of the expectation that a response will lead to particular consequences.

7.   Observational learning also has an early foundation. Newborns can imitate some simple movements (for example, tongue protrusion) and may be able to imitate facial expressions corresponding to happiness and sadness.

8.   Freud and Bowlby emphasized that attachment, the formation of an enduring bond with the available and sensitive caregiver, is a critical developmental milestone. Learning theorists attribute attachment to different causes, but they nevertheless consider it important.

9.   Attachment develops gradually over the first year. By 1 month, the infant has differentiated people and objects; by 6 months, the infant discriminates familiar people from unfamiliar people, and shortly thereafter, infants orient selectively to the mother. By 6 to 8 months of age, the attachment relationship is in place.

10.   Although virtually all infants become attached to their mothers, the quality varies. Babies have shown secure, avoidant, or resistant attachment in the Strange Situation experiment. Secure attachment is more likely when mothers respond sensitively to their infants, which means that they

respond predictably and appropriately. Secure attachment is slightly less likely when mothers are employed full time outside the home, apparently because the quality of mothering sometimes suffers.

11. Infants also become attached to fathers, but the relationship often has a different basis. Fathers are more playful, whereas mothers are more concerned with child care.

12. Secure attachment is related to later adaptive behaviors: Children who form secure attachments interact with their peers more successfully and seem happier. This may be a direct consequence of the trust associated with attachment. Alternatively, parents who support secure attachment may continue to provide positive support.

13. Temperament refers to an infant's "personality"—stable patterns of behavior that are biologically based. Dimensions of temperament include emotionality, activity, and sociability.

14. Temperament alone does not influence the nature of attachment relationships. However, when an infant's temperament conflicts with the mother's personality, insecure attachment may result.

15. Temperament influences the impact of experience on infants. Active infants prefer to explore without adult guidance, and they resist such guidance. In contrast, less active infants benefit from such parental guidance.

Physical and Motor Development

Count Philibert Guéneau de Montbeillard (1720–1788) was a French physician who measured his son's height every several months, from soon after his birth until he was a young man. Graphs depicting the young Montbeillard's steadily increasing stature, shown in Figure 4-1, represent one of the first efforts to track development from birth to maturity. Of course, height is simply one convenient way to document the physical growth that occurs between birth and adulthood: Head, trunk, and limbs all become larger, as do the internal organs, including the brain. Accompanying the body's growth is a greater control over the body: Muscles come to regulate the head, trunk, and limbs with ever greater precision. All these physical changes are intimately related to psychological development. Let's look at some examples.

▶ A typical seventh-grade dance will include several bizarre-looking couples: Thirteen-year-old girls standing inches taller than their partners, 13-year-old boys who remain shorter and childish in appearance. What factors are related to the onset of physical changes at adolescence? How does the body change in other phases of development? And, how do these physical changes affect children's psychological development? Answers

FIGURE 4-1
This record of change in height from birth to maturity is based on measurements that Montbeillard made of his son in the eighteenth century.
(From J. T. Falkner & J. M. Tanner, Human Growth, Vol 2: Postnatal Growth. New York: Plenum Press, 1979, p. 518. Reprinted by permission of Plenum Press.)

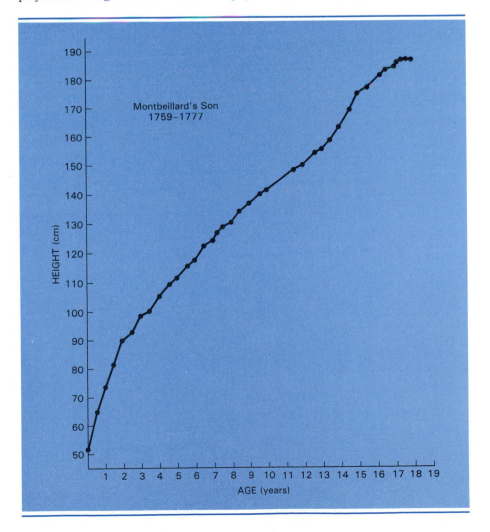

to these questions will come in the first two sections of this chapter when we examine physical growth and the development of the nervous system.

▶   Newborn babies cannot locomote, nor can they use their hands to grasp objects. But in just a few months, virtually all infants are able to scoot or crawl with ease, allowing them to get to interesting objects, which they can then examine with their hands. What is the sequence in which motor skills like these develop? Are experiences important in the development of these skills? To answer these questions, we need to study motor development, which is the focus of the last part of this chapter.   ◀

PHYSICAL GROWTH

Physical growth in humans follows standard, orderly patterns. It proceeds in two directions: from the top down, and from the center outward. As Figure 4-2 shows, the young child is top heavy, and not until adolescence do the proportions of adulthood appear. Function generally follows physical growth. Infants are able to lift their heads within the first weeks of life, but they cannot stand until the end of the first year. The refined motion of the fingers requires a longer time to develop than do the movements of the arm.

Patterns of Growth

Growth occurs through approximately the first 20 years of life in humans. This period is generally divided into three major times: infancy and early childhood (until about the fifth year of life), middle and late childhood (until about age 12), and adolescence (until about age 20). Growth is more rapid and more likely to show spurts during both the infancy and early childhood period and the adolescent period than during middle childhood.

FIGURE 4-2
Changes in body form associated with age. During infancy, the head and trunk are disproportionately large. *(Adapted from C. M. Jackson, "Some aspects of form and growth," in W. J. Robbins et al., Growth. New Haven: Yale University Press, 1929, p. 118. By permission.)*

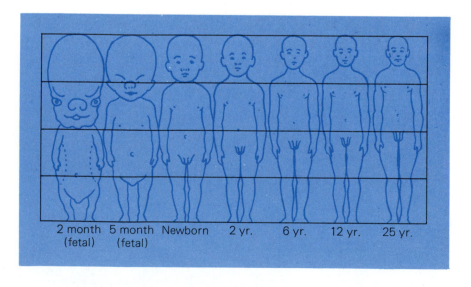

2 month   5 month   Newborn   2 yr.   6 yr.   12 yr.   25 yr.
(fetal)   (fetal)

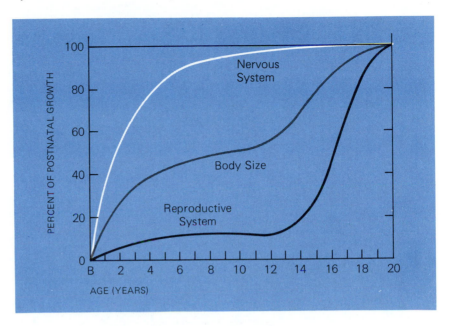

FIGURE 4-3
Growth patterns of three body systems. The nervous system develops most rapidly, followed by overall body size, and by the reproductive system. *(Adapted from J. M. Tanner, "Physical growth," in P. H. Mussen (Ed.), Carmichael's Manual of Child Psychology, 3rd ed., vol. 1. New York: John Wiley & Sons, 1970.)*

However, different parts of the body show different growth patterns relative to age. Figure 4-3 depicts the growth curves of three body systems. The nervous system is almost fully developed by the age of 6. Body size, which includes the skeleton, the muscles, and internal organs, shows moderate early growth but then slows down until adolescence, when it increases again. The reproductive system grows very slowly until puberty, and then undergoes rapid development.

The development of the nervous system is so important to psychological functioning that we examine it separately in the second section of this chapter. Here, let's examine changes in body size and changes associated with puberty.

BODY SIZE. The rate of growth in body size is faster during the first 6 months after birth than it is in any other period of life. Birth weight doubles in about 3 months and triples before the first birthday. Thereafter, weight and height continue to increase, but more slowly. Figure 4-4 shows the average weight and height for 2- to 18-year-olds in the United States. The curves depict well-known differences between the sexes in growth rates. Boys are generally taller and heavier than girls; however, between approximately 10 and 13 years of age, girls are larger on both these measures. Overall, increases in height taper off during childhood, but they accelerate dramatically between the ages of 11 and 13 in girls and between the ages of 13 to 15 in boys (Figure 4-5). This adolescent growth spurt levels off, and growth largely ceases at age 17 in girls and 19 in boys. By this time most people have reached about 98 percent of their mature height. From about 30 to 45 years of age height remains constant; then it begins to decline very slowly (Tanner, 1970).

The patterns shown in Figures 4-4 and 4-5 represent averages for

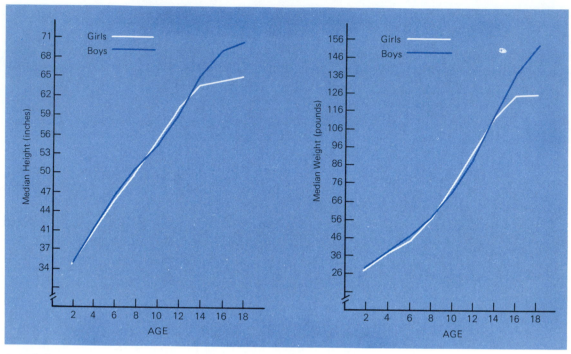

FIGURE 4-4

Changes in height and weight for both sexes from early childhood through maturity. Boys and girls develop at about the same rate through childhood. Because girls usually enter puberty earlier, they are slightly taller and heavier than boys between 10 and 12 years of age. By midadolescence, boys are taller and heavier, a difference maintained in adulthood.

(From National Center for Health Statistics, as cited in The World Almanac & Book of Facts. *New York: Newspaper Enterprise Association, 1984, p. 911.)*

growth at different ages. However, individual variations occur and are sometimes quite striking (Figure 4-6). Each individual's size and timing of growth probably have relatively strong biological determinants (Tanner, 1970). The correlation between weight as an adult and height at 1 year of age is greater than 0.70 (Plomin, 1984).

The change in overall size of the body reflects increases in the size of most body organs: The heart, lungs, stomach, and intestines all become larger with age. Muscle mass also increases with age. This does not reflect an increase in the number of muscle fibers, which is fixed soon after birth. Instead, the individual fibers become larger with development, providing the steady age-related increase in strength that is depicted in Figure 4-7 on page 118 (Malina, 1986).

Growth also reflects an increase in the size of bones. In fact, the relative maturity of the bones, known as **skeletal age**, is a common index of physical growth. In principle, any of the bones could be used, but in practice, the bones in the hands and wrist are evaluated most commonly. X-rays of the hand and wrist are taken to determine the shape of individual

Skeletal age A measure of physical growth based on the relative maturity of the bones.

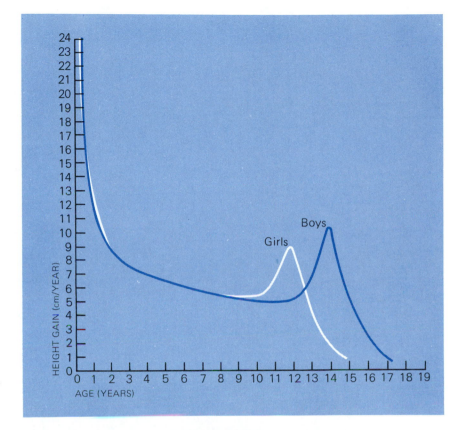

FIGURE 4-5

Increase in height per year for typical boys and girls. Both boys and girls have a growth spurt that coincides with adolescence, but the spurt usually occurs at a younger age in girls. *(From J. M. Tanner, "Physical growth," in P. H. Mussen (ed.), Carmichael's Manual of Child Psychology, 3rd ed. vol. 1. New York: John Wiley & Sons, 1970.)*

FIGURE 4-6

Individuals differ in the timing of the adolescent growth spurt. Although one of these girls appears to be much older than the other, they are actually the same age.

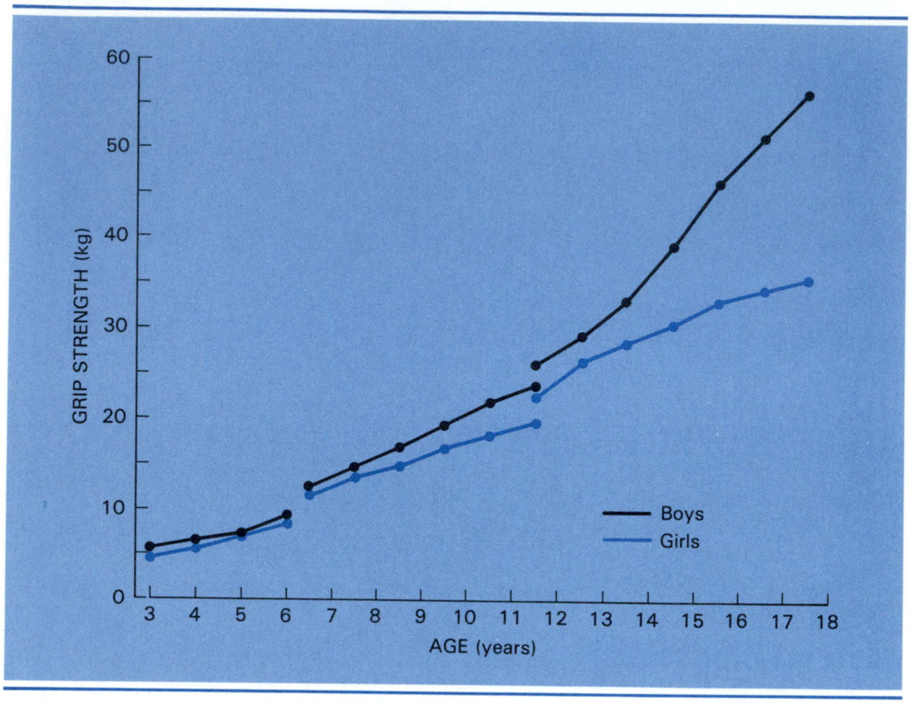

FIGURE 4-7
Strength increases
steadily through
childhood and
adolescence. Throughout
childhood boys are
slightly stronger than
girls; this difference
becomes much larger in
midadolescence.
(From J. Falkner &
J. M. Tanner (Eds.),
Human Growth: A
Comprehensive Treatise,
2nd ed., Vol. 2: Postnatal
Growth, Neurobiology.
New York: Plenum Press,
1986, p. 93. Reprinted by
permission of Plenum
Press.)

bones and their relative positions; this information is then used to calculate skeletal age (Roche, 1986).

PUBERTY, THE GROWTH SPURT, AND MATURATION OF THE REPRODUCTIVE SYSTEM. Adolescence is often used loosely to refer to the "teenage" years. A more precise meaning is to associate the beginning of adolescence with the onset of **puberty**, which denotes a collection of physical changes in boys and girls. For girls, the onset of puberty is marked by the enlargement of the breasts and the start of the adolescent growth spurt. Pubic hair appears later, followed by hair in the armpits. The onset of menstruation, **menarche**, occurs later, typically after the growth rate has begun to slow down. Early menstrual cycles are often not regular and may occur without an egg being released from the ovary. The average age of menarche is about 13 years among North American girls, but the normal range extends from 11 to 15 years. This variability is largely under genetic control (Marshall and Tanner, 1986). However, the environment is also a factor: Menarche is earlier in girls who experience much childhood stress (Moffitt, Caspi, Belsky, and Silva, 1992).

For boys, the first sign of puberty is that the testicles enlarge. Later, pubic hair appears and the growth spurt starts. At about the same time, the penis, prostate gland, and seminal vesicles begin to enlarge. Spontaneous ejaculations of semen, which is made up largely of secretions from the prostate gland, occur about one year after the penis starts to enlarge (Marshall and Tanner, 1986).

The events of puberty usually appear in these sequences, though exceptions are not uncommon. The age of onset of puberty is unrelated to ultimate stature: Children who mature early are not taller than those who mature later. Also, the size of the growth spurt is unrelated to ultimate

Puberty The point in development, usually in early adolescence, when body characteristics typifying adulthood (for example, pubic hair) emerge.

Menarche The beginning of menstruation, typically at approximately 13 years of age.

stature: Children who have a growth spurt that is particularly large are not necessarily taller than those who have had a smaller growth spurt (Marshall and Tanner, 1986).

SECULAR TRENDS: GROWING BIGGER AND FASTER. Growth occurs more rapidly in children and adolescents today. People in general are both taller and heavier than they were in the past (Muuss, 1972), probably due to better diet and health care. The armor of medieval knights seems to fit the 10- to 12-year-old American boy today; seats constructed in the La Scala opera house in Milan about 1788 were 13 inches wide; the average height of American sailors in the War of 1812 was 5 feet 2 inches.

Today the average girl reaches her adult height 2 years earlier than did females at the turn of the century; a similar comparison in boys is even more striking. Given the relation between general body growth and the maturation of the reproductive system, it is not surprising to find a lowering of the age of puberty. Figure 4-8 illustrates this pattern by indicating the earlier onset of menarche over the past 125 years.

What does the trend mean? Muuss (1972) suggests that we might expect several changes in the interests, attitudes, and social sophistication of today's adolescents compared with those of the past. Studies indicate earlier interest in sex, love, and marriage; greater tolerance of others; and increased seriousness and social awareness. Perhaps earlier maturation is also related to increases in premarital sex, venereal disease, and the number of children born to unwed mothers (Dreyer, 1982). The social calendar of youth seems to have moved ahead, much to the dismay of many parents. It is not possible, of course, to draw a cause-and-effect relation between these facts and trends in physical development. Still, the overall picture is one of a consistent downward extension of adolescence into the years we previously might have considered childhood. Whether adolescent psychosocial development has kept pace with this change is a topic we'll pursue in Chapter 14.

FIGURE 4-8
In countries throughout the world, the average age of menarche, the onset of menstruation, has declined steadily over the past century. *(From J. Falkner & J. M. Tanner (Eds.), Human Growth: A Comprehensive Treatise, 2nd ed., Vol. 2: Postnatal Growth, Neurobiology. New York: Plenum Press, 1986, p. 196. Reprinted by permission of Plenum Press.)*

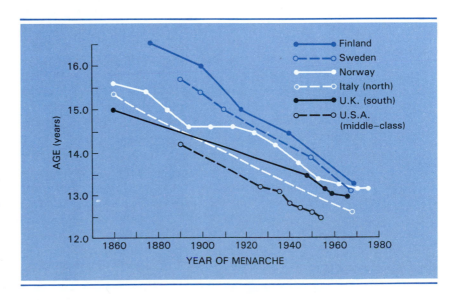

The Role of Nutrition

The human body needs energy to function, energy that is supplied by the food and liquids that people consume. This energy is needed for three functions. First, from infancy through adulthood, most of the energy is required to maintain **basal metabolic rate**. That is, most energy is consumed by basic bodily and cellular functions. A smaller portion is used for physical activity. The third portion is used for growth. In the first few months after birth, approximately 40 percent of the body's energy needs are directed to growth. This figure drops to 5 percent by the first birthday and to 3 percent at age 2.

To provide the necessary energy for growth, infants must consume more than twice as many calories per pound of body weight as adults. For example, a typical 3-month-old who weighs 12 pounds needs to consume about 600 calories daily, which is about 50 calories per pound of body weight (600 calories ÷ 12 pounds). In contrast, a 14-year-old who weighs 110 pounds needs 3020 calories daily. Although the total number of calories is much larger in the 14-year-old, the number of calories per pound of body weight is much less—about 27 (Holliday, 1986).

The calories that an infant needs are supplied by a combination of proteins, fats, and carbohydrates. The optimum combination of these nutrients is still debated. However, human breast milk, which many consider to be the ideal source of infant nutrients, is approximately 55 percent fat, 38 percent carbohydrates, and 7 percent protein (Alford and Bogle, 1982).

In addition to calories, vitamins and minerals are essential for normal physical development. Here, too, older children and adults require a larger quantity of most vitamins and minerals. However, when expressed relative to body weight, the infant's needs are substantially greater. Typical is vitamin A, which is essential for the retina of the eye to adapt to reduced light. A 16-pound infant needs 300 micrograms of vitamin A daily, compared to 750 micrograms for an adult. However, the infant's needs translate into nearly 20 micrograms per pound of body weight, compared to 5 or 6 micrograms for an adult (Alford and Bogle, 1982).

Unfortunately, in the 1990s, meeting these nutritional needs is a human problem of immense proportions. Approximately one-half of the world's children suffer at least mild **malnutrition**; about 5 percent are severely malnourished. Most of these children live in Third World countries, but a substantial number grow up in industrialized nations like Canada and the United States (Lozoff, 1989).

Children who are malnourished tend to lag behind their peers in physical development by an amount that varies directly with the length and degree of their malnutrition. Malnourishment also causes the adolescent growth spurt to be delayed and to be smaller than normal. Malnourishment is particularly harmful during the first 3 years of life, an outcome that is not surprising given the extraordinarily rapid growth that occurs during this period and the large amount of energy needed to sustain this growth.

The solution to malnutrition would appear to be simple: Provide children with an adequate diet. In reality, this is necessary but not suf-

Basal metabolic rate The rate with which energy is consumed to support basic bodily and cellular functions.

Malnutrition The lack of sufficient nourishment to support growth properly.

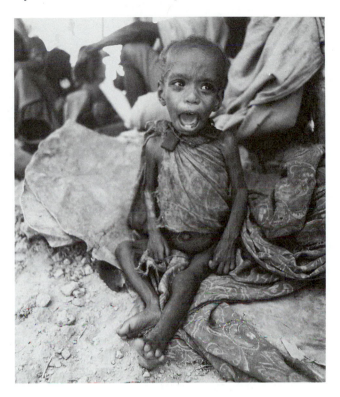

FIGURE 4-9

Many children are malnourished in the United States, Canada, and throughout the world. If the malnutrition is neither extended nor severe, children may experience "catch-up" growth, thereby achieving normal stature by maturity.

ficient. Malnourished children are typically lethargic and withdrawn. This behavior does conserve the child's limited energy, but it can also isolate the child from experiences that foster development. For example, this behavior may diminish the parents' belief that they can influence their children's development, creating a vicious cycle in which malnourished children are abandoned to their fate by parents who feel powerless. Programs in which children's diets are supplemented *and* in which parents are taught how to stimulate children's development may be the most effective in ameliorating the effects of malnutrition (Super, Herrera, and Mora, 1990). In these cases, the children's rates of growth may "catch up" as a result of these changed circumstances. However, even this sort of intervention may be inadequate in cases of sustained severe malnutrition. For these children, physical development may be affected permanently (Holliday, 1986).

Psychosocial Effects

Physical attributes influence psychosocial functioning; this is true for both the quality of the psychosocial characteristics and the rate at which they develop.

IS BEAUTY ONLY SKIN DEEP? Research tells us that people generally prefer physical attractiveness in adults and that they associate it with likability, goodness, and competence (Dion and Stein, 1978). Does this relation hold when it comes to children? It seems so. In one investigation,

FIGURE 4-10
Mothers of infants with deformities behave differently towards their infants than do mothers whose infants are not deformed. Mothers of infants with deformities are less likely to (a) engage in face-to-face interactions, (b) stimulate their infants through touch, (c) vocalize to their infants, (d) engage in affectionate touching, (e) smile at their infants, and (f) demonstrate toys to their infants.
(From R. C. Barden, et al. "Effects of craniofacial deformity in infancy on the quality of mother-infant interactions," in Child Development, 60, 1989, p. 822.)

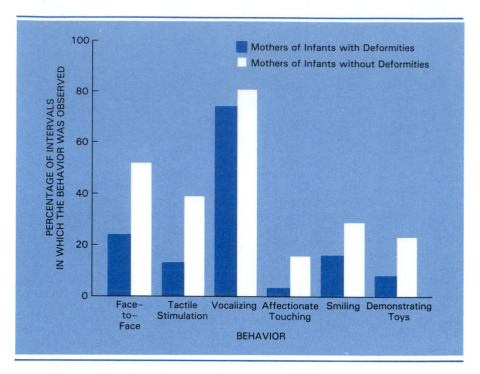

undergraduate students evaluated photographs of infants less than 1 year old; the attractive babies were seen as more likable, good, and smart (Stephan and Langlois, 1984). Given the strong tendency for adults to act as if beauty is more than skin deep, it is not surprising to find that children also perceive attractive children as friendlier, more likable, smarter, more altruistic, and less mean than unattractive children (Langlois and Stephan, 1977). Even 1-year-olds prefer to play with an attractive adult rather than an unattractive one (Langlois, Roggman, and Rieser-Danner, 1990). And 6-month-olds prefer to look at faces of attractive people, regardless of the race or age of the person (Langlois, Ritter, Roggman, and Vaughn, 1991).

The significance of these findings is that from early in life children may be treated quite differently on the basis of their physical appearance. In fact, there is research to support this view. For example, when adult females delivered penalties to children for making errors on a task, they treated the attractive boys with more tolerance than the attractive girls and the unattractive children of both sexes (Dion, 1974). Along these same lines, mothers of 4-month-olds with deformities such as a cleft palate interact with their infants in a less nurturant manner. As you can see in Figure 4-10, all nurturant behaviors were observed less often in mothers of deformed babies, despite the fact that these mothers reported that they found parenting more satisfying than did mothers of babies without deformities (Barden et al., 1989). To the extent that differential treatment of this sort occurs, children can be expected to behave differently and to feel differently about themselves (Stephan and Langlois, 1984).

TIMING OF MATURATION. Individuals mature at varying rates, due to heredity, diet, health, and other factors. Early maturation appears to be advantageous for boys (Jones, 1965). Early maturers are more likely to be elected class officers, have their names in the school newspaper, be rated as attractive, excel in athletics, and be less impulsive. Late maturers seem to be restless, talkative, tense, and attention seeking. These adolescents are less popular, less dominant, more dependent, and more rebellious. They seem to feel inadequate and rejected. Superior size and the physical strength that goes with it are in accord with male sex-role expectations. Early maturers may also be given tasks, privileges, and responsibilities typically assigned to older persons—and thus special opportunities for personal satisfaction and reward (Eichorn, 1963).

Differences between early and late maturing males gradually diminish as size contrasts lessen. Moreover, the overall picture begins to change (Siegel, 1982). As adults, early maturers are poised, responsible, and achieving in a conventional way. But they are also somewhat unflexible and emotionally restricted. Those who mature later are relatively more active, exploring, insightful, perceptive, independent, impulsive, and flexible. It seems that in coping with being behind their peers, late maturers develop many valuable behaviors.

The effects of timing on females are less clear-cut. Among 9- to 11-year-old girls who have not yet started to menstruate, breast growth is positively related to better peer relations and to better psychological adjustment (Brooks-Gunn and Warren, 1988). However, among adolescents, late maturers played more prominent roles in school and were rated higher on poise, sociability, cheerfulness, leadership, and expressiveness (Weatherley, 1964). When these adolescents were older (17 years of age), however, they showed few differences on projective tests, though the early maturers seemed to have a slight advantage (Jones and Mussen, 1958). The picture that emerges is complex. Early-maturing girls may initially suffer some disadvantages because they are not only larger than their male peers, but also tend to be stocky. They may date older males while lacking the adequate emotional and social sophistication necessary to deal with such relationships. They may be looked on with jealousy by their female peers. Even if this is so, however, the disadvantages appear to vanish rapidly, or perhaps to reverse themselves. The most consistent result is that the timing of maturation is simply not as powerful for females' social development as it is for males' social development.

DEVELOPMENT OF THE CENTRAL NERVOUS SYSTEM

Neuron A cell in the body that can transmit information and that is the basic unit of the nervous system.

Cell body The part of the neuron, in the center of the cell, that contains life-supporting structures.

The nervous system consists of the brain, the spinal cord, and the nerves that transmit impulses to and from the body. The basic building block of the nervous system is the nerve cell or **neuron**. An infant's feeling of affection for its mother, a child's travel from home to school, or an adolescent's efforts to solve an algebra problem all involve many neurons communicating with one another. Neurons come in many shapes and sizes, but the one shown in Figure 4-11 is typical. Neurons have three basic components: the **cell body**, in the center of the cell, flanked by a

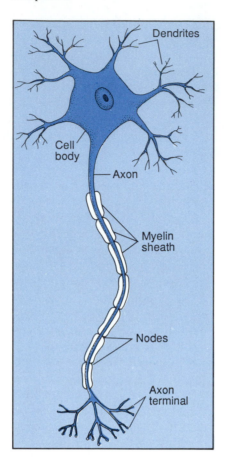

FIGURE 4-11
A nerve cell consists of a cell body, a dendrite that receives information from other nerves, and an axon that transmits information to other nerves. Axons in the brain are coated with myelin, which allows them to transmit information more rapidly.
(From J. M. Darley, S. Glucksberg, & R. A. Kinchla, Psychology, *5/e, © 1990, p. 38. Reprinted by permission of Prentice Hall, Englewood Cliffs, New Jersey.)*

Dendrite A tree-like structure that extends from the cell body of a neuron and receives information from other nerves.

Axon The part of the neuron that carries information from the cell body to other neurons.

Synapses The small spaces between neurons, across which information (nerve impulses) is transmitted by neurotransmitters.

Neurotransmitters Chemicals that are released by one neuron into a synapse, carrying

dendrite and an **axon**. The cell body contains much of the basic machinery needed to keep the neuron alive. The dendrite receives information from other nerves. Dendrites are usually very short: Laid end to end, several thousand dendrites would measure no more than an inch. However, they often consist of many branches, allowing one neuron to receive information from as many as 100,000 other neurons. Axons carry information from the cell body to other neurons. Axons do not branch as extensively as dendrites but they are much longer, with some being several feet long.

Neurons are responsible for the transmission of nerve impulses, although they are not in direct contact with each other. The nerve impulses are carried across the small spaces between the neurons—called **synapses**—by the release of chemicals called **neurotransmitters**.

The nervous system originates in the outer layer of the embryo when a group of cells, the **neural plate**, thickens very soon after conception. The plate folds, and its edges meet to form the neural tube. The entire nervous system arises from this structure (see Figure 4-12). At birth the brain is about 25 percent of its adult weight, forming a large part of the body at birth (Tanner, 1978). The brain attains 50 percent of its eventual weight by 6 months of age, 75 percent by 2 years, 90 percent by 5 years, and 95 percent by 10 years.

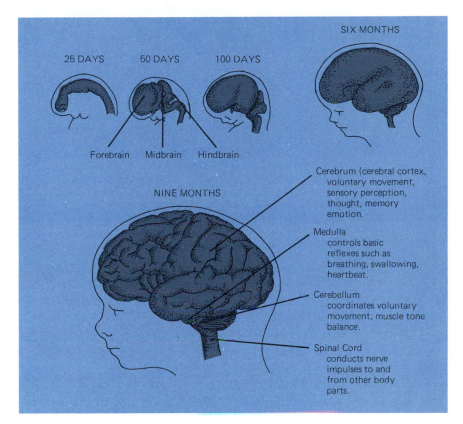

SIX MONTHS

25 DAYS   50 DAYS   100 DAYS

Forebrain   Midbrain   Hindbrain

NINE MONTHS

Cerebrum (cerebral cortex, voluntary movement, sensory perception, thought, memory emotion.

Medulla controls basic reflexes such as breathing, swallowing, heartbeat.

Cerebellum coordinates voluntary movement; muscle tone balance.

Spinal Cord conducts nerve impulses to and from other body parts.

FIGURE 4-12
A side view of prenatal development of the brain. The brain originates at the head end of the neural tube. Shortly before birth, all the major structures of the brain can be recognized.

This increase in weight is simply one manifestation of a series of intricate changes that occur in the brain's development. Let's examine structural change in the brain.

Structural Change

Neurons are formed between the tenth and twenty-sixth week of pregnancy, reaching a peak at 18 weeks. The number of neurons is virtually fixed at birth. However, individual neurons do grow. Axons grow rapidly, sometimes as much as 1 millimeter per day. Dendrites grow much more slowly, but they develop extensions that resemble the branches of a tree. This process of **arborization**, which continues throughout childhood and adolescence, means that a single neuron can receive information from thousands of other neurons (Morgan and Gibson, 1991). Interestingly, the number of synapses grows during the first two years, then slowly declines. The early connections apparently are flexible; there are many that do not become parts of functional neural circuits and that are lost (Huttenlocher, 1990).

Axons of neurons in the brain and spinal cord become wrapped with a fatty sheath known as **myelin**. This sheath acts like insulation, with the result that messages are transmitted much more rapidly in neurons that are myelinated than those that are not. Myelination begins in prenatal

the neural signal to an adjacent neuron.

Neural plate A group of embryonic cells that folds to form the neural tube.

Arborization Growth of dendrites that resembles the branching of a tree.

Myelin A fatty sheath that surrounds axons in the brain and spinal cord, resulting in faster transmission of information.

Cerebral hemispheres
The largest and most recently evolved part of the brain, responsible for those functions that distinguish humans from other animals (such as personality).

Corpus callosum A bundle of nerve fibers that link the left and right cerebral hemispheres.

Fissures Grooves in the hemispheres that are used to identify specific regions in the brain.

Lobes Areas of the brain typically set apart by fissures.

development. Neurons in the brain that control motor functioning are the first to become myelinated; nerves that carry sensory information are next. The remaining nerves acquire myelin only gradually, with some regions of the brain not being completely myelinated until adolescence or even young adulthood (Konner, 1991).

Emergence of the Functioning Brain

The changes in neurons that we have just described allow the brain to function more powerfully. To understand how different brain functions emerge with development, we need to examine the functioning of the mature brain.

THE MATURE BRAIN. The **cerebral hemispheres** represent the largest part of the human brain; they form the upper parts of the brain. The cerebral hemispheres represent the most sophisticated evolution of the nervous system. The cerebral hemispheres dominate the human brain; in other animals, they are much smaller. Not surprisingly, most of the abilities that we consider distinctly human—sophisticated reasoning, complex language skills, elaborate personalities—are controlled by the cerebral hemispheres.

The two cerebral hemispheres are linked by a bundle of nerves called the **corpus callosum**. The cortex of each hemisphere is covered by grooves called **fissures**. Some are so deep that we use them as landmarks to identify different regions or **lobes** of the hemispheres. Figure 4-13 depicts the four lobes of the human brain: frontal, parietal, occipital, and temporal. These

FIGURE 4-13
The cortex of the brain is divided into four lobes. (*From J. M. Darley, S. Glucksberg, & R. A. Kinchla, Psychology, 5/e, © 1990, p. 52. Reprinted by permission of Prentice Hall, Englewood Cliffs, New Jersey.*)

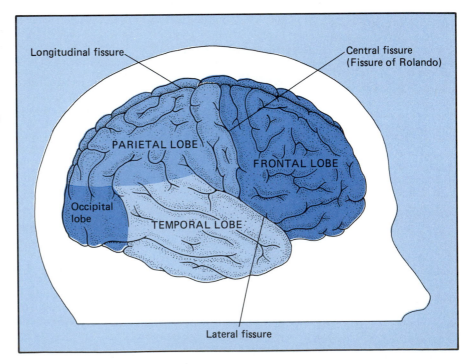

and other parts of the brain are linked by complex circuits that are responsible for distinct components of behavior.

How do these different lobes of the brain function? Many of the answers to this question have come from studies of the impact of disease (for example, stroke) or injury on brain-damaged adults. Damage to a particular location in the brain often yields consistent, specific deficits in perception, thought, or emotion. When this happens, we can conclude that the damaged portion of the brain is an essential part of the neural circuitry for the behavior that is affected.

Work of this sort reveals that the **frontal lobe** is the seat of personality. In addition, the frontal lobe plays a critical role in goal-directed behavior, such as seen in planning activities. The frontal lobe also functions in a way that inhibits impulsive responses.

At the junction of the frontal and parietal lobes is the **somatosensory cortex**, made up of two strips of tissue. The frontmost of these two strips is the **motor cortex**, which plays an important role in regulating muscle movements. The strip directly behind the motor cortex is the **sensory cortex**, a region that receives sensory input concerning touch, temperature, and the position of body parts.

The sensory cortex does not receive input from your eyes or ears. Information from these senses is so complex that special areas of the brain are set aside for each. Neurons from the eyes end up in the occipital lobe, at the back of the brain. Neurons from the ears are connected to large areas known as the **speech center** that cut across the frontal, parietal, and temporal lobes.

Thus far, we have treated the two hemispheres as equal. In fact, they are not. For most people, the left hemisphere plays the more important role in understanding and producing language. The right hemisphere does have some limited language skills: Understanding humor and intonation seem to be right-hemisphere functions. Also under the control of the right hemisphere are the abilities to understand spatial relations, to identify faces, and to recognize emotions. All these seem to be functions that are primarily the domain of the right hemisphere (Kinsbourne, 1989).

DEVELOPMENT OF FUNCTION. Our understanding of the development of brain function is meager. Much of the research has attempted to determine when functions become lateralized in the left and right hemispheres. The consensus is that language is a left-hemisphere function from early in life, perhaps from birth (Hahn, 1987). A variety of evidence supports this conclusion: As with adults, damage to the left hemisphere of a child's brain is more likely to result in loss of language than is comparable damage to the right hemisphere (Witelson, 1987). Consistent with these findings are results of laboratory studies: In **dichotic listening** experiments, verbal materials (for example, words or syllables) are presented with headphones to both ears; children are then asked to report what they have heard. The logic behind this paradigm is that nerves link each ear primarily to the hemisphere on the other side of the brain. Thus, material presented to the right ear is processed primarily by the left hemisphere, whereas material presented to the left ear is processed by the right hemisphere. By age 3 years, children typically recall more verbal information

Frontal lobe The part of the brain that controls personality and goal-directed behavior.

Somatosensory cortex An area of tissue at the junction of the frontal and parietal lobes that is central to sensory and motor functioning.

Motor cortex A part of the brain that plays a key role in regulating muscle movements.

Sensory cortex A part of the brain that receives sensory input concerning touch, temperature, and the position of body parts.

Speech center A large area in the brain responsible for understanding and producing language.

Dichotic listening A task used to assess brain organization in which different information is presented to the left and right ears.

Electroencephalogram (EEG) A record of the electrical activity of the brain, obtained from electrodes placed on the scalp.

Positron emission tomography (PET-scan) A technique used to evaluate brain activity by tracing through different areas of the brain, the presence of a radioactive form of glucose that has been injected into the bloodstream.

from the right ear than from the left, indicating a left-hemisphere advantage for verbal information (Hahn, 1987).

To examine the onset of lateralization in even younger children, investigators have placed metal electrodes on the scalp to record ongoing electrical activity. Each electrode measures the sum of the activity of thousands of nerves in that region of the brain. The output from the electrode yields a pattern of waves known as an **electroencephalogram— EEG** for short. Typically, presentation of speech produces more electrical activity in the left hemisphere of a newborn infant's brain than in the right hemisphere (Molfese and Burger-Judisch, 1991). Thus, the primary role of the left hemisphere in language processing seems to be established at birth.

The development of specialization in the right hemisphere has been more difficult to determine. In dichotic listening studies, some investigators have reported a left-ear advantage for nonspeech sounds. Saxby and Bryden (1984), for example, reported that 5- and 6-year-olds were better able to determine a speaker's emotion (happy, sad, or angry) in sentences that were presented to the left ear. Similarly, some investigators have reported greater activity in the infant's right hemisphere when music is presented to the left ear (Hahn, 1987). However, other investigators report no left-ear advantage in studies such as these. Part of the problem in these studies is that the skills lateralized in the right hemisphere are more heterogeneous than those lateralized in the left. The skills may not become lateralized at the same points in development, which would explain some of the inconsistency in these experiments.

The frontal lobe begins to function during the latter part of the first year of life. The Close-Up features research in which frontal lobe functioning is revealed by comparing an infant's performance with that of a monkey with damage to this part of the brain. Another way to study frontal lobe functioning is to use **positron emission tomography** or **PET-scan** for

FIGURE 4-14
Throughout childhood, the frontal lobe gradually becomes more effective at inhibiting responses. This explains why young children often are unable to inhibit responses.

CLOSE-UP

Frontal Lobe Functioning in Monkeys and Human Infants

Case studies of brain-damaged patients have provided many insights into brain functioning. In these patients, scientists have no control over the location or amount of brain damage. However, studies in which small portions of the brain are removed surgically from a live monkey indicate that the general organization of the monkey's cortex is similar to that of humans. Consequently, a useful strategy for understanding some aspects of human development is to compare the performance of infants, children, and monkeys with intact brains, and then to compare these findings with the performance of monkeys with parts of their brains removed.

Adele Diamond and her colleagues (1991) have used this strategy to trace the development of frontal lobe functioning in human infants. The first step in the research is to use monkeys to identify links between parts of the brain and specific behavior. In Diamond's research, monkeys watched as food was hidden under one of two identical containers. After a few seconds, adult monkeys were allowed to find the food. They invariably reached for the correct container. This procedure was repeated for several trials in which the food was hidden in the same container, then the food was hidden in the other container. On all trials, adult monkeys reached for the correct container.

The behavior of adult monkeys whose frontal cortex had been removed surgically presents an interesting contrast. They, too, found the food in its initial hiding location. However, when the location was changed, they continued to look for the food in the initial location, not in the new location. Apparently, without a frontal cortex, the adult monkey cannot inhibit the dominant response in this situation, which is to reach for the food where it has previously been hidden. Furthermore, this deficit is linked specifically to the frontal lobe because monkeys with a portion of the parietal lobe removed had no difficulty whatsoever—they consistently found the food.

The next step is to test infants with these procedures. Diamond found that 1-year-olds would typically find the hidden object (a toy) both in the initial and new hiding locations. In contrast, the majority of 7- to 9-month-olds behaved exactly like the monkeys who lacked a frontal cortex. Even though they saw the toy hidden in a new location, they continued to reach for the toy in the location where it had previously been hidden.

Thus, Diamond's work has demonstrated parallel differences in performance between (a) monkeys with intact frontal cortex and those lacking frontal cortex, and (b) 7- to 9-month-old and 12-month-old human infants. These parallel differences suggest that age differences in infant behavior on this task reflect a frontal cortex that matures gradually during infancy.

short. The basic idea here is that the brain needs fuel—glucose—to work. The parts of the brain that are working hardest at any given time need more glucose. To measure the brain's consumption of fuel, a radioactive form of glucose is injected into a person's bloodstream. This radioactive glucose is traced through the brain, and a computer generates color-coded images of the brain that indicate the concentration of glucose in different regions. Chugani and Phelps (1986) found little activity in the frontal cortex of 1-month-olds; activity had increased by 3 months of age, and resembled adult levels by the first year.

Of course, adultlike levels of activity do not necessarily mean that the frontal lobe is functionally mature. In fact, the skills associated with the frontal lobe seem to develop in childhood and into adolescence. Insights into the nature of frontal-lobe functioning have come from comparing children's performances with those of brain-damaged adults. When adults with damage to the frontal cortex sort cards according to color and then need to sort on the basis of shape, they will often persist in incorrectly sorting cards by color. These perseverative errors in sorting indicate that people lacking a frontal cortex are unable to inhibit a previously learned response. Young children behave in much the same way as patients lacking a frontal cortex, making perseverative errors frequently. By 10 years of age, children's performances match those of normal adults, which may indicate that the inhibitory functions of the frontal cortex mature during middle childhood (Welsh, Pennington, and Groisser, 1991).

We have only recently begun to understand how brain functions emerge with development. The current view is one in which, by the first birthday, many distinguishing features of the mature brain can be recognized: Organized, goal-directed behavior emerges under the control of the frontal cortex, and speech is being processed by the left hemisphere. However, the brain is far from functionally mature at this point. Neurons grow, synapses are eliminated, and the functioning of the cortex becomes more specialized.

MOTOR DEVELOPMENT

As children mature physically, their ability to move about and to manipulate the environment also develops rapidly. Well before adolescence is reached, they can thread a needle, operate a jig saw, and throw a basketball through a hoop. We call the process of mastering these skills *perceptual-motor development* because it involves complex perceptual and motor processes that gradually build on themselves.

Basic Principles

Differentiation The progressive refinement of motor development, usually in reference to infants or young children.

Hierarchic integration The combination of individual actions into more complex and sophisticated patterns of behavior.

Motor development follows a predictable pattern. Babies cannot walk before they sit, or write before they grasp voluntarily. One principle guiding motor development is that gross motor control, involving large areas of the body, is achieved more easily than fine motor control, involving smaller muscle groups. Children can hold their bottles during the latter part of their first year of life, but lack the ability to play a flute. In other words, over time mass movement becomes specific or differentiated. A second principle is that complex motor skills develop progressively through **differentiation** and **hierarchic integration** (Werner, 1948). Once specific control (differentiation) is achieved, the individual actions can be put together or integrated into larger, complex, and more coherent whole movements. After gaining greater and greater control over arm, leg, and

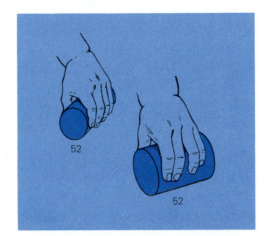

FIGURE 4-15
The pincer movement, in which the thumb functions in opposition to the remaining fingers, allows humans to manipulate objects with great precision.

neck movements (differentiation), the infant will begin to put these relatively simple actions together and perform the more complex and integrated act of sitting up without support.

Of course, humans are not the only animals capable of motion. In fact, the ability to move autonomously is one of the characteristics that distinguishes animals from plants. However, human motor skills are unique in two aspects: First, only adult humans rely exclusively on bipedal (two feet) locomotion to move in their environment; in other animals, quadrupedal (four feet) locomotion is the norm. Second, humans excel at the use of tools, a skill made possible by fully independent fingers (instead of a paw) and a thumb placed in opposition to fingers so that objects can be grasped (see Figure 4-15). This ability to manipulate objects brings information to children about the shapes, textures, and other features in their environments.

In the next few pages, we trace development in each of these two aspects.

Posture and Locomotion

Within a little over one year's time, changes in posture and locomotion transform the child from a relatively immobile bit of humanity into an upright organism that moves through space by crawling, climbing, and walking. The nature of these changes and the approximate times at which they are achieved are shown in Figure 4-16. The figure cannot show, however, the practice, the waverings, and the failures that are the foundations for progress. Shirley (cited by Eckert, 1987), who followed the growth of upright locomotion, suggested that it occurs in five fundamental stages. In the first stage the infant achieves control of the upper body, and in the second, of the entire trunk. During the third stage the infant makes an active effort toward locomotion. In the fourth stage the baby is able to crawl. And in the fifth stage the infant can control posture and coordination for walking. Let's examine some of these developments in more detail.

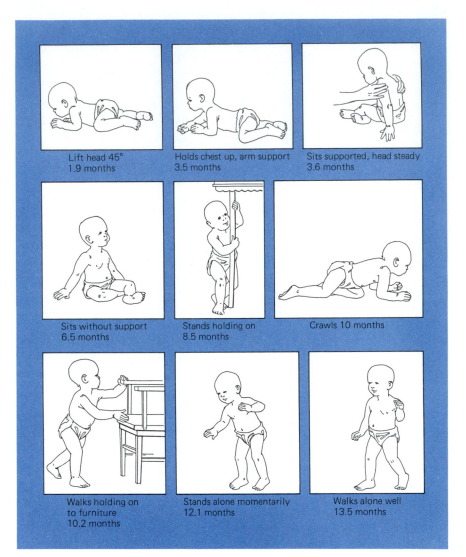

FIGURE 4-16
Ages at which 75 percent of babies achieve specific motor milestones for posture and locomotion. Although individuals may achieve these milestones at different ages, the sequence holds for virtually all infants. *(Primary source: W. K. Frankenburg, and J. B. Dodds (1969), "The Denver Developmental Screening Test" in Journal of Pediatrics, 71, 181–191.)*

Lift head 45°
1.9 months

Holds chest up, arm support
3.5 months

Sits supported, head steady
3.6 months

Sits without support
6.5 months

Stands holding on
8.5 months

Crawls 10 months

Walks holding on
to furniture
10.2 months

Stands alone momentarily
12.1 months

Walks alone well
13.5 months

PREREQUISITES FOR WALKING.   The onset of walking soon after the first birthday reflects the maturity and coalescence of a number of discrete skills, each of which is essential in order to walk. One basic skill is the ability to maintain an upright posture. Newborns are ill prepared to do this; the newborn's body simply does not lend itself to standing upright, much less walking. The problem is that the newborn's body is top heavy, with the head and trunk disproportionately large. The young baby is like a tower of blocks with the smallest block at the base and largest at the top; this sort of a structure is inherently unstable. With growth of the legs and muscles over the several months following birth, it becomes physically possible for infants to maintain a standing posture around their first birthday (Thelen, Ulrich, and Jensen, 1989).

Once upright, posture must be adjusted constantly to maintain that upright status. Maintaining balance in this way depends upon cues from the eyes and the inner ears. Even by four months of age, infants are beginning to use this information to maintain posture: At this age, if a seated infant pitches forward or backward, muscles in the back of the neck will keep the head upright. Surprisingly, young infants are much better able to make these adjustments when they are blindfolded (Woollacott, Shumway-Cook, and Williams, 1989). Similarly, 1-year-olds stand upright equally well in the dark and in the light (Ashmead & McCarty, 1991). Apparently, infants do not need visual cues to maintain an upright posture. The sense of balance provided by cues in the inner ear is sufficient. For young infants, visual cues may actually interfere with their efforts to sit upright.

The stepping motions that are central to walking have a fascinating developmental history. When newborns are held upright, they make stepping movements, but this reflex then disappears in about two months. It is not until many months later that voluntary stepping is observed. However, reflexive and voluntary stepping may be linked by kicking. When infants lie on their backs they often make spontaneous kicking movements. Thelen and Fisher (1982, 1983) suggest that kicking and the stepping reflex involve the same muscle functioning. They believe that the reflex disappears because muscle growth does not keep up with leg growth. That is, in the upright position the muscle is not strong enough to lift the leg, but in the lying-down position the pull of gravity lessens, and kicking can then occur. This suggests that the stepping reflex is actually connected to later walking through spontaneous kicking.

Another major component of walking is moving the legs in alternation, repeatedly transferring the body's weight from one foot to the other. Experiments by Thelen and Ulrich (1991) have revealed in very young babies the rudiments of stepping with alternate legs. In Thelen and Ulrich's procedure, shown in Figure 4-17, infants were placed upright on a

FIGURE 4-17
Esther Thelen and her colleagues use this apparatus to investigate infants' stepping. An adult supports the infant while the belts on the treadmill move.

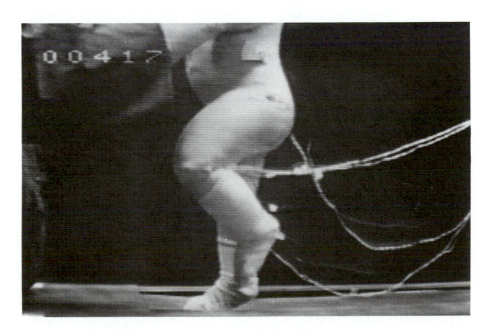

treadmill and supported by an adult. When the belt on the treadmill started to move, even some 3-month-olds demonstrated the mature pattern of alternating steps on each leg. In other babies, alternate stepping was not common until 6 or 7 months of age. On some trials, the treadmill was designed to provide separate belts for each leg, and these belts were then moved at different speeds. Infants adjusted to this change, stepping more frequently on the fast-moving belt and less often on the slow-moving belt.

In these experiments, the treadmill did not *cause* stepping. Because the infants were held by an adult, they could, without fear of falling, simply let their legs be dragged by the belt. Or they might "hop" with both legs. Alternate stepping was not a necessary byproduct of the treadmill. Instead, the treadmill task showed that when the task is simplified so that infants are not responsible for maintaining balance, the alternate stepping motion that is essential for walking is evident long before infants walk by themselves.

These components, along with others, such as the desire to move independently in one's environment, follow specific developmental trajectories through the first year of life. As we have seen, many components function in rudimentary form early in the first year. However, not until 12 to 15 months is a sufficient level of control achieved so that the component skills can be coordinated with enough precision for independent, unsupported walking.

DEVELOPMENT AFTER WALKING. In the months that follow the first tentative steps, walking becomes more skilled. The limbs become better coordinated and children become better able to make the adjustments needed to traverse uneven surfaces and to compensate for unexpected body movements (Clark, Whitall, and Phillips, 1988). By about 2 years of age children can jump. Soon afterward they are able to walk up and down stairs by placing both feet on each step, and then to hop and eventually to skip. With each achievement, the world widens and becomes a more exciting place.

By the time children enter elementary school, they walk, run, and jump with great prowess. Of course, motor performance continues to improve during the school years—children run faster and jump further. These changes can be linked to increased muscle mass with age and to age-related improvements in the intake, transportation, and use of oxygen (Keogh and Sugden, 1985).

Beginning in the elementary school years, boys typically run slightly faster and jump somewhat farther than girls. These differences, shown in Figure 4-18, are small in early childhood but become progressively larger (Thomas and French, 1985). Of course, the data in Figure 4-18 are simply averages for groups of boys and girls; at each age a large number of girls can perform better than some boys. And, with training, some girls' performances can surpass that of most boys (Keogh and Sugden, 1985). Furthermore, most of these differences in the average level of performance of girls and boys can be explained in terms of differences in physical development of girls and boys, differences that become accentuated in early adolescence. Let's take body fat as an example. Superior jumping

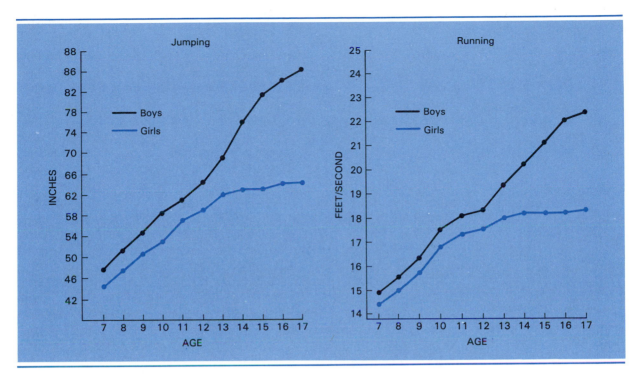

FIGURE 4-18

During childhood, boys run slightly faster and jump further than girls. These differences become larger in adolescence, a change reflecting the composition of adolescent boys' and girls' bodies.
(From J. Keogh and D. Sugden, Movement Skill Development. New York: Macmillan, 1985, Figs. 5-1 and 5-3. Reprinted with permission of Macmillan Publishing Company. Copyright © 1985 Macmillan Publishing Company.)

and running is more common in individuals whose body weight consists of a relatively small amount of fat and a large amount of muscle. Fat constitutes a greater percentage of body weight in girls than in boys, and the differences become even greater in late childhood and in adolescence. This difference, along with differences in other physical variables such as height, explains why boys excel at jumping and running (Smoll and Schutz, 1990). Put another way, boys and girls who are similar in height and in the ratio of body fat to muscle mass should be similar in running and jumping performance.

Bipedal locomotion allows humans to move about in an upright posture. We have seen that the major "hurdles" in the development of this skill are crossed early in life; certainly by the time children enter school their locomotor skills are very functional, allowing them to move effectively, whether from bedroom to kitchen or from home to school.

Often the purpose of locomotion is to place children closer to an object—a toy, tool, or another person—so that they can grasp it. The fine-motor skills that are necessary for grasping are the focus of the next few pages of this chapter. We shall see that here, too, extraordinary development takes place early in life.

Fine-Motor Coordination

Newborns move their limbs in ways that were once thought to be haphazard and reflecting an excess energy. Now it is clear that newborns actually control and coordinate the movement of their arms and hands. When newborns are fed sucrose, they typically bring one hand to their mouth, where it remains while the infant feeds (Blass, Fillion, Rochat, Hoffmeyer, and Metzger, 1989). These movements are coordinated with the control of the mouth. When a newborn begins moving a hand toward his or her face, he or she will open the mouth before the hand makes contact, as if the infant anticipates the hand's arrival. Furthermore, this hand-mouth coordination does not require visual guidance—infants bring their hands directly to their mouths just as effectively when their eyes are closed as when their eyes are open (Butterworth and Hopkins, 1988).

From these early coordinated movements, infants rapidly learn to use their hands to explore their environment (Karniol, 1989). In the first month or so after birth, infants begin to hold objects in one hand. By 1 or 2 months, an infant will move the object, twisting the wrists, for example, so that a held object rotates in space. More complex exploratory motions, such as shaking, emerge at 3 to 4 months of age.

At about 4 months, infants first use both hands simultaneously. Initially, the movements of the two hands are not coordinated; instead, one hand will be used to hold an object passively while the other is used to play with another object. A baby might shake a rattle with one hand, while holding a block motionless in the other. In a short time, infants begin to

FIGURE 4-19
Infants who are just a few months old will use their hands to grasp an object.

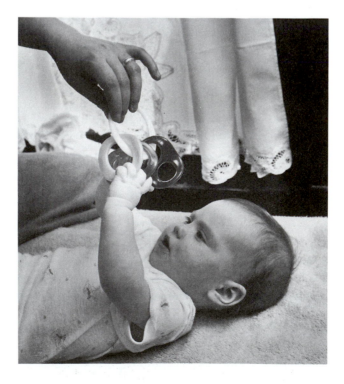

use both hands together, to steady objects or to hold larger objects. An infant will also use both hands to bring an object to his or her face, where it can be examined by mouthing it (Rochat, 1989).

By 5 or 6 months of age, infants start to coordinate the actions of the two hands. One hand may be used to hold an object while the other is used to perform some action involving the object. For example, one hand may be used to support a doll while the other hand is used to stroke the doll's hair. The complexity of these movements increases, so that, at 7 or 8 months, infants move the hands in sequence to achieve some goal. An infant may use one hand to open a box, then use the other to retrieve the contents out of the box.

These qualitative changes in infants' use of their hands are accompanied by quantitative changes in the precision of their movements. Mathew and Cook (1990) videotaped 4½-, 6- and 7½-month-olds as they reached for an attractive, stationary toy. A number of measures indicated that level of skill increased with age. The older infants grabbed the object for which they were reaching more often and did so more rapidly than younger babies. Also, older infants usually moved their hands directly to the object; younger infants moved their hands in the general direction of the object, then slowed their hands and corrected the direction of movement. This recalibration of the route to the object was repeated until the infant's hands finally reached the object.

Eating is one common task in which infants' growing motor skills can be illustrated. By 6 months of age, many babies will feed themselves "finger food." Their initial efforts are clumsy, with the hand placing the food at the cheek instead of in the mouth. Rapidly, however, infants become adept at picking up foods of a variety of sizes, shapes, and textures, and placing them directly in the mouth. Accomplishing this same task with a spoon is much more challenging. When 1-year-olds are given a spoon and dish of food, they spend most of the time playing—dipping the spoon in the food or putting an empty spoon in their mouth. Gradually, infants master the many components of using a spoon successfully.

To illustrate the complexity of this skill, which most adults take for granted, and to see infants' progress, let's consider two aspects of using a spoon that were studied by Connolly and Dalgeish (1989): filling the spoon and guiding it to the mouth. One-year-olds usually fill a spoon by placing it directly over the dish and lowering it until the bowl of the spoon is full. Two-year-olds more often use the adultlike technique in which the spoon and hand rotate around the wrist to scoop food from the dish. After the spoon is full, the journey to a 1-year-old's mouth is filled with course corrections, many of them major; among 2-year-olds, the route is much more direct. Part of this difference reflects the fact that 2-year-olds watch the spoon almost constantly from the time it is filled until it enters the mouth; 1-year-olds watch the spoon part way, then look elsewhere.

This analysis of using a spoon is typical of skilled actions: Many component movements are involved, each of which must be done properly and in the right order, for the action to be completed successfully. Development involves mastery of both the individual motions and the assembling of them to form a smoothly functioning unit.

FIGURE 4-20
Infants gradually master the precise motions needed to successfully maneuver a fully-laden spoon from dish to mouth.

Beyond infancy, dramatic change continues. By 18 months, children can scribble spontaneously, fill a cup with cubes, and build a tower with a few blocks. Before they go to kindergarten, most youngsters can reasonably copy a circle and square, draw some semblance of the human figure, and use crayons with confidence (Frankenburg and Dobbs, 1969).

During the elementary-school years, development involves gradual refinement of existing skills: Handwriting, for example, becomes faster and more legible (Hamstra-Bletz and Blote, 1990). The advanced motor skills of young children were shown by van der Meulen and his colleagues (1990). In their study, a green light moved rapidly but haphazardly from left to right; subjects were asked to keep a red light as close as possible to the green light by moving a handle left and right in unison with the green light's movement. For adults, the correlation between the movements of the two lights was 0.97, indicating that adults tracked the green light's motion nearly perfectly with the red light. For 6- to 8-year-olds, the correlation was 0.87. Although this value was less than for the adults, it indicates that children moved the handle with a high degree of precision in their efforts to track the green light's movements.

By the middle elementary school years, skills are so well-developed that, with practice, children can achieve adultlike levels of performance. A familiar example would be the extraordinary skill with which some children play video games. Laboratory studies document this example: With many trials, children's performances can equal or even surpass that of unpracticed adults (Kail and Park, 1990).

HANDEDNESS. For most children and adults, movements are not equally precise with both hands. Instead, most people prefer to use one hand over the other and perform better with the preferred hand. Handedness is not absolutely consistent across activities; that is, some people may write with their left hands and eat with their right. Nevertheless, approximately 90 percent of the adult human population all over the world shows a preference for the right hand.

By 3 years of age, most children prefer to use their right hand, though not with the consistency seen in adults (McManus et al., 1988). The onset of handedness is less certain. Most investigators find that 6- to 9-month-olds do not consistently use one hand more than the other; when a preference is found at this age, it is usually for the right hand and is more likely to be found in female infants than in males (McCormick and Maurer, 1988).

Soon after the first birthday, preference for the right hand begins to stabilize. For example, Cornwell, Harris, and Fitzgerald (1991) videotaped youngsters as they played with toys that could be manipulated with two hands (for example, a plastic nut and bolt, a ball in a clear plastic box). Among 13- and 20-month-olds, nearly two-thirds of the infants would first grasp the toy with their right hand, then use the left hand to steady the toy while the right hand was used for actions such as unscrewing the nut or removing the lid. At both ages, the left hand was preferred by about 20 percent of the infants.

Theories of handedness range from the social-psychological (that is, children simply acquire the habit) to the genetic. Heredity may indeed be involved: Many investigators find that an infant's handedness can be predicted from family histories. In the study by Cornwell and her colleagues described previously, three-fourths of the 20-month-olds with a family history of right-handedness used their right hand consistently; half of the 20-month-olds with a family history of left-handedness used their left hand consistently. But preference can be affected by educational practices as well as by family and cultural values. Contemporary North American culture is definitely designed for right-handed persons. Tools like scissors and can openers are designed for right-handed people, as are classroom desks. These social pressures certainly contribute to the development of hand preferences. Illustrative are comparisons of Chinese children growing up in Taiwan versus Chinese children growing up in the United States. Virtually no children in Taiwan write with the left hand because this practice is forbidden according to Chinese custom; yet among Chinese children growing up in the United States, the percentage of children who write with their left hand is the same as for non-Chinese children (Harris, 1983). Thus, cultural taboos can, no doubt, suppress left-handedness.

Being left-handed is a disadvantage because environments are usually biased towards right-handed people. There is another disadvantage: Left-handedness has long been associated with evil, corruption, dishonesty, and deficiency. The French word *gauche* means left and awkward, and the English word *sinister* means toward the left and evil. One analysis of the Bible revealed eighty positive references to right-handedness and only negative references to left-handedness (Hardyck and Petrinovich,

1977). In fact, problems in social behavior and academic achievement are slightly but consistently more common in left-handed than in right-handed children (for examples, see Whittington and Richards, 1987).

The association between left-handedness and developmental problems may reflect what has been called "pathological left-handedness" (Hiscock, Hiscock, Benjamins, and Hillman, 1989). This explanation has as its starting point the fact that the right hand is under the control of the left hemisphere of the brain. Some right-handed children may suffer damage to the left hemisphere; as a result of their brain damage, they become left-handed and at risk for developmental problems. Because left-handed children are such a minority, a relatively small number of these "pathological" left-handed individuals could explain the greater frequency of problems among left-handed children as a whole. Of course, right-hemisphere brain damage to a left-handed child could create a "pathological" right-handed child who would also be at risk for problems; the problems would not affect the statistical averages of the performance of right-handed children, however, because of the small number of these "pathological" right-handed children relative to the vast majority of normal right-handed children.

Determinants of Motor Development

To what extent is development a function of physical maturation, and to what extent does it rely on experience? This question has continually arisen in inquiries concerning motor behavior, and it has emerged in our discussion of locomotion and fine-motor skill. Maturation refers to an unfolding of the capacities of the organism that is relatively independent of training or experience. That motor development occurs in such an orderly fashion in all cultures argues for the importance of maturation in its development. Moreover, many examples illustrate that practice may not be necessary for the basic growth of some motor behaviors.

A classic animal experiment demonstrating maturational processes in motor development was conducted by Carmichael. Salamanders were divided into a control group and an experimental group. The latter were placed in water containing an anesthetic; the control animals were allowed to develop in fresh water. In time, the control salamanders began to show vigorous movement, whereas those in the anesthetic were immobile. But when the drugged animals were placed in fresh water, they immediately began to swim. Within half an hour they were indistinguishable from the controls, who had been swimming for five days (Carmichael, 1970). Although similar experiments have not always shown such clear effects, this study served to strengthen the belief that motor development reflected built-in processes operating independently of experience.

An early investigation of the maturation-experience issue involving human infants seemed to provide converging evidence. Dennis and Dennis (1940) collected information about Hopi Indian children on the development of walking. Traditionally reared Hopi infants were secured to cradle boards in such a way that they were unable to move their hands, roll over, or raise their bodies. The babies were removed from the cradle boards only once or twice a day to have their clothes changed. Other Hopi infants, whose parents were influenced by European ways, were not restricted in this manner. Dennis and Dennis found that infants in both groups walked at about 15 months. More recently, Chisholm (1983) reported that Navajo infants, who are swaddled as much as 15 hours per day, learn to walk at the same age as other infants growing up in North America.

Results like these lend weight to the view that basic patterns of movement are strongly canalized. Motor behavior is initially controlled by the lower centers of the brain, notably the cerebellum. As the cerebellum and the cortex continue to develop during the first year of life, the cortex takes on the job of controlling voluntary movement. It seems likely that the growth of the motor cortex is directly related to increases in voluntary behavior. However, the exact nature of this reorganization of the brain is not well understood.

None of the previous factors, however, denies a role to experience. To the contrary, in both monkeys and mice physical exercise results in changes in the cerebellum, which is involved with movement (Thelen and Fisher, 1982). And experience and practice cannot easily be ruled out when it comes to complex movement: Most children are biologically capable of swinging a bat to hit a pitched ball, yet traditionally only children growing up in the Western Hemisphere and some countries in Asia develop this skill to a high level of proficiency.

Also indicating a role for experience in motor development are cross-cultural studies of motor development during infancy. Motor skills develop very rapidly in some groups of African children. In these groups,

FIGURE 4-21
Complex skills like hitting a pitched ball depend upon extensive practice.

FIGURE 4-22
Infants in many African cultures are carried on their mothers' backs. This may strengthen muscles in the thighs and back, which may explain why these infants tend to walk at a younger age than infants growing up in most parts of Canada and the United States.

children walk months earlier than their counterparts in North America. The difference can be linked to child-rearing practices that affect walking specifically and motor development more generally. In many African groups, parents or siblings have infants practice walking daily. In addition, compared with infants in North America, infants in African groups spend more time sitting unsupported or riding on an adult's back, activities that develop muscles in the legs and trunk (Super, 1981).

Complementing the cross-cultural findings is laboratory work on the impact of training on motor development. Zelazo, Zelazo, and Kolb (1972) investigated whether exercise of the stepping reflex would affect later walking. One group of male infants received daily active exercise from the second through the eighth week of life. These infants were held upright with their feet touching a flat surface, and they were moved forward when they made stepping motions. A second group of infants received passive exercise: Their mothers moved their legs and arms while they lay in cribs or sat in infant seats. A no-exercise group was tested weekly along with the other groups. A fourth group was tested only once at the end of the study. The results showed that active exercise increased walking responses over time during the experiment. Moreover, later parental reports indicated that walking had occurred earlier for the infants who had actively exercised.

Motor development, then, involves the interplay of maturation and experience. Motor development clearly depends upon changes in the neuromuscular system, particularly during infancy. Environmental influences on motor development include the practice of physical movements and other processes as well (Adams, 1984). Motor development probably relies strongly on observations of others and attempts to imitate them. In learning to play tennis, for example, beginners watch others and then try the movements themselves. Feedback from others and from our own bodies helps shape our behavior. In complex motor sequences, such as tennis playing, a series of known motor acts must also be connected in proper order and with the proper timing. Individuals learn what acts should follow the preceding one, and thereby they are able to construct the sequence. It is likely that a "motor program"—a mental representation of the sequence— is learned. The opportunity for such learning begins early; for example, during the latter part of the infant's first year, play is characterized by games such as pat-a-cake, peek-a-boo, and clapping (Crawley et al., 1978). Infants playing any of these games with an adult receive a good deal of feedback. So it seems that, in general, motor learning depends on physical maturation, the task being learned, and the match between feedback and capacity to process information (for example, Newell and Kennedy, 1978).

SUMMARY

1. Postnatal physical growth usually follows an orderly pattern. The body grows from the head downward, and from the center to the extremities. Overall body size increases rapidly during the first months of life, then slows down until a dramatic acceleration at puberty. Although the age at onset of puberty varies, for each sex pubertal changes occur in a reasonably consistent sequence. Children today develop physically at a more rapid rate than did children in past generations.

2. Infants need a proportionally higher amount of calories, vitamins, and minerals, in part because a large amount of their energy is devoted to growth. When children do not receive adequate nourishment, growth is slowed, particularly in infants and young children. Improved nutrition sometimes produces "catch-up" growth.

3. Physical growth has psychological consequences. Infants, children, and adults prefer attractive people to unattractive people. In addition, infants, children, and adults seem to treat attractive individuals more favorably than unattractive ones. The rate of maturation also has an impact. Early maturation appears to benefit boys, at least initially; the rate of maturation has less impact on girls.

4. At birth, humans have their full complement of nerve cells. With development, the axons and dendrites of the cells become longer, the dendrites develop many new branches, and the axons become surrounded by myelin. The number of synapses increases up to about two years of age. Thereafter, there is a slow decline in synapses.

5. The cortex consists of four lobes—frontal, parietal, occipital, and temporal. Each lobe regulates different behaviors. The frontal lobe is implicated in personality and in goal-directed behavior. The left hemisphere is specialized for language; the right is implicated in a number of functions, such as understanding spatial relations and in identifying emotions. This specificity is present early in life. Lateralization of language in the left hemisphere is seen at birth; frontal lobe functioning emerges towards the first birthday.

6. As a child grows, motor abilities develop in a predictable pattern; they become more proficient, refined, and complex. Differentiation is the increased control and specificity exhibited by an individual. Actions learned individually are then combined, forming more sophisticated behavior. This process is referred to as hierarchic integration.

7. Infants typically walk shortly after their first birthday. This event reflects a mastery of individual skills—maintaining an upright posture, adjusting balance, stepping with alternate legs—and a coordination of them into the ability to walk. After they begin to walk, children soon learn to run and jump. These skills continue to improve with age, due to increased strength and the improved delivery of oxygen.

8. An infant's use of his or her hands follows a consistent sequence through the first year: holding an object in one hand, using both hands independently, then coordinating the use of both hands. After one year, the control of the hands becomes steadily more precise, a change that is reflected in the greater skill with which children can eat, draw, and write. Soon after the first birthday, most children prefer to use their right hand, but not until the school-age years are children as consistently left- or right-handed as adults. Both genetic and environmental factors cause left- or right-handedness.

9. Motor development depends on both maturation and experience. Some age-related changes in motor skills reflect developments in the nervous system and in the muscles that provide control over the head, trunk, and limbs. The learning of movement involves several processes: practice, the observation and imitation of others, feedback from others and from the body itself, and the capacity to understand the feedback.

P·A·R·T T·W·O

Learning
and Cognition

In the 1990s, Americans have experienced an acute lack of confidence in their public schools. This lack of confidence has been fostered by comparisons between U.S. students and those living in the Pacific Rim countries of Japan, Korea, and China. Students in these Asian countries often have far better academic skills than students in the United States, especially in math and science. This is true despite the fact that Japanese classrooms, such as this one,

tend to have more students and a lack of the "high-tech" aids for learning that are found in U.S. classrooms such as the one shown here.

What is the basis for this difference in academic performance? Are Asian youngsters inherently more capable in some academic areas, possibly because they inherit mental skills that aid learning in particular subjects? Perhaps Asian methods of instruction are superior to those used in the United States and Canada. Maybe cultural values with regard to education hold the key: Scholastic success may come about because families emphasize academics and, such as the family depicted here, work with their children to achieve success.

To understand why U.S. students' educational achievement lags behind that of their Asian counterparts requires a firm grasp of the basic processes of learning and cognition, which are the focus of this unit. We begin, in Chapter 5, by considering the acquisition of language, which provides the basis for much human communication and learning. In Chapters 6 and 7, we examine two complementary views of the means by which children gradually achieve greater cognitive skills as they grow older. In Chapter 8 we explore the nature and assessment of intelligence.

C·H·A·P·T·E·R 5

Language and Communication

Phonology The study of human perception, understanding, and production of speech sounds.

Llexical development The child's acquisition of the meaning of words; the growth of vocabulary.

Syntax The aspect of language that concerns how words are combined to form phrases and sentences.

A child's first spoken word is a momentous occasion: It is the beginning of the ability to communicate with others. Speech allows us to express thoughts and feelings to others at home, at school, and at work. Through written language, we are able to preserve our ideas and to benefit from the accomplishments of the past.

At first glance, acquiring language may seem like nothing more than learning words. This is far from accurate and underestimates the complexity of the task that faces the youngster who is trying to learn language. In fact, scientists typically distinguish at least four different dimensions of language that must be acquired. Let's look at each:

▶   All words in English are constructed from a set of approximately 50 different sounds. Some are based on consonants, such as the "p" sound in *pat*, phonetically written as /p/, the /f/ in *fin*, and the /k/ in *kin*. Others are derived from vowels, such as the /u/ in *boot* and the /o/ in *boat*. Distinguishing these sounds is an essential first step in acquiring language. At what age can infants hear these sounds? When can they produce them? We will answer these questions in the first part of this chapter, which concerns **phonology**, the understanding and producing of speech sounds.

▶   One of the most remarkable of all human accomplishments begins at about 1 year of age: Most children say their first words and, in the next several months, learn hundreds of new words. Why do the first words appear so regularly at about the first birthday, and why are they followed by an explosion of new words? Answers to these questions come from the study of **lexical development**—the acquisition of words—which is the focus of the second part of this chapter.

▶   Soon after children begin to speak, they start to form simple sentences. In English, as in most languages, words must appear in a particular order to convey meaning; random sequences of words are nonsensical. The rules that govern correct sentences in English are many and complex. When and how do children learn these rules? We consider this question in the third part of this chapter, which is devoted to **syntax**, the relations that exist among the elements that form sentences.

▶   Effective communication is more than linguistic ability: It involves knowing what to say as well as how and when to say it. The speaker must be sensitive to the person(s) to whom he or she is communicating as well as to the context within which the communication is being made. When youngsters communicate often their words and sentences are correct grammatically but communication is poor because the children do not provide their listeners with enough information. What factors limit children's communications, and how are they overcome? These questions are the focus of the last section of the chapter, which deals with the development of communication skills.   ◀

PHONOLOGICAL DEVELOPMENT

From birth infants make sounds: They laugh, cry, and produce speechlike sounds. This ability to *produce* sounds is distinct from the ability to *understand* sounds. Assessing infants' understandings of what they hear is not a straightforward process, but some ingenious experimentation has revealed that from very early in life infants are able to hear subtle but essential distinctions among speech sounds. Let's begin by examining infants' perception of speech sounds.

Perceiving Speech

To hear speech and other sounds accurately the ears must function properly, as must the nervous system. Many of the structures of the ear reach their mature sizes by birth. For example, the bones of the middle ear, which link the eardrum to receptors in the inner ear, reach adult proportions by approximately 8 months after conception. The nerve pathways leading from the ear to the brain develop in the fetal period, and at birth many of these pathways are even myelinated (Hecox, 1975). All these facts suggest that the infant is well prepared to hear very early in life. In fact, as we saw in Chapter 3, infants do hear remarkably well from birth; indeed, they hear almost as well as adults (Aslin, Pisoni, and Jusczyk, 1983).

The mere fact that infants can hear accurately does not guarantee that they can distinguish speech sounds. To understand how infants understand and produce language, we need to know more about what speech is. The raw materials of language are **phonemes**, which are distinctive sounds that can be combined to form words. Consider, for example, the /p/ in *pin*, *pat*, and *pet*, as well as the /b/ in *bin*, *bat*, or *bed*. Each is a phoneme, an elemental sound that can be combined with other elemental sounds to form words. These two particular phonemes are both examples of **stop consonants**, so called because both are produced by first closing the lips to stop the flow of air from the lungs, then opening the lips to release the trapped air.

The difference between these stop consonants is subtle, having to do with the amount of time that the flow of air is stopped. Nevertheless, infants can perceive these very subtle differences in adult speech. If a 1-month-old infant is presented with the sound *pa* and then with successive versions of *pa* that gradually sound more like *ba*, the infant will respond as if the sound had suddenly shifted from *pa* to *ba* rather than as if the shift had been gradual. Moreover, the shift seems to occur at the same phonemic boundary as it does when adult listeners discriminate the two sounds in normal conversation (Jusczyk, 1981).

Much the same is true for perception of vowel sounds. For example, in a study by Grieser and Kuhl (1989), recordings of the vowel sounds /i/ as in *peep* and /ɛ/ as in *pep* were presented to 6-month-olds. These babies were trained by using a mechanical animal that would become active (move and make noises) if they turned toward it upon hearing one of the vowels (for example, /i/). That is, head turning to a particular vowel sound was conditioned using the mechanical animal's activities as the reinforcer. After training was complete, versions of /i/ and /ɛ/ were presented in which some of the sound frequencies were changed so that the vowels no longer corresponded exactly to the sounds used in training. Nevertheless, infants almost always turned their heads upon hearing variations of the trained vowel, and they rarely turned when a variant of the nontrained vowel was presented. Thus, infants are able to distinguish

Phonemes Distinctive speech sounds that can be grouped together to form words.

Stop consonants Consonant sounds produced by briefly stopping the flow of air over the vocal tract and through the mouth.

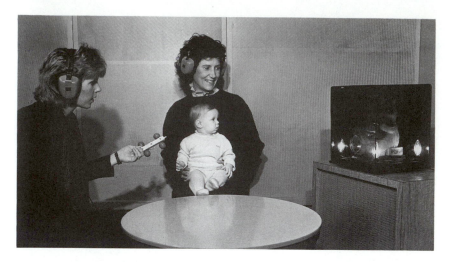

FIGURE 5-1
A typical laboratory set up to study infants' understanding of language sounds.

vowel sounds early in life and respond as if they recognize different categories of vowel sounds.

Infants do not need to experience speech sounds in their environments to be able to discriminate among them. An example would be the distinction between nasal and nonnasal vowels. The nonnasal form is illustrated by the *o* in *cod*; the nasal form is demonstrated by saying *cod* while holding your nose. Some languages, like French and Polish, distinguish nasal and nonnasal vowels. English does not. Young infants with English-speaking parents have no experience with the contrast between nasal and nonnasal vowels, but they can hear the differences between them when tested in the laboratory (Trehub, 1976).

This finding is characteristic of many other speech contrasts as well: Infants are able to distinguish speech sounds that are not differentiated in their native languages. However, with greater exposure to sounds that are specific to their language environments two changes occur. First, infants can recognize variants of language sounds that they hear commonly (Kuhl et al., 1992). Second, infants actually lose this ability to discriminate among sounds in other languages. Werker and Lalonde (1988) found that speech sounds used in Hindi but not in English were distinguished by 6- to 8-month-old infants of English-speaking Canadian parents, but by 11 to 13 months of age, the infants, like their parents, could no longer distinguish these sounds.

Research of this sort indicates that sustained experience with speech sounds is necessary for infants to be able to continue to distinguish speech sounds. One form of early language experience that may be beneficial is **motherese**. When talking to infants and younger children, parents typically speak more slowly, in higher pitches, and with greater variation in pitch and loudness. Use of motherese is not specific to English-speaking parents and is found among parents who speak other languages, too (Grieser and Kuhl, 1988). Infants prefer motherese to speech that is directed toward adults. In one study (Cooper and Aslin, 1990), newborns could activate a tape recording of their mother's speech by looking at a checkerboard

Motherese Speech by adults to infants and children that is slower and higher pitched than normal speech.

pattern. Babies looked significantly longer at the pattern when the recording was of their mother speaking motherese than when the recording was of her speaking to adults.

The exact benefits associated with motherese have not been established. One idea is that motherese may provide a distinct cue to infants that speech is directed to them. Thus, motherese may simply promote an infant's attention to mother's (or, presumably, father's) speech. Another hypothesis is more linguistic in nature. The slower tempo and exaggerated pitch associated with motherese may make it easier for infants to identify speech sounds, just as listening in a foreign language is easier when the speaker talks slowly and carefully.

Regardless of the exact impact of motherese, it is clear that the earliest phases of language acquisition reflect a complementary blend of nature and nurture. On the one hand, soon after birth—and thus with negligible linguistic experience—infants are able to distinguish sounds that are fundamental to many languages. Newborns also seem to prefer motherese to speech directed toward adults. On the other hand, by the first birthday, infants' perceptual skills have been modified by experience: Now they can distinguish only those speech sounds that are present in their own environment.

This interplay between nature and nurture is a recurring theme in the study of language acquisition, as we'll see in examining infants' production of speech sounds.

FIGURE 5-2

When mothers talk to their infants, they often use motherese, in which they speak slowly with exaggerated pitch changes.

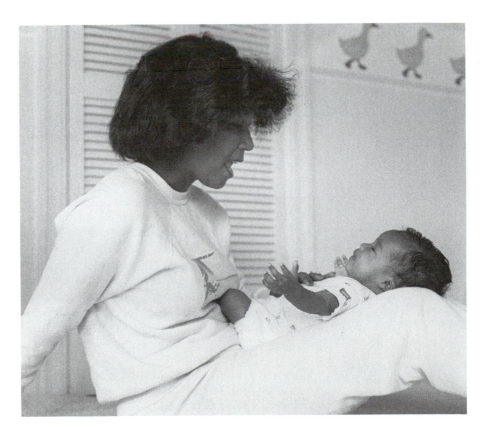

Producing Speech

The first words of a child are preceded by various forms of vocalization, some of which seem to be stepping stones to "real" speech. For the first 2 or 3 months, cries and grunts predominate; then, when the infant is about 3 months of age, **cooing** begins. Coos are shorter than cries, typically lasting less than one second. Also, whereas crying seems to be little more than the blowing of air along the vocal tract, the articulatory organs, mainly the tongue, move during cooing. The results are sounds that resemble vowels ("oooo," "ahhhhhhh").

Cooing is followed by **babbling**, which often sounds like an effort to communicate in a foreign language. One early investigator's report of babbling included infant pronouncements such as "uggle-uggle," "erdah-erdah," "oddle-oddle," "a-bah-bah," and "bup-bup-bup" (Shirley, 1933).

As the infant develops, babbling becomes more and more like human speech. It shifts from odd single sounds to sequences of sounds that are like syllables. A 4- or 5-month-old's babbling often consists of a single consonant and vowel, like *da*. By 7 or 8 months of age, this sound will be repeated to form a string, such as *dadada*. At the most advanced level, normally achieved by 10 months of age, an infant will produce a string of different syllables, as in *dabamaga* (Oller, 1986).

Another early developmental change is an increase in the number of distinct sounds, which emerge in a predictable sequence. For example, babbling usually contains stop consonants (for example, /p/, /t/) before it contains **fricatives** (for example, /f/, /z/). These and other changes in the specific sounds of babbling are probably best explained in terms of growing control over the vocal tract. The "hissing" sound common to all fricatives requires greater control over the lips, tongue, and teeth, which probably explains why fricatives are not produced until after the stop consonants (Stark, 1980).

A further change in babbling between 4 and 12 months of age is the appearance of **intonation**, the pattern of rising or falling pitch. For adults, intonation is often the basis for interpreting a sentence. This is the difference between "You're hungry?" and "You're hungry." Pitch variations in babbling are first noticed at approximately 4 to 6 months of age. Around the first birthday children sometimes use intonation to indicate commands and later to indicate questions (Greenfield and Smith, 1976).

Language experience is an essential ingredient for the normal development of oral babbling. In a sample of deaf infants whose hearing losses ranged from severe to profound, none of the infants had reached the advanced level of babbling by age 10 months (Oller and Eilers, 1988). Only one deaf infant reached this level prior to 1 year of age, and some did not reach it until after their second birthday. Thus, with the extremely limited exposure to language brought on by deafness, the development of advanced oral babbling was delayed.

Interestingly, deaf infants who are learning American Sign Language from their parents go through a babbling phase in their use of signs. That is, at about 7 to 10 months of age, deaf infants produce parts of signs—the manual analogs of syllables. And, at about 12 to 14 months, they

Cooing Vowel-like sounds made by infants, typically starting at about 3 months of age.

Babbling Infant speech, common from 4 to 12 months of age, that consists of alternating vowel and consonant sounds.

Fricatives Consonants that involve hissing sounds, which are produced when air from the lungs is forced through narrow openings formed by the lips, teeth, and tongue.

Intonation A pattern of rising or falling pitch that often indicates whether the utterance is a statement, question, or command.

produce sequences of signs that, although meaningless, match the tempo and duration of real signing (Petitto and Marentette, 1991).

Babbling seems to represent active experimentation with newly acquired units of language. Labov and Labov (1978) describe one child, J, who frequently babbled this way. During one week, for example, J babbled a number of different sequences that included the syllable *da* as in *dat*. After several days J said *daddy* for the first time, and within a few weeks the word was part of her vocabulary.

This gradual movement toward correct production of speech sounds in one's native language is thought to reflect a type of learning based on hypothesis testing (Macken and Ferguson, 1983). This view assumes that children are motivated to produce the "correct" sounds required by their language and that they try out various versions in an effort to produce the right ones. A child may first say *dodi* and then shift to *goggie* before finally learning to produce a recognizable version of the adult *doggie*. According to the hypothesis-testing view, by imitating sounds in their environment and by modifying these sounds based on feedback, infants gradually learn to produce sounds that are recognizably close to actual words (Poulson et al., 1991).

LEXICAL DEVELOPMENT: LEARNING WORDS AND THEIR MEANINGS

First Words

As children near their first birthdays, they often seem to be able to understand what others say even though they are not yet speaking themselves. If a parent asks, "Where is the ball?" a child will often look for it. A child seems to understand the question, even though he or she has never spoken the words *where* or *ball*.

The lag between understanding and producing speech was demonstrated clearly by Oviatt (1980, 1982). Young children were shown an unfamiliar but highly interesting object, such as a hamster in a cage. The object was named many times in each child's presence. Later the experimenter distracted the child's attention from the object and asked about its location (for example, "Where's the hamster?"). Oviatt defined a correct answer to this question as a child's looking at the object for five seconds immediately after the question. Only one 10-month-old responded correctly, compared to half of the 13-month-olds and most of the 16-month-olds.

A few months after demonstrating comprehension, most youngsters will begin to speak. The first word that most children produce sounds very much like *mama*. It is believed that this happens because *mama* is derived from the natural murmur that infants make when sucking (*mmmh-ah*). This and other meaningful words usually appear around a child's first birthday (McCarthy, 1954). The three categories most common in the first ten words of children are animals, food, and toys (Nelson, 1973). Action words (such as *go*) also appear quite early, and they are used to

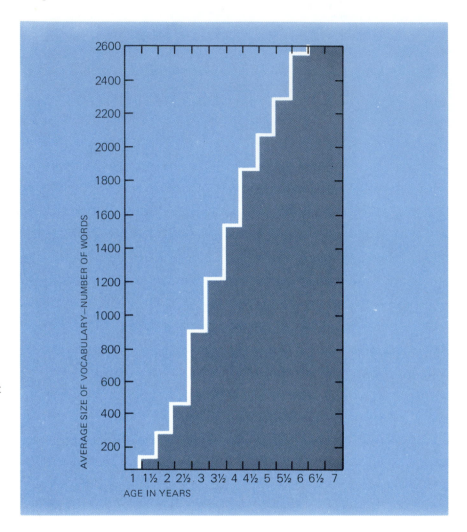

FIGURE 5-3
Size of average vocabulary of children at various ages.
(Data from M. E. Smith, "An investigation of the development of the sentence and the extent of vocabulary in young children," in University of Iowa Studies in Child Welfare, *3, no. 5, 1926.)*

describe a child's own actions before describing the actions of others (Huttenlocher, Smiley, and Charney, 1983). By 24 months of age vocabulary has multiplied 200 to 300 times. The number of words used continues to increase thereafter at a rapid rate (see Figure 5-3).

PHONOLOGICAL LIMITS. The ability to produce speech sounds, discussed in the first part of this chapter, improves gradually throughout the preschool years (Ingram, Christensen, Veach, and Webster, 1980). For very young children, limited phonological skills influence lexical growth because children avoid using words containing sounds they cannot easily say. To verify this, Schwartz and Leonard (1982) taught 14- and 15-month-olds two types of nonsense words. Some words consisted of sounds a particular child had already mastered, whereas other words consisted of sounds the child had never attempted to produce. For example, one child had produced the consonant sound *m* but not *sh*. For this child a nonsense word using familiar sounds was *moemoe*; a word using sounds not yet mastered was *oashoash* (as in *ocean*). Each nonsense word was paired randomly with an action or object whose real name the child did not know. Thus, several times during each training session the experimenter might have said, "Here's an oashoash" while holding a baster. Once in each session the child was shown the action or object and was asked, "What's this?"

Children were more likely to learn words consisting of sounds they had already mastered. Furthermore, children's learning of words with new sounds occurred more slowly than their learning of words with familiar sounds.

WORDS AS SYMBOLS. The emergence of the first words at 12 months of age can be traced, in part, to children's growing facility with symbols. Words are symbols that can be used to refer to objects, actions, properties, and the like. The ability to use symbols is a prerequisite for language. Much evidence links the onset of symbol use to the end of the first year of life. For example, late in the first year children begin to imitate actions they have seen before (McCall, Parke, and Kavanaugh, 1977). Children are capable of making mental representations of past events—that is, they are capable of using their first symbols. According to this argument, the use of symbols in imitation should be closely related to the use of words to symbolize objects. In fact, 9- to 12-month-olds who are more advanced in language are also more likely to imitate (Bates et al., 1979).

The gesture is another symbol, and it, too, is typically observed shortly before the first birthday (Acredolo and Goodwyn, 1988). Young children may smack their lips to indicate hunger or wave "bye-bye" when leaving. In these cases gestures and words convey a message equally well. Both reflect the child's developing ability to use symbols to represent actions and objects. Development in these domains is strikingly similar: At 20 months of age an utterance averages 1.1 words and 1.3 gestures; the longest utterance averages 2.4 words and 2.6 gestures (Shore, O'Connell, and Bates, 1984).

FIGURE 5-4

Pointing is an early and highly effective form of communicating.

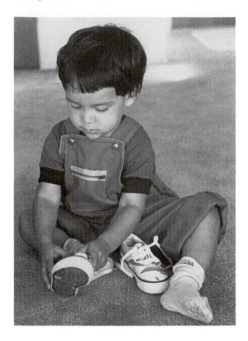

FIGURE 5-5

Words that refer to objects that engage children actively, such as articles of clothing they must put on, are among the first to enter their vocabularies.

This view is also supported by an analysis of the words in children's early vocabularies. The outstanding characteristic of these few words is that they refer to things that move or change by themselves or that can be acted on by the children. As Nelson (1974) points out:

> "Dog," "cat," "car," and "ball" are the most common "thing" words produced by young children. . . . Of the clothing items found in early vocabularies, two-thirds are shoes and other footwear that the child acts on. . . . Early vocabularies do not include items that are just "there," that the child sees but does not interact with and that do not themselves move, for example, furniture. (p. 279)

This finding suggests that a child's first words are based on the child's formation of functional concepts out of his or her own experience and the identification of words that seem to fit the concept. That is, children have identified concepts prior to language; words are then used as symbols to denote these concepts.

Evidence concerning children's early vocabularies, their gestures, and their imitative skills converges on a single conclusion: Near the end of the first year, children are able to use symbols to represent objects, actions, and past experiences. This is a grand landmark in human development, for it allows the development of gestures, imitation, and, notably, spoken language.

WHAT'S WHAT? FAST MAPPING OF WORDS. Understanding that a word can symbolize an object or action is a tremendous achievement, but the task that remains for the child is immensely challenging. To see why, let's imagine a typical situation in which a parent is trying to teach a youngster a new word. A parent shows a toy airplane to a child and labels it several times: "Airplane. This is an airplane. See the airplane." In this example, children could associate the new word with the object, but it would be just as reasonable for them to associate the word with some feature of the object (for example, a wing), its color, or perhaps the parent's actions in demonstrating the new object. These are just a few of the plausible hypotheses that youngsters might formulate upon hearing a new word.

In fact, with just a few presentations of a new word most children will learn the correct referent. This **fast mapping** of words to objects, actions, or properties (Carey, 1978) is so rapid that it is unlikely that children are systematically evaluating all plausible hypotheses. Instead, they seem to follow a series of rules to simplify the task of linking words to their referents. One rule that limits the number of hypotheses children must consider is what Markman (Markman and Wachtel, 1988) calls the "assumption of taxonomic organization." She proposes that

> when children hear someone label an object, they assume that the label refers to the object as an exemplar of a taxonomic category. That is, the child takes the label to refer to the object category . . . and not to the object as a specific individual . . . and not one of its parts, or its substance, or to a property or attribute of the object, or to its relation to other objects. (p. 122)

Another useful rule is **mutual exclusion** (Merriman and Bowman, 1989). According to this rule, objects have only one label; consequently, if children hear a novel word in the presence of familiar and unfamiliar objects, the novel word must apply to the unfamiliar object (Golinkoff, Hirsch-Pasek, Bailey, and Wenger, 1992).

Children's use of this rule was demonstrated by Au and Glusman (1990). Youngsters were first taught a nonsense name for a novel stuffed animal. The experimenter might show children a stuffed lemur (a monkey-like animal) with pink horns and say, "This is a *mido*." The novel term would be repeated several times. Later, children were asked if they could find a *theri* in the set of stuffed animals. Almost no child chose a lemur with pink horns. Instead, they chose the other stuffed animals. They had learned that *mido* was the name for lemur, so they reasoned that *theri* had to refer to one of the other stuffed animals.

Research of this sort has revealed a number of other rules that children use to map words to objects. If children already know a name for an object and they are taught a second name, they interpret the second name as indicating a subcategory of the original name. Children also follow a rule that a word following *a* or *the* (*a tiv*, *the tiv*) probably refers to an object, whereas words appearing before a noun (*the tiv* one) denote a property of an object (Taylor and Gelman, 1988, 1989).

Rules like these allow children to zero in on likely referents of words. Of course, sometimes the process goes awry, with a common example being the tendency to overextend meanings. Young children often call all four-legged animals "dogs" or all adult males "Daddy" (Bowerman, 1976). More often than not, however, these rules allow children to eliminate many potential meanings for words, simplifying the task of learning new words.

Fast mapping The processes whereby young children rapidly associate new words with the correct referents.

Mutual exclusion A linguistic rule intuitively used by young children which says that a new word cannot denote an object whose name is already known but that, instead, it must denote a novel object.

FIGURE 5-6
Young children often overgeneralize the meaning of words—for example, they may initially call all four-legged animals "dogs."

Environmental Influences on Lexical Growth

Exposure to language from parents, siblings, other people, or even television is necessary for children to expand their vocabularies. For example, the total amount of parental speech to children is correlated positively with children's vocabulary size (Huttenlocher et al., 1991). Apparently, parents who speak frequently to their children provide them with more opportunities to learn words than do parents who speak less frequently. Of course, more than sheer quantity of parental speech is important. Parental speech is most likely to foster lexical growth when it refers to objects or activities that are the child's current focus of attention. Also beneficial is speech that is both responsive to the child's speech and encourages further speech by the child (Hoff-Ginsberg, 1991; Whitehurst et al., 1988).

FIGURE 5-7
Adult speech is most likely to benefit children when it is directed toward the child's activities, as is seen when an adult reads a book to a child.

Television, too, can promote children's vocabularies, at least under certain conditions. Researchers found that 3-year-olds who watched *Sesame Street* frequently had larger vocabularies at age 5 years than did 3-year-olds who watched *Sesame Street* infrequently (Rice, Huston, Triglio, and Wright, 1990). It is noteworthy that the frequency with which 3-year-olds watched other television programs, primarily cartoons, was unrelated to vocabulary size at age 5. This difference is probably linked to the fact that, unlike cartoons, *Sesame Street* typically encourages viewer participation. The child viewer is addressed directly and is encouraged to become involved in language-related activities (for example, labeling objects) that are the focus of programming.

Research on the impact of parents and the impact of television point to a common conclusion: Passive exposure to language—illustrated by most television programs as well as by parental speech that is unrelated to children's activities or to their speech—probably has minimal impact on children's language development. Active exposure, in which children are challenged to use their emerging language skills, is more likely to enhance language growth.

Language-Learning Styles

For many years it was thought that the early phases of learning words were much the same for all children. Although the specific words learned would vary from child to child, as would the exact age at which they were acquired, the same processes were thought to be at work in all children. Beginning in the 1970s, it became clear that this view was not entirely accurate. Katherine Nelson (1973) was the first investigator to reveal systematic differences among children in acquisition of language. Nelson studied a group of 18 children for about a year, from their first to their second birthdays, a period during which the children's vocabularies increased from fewer than ten words to nearly 200. Each child was visited monthly for about an hour. The experimenter tape-recorded a large sample of spontaneous speech in addition to giving various tests of language development.

By the time children had 50-word vocabularies—typically at about 1½ years of age—two distinct groups had emerged. Some children, whom Nelson called the Referential group, had vocabularies dominated by words that were the names of objects, persons, or actions. The remaining children, the Expressive group, also learned some names but knew a much higher percentage of words that were used in social interactions (*go away, I want it*) and in asking questions (*what, where*). For example, Rachel, a Referential group child, had 41 name words in her 50-word vocabulary but only two words in the categories of social interaction or question-asking; Elizabeth, an Expressive group child, had a more balanced vocabulary: 24 name words and 14 in the social interaction and question-asking categories.

These two groups of children also differ in later language development. Expressive children typically have smaller vocabularies than Referential children, and are more likely to use pronouns than nouns (Nelson,

1975). In addition, Expressive children often use "dummy" terms—words that have no apparent meanings but instead simply fill places in sentences—perhaps in order to substitute for words they do not know.

SYNTAX: COMBINING WORDS

Within a few months after uttering the first meaningful one-word sentence, youngsters will begin to produce pairs of words that make some type of statement. The transition from two one-word sentences to a functional two-word sentence is gradual. After beginning to use a few single words, the child will string them together, pausing between each. Then the location of the pause will gradually change. For example, the child will begin by saying "baby" and "chair" with a pause separating the words, but will soon combine them to form "baby chair" (Bloom, 1973). Such constructions may be intoned as statements of fact or requests (see Table 5-1).

The Two-Word Sentence

Once the child begins to produce two-word sentences, he or she expands their use rapidly. It is as if the child suddenly discovers the power to express an almost unlimited set of ideas and cannot resist doing so. One early case study showed that more than 1,000 new and distinct two-word utterances per month appear during this phase of development (Braine, 1963). By age 3 years most children are able to produce all the different types of simple sentences that appear in English, and 10- and 11-word sentences are not uncommon (Brown, 1965).

Braine (1976) has argued that these two-word sentences are based on "formulas" that are devised from past experiences and current needs. Some of the formulas are fairly general, such as actor + action ("Mommy sleep," "Melissa walk") or possessor + possession ("Daddy book," "Kimmy

---

TABLE 5-1
Assertions and Requests at the Two-Word Stage

Speech Act	Utterances
Assertions	
Presence of object	See boy. See sock. That car.
Denial of presence	Allgone shoe. No wet. Byebye hot.
Location of object	Bill here. There doggie. Penny innere.
Possession of object	My milk. Mamma dress.
Quality of object	Pretty boat. Big bus.
Ongoing event	Mommy sleep. Hit ball. Block fall.
Requests	
For action	More taxi. Want gum. Where ball?
For information	Where doggie? Sit water?
Refusal	No more.

Source: Adapted from H. H. Clark and E. V. Clark, *Psychology and Language.* New York: Harcourt Brace Jovanovich, 1977.

Grammar The rules that specify how the words in a particular language can be arranged to form phrases and sentences.

Grammatical morphemes Words, such as prepositions and articles, that are not essential to the meaning of a sentence but make the sentence grammatically correct.

pail"). In the early phases not every child invents the same formulas, nor do the formulas develop in a predictable order. However, as more and more formulas are acquired, children begin to converge on a simple **grammar** for their language, based on a common set of formulas for two-word speech.

Grammatical Morphemes

Although children move rapidly beyond two-word speech, their early speech still contains very few sentences that are well formed by adult standards (see Table 5-2), and most articles and auxiliary verbs are missing, as in phrases like "Put suitcase . . . for?" "Where birdie go?" "What inere?" and "Yep, it fit."

Because the pared-down verbal statements of young children resembled telegrams, many writers described youngsters' speech as *telegraphic*. Only words essential to meaning are included. The refinements that make this speech grammatical by adult standards are **grammatical morphemes**

TABLE 5-2
Typical Conversation between Adult and a Young Child

Child (28 Months)	Adult
What dat . . . somebody pencil	Whose pencils are they?
Floor	Floor?
Where birdie go?	
Birdie	
Birdie up dere	
Birdie	
Read dat?	
Read dat?	Will you read it to me?
What inere?	Is that a hammer, Adam?
Hammer	
Hit hammer, mommy	
No Cromer _____,	
mommy?	
Hurt	Poor Adam, Did you hurt yourself?
	What happened, Adam?
Screw (did) happen	Screw happened? You didn't even have a screw.
have screw	
_____ no down there . . .	
table . . . get broom	Does that one fit?
Yep, it fit	
Yep, it fit	Does it fit?
No . . . fit	
Put suitcase . . . for?	What did you put it in the suitcase for?
What dat?	That's tape. We'll use that one tomorrow.
All right 'morrow	Shall we use it tomorrow?
Yep	
Use morrow, yep	
Sure, use morrow	

Source: R. Brown and U. Bellugi, "Three processes in the child's acquisition of syntax," *Harvard Educational Review, 34,* 1964, 133–151. Copyright 1964 by the President and Fellows of Harvard College.

FIGURE 5-8
An example of the pictures used by Berko to demonstrate that children know and use morphological rules even in the preschool years. Although the child has never heard the word *wug* before, he or she will "correctly" pluralize it into *wugs*.
(Adapted from J. Berko, "The child's learning of English morphology," in Word, 14, *1958, 150–177.)*

This is a wug.

Now there is another one.
There are two of them.
There are two _____

like prepositions, articles, and auxiliary verbs. These are acquired during the preschool years (Brown, 1973). Another type of grammatical morpheme emerging during this period is the **inflection**, a change in a word that alters sense without altering fundamental meaning. For example, adding *-ed* to *walk* indicates the past tense, as does converting *swim* to *swam*.

A child's use of grammatical morphemes is based on rules, not just memory. In a classic study, Berko (1958) presented children with totally unfamiliar words that required inflection. The children could not rely on direct past experience. More specifically, Berko showed children some pictures of nonsense objects, such as the one in Figure 5-8, and said, "This is a wug." She then showed each child a picture of two such objects and said, "These are two _____," providing the child with an opportunity to supply the plural form of *wug* (by application of the rule, the plural of *wug* ought to be *wugs*). Her subjects, preschool children, were able to perform remarkably well.

We can see patterns of rule-regulated language of the type identified by Berko even in casual observation of young children's language. For example, Bowerman (1982) described how two preschoolers learned the grammatical morpheme *un-*. When these children first used *un*, they appeared to be imitating specific verbs they had heard (*untangle, unbuckle, uncover*). Later, the children apparently learned a rule that *un + verb* means to reverse or stop the action of a verb, for they created a number of novel verbs (see Table 5-3).

Mastery of plurals reveals the same emphasis on rules. A number of common errors reveal the extent to which youngsters attempt to adhere to new rules (Mervis and Johnson, 1991). They will add *s* instead of using irregular plurals (two *mans* instead of two *men*) or sometimes add *s* to irregular forms (two *mens*), or to words whose singular and plural forms are the same (two *sheeps*). One particularly interesting error involves words whose singular form ends in *s*: Children will often delete the final *s* when using the singular construction, saying, for example, *plier* for *pliers*.

Inflection A suffix that changes the sense of a word without changing its basic meaning; for example, a suffix may make a word plural or change its tense.

TABLE 5-3
Christy's Novel Use of the Prefix *un-*

Age (In years, months)	Utterance
4, 5	[Christy has asked her mother why pliers are on the table.] Mother: I've been using them for straightening the wire. Christy: And *unstraightening* it?
4, 7	Christy: I hate you! And I'll never *unhate* you or nothing! Mother: You'll never unhate me? Christy: I'll never like you.
5, 1	Mother [working on strap of Christy's backpack]: Seems like one of these has been shortened, somehow. Christy: Then *unshorten* it.
6, 0	Christy [watching a freshly poured, foamy Coke]: Wait until that *unfizzes*.
7, 11	Christy [taking a stocking down from the fireplace]: I'm gonna *unhang* it.

Source: Adapted from M. Bowerman, "Reorganizational processes in lexical and syntactic development," in E. Wanner, and L. R. Gleitman (Eds.), *Language Acquisition: The State of the Art.* Cambridge: Cambridge University Press, 1982, Table 11.1.

Errors like these from children's spontaneous speech corroborate Berko's experimental findings: From specific language examples, young children infer rules that are used to apply grammatical morphemes generally.

ORDER OF ACQUISITION. Different grammatical morphemes are acquired gradually, in a reasonably consistent order. Among the first to be acquired are the addition of -ing to verbs to indicate ongoing action, the addition of -s to nouns to indicate plural, and the use of the prepositions *in* and *on* (deVilliers and deVilliers, 1985). Articles (*a, the*) appear later, as do possessives (-'s). Among the last to be acquired are verb contractions (-m as in *I'm* or -re as in *they're*). This order seems to reflect the complexity of the grammatical morpheme, for children first master the least complex forms (Block and Kessell, 1980). According to this explanation, -ing is acquired early because it is always added to a verb to refer to an ongoing event. By way of contrast, rules governing the correct use of *a* and *the* are more complicated. The correct article is *the* when referring to a specific experience or object, but *a* if the referent is unspecified and general. For example, a child would correctly say, "I saw a new girl in school today," if simply reporting an event for the first time. If the topic had been discussed before, "the new girl" would be the correct usage.

Mastery of each grammatical morpheme also occurs in a predictable sequence. Children's acquisition of the past tense, which has been studied extensively, is typical. You would probably assume that the first tendency is to regularize irregular words, and that the error is corrected later after overhearing adult speech. In fact, this is not the sequence at all. Children usually begin by using the correct form of irregular verbs, such as *came* and *broke*, probably because they are imitating frequently heard adult forms. Then, perhaps weeks or even months later, the child will shift from correct to incorrect usage by regularizing all verbs. The child who begins by saying *I broke it* will "advance" to the stage of saying *I breaked it*, rather than the other way around. By the time they start elementary school, of course, most children will have returned permanently to common irregular forms (Ervin, 1964).

It was once thought that this process involved distinct stages (Cazden, 1968), but we now know that children use both incorrect and correct verb forms at the same age. For instance, children sometimes use *goed*, *went*, and *wented* at the same time (Kuczaj, 1981). In addition, children first learn to use the past tense with verbs that refer to actions with well-defined endpoints (Bloom, Lifter, and Hafitz, 1980).

Questions

Children constantly ask questions, but the questions differ in structure and content as children mature. Children's first questions are marked by intonation alone. Soon after a child can declare, "My ball," he or she can also ask, "My ball?" Then comes experimentation with the *wh* words (*who, what, when, where, why*). However, although the use of the *wh* words as a part of questions appears quite early, it does not follow adult form. The young child merely attaches the needed word to the beginning of a sentence—"Why him go?" or "What her eat?"—without altering the base sentence at all. Even when the base sentence already has a negative form, the first questions are produced by simply adding *why not* and the questioning intonation while leaving the base sentence intact, as in "Why not Susie can't walk?" (deVilliers and deVilliers, 1985).

Children begin to use *wh* questions in a distinct order: *what* and *where* emerge early, followed by *why* and *how* (Wootten, Merkin, Hood, and Bloom, 1979). This sequence, like the sequence for grammatical morphemes, reflects the complexity of the questions. Forms that are mastered early—*what* and *where*—ask information about an individual component of a sentence, whereas the later forms ask information about relations among several components.

Nature and Nurture in the Acquisition of Grammar

At one time we thought that children learned to speak grammatically by listening to and then copying adult sentences. A problem with this explanation is that children produce many more sentences than they have ever heard. In fact, most of children's sentences are novel, which is difficult to explain if children are simply imitating adult speech. In addition, it is difficult to explain why children, even when they imitate adult sentences, do not imitate adult grammar. In simply trying to repeat "I am drawing a picture," young children will say, "I draw picture."

Some linguists, notably Noam Chomsky (1959, 1982), proposed that the rules underlying language are too many and too complicated for youngsters to derive them from experience. They proposed that the acquisition of grammar must be guided by innate mechanisms. The general argument of these linguists is that

> the child's mind is somehow "set" in a predetermined way to process the sorts of structures which characterize human language, arriving at something

FIGURE 5-9
In foreign-language immersion programs, much of children's instruction in regular school subjects takes place in a foreign language. By beginning to learn a foreign language early in life, children can ultimately acquire the proficiency of native speakers of the language.

like a . . . grammar of his native language. This is not to say that the grammatical system itself is given as innate knowledge, but that the child has innate means of processing information and forming internal structures, and that, when these capacities are applied to the speech he hears, he succeeds in constructing a grammar of his native language. (Slobin, 1971, p. 56)

Most of the evidence in support of this argument is indirect. First, as we described in Chapter 4, there are regions of the brain that are specialized for processing language, and such specialization seems to be present very early in development (Witelson, 1987). Second, only humans acquire syntax. Chimpanzees have been taught to communicate using gestures taken from sign language (Gardner and Gardner, 1969) or with plastic chips as words (Premack, 1976). However, there is no evidence that chimpanzees can master anything but the simplest of grammatical rules (Berko Gleason, 1989), a result that is consistent with the idea of innate language mechanisms that are unique to humans. Third, there seems to be a critical period for learning language: Only if language is learned early in childhood do individuals achieve normal levels of skill. Individuals who learn language later in life typically have clear deficits in syntax. In one well-known case study, a girl was deprived of language until 13 years of age; after several years of training, her mastery of syntax remained limited (Curtiss, 1977). Similarly, individuals learning sign language or a foreign language achieve the proficiency of native speakers only if they are exposed to the language very early in life (Johnson and Newport, 1989).

Do these findings prove the existence of an innate language acquisition device? No. However, there is definitely an important biological component to language acquisition. Certainly, the regions of the brain that are responsible for language are more plastic during childhood than later in life (Witelson, 1987), which may explain why language experience is so important during childhood. Let's look at some experiences that help children to master syntax.

Controlled laboratory experimentation makes it clear that children can learn syntactic rules from adults' speech. Leonard (1975), for example, found that 2- and 3-year-olds were more likely to use novel grammatical two-word sentences after they had watched an adult model who had been rewarded for using two-word, subject-verb sentences. To determine if similar processes may operate in the natural environment involves several matters: First, if children learn language from adult speech, then we need evidence that adults are easily imitated models, that they in fact adjust their speech to help children learn. Second, adults should provide feedback to children, responding differentially to children's speech, depending upon whether the speech is grammatically correct or incorrect. Third, there should be significant correlations between the parental or adult speech that serves as input and the children's language acquisition (output). Let's examine the evidence for each.

ADULTS TALKING TO CHILDREN. That adults modify their speech to children is well documented. One problem in talking with a young child is simply getting the child's attention. We use various devices to do this, such as saying the child's name at the beginning of a sentence ("Bobbie, look at the horse"), using exclamations (such as "Hey!"), repeating portions of what children have said in order to capture and hold the child's attention ("Yes, horsie!"), or looking and pointing at the objects about which they are talking (Collis, 1977). Adults also monitor children carefully to be sure their attention is sustained. Sachs, Brown, and Salerno (1976) found that adults raise the pitch of their voices at the end of sentences when they are telling a story to young children. This is the same device adults generally use when asking questions; it presumably signals to children that adults want some type of feedback (Clark and Clark, 1977).

Adults also often simplify their speech in various ways when talking to young children (Maratsos, 1983). Articles and possessives are omitted so that these words occur least frequently when adults talk to 2-year-olds, more frequently when they talk to 10-year-olds, and most frequently when talking to other adults. Adults also avoid pronouns when talking to young children, repeating the relevant noun instead. Furthermore, parents adjust vocabulary and grammar, depending upon the ages and perceived language facilities of their children (Rogoff, Ellis, and Gardner, 1984).

PARENTS' RESPONSE TO CHILDREN'S SPEECH. Adults frequently rephrase or expand something a child has said (see Table 5-4). For example, the child's question "Read da?" may be recast by the adult into "Will you read it to me?" and "Put suitcase . . . for?" may be expanded into "What did you put it in the suitcase for?" In using expanded repetition, the adult adds to the child's message, making the utterance clearer as well as more grammatically correct.

These responses generally follow a child's ill-formed sentence, thereby transforming an ungrammatical structure into one that is grammatical.

TABLE 5-4
Imitation with Reduction (by the Child) and Imitation with Expansion (by the Mother)

Imitation with Reduction	
Mother	Child
Daddy's brief case.	Daddy brief case.
Fraser will be unhappy.	Fraser unhappy.
He's going out.	He go out.
No, you can't write on Mr. Cromer's shoe.	Write Cromer shoe.

Imitation with Expansion	
Child	Mother
Baby highchair.	Baby is in the highchair.
Mommy sandwich.	Mommy'll have a sandwich.
Pick glove.	Pick the glove up.

Source: Adapted from Roger Brown, *Social Psychology*. New York: The Free Press, 1965, a division of Macmillan, Inc. Copyright © 1965 by The Free Press. Reprinted with permission of the publisher and the author.

Bohannon and Stanowicz (1988), for example, found that more than 70 percent of recasts and expanded repetitions followed ill-formed sentences. Thus, use of these forms indicates to children, first, that their statement was incorrect and, second, the nature of a correct statement. Bohannon and Stanowicz (1988) also discovered that parents use exact repetition of their children's speech to provide positive feedback: Over 90 percent of the exact repetitions occurred after a child's grammatically correct remark.

Thus, parents, as well as other adults, do provide feedback by repeating well-formed statements and by recasting poorly formed ones. This does not occur for every utterance; in fact, a majority of children's errors—about two-thirds—go uncorrected. However, the amount of feedback is sufficient for children to reject incorrect hypotheses about syntactic rules and retain correct hypotheses (Bohannon, MacWhinney, and Snow, 1990).

CORRELATIONS BETWEEN ADULTS' AND CHILDREN'S SPEECH. Do children profit from the special models of speech that adults provide for them? The answer seems to be "sometimes." In recent years researchers have tried to identify the situations in which parental speech is most likely to affect children's language acquisition. Newport, Gleitman, and Gleitman (1977) computed correlations between the frequency of various constructions in mothers' speech (for example, *wh* questions) and the language development of children between 12 and 27 months of age. They measured two general components of children's language. Some, such as the use of nouns and verbs, were considered to be language universals; that is, they are found in all known languages. Other components, such as auxiliary verbs and noun inflections, were not universal but were language specific. The researchers found that maternal speech was not related to the acquisition of the universals but that it was related to the growth of the language-specific components. One interpretation of these findings is that experience is important only for the language-specific components.

Not all investigators have found this same pattern. Furrow, Nelson, and Benedict (1979) found that a number of characteristics of maternal speech were related to the growth of both universal and language-specific components. The two studies are difficult to compare directly because they differ along many dimensions, including the types of maternal speech that were measured, the methods of statistical analysis, and the age of the children (Hoff-Ginsberg and Shatz, 1982). But the underlying message is clear: As was the case with lexical development, simple exposure to a particular class of parental speech does not automatically lead to increases in the child's use of that same class.

Several investigators have shown that use of recasts is associated with more rapid language acquisition. For example, in a study by Nelson (1974), 2-year-olds received five 1-hour training sessions in which an experimenter conversed informally with each child. The method was simple: In one condition the experimenter often responded to the child's statements by reworking them into questions:

> CHILD: You can't get in!
> EXPERIMENTER: No, I can't get in, can I?

In another condition the experimenter recast many of the child's statements to represent more advanced verb forms:

> CHILD: Where it go?
> EXPERIMENTER: It will go there.

By the end of training, all children had made significant gains: They were more likely to use the constructions that had been recast by the experimenter.

Naturalistic studies also point to the beneficial effects of parental expansions on language acquisition. Newport et al. (1977) found that the frequency with which mothers expanded their children's utterances was positively related to the children's use of auxiliary verbs. And children imitate parents' speech more often when it is presented as recasts than as other conversational forms (Farrar, 1992). But only simple recasts are beneficial; complex recasts, in which more than a single element in a sentence is changed, actually impede language acquisition (Nelson, 1982).

Thus, linguistic experience is most likely to benefit the acquisition of syntax when it provides a few specific examples that allow children to discover particular rules. One experience that has some unique consequences is bilingualism, which we discuss in the Close-Up. With these gains in syntax the child is increasingly better prepared to use language as a tool to communicate with others. Let's turn now to children as conversationalists and communicators.

CLOSE-UP

Impact of Bilingualism

It is estimated that at the turn of the century there will be 5 million children in the United States for whom English is not the primary language at home. In some states in the United States 25 percent or more of the children come from these homes, and the percentages are even higher in some urban areas (Hakuta and Garcia, 1989). How such children should be taught is a volatile issue in many sections of the United States. The view that all Americans should speak English has produced laws mandating instruction exclusively in English and making English an "official language" in 18 states. The view that children will learn more effectively in their native tongue than in English has led to proposals that instruction be offered in both languages concurrently.

Much of the debate over the proper language of instruction is political, reflecting people's preferences either for a society with a universal cultural heritage and language or for a society with pluralistic heritages and languages. Where research in developmental psychology *can* inform the debate, however, is on the impact of bilingualism on children's linguistic and cognitive development. For much of the twentieth century the general assessment was that bilingualism harmed children's development. One child psychology text published in 1952 surveyed the research and concluded, "There can be no doubt that the child reared in a bilingual environment is handicapped in his language growth. One can debate the issue as to whether speech facility in two languages is worth the consequent retardation" (Thompson, 1952, p. 367).

More recent investigators have questioned this conclusion, pointing out numerous flaws in the studies upon which it was based. To illustrate, in many of the studies poor immigrant children performed poorly on standard tests of intelligence. In retrospect, it is clear that poor performance had more to do with their poverty and unfamiliarity with a new culture than with their bilingualism. In fact, modern studies lead to a different conclusion: Bilingual children tend to be more advanced linguistically than their monolingual peers. Bialystok (1988), for example, compared two groups of first graders from middle-class to upper middle-class homes in Toronto. The bilingual subjects attended a French school where instruction was in French, and most had relatives who spoke French. However, the general language environment was English, and English was the common language on the school playground. The monolingual children came from homes where English was spoken, and their instruction was entirely in English.

The groups of children did not differ in their performance on measures of intelligence or achievement, yet the bilingual children surpassed the monolingual children on measures of language skill. For example, the bilingual children better understood the arbitrariness of language (for example, understanding that *sun* and *moon* could be exchanged). Bilingual children were also better able to identify and correct grammatical errors in sentences read aloud.

The upshot of this and other research (Hakuta, 1987) is that bilingualism per se results in no obvious harm to children's developing language and cognitive skill; to the contrary, it actually appears to have benefits. Thus, in the emotional debate that can accompany education for children whose native language is not English, bilingualism cannot be construed as a burden that must be lifted. There is no need to replace the child's native language with English. Rather, skill in one's native tongue and in another language benefits children.

COMMUNICATION SKILLS

Early Skills

We all need to communicate through spoken and written language as well as by using nonverbal signs and signals. Communications specialists have increasingly come to view communication as involving an implicit contract between communicator and communicatee. Mastering the art of communication involves not only complying with this contract, but refining it, which in turn requires understanding its rules. Adult conversations, for example, are guided by a number of implicit rules: People should take turns speaking, their remarks should relate to the conversation, they should be understandable, and so on.

Children master many of these rules at a surprisingly early age. As soon as children begin to talk at all, parents seem to promote the idea of taking turns and alternating the roles of speaker and listener. In fact, many parents begin to teach their children the idea of taking turns long before the children are producing any words of their own:

> The adult asks, "Do you want to tell me a story?"; the infant coos, and the adult responds, "Oh, yeah? And then what happened?"; the infant coos again, and the adult replies, "Oh, that's funny!" (Field and Widmayer, 1982, p. 689)

As soon as an infant is able to produce words, he or she is required to use words, rather than gestures alone, to keep a conversation going. To assist in this form of training, parents often model both sides of a conversation so that their children can learn how the game should be played (Ervin-Tripp, 1970). In an effort to teach turn taking, for example, parents may model the child's role as well as their own by creating dialogues like this one:

> PARENT: (initiating conversation in role of parent) What's the doggie doing?
> PARENT: (modeling appropriate reply for child) The doggie is eating!

During the second year, children become much better conversational partners, and they are more likely to respond to an adult's utterance with a pertinent remark. Barton and Tomasello (1991) videotaped conversations between mothers, their 4-year-old children, and their 19- to 24-month-old children. Conversations were more likely to involve all three people when the infants were 24 months old than when they were 19 months old, reflecting the infants' greater conversational skill. Even at this young age, when infants entered a conversation, they usually maintained the topic; only rarely did they shift to a new topic.

Somewhat older preschoolers can be quite sophisticated in their understanding of the conventions governing conversations. When preschoolers talk to one another, more often than not they will follow a speaker's comment with a relevant remark or action (Garvey and Hogan, 1973). They typically do so promptly—in less than two seconds. If a

FIGURE 5-10

Conversations between young children, their older siblings, and parents become increasingly common as children grow older.

listener does not respond promptly, preschoolers use a number of tactics to encourage a response. Sometimes they repeat their remarks or paraphrase them to make explicit the need for a response (Garvey and Berninger, 1981).

Preschoolers converse differently with younger children than they do with peers or adults. When 4-year-olds talk to 2-year-olds, they use more attention-getting devices than when they talk to peers or adults. In addition, preschoolers' speech to younger children includes shorter and less complex sentences and avoids topics that 4-year-olds believe are too complicated for 2-year-olds (Shatz and Gelman, 1977).

Preschoolers' conversations with one another are more likely to succeed if both children are familiar with the topic. Furman and Walden (1990) studied 3- to 5-year-olds who had been asked to play with toys associated with highly familiar activities (for example, going to the grocery store), as well as with toys associated with less familiar activities (for example, traveling by train). With the unfamiliar activities, children took fewer conversational turns and were more likely to deviate from the topic.

PRAGMATIC SKILL. Adults often indicate requests indirectly rather than directly: "Your ice cream looks delicious" is preferred over "I want some of your ice cream." These *pragmatic* aspects of language typically develop during the elementary school years. This is illustrated by the manner in which children make requests. For example, Grimm (1975) reported a dramatic difference between the way in which 5- and 7-year-olds grant permission to peers. Whereas the permissions issued by 5-year-olds sounded much like commands (such as "You can swing"), 7-year-olds were more likely to say something softer, such as "I don't mind your swinging." Likewise, 5-year-olds would forbid the action by saying, "You mustn't swing!" whereas 7-year-olds were more likely to say something such as "I'd rather you didn't swing." The older children were also more likely to add "please" when making requests.

Wilkinson, Wilkinson, Spinelli, and Chiang (1984) have shown that older children are more indirect in their requests for help on schoolwork. Eight-year-olds typically said, "Please help me spell this word" or "Can you help me spell this word?" They rarely said the more abrupt, "Help me spell this word." Most 6- and 7-year-olds also used indirect methods, but a sizable minority relied upon direct methods.

Even 2½-year-olds occasionally use indirect methods of communication. Newcombe and Zaslow (1981) studied the way in which 2½-year-olds requested an adult to do something. Typically they used imperatives (simply saying "juice" to request juice). Occasionally, however, children's requests were more subtle. In a few instances children hinted to adults:

> SAMANTHA: (holding a can of Playdough) What's in this?
> ADULT: Hm?
> SAMANTHA: What's in this? (Adult does not respond.)
> SAMANTHA: Open it.

Effective Communication

By the time children reach the age of 5 or so, their literal face-to-face conversations are impressively like communications among adults. Most major grammatical forms have appeared, and the youngsters have adequate vocabularies. They take turns speaking and usually share a common topic of conversation. Of course, two individuals may converse, yet not communicate. Misunderstandings are not uncommon in speech among adults, so it is not surprising to learn that children often do not communicate with one another very effectively.

Constructing an effective message means that speakers must consider the aim of the message as well as the characteristics of the intended listener (Schmidt and Paris, 1984). In fact, with increasing age and experience children gradually master both these aspects of effective communications.

CHARACTERISTICS OF MESSAGES. Sometimes, messages are vague or confusing, and in these situations a listener needs to ask the speaker to clarify the message. Frequently, preschool children have difficulty recognizing when a message is ambiguous, and therefore they may not realize that they are responding incorrectly. In one study (Beal and Belgrad, 1990) children were asked to indicate how they could denote a specific object from a set of similar objects. For example, in a set of Christmas trees, the target tree had a gold star and red ornaments, a second tree had red ornaments, and a third tree was surrounded by presents. As shown in Figure 5-11, at all ages children knew that an effective clue would be to refer to a feature uniquely associated with the target (for example, "the tree with the gold ornament"). Notice, however, that most 4- and 5-year-olds thought that ambiguous features (for example, "the tree with the red ornaments") would be useful clues, and many 4-year-olds even judged that unrelated features (for example, "the tree with presents under it") would be helpful.

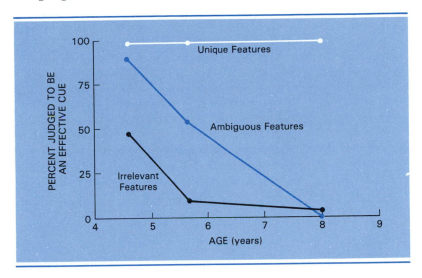

FIGURE 5-11

In the study by Beal and Belgrad (1990), it was found that all children felt that the unique features of objects would be useful as cues in describing those objects when communicating. However, many younger children believed that ambiguous or even irrelevant features of objects could also be used as cues to describe those objects.
(From C. R. Beal and S. L. Belgrad, "The development of message evaluation skills in young children," in Child Development, 61, *1990, 705–712.)*

Part of the problem here is that young children seem unwilling to focus exclusively on the message per se. Instead, they often assume that they know what the speaker meant; if the message is inadequate, pre-schoolers will nevertheless confidently infer what the speaker must have meant. Moreover, when questioned afterward, these youngsters will maintain that they evaluated the message per se and that the speaker had done a good job of communicating. Only when messages almost defy comprehension—they are too soft to be heard or provide obviously ambiguous or even conflicting information—are preschoolers likely to detect the shortcomings of messages. Older children and adults would, of course, recognize the problem in the message and realize that the communication itself was faulty (Singer and Flavell, 1981).

Sometimes messages are *not* to be taken literally. Sarcasm, for example, represents a situation in which the literal meaning of a message is exactly the opposite of the intended meaning. If a soccer player misses the ball entirely and a teammate says, "Nice kick," the speaker's intended meaning is missed entirely if the listener attends only to the literal meaning of the remark.

Understanding of sarcasm should develop relatively late because it involves a collection of subtle skills. For sarcasm, the speaker must express a literal meaning that differs from the intended meaning, but the difference must be obvious to the listener, otherwise the communication fails. Adults typically detect sarcasm from the intonation of the utterance: Sarcastic remarks are often made in mocking or overly enthusiastic tones. The context of a remark is also an important cue to sarcasm: If the speaker's comment is the opposite of what the situation would logically call for, the interpretation of sarcasm is likely to be correct.

Use of these cues to detect sarcasm develops at different rates. Capelli, Nakagawa, and Madden (1990) read brief stories to 8- and 11-year-olds and to adults. A nonsarcastic story was created first. In one story, Matt introduces a friend to his younger sister, who greets the friend politely. The friend remarks that Matt is lucky to have such a nice sister. Another version was created in which the sister first kicks the friend, thereby establishing a distinctive context in which the friend's remark could be interpreted as sarcasm. In addition, each story was read in two ways: with and without the friend's remark said in a sarcastic tone.

Adults judged the friend's remark to be sarcastic if either the contextual cue or sarcastic tone were present. In contrast, children (and particularly the 8-year-olds) relied almost exclusively on tone to detect sarcasm; when only the context of the story provided a cue, children were unlikely to detect sarcasm.

CONSIDERING THE LISTENER. An important element is missing thus far in our discussion of messages: the listener. The clarity of messages cannot be judged without considering the listener. Messages that may be perfectly clear to one listener may be woefully inadequate for another. As a general rule, if listeners are familiar with both the topic of conversation and the general context of the conversation, messages can be briefer than when listeners are unfamiliar with topic and context.

Children's sensitivity to the listener's knowledge was studied by Sonnenschein (1988). Each child in the study was asked to describe a toy so that a listener could find it in the child's house. Both 6- and 9-year-olds' messages included more information when the listener was an unfamiliar child or a familiar child who had never been in the child's house than when the listener was a friend who had played in the child's home frequently. In the latter case, the speaker knew that the listener was familiar with the house and the child's toys, so a less elaborate message was sufficient.

Other work also indicates that 5- and 6-year-olds are capable of considering the conversational setting when formulating messages. Pratt, Scribner, and Cole (1977) asked individual nursery school, first-grade, and third-grade children to describe the rules of a new game to another child. At all ages children gave more elaborate descriptions of the game when the playing board was not visible to the peer. Experimentation of this sort suggests that by the time they enter school, children realize the need to modify their messages depending upon the listener's knowledge of the topic and the general context of the conversation.

This awareness is also revealed in analyses of children's spontaneous speech. Adults frequently use the definite article, *the*, to indicate information that the listener presumably knows already; the indefinite article, *a* (or *an*), is used to indicate new information, as yet unknown to the listener. For example, an adult may say, "I found a key yesterday, and it turned out to be the key to my old suitcase." In one study, 3-year-old

FIGURE 5-12
In conversations between friends, much information is assumed rather than stated.

children who told stories to peers used definite and indefinite articles almost indiscriminantly (Warden, 1976). Five- and 7-year-olds were somewhat more likely to use the indefinite article on the first mention of a piece of information, and 9-year-olds typically used the indefinite article when first mentioning a piece of information most of the time.

TRAINING CHILDREN TO COMMUNICATE BETTER. Even brief training can markedly improve children's communications. To succeed, it is necessary to present appropriate rules for communicating effectively, to encourage children to apply the rules, and to give them specific feedback about how well they are doing.

Pratt, McLaren, and Wickens (1984) presented a series of communication tasks to first-grade children, and then taught some of the children to apply the rules of good communication by reminding themselves of the rules as each task began. Children were first taught to say both a general comparison rule and a specific comparison rule aloud: "First I'll figure out all the different things my clues could mean to you. . . . Then I'll tell you how the one I mean is different from the rest." After practice saying the rules aloud, children practiced whispering the rules to themselves at the beginning of each task. Finally, they practiced saying each rule silently to themselves. Feedback was given after each task. Compared with a control group that practiced the task without rules or feedback, children in the training group showed marked improvement in their referential communication.

Listening critically can also be improved through training. Sonnenschein (1984) had 5-year-old children watch a speaker doll and a listener doll play a game in which the speaker identified one of two common objects that had a hidden star on it and could be seen by the speaker but not by the listener. The two objects presented on any trial were always of the same class (clowns, chairs, triangles), but differed on one dimension (such as color or size). The speaker always gave ambiguous messages. Depending on the group to which they had been randomly assigned, the children heard the listener respond correctly (pick the object with the hidden star), respond incorrectly, or note the ambiguity explicitly without responding by saying "They're both _____. Do you mean the _____ or the _____?" (p. 289). One week later the children themselves interacted as both speaker and listener. Those who had heard the ambiguity pointed out to them the week before now performed significantly better than those in the other groups. So even at this age appropriate training can lead children to monitor their own communications more closely.

SUMMARY

1. Language is recognized as central to human social behavior and communication. The course of language development is best thought of as a number of emerging competencies in distinct aspects of language.

2. In many ways, the infant is well prepared to learn language: The auditory system functions well at birth. Perception of the acoustic characteristics of consonants and vowels, the "raw materials" of speech, is well established in young infants.

3. Parents often speak to infants in "motherese," speech that is slower in tempo and more exaggerated in pitch. The impact of motherese on infants' language development has not yet been determined.

4. For the first 2 months of life, cries and grunts are common. Cooing begins at about 3 months of age. Babbling emerges at approximately 4 months, and progressively becomes more like human speech: The number of distinct sounds increases and intonation emerges. These changes are thought to reflect infants' testing of hypotheses about correct sounds in their language.

5. Toward their first birthdays, infants are able to understand adults' speech, even though they cannot talk themselves. This lag between the comprehension of language and the production of words is typical throughout development.

6. Children typically say their first words around the time of their first birthdays. In the year that follows, the size of their vocabularies increases dramatically. After children learn to talk, there is additional improvement in their production of speech sounds. Children are more likely to imitate words with sounds they already know.

7. Children's first words represent an intellectual accomplishment that is not specific to language. Instead, the onset of language is due to a child's ability to interpret and use symbols. Consistent with this view, there are parallel developments by children in the use of gestures and words in sentences.

8. Children use several rules to limit the possible referents for a new word. Included among these rules are the assumptions by children of taxonomic organization and mutual exclusion with regard to words and language. Word learning can be fostered by parents and by television, particularly when these experiences involve the active use of language by children.

9. For children with referential language-learning styles, names dominate the early vocabulary. For those with expressive language-learning styles, different types of words are represented.

10. Not long after the first birthday, children produce two-word sentences that seem to be formulas for expressing ideas or needs. As children gradually learn the rules that govern the use of grammatical morphemes like prepositions, articles, and auxiliary verbs, their sentences become longer and more sophisticated. They first learn simple grammatical morphemes and later master more complex forms.

11. Young children often ask questions by changing intonation, but soon they begin to use different *wh* questions. The ease with which children learn how to ask questions depends, in part, on the verbs used in the questions.

12. Some linguists believe that language rules are much too complex for children to learn them from experience alone. Consequently, they propose that the child's mind is innately predisposed to learn language. Consistent with this argument are the specialized regions in the human brain for processing language, the inability of chimpanzees to master syntax, and the critical periods in language acquisition seen in human development.

13. Experience can be an important factor in acquiring syntax. Adults speak to children in ways that should help children to learn language. They modify their speech when talking to children and provide children with feedback. Direct relations between children's language experiences and their language development are often difficult to find; one exception to this is parents' use of imitation with modification when speaking to their children, which does aid language growth.

14. Mastering the art of communication involves recognizing and understanding the implicit contract between speaker and listener. Children first learn about this contract during infancy. By the preschool years, children have mastered many of the conventions concerning turn taking when conversing with others, including ways to get responses from listeners.

15. Beginning in the preschool years, children gradually become much more skilled at constructing efficient messages. They are better able to consider the needs of listeners, becoming skilled in the use of indirect methods of communicating. They also become able to determine if a message is vague or ambiguous.

C·H·A·P·T·E·R 6

Piaget's Approach to Cognitive Development

People reason, think, and solve problems daily. Sometimes these intellectual skills are brought to bear on routine problems such as deciding what to wear or what to eat; sometimes they may be used to advance knowledge in science or literature. In any case, intellectual or cognitive skills are essential for human existence.

Of course, the mature intellectual skills of an adult do not emerge overnight. Instead, they are the products of a continuous developmental process that begins at birth. Let's consider some examples:

▶ Suppose you show a jack-in-the-box to a 6-month-old, then demonstrate how it works. The infant will watch you intently and may well smile or laugh when the box top pops open. However, the 6-month-old will probably not repeat any of your actions to make the box open again. But the same infant just a few months later behaves quite differently: Now he or she is eager to take the box and turn the crank, opening the lid. What has happened in those few months so that the infant has begun to imitate actions?

▶ Suppose you lay out two rows of candy. Each row has five pieces of candy, but the candies in one row are spaced further apart, making one row longer than the other. If you ask 3-year-olds which row they would prefer, most would select the longer row; but by age 7 years, children have no preference based upon merely the length of the row. What happens in the early childhood years so that youngsters realize that the number of candies is the same regardless of the length of the row?

▶ Suppose you give children some containers filled with colorless liquids and ask them to find a combination that will produce a yellow liquid. During middle childhood—8 or 9 years of age, for example—children will typically combine the liquids haphazardly. They show little indication of using a systematic approach to the problem. Adolescents, in contrast, usually formulate a plan for considering all possible combinations of liquids so that the right mixture can be isolated. What happens between middle childhood and adolescence that makes problem solving so much more systematic and effective? ◀

What mechanisms are responsible for this steady progression toward the mature intellectual skills demonstrated in these examples? For many years our best answer to this question was provided in a theory formulated by Jean Piaget (1896–1980). Piaget began to study intellectual development in the 1920s and spent nearly 60 years revising and elaborating his theory. As we see in the first section of this chapter, Piaget's theory draws heavily on concepts from biology and formal logic.

Beginning in the late 1960s, many developmental psychologists conducted research that revealed some shortcomings in Piaget's theory. These criticisms are examined in the second section of the chapter. Other psychologists used this new evidence to propose variations on Piaget's theory of intellectual development. These extensions and refinements of the orig-

Epistemology Branch of philosophy that deals with the origin and nature of knowledge.

inal theory are now so numerous that they are often collectively referred to as the neo-Piagetian approaches to cognitive development. We discuss them in the last section of this chapter.

PIAGET'S THEORY

Piaget was a biologist by training but he had a keen interest in **epistemology**, the branch of philosophy dealing with the origin and nature of knowledge. Early in his life, Piaget decided to study epistemological issues. However, rather than debating these issues as philosophers had, he sought answers to epistemological questions in evidence from scientific research. In particular, he hoped to answer these philosophical questions by studying how humans acquire knowledge.

To gain experience with psychological research, Piaget visited different psychological laboratories in Europe, including the laboratory of Theophile Simon, a collaborator on the first intelligence tests (a topic we discuss more in Chapter 8). Piaget was asked by Simon to administer some new reasoning tests developed in England. As a result, Piaget was impressed by the parallels between children's reasoning on these tests and the principles of formal logic. In addition, Piaget saw parallels between biological adaptation and intellectual development: Intellectual growth seemed to involve interplay between children and their environment, just as biological adaptation involves adjustments between organisms and their environments. These initial insights—that biology and logic could be used to understand intellectual development—provided the core of a theory that Piaget elaborated for the next 60 years of his life.

FIGURE 6-1

Jean Piaget, the Swiss psychologist whose stage theory of cognitive development focuses on qualitative changes in the nature of thinking with increasing age.

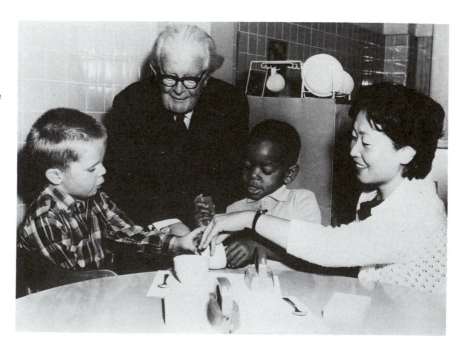

Contents, Functions, and Structures

Contents Piaget's term for the outward, observable manifestations of the intellect.

Functions Piaget's term for the two basic processes—organization and adaptation—that direct cognitive development throughout the life span.

Structures Organized schemes that provide the distinguishing characteristics of thought for each of Piaget's four periods of cognitive development.

Adaptation A function in Piaget's theory that denotes the adjustments that occur between perceived stimuli and the mental structures used to interpret these stimuli.

Assimilation Piaget's term for the interpretation of reality in terms of one's internal model of the world, which is constructed from previous knowledge.

Accommodation Piaget's term for the act of improving one's cognitive model of the world by adjusting it to external reality.

Scheme For Piaget, the mental structure underlying a sequence of behaviors.

Organization A function in Piaget's theory denoting the fact that, at any age, schemes are always linked to form a cohesive mental structure.

Piaget (1952) distinguished three components of intellect: **contents**, **functions**, and **structures**. The contents of the intellect are simply raw, observable behavioral acts. Examples would include the infant's ability to reach for and grasp an attractive object, the preschool child's ability to distinguish different animals, and an adolescent's ability to reason abstractly. These examples indicate that Piaget's definition of intelligent actions is broader than the typical definition: Included would be any action that reflects some thinking. The contents of intelligence per se did not interest Piaget. Instead, he used the contents of intellect to determine the nature of the other two components of intellect: functions and structures.

For Piaget, functions are the basic principles that apply to intelligent acts throughout the life span. One function is **adaptation**. In biology, adaptation refers to changes in structures or forms that result in a better fit of an animal or plant to its environment, resulting in a greater likelihood of survival. To maintain a favorable balance with their environments, all animals must adjust to ecological change: Herds instinctively seek new grazing areas in a drought, and chameleons change color to conceal themselves from predators.

Piaget argued that adaptation of this sort is also fundamental in human intelligence. There is constant give and take between the knowledge that people have and new experiences. People constantly interpret new information in light of what they already know. Elementary school children learning to add and subtract try to relate these operations to their experiences in counting; adolescents learning about the history of racial and ethnic groups may reexamine and discard racial or ethnic stereotypes.

Piaget believed that intellectual adaptation always involves two complementary processes, **assimilation** and **accommodation**. To understand these processes, imagine a toddler in a garden with his father. Seeing a rose, violet, and tulip, the youngster names each a "flower." The child's word *flower* represents assimilation. The child's concept of a flower—what Piaget called a **scheme**—is used to interpret and organize incoming information.

Now suppose the child called a dandelion a flower. Apparently the child's scheme for flower referred simply to small, colorful plants. If the father said the dandelion was a weed, the child might then refer to dandelions as weeds. This would represent accommodation. What was once one scheme is now two, as the original scheme is modified to incorporate this new information.

Another function, **organization**, concerns relations among different schemes and leads us to the third component of intelligence, mental structures. Piaget held that schemes are always organized to form integrated mental structures. These mental structures change as children develop, but they are always organized. The 10-month-old's schemes, which might include grasping, sucking, and waving, form an organized whole, as do the adolescent's schemes for emerging scientific concepts.

Because schemes are linked together, changing one scheme influences others as well. Development will be marked by reorganization of these overarching mental structures. Piaget believed that an organism periodically "outgrows" the existing mental structure, which is then replaced by a qualitatively different, more sophisticated structure. That is, accommodation and assimilation are usually in balance, creating a state of cognitive equilibrium. There are critical times, however, when so many schemes are forced to accommodate to new information that the result is a state of disequilibrium. Resolving the problem and restoring equilibrium leads to more advanced mental structures and intellectual growth.

Piaget proposed that these states of disequilibrium occur three times during childhood and adolescence, which means that intellectual development consists of four periods, each with a distinctive mental structure:

1. Sensorimotor period (birth to 2 years)
2. Preoperational period (2 to 7 years)
3. Concrete operational period (7 to 11 years)
4. Formal operational period (11 years through adulthood)

The ages given are only averages and vary considerably depending upon the environment and background of each child. However, Piaget claimed that the sequence of the stages is constant. Intellectual development always consists of this sequence of sensorimotor, preoperational, concrete operational, and formal operational periods, regardless of environment or ability of the person. Children cannot "skip" a period and move directly, for example, from preoperational to formal operational thought.

In the next few pages, we examine the periods of intellectual development in detail.

The Sensorimotor Period (Birth to 2 Years)

The newborn infant cannot talk, has little control of its limbs and head, and depends upon adults for nourishment. Yet the newborn infant is not completely helpless because he or she is born with inherited reflexes and a number of innate perceptual abilities. During the first two years of life these inborn abilities evolve so that the child is able to engage in increasingly flexible and purposeful actions.

Piaget calls the first two years of life the **sensorimotor period**, which he divides into six stages. Like the larger periods described in Piagetian theory, the chronological ages associated with each stage are approximations. However, the sequence of stages is the same for all infants.

THE FIRST MONTH OF LIFE (STAGE 1). In Chapter 2 we saw that the newborn is endowed with a number of reflexes, such as the stepping reflex and the grasping reflex. During the first stage of the sensorimotor period, reflexes become increasingly smooth and systematic as infants engage in what Piaget calls "reflex exercise." For example, sucking becomes noticeably more coordinated during the first month of life (Flavell, 1963).

Modification of a reflex is the first evidence of accommodation; there is also evidence of assimilation during this stage. At first, infants suck

Sensorimotor period The first of Piaget's four stages of intellectual development, corresponding to infancy.

FIGURE 6-2
During the sensorimotor period, infants begin to construct reality by integrating sensory and motor experience.

only the nipple of the breast or bottle, but soon they suck toys and blankets as well. By sucking a range of objects, infants begin their initial assimilations with the environment. They learn that some objects yield nourishment but others do not.

THE SECOND TO THE FOURTH MONTH (STAGE 2). During the first stage of sensorimotor thought, reflexes become more finely tuned; in the next few months they change through experience. The chief means for change is the **primary circular reaction**, in which some event triggers a reflex by chance. Infants, for example, may accidentally touch their lips with their thumbs, thereby initiating sucking and the pleasant sensations that accompany sucking. Later, they try to repeat the event to re-create those pleasant sensations.

Circular reactions are a critical component of sensorimotor development. They become the basis for the first instances of deliberate, intentional behavior. They provide the first insights into causality because the infant learns that actions yield predictable outcomes. This sequence of cause and effect also provides insights into time as the infant learns that the effect follows the cause. Of course, all these achievements do not occur in Stage 2, but the emergence of the primary circular reaction provides the foundation for these later achievements.

Primary circular reaction A chance event involving direct sensory stimulation that infants find pleasing, which then leads them to try to repeat the event.

Secondary circular reaction A chance event involving indirect sensory input that is pleasing to infants, who then try to repeat the event.

THE FOURTH TO THE EIGHTH MONTH (STAGE 3). Between the fourth and eighth months of life, **secondary circular reactions** appear. The secondary circular reaction has many of the properties of the primary circular reaction: It first occurs by chance, the outcome is pleasing, and the infant strives to repeat the event. The critical difference is that primary circular reactions result in direct sensory stimulation and so often involve the infant's body, whereas the secondary circular reactions produce indirect sensory input and so are usually oriented toward objects and activities beyond the infant's body. For example, suppose that an infant accidentally shakes a rattle and hears a noise. The infant will repeatedly shake the rattle, trying to produce the noise again. This secondary circular reaction, unlike a primary circular reaction, involves an object rather than the infant's own body.

THE EIGHTH TO THE TWELFTH MONTH (STAGE 4). When an infant shakes a rattle and seems to enjoy the result, it is tempting to conclude that the infant is at least on the threshold of deliberate, intentional behavior. However, Piaget believed that truly intentional behavior involves a separation of the goal from the means used to achieve that goal. According to this definition, secondary circular reactions are not really deliberate because the goal and the means to achieve the goal are closely intertwined in the repetition of the act. Not until Stage 4 is there truly purposeful behavior. Now, different secondary circular reactions are coordinated so that one circular reaction is a means to achieve a second. For example, Piaget (1952) showed an attractive toy to an infant, but placed his hand in front of the toy to prevent the infant from grasping it. He observed that it was not until 7 months of age that the infant would systematically move the hand out of the way to grasp the toy. This simple sequence—move the hand, then clutch the toy—represents the first sort of intentional behavior. Removing the barrier is unrelated to the goal per se, but is necessary to achieve it. Thus, infants combine secondary circular reactions to produce new behavior that appears to be deliberate and goal directed.

THE TWELFTH TO THE EIGHTEENTH MONTH (STAGE 5). Variation is first systematically introduced into circular reactions with the **tertiary circular reaction**. As in the case of primary and secondary circular reactions, the tertiary reactions begin with chance events that infants try to repeat. The critical difference is that infants now systematically vary the reactions as they are repeated, as if trying to understand why different objects yield different outcomes. For example, at 10 months of age, an infant may accidentally drop an object from his or her crib. Soon thereafter he or she will begin to drop different toys and objects and intently study each as it falls (Piaget, 1952). This and other tertiary circular reactions represent an extension of the intentional behaviors that were first seen in Stage 4. Tertiary circular reactions are active efforts to adapt to new situations, rather than to simply repeat or combine old behaviors.

THE EIGHTEENTH TO THE TWENTY-FOURTH MONTH (STAGE 6). This is the climax of the sensorimotor period, for infants are now capable of **mental representations**. The child is now able to use symbols, such as words, to refer to objects not present. For Piaget, several events signal the child's use of mental symbols, beginning at approximately 18 months of age. One is that children are capable of **deferred imitation**. Younger children will imitate the actions of other children and adults, but only at the

Tertiary circular reaction The most advanced form of a circular reaction in which infants systematically vary their actions, in an apparent effort to understand more about the properties of objects.

Mental representation The child's internal, symbolic depiction of the world.

Deferred imitation Repetition of actions some time after they have occurred.

time the actions happen. Deferred imitation occurs some time after the children have seen the others' acts (for example, Abravanel, 1991).

Perhaps the most impressive feat of Stage 6 is that the active experimentation characteristic of Stage 5 is now carried out mentally rather than behaviorally. No longer must children literally try out all possible events to determine their consequences; they can anticipate some of these consequences mentally:

> Jacqueline, at [age 20 months] arrives at a closed door—with a blade of grass in each hand. She stretches out her right hand toward the knob but sees that she cannot turn it without letting go of the grass. She puts the grass on the floor, opens the door, picks up the grass again and enters. But when she wants to leave the room things become complicated. She puts the grass on the floor and grasps the doorknob. But then she perceives that in pulling the door toward her she will simultaneously chase away the grass which she placed between the door and the threshold. She therefore picks it up in order to put it outside the door's zone of movement. (Piaget, 1952, pp. 338–339)

This capacity to use mental symbols signals the end of the sensorimotor period. The child has progressed in 2 years from using reflexive acts to using mental symbols. This progression coincides with the major changes in language described in Chapter 5. This is particularly true for intentional behavior, which emerges in Stage 4 and is extended in Stages 5 and 6. Piaget's interpretation of these parallel developments was once controversial: He claimed that the development of language reflected the child's growing ability to use symbols. For many years psychologists and sociologists believed the reverse to be true: Increased intellectual ability was due to the acquisition of greater language skill. However, as we saw in Chapter 5, even psycholinguists now share Piaget's view that the transition from infancy to childhood reflects the ability to use symbols to represent events and objects mentally.

The Preoperational Period (2 to 7 Years)

Preoperational period
The second of Piaget's four stages of intellectual development, corresponding approximately with 2 to 7 years of age.

Egocentrism A characteristic of preoperational thought in which children believe that others see the world, literally and figuratively, as they do.

The end of the sensorimotor period is also the beginning of the **preoperational period**. The young preoperational child's first forays into the world of symbols are tentative and sometimes unsuccessful. The Close-Up shows how fragile these skills are. However, children gradually begin to deal with increasingly complex problems and gradually come to rely on mental representations to solve them.

During the preoperational period, the child begins to develop a perspective of the world and displays an increased ability to accommodate to new information and experience. Although young children can use symbols, their mental representations differ systematically from those of older children and adolescents. In particular, young children are often unable to grasp the fact that their view of the world—both literally and figuratively—may be but one of many. Piaget used the term **egocentrism** to refer to this inability to see the world from another's perspective. Piaget

CLOSE-UP

Early Use of Symbols—The Case of Scale Models

Words and gestures are common, powerful symbols. Other examples of symbols include graphs, maps, and models. In each case, elements of the graph, map, or model are used to represent or symbolize other entities. A scale model of a university campus (or other large physical space), for example, is often available for visitors to use. By looking at the scale model, individuals can identify the locations of landmarks on the campus, understand relations between landmarks, and generally see the "lay of the land."

The ability to use scale models in this fashion develops rapidly in the early preoperational period. In a series of experiments, Judy DeLoache (1987, 1989, 1991) has shown that 2½-year-olds find it very difficult to use the symbolic information contained in a scale model, yet 3-year-olds do so readily. The basic method in this research is for children to watch an adult hide a toy in a scale model of a room; then children are asked to find the toy in the actual full-scale room. The model, with dimensions of approximately 28 inches by 26 inches by 13 inches, contains all the principal features of the full-scale room, including carpet, window, and pieces of furniture. Before the toy is hidden, children are shown both the room and the scale model; the experimenter notes the corresponding features of the two rooms, including the items of furniture that could be used to hide the toy.

When 3-year-olds were asked to find the hidden toy, most did so (see Figure 6-3); in contrast, only a handful of 2½-year-olds could do so. One possible explanation for these results is that the younger children simply had forgotten the location of the toy by the time they were asked to find it in the large-scale room. This explanation can be eliminated, however, by two features of DeLoache's results. First, after children had tried to find the toy in the full-scale room, they were asked to find the toy in the scale model. Most

younger children did so, indicating that simple forgetting was not implicated in their poor performance in the full-scale room. In addition, conditions that are known to improve 2- and 3-year-olds' remembering—such as labeling or pointing to the location as the toy is hidden there—had virtually no impact on younger children's ability to find the toy in the full-scale room (see Figure 6-3).

DeLoache believes that the younger children perform poorly on this task because of some characteristic properties of scale models.

> A scale model is a symbol; it represents a larger space. Unlike many other kinds of symbols, however, a model is both a salient real object (or set of objects) itself and a symbol of something else. In the model task, one must think about the model in two different ways at the same time—as the object that it is and as a symbol for something.
>
> According to this line of reasoning, the 2½-year-old children . . . performed so poorly because they did not represent the model in two different ways at the same time. . . . Thinking of the model only as an interesting object, they failed to appreciate its relation to the room; as a consequence, they did not understand that what they saw happen in the model had implications for the . . . room. (DeLoache, 1991, p. 737)

According to this hypothesis, younger children would perform much more accurately on this test if they were shown the toy hidden behind a photograph of one of the pieces of furniture in the full-scale room. The reasoning here is that although photographs are real objects, they function primarily to represent other objects. This characteristic of photographs should make it easier for younger children to understand the correspondence between hiding the toy behind the picture and its location in the full-scale room. In fact, as shown in Figure 6-3, 2½-year-olds readily found the toy in the full-scale room when they were shown

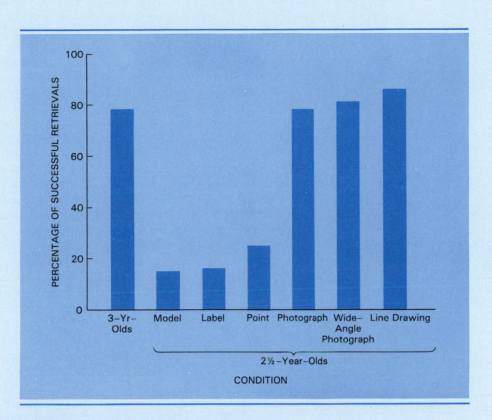

FIGURE 6-3

This graph illustrates the success of young children in finding a toy hidden in a room. A scale model is useful to 3-year-olds but not to 2½-year-olds. Younger children are not helped by memory aids such as labeling or pointing, but they can find the toy when shown a picture of its hiding place or when the experimenter points to its location in a photograph of the room or in a drawing of the room.

(Data from J. S. DeLoache, "Rapid change in the symbolic functioning of very young children," in Science, 238, 1987, 1556–1557; also DeLoache, "Young children's understanding of the correspondence between a scale model and a larger space," in Cognitive Development, 4, 1989, 121–139; also DeLoache, "Symbolic functioning in very young children: Understanding of pictures and models," in Child Development, 62, 1991, 736–752.)

the toy hidden behind photographs of individual pieces of furniture. They also found the toy easily when the experimenter pointed to a particular piece of furniture in a wide-angle photograph of the room or a drawing of the room.

These experiments indicate that the transition to preoperational thought does not guarantee robust use of symbols. On the contrary, the symbol-use skills of 2½-year-olds are flimsy. As DeLoache (1991) notes,

. . . young children who understand a great deal about pictures were not flexible enough to treat them as symbols and objects. A mature symbol user can adopt an "as if" stance to virtually anything; a fledgling symbol user cannot. (p. 751)

In the remainder of this chapter, we shall see that the proficient use of symbols develops considerably over the course of childhood and adolescence.

FIGURE 6-4
The three-mountains problem devised by Piaget to study perspective taking. The child's task is to judge how the mountains would appear to the doll. *(From R. Kail and J. W. Pellegrino,* Human Intelligence, Perspectives and Prospects. *New York: W. H. Freeman, 1985. Reprinted by permission.)*

believed that when preschool children ignore the opinions or views of others, this does not reflect stubbornness that they want their own way. Instead, preoperational children literally cannot understand that there is another way, that other people have views, opinions, and feelings differing from their own. Thus, the preoperational child is an unknowing prisoner of his or her own egocentric point of view.

Chapter 5 included one instance of egocentrism: In children's early efforts to converse, they occasionally disregard what others have said already, moving conversations in completely new and unanticipated directions. Another classic demonstration of egocentrism involves what has come to be known as the three-mountains problem (Piaget and Inhelder, 1956, chap. 8). Children were seated on one side of a display consisting of three toy mountains. They were asked to select a photograph that depicted how the display looked to a doll seated elsewhere (see Figure 6-4). Children under the age of 7 or 8 generally indicated that the doll saw what they themselves saw. Preoperational children apparently assume that their own vantage point is the only view of the mountains; anyone viewing the mountains must see them as they do.

According to Piaget, this egocentric view of the world is responsible for many of the engaging behaviors characteristic of preschoolers. At this age, children sometimes practice **animism**, which means that they attribute life and lifelike properties to inanimate objects (Piaget, 1929). Children may claim that a cloud moves because it wants to and that a car hurts when driven on a bumpy road. Preoperational children, locked in their own egocentric view of the world, suppose that inanimate objects have thoughts and feelings just as they do.

Another characteristic of preoperational children is that they sometimes are unable to distinguish appearance from reality. A typical example occurs at Halloween, when many 3-year-olds are frightened by other children in costumes. This happens despite reassurances from their parents and, perhaps, even after seeing one's older sibling don his or her costume.

Animism Attributing lifelike properties to inanimate objects.

Reality and appearance are not distinguished—the frightening appearance of the costumed sibling is reality for the young child.

Much the same pattern is revealed in simple (and less frightening) experiments in which children are shown objects that are not what they appear to be. For example, children might see a glass of milk be wrapped with transparent, red plastic, making the milk appear red. Typically, 3-year-olds claim that the milk looks red and that it is "really and truly red" (Flavell, Green, and Flavell, 1986). Similarly, if 3-year-olds are shown one pencil that is held behind a prism so that it appears to be two pencils, the youngsters will report that the adult is "really and truly" holding two pencils (Flavell, Green, and Flavell, 1989).

In these examples, children believe that appearance is reality, an error known as **phenomenism**. Another common error is **intellectual realism**. This error is demonstrated when children describe the real nature of an object when asked only about its appearance. Shown an eraser that looks like a banana, 3-year-olds will commonly say that the object really is an eraser and that it looks like an eraser (Flavell et al., 1986).

Both phenomenism and intellectual realism can be understood by returning to young children's difficulties in perspective taking. Recall that in the three-mountains problem, preoperational children often assert that the doll's view of the mountains is the same as theirs. Successful performance on both the three-mountains problem and appearance-reality problems requires the understanding that a single object can have multiple mental representations. The egocentrism of the preoperational children usually limits them to a single mental representation, which means that appearance and reality are sometimes fused.

The Concrete Operational Period (7 to 11 Years)

Egocentrism lessens during the preoperational period, in part through contact with friends, siblings, and classmates who have their own perspectives (LeMare and Rubin, 1987; Piaget and Inhelder, 1969). The decline in egocentrism is apparent in children's performances on many tasks: Youngsters are now unlikely to confuse appearance and reality; they are better able to take the perspective of another person. By the time they enter school, most children have begun the transition to the **concrete operational period** of thought.

What change has freed children from their earlier egocentrism? According to Piaget, the key is the **mental operation**. As the names of the two periods imply, school-age children are capable of something called operational thought, but preschoolers are not. What are these operations? Piaget proposed that psychological operations are much like arithmetic operations such as addition and subtraction. Mental operations are actions that can be performed on objects or ideas and that consistently yield a result. One important property of operations is that they can be reversed. In arithmetic operations, adding 2 to 4 yields 6; reversing the operation, subtracting 2, returns us to the starting value of 4.

Piaget's use of reversibility is demonstrated in one of his best-known experiments: the conservation of liquid quantity. In this experiment, chil-

Phenomenism A common error among preoperational children, who claim that an object is always what it appears to be.

Intellectual realism A common error during the preoperational period in which children claim that the object has its normal appearance even though they have been told the object has been disguised as something else.

Concrete operational period The third of Piaget's four stages of intellectual development, corresponding approximately with 7 to 11 years of age.

Mental operation Mental actions that are the psychological analogs of arithmetic operations and that emerge during the concrete operational period.

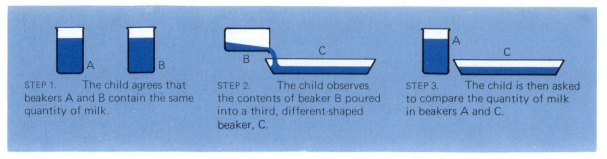

STEP 1.   The child agrees that beakers A and B contain the same quantity of milk.

STEP 2.   The child observes the contents of beaker B poured into a third, different-shaped beaker, C.

STEP 3.   The child is then asked to compare the quantity of milk in beakers A and C.

FIGURE 6-5
A typical sequence for studying conservation of liquid quantity.

dren are shown two identical beakers, both filled with the same amount of liquid (see Figure 6-5). Water from the second beaker is poured into a third beaker, which differs in shape from the first two. Concrete operational children would say that the first beaker and the third beaker still contain the same amount of liquid. They would justify their answers by saying that the water could be poured back into the second beaker. They realize that the pouring can be reversed. In contrast, preoperational children usually claim that there is more water in the third beaker, in which the water level is visibly higher. Unable to reverse the pouring operation mentally, they base their answer on the dramatic difference in the appearance of the water in the first and third beakers.

Reversible mental operations are also the key to success on Piaget's class-inclusion problem. Here, children are shown objects from two categories—pictures of five boys and four girls, two dogs and three cats, or seven roses and four tulips. Each problem consists of two subsets, one larger than the other. After children are shown the sets, they might be asked, for example, "Are there more roses or flowers?" Concrete operational children answer these problems correctly. They first add the two classes, roses and tulips, to form the class of flowers. Then they reverse the operation, dividing the flowers into the two original classes. Because roses are a subset of flowers, there must be more flowers.

In contrast, preoperational children typically respond, "More roses." They cannot simultaneously conceive of roses as a distinct subset and as a member of the larger set of flowers. That is, as was true for the perspective-taking and appearance-reality problems, preoperational children are unlikely to solve class-inclusion problems correctly because they require multiple mental representations of the roses. Instead, they erroneously equate flowers with the smaller set of tulips, then conclude that there are more roses than flowers.

Reversible mental operations give flexibility and coherence to thought. But concrete operational children are still bound up with the world as it is, and they cannot get any further in problem solving until they begin to delineate all possible explanations at the outset of considering a problem. This ability to appreciate the possible, as well as the real, characterizes the transition to formal operational thought. It is not that the concrete operational child is unintelligent; by middle childhood, youngsters have at their command an impressive array of cognitive tools. However, in Flavell's colorful words, the concrete operational child takes "an earth-bound, concrete, practical-minded sort of problem-solving approach, one that persistently fixates on the perceptible and inferable reality right there in front of him. . . . A theorist the elementary-school child is not" (Flavell, 1985, p. 98).

CHILDREN'S HUMOR. Piaget's developmental periods are not limited to logical, scientific, and mathematical reasoning. On the contrary, Piaget believed that the mental structures associated with each stage of intellectual development are the means by which children interpret all experiences, including, for example, interpersonal experiences (Barenboim, 1977). Piaget's stages have even been used as the basis for understanding children's humor. Many theories of humor claim that children's

> comprehension and appreciation of ludicrous situations will depend to a great extent . . . on the match between the individual's existing developmental level and the cognitive demands placed upon him by the humorous event. All things being equal, the individual's appreciation of humor is expected to increase as cognitive demands . . . [of] the humor increase, up to the point where the stimulus becomes too difficult, complex, or novel to be assimilated by the individual's cognitive structures. (Brodzinsky and Rightmyer, 1980, pp. 187–188)

One prominent theory, proposed by Paul McGhee (1979, 1983), takes these general ideas and links them directly to Piaget's developmental stages. According to McGhee, children's understanding and appreciation of humor is determined, in large part, by their level of cognitive development. For example, a child who has just entered the period of concrete operations should particularly enjoy humor that taps these newly acquired mental structures. This child would find preoperational jokes silly and would also not understand formal operational humor.

In one study McGhee (1976) examined the relation between children's understanding of conservation and their appreciation of jokes based on the concept of conservation. An example would be the following:

> Mr. Jones went into a restaurant and ordered a whole pizza for dinner. When the waiter asked if he wanted it cut into six or eight pieces, Mr. Jones said: "Oh, you'd better make it six! I could never eat eight!" (McGhee, 1976, p. 422)

As predicted by McGhee's theory, the children most likely to enjoy such jokes were in the transition from preoperational to concrete operational thought, when the humor was challenging for their newly acquired mental structures. Children enjoyed these jokes significantly less prior to the onset of concrete operational thinking and also after such thinking has become well established.

Thus, understanding some forms of humor is really nothing more than a distinctive, particularly pleasant form of solving problems. People are most likely to appreciate humor when their levels of cognitive development make resolving the incongruity neither so transparent that there is no challenge, nor so complex that it becomes tedious.

Formal operational period The fourth of Piaget's four stages of intellectual development, beginning at approximately 11 years of age and extending through adulthood.

Hypothetical-deductive reasoning Reasoning that starts with a fact or premise and leads to conclusions.

The Formal Operational Period (11 Years through Adulthood)

Beginning with preadolescence, people can reason abstractly. They can draw hypotheses from their observations, imagine hypothetical as well as real events, and deduce or induce principles regarding the world around them. They begin to consider all possible explanations for a problem, and only then do they try to discover, systematically, which explanation really applies. Collectively, these changes signal the onset of the **formal operational period**.

Adolescents' more sophisticated thinking represents significant advances on two fronts. The first concerns **hypothetical-deductive reasoning**, which is any type of reasoning that starts with a fact, a premise, or a hypothesis and then draws conclusions based upon one of these elements. For example, consider the following:

1. If an animal has gills, it is a fish.
2. A trout has gills.

From the premise, an adolescent will reach the logical conclusion "A trout is a fish."

Sometimes concrete operational children will also reach this conclusion, but not via deductive reasoning. To see why, suppose we replace the second statement in our example with the following:

2. A giraffe has gills.

The conclusion "A giraffe is a fish" follows from the premise just as necessarily as the first conclusion about a trout, and formal operational adolescents would understand the validity of this latter conclusion. For concrete operational children, however, conclusions are derived from experience. Hence, they would draw the first conclusion but not the second.

These changes in reasoning ability are illustrated in research by Markovits and Vachon (1989). These investigators examined people's ability to reason from factually correct statements and factually incorrect statements. One factually correct statement was "If an object is put into snow, it will become cold," while the corresponding factually incorrect

FIGURE 6-6

As children approach adolescence, they are able to appreciate the operation of formal principles of reasoning and become able to reason abstractly.

Implication A logical statement in which, if the premise is true, then a specific conclusion follows.

Equivalence A logical statement in which the conclusion follows only when the stated premise is true.

Inductive reasoning Reasoning that involves determining facts from different experiences.

Separation of variables A formal operational scheme used to identify causal relations between events.

statement was "If an object is put into boiling water, it will become cold." Given either the factually correct or the factually incorrect premise, 15- and 18-year-olds—who should be solidly established in the formal operational stage—typically agreed that the object would become cold. However, 10- and 13-year-olds reached this conclusion less often when the statement was factually incorrect. These children show the influence of concrete operational thinking, in which conclusions are based on experience, not logical necessity.

The example we have used here illustrates a type of reasoning that logicians call **implication**, represented by "if P then Q." Actually, this is only one of 16 forms of deductive reasoning that Piaget identifies with the formal operational period. For example, **equivalence** is defined as "if and only if P, then Q." These 16 operations form an integrated system that affords flexibility of thought that is not possible in the concrete operational period. In addition, the Ps and Qs of propositional logic can denote concrete entities such as objects or people, but they can just as easily refer to abstractions such as ideas, values, or even thinking itself.

Another important component of reasoning, determining the validity of premises, is known as **inductive reasoning**. Inhelder and Piaget (1958) proposed that several schemes emerge during the formal operational period that allow adolescents to induce correct generalizations across different problems that are similar in structure. One of these general-purpose schemes is the **separation of variables**, which is useful for understanding causal relations. Piaget's research on the pendulum problem demonstrates the use of this scheme. In this experiment, the subject is presented with a pendulum consisting of an object hanging from a string. He or she is permitted to vary the length of the string, change the weight of the suspended object, alter the height from which the pendulum is released, and push the pendulum with varying degrees of force. The problem that must be solved is a classical one in physics: to discover which of these factors alone or in combination will influence how quickly the pendulum swings back and forth. (In fact, length of the string is the critical variable: The shorter the string, the faster the pendulum swings.)

Concrete operational children approach the problem unsystematically and soon give up because their chaotic approach leaves them without any real clue to the answer. Formal operational children, in contrast,

FIGURE 6-7
Youngsters enter into the period of formal operations about the time when adolescence begins. According to Piaget, the ability to conduct scientific experiments depends on formal operations.

handle the problem quite systematically. First, the adolescent envisions all the possible factors and combinations of factors that could influence the speed of the pendulum: string length, weight, height of release, force, length and weight, length and height, length and force, and so on. The formal operational child can cast the possibilities into the form of propositions, which function as hypotheses. Finally, these hypotheses are tested empirically. To construct a valid test of each hypothesis the child varies one dimension, such as length of string, while holding all other dimensions constant. For example, a 100-gram weight with a long string will be compared with a 100-gram weight with a short string. Formal operational thinkers realize that an experiment would yield inconclusive results if both weight and string length were varied together because they would be unable to deduce which factor produced the difference in pendulum speed.

Formal operational schemes like this one allow adolescents to explore and discover relations that exist in the world. It is important to keep in mind, though, that formal operational reasoning is something most older adolescents and adults are capable of, but not necessarily something they do all, or even most, of the time. Adolescents and adults may often fail to think logically, even when they are capable of doing so and when such thinking would be highly beneficial.

CRITICISMS OF PIAGET'S THEORY

In the 1960s and the 1970s, literally hundreds of studies were published in which the aim was to probe various facets of Piaget's theory. This research provided support for many of Piaget's claims but also revealed some important shortcomings in his theory. In the next few pages, we describe some of the problems with his theory that were encountered.

Alternative Explanations of Performance on Piagetian Tasks

Some researchers believed that children's performances on Piagetian tasks could not be explained by the processes that Piaget described. Consequently, the results from these tasks did not necessarily provide support for Piaget's theory. To illustrate why some researchers have come to this conclusion, we can reconsider four phenomena: object permanence, conservation, perspective taking, and animism.

OBJECT PERMANENCE. Piaget argued that one of the milestones of infancy is the understanding that objects exist independently of oneself and one's actions. For very young infants who lack this understanding, objects cease to exist when they disappear from view. Piaget traced the development of the perceived permanence of objects using a task in which an attractive toy was placed, in full view of the child, under a container. By about 8 to 10 months of age, children will readily reach under the container to retrieve the toy. However, Piaget found that if after a few hidings the toy is now placed under a second container, 8- to 10-month-olds would routinely look for the toy under the first container. Piaget claimed that this showed the fragmentary nature of object permanence at 8 to 10 months of age: Infants could not dissociate the object per se from the actions they had used to locate the object (for example, lifting a particular container).

Other investigators have questioned this interpretation. A number of relatively minor procedural changes can affect an infant's success on this task: An infant is more likely to look under the correct container, for example, if the interval between hiding and looking is brief and if the containers are readily distinguished from each other. One interpretation of these results is that an infant's usual lack of success on this task reflects a poor memory rather than inadequate understanding of the nature of objects (Wellman, Cross, and Bartsch, 1986).

Also inconsistent with Piaget's claims is work by Baillargeon (1987) in which object permanence was assessed using habituation procedures like those illustrated in Figure 6-8. Infants first saw a silver screen that appeared to be rotating back and forth. After they had habituated to this display, on alternative trials they were shown two new displays. In the *possible event*, a yellow box appeared in a position behind the screen, making it impossible for the screen to rotate as far back as it had previously. Instead, the screen rotated until it made contact with the box, then rotated forward. In the *impossible event*, the yellow box appeared, but the screen continued to rotate as before. The screen rotated back until it was flat, then rotated forward, again revealing the yellow box. The illusion was

FIGURE 6-8

The procedures used in the habituation phase of Baillargeon's (1987) study are shown in the top row. The screen rotated away from and back toward the infant. In the *possible event*, the screen rotated away from the infant until it rested on a box, then rotated back toward the infant. In the *impossible event*, the screen rotated away from the infant, then passed through the box as if it had disappeared. When the screen rotated toward the infant, the box reappeared. The chicanery in the impossible event was achieved because the box was mounted on a movable platform that dropped out of the way of the moving screen at the appropriate time.

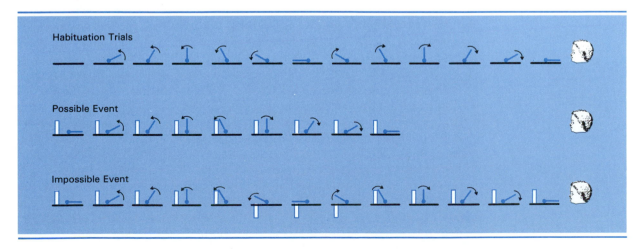

possible because the box was mounted on a movable platform that allowed it to drop out of the way of the moving screen. However, from the infant's perspective, it appeared as if the box vanished behind the screen, only to reappear.

The disappearance and reappearance of the box violates the idea that objects exist permanently. Consequently, an infant who understands the permanence of objects should find the impossible event a truly novel stimulus and look at it longer than the possible event. Baillargeon (1987) found that 4½-month-olds consistently looked longer at the impossible event than the possible event; among 3½-month-olds, those who had habituated rapidly to the initial display also looked longer at the impossible event. Evidently, infants have at least rudimentary understanding of object permanence long before this should be possible according to Piaget's account of sensorimotor development.

CONSERVATION. Upon close examination, it can be seen that the difficulty of the traditional conservation of liquid quantity problem (shown in Figure 6-5) can vary with subtle changes in experimental procedures. For instance, the way in which the conservation question is phrased turns out to be critical (Winer, Craig, and Weinbaum, 1992). In the standard procedure, children are asked twice about the similarity of the two quantities, once before and once after the liquid is poured. When questions are repeated in everyday conversation, however, it usually means one of two things: Perhaps the first answer was wrong, as when a parent questions a child a second time about some misdeed, suspecting that the first answer may have been less than truthful. Or perhaps something has happened in the interval between the questions that should change the child's response. An example would be when parents ask children about their hunger before and after a meal. Thus, children may interpret the repeated question in the standard conservation procedure as an implicit request that they should change their answers. If this argument is correct, asking children about the quantities once—after the liquid has been poured—should increase the likelihood that children understand the concept of conservation. And usually, it does (Silverman and Rose, 1979). Thus, although Piaget believed that young children perform poorly on conservation tasks because they lack reversible mental operations, they may simply be following the usual conversational rule for answering questions that are repeated.

PERSPECTIVE TAKING. Recall that in Piaget's three-mountains problem, children must decide how others view the mountains. A number of investigators suggested that this task is so difficult that it may lead us to underestimate young children's perspective-taking skills. Imagine, for example, if a college student were asked to describe, in detail, how a classroom looks to a professor. The student would understand that the professor's view differs, but the student's description would probably still be incorrect in some ways. The student might, for example, suppose that the professor cannot see students in the back of the room when, in fact, the professor can. In this case and in the three-mountains problem, the difficulty of the task may lead us to conclude, incorrectly, that an understanding of perspective taking is missing.

FIGURE 6-9

Performance on Level 1 and Level 2 perspective-taking tasks. The dog and cat picture measured Level 1 perspective taking. The turtle picture measured Level 2 perspective taking. Level 1 tasks can be solved by 3 years of age; Level 2, by 5 years.

(Data from Z. S. Masangkay et al., "The early development of inferences about the visual percepts of others," in Child Development, 45, 1974, 357–366.)

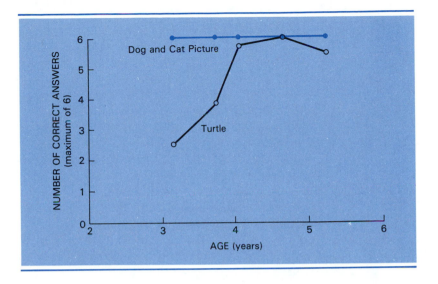

A solution to this problem, provided by Flavell and his coworkers (Masangkay et al., 1974), is to devise the simplest conceivable tasks that still require the subject to judge what others see. In one task, children were shown a piece of cardboard with a picture of a dog on one side and a picture of a cat on the other. Children were asked to describe what they saw as well as what the experimenter saw. In another task, a picture of a turtle was held horizontally between the child and experimenter. Children were asked how the turtle looked—upside down or right side up—to them and to an experimenter. Typical results are shown in Figure 6-9: Three-year-olds are quite accurate on problems like the first one; they consistently report that they would see a dog but the experimenter would see a cat. However, on the turtle picture, 3-year-olds usually respond egocentrically. They believe that they and the experimenter would see the turtle in the same way. In contrast, 4- and 5-year-olds usually perform flawlessly on both problems.

Based on these and similar results (Flavell, Everett, Croft, and Flavell, 1981), Flavell proposes two distinct levels of understanding of perspective taking. At Level 1, corresponding to 2 to 3 years of age, children understand that others do not always see what they see. They realize, for example, that an object they can see may be hidden from another person. Not until Level 2, however, do children acquire the understanding that an object may look different to two individuals. By age 5, most children know that an object will look the same to people viewing it from the same position and that an object will look different to people viewing it from different positions (Flavell, Flavell, Green, and Wilcox, 1981).

ANIMISM. Recall that young children are sometimes animistic, meaning that they attribute lifelike properties to inanimate objects. For Piaget, animism reflected the young child's egocentrism: The child assumes that other people and inanimate objects think and feel much as he or she does. As the child's thinking becomes less egocentric, animism subsides.

More recent investigators have questioned the extent of the role of animism in children's thinking. Although Piaget claimed that young children attribute human properties, such as feelings and motives, to inanimate objects, modern studies have raised doubts as to this idea's validity. Springer and Keil (1989, 1991), for example, have studied youngsters' understandings of causality in animate and inanimate objects. Their research indicates that by 7 years of age, children distinguish the causal forces typically associated with animate objects from those generally associated with inanimate objects. For example, preoperational children believe that "natural agents" like a mother's color determine a puppy's color, but they believe that mechanical factors like a machine determine the color of an inanimate object such as a can.

Thus, in the case of animism, as well as in the cases of object permanence, conservation, and perspective taking, performance on Piaget's tasks sometimes is better explained using concepts that are not part of Piaget's theory. Furthermore, when tasks are simplified without changing their fundamental nature, they are solved by children at younger ages than predicted by Piaget's theory.

Training Piagetian Concepts

Another implication of Piaget's view of the mind is that efforts to teach children advanced concepts should be unsuccessful. For example, it should be impossible to teach concrete operational concepts such as conservation or class inclusion to preschoolers because they lack the necessary mental apparatus to profit from the teaching experience.

Beilin (1965) was among the first to try to teach preoperational children to conserve. His approach was simply to teach the rule itself. In teaching conservation of length, for example, when children erred, they were told the correct rule:

> Whenever we start with a length like this one (pointing) and we don't add any sticks to it or take away any sticks . . . it stays the same length even though it looks different. See, I can put them back the way they were, so they haven't really changed. (p. 326)

While reciting the rule, the experimenter made the appropriate changes in the object so that the child would have a physical as well as a verbal representation of it. This procedure was quite successful in inducing specific conservation on the training task. But this approach failed to produce significant generalization to other conservation tasks. That is, training led to better performance on specific conservation tasks, but not to a general understanding of the concept of conservation.

General understanding of conservation can be taught, however, by directing children's attention to the fact that the quantity remains the same despite transformations. That is, Gelman (1969) argued that a preschooler's attention is drawn to many cues in a conservation task, such as the size, height, and diameter of the beakers, and the level of the liquid in the beakers. Most of these cues change as the liquid is poured from one beaker to another, which probably prompts youngsters to believe that the amount of liquid has changed. To direct the child's attention to the

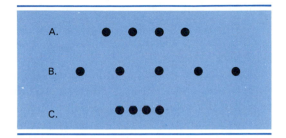

FIGURE 6-10

In Gelman's (1969) experiment, children
were trained to ignore the length of the rows
of circles and to attend only to the number of
circles in each row.
*(From R. Gelman "Conservation acquisition:
A problem of learning to attend to relevant
attributes," in* Journal of Experimental Child
Psychology, 7, 1969, 167—187*)*.

fact that the quantity can remain the same despite differences in many
other cues, Gelman (1969) had preoperational children solve nearly 200
problems in which two quantities were the same but a third differed. For
example, in the problem shown in Figure 6-10, the child would be asked
to select the two rows that had the same number of circles in them. To
answer correctly, children must learn to ignore the fact that the top and
bottom rows differ in length and attend, instead, only to number.

After this training, almost all children solved conservation tasks that
were similar to the training tasks. Even more impressive, many youngsters
were also able to solve conservation tasks that were quite different from
the training experience. In other words, provided with many different
examples and with feedback, children learn to ignore misleading cues
and to attend to the relevant feature, quantity.

Training procedures such as Gelman's, although successful, may
seem artificial. However, cognitive change can also be achieved using
experiences common to childhood: conflict with peers! When nonconservers solve conservation problems together with children who did conserve, their joint answer is likely to be a conservation response. More
important is the fact that subsequently, if tested alone, children who
formerly failed to conserve will now conserve. These children are not
simply parroting the conservers' answers because they explain the conservation response correctly and the training generalizes to new conservation tasks (Ames and Murray, 1982; Miller and Brownell, 1975).

Training has not been restricted to conservation; investigators have
also asked whether children below the age of formal operations can learn
to master formal operational problems. For example, many 10- and 11-
year-olds can solve the pendulum problem following instruction that includes definitions of key scientific concepts, application of these concepts
to particular problems, and demonstration of the use of precise measuring
instruments (Siegler, Liebert, and Liebert, 1973). Similarly, some 9- to 11-
year-olds can solve the pendulum problem if they are prompted to pay
attention to all variables and to hold all variables constant except the one

being tested (Danner and Day, 1977). Clearly, children in the concrete operational period can learn formal operational concepts—although, in line with Inhelder and Piaget's findings, these children rarely solve the problems without instruction.

Simply finding that Piaget's stages can be demonstrated in younger children if they are trained does not make Piaget's theory wrong. After all, many of the children in these studies were near the age when they would acquire the concepts associated with the various stages anyway. Training may have simply induced a cognitive change sooner. This interpretation does have a testable implication—that "children at more advanced stages should derive greater benefit from training than should children at less advanced stages—or more simply, the higher the stage, the greater the learning" (Brainerd, 1977, p. 921). For example, suppose we tested a large number of 5- and 6-year-olds on conservation tasks and divided the children into those who never conserve versus those who are "transitional"—that is, they sometimes conserve but more often do not. If previous training studies have simply facilitated an incipient cognitive change, then transitional children should profit more from training than nonconservers. In fact, both groups are equally likely to learn to conserve from training (Brainerd, 1977), and this outcome does not follow from Piaget's theory.

Consistency of Thought within Stages

For Piaget, each period of intellectual development consists of a unified set of mental operations that is implicated in all aspects of a child's thinking. This view leads to obvious experimental tests. According to Piaget, preschool children should perform at the preoperational level across all cognitive tasks. If they do not, this would be inconsistent with Piaget's view that the children's thinking is unified at each stage.

In fact, children's performances on Piaget's tasks are often not consistent in the way suggested by the theory. Research by Siegler (1981) illustrates this inconsistency on the three Piagetian tasks shown in Figure 6-11. In the balance scale task, individuals are shown a balance scale in which weights have been placed at various distances on either side of a fulcrum. Individuals must decide which side of the balance scale will go down, if either, when the supporting blocks are removed. On the projection of shadows task, the T-shaped bars are placed at various distances from the light source, and the horizontal part of the T varies in length. Subjects are asked to judge which of the two bars will cast a longer horizontal shadow. In the probability task, subjects are shown two piles of marbles, each containing red and blue marbles. They decide which pile would be more likely to produce a red marble if they must choose a marble with their eyes closed.

Despite apparent differences in the nature of the tasks, the underlying structure is the same for each: It involves a comparison of ratios. The scale will balance when the ratio of weight to distance is the same on the two sides of the fulcrum. The shadows will be the same size when the ratio of the length of the horizontal part of the T-bar to the distance of the bar from the light is the same for both bars. The probability of selecting

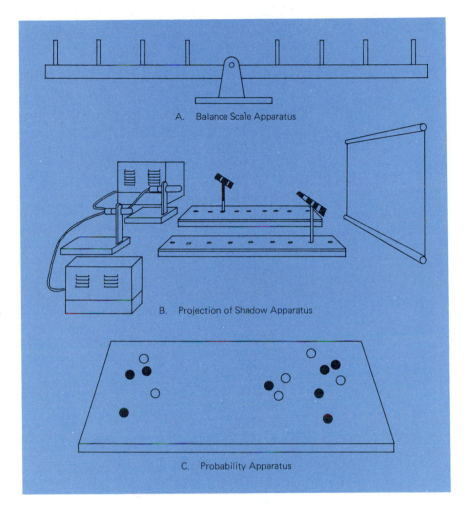

A.   Balance Scale Apparatus

B.   Projection of Shadow Apparatus

C.   Probability Apparatus

FIGURE 6-11
Apparatus for balance scale, projection of shadows, and probability tasks.
(From R. S. Siegler, "Developmental Sequences within and between Concepts," in Monographs of the Society for Research in Child Development, 46, *no. 189, 1981, 1–70. Reprinted by permission of the Society for Research in Child Development, Inc.)*

a red marble will be the same when the ratio of the number of red marbles to the total number of marbles is the same for both piles.

Because the underlying structure of the tasks is fundamentally the same, we would expect consistency in performances across the three tasks. In fact, Siegler (1981) found that only one-third of the subjects performed at the same level on all three tasks. The remainder differed in performance, sometimes considerably, depending upon the task performed. For example, all 11 subjects whose level of performance on the balance scale task corresponded to the formal operational period were found to be only at the level of the concrete operational period on the shadows task. Such variability across tasks is far from what one would expect to find from the homogeneous mind that is described in Piaget's theory.

NEO-PIAGETIAN APPROACHES

In the face of these criticisms, many theorists have tried to modify Piaget's theory. The general approach has been to retain Piaget's claim of important qualitative changes in thinking at approximately 2, 7, and 11 years of age.

However, reflecting the research we have described in the last few pages, the new theories also allow for much greater variation in performance from task to task.

Case's Stage Theory

One major neo-Piagetian theory has been developed by Robbie Case (1985, 1986; Case and Sowder, 1990). Some features of the theory are strikingly Piagetian: there are four qualitatively different stages of development; transitions between stages typically occur at roughly 2, 5, and 11 years; and all individuals progress through all four stages. Case's theory begins to diverge from Piaget's theory in the means by which thinking progresses from one stage to the next. Recall that Piaget explained the phenomena of transition from one period to another in terms of accommodation and assimilation. Case, in contrast, believes that cognitive change is brought about when two distinct schemes become integrated, with one subordinate to the other. For example, suppose a child is asked to decide which side of a balance beam is heavier. The child might resort to counting the weights on the two sides. Finding that this method works (at least on some problems!) the child integrates the "weight-determining scheme" with the "counting scheme." The "weight-determining scheme" is dominant in that it triggers the "counting scheme," not vice versa.

Integration of schemes in this manner could lead to a great deal of variation in the age at which children master specific tasks. Through exploration, imitation of peers or adults, or specific instruction, they may become proficient in some domains earlier than in others. The problem now is to explain why there is *some* consistency in the ages at which children master skills. Although thinking at each stage in cognitive development is not as unified and homogeneous as Piaget claimed, there definitely is some consistency in thinking across domains. Integration of schemes per se does not guarantee this consistency. To explain this consistency, Case proposes that only a limited number of schemes can be kept in mind at once, and that this number increases with age. Specifically, schemes are kept in a **short-term storage space**, and the size of this space increases with age. Thus, even though the specific integrations that may occur at a particular age may differ from one child to the next, the complexity should be similar for all children, reflecting the limit imposed by the available short-term storage space.

A study by Marini and Case (1989) illustrates how complexity can provide an upper limit to performance on dissimilar tasks. Preschool children between 1½ and 4 years of age were tested on a balance task similar to the one described on page 200, as well as a task in which puppets interacted. Several variations were created for each task, ranging from quite simple to very difficult. To illustrate, in the simplest version of the balance task, children only had to move the balance beam far enough to hit a bell, making it ring. In the simplest puppet task, children were told that although Kermit the Frog was sad, he would become happy (smile) if they patted him on the forehead.

Marini and Case (1989) argued that these versions are equally complex because each involves understanding a single relation. For the bal-

Short-term storage space In Case's theory, a temporary, working memory of limited capacity.

ance task, the relation is "move beam → bell rings." For the puppet task, the relation is "pat forehead → Kermit smiles." More complex versions of the tasks were created by increasing the number of steps needed to achieve the end results of ringing the bell or making Kermit smile. In the next level of difficulty, for example, children had to remove supporting blocks prior to moving the beam, and they had to pick up a blanket to use to pat Kermit on the forehead. Using procedures like these, five levels of complexity were created.

Marini and Case found considerable consistency in children's performance on the two tasks. Nearly two-thirds of the children performed at the same level of complexity on the two tasks. In other words, if children could solve the balance task at the fourth level of complexity but not the fifth, they typically solved the fourth but not the fifth level on the puppet task. Of course, older children tended to solve more complex versions of both tasks, reflecting the fact that as storage space increases with age, individuals are able to integrate more complex schemes.

Why should storage space increase with age? Case proposes two explanations. One is that individual schemes may require less storage space as children develop. For example, as children develop, they count more proficiently. Case suggests that one consequence of this proficiency is that the counting scheme takes less storage space in older children than younger children. Thus, after the counting scheme has been stored, there would be more storage space remaining in older children than in younger children.

Another explanation for increased storage space involves change in the central nervous system. Recall, from Chapter 4, that some nerve cells in the brain are covered with myelin. This fatty substance acts as an insulator, allowing nerve impulses to be transmitted more rapidly. Myelinization of neurons is not complete until adolescence and seems to occur in cycles that apparently coincide, roughly, with the cognitive changes noted by Piaget and Case. Consequently, Case proposes that myelinization may be responsible for developmental changes in short-term storage space.

Many aspects of Case's theory are quite speculative, and many are controversial. However, the theory is attractive because it allows for both general developmental changes as well as those that are specific to individual skills.

Fischer's Skill Theory

Another example of a neo-Piagetian theory is Kurt Fischer's (1980, 1983) skill theory. According to Fischer, cognitive development involves the acquisition of complex skills. However, the complexity of skill that children can master is determined by their optimal level, "the upper limit of a person's general information processing capacity" (Fischer and Pipp, 1984, p. 47). Fischer proposes ten distinct levels of cognitive development that he groups into three **tiers**. The **sensorimotor tier** corresponds directly to Piaget's sensorimotor period; in this tier, skills are limited to actions. It is not until the **representational tier**, which includes both the pre-operational and concrete operational periods of Piaget, that children are able to understand and reflect on their skills. The final tier is the **abstract**

Tier A stage of cognitive development in Fischer's theory that encompasses several cognitive levels.

Sensorimotor tier The first stage of cognitive development in Fischer's theory, corresponding to the sensorimotor stage in Piagetian theory.

Representational tier The second stage of cognitive development according to Fischer, including both the preoperational and concrete operational periods of Piaget's theory.

Abstract tier The final stage of cognitive development in Fischer's theory, corresponding to Piaget's period of formal operational thought.

tier, corresponding to Piaget's formal operational period. In this tier, individuals can understand relations between two sets of facts. For example, at this tier individuals could formulate a general understanding of conservation from two specific facts: (1) The amount of water is unchanged by pouring it from one container to another, and (2) the amount of clay is unchanged by molding it into different shapes.

The tiers and levels of Fischer's theory can be used to explain why there is some consistency in thought: The levels limit the complexity and sophistication of thought at a particular age. However, by emphasizing that this is an upper limit—meaning that many skills may not be developed to this limit—it is possible to understand why children may be highly skilled in some domains but novices in others.

Another important contribution of skill theory concerns cognitive development in adolescence. In Piaget's theory, adolescence is effectively the end point of cognitive development, since children are thought to enter the formal operational period at approximately 11 or 12 years of age. Many theorists (for example, Arlin, 1975) have criticized this aspect of Piaget's theory and have proposed ways that cognitive development might continue during adolescence and adulthood.

In skill theory, individuals enter the abstract tier at approximately 10 to 12 years of age. However, this tier consists of four distinct levels, marked by greater and greater degrees of abstraction. Individuals do not reach the last two tiers until early adulthood. For example, at the second level in this tier, adolescents are capable of **abstract mappings**, which means they can relate abstract concepts to one another. A teenage girl, for example, could notice that she wants a job with an excellent salary and pressure to succeed, while her mother was happy with a modest salary but little pressure. In the final level of the abstract tier, what Fischer calls **systems of abstract systems**, people are able to coordinate several abstract systems of thought. The same teenage girl, having now become an adult, might compare changes over the years in her occupational identity and aspirations.

Fischer's skill theory, like Case's stage theory, illustrates the important characteristics of neo-Piagetian theories of cognitive development. These theories share Piaget's effort to provide a general account of cognitive development, one that has at its core the claim that thinking changes qualitatively with development. However, each theory incorporates a mechanism to explain why a child's thinking may be mature in some areas but not others.

Abstract mappings A mental relation between concepts, an ability achieved in the second level of Fischer's abstract tier.

Systems of abstract systems Coordination between sets of abstract concepts, usually not achieved until the final level of cognitive development, according to Fischer's theory.

SUMMARY

1.   The work of Piaget on cognitive development distinguishes the contents, functions, and structures of the intellect. Contents refer to behavioral acts. The functions of intelligence are constant throughout development and include organization and adaptation. Adaptation, in turn, consists of

assimilation, the use of schemes to interpret and organize information, and accommodation, the modification of schemes to reflect the acquisition of new knowledge.

2. Piaget identified four distinct intellectual structures that form an invariant developmental sequence: the sensorimotor, preoperational, concrete operational, and formal operational periods.

3. The sensorimotor period lasts approximately from birth to 2 years of age. A key component of this period is the circular reaction, which refers to an event that first happens by chance and produces pleasant consequences for the infant, who then tries to repeat the event.

4. The preoperational period lasts from approximately 2 to 7 years of age. Children now use symbols, but their thinking is marked by egocentrism: They are unaware that others view the world differently than they do. Younger preoperational children are also limited in their ability to distinguish appearance from reality.

5. The concrete operational period lasts from 7 to 11 years of age. Children's thinking is no longer egocentric but is based on mental operations like reversibility. However, thought at this level is based on the concrete and real; abstract reasoning is not yet possible.

6. The formal operational period begins at approximately 11 years of age and continues into adulthood. At this stage individuals are able to think abstractly and hypothetically. These advances are reflected in the ability to reason deductively, which involves starting with premises and drawing appropriate conclusions. They are also reflected in inductive reasoning, the ability to make valid generalizations from experience.

7. Piaget's theory has been criticized on a number of grounds. First, performance on Piaget's tasks can be explained using concepts that are not part of his theory. Second, children can learn individual Piagetian concepts with relatively brief training; but according to the theory, such changes should only occur spontaneously following states of disequilibrium. Third, the Piagetian theory predicts that thinking within a particular stage should be relatively similar on all tasks, but researchers often find that a child will show considerable diversity in thinking across tasks.

8. Neo-Piagetian theorists adhere to many of the basic claims of Piaget's theory but differ in their explanations of the specifics of cognitive development. In Case's theory, cognitive change occurs when schemes become integrated. Schemes are kept in a short-term storage space, which increases in size with age. This increase in size means that older individuals are able to integrate more and more complex schemes. Storage space increases with age because schemes require less storage space as individuals use them more often, and because of the myelinization of nerve cells in the brain.

9. Another neo-Piagetian theory is Fischer's skill theory, in which there are three distinct tiers of cognitive development, each consisting of several different cognitive levels. An attractive feature of Fischer's theory is that it suggests ways in which cognitive skills continue to develop during adolescence and adulthood.

C·H·A·P·T·E·R   7

The Information-Processing Approach to Cognitive Development

The aim of Piaget's theory was to capture the general features of thought at different phases of development. Key concepts in the theory, such as egocentrism and adaptation, were said to apply to children's thinking across a wide range of activities, tasks, and problems. A contrasting approach to cognitive development is one in which the analysis starts with a particular intellectual task. The aim of the analysis is to identify the specific cognitive processes that are needed to perform this task successfully and to determine how these processes change with age. This sort of detailed analysis may be repeated for several tasks. The analyses can then be compared to determine cognitive processes that seem to be general—that is, they are used in many intellectual tasks—as well as those that seem to be specific to particular tasks.

These two approaches are complementary. Just as some artists may start a painting with a complete overall sketch, whereas others like to concentrate on details from the beginning, there is more than one way to create a theory of cognitive development. Theories can be constructed by starting with a handful of general properties that become more elaborated as the theory evolves. Or, investigators may chart in detail the development of specific skills, then determine if general properties emerge.

The analysis of processes specific to particular tasks has been the aim of the **information-processing** approach to cognitive development. The approach began in the 1960s and is now a dominant view of cognitive development in the 1990s. The term information processing is drawn from computer science, and the approach draws heavily on computer operations to explain mental activities. Let's begin with some illustrations of the information-processing style of analysis.

▶ An adult slowly pronounces a set of digits to a child, who tries to repeat them in order. A typical 3-year-old remembers a sequence of 2 or 3 digits but cannot recall longer sequences accurately. By 12 or 13 years of age, a child can remember sequences of 6 and sometimes 7 digits. What has happened in the intervening 9 to 10 years that has allowed the child to double or triple the number of digits that he or she can remember? Information-processing analyses of memorization have revealed that a number of independent processes contribute to a gradual age-related increase in retention.

▶ A child is shown a card with 4 + 5 = ? printed on it. Of course, for adults, the number 9 comes to mind effortlessly. Information-processing analyses have shown that children may solve this problem several ways. Older children will, like adults, sometimes retrieve the sum from memory, a process that is rapid and seemingly automatic. Younger children are more likely to use other approaches that, although slower and more cumbersome, can be just as effective.

▶ Most weekday mornings, 6-year-olds and older children walk from home to school and back without getting lost. In contrast, 3- and 4-year-olds are rarely permitted to make such journeys, despite precautions like stop lights and street-crossing guards. Recent research has identified some

Information processing
An approach to cognitive development that emphasizes the similarities between human thinking and the processes of a modern computer.

of the sophisticated mental navigation skills that allow a person to travel to a distant location, and these studies have also revealed that these "way-finding" skills develop rapidly during the school-age years. ◀

In this chapter, we examine some of the specific contributions of the information-processing approach to an understanding of how children's thinking changes as they develop. We start by considering some of the properties of this approach in more detail. Then we examine attention and memory, two categories of processes that are implicated in many cognitive tasks. The third section of the chapter traces mental development in three specific domains: quantitative thinking, way-finding, and reasoning. In the final section, we discuss some general explanations of mental development that have emerged from the information-processing approach.

PROPERTIES OF THE INFORMATION-PROCESSING APPROACH

A microcomputer fresh out of the box includes hardware—disk drives, random-access memory, and a central processing unit—as well as an operating system that allows these pieces of hardware to function. Of course, computers achieve their real power through the software that is written to achieve particular tasks, such as word processing, creating graphs, or playing games.

Information-processing theorists believe that human cognition, too, consists of both mental "hardware" and mental "software." Human cognition consists of mental and neural structures that are built-in and allow the mind to operate. However, cognitive growth is marked by the acquisition of skills in particular domains—writing poetry, playing the flute, and kicking a soccer ball are just a few examples. In the information-processing view, mastery of skills like these can be understood as the acquisition of ever more complex and efficient software that is designed to accomplish an ever increasing array of tasks and functions. That is, at any point in development, thinking consists of an organized set of cognitive processes, many of which can be broken down into even more elementary processes, just as computer software consists of modules that can be broken down into other modules or into individual commands. Thinking at different phases of development is distinguished by the amount, complexity, efficiency, and power of this mental software.

Information processing represents a general approach to cognition and development that encompasses many specific theories (Kail and Bisanz, 1992; Klahr, 1989). An early and still influential view of human information processing is depicted in Figure 7-1. The hardware consists of three components. The first component is sensory memory, where information is held in raw sensory form for no more than 1 to 2 seconds. Information is then categorized and passed on to the second component, the short-term store; or it is forgotten altogether. The short-term store is

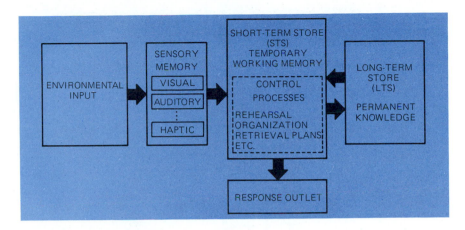

a temporary working memory of limited capacity. The third component
is the long-term store, a limitless, permanent storehouse of knowledge of
the world. Once information reaches the long-term store, very little is lost.

Mental processes are used to transfer information from the short-
term to the long-term store. They are also used to retrieve information
from the long-term store so that it can be used in ongoing thinking.

In the next section, we examine two cognitive processes that are
fundamental to the successful completion of most mental activities—
attention and memory.

DEVELOPMENT OF BASIC PROCESSES

Attention

Our perceptual systems are marvelously powerful. They provide us with
far more information at any time than we could possible interpret. The
function of **attention** is to help select information that will be processed
further. In the general framework depicted in Figure 7-1, attentional mechanisms are involved in directing a small amount of the information that
arrives at the sensory registers to the short-term store.

Attention is made up of several discrete processes, many of which
correspond to everyday definitions of attention (Enns, 1990). To illustrate,
let's consider the common situation in which teachers admonish their
pupils to "pay attention." Usually some well-defined stimulus—a teacher's explanation of an assignment, for example—that should be the focus
of a student's attention is competing with other equally well-defined stim-

Attention Selection of
information to be
processed.

FIGURE 7-2
Attention is required when searching for specific information that is part of a complex stimulus, such as looking for a newspaper article on a particular topic.

uli that are irrelevant to the task at hand. A student's new digital watch, a friend in the hallway making faces, or the odor of pizza being cooked for lunch all compete for attention with the teacher's explanation of the homework assignment. The task here is to **filter** the irrelevant stimuli to prevent them from entering the limited mental workspace that is available in the short-term store.

Another example illustrates a second aspect of attention. Often people are asked to find a particular stimulus. A youngster may scan the sports pages of a newspaper looking for the outcome of a particular game, or scan the shelves in a grocery store looking for a favorite brand of cereal. Each of these tasks involves **search** for a stimulus that is embedded in a complex array of stimuli. Most of the other printed words or bland-tasting adult cereals are to be ignored—passed over as rapidly as possible—in the effort to find the desired stimulus.

Children become more adept at both aspects of attention as they grow. Let's see how.

FILTERING. The pioneering work on filtering was done by John Hagen and his colleagues (Hagen and Hale, 1973). In their research, children were shown the cards depicted in Figure 7-3. One card was presented at a time and the children were asked to remember the names of the animals; they were also told that the household objects were irrelevant and could be ignored. Thus, the animal on each card was a well-defined stimulus that was relevant to task performance; the household object was irrelevant to task performance. After several trials in which the children's recall of animals was tested, children were given a set of cards with the eight animals and another set with the eight household objects. They were asked to match each animal with the corresponding household object. At all ages, children matched only a few pairs correctly, indicating that children had filtered out the irrelevant stimuli, but not perfectly. The oldest sub-

Filter Removing irrelevant information so that only relevant information is processed.

Search Scanning an environment to find a specific stimulus.

FIGURE 7-3
Stimuli used by Hagen
and his colleagues in
their studies of filtering.
Children were told to
remember the animals
but to ignore the
household objects. Later,
they were asked to pair
animals and household
objects that had appeared
together.
*(From J. W.
Hagen,"Strategies for
remembering," in S.
Farnham-Diggory (ed.),*
Information Processing in
Children. *New York:
Academic Press, 1972.
Reprinted by permission
of the publisher and the
author.)*

jects—12- and 13-year-olds—were the most skilled at filtering irrelevant information.

This general pattern of a gradual age-related improvement in filtering is now well established (Enns, 1990). How can we help children, particularly younger ones, to filter more effectively? The most straightforward solution would be to reduce or eliminate the irrelevant information, but this may not be practical. An alternative is to heighten the contrast between relevant and irrelevant information, so that youngsters can readily distinguish them. On a blackboard or computer screen, for example, relevant and irrelevant information can be separated spatially. Color coding can also be used to differentiate the two types of information. And children can be reminded of the need to attend only to the task-relevant information. For preschool children, all of these aids are often necessary to achieve effective filtering (Woody-Ramsey and Miller, 1988).

SEARCH. Children often need to search a complex pattern for a specific stimulus. Examples would include searching the faces in a crowded auditorium to find a father or mother, or searching a box of toys to find a favorite toy car. As children grow older, they search more rapidly and more accurately, a change that seems to come about because children learn to use information to direct the search more effectively. Let's return to our example of a child looking for a father's face in a crowd. Suppose the father is clean shaven, wears glasses, and has dark hair. These facial features can be used to expedite search. Locating a beard means that the face need not be processed further, as would the absence of glasses or light-colored hair or baldness. In each of these cases, one facial feature is

FIGURE 7-4
Children can search for stimuli rapidly when the stimulus is distinct.

enough to tell the child that this is not the father's face. School-age children take advantage of cues in this fashion, but preschool children often do not. Instead, these youngsters will consider many of the elements of a stimulus, despite the fact that they provide redundant information (Shepp, Barrett, and Kolbet, 1987).

All children find the target of search more rapidly when it can be readily distinguished from surrounding stimuli. A distinctive color can be used: Children will quickly find the only person in a crowd wearing a neon-pink hat. A distinctive shape also works: Children will have no trouble locating the person wearing a cowboy hat in a crowd of hatless people (Kaye and Ruskin, 1990).

Search and filtering, then, both improve as children grow. However, in some settings, we can improve youngsters' attention by creating environments in which irrelevant information is minimized and in which the critical information is readily distinguished.

Memory

The development of memory in children and adolescents has been studied extensively since the 1970s (Kail, 1990, 1992). We now know that age-related change in memory can be traced to two related factors. First, as children grow, they use more effective strategies to improve memory. Second, children's growing factual knowledge of the world allows them to organize information more thoroughly, improving memory. Let's begin our study of memory by focusing on the first of these factors.

MEMORY STRATEGIES. The Edmonton *Journal* reported the following story:

A nine-year-old boy memorized the licence plate number on a getaway car

Rehearsal A memory
strategy in which stimuli
are named repeatedly.

mnemonics Strategies
that are used to aid
memory.

following an armed robbery, a court was told Monday. . . . The boy and his
friend . . . looked in the [drug] store window and saw a man grab a 14-year-
old cashier's neck. . . . After the robbery, the boys mentally repeated the
license number until they gave it to police.

These boys used **rehearsal**, a strategy of repetitively naming stimuli that
are to be remembered. Rehearsal is only one of many memory strategies
or **mnemonics** that can be used to transfer information from short- to long-
term store, or to retrieve information from long-term store.

Children begin to rehearse on many memory tasks at approximately
7 or 8 years of age, and they rehearse an increasingly large number of
words as they grow older (Flavell, Beach, and Chinsky, 1966). Younger
children's use of memory strategies seems to be limited to "simple" strategies such as looking at or pointing to an object that is to be remembered
(DeLoache, 1984).

Adolescents use strategies more flexibly than children, modifying
the strategies as needed to meet the demands of particular problems. A
parent might ask a child to help remember the food to buy for a picnic:
hot dogs, pretzels, soda, potato chips, lemonade, and hamburger. Rehearsal is more effective if the same-category members are rehearsed together: hot dog, hamburger, pretzels, potato chips, soda, and lemonade.
Adolescents will modify their rehearsal in this manner to fit the structure
of the material to be remembered; normally, younger children do not do
this (Ornstein, Naus, and Liberty, 1975).

FIGURE 7-5
As children grow older, the ability to "operate" their own memory increases
dramatically.

FIGURE 7-6

When the aim is to recall the important features from a large body of information, such as that found in a textbook, useful strategies are underlining and outlining.

Even greater flexibility is needed when trying to remember detailed information of the sort presented in textbooks or newscasts. Literal recall of individual sentences or individual words is no longer the objective; instead, the aim is to recall the main points. An effective mnemonic must identify the key ideas in the text. Examples would be outlining text material and highlighting key phrases. College students and high school students often use these strategies to learn from texts. Junior high students use these strategies infrequently and upper elementary school students rarely do. The quality of outlining and highlighting also improves with age: Only older adolescents identify the key points in text with reasonable consistency (Brown and Smiley, 1978; Drum, 1985).

Successful use of strategies like rehearsal and outlining usually is the byproduct of analysis of the memory task to determine exactly what is required and how difficult it may be. This appraisal then dictates the choice of a strategy that suits the objectives: Rehearsal is well suited for remembering telephone numbers and brief lists but outlining is a more appropriate strategy for recalling the gist of text.

This sequence of events is shown in Figure 7-7: understand the memory task, select an appropriate strategy, and use it. Figure 7-7 also includes a fourth step: monitoring. Intelligent use of a mnemonic requires that children evaluate its effectiveness. If a strategy is working, then children can apply it to the information that they have yet to learn; if it is not, then they need to reanalyze the memory task and come up with a better approach.

As you might anticipate, youngsters often err in each of the steps depicted in Figure 7-7. Younger children often misjudge the goal or difficulty of a memory task, and they choose less than optimal strategies. Often they do not routinely check their progress (Kail, 1990).

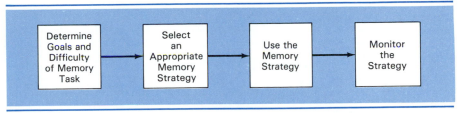

FIGURE 7-7

Successful memorizing begins with an analysis of the problem to determine the goal of the memory task and the difficulty in achieving this goal. This determines the choice of an appropriate strategy. As the strategy is used, its performance is monitored to determine its effectiveness.

Choosing an appropriate strategy illustrates changes with age that are common to all of the skills depicted in Figure 7-7. In research on this topic, children are asked to learn to associate ten pairs of stimuli, for example, *airplane* with *couch*, *lion* with *mirror*. Upon presentation of *airplane*, children are to respond with *couch*. On one trial, children are told that a good way to remember the items in a pair is to say their names together aloud, repeatedly (a simple rehearsal strategy). On another trial, with ten different pairs, children are taught to use an **elaboration** strategy in which they think of a sentence or a mental image that links the words in a pair (for example, an image of a comfortable couch in an airplane). Repetition and elaboration strategies were chosen because the first should be a much less effective mnemonic in this task than the second: Children typically recall approximately twice as many pairs when using the elaboration strategy as when using the repetition strategy. When children are allowed to use either strategy, most 10-year-olds choose the elaboration strategy. However, despite experience that demonstrates the relative power of the two mnemonics, many 7-year-olds use repetition (Lodico et al., 1983).

Matching strategies to particular memory tasks develops gradually through the elementary school years (McGilly and Siegler, 1990), as do the other skills shown in Figure 7-7. Clearly, a youngster's effort to remember demands proficiency in several component skills. During the elementary-school years, children gradually acquire proficiency in each of these skills, as well as proficiency in coordinating them. Paralleling these changes is the child's growing understanding of the world; this increased factual knowledge also contributes to improved memory, as we shall see in the next few pages.

CONSTRUCTIVE ASPECTS OF MEMORY. In an unusual experiment by Chi (1978) in which children and adults were asked to remember the positions of stimuli in a matrix, the recall by 10-year-olds was nearly twice that of adults. What was responsible for this remarkable reversal of the usual age difference? The task was actually to recall the positions of chess pieces on a board. The children were skilled chess players but the adults were novices. The positions of the pieces were taken from actual games, so they represented familiar configurations for the child chess players. For the

Elaboration A memory strategy in which information to be remembered is linked by a mental image or a vivid sentence.

Script A part of
knowledge describing
events that occur in a
particular order.

adults, who lacked an in-depth knowledge of chess, the task was one of
remembering an arbitrary pattern. Just as remembering the letters

n n c c b a s b c c b n

becomes much easier for adults when reversed and seen as

n b c   c b s   a b c   c n n,

only children expert in chess had the knowledge to organize and give
meaning to a complex pattern of chess pieces. Consequently, children
could remember one configuration instead of many isolated pieces.

Usually, of course, the knowledge that allows one to organize information and give it meaning increases gradually as children develop. Psychologists often depict this knowledge as a network in which entries are
related to one another. An example of such a network, depicting part of
a 13-year-old's knowledge of animals, is shown in Figure 7-8. The entries
in the network are shown as ellipses that are linked by different types of
associations. Some of the links denote membership in categories, others
denote properties, still others denote **scripts**, which are rules for performing acts in a particular sequence (Kail, 1990).

A diagram like Figure 7-8 for a younger child would have fewer
entries, as well as fewer and weaker connecting links. This means that

FIGURE 7-8

A hypothetical portion of
a child's knowledge
about dogs. The lines
between the ellipses
denote different types of
associations, such as
those denoting
membership in categories
or those denoting
properties.
*(Adapted from R. Kail,
The Development of
Memory in Children, 3rd.
ed. New York: W. H.
Freeman, 1990.
Reprinted by
permission.)*

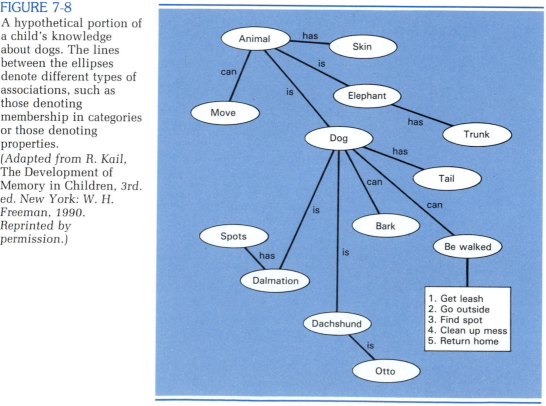

FIGURE 7-9
In children's remembering, information is often distorted so that it conforms to the child's understanding of what usually happens. Told a story about this helicopter, many children would remember its pilot as a man not a woman, reflecting conventional sexual stereotypes.

younger children can organize information less extensively, which makes remembering more difficult for a younger child than for an older child. Nevertheless, the knowledge that young children have *is* organized, and this turns out to be a powerful asset. In the case of events that fit scripts, for example, they needn't try to remember each individual activity; instead, they simply remember the script. When a preschooler returns from lunch at McDonald's with a friend's family and is greeted by parents eager to hear about the events, the script guides retrieval: The general sequence can be retrieved from long-term store and used to structure a recall of specific events of interest.

Knowledge can often distort a child's memory. If experiences differ from the generic version that is held in long-term store, the experiences may be forgotten or may be remembered in the way specified by long-term memory. Superheroes may be depicted as weak in stories, but children often remember them as strong (Stangor and McMillan, 1992). Another common distortion is that children, particularly preschoolers, cannot distinguish what they experienced from what is specified in the script from long-term memory: Youngsters may remember throwing trash in the waste basket simply because this is part of the after-dinner script, not because they actually did so (Farrar and Goodman, 1992).

These distortions are less likely when children are recounting the first experience of some new activity, because they will lack a script at

CLOSE-UP

Children on the Witness Stand

The Chicago *Tribune* carried the following story on March 21, 1989:

> A soft-spoken 5-year-old girl sat in the witness chair Monday and pointed out Sandra Fabiano, the woman she says sexually molested her during nap time at a day-care center the girl attended.
>
> The center's owner "took down my pants" and touched her genitals, the blond-haired girl said as she testified . . .
>
> The girl's riveting testimony was vital to the prosecution's case, and apparent contradictions in that testimony were seen as grist for the defense contention that nothing ever happened and that the allegations were just a fantasy.

This story illustrates a phenomenon that is all too common in North America today. Children, many of them very young, are serving as witnesses, typically in cases of alleged child abuse. Traditionally, courts have been cautious concerning children's testimony. Today, however, courts decide on a case-by-case basis if children are competent to testify. Psychologists studying children's memory have been asked to determine when children's memory for these experiences is most accurate. For these researchers, the validity of experimental results has been a thorny issue. The research would be most useful if children's memory was assessed in situations such as those in which abuse occurs. Of course, research conducted under such conditions would be unethical. Consequently, most investigators have created paradigms that are designed to capture some of the important features of the abusing situation: Children may interact with an adult who is a stranger, sometimes in games where they perform unusual behaviors. Later, children are asked to describe their interaction.

Typical results come from a study by Goodman and Aman (1990). Children played several games with an unfamiliar adult—they had a tea party, played with puppets, and played a game of Simon Says in which children were asked to touch

that time. A child's first trip to a museum or first ride in an airplane may be recalled vividly; additional, similar experiences will cause children to formulate a script that includes the common features of these experiences and will also allow distortions to occur. Hudson (1990), for example, compared recall by 3- to 6-year-olds who had participated in either one or four creative movement workshops, each with the same structure of singing, dancing, exercising, and related activities. Children who had participated in four workshops could recall more about what happened during the first workshop than in subsequent ones, and they more often recalled the events in the correct sequence. However, their recall was more prone to distortions, such as recalling events from other workshops.

The findings from Hudson's study capture the essence of constructive processes in memory. Knowledge allows all children, even infants and toddlers, to remember elaborate experiences and complex stimuli that children would forget readily if they could only be remembered as individual, isolated elements. The cost associated with this memory benefit is that children's memory is sometimes distorted.

parts of their bodies and to touch the adult's knee. One week later, children were asked to describe what had happened. The subjects, 3- and 5-year-olds, recalled very little in response to this general prompt. However, when asked a series of questions that could be answered with either yes or no, 3-year-olds answered 59 percent of the questions accurately and 5-year-olds answered 76 percent accurately. Clearly, questions about specific actions or behaviors are more revealing than are general requests for descriptions of events.

The drawback to specific questions is that they tend to "lead" to an answer. Compare "And what happened during nap time?" to "During nap time did the teacher touch you?" A youngster asked the second question might answer yes even though nothing had happened during nap time. The child might simply decide that it *could* have happened, and the nature of the question suggests that it did happen.

People of all ages can be influenced by leading questions but young children are particularly influenced by them. For example, in the Goodman and Aman (1990) study, children were asked questions such as "He asked you to put on a costume, didn't he?" The correct answer to this question was no. The 3-year-olds answered 47 percent of these questions incorrectly, compared to 19 percent for 5-year-olds. A few of the misleading questions dealt directly with behaviors related to abuse: "He took your clothes off, didn't he?" Here, 3-year-olds answered 24 percent of the questions incorrectly compared to only 3 percent for adults.

Findings like these indicate that preschoolers can be influenced by leading questions. Other research (Goodman, Rudy, Bottoms, and Aman, 1990; Kail, 1990) indicates that these youngsters are often inaccurate in identifying faces that they have seen in the past and that their memory for past events sometimes is biased by subsequent experiences, including their own thoughts. This work indicates that preschoolers' testimony needs to be corroborated because their memory can easily be distorted. School-age children are far less prone to these distortions, but we cannot yet offer precise guidelines concerning the circumstances under which their testimony is likely to be reliable. Research is underway that should help to sharpen current guidelines and produce more precise ones. At the same time, we can hope that research on abuse itself, which we describe in Chapter 9, will yield a greater understanding of abuse and help to eliminate the circumstances that lead to it.

DEVELOPMENT OF COMPLEX SKILLS

Attention and memory represent two processes that are very general: They play a role in virtually all intellectual tasks. In this section, our focus shifts to those aspects of cognitive development that are specific to particular domains. We will examine three cognitive skills that seem to develop in cultures worldwide: quantitative knowledge, way-finding, and problem solving.

Quantitative Knowledge

Quantitative skills range from simple counting to calculus and beyond. Few individuals progress to the most advanced levels, but knowledge of numbers and simple mathematical operations is widespread in most cultures (see Figure 7-10).

ORIGINS OF NUMBER SKILLS. Counting is perhaps the first obvious

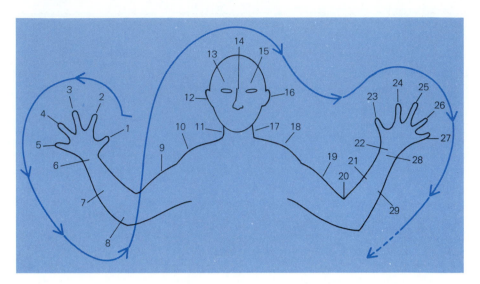

FIGURE 7-10
The Oksapmin of New Guinea count by using the parts of the body, in the
order indicated.
(From G. B. Saxe, "Culture and the development of numerical cognition:
Studies among the Oksapmin of Papua, New Guinea," in C. J. Brainerd, Ed.,
Children's Logical and Mathematical Cognition. New York: Springer-Verlag.
Copyright 1982 by Springer Verlag. Reprinted by permission.)

indicator of quantitative skill. However, counting is actually the crowning
achievement in a developmental sequence that begins soon after birth:

> Infants lie in cribs with a certain number of bars. The walls in their rooms
> display repetitions of bricks or wooden boards or regularity in the pattern
> of wallpaper. Their parents go into the room and out of it over and over
> again. Some of their toys are bigger than others; some are identical and
> others are equivalent in size. If they push a toy it moves; and the harder
> they push, the harder it moves. Infants thus have ample opportunity to learn
> about number, repetition, regularity, differences in magnitude, equivalence,
> causality, and correlation. (Ginsburg, 1977, p. 30)

For many years psychologists could only speculate about what infants might learn about number from experiences such as these. Beginning
in the early 1980s several investigators used habituation (described in
Chapter 3) to demonstrate that infants can discriminate between sets of
objects that differ only in quantity. The general approach is illustrated in
Figure 7-11. Infants are shown sets of stimuli that vary in the specific
objects presented, their size and color, and how they are arranged. Only
the number of stimuli is constant from one trial to the next. For example,
an infant might see a picture of two small dogs aligned horizontally,
followed by two large butterflies presented along a diagonal, and so on.
After infants have habituated, they are shown a pattern consisting of either
one more or one fewer element than they had previously seen. These
procedures mean that infants could discriminate stimuli only on the basis

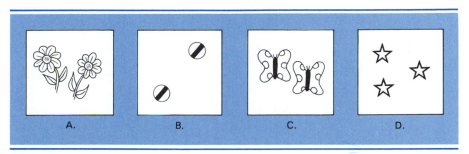

FIGURE 7-11
Stimuli representative of those used to study infants' perception of numerosity. Infants first saw the stimuli, such as those labeled A, B, and C. After they had habituated, they saw the stimulus labeled D, which differs from the others only in terms of the number of objects depicted.

of number. The typical outcome is that 5-month-olds can distinguish sets of two objects from sets of three, and sometimes sets of three objects from sets of four (Curtis and Strauss, 1983; van Loosbroek and Smitsman, 1989).

How do infants do this? Older children and adults might do so by counting, but of course infants have not yet learned number names. Instead, the process is probably more perceptual in nature. As we noted in Chapter 3, we know that the infant's perceptual system is designed to be sensitive to certain characteristics of stimuli such as color (Bornstein, 1981). Quantity may well be another characteristic to which infants are sensitive. That is, just as colors (reds, blues) and shapes (triangles, squares) are basic and salient perceptual categories, small quantities ("twoness" and "threeness") may be a perceptually salient property (Strauss and Curtis, 1984).

COUNTING. Not long after children have learned to talk, they begin to learn number names. Some of these number names are learned in isolation, but many are probably learned in the context of counting. Parents and teachers sing counting songs and television programs like *Sesame Street* emphasize counting.

Rochel Gelman and her colleagues have traced the acquisition of counting from its origins in 2-year-olds to its near-mature form in 5- and 6-year-olds (Gelman, and Meck, 1986; Gelman and Gallistel, 1978). Gelman believes that successful counting involves mastering three principles:

One-to-one principle In Gelman's theory, the idea that each object to be counted must have just one number name.

Stable-order principle In Gelman's theory, the requirement that number names be used in the same order.

Cardinality principle In Gelman's theory, the understanding that the final number name denotes the number of objects counted.

1. The **one-to-one principle**: There must be one and only one number name for each object in a set to be counted.
2. The **stable-order principle**: Names for numbers must be used in the same order every time a person counts.
3. The **cardinality principle**: The last number name is distinctive in denoting the number of objects in a set.

Children begin to acquire these principles as 2- and 3-year-olds. In Gelman's research, she placed plates with varying numbers of objects in front of a child, who was simply asked: "How many?" A child was credited

Abstraction principle In Gelman's theory, the realization that objects need not be similar or related to be counted.

with following the one-to-one principle if there were as many number words as items. Thus, counting four objects as "1, 2, 3, 4" or "1, 2, 2, 3" or even "1, 2, A, B" would each be consistent with the one-to-one principle.

The stable-order principle required that the child use number names— whether the correct names or idiosyncratic ones like letters of the alphabet—in a consistent order on each counting trial. That is, children might be asked to count six different sets of five objects. They would receive credit for the stable-order principle only if they used the same order of names in counting four of the six sets.

Finally, there were several ways that children could demonstrate the cardinality principle. One way—most frequent among the older children—was that they simply responded immediately with the proper cardinal value without counting aloud. Other criteria for exhibiting the cardinality principle were stressing the last number word or repeating the last number word. For example, counting five objects as "one, two, three, four, *five—five*!!" illustrates both stress and repetition.

Figure 7-12 shows the percentages of 3-, 4-, and 5-year-olds who followed all three principles. Most 3-year-olds followed all three when counting a small number of objects. As children grow older, they apply the principles when counting ever larger numbers of objects.

Gelman considers the how-to-count principles the "nuts and bolts" of counting. She has also studied preschoolers' understanding of two more conceptual properties of counting. The **abstraction principle** refers to the fact that any set of distinct objects can be counted regardless of their relation (or lack of relation) to one another. The set "giraffe, zebra, cat, dog" is counted just as readily as the set "transistor, Corvette, Democrat,

FIGURE 7-12

Percentage of 3-, 4-, and 5-year-olds who adhered to all three "how-to-count" principles, as a function of set size. Many 3-year-olds adhere to all principles with small sets; 4- and 5-year-olds do so with larger sets, but even 5-year-olds have trouble counting sets greater than 10.

(Data from R. Gelman and C. R. Gallistel, The Child's Understanding of Number, Cambridge, Mass.: Harvard University Press, 1978.)

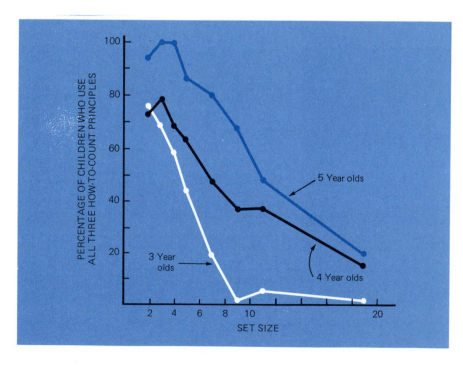

eraser." In fact, preschoolers are equally likely to count heterogeneous sets of objects as homogeneous sets, indicating they apparently understand that "counting can be applied to any collection of real and imagined objects" (Gelman, 1982, p. 183).

A second conceptual principle is **order irrelevance**, the fact that as long as one obeys the how-to-count principles, the order in which items in a set are counted does not matter. Gelman tested preschoolers' understanding of this concept by asking them to count the same set of objects repeatedly. Only rarely did children count the objects in exactly the same order each time; usually they counted them in different orders. Another procedure was to ask children to recount a set making a particular object the first, second, or third item. The most frequent response among 3-year-olds was to ignore the experimenter's request! However, many 4-year-olds and most 5-year-olds were capable of altering their counting so that an item would be counted at the requested point in the sequence. In other words, by the time most children enter school, they have mastered the abstraction and order-irrelevance principles, as well as the how-to-count principles.

This understanding of quantitative properties arises from children's experiences with numbers. By 2 years of age, children are already involved in many number-related activities: Counting, reading number books, and watching *Sesame Street* are all common activities for many 2-year-olds growing up in North America. Children initiate many of these activities spontaneously, but mothers also deliberately play many number-related games with their children. Mothers gradually adjust the type of games that they play, making them more challenging as children master basic skills. However, children do not simply absorb knowledge passively from number-related activities. Instead, children seem to be inherently motivated to understand variation in quantity as part of their desire to understand more about their world generally. Consequently, they profit more from number experiences that relate to their own numeric goals (Saxe, Guberman, and Gearhart, 1987).

ADDITION AND SUBTRACTION. Counting is the starting point for children as they learn to add. In fact, most preschoolers first add by counting. Suppose children were told to imagine that they have four oranges and they then get two more. Asked to determine the total number of oranges, many children first count out four fingers—1, 2, 3, 4—then two more— 5, 6 (Siegler and Shrager, 1984). To subtract, they reverse these acts.

Young children often abandon this approach for a more efficient method. Instead of counting out the fingers on the first hand, they simultaneously extend the number of fingers on the first hand corresponding to the larger of the two numbers to be added; then they count out the smaller number, using fingers on the second hand (Groen and Resnick, 1977).

In school, children start to receive formal instruction in arithmetic. Addition problems are solved less and less by counting aloud or by counting one's fingers. Instead, children add and subtract by counting mentally. However, early mental addition is still closely linked to counting. Children behave as if they are counting *silently*, beginning with the largest number

Order irrelevance A principle in Gelman's theory that objects can be counted in any order.

CLOSE-UP

Math Achievement in Japan, Taiwan, and the United States

Asian children often excel in mathematics; children in the United States, by comparison, fare poorly. The differences, shown in Figure 7-13, are stunning. With regard to both computational skill and the use of mathematics to solve problems, children in the United States lag far behind their counterparts in Japan and Taiwan.

Why are there such striking differences in achievement? We can rule out cultural differences in general intelligence and in general cognitive skills: Children growing up in Japan, Taiwan, and the United States do not differ systematically in any of these domains (Stevenson and Lee, 1990). A more likely source of the difference is to be found in the nature of children's experiences at school and at home. Stevenson and Lee (1990) conducted a comprehensive evaluation of first- and fifth-grade children living in Japan, Taiwan, and the United States. They identified a number of ways in which experiences at school and at home foster math achievement in Japan and Taiwan, but not in the United States. Let's examine some of these factors revealed in Stevenson and Lee's analysis.

1. *Time in school and how it is used.* First graders in all three countries spend about 1,000 hours in school each year. This figure is about the same for fifth graders in the United States but jumps to about 1,500 hours for fifth-grade children in Japan and Taiwan. Furthermore, at both grade levels, less time in U.S. schools is devoted to academic activities: U.S. children spend 67 percent of each day in academic pursuits, compared to more than 80 percent of each day in Japan and Taiwan.

2. *Time spent doing homework and attitudes towards it.* Fifth graders in the United States spend about 4 hours each week doing homework. Fifth graders in Japan spend about six hours, and those in Taiwan, nearly thirteen hours. In Japan and Taiwan, teachers and students value homework much more than teachers and students do in the United States.

3. *Parental attitudes and expectations.* Nearly half of the parents of U.S. students reported that they were "very satisfied" with their child's schoolwork. In contrast, fewer than 5 percent of the parents in Japan and Taiwan reported this level of satisfaction. In addition, parents in Japan and Taiwan had a stronger belief in the role that effort

and adding on. By 8 or 9 years of age, children typically have learned the addition tables so well that sums of the single-digit integers (0 to 9) are facts that are simply retrieved from memory (Ashcraft, 1982).

These strategies do not form a lock-step, in flexible developmental sequence. On the contrary, individual children will use many or all of these strategies, depending upon the problem. Siegler (1987, 1988) has shown that children first try to retrieve the answers to arithmetic problems. If they are not reasonably confident that the retrieved answer is correct, then they resort to back-up strategies—counting aloud or on one's fingers—to verify the answer.

Solutions to problems with small addends (for example, 1 + 2, 2 + 4) are likely to be retrieved because these problems are presented to children in textbooks and by teachers. As a result, the answer is highly associated with the problem, which makes the child confident that the retrieved

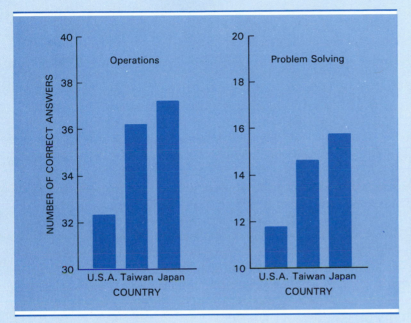

FIGURE 7-13
Number of correct responses by fifth graders on measures of mathematical operations and mathematical problem solving. On both measures, fifth graders in the United States have lower scores than students in Japan and Taiwan.
(Data from H. W. Stevenson and S. Lee, "Contexts of achievement," in Monographs of the Society for Research in Child Development, 55, 1990, *no. 221.)*

plays in their child's achievement in school; parents in the United States accorded a greater role to their child's native ability in determining academic achievement. Thus, unlike parents in Japan and Taiwan, parents in the United States may see little reason to encourage their children to become involved in activities that would foster mathematical skills because (a) they are satisfied with their child's current success, and (b) they believe that native ability, not effort or experience, is a critical determinant in math achievement.

These and other findings from Stevenson and Lee's work (1990) make it clear that differences in math achievement stem from cultural differences in standards for successful performance and from the degree of effort by schools, parents, and children in achieving those standards. The implication is that, for American children to excel in math, parents in the United States need to revise their attitudes and expectations concerning achievement in mathematics, and to urge children to spend more time in math-related activities.

answer is correct. In contrast, problems with larger addends (for example, 8 + 9) appear less frequently. The result is a weaker link between problem and answer, and, consequently, a greater chance that children will double-check the accuracy of the retrieved answer with a back-up strategy.

Of course, arithmetic skills continue to improve after age 8. Children gain greater proficiency in addition and subtraction, learn multiplication and division, and extend these skills to quantities other than integers. These skills lead to the more sophisticated quantitative thinking that is the basis for algebra, trigonometry, and calculus (although not to the same extent in all cultures, as we can see in the above Close-Up). These more advanced mathematical skills are impressive. Yet what is perhaps just as impressive is how early in life children master the essentials of quantitative knowledge. As we shall see in the next section, much the same can be said for way-finding abilities.

Way-Finding

As soon as infants can crawl, they begin to explore their environments. These explorations are usually limited to relatively circumscribed areas, such as a single room or adjacent rooms. In these settings, finding the way to a particular location is not complicated because the destination can usually be seen from the outset. Within a few years, however, children begin to explore much larger realms. They may move freely within an entire house or apartment building and in the surrounding environs. Now **way-finding** skills become essential because the child's destination often cannot be seen from the start. When a 3-year-old playing outdoors realizes that she's hungry, the kitchen may not be in sight. To get there, she must know a route that will lead her indoors and into the kitchen.

Learning to find one's way in an environment involves three related skills, which we consider in the next few pages. First, children must identify **landmarks**, distinctive locations in an environment. Second, a child uses landmarks to form **routes**, sequences of action that lead from one landmark to another. Third, landmarks and routes are formed into clusters, or configurations. These ultimately form a **cognitive map**—a unified mental configuration of an environment that integrates many landmarks and routes (Anooshian and Siegel, 1985; Siegel and White, 1975).

LANDMARK KNOWLEDGE. Landmarks are salient objects or points of decision in the environment that are noticed and remembered and around which the child's actions and decisions are coordinated. For children, landmarks might be a candy store, a playground, and a school crossing. Children move and travel to and from these landmarks, and they are used to maintain one's course during travel.

Learning about landmarks begins very early in life. Before children can walk, they move through environments in parents' arms, in strollers, and in automobiles. Even when they are still, infants see people and objects move in their environments. According to Piaget (Piaget and Inhelder, 1967), a child first thinks of the position of an object in space exclusively in terms of the object's position relative to the child's own body—what Piaget called an **egocentric frame of reference**. Only later do children acquire an objective frame of reference in which an object's location is thought of relative to the positions of other objects in space.

One research technique has been particularly useful in tracing the development of these two ways of locating objects in the environment. Subjects are seated in a room in which there are two identical objects, one to the subject's left and one to the right. On each of several trials, a particular event always occurs at either the left or right object (see Figure 7-14). For example, the objects might be identical windows on the left and right sides of a room. When the infant is looking straight ahead, an experimenter sounds a buzzer. Shortly thereafter a person appears always in the left window, saying the infant's name and showing toys (Acredolo, 1978, 1979). Infants quickly learn to anticipate the appearance of the person in this window when they hear the buzzer.

After infants have learned to anticipate the face, they are turned 180

Way-finding Movement in large environments in which the destination cannot be seen at the start.

Landmarks Salient, distinctive objects in an environment.

Routes Sequences of actions that link landmarks.

Cognitive map A mental configuration of an environment that includes landmarks and routes.

Egocentric frame of reference A framework, typical until about one year of age, in which objects are located by their position relative to the infant's body.

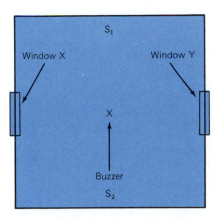

FIGURE 7-14

Experimental situation used to distinguish objective and egocentric frames of reference. In this example, S_1 refers to the position of the infant on the learning trials; S_2, the infant's position after being rotated 180 degrees.
(From L. P. Acredolo, "Development of spatial orientation in infancy," in Developmental Psychology, 14, 1978, 224–234. Copyright 1978 by the American Psychological Association. Reprinted by permission.)

degrees, so that they are facing exactly the opposite direction. Once again the buzzer sounds. The crucial question is, Which way will the infant look? Let's first consider infants whose understanding of objects in the environment is still egocentric. What they have learned in the initial phase of the experiment is that the face appears to their left. Turned 180 degrees, this means that they will look in the wrong direction. An infant whose understanding of locations is objective realizes that even though he or she has moved, the object has not. So, the infant will look to the same window as before, even though this means turning in a different direction.

It turns out that infants respond egocentrically for much of the first year. At the first birthday, egocentric and objective responses are equally likely; during the second year, objective responses become more frequent (Acredolo, 1978; Wishart and Bower, 1982).

When objects in an environment are located in terms of an objective frame of reference, they can be used to locate other objects. That is, some objects become landmarks that help to identify the position of other sites. Children learn environments more rapidly if landmarks are established for them. Cornell, Heth, and Broda (1989), for example, found that 6- and 12-year-olds were better able to learn their way around an unfamiliar university campus when prominent landmarks were shown to them.

Not all elements in an environment are equally suited to be landmarks. An essential skill in way-finding is to identify distinctive landmarks that will be recognized when one travels the route again. For example, suppose a child were walking down the street shown in Figure 7-15 and wanted to remember to turn right at the intersection, which is one of many crossing this street. The stoplight would be of little value as a landmark, because many intersections have stoplights. The parked car would be equally poor as a landmark, because it will not always be in this location. However, the store on the corner would be an excellent choice: It is a distinctive storefront that children would probably notice whenever they walked along this street.

Allen, Kirasic, Siegel, and Herman (1979) examined developmental change in children's choices of landmarks. They took photographs of the walk shown in Figure 7-16, depicting what people would see if they walked along the sidewalk always looking straight ahead. Some of the

FIGURE 7-15
Distinctive landmarks,
such as familiar
storefronts, help children
to learn routes.

photographs (those in locations that are colored in Figure 7-16) showed no intersections where subjects might turn. Other photographs (those in locations that are white in Figure 7-16) included intersections that represent a potential change in heading. These photographs were shown to 7-year-olds, 10-year-olds, and adults in succession, to give them the impression of taking a walk through an unfamiliar neighborhood. Then all 52 photographs were presented at once, and subjects were asked to select nine pictures that would be most helpful in reminding them of their location.

Virtually all the photographs that adults chose included intersections at which one would need to know whether to continue straight ahead or to turn. The 10-year-olds were less likely to choose these key photographs, but they still selected a substantial number of them. The 7-year-olds selected even fewer of these photographs—62 percent—but this figure is greater than would be expected if these children were simply guessing. In other words, by 7 years of age children are beginning to understand that landmarks are most useful if they are prominent or located at decision points along a route.

ROUTE LEARNING. Landmarks are essential to way-finding in large environments, but alone they are not sufficient for travel. Instead, landmarks must be linked in a particular sequence, forming a route in which the last landmark is the destination. If the sequence of landmarks does not conform to our expectations, we quickly have the feeling of "being lost." Routes can thus be considered a kind of spatial "glue" that links environmental landmarks.

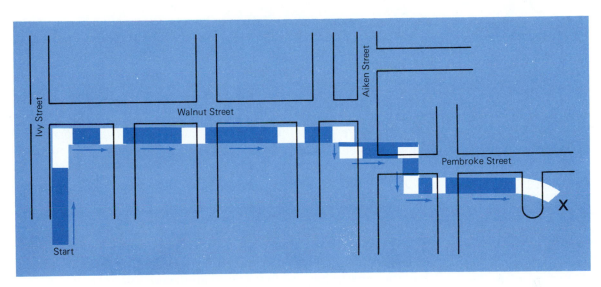

FIGURE 7-16
Schematic diagram illustrating the walk used by Allen, Kirasic, Siegel, and
Herman to study the choice of landmarks. The portions of the route in white
indicate standpoints from which critical areas were visible in the slide
presentation.
(From G. L. Allen, K. C. Kirasic, A. W. Siegel, and J. F. Herman,
"Developmental issues in cognitive mapping: the selection and utilization of
environmental landmarks," in Child Development, *50, 1979, 1062–1070.*
Reprinted by permission.)

The ability to learn routes improves consistently throughout the preschool years. Hazen, Lockman, and Pick (1978) found that 3-year-olds
needed 50 percent more trials than 5-year-olds to learn a route through
four rooms. By school age, children have acquired considerable skill in
route learning. In one study (Cohen and Schuepfer, 1980), subjects saw a
sequence of photographs depicting a walk through hallways. Each photograph contained an intersecting hallway, and the subject's task was to
learn the sequence of left and right turns that would lead to the end of
the corridor. Seven-year-olds and adults learned this sequence at approximately the same rate. In addition, school-age children and adolescents
are very good at arranging photographs of landmarks in the order in which
they were encountered along a route (Cousins, Siegel, and Maxwell, 1983).

Although children can readily learn the sequences in which landmarks appear, they are less skilled than adults in estimating the distances
between landmarks (Cohen and Weatherford, 1980). Judging distance is
important because it allows people to estimate the time needed to travel
between two points. This, in turn, allows a traveler to estimate when a
landmark should appear along a journey; we feel "lost" when a landmark
that is expected after a certain distance fails to appear.

A number of factors influence the accuracy with which people judge
distances. For instance, both children and adults overestimate a distance
that is covered slowly and underestimate one that is covered rapidly
(Herman, Roth, and Norton, 1984). Estimates of distances are also distorted

if the landmarks are segregated in clusters. When a barrier separates two landmarks so that one is not visible from the other, children and adults usually overestimate the distance between them (Cohen and Weatherford, 1980).

When adults first encounter a novel environment, they often use maps to guide them. Children, too, can learn about environments from maps. In one study (Uttal and Wellman, 1989), 4- and 5-year-olds were asked to learn a specific route that connected six landmarks. Children who had memorized a map beforehand learned the route more rapidly than children who had not seen the map. Giving a map to children may help them to form their own cognitive map of the environment, which is our next topic in way-finding.

COGNITIVE MAPS. Learning 10 or 100 or 1,000 different routes through an environment is tedious. A cognitive map is the mental structure by which humans apparently store all the way-finding information about an environment (where routes cross, landmarks common to two or more routes, which routes are parallel and so forth).

It might seem that an easy way to examine children's cognitive maps would be to ask them to draw maps of familiar environments. Actually, this method is not satisfactory because children know much more about their environments than they can draw accurately (Siegel, Kirasic, and Kail, 1978). Investigators have used a number of ingenious approaches to probe configurational knowledge. Consider the two routes shown in Figure 7-17. A child's knowledge of that neighborhood would be called configurational when, regardless of his or her position in the environment, the child would know the relative location of all four houses. If, for example, a child is walking east past the bank, his or her knowledge is configurational if the child knows that (1) house D is straight ahead; (2) house C is directly behind; (3) house B is ahead, off to the left; and (4) house A is behind, off to the left.

When people's knowledge of environment is assessed in this manner, accuracy is seen to improve gradually throughout childhood. In several studies, subjects have been taken to various locations in an environment and asked to use a telescopelike sighting tube to locate other landmarks that are not visible. By 7 years of age, children's estimates of the heading to a landmark indicate that they are aware of the general locations of landmarks. Anooshian and Young (1981), for example, found an average error of 27 degrees for 7-year-olds. This is less accurate than the estimates of 10- and 13-year-olds (17 and 14 degrees, respectively), and it is certainly not the sort of precision that would allow one to navigate accurately from Vancouver to Honolulu. However, for 7-year-olds' needs for traveling within a neighborhood, this degree of precision is more than adequate.

Knowing the direction of a landmark is only one part of configurational knowledge. Children must also know the approximate distance of that landmark. Children could well know that a landmark is in a particular direction and at the same time have a relatively poor idea of how far to travel in that direction. Children estimate distances between landmarks along familiar routes more accurately than distances between land-

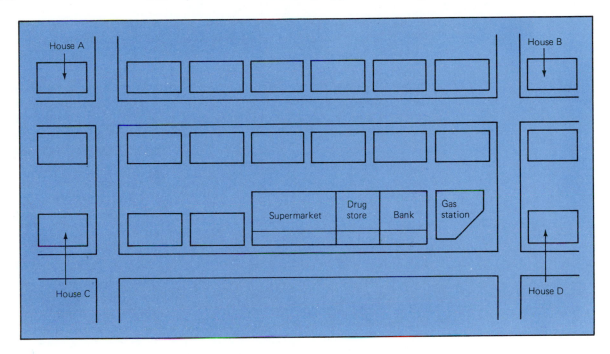

FIGURE 7-17

A cognitive map of this environment includes the distinctive landmarks
(houses, stores), routes that link the landmarks, and the overall configuration of
the environment.

marks that are not connected by routes. But estimates of these latter distances become increasingly accurate with age (Herman, Cachuela, and
Heins, 1987).

The research we have described thus far indicates that configurational knowledge is present by 6 or 7 years of age and that it becomes
increasingly more precise thereafter. Are younger children capable of configurational knowledge? Preschoolers are capable of at least limited forms
of configurational knowledge. Lockman and Pick (1984), for example, used
the sighting technique with preschoolers in their own homes. Asked to
locate landmarks that were out of sight but on the same floor of the house,
preschoolers were just as accurate as their parents. Preschoolers are typically much less accurate when asked to judge locations in less familiar
environments. It may well be, then, that youngsters' cognitive maps begin
with the layout of their home, an environment that includes most of their
early travels. The map expands in all directions as children's explorations
move beyond the confines of home.

Problem Solving

The information-processing approach was first used by developmental
psychologists to discover how children solve some of the tasks that Piaget
devised to assess preoperational, concrete operational, and formal oper-

ational thought. The aim of the initial studies was to provide an explicit step-by-step account of the rules or strategies that children use in their efforts to solve these problems. This approach is illustrated in work by Siegler (1976) on balance-scale problems. Here subjects are shown a balance scale in which differing numbers of weights have been placed at various distances to the left and right of a fulcrum. The subject's task is to determine which side of the balance (if either) will go down when supporting blocks are removed. By varying the numbers of weights and their distances from the fulcrum, it is possible to identify the rules that subjects use to solve the problem.

Typically, 5- and 6-year-olds follow a rule in which only the number of weights is considered. If the weights on the two sides are equal, the child predicts that the scale will balance; otherwise, the child predicts that the side with the greater number of weights will go down.

For 9- and 10-year-olds, two rules are common. The first is a variation of the rule that 5- and 6-year-olds use: As before, when the number of weights on the two sides is unequal, children always predict that the side with more weights will go down. But when the weights are equal, children no longer automatically predict that the scale will balance. Instead, they accurately consider the distance of the weights from the fulcrum.

The second rule used frequently by 9- and 10-year-olds involves a consideration of both weight and distance on every problem. When values on one variable (for example, weight) are the same, children will correctly base their judgments on the other variable (for example, distance). Where children using this rule err is when more weights are on one side but the distance from the fulcrum is greater on the other side. This rule has no provision for combining information about distance and weight, so children simply guess.

Using this approach on the balance scale and on other problems has revealed that even very young children follow rules when they solve problems. The rules are limited in scope, but young children are not behaving inconsistently or capriciously as had once been assumed.

In work like Siegler's, the rules are linked to an understanding of specific problems (for example, an understanding of the concept of balance). Other investigators have been interested in aspects of problem solving that apply more generally. **Heuristics** are important rules of thumb that often help people to solve problems. **Trial-and-error** is one heuristic: If an adolescent is trying to find the house key on a dark night, the best approach may simply be to try each key on the key ring until he or she finds the one that fits. Another common heuristic is **means-ends analysis**. According to this rule-of-thumb, a person identifies the difference between the current state of affairs and the goal, then searches for actions that will reduce (or eliminate) the difference. For a hungry child, going to the kitchen is a good first move; going to the bathroom is not.

Preschool children's use of heuristics has been revealed in their solutions to the Dog-Cat-Mouse problem, shown in Figure 7-18 (Klahr, 1985). Food (bone, fish, cheese) is placed on three of the four corners. Animals (dog, cat, mouse) are also placed on three of the four corners, but not matching their favorite food. The child's task is to move the

Heuristics Rules-of-thumb that can help to solve problems.

Trial-and-error One heuristic in which approaches are tried in a haphazard order until the solution is found.

Means-end analysis An heuristic in which the action that is taken is one that reduces the difference between the current situation and the goal.

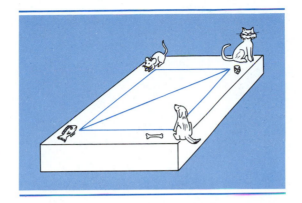

FIGURE 7-18
In the Dog-Cat-Mouse puzzle, children must move the animals, one at a time along the paths, until each is with its preferred food.

animals along the paths, one at a time, until each animal is paired with its favorite food.

Let's first look at means-ends analysis, in which the quality of a move is determined by comparing the extent to which it matches the goal. To illustrate, consider the problem shown in Figure 7-18. The child could move any of the animals to the open position, where the fish is located. Moving the cat would put it at its goal, and this was the move the children usually made.

Another useful heuristic is to look ahead, to project a series of moves to determine whether they will lead to a solution. In games like chess and checkers, players will often plan ahead two or three moves in order to take the opponent's piece. In the Dog-Cat-Mouse problem, performance at various distances away from the goal can be used to measure looking ahead. Most children looked ahead at least two moves because they never made wrong moves when they were two moves away. That is, if children look ahead two moves, then from two moves away they should always proceed directly to the goal. For example, when the animals were in the configuration shown in Figure 7-18, most children would move the cat along the diagonal to the fish, then move the mouse to the corner with the cheese, just vacated by the cat.

These analyses reveal that preschool children often use many of the same heuristics that adults use when trying to solve problems. Older children and adults often use heuristics more effectively, for example, looking ahead further. Nevertheless, the roots of skilled problem solving are clearly planted by the preschool years.

Collaboration. Children solve many problems alone, but collaboration is often necessary to solve some problems: Youngsters planning a birthday party may engage in give-and-take with their parents over the party of their dreams versus one that is practical; scouts planning a camp-out need to agree upon a menu that is filling, has some nutritional value, and is sensitive to everyone's likes and dislikes.

Developmental psychologists have only recently begun to study such collaborative problem solving. An example is work by Radziszewska and Rogoff (1991) in which subjects were given a list of errands and asked to plan the shortest route between stores related to the errands. When pairs

FIGURE 7-19
Children profit more
from collaborative
problem solving with
adults, because adults
allow them to play a
greater role in planning
and decision making.

of 9- and 10-year-olds worked together, their planning was less sophisticated than when 9- and 10-year-olds worked with their parents. Pairs of children devised longer routes because many of their moves considered only one destination at a time and because they were less likely to explore and compare alternative routes.

Particularly revealing was the performance of another group of pairs of children in which one child had previously been shown the optimal strategy to the problem. These pairs performed nearly as well as parent-child pairs, but the nature of their collaboration was quite different. Parents sought to involve their children in planning and decision making, and often discussed optimal strategies with their children. Children who had been taught the strategy simply concentrated on the task and effectively ignored the untrained partner.

The impact of these differing interactions was revealed in the last phase of the study, when children solved more of the problems, but alone. Children who had worked with trained peers planned more effectively than children who had worked with untrained peers but less effectively than children who had worked with their parents. Apparently, children can learn some of the properties of an effective strategy simply by watching a skilled peer. However, active participation in planning and evaluating leads to greater insights into the best way to solve problems.

MECHANISMS FOR CHANGE

As children grow, they develop ever-greater cognitive skills. What is responsible for this steady march towards mature intellectual skill? Experience certainly plays a role, but alone it cannot provide the answer. Instead, we need to explain how changes in mental structures interact with experience to produce cognitive change. You may recall from Chapter 6 that disequilibrium was the mechanism underlying all cognitive change in Piaget's theory: Children cannot accommodate schemes to their current way of thinking, which must then lead to a reorganization of the child's mental structures.

The information-processing approach has led to a number of possible mechanisms for change (Kail and Bisanz, 1992). Let's look at three.

Increased Processing Resources

All people are limited in the amount of mental activity that they can perform at one time. People can usually concentrate their efforts on one or two activities; if they try to do more, performance deteriorates rapidly. This limit on mental activity has been referred to as a limitation in **processing resources**. Most intellectual tasks require effort and all individuals are limited in the effort that they can make available (Bjorklund and Harnishfeger, 1989).

Applied to development, the resources available for mental activity may simply increase with age. Adolescents may have more processing resources than children, who in turn may have more resources than preschoolers and infants. Just as more electrical power makes it possible to run a more complex machine, more mental power may allow for children to tackle more complex cognitive tasks.

Automatization

In a second view, processing resources are used in a slightly different way to explain development. As individuals acquire more experience on a particular task, fewer resources may be required for successful performance on that task. Ultimately, performance may become so refined that the task is performed effortlessly. **Automatization** has occurred when a process can be performed automatically, requiring no processing resources at all. For example, beginning drivers are told neither to talk with passengers nor to listen to the radio; both activities would divert resources needed for driving. However, with more experience behind the wheel, fewer resources are needed for safe driving, so adolescents can converse or listen while maintaining the same level of driving skill.

When applied to development, children are seen as "universal novices." Whatever the task, their experience is limited compared with adults. With age, children gain greater experience, so that processing requires fewer and fewer resources. Thus, although the total amount of resources does not change with age, greater experience means that children gradually have more resources available to be allocated to novel or particularly challenging tasks.

Processing resources Mental energy that is needed to perform cognitive tasks and that is limited in supply.

Automatization A state achieved after much practice in which a task can be performed without processing resources.

Increased Speed of Processing

As children develop, they complete most mental processes at an ever-faster pace (Hale, 1990). This change is obvious on tasks in which we can measure the speed with which children respond. A useful rule of thumb is that 4- and 5-year-olds will respond three times as slowly as adults; 8-year-olds will respond twice as slowly (Kail, 1991). The impact of these differences in the speed of mental processing is not limited to tasks in which we can measure speed of response. On the contrary, speed of processing will play a role whenever a specified number of actions must be completed in a fixed period of time. Thus, on any task in which children must answer in a specified period, age differences in performance may be due to the fact that younger children could not complete all of the processes responsible for successful task performance in the time allotted.

The mechanisms described here are not mutually exclusive; all could be involved. Combined, they yield a steady, age-related increase in cognitive skill. However, unlike Piaget's concept of disequilibrium, the process of change is continuous. There are no abrupt or qualitative changes in development. Instead, increased resources, automatization, and processing speed result in constant but gradual cognitive change.

SUMMARY

1.   The information-processing approach to cognitive development likens the mind to a computer consisting of mental "hardware" and "software." The hardware consists of sensory memory, short-term store, and long-term store; the software consists of strategies used to transfer information between the hardware components.

2.   Attention is required for successful performance on many tasks. The two aspects of attention, filtering irrelevant information and searching for specific information, both improve with development.

3.   Memory increases with age because children more often use strategies such as rehearsal to improve retention. Successful use of strategies, in turn, depends upon an accurate analysis of the memory problem, selection of an appropriate strategy, and the monitoring of the strategy. Each of these processes becomes more effective as children develop.

4.   Knowledge that is acquired with development improves memory by helping to organize the information to be remembered. Sometimes knowledge distorts memory because children remember events as they usually happen, and they tend to forget events that are not a part of a regular script. Distortion of this sort is infrequent for novel events but is more likely as events become familiar.

5.   Today children often testify in court, usually in cases involving child abuse. A preschooler's memory is best revealed by asking questions about specific events, but these questions can introduce distortions into a child's recall of the past.

6. Quantitative skill emerges in the first year of life: Infants are able to distinguish sets of different sizes. Counting involves a number of distinct procedures, including the one-to-one principle, the stable-order principle, and the cardinality principle. Even 3-year-olds can apply many of these principles as long as the sets to be counted are small. Two other principles—the abstraction and order-irrelevance principles—are also mastered by school age.

7. Counting is the starting point for addition and subtraction. Children quickly resort to more efficient modes of counting, ultimately doing all their counting mentally. Finally, by 8 or 9 years of age, children no longer determine sums and differences by counting, but instead by simply retrieving them from memory.

8. Children in Japan and Taiwan surpass those in the United States on measures of achievement in mathematics. This difference can be traced to cultural differences in the time spent on math in school and at home, and to cultural differences in attitudes towards, and expectations for, success in mathematics.

9. Way-finding involves learning about landmarks, routes, and configurations. Landmarks are salient objects in the environment that form the basis of the child's spatial knowledge. By the preschool years, children are quite capable of recognizing landmarks and anticipating their appearances on routes. Ultimately children form cognitive maps, which are mental configurations of an environment that integrate many landmarks and routes.

10. Even preschool children use rules to solve problems, such as those involving the concept of balance. They also use heuristics like means-ends analysis. Children solve problems more effectively when collaborating with an adult than with a peer. Children also learn more from their collaborations with adults because adults involve them in decision making and planning.

11. Information-processing mechanisms for change include increased processing resources, automatization, and increased processing speed. Combined, these mechanisms provide for gradual increases in cognitive skill as children develop.

C·H·A·P·T·E·R 8

Intelligence

In previous chapters we described the basic processes through which the child comes to know and to adapt to the world. Learning, perception, memory, and the construction of a vision of reality in the ways described by Jean Piaget and others are fundamental aspects of the overall process of intellectual development. In this chapter we examine intelligence from another point of view. We look at how individual children differ from one another in intelligence. Several questions will guide our study of intelligence and the tests that measure it:

▶   Intelligence tests have been part of North American culture since the beginning of the twentieth century. Tests were once hailed as psychology's greatest contribution to society, but now their value is questioned by many. What do current intelligence tests measure? How were they created? We begin this chapter by examining the construction and contents of intelligence tests.

▶   At any point in infancy, childhood, and adolescence, there is much variation in intelligence among individuals of the same age. Are these differences between individuals stable over time? That is, is a precocious baby destined to be a gifted child? And what causes these differences between individuals? Can intelligence be attributed primarily to one's heredity, to one's upbringing, or to some combination of the two? We will address each of these questions later in this chapter.

▶   Throughout development there are truly exceptional individuals—those who do not achieve the typical standards of intelligence as well as those who substantially surpass them. What is the cause for this exceptionality? For retarded individuals, how can we improve their abilities so that they may lead fuller lives? For especially gifted and creative people, what can we learn from them that would allow all people to be better able to achieve? These questions provide the focus of the final sections of this chapter.   ◀

WHAT IS INTELLIGENCE?

Although everyone has some notion of what is meant by intelligence, the idea is difficult to define. The difficulty occurs, in part, because intelligence is not a "thing" but an idea. Intelligence is not something concrete that you can possess a specific amount of, such as money; instead, intelligence is an abstraction (Gould, 1981).

Psychometric Theories

Professionals and laypeople alike agree that intelligence encompasses both *verbal ability* and *problem-solving ability* (Sternberg, 1985b). Moving beyond these labels to characterize the structure of intelligence has been the goal of *psychometricians*, psychologists who specialize in tests and measurement. The approach that they use is to administer a large number of tests to groups of individuals. It is assumed that success on some of the

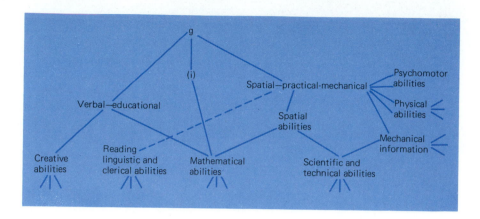

FIGURE 8-1
Vernon's hierarchical
theory of intelligence.
*(Adapted from H. J.
Eysenck,* The Structure
and Measurement of
Intelligence. *New York:
Springer-Verlag, 1979.
Used by permission.)*

tests requires skill in one area, whereas success on other tests requires skill in other areas. For example, some tests might require skill in memorizing verbal material; others might require the ability to work effectively with abstract mathematical concepts.

Investigators use a technique called **factor analysis** to discover different groups of tests, each of which measures a different skill. The logic underlying this technique is similar to the logic a jungle hunter might use in deciding whether a set of dark blobs in a river is three separate rotting logs or a single alligator (Cattell, 1965). If the blobs move together, the hunter decides that they are part of the same structure, an alligator. If they do not move together, they are three different structures, three logs. Similarly, if changes in performance on one test are accompanied by changes in performance on a second test—that is, if they move together—one could assume that the tests are measuring the same attribute or factor. It remains for the investigator to give a name to each factor.

Some research, beginning with the work of Charles Spearman (1904), supports the idea that a general factor, or g, is responsible for performance on all mental tests. Other results are more consistent with the belief that intelligence consists of distinct abilities. For example, Thurstone and Thurstone (1941) concluded that there are seven primary abilities: perceptual speed, word comprehension, word fluency, space, number, memory, and induction. They also acknowledged a general factor that operated in all tasks but emphasized that analysis of the several factors is more useful in assessing intellectual ability.

These conflicting findings have led many theorists to propose hierarchical theories of intelligence that include both general and specific components. Vernon (1965), for example, proposed the theory shown in Figure 8-1. At the top of the hierarchy is g. The first major distinction is between verbal-educational ability (v:ed) and spatial-practical-mechanical ability (k:m). Each of these factors can be subdivided. The verbal-educational factor includes verbal and numerical skills; the spatial-practical-mechanical factor includes perceptual speed and spatial ability.

The Theory of Multiple Intelligences

The **hierarchical theory of intelligence**, like most psychometric theories of intelligence, evolved independently of the theories of intellectual de-

Factor analysis A statistical technique used to identify clusters of abilities or skills.

Hierarchical theory of intelligence A theory in which intelligence includes a general ability that can be further differentiated into even more specific skills.

velopment discussed in Chapters 6 and 7. Only recently have developmental psychologists tried to integrate psychometric theories with developmental theories derived from Piaget and information-processing psychology. These new theories draw on the assets of the traditional approaches to create a much broader theory of intelligence and its development. One ambitious theory of this sort is Howard Gardner's theory of multiple intelligences (1983). Instead of using test performance as the basis for his theory, Gardner proposes several "signs" that can be used to identify distinct intelligences:

1. *Isolation by brain damage.* Often injury to the brain impairs a specific intellectual skill but leaves other skills intact.

2. *The existence of exceptional talent.* Some individuals are truly extraordinarily skilled in one intellectual domain, but ordinary—or even retarded—in most other domains.

3. A *distinct developmental history.* If an intelligence is independent, it should develop as a reliable sequence of initial, intermediate, and advanced levels of proficiency.

4. *An evolutionary history.* Intellectual skills have emerged as the human species has evolved. Hence, a well-defined evolutionary sequence helps to identify autonomous intelligences.

5. A *set of core operations.* If an intelligence is independent, associated with it should be a distinct set of mental operations.

Using these signs, Gardner identifies six distinct intelligences. Some are common to psychometric theories of intelligence: linguistic intelligence, logical-mathematical intelligence, and spatial intelligence. However, three intelligences are not: musical intelligence, bodily kinesthetic intelligence, and personal intelligence.

A glimpse at musical intelligence reveals some of the unique features of this approach to characterizing intelligence. Gardner notes that studies of individuals with brain damage demonstrate the independence of musical intelligence. For example, Shebalin, a Russian composer, was afflicted with Wernicke's aphasia, in which speech remains fluent but comprehension is impaired. Nevertheless, Shebalin could understand and compose music as skillfully as ever.

Also supporting Gardner's proposed musical intelligence are the legendary musical prodigies. The best known is Mozart, whose talent as a performer and composer was evident early in childhood. Less known are *idiot savants*, individuals who may suffer from extreme mental retardation, yet are musically quite talented. Many idiot savants can play a tune correctly after a single hearing and do so without any formal musical training (Shuter-Dyson, 1982).

Musical ability along with the other distinct domains of intelligence revealed in Gardner's analysis presents a much broader view of intelligence than that offered by traditional psychometric theories. An equally broad, but different, view of intelligence comes from another new theory, the *triarchic theory.*

FIGURE 8-2
The existence of
prodigies, children who
show exceptional talent,
is one of the signs that
Gardner (1983) uses to
identify a distinct
intelligence.

The Triarchic Theory

Robert Sternberg first studied how adults solve problems on intelligence
tests (Sternberg, 1977). He devised a theory to explain test performance,
which he later elaborated to explain the development of intelligence. The
elaborated theory is called the **triarchic theory** because it includes three
subtheories (Sternberg, 1985a).

According to the *contextual subtheory*, intelligent behavior always
involves skillful adaptation to an environment in an effort to achieve one's
goals. The starting point for an analysis of intelligence must be the individual's culture because this will influence the goals that individuals
select. By this line of reasoning, intelligence test scores will be valid only
if they are based on items that are relevant to individuals' skillful adaptations to their environments.

The *experiential subtheory* considers children's familiarity with test
items. At one extreme are items that are so unfamiliar that they are completely outside the child's range of experiences. At the other extreme are

Triarchic theory A
theory of intelligence,
proposed by Robert
Sternberg, that includes
contextual, experiential,
and componential
subtheories.

items that involve cognitive skills that have become highly automated: After considerable practice, children can execute mental processes effortlessly. According to Sternberg, neither of these items provides a useful assessment of intelligence: Asking a 9-year-old to solve $1 + 1$ is just as uninformative as asking the same child to solve a calculus problem. The addition problem is so familiar that it is probably solved automatically; the calculus problem is so novel that the child has no way of knowing how to proceed.

Sternberg claims that the best test items are intermediate. They should be neither totally novel nor totally familiar. Instead, they should be sufficiently novel so that they assess an individual's ability to apply existing knowledge to new problems. Given two individuals with equivalent experience in a novel situation, the more intelligent individual will be the one who more rapidly copes with the demands of the problem and more rapidly automates the skills required to solve the problem.

Finally, according to the *componential subtheory*, which is closely related to the information-processing perspective discussed in Chapter 7, all thought is composed of basic cognitive processes called components. Successful task performance—whether solving an item on an intelligence test, reading a newspaper, or understanding a television program—requires that components be selected and organized in the proper sequence. In this subtheory, intelligence is associated with more efficient organization and use of components (similar to the strategies discussed in Chapter 7).

Compared with traditional psychometric theories, which are based on factor analysis of test scores, Sternberg's theory is very broad indeed. The triarchic theory highlights that people may differ in the procedures they use to solve the test items (the componential subtheory), the familiarity of the items (the experiential subtheory), and the relevance of the items to personal and cultural goals (the contextual subtheory).

The triarchic theory also underscores the difficulties and dangers involved in comparing test scores for different cultural, ethnic, or racial groups. Comparisons between two groups from different cultural contexts are usually invalid because the test items are not equally relevant to individuals' goals in both cultures. In addition, test items will typically not be equally novel in different cultures. A vocabulary test, for example, will be useful in assessing intelligence in cultures where formal education is essential to skilled adaptations, because the skilled use of language is a prerequisite for success in schools. In cultures where schooling is not a key to success, a vocabulary test would not provide useful information for assessing intelligence because it would be irrelevant to the cultural goals and would be much too novel.

As Gardner's work and Sternberg's work make clear, the question "What is intelligence?" is still being debated. However, it is clear that among people who share a common culture, individuals differ substantially in how well they adapt to and deal with their environments. Numerous tests have been devised to assess these differences. The construction and limits of these tests are the focus of the next section of this chapter.

MEASURING INTELLIGENCE

For much of the twentieth century, intelligence tests have been used in schools. These tests are designed to determine the intellectual tasks individuals can perform. With this information, educators have tried to match instruction with ability. Poor test performance, sometimes combined with other information, has often been used as a reason for placing a child in a special class. Intelligence tests have also been used in the armed services to evaluate the success of educational programs and institutions and to select employees. To understand and evaluate this mental-testing movement, we must first know how the tests are constructed.

Test Construction Principles

INITIAL SELECTION OF ITEMS. The first step in constructing any kind of psychological test is to select appropriate items—that is, the test questions. The choice depends on the purpose of the test and the theoretical approach of the people constructing it. However, the general principle is that the items should be a representative sample of the behaviors or skills of interest.

> In this respect, the psychologist proceeds in much the same way as the biochemist who tests a patient's blood or a community's water by analyzing one or more samples of it. If the psychologist wishes to test the extent of a child's vocabulary, a clerk's ability to perform arithmetic computations, or a pilot's eye-hand coordination, he or she examines their performance with a representative set of words, arithmetic problems, or motor tests. (Anastasi, 1982, pp. 22–23)

NORMS AND STANDARDIZATION. Next, the test items must be administered to a representative group of individuals in order to establish normative performance. This group, the standardization sample, must be chosen carefully because its scores will be used as a standard against which later scores will be compared. For example, if the test is being designed for children of varying ages and socioeconomic backgrounds, the standardization group should include appropriate proportions of individuals reflecting these backgrounds.

Still another part of standardization procedures concerns the context within which the test is administered. When classroom tests are given in school—for example, spelling or arithmetic tests—individual teachers may differ widely in their selection of content, their allotment of time for taking the test, their policy on using notes, and so forth. Such tests do not permit direct comparisons from one classroom to another. A child who correctly answered 80 percent of the questions on Mr. Jones's arithmetic test might very well have learned less—or more—than one who earned the same score on Ms. Smith's test. If we are to compare many children from different parts of the country successfully, this problem must be overcome. Standardization of test procedures is used for this purpose. A **standardized test** is one in which the apparatus, procedure, and scoring have been fixed so that exactly the same test is given at different times and places.

Standardized test A test in which the apparatus, procedure, and scoring have been fixed so that exactly the same test is given at different times and places.

FIGURE 8-3
Intelligence tests are administered in a standard format for every child so that scores can be compared accurately with the norms derived from the standardization sample.

Some people feel that one of the weaknesses of psychological tests is this standardization, which does not allow the examiner to provide the best conditions for any one individual. But if we want to use the test for comparison with others, it must be conducted in a standardized way for all who take it.

RELIABILITY. After a test has been standardized, efforts must be made to check its reliability. **Reliability** is a measure of how closely sets of scores are related or how consistent the scores are over various time intervals. One common method of determining reliability is to administer a test to the same individuals on two different occasions. Another consists of administering equivalent forms of the test or items from the same test form on separate occasions. In either case, the two sets of scores are then correlated. The higher the correlation coefficient, the higher the reliability.

VALIDITY. According to many psychologists, questions of validity are the most important that can be asked about any psychological test. Simply, the **validity** of a test is the degree to which it actually measures what it purports to measure.

How does one determine validity? Usually, one or more independent criterion measures are obtained and correlated with scores from the test in question. Criterion measures are chosen on the basis of what the test is designed to measure. Anxiety exhibited in a public-speaking situation, for example, might be a criterion measure for a test to evaluate self-consciousness. If individuals who are visibly nervous when they speak publically have higher test scores than people who are relaxed while speaking, then evidence exists that the test enjoys some validity.

The validity of intelligence tests is usually determined by using as criterion tasks measures of academic achievement, such as school grades, teacher ratings, or scores on achievement tests. The reported correlations for the more widely used intelligence tests and these criterion tasks are

Reliability A measure of the consistency with which a person will receive the same score on successive administrations of a test.

Validity The degree to which a test actually measures what it purports to measure.

reasonably high, typically falling between 0.4 and 0.8. Furthermore, children who have been accelerated or "skipped" one or more grades do considerably better on intelligence tests than do those who have shown normal progress. Youngsters who were held back one or more grades exhibit considerably lower than average scores (McNemar, 1942). Low scores on intelligence tests also predict poor performance in school, and this is true regardless of race or socioeconomic background (Cleary, Humphreys, Kendrick, and Wesman, 1975).

Thus, most tests of intelligence are reasonably valid, at least insofar as intelligence is reflected in school performance, and most are relatively successful in predicting school achievement. This *predictive validity* is the major reason for the wide use of tests of intelligence. You should keep in mind, however, the limits associated with the use of school achievement as the criterion measure. The evidence that we have described demonstrates that modern tests provide valid assessments of intelligence as it is required for school achievement; tests do *not* necessarily accurately measure aspects of intelligence that are necessary for success in activities in other contexts.

Individual Tests for Children and Adults

All the widely used tests discussed in this section are administered to individuals rather than to groups. Group tests have the advantage of providing information about many individuals quickly and inexpensively, often without the need of highly trained psychologists. However, individual testing optimizes the motivation and attention of the examinee and provides an opportunity for a sensitive examiner to assess factors that may influence test performance. The examiner may notice that the examinee is relaxed and that therefore test performance is a reasonable sample of the individual's talents. Or the examiner may observe that intense anxiety is interfering with performance. Such clinical judgments are not possible with group tests.

THE BINET SCALES. In 1905 Alfred Binet and Theophile Simon, commissioned by the minister of public education in Paris, devised the first successful test of intellectual ability. It was called the Metrical Scale of Intelligence and was made up of 30 problems ordered according to difficulty. The goal was to identify children who were likely to fail in school so that they could be transferred to special classes. Revisions of the test, in 1908 and 1911, were based on the classroom observations of students that teachers called "bright" and "dull," as well as on trial-and-error adjustments. Test scores agreed strongly with teacher ratings of intellectual ability.

Beginning with the 1908 revision, the Binet-Simon test was categorized according to age levels. For example, the investigators placed into separate groups all tests that normal 3-year-olds could pass at the three-year level, all tests that normal 4-year-olds could pass at the four-year level, and so on up to age 13. This arrangement gave rise to the concept of **mental age**, **MA**. A child's mental age is equivalent to the **chronological**

Mental age (MA) On intelligence tests, the average chronological age of individuals whose test performance the person equals.

Chronological age (CA) Age as measured by time (months or years) since birth.

age, CA, of children whose performance he or she equals. A 6-year-old child who passed tests that the average 7-year-old passed would be said to have an MA of 7. This simple procedure did much to popularize the mental-testing movement generally.

THE STANFORD-BINET TESTS. The Binet-Simon tests attracted much interest, and translations soon appeared in many languages. In the United States, Lewis Terman at Stanford University revised the test into the first Stanford-Binet test in 1916. The Stanford-Binet was a new test in many ways. Items had been changed, and it had been standardized on a relatively large American population, including about 1,000 children and 400 adults. Furthermore, Terman and his associates used the notion of the **intelligence quotient** or **IQ**—the ratio of an individual's mental age to his or her chronological age, multiplied by 100 to avoid the use of decimals. Thus:

$$IQ = MA/CA \times 100$$

This quotient was a really clever idea at the time. If a child's mental age and chronological age were equivalent, the child's IQ, regardless of actual chronological age, would be 100—reflecting average performance. The procedure also made it possible to compare the intellectual development of children of different chronological ages. If a 4-year-old boy has a mental age of 3, his IQ will be 75 (3/4 × 100), as will that of an equally retarded 12-year-old with a mental age of 9 (9/12 × 100 = 75).

The Stanford-Binet test was revised in 1937, 1960, 1972, and 1986. Since the 1960 revision, an individual's IQ is calculated by comparing test results with the average score earned by those of the same age in the standardization group. Statistical procedures allow the average score for each age group to be set at 100, with approximately the same number of scores below 100 as above it. An IQ score thus reflects how near or how far, and in what direction, the individual is from the average score of his or her age group. Moreover, it is possible to calculate the percentage of individuals who will perform higher or lower than any particular IQ score. This kind of comparison is now used in many intelligence tests.

Like the earlier versions, the Stanford-Binet today consists of many cognitive and motor tasks, ranging from the extremely easy to the extremely difficult. The test may be administered to individuals ranging in age from approximately 2 years to adulthood, but not every individual is given every question. For example, young children (or older retarded children) may be asked to recognize pictures of familiar objects, string beads, answer questions about everyday relations, or fold paper into shapes. Older individuals may be asked to define vocabulary words, find the solution to an abstract problem, or decipher an unfamiliar code. The examiner determines, according to specific guidelines, the appropriate starting place on the test and administers progressively more difficult questions until the child or adult fails all the questions at a particular level. An IQ score is assigned on the basis of how many questions the individual passed compared with the average number passed by people of the same age.

Intelligence quotient (IQ) Traditionally, the ratio of an individual's mental age to his or her chronological age, multiplied by 100.

THE WECHSLER SCALES. A second set of intelligence scales widely used in assessment and research with children is based on the work of David Wechsler. The original Wechsler scale, the Wechsler-Bellevue, was published in 1939 and was geared specifically to measure adult intelligence for clinical use. Later revisions resulted in instruments for adults (Wechsler Adult Intelligence Scale, or WAIS), for schoolchildren (Wechsler Intelligence Scale for Children-III; or WISC-III), and for children 4 to 6 years of age (Wechsler Preschool and Primary Scale of Intelligence-Revised, or WPPSI-R). All these tests follow a similar format.

The WISC-III was published in 1991 and is the third edition of the WISC, which was first published in 1949. Unlike the Stanford-Binet, the WISC-III includes subtests that are categorized into verbal or performance subscales; the latter taps nonverbal symbolic skills. Children are thus assessed on verbal IQ, performance IQ, and a combination of the two, the full-scale IQ. A second major difference between the WISC-III and the Stanford-Binet is that each child receives the same subtests, with some adjustment for either age level or competence or both. The subtests include puzzles, tests for vocabulary, knowledge of the social environment, and memory tasks.

THE KAUFMAN ASSESSMENT BATTERY FOR CHILDREN. Alan Kaufman directed the 1974 revision of the WISC, the WISC-R, and he wrote a well-known book on the proper use of the WISC-R (Kaufman, 1979). From these experiences with the WISC-R, he and Nadeen Kaufman developed a new test of intelligence, the Kaufman Assessment Battery for Children, or K-ABC, for short (Kaufman and Kaufman, 1983a, b). The starting point for the K-ABC was the distinction, derived from cognitive psychology and neuropsychology, between **simultaneous** and **sequential processing**. Simultaneous processing requires that a child integrate different information simultaneously. Typifying this sort of mental synthesis would be understanding pictures, in which many elements must be integrated to form a cohesive whole. In contrast, sequential processing requires that information be integrated in sequence. An example would be language comprehension, where meaning hinges upon the particular order of words.

The K-ABC consists of three scales—sequential processing, simultaneous processing, and achievement—that can be administered to 2- through 12-year-olds. Scores on these scales can be compared with norms to determine a child's level of performance relative to other children of the same age. Measures of children's ability derived from the K-ABC in this fashion are highly correlated with IQ scores derived from the Stanford-Binet and the WISC-R (for example, Knight, Baker, and Minder, 1990).

The different subscales of the K-ABC are particularly useful in diagnosing children's academic difficulties. To see how this can be done, let's consider a typical case in which the K-ABC might be administered to a youngster who is struggling in school. If the child had higher scores on the simultaneous scale than on the sequential scale, one recommendation might be that the child is more likely to learn from instruction that emphasizes synthesis of information rather than step-by-step analysis (for example, learning to read whole words rather than parts of words pho-

Simultaneous processing A type of mental activity, as assessed on the K-ABC test, in which different information must be integrated simultaneously.

Sequential processing A type of mental activity, as assessed on the K-ABC test, in which information is integrated sequentially.

netically). Suppose, instead, that the child had above average scores on both the simultaneous and successive scales, but below-average scores on the achievement scales. Here the interpretation might be that the child has the general intellectual skills to succeed in school; the child's failure to achieve, therefore, may be traced to motivation or attitudes toward school.

The K-ABC illustrates that more precise assessment of a child's strengths and weaknesses is possible when (a) scales are derived from a theory of mental processing and (b) achievement is distinguished from processing. In the future, these features may well be standard fare in all intelligence tests (Pellegrino, Hunt, and Yee, 1989).

CONSTANCY OF IQ SCORES. One reason that intelligence tests were devised was to predict the outcome of each individual's development. The hope was that a test administered early in a child's life could be used to predict that child's intelligence as an adult (McCall, 1989). What happens when test scores obtained by children are correlated with later performance? Figure 8-4 shows, on the basis of several studies, the correlations of scores obtained at maturity with those obtained earlier. These studies clearly show that although the relation increases progressively as time of testing approaches maturity, even tests obtained during childhood predict later performance when data for groups of people are examined.

FIGURE 8-4

Correlations between intelligence (as measured by test scores) obtained at each age and intelligence at maturity. The graph lines represent data from different investigations, and they illustrate the substantial power of tests obtained during early childhood to predict later performance.
(Adapted from B. S. Bloom, Stability and Change in Human Characteristics. New York: John Wiley & Sons, Inc. Copyright 1964. Reproduced by permission of John Wiley & Sons, Inc.)

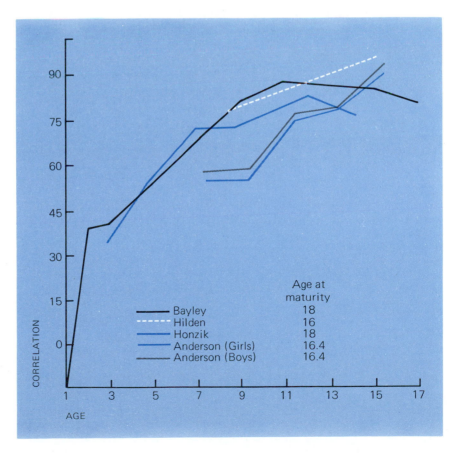

	Age at maturity
Bayley	18
Hilden	16
Honzik	18
Anderson (Girls)	16.4
Anderson (Boys)	16.4

These results at first appear to support the idea that intelligence is relatively fixed. However, when individual performance over time is examined, we see that constancy is not a hard-and-fast rule. For example, in one study in which children were tested several times between 6 and 18 years of age, almost 60 percent of the children changed by 15 or more IQ points (Honzik, MacFarland, and Allen, 1948).

In another study that involved repeated assessment of subjects' IQ scores, nearly half the children had approximately the same IQ scores at each assessment. For the remaining children, some had IQs that increased during childhood but decreased in adolescence; others declined steadily throughout childhood and adolescence; still others declined during childhood but increased in adolescence (McCall, Appelbaum, and Hogarty, 1973).

Thus, although IQ is often relatively stable throughout childhood and adolescence, this is definitely not the only pattern. For many children, IQ will change—both up and down—as they develop. As we shall see later in this chapter, heredity and environment are both implicated in these patterns.

Infant Tests

The Stanford-Binet, WISC-III, and K-ABC cannot be used to test intelligence in infants. For this purpose, several individual tests have been developed during the last 50 years, including the Gesell Developmental Schedules and the Bayley Scales of Infant Development.

FIGURE 8-5
Illustrations from the Gesell Developmental Schedules of behaviors typical at 28 weeks of age.
(Adapted from A. Gesell and C. S. Amatruda, Developmental Diagnosis. New York: Paul B. Hoeber, Inc. Copyright 1941, 1947, by Arnold Gesell. Used by permission.)

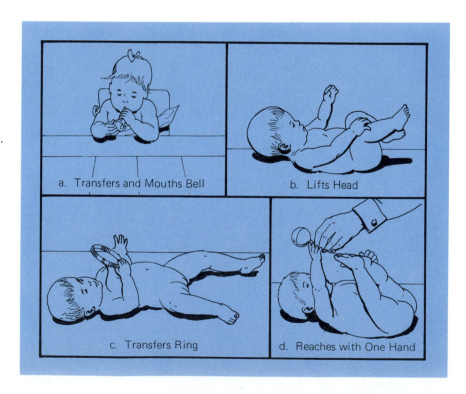

a. Transfers and Mouths Bell

b. Lifts Head

c. Transfers Ring

d. Reaches with One Hand

Developmental quotient (DQ) A measure of an infant's performance on an intelligence test.

When published in the 1920s, Arnold Gesell's test was the first specifically designed to measure mental ability in early infancy. Now in its third edition, the Gesell schedules are used widely by clinicians and researchers (Francis, Self, and Horowitz, 1987). The Gesell schedules evaluate behavior in four basic areas: motor, adaptive, language, and personal-social (Figure 8-5). The first three scales are based on the examiner's observations of the infant; the last scale is scored mainly from a parental interview. The child's performance, labeled **DQ** for **developmental quotient**, is compared with norms derived from a relatively small group of middle-class children who were followed longitudinally.

The Bayley Scales of Infant Development (Bayley, 1970) are designed for infants 2 to 30 months old. They consist of mental and motor scales and an Infant Behavior Record. The mental scale, designed to assess the development of adaptive behavior, includes measures of such behaviors as attending to visual and auditory stimuli, following directions, looking for a fallen toy, and imitating. The motor scale measures such items as holding the head up, walking, and throwing a ball. The Infant Behavior Record is a rating of the child's orientation toward its environment in terms of fearfulness, endurance, responsiveness, and goal directedness.

Infant scales like these were devised, in part, because psychologists hoped to be able to predict adult intelligence from infants' behavior. How well do early tests predict scores on tests given at later times? A strong positive relation would indicate that assessment early in life does provide information about later performance. In one study, correlations were calculated between Bayley scores obtained from tests given at 3, 6, 9, 12, 18, and 24 months and Stanford-Binet scores obtained at 9 years (Humphreys and Davey, 1988). As shown in Table 8-1, the correlations were small for scores obtained in the first year but increased for those obtained in the second year. Investigators have occasionally reported higher correlations between infant scores and IQ scores in childhood and adulthood: Roe, McClure, and Roe (1983), for example, reported a correlation of 0.65 between Gesell DQs at 5–9 months and scores at age 12 years on the WISC-R performance scale. However, the average correlation between test scores obtained in the first year and child or adult IQs is approximately 0.15 (McCall, 1989). The consensus is that children must be at least 18 to 24 months old before their Bayley scores, or scores from similar scales, can predict later IQ scores on the Wechsler or Stanford-Binet scales (Kopp and McCall, 1982).

TABLE 8-1
Correlations between Scores on Infant IQ Tests and IQ at Age 9

Age (in months)	Correlation
3	0.30
6	0.31
9	0.20
12	0.33
18	0.48
24	0.56

Source: Data from L. G. Humphreys and T. C. Davey, "Continuity in intellectual growth from 12 months to 9 years," in *Intelligence, 12*, 1988, 183–197.

Why isn't prediction of childhood or adult IQ more accurate? One reason is that there is relatively little room for the display of individual differences during the early months of life (Ames, 1967), so infants can be differentiated only in a global way. Another explanation, perhaps the most important, is that infant tests tap abilities other than those evaluated on tests administered to children, adolescents, and adults: Infant tests place more emphasis on sensorimotor items and less on tasks involving cognitive processes such as language, thinking, and problem solving.

According to this reasoning, a measure of infant cognitive processing might yield more accurate predictions of later IQ. In fact, habituation (described on page 86 in Chapter 3) is one such measure that does seem to predict later IQ more effectively than do scores from the Bayley or Gesell Tests (Rose, Feldman, Wallace, and Cohen, 1991). The average correlation between habituation and later IQ is approximately −0.5 (Bornstein, 1989). That is, 1- to 6-month-olds who habituate to visual stimuli more rapidly—they look less—tend to have higher IQs as children.

Why does infant habituation predict childhood IQ? To answer this question, let's review what habituation represents. When infants are shown a new stimulus, they will stare intently, as if studying it. After several presentations, they glance at it briefly and then look away, apparently spending only enough time to determine that nothing has changed, that this is the same, familiar stimulus. Thus, habituation tells us that the infants have constructed a mental representation of the stimulus, have compared the stimulus to the mental representation, and have determined that they are the same. Infants who habituate rapidly may well be more efficient in the processes of constructing mental representations, a process that is essential to intelligent behavior throughout childhood, adolescence, and adulthood (Bornstein, 1989). Not all psychologists are convinced by this explanation (for example, Kagan, 1989), so additional research is ongoing to understand the mechanism that allows prediction of IQ from habituation scores.

If scores on the Bayley and Gesell scales do not predict later IQs, you may wonder why these tests would be used. The reason is that both measures are valuable in assessing an infant's development early in life. For example, the impact of exposure to toxins during prenatal development can be detected with the mental scale of the Bayley (Bellinger et al., 1987) as can the impact of variety and organization in an infant's home environment (Bradley et al., 1987). Consequently, infant tests are important diagnostic tools: They can be used to determine if development is progressing normally or if development has gone awry.

FACTORS INFLUENCING INTELLIGENCE TEST SCORES

Hereditary and Environmental Influences

How are we to explain that children of the same age can differ so much in IQ? And why does IQ remain stable over some children's lifetimes but vary for others? Historically, answers to these questions have emphasized heredity, the environment, or some combination of the two. Let's begin with genetic factors.

The notion that human intelligence is at least in part genetically determined may be distasteful to a society that cherishes the belief that all people are created equal. But a great deal of research suggests that intellectual variations within the normal range of functioning seem to involve both inherited and environmental influences.

Probably the best known way to evaluate the impact of heredity is to study twins. Identical, or *monozygotic*, twins develop from a single union of egg and sperm, so they have identical genotypes. Fraternal, or *dizygotic*, twins develop from two separate unions, so on the average, they share 50 percent of their genes. Genetic influence is indicated when identical twins are more similar on a characteristic than are fraternal twins. In fact, the performance of identical twins on IQ tests is more alike than that of fraternal twins (Scarr and Kidd, 1983). A typical result, reported by Sundet and his colleagues (1988), was that test scores were substantially more similar for identical twins, $r = 0.83$, than for fraternal twins, $r = 0.51$.

Some of this greater similarity may be accounted for by identical twins having more similar environments than fraternal twins, especially when the fraternal twins are of the opposite sex. However, research on the intelligence of identical twins reared in different environments suggests that even when identical twins are separated, they tend to be similar (Bouchard, 1983).

This research approach can be extended by including other individuals who differ in their genetic similarity. If heredity plays an important role in IQ, then IQs should become more alike as genetic similarity increases. As you can see in Table 8-2, this pattern is found: IQs are most alike for identical twins and least alike for a child and an adopted sibling.

Interestingly, the impact of heredity is not the same for all aspects of intelligence. Verbal abilities and spatial abilities are more influenced by heredity than are memory skills (Thompson, Detterman, and Plomin, 1991).

Heredity can also influence patterns of development. Genes may turn on and off, thereby having more influence in some phases of development than others (Plomin, DeFries, and McClearn, 1990). The Louisville Twin Study traced similarity in twins and their siblings from 3 months to 15 years of age (Wilson, 1983). Children's IQ scores showed distinctive pat-

---

TABLE 8-2
Correlations between IQ Scores for Individuals Differing in Genetic Similarity

Relationship	Correlation
Identical twins	0.86
Fraternal twins	0.60
Siblings	0.47
Child and adopted sibling	0.29

Source: From T. J. Bouchard and M. McGue, "Familial studies of intelligence: A review," *Science, 212,* 1981, 1056.

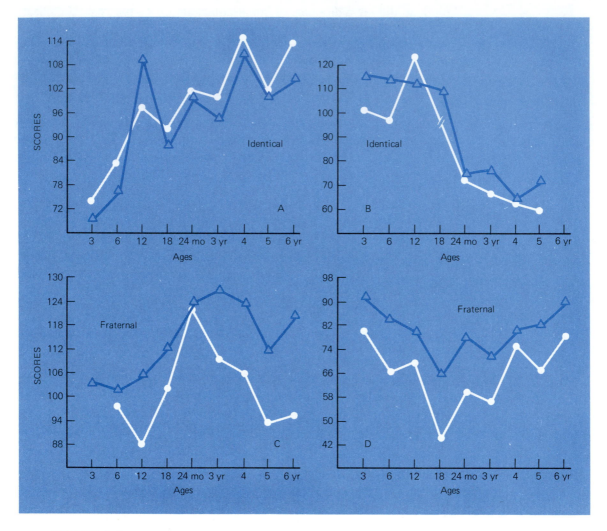

FIGURE 8-6

Trends in mental development in early childhood for two pairs of identical
twins and two pairs of fraternal twins.

*(Adapted from R. S. Wilson, "The Louisville twin study: Developmental
synchronies in behavior," in* Child Development, 54, 1983, 298–316. © The
Society for Research in Child Development.)

terns of spurts and lags that were regulated genetically. Furthermore,
patterns of development, reflected in IQ scores, are more alike for identical
twins than for fraternal twins. Shown in Figure 8-6 are typical profiles of
IQ scores for four pairs of twins. The identical twins in Graphs A and B
develop with more synchrony than do the fraternal twins shown in Graphs
C and D. Thus, identical twins are more alike not only in IQ but also in
developmental paths as well.

　　And there is more to the story. Across time, identical twins are more
consistently alike. In contrast, fraternal twins become less similar over
time (McCartney, Harris, and Bernieri, 1990). By age 15, they are no more

alike to each other than they are to their nontwin siblings (Wilson, 1983). One interpretation of these findings is that fraternal twins and siblings increasingly select different environmental niches based on different genetic dispositions; identical twins select similar niches based on genetic similarity (Scarr and McCartney, 1983).

Studies of adopted children also suggest that hereditary effects increase during childhood and adolescence: Here, investigators examined the correlation between adopted children's IQ scores and those of their biological parents and those of their adoptive parents. Children get 50 percent of their genes from each of their biological parents, but they receive no genes from their adoptive parents. Hence, if heredity helps to determine IQ, then children's IQs should be more like their biological parents' IQs than their adoptive parents' IQs. These correlations were computed in the Colorado Adoption Project (Fulker, DeFries, and Plomin, 1988), which included 245 adopted children as well as their biological and adoptive parents. At age 3, adopted children's IQs resembled both sets of parents equally. However, by age 7, the correlation was higher for biological parents ($r = 0.28$) than for adoptive parents ($r = 0.06$). In other words, 7-year-olds with high test scores tended to have biological parents with high test scores but not necessarily adoptive parents with high test scores. Such

FIGURE 8-7
Typically, adopted children as a group have IQ scores more similar to those of their adoptive parents than those of their biological parents.

a finding is evidence for an increasing impact of inheritance on IQ as a child grows.

Adoption studies also provide evidence that the environment influences mental development. Typically, the average IQ of the adopted children, as a group, is more similar to the average IQ of the adoptive parents than to the average IQ of the biological mothers (Lucurto, 1990). That is, biological mothers score the lowest, adoptive parents score the highest, and the adopted children scored in between, but their scores are closer to their adoptive parents than to their biological mothers (Scarr and Weinberg, 1983). So although the children are influenced by genes transmitted to them from their mothers, they also are influenced by the environmental advantages provided by the adoptive parents.

The features of the environment that are associated with higher IQs are not addressed in most adoption studies, but they have been identified in other research. Caldwell and Bradley (1984) developed the HOME inventory to measure the type and amount of stimulation available to children in their homes. From interviews with parents and observations in the home, scores are obtained on six scales that measure such characteristics as parents' responsivity to their children and their acceptance of their children. Also measured is the organization and variety in the child's environment.

High scores on the HOME scales have been linked to higher IQs for children. Bradley, Caldwell, and Rock (1988), for example, determined HOME scores when children were 6 months and 2 years old. Both HOME assessments predicted children's IQs at age 3. That is, children with high IQ scores tended to have responsive and involved parents and lived in organized, stimulating homes that included plenty of age-appropriate toys. However, conclusions from this result need to be made cautiously because, as we show in the Close-Up on pages 258–59, characteristics of parents and environments that are associated with higher IQ scores may not be the same for all ethnic groups.

Socioeconomic Status, Race, and Ethnicity

There is a positive relation between **socioeconomic status (SES)** and IQ. Children from middle-class homes tend to have higher IQ scores than children from lower-class homes. In one study, the correlation between SES and Stanford-Binet IQs was 0.47 (Bradley et al., 1989). Another way to illustrate these differences is in terms of parental occupation. For example, children whose fathers were classified as professionals obtained an average WISC score of 110, whereas children whose fathers were manual laborers obtained an average score of 94 (Seashore, Wesman, and Doppelt, 1950). In general, a 15- to 25-point difference exists between the scores of children of professionals and those of laborers.

Race is also related to IQ. Blacks do less well on standard IQ tests than whites (Vernon, 1979). The usual difference is in the range of 15 to 20 points—that is, the average score for blacks is about 80 to 85, compared with the average score for whites of 100. The size of the black-white difference depends upon SES: Differences are smallest between lower-

Socioeconomic status (SES) A measure of social class reflecting occupation, income, and education.

class black and white children but are larger between higher-SES black and white groups (Broman, Nichols, and Kennedy, 1975). Differences also tend to be largest on tests that primarily measure the general intelligence factor, g (Naglieri and Jensen, 1987).

In addition, ethnic and racial groups show distinct patterns of performance on intelligence tests. One study tested first-grade children from middle- and lower-class families with Chinese, Jewish, black, and Puerto Rican cultural backgrounds (Lesser, Fifer, and Clark, 1965). Tests measured verbal ability, reasoning, number facility, and space conceptualization. Jewish children performed best on the verbal tasks and least well on reasoning and spatial tasks. Puerto Rican children performed best on spatial tasks and least well on verbal ones.

Another study (Nagoshi and Johnson, 1987) involved comparisons of Hawaiians of differing backgrounds. In this study, Hawaiians of European ancestry had higher scores on verbal and visual memory tasks. Hawaiians of Japanese ancestry had higher scores on spatial and perceptual-speed tasks.

Differences in intelligence associated with SES and race often increase with age. Bradley and his colleagues (1989), among others, found that starting at about 2 years of age, measures of SES correlated more and more positively with IQ. Before that age, there is either no relation or a negative one. Similarly, black infants do as well as whites on the kinds of skills required by infant tests; differences between blacks and whites generally do not show up until the preschool years (Montie and Fagan, 1988).

FIGURE 8-8

Use of intelligence test scores for different racial and ethnic groups remains a controversial practice. Test scores do predict scholastic success for most groups, but may tell little beyond this.

CLOSE-UP

Features of Home Environments that Predict Intelligence in Three Different Ethnic Groups

The characteristics of the home environment that are associated with intelligence need not be the same in all cultures. On the contrary, according to contextual approaches to development and intelligence, the expected pattern would be for each culture to have a unique set of environmental factors that predict high IQ scores.

This variety was demonstrated in a study by Bradley and his colleagues (1989). This project was unique in that it included a large number of families (more than 900) from three different ethnic groups living in six different cities in North America. The investigators originally began their work as separate studies, but they were able to pool their data because each project used the HOME inventory and measured IQs in the same way.

Some of the results of the collaborative study are shown in Figure 8-9. Shown here are correlations between children's Stanford-Binet IQ scores at age 3 and scores on different subscales of the HOME inventory. These correlations are pre-

sented separately for white, black, and Mexican-American children. For each group, parental involvement is related to intelligence: Greater parental involvement is associated with higher IQ scores. However, the remaining scales are not related to intelligence in a consistent manner for the three ethnic groups. For white children, high IQ scores are more likely when parents are responsive and when the environment is varied and includes appropriate play materials. In contrast, for black children, high IQ scores are linked to organized environments. Finally, for Mexican-American children, none of the other subscales of the HOME inventory is linked strongly to IQ scores.

Thus, parental involvement predicts IQ in each group but the other factors associated with IQ are unique to each ethnic group. Creating above-average intelligence includes a healthy dose of parental involvement, but otherwise each ethnic group has its own set of preferred ingredients.

How do we interpret these differences in IQ scores associated with SES and race? Since individual differences in IQ are thought to reflect the combined effects of heredity and environment, it should not surprise you that these factors have been invoked to explain differences associated with SES and race. In other words, theorists attribute the differences to the cumulative influence of the environment, the appearance of genetically based abilities, or a combination of these factors. The relative contributions of the two factors, as well as the exact way in which they

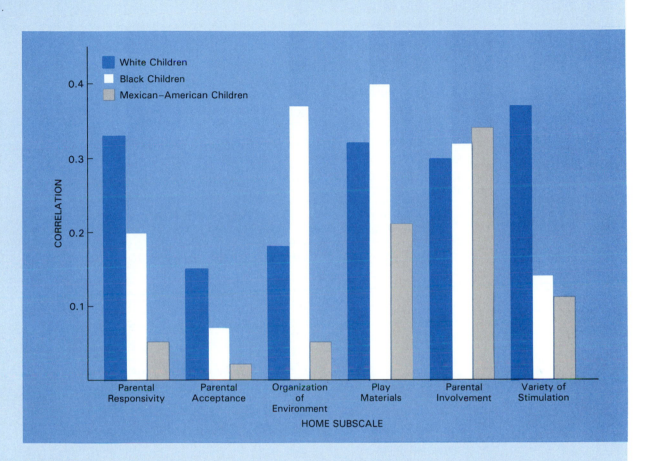

FIGURE 8-9
Correlations between children's IQ scores and six subscales of the HOME
inventory, separately for white, black, and Mexican-American children.
*(Data from Bradley et al., "Home environment and cognitive development in
the first 3 years of life: A collaborative study involving six sites and three
ethnic groups in North America," in Developmental Psychology, 25, 1989,
217–235.)*

interact, continue to be topics extensively researched and much debated
(Wachs and Gruen, 1982). Another factor that needs to be considered,
however, is the claim that tests are biased against children from certain
groups.

THE CULTURAL BIAS OF INTELLIGENCE TESTS. Psychological testing has
come under increasing criticism since the 1950s. Many critics assert that
conclusions about the intelligence of various minority groups are based

on tests that are biased against them. Consider the following informal description of cultural bias as suggested by Kenneth Eells (1953):*

> Let us suppose for a moment that you have a friend in Australia and that you have gone to visit him in his home country. He has told you that he is to take an intelligence test that afternoon and suggests that you take it too, just for the fun of it. . . . When you first open the test booklet you say to yourself, "Well, I'm in a foreign country, but since they speak English, I shouldn't have any special difficulty with this." But soon you are in trouble. . . . You realize that because of the mutton and the kangaroo, the strange words, the local information, and the variations in word connotations your friend had an advantage over you. If he thinks this is a good measure of your intelligence you are glad that he cannot compare your score with his. . . . As a measure of your ability to get along in a certain portion of the Australian culture the test might be excellent and you might willingly accept your low score as an accurate reflection of your "current ability." It is the labeling of the test as an "intelligence" test, with its accompanying implication that this is somehow a measure of some basic ability or potentiality of yours, that disturbs you. . . . You wouldn't object to being told you couldn't understand Australian newspapers very well; but to be told you're not very "intelligent" implies something more serious, doesn't it? (pp. 284–285)

Eells goes on to note that children from poor areas in America are in the same situation. They are judged on the basis of test items requiring cultural experiences different from their own. Consider, for example, a test item such as this:

> A symphony is to a composer as a book is to what?
>
> paper   author   musician   man

It would surprise no one if children from middle-class homes chose the correct answer, simply on the basis of experience, more often than those from the lower-class homes. And yet this outcome is frequently used to argue that individuals from lower-class homes lack some inherent ability called intelligence.

The pitfalls of standard IQ testing are easier to understand if you remember two ideas discussed earlier in this chapter. Recall that according to Sternberg's triarchic theory intelligence always reflects adaptation to a particular environment or context. Also recall that the validity of intelligence tests rests largely on the finding that they predict success in school; intelligence tests measure successful adaptation to a school environment that often reflects the values of the middle class. Typically, tests predict success about as accurately for black and Hispanic students as for white students. What this means is that a child with an IQ score of 85, regardless of race or SES, is unlikely to fare well in school.

Outside of school, IQ scores may have little meaning. Tests that measure IQ were not designed to measure successful adaptation to non-

---

school environments and they often do not. A dramatic example of the limitations of standard IQ testing was offered by Mercer (1971). Mercer developed a system of assessment that included direct measures of children's ability to adapt to their nonschool environments. Included were relatively simple tasks such as dressing oneself, as well as more complex tasks such as shopping. She administered her measure and a standard Wechsler IQ test to over 600 Chicano, black, and white children in California. As might have been predicted, white children with standard IQ scores below 70 invariably failed her adaptive behavior scale. The same was not true of black and Chicano children with IQ scores below 70. A clear majority of these children passed the skills test despite their supposedly low IQs. These results suggest that for minority children, low IQ scores should not be considered a measure of adaptive skill or potential, although for middle-class white children they may be interpreted that way.

Another approach to the problem of cultural bias has been the attempt to construct tests that eliminate cultural differences, such as those found in content and language (Anastasi, 1968). Today several "culture-fair" tests are relatively good predictors of academic success. Raven's Progressive Matrices, for example, consist of designs, each of which has a missing section (Figure 8-10). Examinees are required to select the missing part of the design from several alternatives. There is no time limit and

FIGURE 8-10
Materials similar to those used in Raven's Progressive Matrices Test.

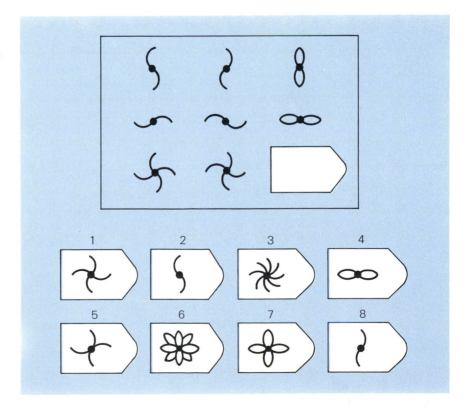

the instructions are simple. The Goodenough-Harris Drawing Test requires subjects to draw a picture of a man, a woman, and themselves. It is reasonably reliable and correlates with other intelligence tests.

The drawback to these and similar tests is that they are more culture-laden than originally expected. Scores on the Raven's Progressive Matrices reflect the amount of education (Anastasi, 1968), and those from the Goodenough-Harris Drawing Test are related to the degree to which representational art exists in particular cultures (Dennis, 1966). For example, a study of the Goodenough-Harris Drawing Test showed that aboriginal Australian boys, but not girls, outperform the average U.S. child (Money and Nurcombe, 1974). This outcome can be traced to specific cultural experiences for aboriginal boys who are exposed to a strong cultural heritage of painting totemic designs.

It does not seem possible, at this time, to construct tests that are free of cultural content. Consequently, always bear in mind that tests assess successful adaptation to a particular culture, environment, and context; test scores are useful only as indices of adjustment in that context and *not* as all-purpose measures of success and ability.

Effects of Intervention on IQ Scores

"SES predicts IQ which predicts school success." This sterile summary captures the gist of the research described in the last few pages, but it falls far short of capturing the bitter implications for the lives of many children. Roughly one child out of every four in the United States grows up in a home where the income is below the federal poverty line. And this figure is higher for black, Mexican-American, and other minority children. In conditions of never-ending poverty, the consequences for children are predictable and tragic: Low IQ scores accurately predict school failure, which is followed by unemployment and resentment toward society. Later unemployment and feelings of resentment may lead to crime and violence. Although this life script is not necessarily unavoidable, it is far too common; and it typically results in successive generations of lives spent in poverty with all its attendant problems (Ramey and Ramey, 1990).

For more than 25 years, intensive educational intervention has been advocated as a means to break out of this intergenerational cycle of poverty. When President Lyndon Johnson began Project Head Start in 1965 as part of his War on Poverty, he said that the program would "rescue [disadvantaged] children from the poverty which otherwise could pursue them all their lives. The project is designed to put them on an even footing with their classmates as they enter school" (Zigler and Valentine, 1979, p. 69).

Do programs like Head Start work? With massive intervention can we change development that is otherwise destined for scholastic failure? Yes, according to most studies: Intervention can produce higher IQ scores, which means that children should be more likely to succeed in school. The typical result, phrased more precisely, is that intervention programs usually increase IQ scores by about ten points as well as produce similar increases on measures of school readiness and achievement (Clarke and Clarke, 1989).

There are two essential qualifications for this conclusion (Ramey and Ramey, 1990): First, it holds only for programs that have *massive* intervention. These programs may operate during the summer and school year, may include structured curricula for both children and their parents, and may be coordinated with other social services provided for children. Modest, small-scale programs that have only some of these components are unlikely to affect children's development. The second qualification is that the gains associated with intervention programs erode gradually unless children receive supplemental educational and social services. Providing one or two years of enrichment experiences helps children (and their parents) to get established on the road to scholastic success but, alone, does not guarantee that they will be able to follow it.

MENTAL RETARDATION

Throughout history, society has recognized that there are individuals whose abilities to learn and think are substantially less than would be expected based on their age. Today, approximately 1 percent of the population is classified as mentally retarded, with boys almost twice as likely to be retarded as girls (McLaren and Bryson, 1987). Intelligence, as it is assessed on standard tests, is crucial to the definition of **mental retardation**. The American Association on Mental Retardation (AAMR) defines mental retardation as "significantly subaverage general intellectual functioning existing concurrently with deficits in adaptive behavior and manifested during the developmental period [that is, before the age of 19]" (Grossman, 1983, p. 1). By "significantly subaverage" the AAMR means a score of 70 or below on standard intelligence tests.

What is meant by "deficits in adaptive behavior"? The AAMR provides examples of levels of deficits at different ages (Grossman, 1983). It also distinguishes what is needed for adaptive functioning at different ages. During infancy and early childhood, the emphasis is on sensorimotor skills, speech, and language. Also emphasized are self-help skills and the ability to interact with others. During childhood and early adolescence, the focus is the application of basic academic skills in daily life activities, appropriate reasoning in mastering the environment, and participation in group activities and interpersonal relationships (Grossman, 1983).

Children who show marked deficiencies in these areas *and* whose mental test performance is subpar may be mentally retarded. That is, a very important aspect of the AAMR definition is that the retardation label should be applied only if the individual shows significant subaverage intelligence *and* deficits in adaptive behavior.

Causes

Mental retardation
Intellectual functioning that is significantly below average and that exists concurrently with deficits in adaptive behavior.

Although the causes of mental retardation vary considerably, two distinct categories have been identified, and they can help us understand the range of characteristics and abilities displayed by retarded individuals.

Familial mental retardation is said to account for roughly 80 percent of all mental deficiency. A familially retarded child may be viewed as having an IQ within the lower range of the normal IQ distribution. As we would expect from this distribution, most children in this category are only mildly retarded. They are physically normal and have no history of brain damage or neurological defect.

Biologically caused mental retardation stems from some particular damage or defect. These include chromosomal anomalies such as Down syndrome and gene defects such as PKU, both of which were discussed in Chapter 2, as well as brain damage caused by infectious disease, oxygen deprivation, or physical trauma. Most, though not all, individuals with IQs below 50 appear to be in this category.

Levels and Measurement

Historically, retardation has been classified according to severity. Over the years three or four categories have generally been recognized, although the labels associated with them have varied with the time and the setting. The terms *moron, imbecile,* and *idiot,* for example, were once standard designations for retarded individuals. Current labels used by educators in the United States reflect the school capabilities of each group: *educable* (EMR), *trainable* (TMR), and *custodial* levels. Today the AAMR uses the terms *mild, moderate, severe,* and *profound.* Table 8-3 shows the parallel between the AAMR classification scheme and the accepted IQ range for each category.

Variations in labels are not due simply to current fashion. They reflect a specific orientation toward retardation. Changes in labels have also served the beneficial purpose of helping to overcome prejudices and stereotypes. Today most of us would be horrified to hear a mentally retarded person referred to as an imbecile or idiot. And children labeled slow learners are judged more favorably than those labeled mentally retarded (Hollinger and Jones, 1970).

Identifying levels of retardation on the basis of adaptive functioning is nowhere near as precise as using intelligence test scores. Ideally, such identification would involve numerous observations of the individual in various settings. In practice, it is based on interviews and rating scales. The Vineland Adaptive Behavior Scales (Sparrow, Balla, and Cicchetti, 1984) measure behavior in four broad domains: motor skills, communication, socialization, and daily living skill. The Adaptive Behavior Scale

---

TABLE 8-3
Categories of Mental Retardation and the Associated IQ Ranges

Term	IQ Range for Level
Mild mental retardation	50–55 to approx. 70
Moderate mental retardation	35–40 to 50–55
Severe mental retardation	20–25 to 35–40
Profound mental retardation	Below 20 or 25

Source: H. J. Grossman (Ed.), *Classification in Mental Retardation.* Washington, D.C.: American Association on Mental Deficiency, 1983, p. 13. Reprinted with permission.

TABLE 8-4
Behavioral and Personality Domains Evaluated by the Adaptive
Behavior Scale Used by the AAMR

Part I	Part II
Independent functioning	Violent and destructive behavior
Physical development	Antisocial behavior
Economic activity	Rebellious behavior
Language development	Untrustworthy behavior
Numbers and terms	Withdrawal
Domestic activity	Stereotype behavior and odd mannerisms
Vocational activities	Inappropriate interpersonal manners
Self-direction	Unacceptable vocal habits
Responsibility	Unacceptable or eccentric habits
Socialization	Self-abusive behavior
	Hyperactive tendencies
	Sexually aberrant behavior
	Psychological disturbances
	Use of medications

Source: Adapted from J. M. Kauffman and J. S. Payne (Eds.), *Mental Retardation: Introduction and Personal Perspectives.* Columbus, Ohio: Charles E. Merrill, 1975, pp. 99–101.

used by the AAMR is composed of two major sections and subdivisions, shown in Table 8-4. These two scales are among the most frequently used to evaluate adaptive behavior and to plan remedial programs.

As a group, mentally retarded children are slow to walk, talk, and feed themselves. They also take unusually long periods of time before they are toilet trained. In the more severe cases, retardation extends to almost all areas of anatomical, motor, and verbal development. Because intellectually normal children may also display one or more of these indicators, it is usually not assumed that a young child is retarded unless a pattern of deficits is present.

By far the largest group of retarded individuals are classified as mildly or educably mentally retarded; these people are rarely institutionalized. Of course, even with a mild level of retardation a child will have a difficult time in school and is likely to lag behind average children of the same age. An educably retarded youngster can acquire many of the academic skills mastered by elementary school children but reaches this level of achievement at a later age. There are many jobs the mildly retarded are quite capable of filling; they have become welders, miners, painters, and tailors. Because success depends more on social skills than on occupational ones (Telford and Sawrey, 1972), parents of these children must avoid the temptation to keep such children dependent or to make excuses for them because of their intellectual deficit.

The moderately or trainably retarded are usually unable to hold jobs except within sheltered workshops; they rarely marry and often are institutionalized. For the profoundly retarded—with IQs below 25—institutionalization is almost inevitable. Among these individuals, interpersonal communication is minimal or lacking. Learning even the simplest kind of self-care often proves extremely difficult or downright impossible.

Deficits in Cognitive and Social Skills

Retardation literally means *slowness* in development. In fact, mentally retarded individuals often perform like younger nonretarded children who are their intellectual peers. These similarities have lead to the *similar sequence* and *similar structure* hypotheses. According to these hypotheses, retarded children go through the same sequence of development as nonretarded children, but they do so more slowly. In addition, the structure of retarded children's thinking resembles that of younger nonretarded children (Hodapp, 1990).

Consistent with these hypotheses, retarded adolescents and younger nonretarded children perform similarly on Piaget's conservation tasks (Mundy and Kasari, 1990): Individuals in both groups with a mental age of 5 years typically fail the conservation tasks, but those with a mental age of 9 years pass them (Gruen and Vore, 1972). In addition, on memory tasks, retarded adolescents whose mental age is 6 years perform like nonretarded 6-year-olds (Kail, 1990).

Similar results are obtained with measures of social skill. Adams and Markham (1991), for example, studied the ability to recognize emotions in facial expressions. Retarded and nonretarded children were shown three pictures of faces and asked to select the face whose expression corresponded to a specific emotion (for example, happiness, sadness, anger). Retarded 10-year-olds selected the correct face less often than nonretarded 10-year-olds. However, the retarded 10-year-olds, whose mental age was nearly $6\frac{3}{4}$ years, performed at the same level as nonretarded 7-year-olds.

These similarities in performance are so widespread that Piaget's associate Barbel Inhelder (1968) described levels of retardation in terms of Piaget's stages. The mildly retarded are viewed as functioning no higher than the concrete operational stage; the moderately retarded as not surpassing the preoperational stage; and the severely and profoundly retarded as functioning at the sensorimotor stage (Robinson and Robinson, 1976). Retardation can thus be considered a failure to progress beyond certain stages. The retarded child passes through the usual stages of cognitive development more slowly than the nonretarded child and finally reaches a lower level of development than the nonretarded child (Hodapp, Burack, and Zigler, 1990).

Personality and Motivation

Retarded persons often differ from nonretarded persons in personality and motivation. One common characteristic, called the "positive-reaction tendency" (Merighi, Edison, and Zigler, 1990) refers to the fact that retarded children crave attention and praise to a greater degree than would nonretarded children of the same chronological or mental age. Evidence for this tendency came from a study by Zigler and Balla (1972), who compared the influence of social praise on the behavior of retarded and nonretarded children of mental ages 7, 9, and 12 while they were performing a boring task. Retarded children performed the boring task longer than nonretarded ones. Even the oldest retarded individuals performed the boring task for a longer time than did the youngest nonretarded children. For retarded children, the continued praise from the adult more than compensated for the boring nature of the task.

Another motivational factor to be considered with retarded children is that many have often experienced situations for which their intellectual skills were insufficient, leading them to failure and perhaps embarrassment or humiliation. A byproduct of these experiences is that retarded individuals have low expectations of success and are not motivated to succeed. Instead, the desire to avoid failure is particularly important for them when faced with new problems. Retarded children are therefore more likely than nonretarded children of the same mental age to "settle for" poor performance even when they can do better (Balla and Zigler, 1979). Building positive self-concepts should be a high-priority goal for anyone teaching retarded children.

Training Retarded Individuals

The developmental approach to mental retardation has had an enormous impact on educational practices for the mentally retarded. The approach provides three basic ideas to guide the education of the retarded: (1) The growth of intellectual skills follows a developmental path that is largely the same for all children. (2) The development of these skills always proceeds from the simpler to the more complex. (3) The more complex skills are created or "built" from combining and coordinating the simpler ones (Haring and Bricker, 1976).

FIGURE 8-11
With well-planned instruction, some severely retarded children can learn important academic skills.

Using this approach, mentally retarded children have been taught many of the cognitive and social skills that they lack. Poor performance on memory tasks, for example, can be traced to retarded youngsters' failure to use mnemonic strategies. Through teaching the components of rehearsal (and other strategies), retarded children's memory can be improved (Kail, 1990). As another example, through role playing, discussion, and modeling, retarded children have been taught to shop in department stores (Westling, Floyd, and Carr, 1990).

Successful training is difficult because retarded children do not always maintain the skills acquired through training. In addition, retarded children may not generalize the skills to appropriate situations that differ from those used in training. For example, the retarded children who were trained to shop in department stores such as Sears and K-Mart were unable to apply their new skills to shopping in convenience stores such as Seven-Eleven (Westling et al., 1990).

Researchers do not yet fully understand all the factors required for skills to be maintained and generalized to new settings, but some useful rules of thumb have been established. First, amount of training is one key to success. Brief training can improve skills substantially, but the improvement is short lived. Thorough training, to the point where individuals have mastered the skills, is more likely to lead to success (Kail, 1990). Another important element is the individual's understanding of the skill: Skills are more likely to be maintained and generalized when retarded youngsters are taught the goal of the skills, why the skills are to be used, and typical characteristics of situations where the skills should be used (Belmont and Mitchell, 1987). Finally, the skills learned often disappear when the experimenter no longer provides reinforcement. Training is more likely to be successful if the retarded youngster is weaned from the instructors' praise. Gradually reducing reinforcement or gradually extending the time between a target behavior and reinforcement are some effective techniques (Demchak, 1990).

These techniques derived from the developmental approach form a guide for educators, not a cookbook with precise instructions (Switzky, Rotatori, Miller, and Freagon, 1979). Nevertheless, the findings also suggest that the aim of training retarded youngsters *can* be accomplished.

THE INTELLECTUALLY GIFTED AND CREATIVE

We now turn to the opposite end of the IQ spectrum, the exceptionally gifted. Because humans have always been fascinated by the unusual, many myths and attitudes have grown up concerning the exceptionally gifted and talented. Historically, the gifted have been associated with either the supernatural or with madness (Albert, 1975). Goethe spoke of poets as "plain children of God," and the word *divine* is often applied to artists. For Aristotle, "there is no genius without madness."

These attitudes still exist today in stereotypes of the gifted as being strange, odd, socially inept, maladapted, and downright "crazy" (Halpern and Luria, 1989). But studies of the gifted paint a strikingly different picture. Several such studies began in the 1920s and 1930s. Among the most influential is the Stanford study of the gifted. Beginning in 1921, Lewis Terman attempted to identify factors that influenced life success among gifted men. The subjects were first rated on life success—the extent to which they made use of their abilities—and then the 150 who rated highest and the 150 who rated lowest were examined. The most spectacular difference, according to Terman, was the greater drive to achieve and the greater mental and social adjustment of the successful group. With regard to the notion that the gifted are strange, Terman said, "In our gifted group, success is associated with stability rather than instability, with absence rather than with the presence of disturbing conflicts—in short with well-balanced temperament and with freedom from excessive frustrations."

In Terman's research, gifted individuals were defined as those with high IQ scores (≥ 140) who had channeled their superior talents into a specialized area. Modern definitions of giftedness include such facets as general intelligence, a specialized skill, and a commitment to excellence and achievement, although how these facets should be integrated is still debated (Sternberg and Davidson, 1986).

Perhaps because of our stereotypes of giftedness, we may think that gifted children's thinking is fundamentally different from that of nongifted children. However, most studies paint a different picture: Thinking develops in much the same way in gifted and nongifted children. Development is more rapid in gifted children, who often solve Piagetian tasks at relatively younger ages and process information more efficiently. However, most results suggest that gifted children behave and think like older nongifted children (Jackson and Butterfield, 1986).

What Is Creativity?

Most people recognize in others and in themselves something that seems to go beyond intelligence, something that might be labeled creativity. An exact definition of creativity, though, is hard to come by. Researchers have begun by asking whether creativity can, in fact, be distinguished from intelligence.

One strategy used to see if there is a distinction between creativity and intelligence has been to compare "average" people with very successful people in various occupations, such as art, scientific research, mathematics, and writing. Are those who have made the most significant adult contributions in their occupations the ones with higher intelligence? Did they have the better grades in school? In one study involving mathematicians (Helson and Crutchfield, 1970), the index of creativity was nominations by other mathematicians for significant accomplishment. The highly creative scholars were compared with others, matched for age (all in their late thirties), who had doctorates from universities of equally high standing. The men in the two groups were approximately equal in terms of the amount of time they spent on their work, yet by agreement of their peers, they differed markedly in terms of the quality of their products. It came as a surprise, then, that the two groups were entirely comparable

Convergent thinking A type of thinking in which people start with established information and arrive at an answer that is known to be correct.

Divergent thinking A type of thinking in which, instead of seeking a known correct answer, an individual considers many alternatives or explores new possibilities.

in terms of IQ as usually measured. At this range of ability, intelligence was unrelated to creativity.

In fact, those who are creatively accomplished as adults are often not identifiable by school grades. "As students," writes researcher D. W. MacKinnon of one sample of creative individuals, "they were, in general, not distinguished for the grades they received, and in none of the samples did their high school grade-point average show any significant correlation with their subsequently achieved and recognized creativeness" (1968, p. 103).

Using a different strategy, Getzels and Jackson (1975) were able to distinguish two groups of adolescents attending a private school. One group was labeled highly intelligent and the other highly creative. The groups were equally superior in academic achievement. However, the highly intelligent students were in the top 20 percent on standard IQ measures but not in the top 20 percent on measures of creativity. The highly creative ones showed the reverse pattern.

Several differences were apparent between the groups. The high-IQ students displayed the desire to possess qualities that would lead to future success. The creative students did not appear to select present goals on the basis of expectations of future success. Also, compared with the high-IQ students, the creative students deemphasized the value of high marks, IQ, pep and energy, character, and goal directedness. They valued instead a wide range of interests, emotional stability, and a sense of humor.

From these studies, as well as a number of others, the conclusion is that, in general, creativity and intelligence refer to different aspects of human ability (Kogan, 1983). One way to distinguish creativity and intelligence is in terms of the difference between **convergent** and **divergent thinking**, as proposed by J. P. Guilford (1957, 1966). Convergent thinking involves integration of established information to arrive at the standard, correct answer. Divergent thinking goes off in many directions to arrive at an answer in cases in which no one answer is necessarily correct. It is this divergent mode that indicates creativity, according to Guilford.

FIGURE 8-12
Creative products display appropriate yet novel use of elements and ideas.

The most commonly used measures of divergent thinking involve ideational fluency—the ability to produce a large number of ideas when asked to be productive (Kogan, 1983). Ideational fluency can be tapped by asking children to name all the things they can think of that can be used for cooking, or all the things they can think of that are round. In more than 70 studies, ideational fluency tests of divergent thinking have been found to correlate positively with various indices of real-life creative activity or accomplishment (Barron and Harrington, 1981).

What characteristics are associated with creativity in children? La Greca (1980) found that the most creative third and sixth graders, as measured by ideational fluency tests, were much better able than other children to verbalize strategies such as scanning the immediate environment for ideas. The less creative children tended to take a passive attitude toward the test; usually they just waited for ideas to come to them.

School-age children and adolescents can be taught to be more creative. Some success has been achieved with training programs that emphasize the use of divergent thinking to solve real problems. Students who participate in these programs are likely to be more creative both in school and outside of school (Starko, 1988).

Creativity in the Preschool Years

Researchers have been particularly interested in trying to understand signs of creativity in the preschool years and in trying to foster creativity by cultivating it early in life. Creativity in young children shows itself as spontaneity, playfulness, and a tendency, even at a young age, to see the humorous side of things (Dansky, 1980). Singer and Rummo (1973), for example, measured creativity in a group of 79 kindergarten children and then correlated the children's ideational fluency scores with teacher ratings of various aspects of the children's classroom behavior. They found, as did Lieberman (1977), that the most creative children, as measured by the test, were generally more playful than other children; they also found the most creative children more erratic in their work and more likely to respond aggressively to frustration than other children. Also, as is the case for older children, creativity in preschoolers is largely unrelated to IQ scores (Godwin and Moran, 1990).

We may wonder whether creativity in children this young is related to creativity as measured or expressed later in their lives. Harrington, Block, and Block (1983) reported the results of a longitudinal study of creativity spanning seven years, from preschool (age 4) to preadolescence (age 11). The preschool creativity test consisted of a question geared toward measuring a child's ability to come up with creative instances ("Tell me all the things you can think of that are round") and an alternative uses test ("Name all the different ways a newspaper, ceramic cup, table knife, and coat hanger can be used"). Answers to the instances tests were considered high quality if they referred to objects that were truly round and not found in the testing room. Answers on the alternative uses test were considered high quality if they referred to possible but unintended uses, such as using a newspaper to start a fire.

Seven years later, when the children were in elementary school, they were all individually rated by their teachers for their degree of creativity. As predicted, highly creative answers given by a child at age 4 significantly predicted high teacher ratings of creativity for that child at age 11. These results show the consistency of creativity in childhood and demonstrate that it is a characteristic that can be separated from general intelligence. They also demonstrate the importance of viewing creativity in terms of the quality as well as the sheer quantity of divergent thinking.

Other researchers have sought to encourage young children's creativity. Pepler and Ross (1981) presented 3- and 4-year-old children with convergent or divergent play materials to see if they could influence performance on a test of divergent thinking. The convergent play materials consisted of colored pieces that fit together into a form board. The divergent play materials consisted of unrelated play pieces, such as an assortment of colored random shapes. The divergent play materials clearly helped subsequent performance on a test of ideational fluency. And the children's other play activities seemed to become more flexible and imaginative, which suggests that encouraging children to play in a creative fashion may produce general advances in tendencies to approach tasks creatively.

SUMMARY

1. Psychometric approaches to intelligence include theories that describe intelligence as primarily a single factor (g), as well as theories that depict intelligence as made up of independent, specific factors. Still other theories combine single-factor and multifactor explanations by viewing intelligence as hierarchical, with g at the top but with various specific skills (such as scientific ability, reading ability, and psychomotor ability) feeding into it.

2. New theories of intelligence are broader than traditional psychometric approaches. Gardner's theory of multiple intelligences relies on signs rather than test scores to advance the claim that there are six different intelligences. These include three intelligences that parallel abilities found in psychometric theories (linguistic, logical-mathematical, and spatial intelligence), and three that are new (musical, bodily kinesthetic, and personal intelligence). Sternberg's triarchic theory includes contextual, experiential, and componential subtheories.

3. Test construction involves selecting a representative sample of test items and administering them to a standardization group. The test must also show consistency (reliability), and its validity must be established by relating scores to school performance or other pertinent criteria.

4. The original Stanford-Binet test became extremely popular because it introduced the concept of the intelligence quotient, or IQ, which allowed individuals of different ages to be compared directly. The Stanford-Binet test consists of many cognitive and motor tasks, ranging from easy to difficult.

5. Other widely used tests are the WISC-III and K-ABC. On these tests, a full-scale IQ is provided as well as more specific IQs based on groups of subtests (for example, the verbal subscale of the WISC-III). IQ scores obtained at age 4 or 5 correlate quite well with IQ as measured when the same child has become an adolescent or an adult. However, for many individuals, test scores fluctuate as they develop.

6. Special tests have been developed for infants. Scores on infant tests do not correlate very well with later IQ scores but are useful in determining if the infant is developing normally. The rate that an infant habituates seems to predict later IQ with some accuracy.

7. Heredity and environment both contribute to individual differences in intelligence. The impact of heredity may increase as children develop. Several characteristics of home environments are associated with intelligence, but most are specific to particular ethnic groups.

8. Race, ethnicity, and SES are all related to IQ. The roles of heredity and environment in these relations have been the subject of debate and experiment, as has the question of cultural bias in IQ tests. Massive intervention programs can raise IQ scores, but gains will be lost unless supplemented by additional instruction.

9. Mental retardation results from the combination of below-average intellectual functioning and the presence of deficits in adaptive behavior. Some retardation occurs simply because a certain percentage of individuals are at the low end of the normal IQ distribution (familial mental retardation), but retardation can also be biologically caused.

10. Mental retardation is usually scaled into three or four levels. Mildly retarded persons are rarely institutionalized and are quite capable of doing many jobs. Moderately retarded individuals can work only in sheltered workshops and are often institutionalized. Those who are severely retarded may be trained to perform very simple tasks and are quite likely to be institutionalized. Profoundly retarded individuals are unable to communicate with others except on a primitive level and are almost always institutionalized.

11. Developmental approaches to retardation state that the development of intellectual skills follows the same course for retarded and nonretarded individuals, so that a retarded child has the cognitive and social skills of a younger nonretarded child. This model has been useful in developing ways to teach new skills to retarded children. With appropriate training and encouragement, many retarded individuals can also be taught relatively advanced skills.

12. People with unusually high IQs were once thought to be peculiar or strange, but actually very bright individuals tend to be better adjusted and more stable than others. Gifted children develop in much the same way as nongifted children, but more rapidly.

13. Creativity can be differentiated from IQ, and it appears to involve divergent thinking—that is, the ability to let one's thought go off in many directions. Creativity has also been shown to be reasonably stable from the preschool years through adolescence to adulthood.

P·A·R·T T·H·R·E·E

Socialization and Social Skills

I n the 1950s and early 1960s, the media customarily depicted women in the role of housewife. Popular television programs like *Father Knows Best*, *Ozzie and Harriet*, and *Leave It To Beaver* depicted families in which men spent the day at work while women stayed at home caring for the children, cooking, and cleaning the house. Today the images of women are not so uniform. The image of a woman as wife, mother, and homemaker is still with us, but it has been joined by others. Television's *Murphy Brown*, now a working mother, portrays a common image, as is the image of a single professional woman. These images correspond to changes in Canada and in the United States concerning women's roles and functions. The range of attitudes and behaviors that are acceptable for today's women is substantially greater than it was for the women of 30 or 40 years ago.

Communicating to children the attitudes and behaviors that their culture considers appropriate is a task that usually falls to parents, at least initially. Teaching the attitudes and behaviors that are expected of boys and girls is just one part of this task. Teaching children how to interact with peers and teaching cultural ideals are other important tasks that parents and others must perform.

These processes of socialization are the focus of this unit. We begin, in Chapter 9, by examining some of the common goals of socialization and the means by which parents try to attain them. In Chapter 10 we study children's interactions with their peers, including the formation of friendships. In Chapter 11 we discuss how children learn to control their behavior and to act in ways that their culture considers to be moral. Finally, in Chapter 12, we consider society's roles for men and women and how children learn these roles.

C·H·A·P·T·E·R 9

Socialization and the Family

We all know the phrases and the routines of socialization: "Don't touch the stove—hot, hot!" "Watch me." "This is the way to do it." "Say please." "Tell Mommy (or Daddy or Grandma) when you want to go to the bathroom." "Let Jackie play with your toys." And we realize that these exchanges are a vital part of development—learning how to live as a member of our group. Socialization is the set of events and processes by which children acquire the beliefs and behaviors of the particular society, and subgroup of that society, into which they are born. It depends in part on cognitive and language skills and in part on biological factors and the physical environment.

Many goals of socialization are common to all societies. At the same time, each society and subgroup evolves some unique or specific practices and goals in order to maintain itself in its particular ecological niche. In most cultures, the tasks of socialization fall initially to parents. By focusing on the nature and impact of parent-child relationships, we can begin to learn how children become members of their social group. Some examples illustrate the host of specific tasks of socialization and the diverse ways that parents try to accomplish them:

▶ Sharon and Stacey, both fifth graders, want to see a movie Friday night with two boys from their class. When they ask their parents' permission, Sharon's mother says that she can't go. Sharon's request for an explanation angers her mother who simply replies, "Because I say so!" Stacey's mother, too, won't allow her daughter to go. When Stacey asks her mother why, her mother explains in a calm and caring voice that she believes Stacey is too young to be involved in boy-girl activities. Stacey's mother offers to take the two girls to the movie if they would like to go without the boys.

▶ Jack has lived with his dad for four years since his parents' divorce; he visits his mother every other weekend. Although Jack was confused and downcast when his parents decided to divorce, he has now come to terms with the new situation. He's excelling in school, where he is well liked by peers and teachers. Troy's parents are married but bicker constantly since his dad lost his job. His parents are unable to agree on anything; arguments are triggered by the pettiest of events or remarks. Troy's grades have fallen and, while he was once a leader among the boys in his class, he now prefers to be alone.

▶ Every day after school, 9-year-old Sanba walks home from school, lets himself in the house, and locks the door behind him. He calls his mother at work to let her know that he's home. For the two hours that he is alone until his parents return from work, he finishes his homework and then watches television. Sanba's mother believes that this arrangement teaches her son to be independent and responsible; Sanba's father sometimes worries about his son's safety and feels that Sanba should be outdoors playing with his friends. ◀

Interacting with members of the opposite sex, achieving in school, making friends, being independent and responsible—these are just a few of the challenges that confront children as their social lives expand and become more complex. Parents adopt different styles in their efforts to help their children meet these challenges and they do so in a range of differing family circumstances (for example, differences among families in the number of parents, relatives and other children present in the home).

To start our study of socialization, we examine the goals of socialization and how these vary in different cultures. Next, we consider the mechanisms by which parents and other individuals socialize children. Finally, we focus on the family, inspecting socialization processes both in the traditional nuclear family and in other common family configurations as well.

CULTURAL INFLUENCES

Culture is the full set of specific attitudes, behaviors, and products that characterize an identifiable group of people. New members of a cultural group must be prepared to live in the culture into which they have been born. So, **enculturation**—teaching children cultural rules and habits—is a major goal of all peoples. Nevertheless, the variation in socialization practices and expectations from one culture to another is enormous. (Wagner and Stevenson, 1982)

The Cultural Context

People have probably always been fascinated by how others live. By the 1920s anthropologists were going into the field and bringing back detailed descriptions of cultures around the world. From Freud they borrowed a theoretical framework, and they began to direct their energies to the issues of child development and personality (Sears, 1975).

Two classic studies are Bronislaw Malinowski's test of Freudian theory conducted in the Trobriand Islands and Margaret Mead's examination of adolescence in Samoa. Malinowski reported that in a culture in which uncles played a dominant role in family life, boys did not appear to come into conflict with their fathers in the way Freud predicted. Mead (1928) concluded that the adolescent years for youth in Samoa were more serene than for youth in the United States. Although these early studies had their methodological difficulties, they drew attention to the cultural context of development.

Of modern anthropological studies, Whiting and Child's (1953) survey of 75 cultures is still considered a classic. One of the main conclusions drawn from the study is that child training involves certain universals. All cultures must deal with eating behavior, evacuation of waste products, and the development of sexuality. Aggressive impulses and the growth of independent and responsible actions also must be shaped.

Another conclusion, however, pointed to the great variability in the specific goals of socialization and the ways in which they are attained. This can be seen dramatically in accounts of toilet-training practices found

Enculturation The processes by which children acquire the rules and habits of their culture.

FIGURE 9-1

Some aspects of child rearing are universal, such as training children to feed themselves.

in two cultures. The Dahomeans of West Africa were rated as severe in their practices:

> A child is trained by the mother who, as she carries it about, senses when it is restless, so that every time it must perform its excretory functions, the mother puts it on the ground. Thus, in time, usually two years, the training process is completed. If a child does not respond to this training, and manifests enuresis [bedwetting] at the age of four or five, soiling the mat on which it sleeps, then, at first, it is beaten. If this does not correct the habit, ashes are put in water and the mixture is poured over the head of the offending boy or girl, who is driven into the street, where all the other children clap their hands and run after the child singing:

> Adida go ya ya ya

> (Urine everywhere.)

> (Herskovitz, as cited by Whiting and Child, 1953, p. 75)

The practices of the Siriono show considerable overindulgence:

> Almost no effort is made by the mother to train an infant in the habits of cleanliness until he can walk, and then they are instilled very gradually. Children who are able to walk, however, soon learn by imitation, and with the assistance of their parents, not to defecate near the hammock.
> When they are old enough to indicate their needs, the mother gradually leads them farther and farther away from the hammock to urinate and defecate, so that by the time they have reached the age of 3 they have learned not to pollute the house. Until the age of 4 or 5, however, children are still wiped by the mother, who also cleans up the excreta and throws them away. Not until a child has reached the age of 6 does he take care of his defecation needs alone. (Holmberg, as cited by Whiting and Child, 1953, pp. 75–76)

Similar differences are found for feeding and weaning practices. The Kwoma tribe, for example, is extremely indulgent:

> Kwoma infants up to the time they are weaned are never far from their mothers. . . . Crying . . . constitutes an injunction to the mother to discover the source of trouble. Her first response is to present the breast. If this fails to quiet him, she tries something else. . . . Thus during infancy the response to discomfort which is most strongly established is that of seeking help by crying or asking for it. (Whiting, as cited by Whiting and Child, 1953, pp. 91–92)

In contrast, Ainu children of Northern Japan have considerably different experiences:

> Put into the hanging cradle . . . the poor little helpless creatures could not get out, and for the rest they were free to do whatever they were able. This usually meant a good deal of kicking and screaming until tired of it, followed by exhaustion, repose, and resignation. (Howard, as cited by Whiting and Child, 1953, p. 93)

Whiting and Child's examples are taken from descriptions of non-industrialized societies, but differences along many dimensions are also found in modern, industrialized ones. In the Israeli kibbutz, children are tended to by many adults and actually live with peers in a building separate from the residence of their biological parents. Infants in isolated communities in Guatemala spend their first year or so in small family huts with no windows. Seldom spoken to or played with, they are given simple toys of corn ears, wood, and clothing (Kagan and Klein, 1973). In contrast, children in middle-class homes in Canada and the United States are stimulated by parents and provided with pets and a large number of toys, including blocks, stuffed animals, dolls, and toy trucks.

FIGURE 9-2
In the Israeli kibbutz, children live with their peers in a separate building and are tended to by many adults, who are not their parents.

Universal Goals of Parenting

From a cultural analysis of child-care customs, Robert LeVine (1974, 1983) has proposed a useful framework for relating child care to the overall setting and development of cultures. LeVine came to his ideas after he noted that a common hazard for African infants of the Gusii (Kenya) and Hausa (Nigeria) people is the cooking fire, especially when the fire is kept burning through the night for warmth. Perhaps, he speculated, this hazard had led to the practice of the child being carried on the backs of adults or otherwise restricted in mobility. Such a limitation might adversely affect the development of certain skills, but it would at least ensure protection from the fire and, thereby, survival, which must be the first priority.

LeVine proposed that many child-rearing customs might have been established to promote survival. Of course, other considerations also determine child-care practices. LeVine, in fact, suggests the following hierarchy of determinants:

1. The physical survival and health of the child including (implicitly) the normal development of his or her reproductive capacity during puberty.
2. The development of the child's behavioral capacity for economic self-maintenance during maturity.
3. The development of the child's behavioral capacities for maximizing other cultural values—for example, morality, prestige, wealth, religious piety, intellectual achievement, personal satisfaction, self-realization—as formulated and symbolically elaborated in culturally distinctive beliefs, norms, and ideologies. (1974, p. 230)

These universal goals are arranged in a definite order. Sheer physical survival during childhood is required before any later capacities can develop and so it assumes paramount importance in environments that pose great danger to the young. In much the same way, economic self-maintenance must be considered before the relative luxury of maximizing one's status and prestige. Do things really work this way? The evidence suggests that they do.

LeVine's review of studies done in African, Latin American, and Indonesian communities with very high infant mortality rates shows that practices in these societies are highly responsive to environmental threats. The general pattern in these cultures is to keep the infant on or near the caregiver's body at all times, day or night, and to respond quickly to crying, usually by feeding. Development of self-maintenance skills receives little attention during this period. By Western standards, these mothers rarely smile at their infants or even make eye contact with them.

In societies in which food and related materials for subsistence are scarce, we would expect that child-rearing customs would emphasize the development of behaviors that would ensure economic self-maintenance. The pattern that is found emphasized obedience, presumably because an obedient child can contribute to food and craft production, or at least baby-sit competently, thereby freeing parents to do productive labor. In the long run, these children benefit from obedience training as much as or more than their parents. "The African parents with whom I have worked," writes LeVine, "want their children to become obedient in part because they believe it is the single most important quality involved in adult economic adaptation, and they are concerned that their children have the capacity to survive in a world of scarce and unstable resources" (1974, p. 237).

Following LeVine's hierarchy, when food, shelter, and safety are assured, societies tend to emphasize the maximizing of achievement, self-realization, and the like. These are important goals for many parents in the United States and Canada. However, like most industrialized societies, these countries are heterogeneous; people live in poverty a stone's throw from middle-class neighborhoods. Consequently, all parents in the United States and Canada do not share the same goals for socialization. Middle-class parents may strive for behavioral goals, whereas poverty parents may favor goals designed to ensure their children's survival.

Although the goals of child rearing may be varied, parents rely upon a common set of tools to achieve them. These processes of socialization are the focus of the next section.

PROCESSES OF SOCIALIZATION

Socialization involves acquiring skills and knowledge. The processes of socialization have been studied from many theoretical perspectives. The ecological view reminds us that parents' efforts to socialize their children are influenced by the multiple contexts in which parents and children live. Biologically-based theories emphasize that many social behaviors (for example, caring for the young) are adaptive to humans because they allow children to reach maturity so they can pass on their genes to future generations (Belsky, Steinberg, and Draper, 1991). However, most of the modern insights into socialization have come from the social-cognitive learning view (Ladd and Mize, 1983), which distinguishes three broad processes: direct instruction (including coaching and exhortation), shaping, and learning from social models. All three processes teach children the social roles that they and others can play in the culture. And all three are mediated by children's social cognition—their understanding of the social world. In real life these processes typically operate together, as when a parent both shows and tells a child what to do in a particular social situation. In the next few pages, we examine each of these processes.

Direct Instruction

Direct instruction may include either specific or general information about what to do or say, and how or when to do or say it. The principal vehicle of direct instruction is language, and so direct instruction deals in concepts and ideas. As we saw in Chapter 5, instructions do not always convey what the communicator intends. In fact, a whole range of cognitive and social processes mediate what is understood, remembered, and believed.

FIGURE 9-3
One common socialization strategy that parents use is direct instruction—they tell their children what to do, why they should do it, and perhaps reward them for doing the appropriate behaviors.

Direct instruction provides both information on what to do and behavioral instigation or exhortation—that is, urging or persuading someone to adopt a particular goal or to follow a particular course of action. Direct instruction can be broken down into parts, two of which seem especially important. First, direct instruction can provide the intent to learn or act differently, by explaining the importance of a particular practice, idea, or way of behaving. Second, direct instruction can provide cognitive structure by identifying relevant and irrelevant attributes of a situation or performance so that children do not need to figure out underlying similarities on their own. For example, you might say to a child who has just made an unkind remark to a peer, "You weren't very nice to make fun of Johnnie. You wouldn't want someone to make fun of you."

Direct instruction is widely used by itself in training academic and occupational skills, but in transmitting social values and behavior it has typically been studied as a partner of modeling or shaping. Exhortations by themselves, such as an exhortation to share with others, are frequently effective in the presence of the authority figure who provides the exhortation, but are often ignored in the absence of such authority. However, providing reasons, explanations, and rationales may do much to facilitate children's adoption of particular beliefs or practices, especially if incentives to do so are given as well.

Shaping

Shaping The application of conditioning processes to achieve social goals.

As we saw in Chapter 3, classical and operant conditioning are learning processes that allow an infant to benefit from experience. These basic conditioning processes continue to play a significant role throughout life. **Shaping** is the application of these processes to achieve social goals.

One of the first psychologists in the United States to think about shaping children was John Watson, the founder of modern behaviorism. Watson was convinced that given certain conditions and stimuli, responses would be orderly and predictable. He enthusiastically advocated that conditioning principles be applied to shape and socialize children, and he was sure it could be done:

> Give me a dozen healthy infants, well-formed, and my own specified world to bring them up in and I'll guarantee to take any one at random and train him to become any type of specialist I might select—doctor, lawyer, merchant, chief and, yes, even beggar-man and thief, regardless of his talents, penchants, tendencies, abilities, vocations, and race of his ancestors. (Watson, 1925, p. 82)

Watson, though, was more effective as an advocate than as an experimenter. His only remembered study, the case of little Albert (Watson and Rayner, 1920), stands as much as a curiosity as a milestone. Albert was an 11-month-old boy with no detectable fear except of loud sounds, such as that made by striking a steel bar behind him. Assuming that the sound was an unconditioned stimulus that elicited fear, Watson and Rayner attempted to show that they could induce or condition fear of a white rat in Albert by systematically pairing exposure to the animal with the sound. After seven such presentations, the rat, which previously had not evoked any fear, elicited a sharp avoidance reaction that included crying and attempts to escape from the situation.

In a follow-up study, Mary Cover Jones (1924) was encouraged by Watson to show that fear responses can be partially extinguished by procedures similar to conditioning. Her subject, Peter, was a boy of 2 years and 10 months, who had previously developed a severe fear reaction to furry objects. Jones first arranged for Peter to play, in the presence of a rabbit, with three children who exhibited no fear of the animal. The treatment appeared to be working well when a setback occurred due to an illness and an accidental exposure to a large dog. Jones then decided to treat the boy with a combination of exposure to fearless others and **counterconditioning**. The latter involved moving the animal progressively closer to Peter while he ate some of his favorite foods, thus pairing the feared stimulus with pleasure. The boy's fear diminished with this treatment until he was even able to hold the rabbit by himself.

Watson's contribution was to pave the way for later generations of behavioral psychologists to study the question of the extent to which children can be shaped, both purposely and accidentally. Central to this work were demonstrations of the effects of consequences on behavior.

THE IMPORTANCE OF CONSEQUENCES. Potential consequences of behavior provide motivation for learning new things and behaving in different ways. Without actual or expected consequences, most socialization efforts would fail.

Counterconditioning
Conditioning in which an aversive response to a stimulus is eliminated by pairing the aversive stimulus with pleasant stimuli.

Consequences can be positive or negative—pleasant or aversive. They can also be manifested as "something given or done" or as "something taken back or removed." The distinction is important. If you want to increase the likelihood that a child will act in a particular way, you can provide something (a smile or a spanking), or you can take something away (a previous restriction or a previous privilege). The effect of the

TABLE 9-1
Types of Consequences and Their Effects

Perceived Nature of the Consequence	Stimulus Presented (Positive)	Stimulus Taken Away (Negative)
"Good"	Example of Positive Reinforcement: Receiving a piece of candy as a reward for finishing one's vegetables.	Example of Negative Reinforcement: Having a curfew lifted for getting better grades.
"Bad"	Example of Positive Punishment: Receiving a spanking for coming home late.	Example of Negative Punishment: Losing television privileges for hitting another child.

consequence does not depend on whether it is given or taken, but only on whether the overall result is reinforcing or punishing. Thus, there are four different types of consequences: positive reinforcement, negative reinforcement, positive punishment, and negative punishment. The four possibilities are shown in Table 9-1.

Positive reinforcement is the application of consequences that, when presented, tend to increase the likelihood of a response. Praise may positively reinforce a child's studying. **Negative reinforcement** also increases the likelihood of the response, but works in a different way. Negative reinforcement involves the ending of some experience or stimulation that is unpleasant, such as when a restriction is lifted for good performance.

Positive punishment refers to the presentation of a stimulus that discourages the recurrence of a response. Almost anyone will show a decline in responses that result in electric shock; shock is a punisher that is almost universally effective. Finally, **negative punishment** involves the reduction of a response by removing some stimulation or experience contingent on the occurrence of the response. An example is not allowing a child to watch television in order to eliminate the child's poor school grades.

Consequences are judged by their effects and not by their intentions. For example, parents, teachers, and even peers may use frowns and various forms of verbal disapproval to discourage particular actions. Nevertheless, attention, even when it is tinged with criticism, often serves as a positive reinforcer. It increases the very behavior it is designed to discourage. And consequences often combine to produce their influence. For example, learning tends to occur more quickly when mild punishment for an unwanted response is used to supplement reinforcement for a desired response (Whitehurst, 1969).

PUNISHMENT. Spankings and other positive punishments (usually simply called "punishment") play an important role for many parents. According to one survey, virtually all parents (98 percent) use such punishment at least occasionally (Sears, Maccoby, and Levin, 1957). Whereas reinforcement is most effective in building new patterns of behavior, the effects of punishment are primarily suppressive; when punishment "works,"

Positive reinforcement Any consequence that, when presented, makes the preceding response more likely.

Negative reinforcement Any consequence that, when ended, makes the preceding response more likely.

Positive punishment A stimulus, such as electric shock, that when presented reduces the likelihood of the preceding response.

Negative punishment Any stimulus that, when removed, decreases the likelihood of a response.

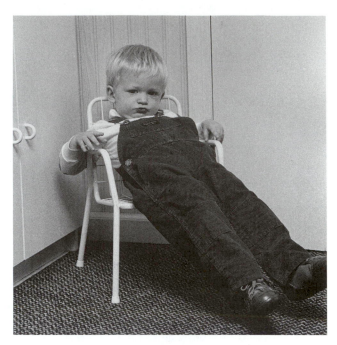

FIGURE 9-4
Time-out is a form of negative punishment in which children are isolated from others, thereby making it impossible for children to continue the undesirable activity. Time-out is also more effective than other forms of punishment because children do not receive adult attention during the punishment.

it reduces the likelihood of certain noxious or potentially dangerous responses.

For ethical and philosophical reasons, many parents seek alternatives to positive punishment. One useful form of negative punishment is **time-out**, which is an abbreviated way of saying "time-out from positive reinforcement" (Sherman and Bushell, 1975). For example, parents can reduce the fighting or arguing between their elementary school-age boys by isolating them in their bedrooms for five minutes (time-out) for each instance of such behavior that they display (Wahler, 1969). Whereas time-out removes the opportunity to continue behavior like fighting or arguing, **response cost** removes some tangible reinforcer already in the child's possession or one that would otherwise be due. Fines are the most obvious examples.

Response-cost and time-out techniques have clearly been shown to be effective when the loss to the individual being punished is substantial enough to outweigh the reinforcers associated with the response to be eliminated. Plainly, however, imposing a small fine on those who are caught engaging in some intrinsically rewarding activity (or, of course, in an activity that produces much extrinsic reinforcement) is not likely to be effective. The effectiveness of negative punishment also increases as the punishment becomes more severe (Burchard and Barrera, 1972).

SIDE EFFECTS OF PUNISHMENT. Punishing a child can have various possible side effects: avoidance of the punishing agent, emotional behavior, and an increased likelihood of aggression, especially the punishment of others, such as a younger brother or sister (Whitehurst and Vasta, 1977). For example, aggressive delinquent adolescents tend to be individuals who were themselves given physical punishment as children (Bandura

Time-out A form of negative punishment in which children are isolated so that they cannot receive positive reinforcement.

Response cost A form of negative punishment in which a valued object is taken from the child.

and Walters, 1959). Such side effects need not occur if punishment is used carefully and in combination with positive reinforcement for alternative activities. Parents and other socializing agents who give a generous reward for one behavior but express a willingness to punish another are usually seen as fair rather than cruel.

Observational Learning (Modeling)

Modeling involves observing and imitating the behavior of others, including parents and other adults, siblings and other children, and people in the electronic and print media. Modeling works by providing children with information that they can then use to guide their own actions in a range of situations. But the notion of the information value of modeling cannot stand by itself, for it is the child's interpretation and understanding of what has been observed that is the real result of any modeling experience (Ladd and Mize, 1983).

FIGURE 9-5
Children can learn a range of specific skills and roles by observing adults.

COUNTERIMITATION. Exposure to a model can lead to relatively exact duplication of the model's behavior, either immediately or when the environmental conditions are right; this is direct imitation. Observing another's behavior also can reduce the probability of matching that behavior. The child who sees a peer burned by a hot stove, for example, typically will become less likely to touch the stove than previously: The model's action and its consequences are a guide for what should not be done. Such an outcome is known as direct **counterimitation**.

INHIBITORY AND DISINHIBITORY EFFECTS. Modeling may also influence actions that fall into the same general class as those observed, but that are different in virtually all details. Youngsters who watch a movie filled with shooting and fighting, for example, may become more likely to yell at or push a younger sibling. In such a case, aggressive responses in general have increased or have been disinhibited. Similarly, a child who, on the first day of class, sees that the teacher punishes a classmate for disrupting the lesson may be less likely to turn in homework assignments late. Failing to turn in homework and carrying on in class, though far from identical, fall into a common category of behavior—disobedience to the dictates of the teacher. The second child's general inhibition with regard to breaking the rules may be traced to the first child's disruption of the class and that child's punishment.

Social Cognition

So far we have spoken of socialization as if it involved little thought on the child's part. This is not so. In fact, children almost never respond automatically or passively to efforts to socialize them. Rewards, punishments, instructions, and modeled examples are affected by children's interpretations of what they mean when they happen. According to the **social-cognitive view**, we must look at the social world from the child's perspective (Bandura, 1986; Mischel, 1979). Children—and adults—respond not to environments or socializing agents themselves; instead, their responses are based on their own social goals as well as their perception about what others know about them and expect from them. A coordinated and cross-referenced system of social understanding underlies children's specific actions and perceptions. Of course, children's thinking in the social domain becomes more sophisticated and elaborate as they develop. This greater knowledge allows them to navigate the social world with ever-greater precision.

Children's understanding of the goals and causes of their own and others' behaviors will be a major theme in many of the remaining chapters of this book. Here our focus is children's perception and interpretation of their parents' behavior, especially behavior that reflects parents' efforts to socialize their children. William Damon (1980, 1983) has identified a gradual developmental progression in children's ideas about parental authority. In his research, children heard stories in which hypothetical children had been told by their parents to perform some chore (for example, cleaning their rooms). Before the chore was finished, the opportunity arose

Counterimitation A form of observational learning in which the consequences to a model's actions indicate a behavior that should not be done.

Social-cognitive view An approach to socialization that emphasizes the roles of children's interpretation of events and children's social goals.

for these hypothetical children to participate in some special event (for example, going on a picnic), but the parent insisted that the children complete the chore. The subjects in Damon's research—4- to 11-year olds—were asked to decide whether the children in the story should obey their parents, and they were also asked to justify their choice.

At all ages children believed that parents should be obeyed, but the reasons for obedience differed for younger and older children. As shown in Table 9-2, preschoolers' close dependence upon parents is the basis for obedience. Slightly older children also consider the consequences of failing to obey. During the elementary school years, children believe parents should be obeyed because of parents' greater experience in human affairs and because they know that most parental requests stem from concern for their children.

Children also gradually form attitudes about different methods of discipline. By 10 or 11 years of age, most children believe that reasoning is more appropriate than withdrawal of love, permissiveness, or physical punishment. In contrast, 6- or 7-year-olds judge these techniques to be equally effective (Siegal and Barclay, 1985; Paikoff, Collins, and Laursen, 1988).

Older children also have acquired a surprisingly sophisticated understanding of the limits to parental authority. To illustrate, imagine that two classmates are trying to decide whose turn it is to feed the class hamster. Suppose a parent is visiting the class, as is a child from another school. Neither the parent nor the visiting child knows the two children

TABLE 9-2
Children's Authority Conceptions

Approximate Age Range	Authority Legitimized by:	Basis for Obedience
4 yrs. and under	Love; identification with self.	Association between authority's commands and self's desires.
4–5 yrs.	Physical attributes of persons.	Obedience is a means for achieving self's desires.
5–8 yrs.	Social and physical power.	Respect for authority figure's power.
7–9 yrs.	Attributes that reflect special ability, talent, or actions of authority figure.	Authority figure deserves obedience because of superior abilities or past favors.
8–10 yrs.	Prior training or experience with leadership.	Respect for authority figure's leadership abilities; awareness of authority figure's concern for subordinate's welfare.
10 yrs. and above	Situationally appropriate attributes of leadership.	Temporary and voluntary consent of subordinate; spirit of cooperation between leader and led.

Source: Based on W. Damon, "Patterns of change in children's social reasoning: A two-year longitudinal study," in *Child Development, 51,* 1980, 1011.

nor the classroom's routine for selecting a child to feed the hamster. If the parent suggests that one child feed the hamster but the visiting child picks the other, most 6- to 7-year-olds believe that the adult should be obeyed. However, 10- and 11-year-olds say that neither person has the authority to make a decision, because both lack the necessary expertise (Laupa and Turiel, 1986).

Thus, children gradually come to understand and evaluate why people—particularly parents—act as they do. This increased understanding means that as children develop they may respond differently to the same parental behavior. And these changing responses may modify parents' behavior, a possibility that we consider in the next section.

Socialization as Reciprocal Influence

The tone of the discussion so far may suggest that socialization is a one-way, completely conscious influence by adults on the behavior of children. This, in fact, was the assumption many developmental psychologists made from the time of John Watson until as recently as the 1960s. In the past few decades, however, developmental psychologists have realized that the process is never simple. Socialization is always complex and multidirectional, and it involves a set of dynamic reciprocal influences between the child and others in the environment.

From the moment of birth, children influence the manner in which others treat them. Children arrive with their own particular temperaments, and the way their temperamental characteristics fit with those of their mothers, fathers, and other family members immediately influences the way they are treated (see pages 108–9). The treatment they receive influences them, of course, and all of this happens not in the isolated context of two (or even three, four, or five) people, but in the context of the total social environment.

Compliance has emerged as one aspect of children's behavior that is particularly influential. A study by Anderson, Lytton, and Romney (1986) illustrates the power of a child's behavior to influence adults. These investigators studied mothers as they interacted with boys during free play as well as during structured tasks that involved doing arithmetic and cleaning up. Each mother was observed in these situations with a boy who had been classified as conduct-disordered and with one who had not. Each of the mother's responses to the boy's behavior was rated during each interaction, as was the degree of the child's compliance or noncompliance to the mother's requests.

Conduct-disordered boys proved to be less compliant than the non–conduct-disordered boys. In turn, more negative responses and requests were directed toward the conduct-disordered boys. Apparently, the behavior of the boys determined the nature of the interactions between mothers and children. That is, children's non-compliance leads adults to be more controlling and punitive; the anticipated byproduct is that children will be even less likely to comply in the future, leading to ever-more coercive parental behavior.

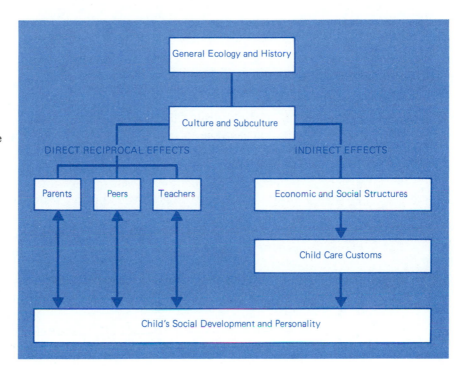

FIGURE 9-6
Socialization involves the transmission of cultural goals directly to children through parents, peers, and teachers, as well as the transmission of these goals indirectly through economic and social structures. However, children are not simply passive recipients of these influences; instead, children influence the manner in which others treat them, creating a pattern of reciprocal influence.

Of course, this cyclical pattern need not always be negative. Cheerful compliance to requests may cause parents to be less controlling and more positive, providing children with an incentive to comply in the future.

Compliance and temperament are but two examples of **reciprocal influence**, which is an integral component of all socialization. Figure 9-6 presents a schematic representation of how various forces interact with children and with each other to influence children's social development and personalities. We will have many opportunities to consider such interactions in the following chapters. We start by focusing on the role of the family.

THE FAMILY

Reciprocal influence The view that socialization involves the interplay of parental influences on children as well as children's influences on parents.

The family has many functions in societies: It serves as an economic unit, it helps satisfy adult sexual drives, and it assumes responsibility for a small number of people as they move through life. But perhaps its most widely recognized function is the care and socialization of new generations.

The exact form of the family may vary from society to society, and even within one society. In no society, however, is there a complete lack of family influence on the developing child, even when the responsibility for child rearing is more diffuse than it is in Canada and in the United States. Parents are, in fact, usually considered the primary agents of socialization because their influence begins so early in life.

Authoritarian A style in which parents exert considerable control over their children but are relatively uninvolved with them.

Authoritative A style in which parents are fairly controlling of their children but also respond to their needs.

Parenting

STYLES. If we were to observe parents as socializers, could we identify dimensions on which they differ? Since the pioneering work of Diana Baumrind (1975, 1991), investigators have attempted to answer this question through studies using interviews, questionnaires, and ratings of parents and children: The overall results suggest that there are important differences in parenting styles, and that these differences are significantly related to children's social and personality development. Investigators now agree that parental behavior differs along at least two important dimensions (Maccoby and Martin, 1983). One is the degree and type of control parents exercise over children's behavior. At one extreme are controlling, demanding parents; at the other, parents who make few demands and rarely exert control. A second dimension refers to parents' responsiveness and involvement. At one extreme, some parents are involved with their children, both emotionally and in their allocation of time and effort; at the other extreme are parents who are relatively uninvolved with their children and who sometimes seem to be rejecting them.

Combining the two ends of these dimensions results in four prototypic styles of parenting, which are shown in Figure 9-7. A parent style that combines high control with low involvement is called **authoritarian**. These parents are strict in the traditional, old-fashioned sense: They lay down the rules and expect them to be followed without discussion or argument. Infractions are punished and debate about the rules is firmly discouraged. Hard work, respect, and obedience are what authoritarian parents wish to cultivate in their children. There is little give-and-take between parent and child because authoritarian parents do not balance their demands in light of the child's needs or wishes.

Authoritative parents are like authoritarian parents in exerting a fair degree of control over their children. They are reasonably firm, but favor giving explanations for rules and encouraging discussion. Further, these parents recognize that children have needs and desires; authoritative par-

FIGURE 9-7
The two dimensions of parenting are control and involvement. When they are combined, four distinct parental styles emerge.

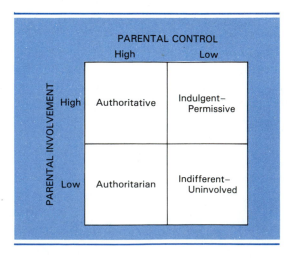

ents try to be responsive to these needs and desires when it is possible and appropriate.

The third style is called **indulgent-permissive**. These parents give their children a great deal of latitude and place few demands or restrictions on them. Indulgent-permissive parents are warm, caring, and involved, but exert little control over their children. They tolerate much of their children's behavior and rarely punish them.

The final style is called **indifferent-uninvolved**. These parents meet the physical and emotional needs of their children only minimally. They do not go beyond these minimal levels; instead, these parents attempt to reduce the time and effort associated with their children. Indifferent-uninvolved parents maintain a psychological distance between themselves and their children.

The classification scheme in Figure 9-7 is also useful in comparing styles that are used by parents from different cultures. Compared to parents in the United States, for example, Chinese parents are more controlling and less emotionally involved with their children (Lin and Fu, 1990).

The behaviors that define these prototypic parental styles are relatively stable over time: Mothers who exert considerable control over their 7-year-olds do the same for their 16-year-olds, just as mothers who feel anger toward their 7-year-olds are likely to feel anger toward their 16-year-olds (McNally, Eisenberg, and Harris, 1991). Also, each style is associated with distinct developmental outcomes. The pattern for school success or failure in children can be summarized easily: Permissive and authoritarian parenting styles are associated with lower grades, whereas authoritative parenting is associated with higher grades. This general pattern is found for African-American, Asian-American, Hispanic-American, and white parents and their children (Dornbusch et al., 1987).

Links between parental style and social development are more complex. The indifferent-uninvolved style can be damaging. Children are more likely to be impulsive and easily frustrated. As adults, they continue to lack emotional control, and do not have goals. Children of indulgent-permissive parents, too, tend to remain immature and display little self-control. Not having been taught responsibility and not having had leadership modeled for them, they also tend to lack these characteristics (Maccoby and Martin, 1983).

Authoritative parents, in contrast, tend to have children who are responsible, self-reliant, and friendly. In contrast, children of authoritarian parents are not very competent socially: They rarely take the initiative in social interactions and often avoid them altogether. Their self-esteem is low. Children may believe their parents' constant control stems from the belief that they are irresponsible. Finally, in reasoning about moral problems, these children often emphasize the importance of authority figures, not ethical or moral codes (Maccoby and Martin, 1983).

A recent comprehensive study of adolescents demonstrates some of these links between parental styles and developmental outcomes. Lamborn and her colleagues (1991) studied more than 4,000 high-school students to determine links between parental style and social development, competence in school, perceived distress, and problem behavior. Some

Indulgent-permissive A style in which warm, caring parents place few demands on their children.

Indifferent-uninvolved A style in which parents are emotionally uninvolved with their children and invest relatively little time with them.

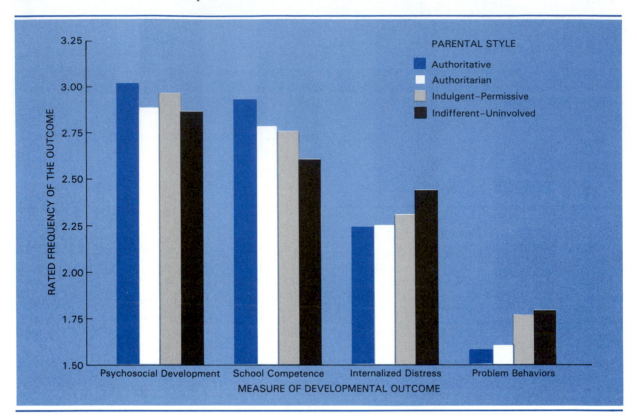

FIGURE 9-8

The influence of the four parental styles on four measures of development.
In every case, authoritative parenting is associated with the best outcome
whereas indifferent-uninvolved parenting is associated with the worst
outcome.
(From S. D. Lamborn, N. S. Mounts, L. Steinberg, and S. M. Dornbusch,
"Patterns of competence and adjustment among adolescents from authoritative,
authoritarian, indulgent, and neglectful families," in Child Development, 62,
1991, 1049—1065, table 3.)

of their results are shown in Figure 9-8. The authoritative and indifferent-uninvolved styles invariably represent the two extremes. Adolescents with authoritative parents have the best scores on all measures; adolescents with indifferent-uninvolved parents have the worst scores.

Teens from the other two groups fall in between and represent a mixture of positives and negatives. Adolescents with authoritarian parents do well in school and do not become involved in problem behavior. However, they do not view themselves as very competent. Adolescents with indulgent-permissive parents are socially competent and well adjusted. They do get involved in some deviant behaviors (usually minor ones) and are only modestly successful in school.

Thus, the cumulative effects of parental style appear in virtually all major arenas of development, with much the same pattern: The authoritative pattern is consistently associated with positive developmental outcomes. Children seem to fare best when parental control is accompanied by parental warmth and affection.

PARENTAL ATTRIBUTIONS. In the approaches to parenting that we have described so far, parental style is akin to a personality trait—the style is viewed as a relatively stable theme that typifies most of a parent's interactions with his or her children. In fact, authoritative parents are not always reasonable; sometimes they command their children without further explanation. Authoritarian parents sometimes change rules to respond to their children's needs. And a great many parents do not fall neatly into any one of the four categories in Figure 9-7. Their parental style may be controlling or lax, involved or uninvolved, depending on the circumstances.

Examples like these make it clear that parental behavior cannot be understood solely by focusing on parenting styles; in addition, we need to examine the causal factors to which parents attribute their children's behavior. How parents respond to their children's behavior does reflect a general orientation or style but it also depends on the parents' judgments of motives underlying their children's behavior, their children's understanding of the situation, and an assessment and determination of the appropriate parental response.

A parent's responses to a child's behavior is linked strongly to his or her judgment of the child's competence. Parents tend to punish children's misbehavior if they believe that children should have known better; if a child's misbehavior stems from ignorance (for example, a youngster unknowingly eats cupcakes that were for a class party), parents usually explain to children why their behavior was wrong. Parents see younger children as less competent, which means that parents have lower expectations for younger children and are less likely to punish them (Dix, Ruble, and Zambarano, 1989).

The view that children's behavior and development is determined by multiple factors is particularly salient for parents who have immigrated and who have functioned successfully in both their original and in their new cultures. For example, Mexican-American mothers who are highly acculturated to life in the United States have a very sophisiticated understanding of the multiple causes of children's behavior. When actively participating in different cultures, it becomes salient for adults that the same behaviors may be attributed to quite distinct and different causes in the two cultures (Gutierrez and Sameroff, 1990).

Mothers

Despite all that has been said about recent changes in the family in Canada and in the United States, and despite the enormous cultural variety that differentiates places, times, and peoples, mothers are still the primary caregivers to children, especially infants and young children. Mothers play so many vital roles that we often do not even stop to think about them—except perhaps on Mother's Day.

Mothers provide nourishment, warmth, and protection. They also provide important cognitive and social input, even when they seem to be only playing with their children. Consider the games mothers in all societies seem to play with their babies (Field and Widmayer, 1982). In addition to contributing to emotional attachment, these games teach cognitive and motor skills ("peek-a-boo") and such rudimentary social skills as turn taking in social interaction ("pat-a-cake").

EMPLOYED MOTHERS. In the past two decades there has been an enormous increase in the number of mothers working outside the home; in fact, a majority of mothers now work. Particularly striking is the number of mothers of very young children who work: Half of the mothers with infants younger than 12 months of age work, as do two-thirds of the mothers of 2- and 3-year-olds (Baydar and Brooks-Gunn, 1991). This important social change raises a question: What are the effects of maternal employment upon children?

The answer to this question depends upon the age of the children. For school-age children and adolescents, maternal employment has several consistent effects. Typically, children of employed mothers are better adjusted, are more independent, and do better in school (Lerner and Hess, 1991). In addition, when mothers are employed, their children typically have less traditional views of sex roles. That is, they are less likely to believe that specific traits, interests, or occupations are uniquely associated with males or females (Hoffman, 1989).

These effects are stronger for daughters than for sons. That is, daughters in particular seem to benefit from maternal employment. For sons the advantages of maternal employment are sometimes negated by other factors. For example, boys are less compliant than girls and day care tends to make children even less compliant. Thus, when mothers are employed and their sons are placed in day care, conflict may develop because sons become less compliant (Hoffman, 1989).

This general pattern, in which maternal employment is positive for

FIGURE 9-9
When mothers of toddlers work full time, the result may be that their children receive lower scores on IQ tests and are likely to be more defiant toward parents.

daughters and benign (or possibly positive) for sons, is subject to a number of qualifications:

1. The impact of employment depends on the number of hours that women work. The positive effects are most evident when mothers work part-time; when mothers work more than 40 hours per week, harmful effects emerge for mothers and children alike. Mothers are more anxious and the quality of interactions with their children may decline. Children, too, more often express negative emotions, such as anxiety and anger, when their mothers work full time, and their school performance may decline as well (Gottfried, Gottfried, and Bathurst, 1988).

2. Effects of employment are linked to mothers' and fathers' attitudes towards the mother's employment. Positive effects associated with employment are common when mothers and fathers favor the mother's employment and change family responsibilities to reflect the mother's commitments outside of the home. When mothers and fathers disapprove of the mother's employment, the stress that results can be harmful (Hoffman, 1989).

3. When a mother works outside of the home, this usually means that other people care for her children. The positive effects of maternal employment hinge upon the fact that the children receive adequate alternative care, either from a baby sitter or a relative or in a day-care center. When children are left unsupervised, positive outcomes are less likely, although, as we shall see in the Close-Up, under some circumstances children are quite capable of self-care.

When we turn to the impact of maternal employment on infants, a murkier picture emerges from research. You may recall that in Chapter 3 we concluded that infants are at slightly greater risk for insecure attachments when their mothers are employed. This is especially true for sons and first borns and when mothers work many hours and the quality of alternative child care is poor.

Other evidence indicates that maternal employment during early years may place children at risk. In one study (Baydar and Brooks-Gunn, 1991), when mothers returned to work prior to their child's first birthday, their children subsequently, as 3- and 4-year-olds, had lower IQ scores and more behavior problems than children whose mothers had not been employed when they were infants. These effects were reduced when mothers worked no more than 10 hours per week and when mothers waited until the infant was at least 9 months old to return to work. In another study (Crockenberg and Litman, 1991), the same degree of negative control (that is, maternal control that is accompanied by feelings of anger or annoyance) produced greater defiance in children of employed mothers than in children of nonemployed mothers.

Based on findings like these, should a mother of an infant or toddler work? If possible, she should avoid returning to full-time employment until her baby is 9 or 10 months old. By this age, the general guidelines are similar to those that we mentioned in Chapter 3. Employment per se is probably not harmful; instead, it only becomes harmful when it reduces the quality of parenting that an infant or toddler receives. When women

CLOSE-UP

Latchkey Children

The term **latchkey** was first used over 200 years ago to describe children who raised a door latch to enter their own homes. At the beginning of the twentieth century, these children were called "dorks" because they carried their own door keys (Robinson, Rowland, and Coleman, 1986). Today the term *latchkey* is used to refer to children who care for themselves after school—approximately 10 percent of all 5- to 13-year-olds in the United States (Galambos and Maggs, 1991). It encompasses a variety of distinct experiences: Children may stay at home alone (sometimes with parental supervision in absentia via the telephone), children may be at friends' homes where adults are sometimes present, or children may be unsupervised in public places, such as shopping malls.

The popular perception is that latchkey children are a frightened, endangered lot. However, research provides little support for this view. To the contrary, the most consistent finding is that children caring for themselves after school fare as well as children in the care of parents or other adults (Lovko and Ullman, 1989). In one study, third, fourth, and fifth graders who cared for themselves were no more anxious, headstrong, or dependent than children cared for by their mothers

(Vandell and Ramanan, 1991). The evidence also indicates that one at-risk group consists of children who have not been exposed to authoritative parenting and who are away from home, unsupervised, after school. This group, compared with children under adult care, children at home or alone, or unsupervised children of authoritative parents, is more prone to the antisocial influences of peers, and they are more likely to engage in problem behavior (Galamabos and Maggs, 1991; Steinberg, 1986).

This generally rosy picture does *not* mean that parents should begin a program of self-care with little planning. Robinson, Rowland, and Coleman (1986) suggest that parents contemplating self-care for their children should ask themselves the following eight questions:

Is the child old enough to be left alone?

Is the child emotionally mature enough, regardless of age, to assume the responsibility of self-care?

Has the child been adequately prepared for the basics of self-care?

Does the child reside in a safe neighborhood where crime is low and community cohesion is high?

who are employed have suitable child-care arrangements and are happy with these arrangements and with their employment, the risks to infants and toddlers are reduced.

Fathers

During the nineteenth century and the first half of the twentieth century, fathers in the United States rarely played more than a minor role in the care and socialization of infants and young children. In fact, most mammals divide responsibility so that the male provides for the protection

Latchkey Used to refer to children who care for themselves after school.

Can neighbors and community facilities be depended upon as support systems?

Does the child stay home for short time periods?

Do the parents have a positive attitude toward the child's latchkey experience?

Does the child's self-care arrangement provide for some type of distal or proximate adult supervision? (p. 59)

If each of these questions can be answered "yes,"

then self-care will probably work. In this case, it is essential that children are prepared for self-care. They need to know after-school routines (for example, acceptable ways of getting home from school and how to check in with a parent), rules for their own behavior after school (for example, acceptable and unacceptable activities), and how to handle emergencies (Peterson, 1989). Simple lists with this information, like the one shown in Figure 9-10, posted conspicuously, often reassure children.

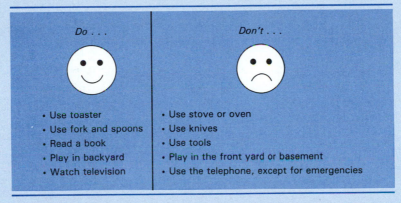

FIGURE 9-10

A check-list that provides rules for children's behavior is useful for children who care for themselves after school.

(Reprinted with the permission of Lexington Books, an imprint of Macmillan, Inc., from Latchkey Kids: Unlocking Doors for Children and Their Families *by Bryan E. Robinson, Bobbie H. Rowland, and Mick Coleman. Copyright © 1986 by Lexington Books.)*

and safety of the female and offspring, but does not share the daily responsibilities of child rearing with the female. But this system is not a biological imperative for humans or for other animals. Primate males from species that ordinarily leave the child rearing to females will assume caregiving responsibilities when females are absent; the same is true of human fathers (Parke and Suomi, 1981). Moreover, fathers in North America and elsewhere are doing more and more caregiving for their children, including quite young children and infants. Recently, with more and more mothers working outside the home, fathers are assuming more responsibility for child care than ever before (Crouter, Perry-Jenkins, Huston, and McHale, 1987).

Research has shown that fathers fill a distinct role in the rearing of children, different from that typically filled by mothers. As we described in Chapter 3, mothers and fathers interact differently with infants. Fathers engage in more physical-social play; mothers concentrate on intellectual activities. In the presence of the father, mothers tend to take a low-key role, verbalizing less with the infants and generally not interfering in father-infant interactions (Clarke-Stewart, 1978).

After infancy, fathers' involvement in child rearing influences the development of both sons and daughters. Boys' intellectual functioning and academic performance are related to the quality of their relationships with their fathers (Lamb, 1986). Fathers also make significant contributions to their sons' self-esteem and social development. Fathers who are involved, while at the same time setting appropriate limits for their sons, appear to have the most socially mature boys during the elementary school years (Gottfried, Gottfried, and Bathurst, 1988). Boys who become the best adjusted and most interpersonally successful adults tend to grow up in families in which parents have compatible views and are both closely involved in the upbringing of their children. Boys who become juvenile

FIGURE 9-11
Developmental psychologists have come to appreciate the important role that fathers play in caring for their children.

delinquents in adolescence tend to come from father-absent homes or to have very poor relationships with their fathers (Block, 1971).

Fathers also play a role in their daughters' psychological development. Girls' intellectual functioning is related to their relationships with their fathers, but to a lesser extent than boys. Fathers who are themselves relatively masculine in their own behavior but who encourage femininity in their daughters tend to have girls who enjoy relatively smooth sex-role development. Like boys, girls who are the most socially mature tend to come from homes in which both parents are positively involved with their children (Gottfried et al., 1988).

Why does paternal involvement influence children's development? When fathers actively participate in child rearing, this usually means that children benefit from two highly involved parents instead of only one. A father's participation may affect children indirectly as well. Mothers in these families may feel more fulfilled because fathers' efforts allow them to pursue other activities that they find rewarding. Both parents, then, may feel more satisfaction because they are engaged in a range of pleasurable and rewarding pursuits. This, in turn, may provide a warmer and richer family environment for the children (Lamb, 1986).

Thus, mothers and fathers influence children directly, but also indirectly, through their interactions with one another and through the family climate that results. Much the same can be said for siblings, which we examine in the next section, and for grandparents, who are the focus of the following Close-Up.

The Influence of Birth Order and Siblings

The number and spacing of children in a family contribute much to the environment in which children develop. A staggering number of different configurations is possible. Each child may have no siblings, just one, or as many as three, four, five, or more. The siblings may be all boys, all girls, or a combination; the siblings may also be separated by age differences as small as 11 months or as large as 20 or more years. Children may be born first, last, or somewhere in between.

A glimpse at the impact of the number, the configuration, and the spacing of siblings comes from the following account of one daughter's experience:

> I had the distinction of having one brother 6 years older than I—who reportedly greeted me with considerable pride and love. I was followed in $3\frac{1}{2}$ years by two more brothers. This was our family until my sister arrived when I was almost 10 years old. My older brother was a model for me. I was able to follow my brother in important ways, primarily by doing well in school and being active and agile physically. The entire family worked in the family business, which required fairly heavy outdoor physical activities. But as the only female besides my mother for many years, I also participated in household tasks and in caring for my younger brothers. In this respect I became a little mother, caring and bossy. This role was so strong that when I had two sons close in age many years later, I occasionally called them by the names of these brothers—in the correct age order. Despite the

CLOSE-UP

The Black Extended Family

Many black families in the United States include adults other than mothers and fathers. Grandparents as well as aunts and uncles are often present in the same household, creating an **extended family**. Although this arrangement is sometimes found in white families, it is three or four times more prevalent among black families, and it often represents an adaptive adjustment to poverty, unemployment, divorce, and adolescent pregnancy (Wilson, 1989).

Grandmothers in an extended family frequently become involved in rearing their grandchildren. When their daughter is an adolescent mother, the grandmother may be the child's primary caregiver. This arrangement benefits both the adolescent mother and the child. Freed from the obligations of child rearing, the adolescent mother often tries to improve her situation by finishing school, for example. The child benefits because the grandmother is frequently a more effective caregiver than is the child's adolescent mother: Grandmothers are more responsive and less punitive (Wilson, 1989).

Even when grandmothers are not children's primary caregivers, they play an active role in caregiving, typically surpassing the role of fathers (Pearson, Hunter, Ensminger, and Kellam, 1990). In this role, they relieve some of the burden from the mother and contribute to a less stressful family life.

The extended family arrangement works well for children. In terms of achievement and adjustment, children living in extended families resemble

FIGURE 9-12
Grandmothers play an important role in caregiving in many black extended families.

children living in two-parent families, and they tend to be better off than children in single-parent families (Wilson, 1989). The key seems to be not the organization of the family but the environment that it provides: Warmth, support, and guidance are important for children, regardless of the structure of the family.

Extended family A household that includes parents as well as other adult relatives such as grandparents.

fact that I consider my childhood happy, I was lonely for a sister. Not another sibling, but a sister. One of the greatest joys of my life occurred early one Monday morning when my older brother returning on his bicycle from a telephone (as we had no home phone) announced, "It's a girl." Because my older brother was already 16 years of age he was able to visit our sister in the hospital; I had to wait several days. On the day she came home I pretended a stomach ache so that my father allowed me to skip school. I rushed to clean furiously so that all would be ready. For years I believed that my father thought that I had had a stomach ache. My sister has always been special to me. We talk sometimes of how different her family experiences were, as the last child with siblings so much older than she. In a real way, she grew up in a different family than I did.

In the discussion that follows we begin by summarizing a few of the major findings concerning the effects of birth order, then we examine sibling interactions.

EFFECTS OF BIRTH ORDER. Possible differences between first-born and later-born children have been among the most studied aspects of family configuration and socialization. First-born children are generally more successful than later-born children in a variety of ways: They speak at an earlier age, are more active physically, tend to perform better on tests of intellectual ability, are more likely to attend college, and are more likely to be recognized as scholars. They also tend to be somewhat conformist, and they adopt the standards and values of their parents. However, later-born children are more popular (Eaton, Chipperfield, and Singbeil, 1989; Shaffer, 1988).

Only children, that is, children without siblings, have been viewed as selfish and egotistical, dependent, lonely, and unsociable. The founder of developmental psychology, G. Stanley Hall, even declared, "Being an only child is a disease in itself" (Fenton, 1928, p. 547). But the research evidence tells a different story. A recent comprehensive analysis revealed that only children are not disadvantaged. In fact, they are significantly *better* off in many ways than children who grow up with brothers and sisters. Falbo and Polit (1986) analyzed 115 published studies in which "onlys" and "non-onlys" were compared on achievement, adjustment, character, intelligence, and sociability. In no case were onlys worse off than other children. Furthermore, only children achieved more than non-onlys and were also found to have higher intelligence and higher levels of leadership, autonomy, and maturity.

Differences between first-born, later-born, and only children can be traced to parenting. Parents place great importance on their first children; they are tense about handling them; they hold high expectations for them; they give them attention and affection. First borns become the "little adults" in the family, garnering knowledge, power, authority, and responsibility (Shaffer, 1988). With the birth of a sibling, first-born children are no longer the sole focus of parental attention; however, only children derive the benefits (and costs) of exclusive parental attention for a lifetime.

INTERACTIONS BETWEEN SIBLINGS. For many first borns, the birth of a sibling causes distress. Children may become withdrawn or revert to less mature forms of behavior. The distress probably stems from the many changes in the child's world that accompany a sibling's birth, notably an altered relationship with the mother. However, not all children are upset by the arrival of a new brother or sister. Children who are older than 3 years of age adjust better than younger children, and children seem to fare better when their parents are warm, approving, and understanding (Gottlieb and Mendelson, 1990).

As the new infant grows older, it begins to interact more often with older siblings. Throughout childhood, younger siblings tend to be the more submissive. Younger siblings initiate fewer interactions and tend to submit to the wishes of the older brother or sister rather than assert their own will (Abramovitch, Corter, Pepler, and Stanhope, 1986). By the time the younger sibling is approximately 12 years of age, these asymmetries have largely vanished. Children at this age report that sibling relationships are more egalitarian and less intense than they were previously (Buhrmester and Furman, 1990).

The diversity of sibling relationships during childhood is extraordinary. Some relationships are marked by warmth and harmony; these siblings are one another's best friends in ways that nonsiblings can never be. Other sibling relationships are dominated by conflict and competition; they produce stress because the unpleasant relationship cannot be easily avoided.

Many factors help to define the quality of interactions between siblings. Generally, relationships between siblings of the same sex are warmer and less conflict prone than those between siblings of the opposite sex (Dunn and Kendrick, 1981). Sibling relationships are generally more harmonious when mothers are equally affectionate, responsive, and controlling toward all children; conflicts arise when siblings perceive that they are being treated differently (Stocker, Dunn, and Plomin, 1989). Finally, the quality of sibling relationships reflects the quality of family relationships generally: MacKinnon (1989) reported a correlation of 0.51 between the quality of sibling relationships and the quality of the husband-wife relationship.

FIGURE 9-13

The birth of a sibling can be a traumatic event for children, particularly for those who are younger than 3 years of age and whose parents are not warm and affectionate.

The Changing Family

DIVORCE. The most striking change in marriage and family patterns in the past few decades is the dramatic increase in the divorce rate. In the 1980s, the proportion of children who experienced their parents' marital disruption grew to nearly 50 percent (Chase-Lansdale and Hetherington, 1990).

The domestic turmoil produced by divorce appears to touch most aspects of children's development. In a recent analysis, Amato and Keith (1991) evaluated the results of 92 separate studies involving a total of more than 13,000 children. They compared children living in intact families with children whose parents had divorced and were now living in single-parent families. Children were compared on seven dimensions: school achievement, conduct, psychological adjustment, self-concept, social adjustment, mother-child relations, and father-child relations. As shown in Figure 9-14, on every dimension, children whose parents had divorced were less well off. They were, for example, less successful in school, had lower self-esteem, and were less well adjusted.

FIGURE 9-14

When compared with children from intact families, children in single-parent families are usually less well off. Shown here are the differences between children in intact families and children in single-parent families for seven dimensions of development. In every case, children from single-parent families have poorer scores than children from intact families.

(From P. R. Amato and B. Keith, "Parental divorce and the well-being of children: A meta-analysis," in Psychological Bulletin, 110, 1991, 26–46.)

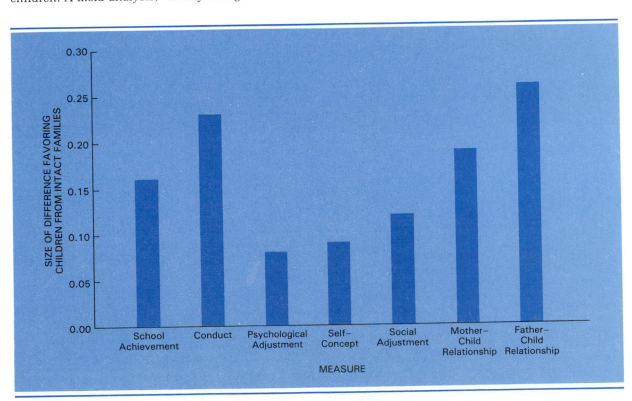

Children and adolescents at all ages were affected by divorce. Generally the pattern was the same for boys and girls, but Amato and Keith (1991) noted two important exceptions: The performance of girls in school was more affected by divorce than the performance of boys. However, divorce was associated with more problems of social adjustment for boys than for girls.

The harm to children associated with divorce stems from several sources (Amato and Keith, 1991). First, the absence of one parent means that children lose a role model, a source of practical help and emotional support, and a supervisor. Second, children in single-parent families experience economic hardship, which can influence their development in many ways. For example, the custodial parent may spend more time away from home earning income. Or money problems may create stress for the custodial parent, draining emotional resources that could be used for parenting.

Third and probably most important, the conflict that gives rise to marital disruption is very painful for children. Among intact families, exposure to marital conflict is associated with maladjustment in children: When the parents' relationship is marked by discord, common outcomes for the children are behavior problems, social immaturity, and poorer grades (Grych and Fincham, 1990). According to this line of reasoning, many of the consequences that we attribute to divorce actually stem from marital conflict that precedes and contributes to the divorce. Supporting this argument are elaborate longitudinal studies of children living in Great Britain and in the United States. In these studies, Cherlin and his colleagues (1991) found that much but not all of the harm associated with divorce was evident prior to the divorce.

We do not want to paint too dark a picture. Divorce does not always make life worse for a child. Children may be better off in a single-parent family than in a two-parent family riddled with conflicts and fights between parents (Amato and Keith, 1991). Moreover, children differ greatly in their reactions to divorce. Those who adjust well appear to come from homes in which there is relatively little change in financial situation, a low level of parental conflict, and agreement between parents on discipline (Hetherington, 1989). Children's adjustment to divorce is also related to their overall adjustment; the better adjusted a youngster is in general, the better he or she adjusts to divorce. Children who live with same-sex parents (boys with their fathers and girls with their mothers) tend to be better adjusted than those living with the opposite-sex parent (Santrock and Warshak, 1986).

Many of the adverse effects of divorce on children are only temporary. Within two years after divorce, most youngsters have overcome their hostility and readjusted to the new situation (Chase-Lansdale and Hetherington, 1991). Additional cause for optimism also emerges in Amato and Keith's (1991) analysis. Compared with studies conducted prior to 1979, more recent studies show that the harmful effects of divorce are smaller. In addition, the effects of divorce are smaller in studies conducted in the United States than in studies conducted in other countries where divorce is less common. Both of these results indicate that as divorce

Socialization and the Family

Remarried families
Families in which at least one of the adults has been married previously and has children from that marriage.

becomes more common, it becomes less harmful. Perhaps the more frequent incidence of divorce has reduced the stigma associated with divorce (Barber and Eccles, 1992). Another possibility is that higher divorce rates have led to a greater awareness among parents and mental-health professionals of the need to reduce the distress that divorce can cause in children.

REMARRIED FAMILIES. It is increasingly common for people to divorce and then marry for a second time, bringing to the new marriage (psychologically or literally) children from the previous marriage. Such families have been referred to as stepfamilies, but the term **remarried families** is a less stigmatizing label for what is inherently a very trying situation for all concerned (Wald, 1981). The first problem to be overcome is that people often remarry with the hope that their new marriage will be an idealized version of the previous, failed marriage. In reality, a remarriage is a far more complex arrangement to manage than a first marriage. It does not simply replace previous relationships, but instead it complicates them. "It has to be more complex," observed Leonard Friedman, "because there are many more relationships. The new ones are added on to the set of old ones, with many more possibilities for triangulation, conflicting loyalties, conflicts of interest, and guilt" (1983, p. 279).

Because relatively few fathers are custodial parents, most of the research on remarriage has focused on single mothers who remarry. When their children are compared with children in intact families, differences usually favor the latter children. What is striking in this research, however, is the different impact on sons and daughters. After an initial period of adjustment to the new marriage, boys sometimes benefit from the presence of a stepfather but girls do not. Apparently many single mothers establish warm, intimate relationships with their daughters. These relationships are often threatened by remarriage, causing daughters to resent their stepfathers (Vuchinich, Hetherington, Vuchinich, and Clingempeel, 1991).

FIGURE 9-15

Step by Step is a current television program depicting the lives of a woman with children who marries a man with children of his own. This program fairly depicts the complex interactions and resultant problems that can be involved in families formed by a remarriage.

Clearly, the task for stepfathers (and, perhaps, stepmothers) is to appear involved with and interested in their stepchildren without intruding on established relationships. The task for newly remarried single mothers (and, perhaps, remarried single fathers) is to be sure that energy and affection for their new spouse does not come at the expense of the children. Unfortunately, research can not yet provide firm guidelines about a proper balance that will best serve both the new marriage and the children of the prior marriage.

Child Abuse

Although the family is supposed to care for, socialize, and optimize the potential of children, it sometimes falls short of these goals. Children may be neglected, both physically and psychologically. And they may be abused—that is, physically, sexually, or psychologically harmed. This grave problem has not been solved, but we are learning more about it and how to deal with it. Child abuse—that is, physically, sexually, or psychologically harming children—has come to be seen as reaching almost epidemic proportions in the United States.

The extent of physical abuse is difficult to estimate. One reason is that confrontations usually occur in the home. Also, some victims are afraid to mention the situation or are not in a position to do so. Preschoolers are often unable to report their troubles and adults may question the credibility of their stories. Abusers, too, are afraid or ashamed to tell the truth about their behavior. Given these considerations, it is understandable that estimates of abuse vary widely, ranging from 500,000 cases annually in the United States to nearly 2.5 million (Widom, 1989).

Some children are more likely than others to be the targets of abuse. Children in the first three years of life seem most vulnerable (Fontana, 1973). Sons are somewhat more likely to be abused than daughters; moreover, a particular child in a family may be the only one to be abused. Children who are born prematurely are at risk for abuse, as are the physically and mentally handicapped and perhaps the temperamentally difficult child (Vasta, 1982).

The effects of abuse are pervasive and long lasting. Of course, severe physical abuse can cause neurological and brain tissue damage. Even when there is no physical damage, abused children suffer from impaired intellectual functioning, as seen in lower performance on IQ tests. They are more likely than other children to have learning disorders, and are consistently behind nonabused peers in language comprehension and production (Trickett, Aber, Carlson, and Cicchetti, 1991). Social development suffers, too. Abused children are often aggressive toward other children, and typically have either hostile or distant relationships with teachers and other adults. They seem to view the world as a mean and scary place (Haskett and Kistner, 1991).

Not too long ago the stereotypic child abuser was cast as a disturbed, nearly deranged individual. In fact, only about 5 percent of all physical abusers suffer from extreme psychopathology. Most parents who abuse cannot be discriminated from nonabusing parents on the basis of standard

FIGURE 9-16
Child abuse is a problem of monumental proportions with grave consequences to the child involved and to society at large.

psychiatric criteria (Wolfe, 1985). However, abusing parents do appear to be more emotionally reactive to child misconduct than are other parents (Wolfe, Fairbank, Kelly, and Bradlyn, 1983), and they appear to perceive their children's behavior and their own lives as worse than they really are (Mash, Johnston, and Kovitz, 1983).

Abusing and nonabusing parents differ in other ways as well. One of the clearest differences appears to be in parenting skills. Abusing parents generally rely upon an authoritarian approach to parenting; they do not seem to know how to set up positive contingencies or how to reason with their children effectively (Trickett and Kuczynski, 1986). Instead, they are likely to yell, make threats, and continuously express annoyance and frustration (Burgess and Richardson, 1984). Abusing parents also tend to engage in many more aversive than positive interactions with their marriage partners than do nonabusers (Lorber, Felton, and Reid, 1984). In short, the picture of the typical abusing parent that has now emerged is a somewhat negativistic person who lacks the social skills needed to deal with other people in positive, cooperative, and friendly ways.

In many cases parental behavior can be linked to a harsh upbringing that the parents themselves experienced as children. Simons and his colleagues (1991) tested this model of "intergenerational transmission of harsh parenting" by assessing more than 900 mothers and fathers of seventh-grade boys and girls. Their findings indicated that mothers whose own childhood was marked by harsh discipline from their mothers tended to be harsh with both sons and daughters. Fathers whose mothers had disciplined them harshly were harsh with their sons but not their daughters. For these adults, harsh discipline from their fathers affected their own disciplinary practices indirectly: It resulted in more hostile personalities and this was associated with harsh parenting.

A comprehensive account of child abuse must also consider broad social factors such as family stress and society's attitudes. Large family size, low income, low educational levels, and unemployment are related to abuse (Gil, 1979). Social isolation of the family and marital conflict are often present (Belsky, 1980; Friedman, Sandler, Hernandez, and Wolfe, 1981). The age-old belief that children are the property of the family, to be dealt with as the family wishes, also contributes to abusive parenting.

SEXUAL ABUSE. In the past few years, child sexual abuse has captured a great deal of media attention. Child sexual abuse runs a gamut of severity from unwanted touching of clothed body parts to forced oral, anal, or genital intercourse. Extreme social disapproval makes it almost impossible to get a reasonable estimate of the prevalence of child sexual abuse, but studies of those who have been abused suggest the problem may be widespread and that the effects are extremely serious for the child, especially when some type of intercourse is involved. In contrast to physical abuse, the majority of victims of child sexual abuse are female and almost all of the perpetrators are male. The most common perpetrators appear to be fathers and stepfathers (Browne and Finkelhor, 1986).

The immediate effects of being the victim of sexual abuse as a child include a complex of strong negative emotions (fear, hostility, and guilt), sleep disturbance, and heightened inappropriate sexual interest, as seen in such behavior as displaying the genitals. Equally serious are the long-term effects. Adults who were abused as children are considerably more likely than nonabused adults to be depressed, suffer from low self-esteem, and to attempt suicide on one or more occasions. Women who have been victims of incest as children often harbor feelings of rage (more often directed toward their mothers than toward their fathers). Virtually all incest victims seem to have later difficulty with their sexuality. Many do not marry, and those who do run a considerably higher than average chance of being abused by their husbands. They are almost five times as likely as other women to repeatedly be victims of rape. They often perceive themselves to be particularly promiscuous, although in fact they are no more promiscuous than other women (Browne and Finkelhor, 1986).

TREATMENT. Only when abuse is reported can parents and children be treated, so the great majority of child abusers (including almost all sexual abusers of children) go untreated. Even among those who receive treatment, the problem is often intractable. Treatment of child abuse typically focuses on parental counseling and parent-child interaction. Reported improvement rates range from 40 percent to 80 percent. A reasonable rule of thumb is that even the best of treatments—a combination of parent aides or Parents Anonymous support groups and the assignment of individual case workers—can be expected to produce the reduction or elimination of abuse in no more than about half of all cases. There is thus great need for prevention. This can come in the form of parental education in child development and management and in the identification, support, and counseling of families at high risk for child abuse.

SUMMARY

1. Socialization is the entire set of events and processes by which children acquire the beliefs and behaviors of the particular society and subgroup into which they were born.

2. Socialization is a complex process, influenced indirectly by the general ecology and history of the group's culture and subculture, by the economic and social structures, and by the child-care customs.

3. Every culture appears to be concerned about enculturation—teaching children the culture's rules and habits. Furthermore, parents everywhere appear to have the same hierarchy of goals for their children, beginning with physical safety and survival of children, then development in children of the capacity for economic self-maintenance, and finally development in children of the ability to strive for higher forms of self-actualization.

4. The three principal modes of socialization are direct instruction, shaping, and modeling. All three are used to teach children about the social roles they and others can play in the culture, and all three are affected by social cognition, the child's understanding of social matters.

5. Direct instruction provides both information on what to do and behavioral instigation—urging or persuading someone to adopt a particular goal or follow a particular course of action. Direct instruction can provide a motive to learn or act differently and the cognitive structure with which to learn or act by identifying the relevant and irrelevant attributes of a situation.

6. Shaping is the application of the basic conditioning processes to achieve social goals. It works by providing consequences that will secure a child's attention and motivate him or her. Consequences can involve either reinforcement or punishment, which in turn may be either positive (when the child receives something from a socializing agent) or negative (when the child has something taken away by a socializing agent). Time-out and response cost are the two major forms of negative punishment.

7. Modeling involves observing and imitating the behavior of others, including an endless array of real people and media characters. Modeling involves more than simple imitation. A model's behavior, for example, can be accepted as a guide for what should not be done (counterimitation); it can also produce more general inhibitory and disinhibitory effects on whole classes of responses.

8. Children are not the passive recipients of efforts to socialize them. Rather, all socialization efforts are mediated by the child's understanding of the complex set of expectations, roles, and events that form the context for all his or her actions.

9. Parents, peers, and teachers act as direct agents of socialization. However, these people not only influence the children with whom they come into contact, but also are influenced by them. Thus, we say that all socialization involves reciprocal influence.

10. The family is the first major force responsible for socializing the child. Marked differences in parenting styles have been noted. Four common styles are authoritarian, authoritative, indulgent-permissive, and indifferent-uninvolved. Of these, the authoritative style is most consistently related to positive developmental outcomes. Parental behavior is also influenced by the attributions that parents make concerning their children's competence.

11. The mother is the single most important person in the life of most infants and young children, and the mother is thus the primary socialization agent. When the mother is employed, her school-age children and adolescents, particularly her daughters, are better adjusted and more successful in school. This pattern depends upon the amount of time that the mother works, her attitudes toward work, and the quality of alternative care. When the mothers of infants and toddlers are employed, their children may obtain lower scores on IQ tests and may show increased defiance of their parents.

12. Latchkey children are without adult supervision after school. Contrary to popular stereotypes, these children are not necessarily at risk; most research shows that they do not differ from children cared for after school by parents. Behavior problems are more likely, however, in children who are unsupervised while away from home and whose parents do not use authoritative parenting.

13. Fathers also make an important contribution to children's social and intellectual development. For both sons and daughters, paternal involvement and warmth is consistently related to more advanced cognitive and social development.

14. The family configuration influences development. First-born and only children tend to be more successful than other children, but later-born children tend to be more popular. Children can be distressed by the birth of a sibling. But this distress is less in older children, and it is less when parents provide emotional warmth toward the older siblings. Sibling interactions are dominated by older siblings at first but become egalitarian by the time the younger sibling is 12 years old. Overall, siblings get along better when they are of the same sex, when they believe they are treated fairly by parents, and when family interactions are generally positive.

15. Almost half of all youngsters in the United States experience a divorce at some time during their childhood or adolescence. Children in single-parent families fare poorly on most psychological measures, reflecting the absence of one parent, economic distress, and marital discord. The harm associated with divorce and marital distress lessens over time and is affected by a number of factors, such as the child's overall adjustment and whether the child resides with the same-sex or opposite-sex parent. Remarriage is also stressful, particularly for daughters living with stepfathers.

16.   Abused children, who are commonly younger children, particularly boys, tend to lag behind in both cognitive and social development. Their parents typically do not suffer from psychopathology but lack the social skills needed to deal with their children. Children who are victims of sexual abuse are generally depressed, have low self-esteem, and have sexual problems later in life. Individuals who abuse are treated through counseling, but recent efforts to curb child abuse have been directed toward prevention through education.

Interacting with Others

We begin learning how to get along with others from the moment we are born, and we never really stop. Very few of us will spend our lives in a mountain cave or a desert hut; we will be with other people most of the time. Humans need other humans—to survive and to function well and to enjoy life to its fullest. The first relationships with other people are established within the family, a phenomenon that we examined in detail in Chapters 3 and 9. However, the scope of social relationships expands rapidly beyond the family, and, in particular, begins to include one's peers. The nature of these relationships is the focus of this chapter. Let's start with some examples illustrating the issues that we will consider.

▶   If two 9-month-olds are together, they will look at each other and maybe smile or vocalize, behaviors that certainly suggest a rudimentary social exchange. If two 9-year-olds are together, they may wrestle and hit each other playfully. This, too, represents a form of social exchange, but of vastly greater complexity than the infants' looking, smiling, and vocalizing. The nature of these developmental changes in peer interactions will be addressed in the first section of the chapter.

▶   School-age children who are best friends will often compete viciously with each other, as if losing would be absolutely unbearable. Adolescent best friends, in contrast, just as earnestly avoid such competition. Apparently the nature of best friendships changes between childhood and adolescence in a way that transforms the role of competition. This phenomenon and other features of friendship provide the focus of the second section of the chapter.

▶   Nerds and geeks are smart but dress poorly, whereas jocks play sports and drink beer. Groups such as these are particularly salient during late childhood and adolescence, and they play a remarkable role in peer interaction during these years. We explore the properties of children's and adolescents' groups in the third section of this chapter.

▶   Every elementary school classroom seems to have at least one "star"— a child whom most everyone wishes to befriend. Sadly, most classrooms also contain children who are rejected by nearly all their classmates. What causes some individuals to become so popular or unpopular at such relatively young ages? Answers to these questions will come in the fourth part of this chapter.   ◀

RELATIONSHIPS WITH PEERS

Interactions with peers begin early in life. Most 6- to 12-month-old infants growing up in the United States and Canada see other infants at least once a week. Some of these encounters come about when parents deliberately bring their babies together to play. Other meetings take place without explicit social intent, as when infants interact at the same day-care center. As you would imagine, "interactions" between young babies are limited by their lack of cognitive, social, linguistic, and motor skills. However, between 6 and 12 months, social overtures become more frequent and more often lead to coordinated but simple social interactions. One infant

FIGURE 10-1
These infants are engaged in parallel play. Each is playing separately but near the other, and each infant frequently looks at what the other is doing.

may smile at another, who responds by vocalizing (Vandell, Wilson, and Buchanan, 1980).

By the first birthday, the infant's growing language and motor skills pave the way for more complex encounters with peers. Between 1 and 2 years of age, coordinated social actions become much more common. Howes (1988; Howes, Unger, and Seidner, 1989) described a sequence of three stages of interaction between 1-year-olds. From 12 to 15 months, **parallel play** is common (see Figure 10-1). Each toddler is involved in his or her own distinct play, but each maintains proximity to and frequent eye contact with the other. The rudimentary social exchanges from the first year continue but are more often successful: A smile or vocalization from one infant will more likely produce a response in the other.

Beginning at about 15 months, toddlers become involved in similar activities and social exchanges become more elaborate. Imitation emerges as an important part of peer interaction: If one toddler throws a ball, another may throw a bean bag. When Eckerman and her colleagues (1989) observed pairs of 16-month-olds at play, they recorded about one imitative act per minute. By the time children were 28 months old, this figure had increased to more than three imitative acts per minute.

At approximately 20 months of age, interactions between youngsters come to be linked by a common play theme. Recognizable games such as "hide-and-seek" or "chase" emerge. Many of these games involve distinct roles (for example, as hider and seeker), and children begin to take turns playing each role.

THE PRESCHOOL YEARS. Between 2 and 5 years of age, children's cognitive and linguistic skills expand rapidly. These changes make possible more sophisticated interactions with peers. A form of play that becomes more common is **cooperative play**, in which play is organized around a particular theme and in which children have distinct roles that relate to

Parallel play A form of interaction common in infancy in which two or more youngsters play independently but near each other, while maintaining eye contact with each other.

Cooperative play A form of play common during the preschool years in which play revolves around a common theme and in which children have specified roles.

FIGURE 10-2
As youngsters near their second birthday, their play becomes linked by a common theme, which may involve distinct roles for the children, such as the "hider" and "seeker" roles depicted here.

that theme (Parten, 1932). The building of a castle of blocks, in which each youngster takes responsibility for constructing a different part of the building, illustrates this form of cooperative play.

Cooperative play complements other forms of play during the preschool years. Parallel play is still common. And many children continue to play alone; such solitary play is frequent and is not necessarily unhealthy. Youngsters who spend time during free play looking at books, solving puzzles, or drawing usually fare quite well. They typically spend time in some forms of social play and, when they do, interact easily with peers (Rubin, 1982).

A hallmark of play during the preschool years is the emergence of make-believe or play that involves pretending (called *pretend play*). Even toddlers will engage in rudimentary pretend play. They will have conversations on toy telephones or drink from toy coffee cups. For these children, however, realistic props are necessary. The toy telephones and coffee cups resemble real phones and cups; it is the conversational partner and the liquid consumed that are imaginary.

Make believe becomes more elaborate over the preschool years. Children become less dependent upon realistic-looking props: A ruler may serve as a dagger, a pencil as a magic wand or a shoe box as a crib. These changes can be traced to the child's growing ability to use symbols (Black, 1989). And solitary pretend play is joined by social pretend play in which

318

FIGURE 10-3
Make-believe is an
important part of
preschoolers' play and
may help them to
understand feelings such
as fear or anger.

playmates make believe together. Children better coordinate their pretend play as they get older, producing an activity of great complexity:

> ...children must become coplaywrights, codirectors, coactors, and vicarious actors, without getting confused about which of these roles they or a playmate are momentarily adopting. Children must (as playwrights) decide on the plot, and as directors decide on role distribution and props in order to (as coactors and vicarious actors) perform the make-believe drama. To do this successfully, they must repeatedly alternate between stage-managing and acting, because the creation of make-believe plots proceeds on an invent-as-you-go principle: negotiations about the plot are interspersed with enactments of it. (Bretherton, 1989, p. 384).

Mastering these many roles is an impressive accomplishment, one that occurs gradually over the preschool years.

Make-believe is more than just entertainment for youngsters. Analyses of the themes of pretend play indicate that children often use make believe to explore emotion-laden topics, such as understanding and conquering their fears. One investigator (Gottman, 1986) described children who were afraid of the dark and who frequently used this theme in their make-believe, comforting their dolls, who were also afraid of the dark. When darkness was no longer distressing to the children, this topic disappeared from their pretend play. Make-believe evidently allowed the children to understand and gain control of their fear of darkness. Other feelings—of anger, joy, and affection—can be probed within the safety of a make-believe world that can, when necessary, be quickly abandoned for reality.

CHILDHOOD AND ADOLESCENCE. Continued cognitive growth in childhood and adolescence allows ever more sophisticated interaction with peers. Social interaction becomes more governed by rules. Children learn social rules that regulate their exchanges with others. They learn to be polite, to take turns, to be good sports, and so on—the list of pertinent cultural rules is long, if not endless. Complex rules also are common in the games that are popular at this age. Elementary school children enjoy board games like checkers and begin to participate in sports, such as soccer and baseball, that have elaborate sets of rules.

To rule-governed play we must add two other distinctive features of peer interaction during childhood and adolescence. School-age children often chase one another, wrestle, and engage in mock fighting. This **rough-and-tumble play** is not aggressive behavior: The children involved are often friends and the interaction is marked by smiles and laughter, not by anger (Pellegrini, 1989). Rough-and-tumble play is not just a boys' activity; girls have rough-and-tumble play as well, although they tend to emphasize running and chasing over wrestling and fighting (see Figure 10-4). These behaviors may be a legacy from evolution. Young monkeys are often seen playing in much the same manner, behavior that is apparently a precursor to more serious fighting later that will establish the dominant individuals within the group.

FIGURE 10-4
Children often enjoy rough-and-tumble play, which can resemble aggressive behavior but is not, and is displayed between friends. Boys often wrestle and mock fight; girls, like the ones shown here, are more likely to chase one another.

Rough-and-tumble play
A form of play common among school-age children that involves chasing, wrestling, or mock fighting, not truly aggressive behavior.

A final noteworthy change is the emergence of groups in children's and adolescents' interactions. For younger children, relations with peers are usually thought of as being between individuals. However, beginning at about 9 or 10 years of age, twosomes become embedded in a larger structure, the social group. For the rest of childhood and most of adolescence, the group plays a critical role in peer interactions, as we shall see later in this chapter (Hartup, 1983).

Parental Influence on Peer Relations

Parents influence their children's peer relationships both directly and indirectly. Parents often exert control over their children's interactions with peers. With infants, this direct control might involve arranging for one's infant to be with other babies for "play time." With older children and adolescents, parents may limit interactions with certain peers or in certain contexts. For example, a mother might prohibit her 13-year-old son from "hanging out" at a mall in a large group of boys (Hartup, 1992).

Parents' involvement often results in more successful social interaction. Preschoolers whose parents arrange frequent contacts with peers have more playmates, and, at least for boys, are better liked (Ladd and Golter, 1988). In addition, parental supervision of children's play often results in more cooperative and longer play between children (Parke and Bahvnagri, 1989).

FIGURE 10-5
Mothers of infants often organize opportunities for their infants to play with other babies.

Just as important as the direct influence of parental management is the indirect impact of the parent-child relationship on the child's peer relationships. Of course, parent-child relationships differ in many respects from peer relationships. For example, relationships between peers tend to be relatively egalitarian, whereas parents exert the greater control in parent-child relationships. Nevertheless, most developmental psychologists believe that parent-child relationships are intimately linked to children's peer relationships because the parent-child relationship sets the stage for peer relationships.

Evidence that supports this view was presented in Chapter 3, in which we mentioned that quality of attachment is related to the quality of children's later peer relationships. Children who are securely attached usually have more successful peer relationships than do children with insecure attachments. For example, Vandell and her colleagues (1988) studied interactions between twins. They compared pairs in which both twins were securely attached to the mother with pairs in which one or both of the twins were insecurely attached. Interactions between twins who were securely attached occurred more often and were longer than were interactions between twins in which at least one child was not securely attached.

Why should the quality of attachment between parent and child predict the success of children's peer relationships? One view is that the child's relationship with his or her parents is the prototype for all subsequent social relationships. It serves as a "working model" of all subsequent relationships. Thus, if the attachment relation is of high quality and is emotionally satisfying, this may encourage children to form relationships with other people. Another possibility is that, with a secure attachment relationship with the mother, an infant feels more confident exploring the environment, which typically provides the child with more opportunities to interact with peers. These answers are not mutually exclusive; both may contribute to the relative ease with which securely attached children interact with their peers (Hartup, 1992).

Enhancing Cooperation

Societies are to a great extent built on cooperation, which refers to behavior in which two or more people work together for mutual benefit. Generally speaking, cooperative behavior increases with age. As children become less egocentric in their views of the world, they come to appreciate the benefits of working with others. They also acquire the cognitive and social skills that are necessary for effective cooperation.

Nevertheless, cooperative behavior is strongly influenced by the context. Cultures differ in the emphasis that they place on cooperation, a difference that can be seen in children's willingness to cooperate with their peers. Orlick, Zhou, and Partington (1990) observed 5-year-olds in kindergarten classes in Beijing, China, and in Ottawa, Canada. All interactions between children were scored as either *cooperative*, in which one child helped or was supportive of a peer, or *conflicted*, in which one child aggressed against or was inconsiderate of a peer. Among Chinese 5-year-

olds, 85 percent of the interactions were cooperative, but only 15 percent were conflicted; for Canadian 5-year-olds, only 22 percent of the interactions were cooperative, whereas 78 percent were conflicted. Apparently, Chinese 5-year-olds have learned the emphasis in their culture on the importance of sharing and helping.

More immediate forces also dictate whether children will cooperate. Whether people behave cooperatively or competitively is likely to be determined both by the structure of the situation and by the attitudes they bring with them. Such situational influences on cooperation were revealed by Brady, Newcomb, and Hartup (1983), who studied the behavior of first-, third- and fifth-grade children as they played a board game in which the aim was to cross colored bridges. The rules of the game were varied so that some children at each grade were told that the number of bridges that they crossed would determine the prize that they received at the end. Other children were told that the number of bridges that they *and* their opponent cross would determine the prize. The other player, who was said to be in an adjacent room, was actually nonexistent. The moves of the other player, transmitted to the child by an intercom, were controlled and programmed by the experimenters. Sometimes the fictitious player's moves were set up to facilitate the progress of the subject (that is, to be cooperative); sometimes the moves were set up to block or impede the progress of the subject (that is, to be competitive).

For all three age groups, the behavior of the fictitious companion had a strong effect on the subject's own behavior: Cooperative companions produced cooperative responses and competitive companions produced competitive responses. The rules linking the prize to performance had virtually no effect on the first graders. They willingly cooperated with a cooperative companion even in a competitive situation in which cooperation would assure that they would lose the game. They were equally likely to impede the progress of a competitive companion even though they hurt themselves by doing so. In contrast, the third and fifth graders were decidedly more sophisticated. They took both their companion's behavior and the rules of the game into account. They made the most cooperative responses when dealing with a cooperative companion in a cooperative situation and the least cooperative responses when facing a competitive companion in a competitive situation.

These results indicate that we can stimulate older children to be cooperative if situations are structured in terms of mutual gain. A "we" rather than an "I" orientation seems to be important, so that children see themselves as working *with* rather than against each other. Not surprisingly, direct experience with the positive consequences of cooperation increases the likelihood that such behavior will occur. Guiding children into practical cooperative relationships and letting them directly experience the benefits markedly increases cooperation.

Finally, modeled examples of cooperative behavior by other children can have a powerful influence. In one study (Liebert, Sprafkin, and Poulos, 1975), children were exposed to a 30-second television spot designed to teach cooperation through a positive example. "The Swing," as this spot was called, opens with a boy and girl running across a field to reach the last remaining swing on a playground; they both reach the swing at the same time and immediately begin to struggle over it. After a moment during which battle seems inevitable, one of the youngsters produces the insight that they should take turns and suggests that the other child go first. Each of the children is finally shown taking her or his turn, joyfully swinging through the air with the help of the other, while an announcer's voice says: "There are lots of things you can do when two people want the same thing. One is to take turns . . . and that's a good one." Children exposed to this example are considerably more likely to exhibit cooperative behavior in a test situation (see Figure 10-7).

Mutually satisfying interactions of this sort are central to friendship, which we discuss in the next section.

FIGURE 10-7

The effects of exposure to a cooperatively oriented television spot, *The Swing*, on children's cooperative behavior. Children in a control group were shown TV spots that did not have cooperative messages. In the test situations, children could cooperate by taking turns or they could compete unfruitfully.

(From Liebert, Sprafkin, and Poulous, "Selling cooperation to children," in W. S. Hale et al., Proceedings of the 20th Annual Conference of the Advertising Research Foundation. © 1975, *reprinted by permission of the Advertising Research Foundation, New York.)*

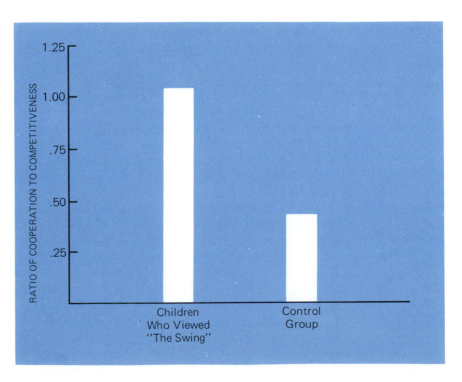

FRIENDSHIP

The ability to establish and maintain friendships lies at the very heart of human social existence. People everywhere seek friends with whom they can share thoughts, feelings, and the meaning of their lives. Over the course of a lifetime, having at least a few people as true friends is one of the great joys of having lived fully and well.

Among the pioneers in the study of friendship was Harry Stack Sullivan, a psychiatrist who suggested that the development of interpersonal relationships follows a stagelike sequence. Between the ages of 2 and 5, children's most important relationships are with adults, on whom they rely for their physical, social, and emotional needs. In the second stage, roughly between the ages of 4 and 8, children turn to peers as playmates and companions. But the relationships are typically short and the interactions superficial and self-serving.

The third stage, which occurs between the ages of 8 and 11, is the stage of **chumship**. In this stage children are able for the first time to form intense attachments to other children of the same sex. Chumships are characterized by intimacy and reciprocity. They are reasonably stable over time, and involve a mutual give and take from which children learn to recognize and appreciate how the thoughts and feelings of others may be different from their own.

In general, research has supported the broad outline of Sullivan's position (Selman, 1981). Let's look at this work in more detail.

Developmental Change in the Meaning of Friendship

As we saw in the first part of this chapter, during the toddler years children begin to offer, accept, and share toys; they copy each other's motor acts in turn-taking fashion; and they interact verbally in more varied and complex ways. From these initial social ventures, children find other children with whom they interact easily and comfortably. They soon prefer interactions with these peers and friendships take root.

This mutual attraction that we associate with friendship can be seen in very young children. Howes (1983) observed 10-, 20-, and 42-month-old children as they interacted with peers in a day-care facility. She defined a pair of children as friends if (a) their overtures to one another to play were successful at least half the time, (b) their interactions together involved complementary play (for example, in playing games, the children would alternate roles), and (c) their interactions included the exchange of positive emotions (for example, one child would smile and the other would laugh). That is, friendship was defined by the presence of mutual preference, skilled interaction, and mutual enjoyment. According to these criteria, 14 percent of the pairs of 10-month-olds were friends, compared to 40 percent of the 20- and 42-month-olds.

Chumship The last of Sullivan's phases of friendship in which children form intimate and reciprocal relationships with peers.

These early friendships tend to be less stable than later ones. Certainly part of this instability stems from the fact that friendships require time spent together but preschoolers rarely are allowed by their parents to roam freely when they are with their friends. Consequently, parents must play an active role in maintaining their preschool children's friendships.

The mutual attraction and time spent together that is the essence of first friendships continues, of course, in friendships among older children and adolescents. But friendships take on an additional dimension as children develop: They understand that friends help one another, especially in times of need (Berndt and Perry, 1990).

As friendships take on more dimensions, children begin to differentiate types of relationships with peers. When kindergarten-age children are asked to name their friends, many will name all of their classmates. In contrast, adults often distinguish among a *best* friend, *close* friends, *good* friends, colleagues, and acquaintances (Berndt, 1988). This sharpening of the distinction between friends and acquaintances and between various degrees of friendship occurs gradually during childhood. Typically, 8-year-olds distinguish friends from acquaintances, expecting greater loyalty and positive behavior from friends than from acquaintances. However, by age 10, these contrasts between friends and acquaintances are much more clear-cut (Berndt and Perry, 1986).

Friendships become more stable over the course of childhood. In one study, Berndt and Hoyle (1985) interviewed first graders and fourth graders during the fall to identify pairs of friends. They returned to the school in the spring, about five months later, and repeated their interviews. Among the first graders, about half the fall friendships lasted until spring; among the fourth graders, however, three-quarters of the fall friendships were intact in spring. These figures, particularly for the older children, undermine the popular folklore that childhood friendships are in a constant state of flux. Some friends drift apart and new friendships are formed, but these changes occur gradually.

ADOLESCENT FRIENDSHIPS. Friendships take on a special importance during early adolescence. Adolescents themselves report spending more time talking to peers than doing anything else; they also report that they are most happy when talking with peers (Berndt and Perry, 1990). Several factors make the increased importance of friendships during adolescence both possible and desirable. One, of course, is that adolescents have increased cognitive abilities. They are better able than younger children to appreciate their friends' feelings, hopes, and uncertainties, and to appreciate differences between their friends' thoughts and their own (Selman, 1981).

Adolescents also have a heightened need for friendship, in part because they are beginning to break the strong ties to home and parents that characterize childhood. Another reason is that they must come to grips with sexual feelings, impulses, and experiences; sharing their thoughts about these things with friends is often helpful and reassuring.

These special needs give friendships between adolescents several important qualities. Intimacy and self-disclosure, the processes of communicating personal information about one's self to someone else, emerge as essential ingredients of adolescent friendships. Adolescents are much more likely than children to mention the sharing of intimate feelings in describing their close friendships. One 13-year-old girl described the value of intimacy by saying, "I can tell Karen (her friend) things and she helps me talk" (Berndt and Perry, 1990, p. 272). Adolescents actually do have

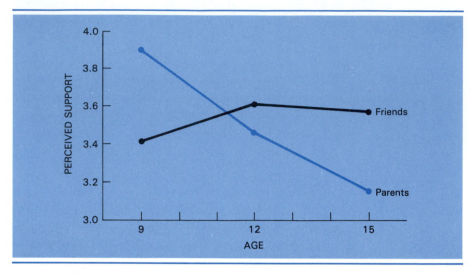

FIGURE 10-8

This graph depicts perceived support from parents and friends at three age levels. The youngest children perceive parents to be more supportive than best friends, but the two oldest groups judge best friends to be most supportive.

(Results from W. Furman and D. Buhrmester, "Age and sex differences in perceptions of networks of personal relationships," in Child Development, 63, 1990, p. 107.)

more intimate knowledge of their close friends than children do (Berndt, 1982).

The greater intimacy and support associated with adolescent friendships coincides with a decline in adolescents' perceptions of parental support. Furman and Buhrmester (1992) asked 9-, 12-, and 15-year-olds to rate their parents' supportiveness as well as their best friend's supportiveness. Figure 10-8 shows that 9-year-olds perceived parents to be more supportive than best friends. However, both 12- and 15-year-olds judged best friends to be more supportive.

Many psychologists believe that the intimate self-disclosures that occur in intimate relationships play a central role in formulating and refining self-concept in adolescence. Sullivan (1953), for example, felt that mutual self-disclosure enables children to reduce distortions in their self-images. They learn to recognize how they are perceived by others and, at the same time, to appreciate the similarities and differences among people.

Adolescent friendships are also characterized by greater emphasis on loyalty and faithfulness (Berndt and Perry, 1990). Much more so than children, adolescents believe that friends should defend one another. And they believe, just as strongly, that friends should not deceive or abandon one another.

The emphasis on loyalty and faithfulness apparently goes hand in hand with the emphasis on intimacy: If a friend is disloyal, adolescents are afraid that they may be humiliated because their intimate thoughts and feelings will become known to a much broader circle of people.

Yet another distinctive aspect of adolescent friendship is a greater willingness to share (Berndt and Perry, 1990). Surprisingly, children are often *less* likely to share with close friends than with other classmates with whom they are not particularly friendly, apparently because a degree of jealousy characterizes most of these friendships. Children almost never like to feel they have less than others with whom they are in close contact (Rubin, 1980). By adolescence, however, the picture changes. Adolescents are more likely to share with, and be helpful to, their friends than other classmates. Berndt (1982) suggests that this development reflects increased preference for equality over competition and is part of passing from childhood to adolescence. "Adolescents," suggests Berndt, "have more mature conceptions of reciprocity and equality than young children [and] may also appreciate that competition between friends makes it difficult to maintain an intimate relationship" (1982, p. 1452).

Berndt and his colleagues (1986) revealed this developmental change in research in which subjects were asked to color geometric shapes such as circles and squares. Each pair of best friends was given one artist's template with which to draw the outline of the shapes. They were also told that the child who colored more shapes would receive a prize. The 13-year-olds who were best friends shared much more than did 9-year-olds who were best friends. Confronted with a situation involving winning or losing, children apparently did not want to look inferior to their friends and so they competed intensely instead of sharing. Adolescents, in contrast, believed that by sharing, they would remain equals with their friends. They also may not have wanted to risk damaging their friendship by competing with each other.

Consistent with this explanation, Buhrmester and his colleagues (1992) reported that 9-year-olds would share with their friends more than with acquaintances if the sharing was anonymous. When there was no need to appear superior to friends, these youngsters were very generous with them.

Some of these distinctive characteristics of adolescent friendships are particularly pronounced in girls. Intimate relationships are more common among girls than boys, and girls are more likely than boys to have one exclusive "best friend." Girls are also more likely to be concerned about the faithfulness of their friends and to worry about possible rejection by them (Berndt, 1981).

Who Become Friends?

Children tend to choose as friends those who are similar to them in age, sex, and race (Hartup, in press). Same-age friendships come about, in part, because children and adolescents spend much of their lives in age-segregated schools, which means that most potential friends are approximately the same age. However, even without this constraint, the norm is for friends to be roughly the same age: The egalitarian nature of friendships is more difficult to maintain between children who differ considerably in age.

Children's preference for same-sex friends emerges in the preschool years and is remarkably consistent throughout childhood and adolescence.

FIGURE 10-9
Children's friends typically are similar in age, sex, and race.

During these years, only about 5 percent of friends are members of the opposite sex (Hartup, in press). This preference for same-sex friends is not surprising, of course, because children play primarily with same-sex peers, making it difficult for friendships to form between boys and girls. Even after heterosexual relationships become important in adolescence, most teenagers retain a same-sex best friend. In fact, romantic relationships are seen by adolescents to be quite different from the relationship that one has with a best friend (Berndt, 1988).

Although both boys and girls prefer same-sex friends, the nature of their friendships differs. Girls have a much stronger tendency than boys to develop exclusive friendships, and they are also much less open than boys to admitting new members into their circle of friends. Perhaps boys are more accustomed than girls to group friendships because of their involvement in group sports. Perhaps girls prefer exclusive friendships precisely because they allow for more intimate relationships (Hartup, in press).

Black and white children usually find friends within their own racial groups. These preferences, which are evident in young children and gradually increase during childhood and adolescence, reflect racial segregation in society at large. That is, segregation limits the number of other-race peers that a child will know well enough to become friends with (Berndt, 1988).

Even when children attend integrated schools, most friendships are between same-race children, but some friendships do form between children from different racial groups. To determine the factors that lead to these friendships, Hallinan and Teixeira (1987) studied black and white students in grades 4 through 7 in several desegregated schools. The racial composition of the students' classrooms ranged from 10 percent black and 90 percent white to 10 percent white and 90 percent black. Students were given a list of their classmates and asked to classify each as "best friend," "friend," "know," and "don't know."

For both black and white students, about one-fourth of the best friends represented other-race choices. Particularly interesting in the Hallinan and Teixeira (1987) results is information concerning the classroom settings that are conducive to the formation of these friendships. Class size was critical: Both blacks and whites had fewer other-race friends in large classes than in small classes. Apparently, when classes are large, children tend to select friends from the ample pool of same-race peers; in smaller classes, fewer same-race children are available, so children are more inclined to form friendships with other-race children.

Two other results clarify the role of academic achievement on friendship formation between children of different races. First, white children had more black best friends in classrooms where much instruction took place in groups based on ability than in classrooms where ability grouping was absent. Second, black children were more likely to claim a white child as a friend if the white child's level of academic achievement was greater than their own.

What do these findings tell us about factors that cause children to form friendships with children from other racial groups? Hallinan and Teixeira (1987) suggest that

> two separate mechanisms appear to influence the cross-race friendship choice of black and white students. For whites, getting to know blacks and working with them may be of primary importance, and assignment to the same instructional group promotes this process. Blacks, on the other hand, may be attracted by high academic status and possibly the power than can be associated with it in the social structure of a classroom. (pp. 579–580)

Thus, Hallinan and Teixeira's work indicates that teaching black children and white children in the same classroom does not guarantee that friendships will form between these youngsters. Instead, these friendships depend upon characteristics of the classroom—its size, whether the teacher instructs students in groups based on their ability, and the relative achievement of students in the class.

Another important message from the Hallinan and Teixeira (1987) study is that if we wish to learn more about how children choose their friends, we need to look beyond similarities in such demographic variables as age, sex, and race. Research reveals that friends usually have similar attitudes toward school and toward contemporary teen culture. Children and adolescents who value and enjoy schoolwork generally have friends who share these views. In like manner, friends typically have similar views on how to spend their time outside of school: Friends will, for example, both agree to participate in extracurricular activities or both agree to avoid parties where drinking alcohol is known to occur (Hartup, in press).

As time goes by, friends become more similar to one another. Kandel (1978), for example, studied adolescent friendships and individual attitudes over a one-year period and found that friends gradually became more alike in their attitudes toward marijuana use, delinquent activity, educational goals, and political identification.

Despite all that we have said about the importance of similarity, children *do not* select photocopies of themselves as friends. Instead, friends often differ from one another in subtle ways that help them maintain positive evaluations of themselves. One way that this occurs is through reflection, which involves taking pleasure in a friend's accomplishments and enhancing feelings about oneself by basking in the reflected glory of friends' reputations, abilities, or deeds. For reflection to be successful, a child must feel psychologically close to the other child and also believe that the other child possesses admirable characteristics. For example, an elementary school child may say such things as, "Sally and I walk to school together every day, and she's the best speller in the whole school" (Tesser, Campbell, and Smith, 1984).

Of course, having a highly successful friend can make a child look relatively less successful by comparison. How can a child enjoy the glow of a friend's success without, at the same time, experiencing some disappointment from standing in the friend's shadow? Tesser and his associates propose that children may choose as best friends those who excel in different domains from themselves, and that each child places less value on the other child's domain of excellence. For example, a child may savor a friend's success as a tennis player but not be troubled by his or her own inability in tennis because athletics are not relevant personally

FIGURE 10-10

Students' ratings of (a) their own performance, and (b) that of their most-preferred classmate. Each student rated activities designated as relevant to them personally and activities rated not relevant. Notice that students rate themselves higher than their friends on personally relevant activities but lower than their friends on irrelevant activities.

(*Adapted from A. Tesser, J. Campbell, and M. Smith, "Friendship choice and performance: Self-evaluation maintenance in children," in* Journal of Personality and Social Psychology, 46, 1984, pp. 561–574. Copyright 1984 by the American Psychological Association. Adapted by permission of the author.*)

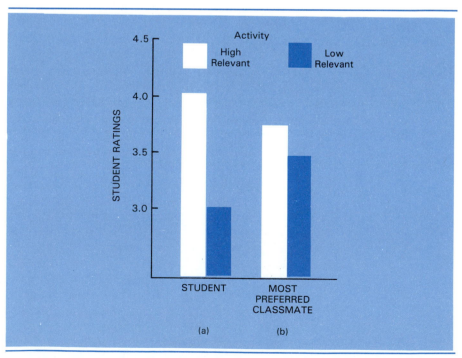

as a measure of success. However, if the child valued his or her dramatic ability, then the child would judge himself or herself to be a better actor than the friend.

To test this hypothesis, Tesser and his associates asked 270 fifth- and sixth-grade children to pick four activities and to select the classmate with whom the child most preferred to spend time. The activities were to be the two each student considered most important and the two each considered least important, as selected from a list provided by the investigators. A week later, students rated themselves and their most-liked classmates on their performance of the chosen activities.

As shown in Figure 10-10, the overall theory received clear support. Students rated themselves as better than their most-preferred classmates on highly relevant activities, but they rated their most-preferred classmates as better than themselves on activities of low relevance.

Impact of Friendships on Development

Friends are valuable resources. From friends, children and adolescents can learn about the physical world, about other people, and about themselves. Friends provide comfort and support during times of stress and turmoil. The functions that friends serve are vital during childhood and adolescence; we could easily imagine that the developmental road would be rocky for children and adolescents with few or new friends. Research generally supports this prediction: Having friends is correlated positively with desirable outcomes. For example, children with friends are generally more willing to share, to cooperate, and to interact with their peers than are children with no friends (Hartup, in press). Also, having supportive friendships is related to successful psychological, social, and academic adjustment (Savin-Williams and Berndt, 1990).

It is not simply the number of friends that matters, but the quality of those friendships. Buhrmester (1990), for example, found that 13- to 16-year-olds who reported more intimate self-disclosure with their best friends were less hostile, less anxious, and had greater self-esteem. Also, adolescents who report that they often argue with their best friend or that their best friend is often annoying are more likely to be disruptive in school (Berndt and Keefe, 1991).

Research of this sort leaves open the question of causality. Friendship might cause these positive outcomes because, for example, children with many friends have multiple sources of information about school and more sources of emotional support. An alternative hypothesis is that a third variable leads some children to have more friends (and better friendships) *and* to be better adjusted. Children whose social skills are well developed, for example, might find their friendships more satisfying and be better adjusted.

Recent longitudinal research makes it possible to determine the causal role of friendship in children's and adolescents' adjustment. In a study by Ladd (1990), kindergarten children with more friends in the fall tended to be better adjusted to kindergarten in the spring. For example, the correlation between the number of friendships that were maintained over the

FIGURE 10-11
The transition to a new junior high or middle school is easier for children who have friends.

first 2 months of kindergarten and children's perception of school in May was 0.39. That is, children who had more stable friendships over the first 2 months of the school year viewed school more positively. They were more likely to believe that teachers were interested in them and that school was fun.

Much the same pattern has been reported for children's transitions from elementary school to middle school or to junior high school. Students with high-quality friendships in elementary school tend to adjust more readily to junior high or middle school. For example, as seventh graders, they are viewed more favorably by their peers and are less often disruptive in school (Berndt and Perry, 1990).

This work indicates that children's and adolescents' friends are more than just favored playmates and companions. Instead, they are valuable assets with whom children and adolescents can endure life's disappointments and savor its pleasures.

GROUPS

In 1954, Muzafer Sherif and his colleagues conducted a landmark study of children's groups. Known as the Robbers Cave Experiment because it was conducted at a camp in Robbers Cave State Park in Oklahoma, the experiment involved two groups of 11 boys who had not known one another previously. The boys in the two groups were matched according to several criteria thought to be important to the camp setting, such as height and weight, athletic ability, and previous camping experience.

For the first week, the two groups were kept apart and did not know of the other's existence. Both groups spent their time in traditional camp activities that required considerable cooperation within groups. Transporting boats and other camping equipment, as well as organizing hikes, camp fires, and meals, were typical activities that demanded that the boys in each group assist one another.

After just a few days, leaders had emerged within each group. Boys acquired nicknames specific to the group, and the groups themselves acquired names, Rattlers and Eagles. Each group established norms to regulate behavior within the group. Boys who complained about minor injuries or being homesick were teased for not being "tough."

At the end of the first week, it was arranged that each group should discover the other. Each insisted that the other had intruded on its "turf," an event that helped to solidify the emerging feelings of group membership within each group. Each group insisted that they be allowed to challenge the other in baseball. A game between the groups was planned, as were competitions in other sports and other camp activities (such as tent pitching and cleaning the cabins). Prizes were announced for the winners.

Preparing for these events further solidified group loyalties and interdependencies. Activities that had once been avoided—cleaning the cabins, for example—were now pursued with vigor because they contributed to the goal of establishing the group's superiority. Also obvious in this phase was growing antagonism toward members of the other group. During the competitions, boys heckled and cursed members of the other group. After losing to the Rattlers in the first baseball game, members of the Eagles found the Rattlers flag at the ball field. They burned it and hung the remnants for the Rattlers to find. One Eagle said, "You can tell those guys *I* did it if they say anything. I'll fight 'em!" Relations deteriorated rapidly between the groups, so that in just a few days the boys had abandoned displays of good sportsmanship, and they now refused to associate with each other. For example, they objected to eating together in the same mess hall. And, stereotypes formed. Rattlers were convinced that Eagles were unfriendly, sneaky, and the like. Of course, Eagles felt the same way about Rattlers.

After about two weeks, the final phase of the experiment began. The objective now was to determine what would be necessary to reduce the hostility between the groups. The first approach involved having the two

FIGURE 10-12

The common goal of starting a stalled truck was one of the techniques that Sherif and his colleagues used to reduce friction between the Rattlers and Eagles.

groups participate together in enjoyable, noncompetitive events, such as watching a movie or shooting off firecrackers together. These failed completely. Each group complained at length about the requirement that it participate with the other; the antagonism that marked recent interactions continued, unabated.

The second approach was more complicated and involved creating common goals for the two groups that required mutual cooperation. In one episode, the boys wanted to see a popular movie but the staff announced that the camp could not afford to pay all of the cost to rent the film. After some debate, the two groups agreed to contribute equally to the cost of the movie. A few days later, a truck that was used to get food to the camp would not start. A Rattler suggested that they use a rope to pull the truck to start it; all group members joined in, and, after a few tries, they successfully started the truck (which, of course, was really in working condition all the time). The boys immediately congratulated one another and the groups intermingled easily.

Yet another situation requiring cooperation was one in which the boys needed to pitch tents. The staff had deliberately mispacked the gear, so that each group had some extra pieces of equipment that were missing from the other group's gear. The Rattlers and Eagles immediately recognized the problem and promptly swapped the necessary equipment without argument.

These and other episodes involving cooperation to achieve common goals effectively eliminated the hostility between the groups just as rapidly as the initial competition had elicited it. By the end of the week, Rattlers and Eagles no longer sat with their own group members in the mess hall but, instead, crossed the imaginary lines that had divided the groups. When camp was over, the Rattlers and Eagles requested that they travel home on the same bus. At a rest stop, the Rattlers used a $5 prize from one of the contests to buy drinks for all of the boys.

The Robbers Cave study, though nearly 50 years old, tells us much about group formation and group functioning. Three conclusions are particularly worth remembering:

1. When groups of children are brought together, a structure emerges rapidly in which individuals have specific roles, for example, as a leader.
2. When groups compete for scarce resources (for example, prizes), individuals' identification with and support for their own group increases. At the same time, they develop negative stereotypes of members of other groups and feel antagonistic toward them.
3. When common goals require that groups collaborate, group boundaries become less pronounced and hostility between groups ceases.

Group Structures

As was the case in the Robbers Cave study, groups are rarely egalitarian or entirely democratic. Instead, some individuals exert more social power than others, producing a hierarchy of leaders and followers. This type of organization is not unique to humans, but instead is common among the groups of many primates. Male baboons, for example, establish strict **dominance hierarchies** based on aggressive encounters with one another. The most successful baboon, called the *alpha male*, is the first to eat and the first to mate. Other males know their position in the hierarchy. They defer to those above them and assert themselves over those below them (Rowell, 1966).

A dominance hierarchy of this sort has obvious benefits to baboons. Fighting is minimized because each baboon knows his status in the group. Equally important is that the most successful males are more likely to mate and thereby pass on their genes to future generations.

Dominance hierarchies can be readily identified in children's groups. In an early study, Strayer and Strayer (1976) observed 3- to 5-year-olds at their preschool center. They recorded instances of antagonistic behavior such as chasing, pushing, or hitting other children. Also recorded were children's responses to these antagonistic behaviors. The Strayers discovered that the frequency of attacks and the nature of the response reflected a well-developed dominance hierarchy. Children at the top of the hierarchy could attack virtually any of the children in the group, who would usually respond submissively (for example, by flinching, cringing, or running away). In contrast, children at the bottom of the hierarchy rarely attacked.

Similar hierarchies have been observed in other studies but they are not always based on physical dominance. Instead, hierarchies are often based on children's characteristics that relate to the group's principal function. In classroom settings, for example, academically talented youngsters usually occupy positions of social power. In camping settings, however, the socially powerful children often have skills that are important in a camp setting; for example, they have camping experience and they play games well. Even the Strayer and Strayer's (1976) findings are consistent with this principle of group structure. Physical play and play with toys and games are central to the function of preschool groups, and a group structure based on physical dominance relates to this function. This type of organization is sensible because children whose skills are most useful to the group tend to have the most social power (Hartup, 1983).

Influences of Groups on Individuals

In the Robbers Cave experiment, the groups quickly established the expectation that boys would be "tough." Complaints about injuries or homesickness were met with ridicule. These implicit rules about acceptable behavior help to give a group its distinctive identity. And they help to influence the behavior of individuals within groups.

However, contrary to popular stereotypes, children and adolescents do not blindly follow the dictates of their groups. When appropriate behavior is clear and well defined, children and adolescents are least likely to be influenced by their peer groups. Groups seem to be most influential when the appropriate behavior may not be obvious. Preferences in music and clothing, for example, are completely subjective; lacking any objective

Dominance hierarchy An ordering within a group from the most socially powerful individual to the least powerful.

way to determine what is appropriate, children and adolescents often turn to their peer group for guidance.

Smoking, drinking, and using drugs represent other instances where the appropriate behavior is not always clear. On the one hand, parental preaching may discourage teens from smoking, drinking or using drugs; on the other hand, modern culture is replete with adolescent and adult models who endorse these behaviors, either implicitly or explicitly. Here, too, the peer group exerts a strong influence on individuals' behaviors. If the group norm is that smoking is acceptable, then adolescents who do not smoke often start (Chassin et al., 1986).

The variable nature of group influence was demonstrated in a study by Hoving, Hamm, and Galvin (1969). Subjects in this experiment were shown slides depicting many dots separated by a vertical line. The subjects— second, fifth, and eighth graders—were allowed 4 seconds to judge which side of the slide had more dots.

Two aspects of the procedure were critical. First, some problems had an equal or nearly equal number of dots on either side of the vertical line, whereas other problems had approximately twice the number of dots on one side of the line as on the other. The problem that showed an equal number of dots represented an ambiguous situation—one in which an appropriate answer could not be determined in the allotted 4 seconds. In contrast, the problem that showed many more dots on one side of the line was nonambiguous—the answer was immediately obvious.

The second critical feature of the procedure is that, on some trials, two lights appeared below the dots, either to the left or right of the vertical line. Subjects were led to believe that these lights indicated the answers of two peers seated in adjacent rooms. In fact, the lights were controlled by the experimenter and were used to make the subjects believe that both of the other children had chosen a particular side of the slide as having more dots.

For problems in which the answer was obvious, the lights indicated that the peers had selected the wrong side. Nevertheless, subjects at all grades typically answered correctly, ignoring the normative influence of the two fictitious peer subjects. In contrast, when the correct answer was ambiguous, subjects' responses generally agreed with those of the fictitious peer subjects. Thus, the group norm—represented here by lights indicating peers' choices—influenced subjects' choices when the correct response was ambiguous but not when it was obvious. Interestingly, these effects were larger for fifth and eighth graders than for second graders, indicating that preadolescents and adolescents were both more independent and more susceptible to group influence than younger children.

POPULARITY AND REJECTION

Observe a classroom of children for a few hours and you'll probably notice a few youngsters who seem to be the "stars" of the room—they stand out by being especially popular with their classmates. Other children seem to vie for the stars' attention (see Figure 10-13). Watch longer and you'll

FIGURE 10-13
Classrooms often contain "stars," youngsters to whom many in the class spontaneously gravitate.

Popular children
Youngsters who are liked by most of their classmates.

Rejected children
Youngsters who are disliked by most of their classmates.

Controversial children
Youngsters who are liked by many classmates and also disliked by many classmates.

Neglected children
Youngsters who are neither liked nor disliked by their classmates.

see other children who are rejected by most of their classmates; their presence is obviously unwanted. You may also spot some neglected children; these are youngsters who have few interactions—either positive or negative—with their classmates.

Observations like these—though more extensive and systematic—represent one method that developmental psychologists have used to study popularity. Another method is to ask children to name classmates that they like a lot as well as those that they don't like very much. Sometimes children are asked to rate each child in the class, using a scale that might range from "I really like to play with ____" to "I really don't like to play with ____." Typically these procedures—observations, nominations, and ratings—yield similar profiles and each is related to measures of independent observers (typically, teachers). The usual outcome is that most children—about two-thirds—fall into one of four categories: (1) **popular children**, those who are liked by many classmates; (2) **rejected children**, those who are disliked by many classmates; (3) **controversial children**, those who are both liked and disliked by classmates; and (4) **neglected children**, those who are neither liked nor disliked by classmates. Children in the remaining third are liked or disliked by some of their peers, but without sufficient frequency or intensity to be placed in one of the four groups; they are simply described as average children (Coie, Dodge, and Coppotelli, 1982).

Who Is Popular?

Why are some children popular whereas others are rejected, controversial, or neglected? The characteristics of popular children are fairly well known. They tend to be more intelligent and more attractive physically than children who are not popular. Later-born youngsters are more likely to be popular than first borns; later-born children may develop more sophisticated interpersonal skills because they are routinely dealing with parents and older siblings in a variety of social situations (Hartup, 1983).

The emphasis on social skill is not restricted to later-born children. Generally, social skill seems to be a key component of popularity in childhood and adolescence. Popular children are better able to learn how to initiate social interactions with other children. They are more skillful at communicating and better able to integrate themselves into an ongoing conversation or play session. Popular children also seem relatively gifted in assessing and monitoring their own social impact in various situations and in tailoring their responses to the requirements of each new social situation (Hartup, 1992).

Among children who are not the "stars," isolated children tend to be more depressed, anxious, and immature than average children (East and Rook, 1992). More is known about rejected children. Some rejected boys are withdrawn but otherwise are difficult to distinguish from popular boys. Another group of rejected boys forms a more deviant group; they, too, are withdrawn but they also tend to be aggressive, have poor self-control, and have behavior problems (French, 1988). Rejected girls are, likewise, heterogeneous. Some rejected girls are primarily withdrawn and lacking in self-control. Others are also aggressive, hostile, and anxious, and they do poorly in school (French, 1990).

Thus, correlational findings link popularity to social skill and link rejection to aggression and withdrawal. As is always the case, determining causal relations from these findings is difficult. Perhaps aggressive behavior causes children to be rejected by their peers. Alternatively, rejected children may resort to aggressive behavior because other more conventional forms of interaction are ineffective. That is, perhaps their peers don't respond to polite, socially acceptable requests, so they resort to aggressive behavior out of necessity.

Longitudinal findings provide some indication that both phenomena may be occurring. Hymel and her colleagues (1990) twice measured children's popularity, aggressive behavior, and social withdrawal: first, when the youngsters were 7 years old, and a second time when they were 10. Aggressive behavior at age 7 was negatively related to popularity at age 10, $r = -0.33$, which suggests that more aggressive behaviors led children to become less popular. However, popularity at age 7 was also negatively related to aggression at age 10, $r = -0.37$, and negatively related to withdrawal at age 10, $r = -0.39$. Children who were unpopular as 7-year-olds were more aggressive and more withdrawn as 10-year-olds. Apparently, children who are aggressive are not popular with peers; lacking popularity, they become withdrawn and rely even more on aggressive behavior in their attempts to influence their peers.

The Consequences of Rejection

Is being rejected by one's peers simply an unfortunate and pathetic phase of some children's development or does it have longer-lasting effects? The evidence clearly indicates the latter. One writer, summarizing the consequences of childhood rejection, concluded that

the socially withdrawn, socially incompetent and aggressive child soon be-

CLOSE-UP

Long-term Effects of Relationships with Peers

Satisfying relationships with peers are often associated with positive developmental outcomes whereas unsatisfying relationships are associated with negative outcomes. That is, youngsters who generally have pleasant and rewarding relationships with other children typically fare better in school and are better adjusted later in life. Results documenting these conclusions come from a longitudinal study reported by Morison and Masten (1991). In the first phase of the study, 207 children in grades 3–6 completed the Revised Class Play. This measures a child's reputation among his or her peers by asking each child in the class to assign his or her classmates to roles in a hypothetical class play. Typical roles would be "a person everyone likes to be with," "a person who gets into lots of fights," or "a person who is often left out of class activities." The number of times that each child in a class is assigned to a role is summed and provides an estimate of the extent to which each child's peers judge him or her to be sociable, disruptive, or isolated.

Approximately seven years later, Morison and Masten (1991) obtained measures of academic achievement, social competence, and adjustment for these subjects, who were now 14- to 19-year-olds. The results indicated that youngsters who had been judged by their peers to be sociable had the best outcomes as adolescents. They were more competent socially, were more successful in school, and were least likely to have behavioral or psychological problems. In contrast, children who were thought to be disruptive or isolated had less desirable outcomes. Disruptive children were less successful in school, had less self-worth, and were more likely to have "externalizing" behavioral problems such as trouble with the law or antisocial behavior. Children who were judged to be isolated were less competent socially and were more likely to suffer internalizing behavior problems such as inhibition or anxiety.

The message here is that the impact of children's experiences with their peers extends far beyond the immediate satisfactions or disappointments of peer relationships. Instead, the quality of a child's peer relationships plays a substantial role in most major facets of a child's development.

comes the socially inept adult social casualty. For example, the most famous mass murderers of almost every country (e.g., Christie, the Black Panther, Blue Beard, the Michigan Murderer, the Boston Strangler, and others) have invariably been found to have had abnormal social experiences in childhood. . . . They are usually found to have been loners, quiet types and unsociable people, often dominated by selfish parents, or hounded by thoughtless classmates. (Duck, 1983, p. 115).

Consistent with this view, Parker and Asher (1987) reviewed an extensive body of research and concluded that poor peer relations can be linked directly to two undesirable outcomes. First, children who are not accepted by their peers drop out of school more frequently than children who are accepted. Most of the studies did not distinguish rejected children from neglected children; but when these groups are distinguished, it appears that only rejected children are at risk for dropping out of school. Second, children who are not accepted by their peers are more likely than accepted children to commit juvenile offenses and to have criminal records as adults. This is particularly true for rejected children who are aggressive, a topic that we will explore in more detail in Chapter 11. In the Close-Up on page 339, we examine a longitudinal study that reveals some of these long-lasting effects of peer relationships.

Antecedents of Peer Rejection

Because of the dire consequences of rejection by peers, understanding why children are rejected is essential. We have already mentioned that rejected youngsters are often awkward in their interactions with peers, which contributes to their lack of popularity. Some of this initial clumsiness may reflect biological factors. Remember from Chapter 3 (pages 101–9) that some children are temperamentally less comfortable when dealing with others. These youngsters may well be more prone to peer rejection than are children who are temperamentally more social. Too, as we'll see in Chapter 11, aggressive behavior may have a biological basis. For some children, periodic use of force to influence others may simply be a physiological imperative.

The most compelling evidence, however, points to family influences on children's popularity and rejection (Hartup and Moore, 1990). Some of this influence comes through observational learning. Children see their parents in a multitude of social situations and observe their parents' responses. Parents who try to resolve conflicts with others through tactful negotiation are demonstrating an effective approach to their children. Parents who rant and rave are illustrating less effective tactics; children may imitate these parents nonetheless, simply because they know of no other ways in which to respond (see Figure 10-14).

FIGURE 10-14
Adults sometimes try to resolve conflicts by intimidating others. When children observe this behavior, it encourages them to use aggression, which is the first step toward being rejected by peers.

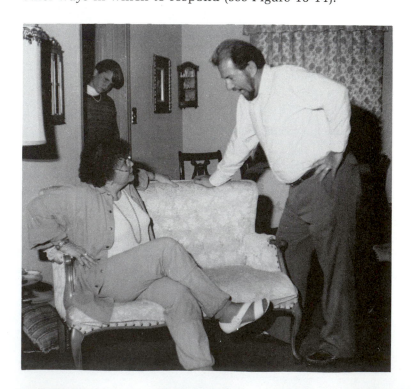

If children imitate their parents' social responses, then we would expect children and parents to respond similarly to the same social stimulus. A study by Keane and her colleagues (1990) provides evidence consistent with this view. Videotaped vignettes were prepared in which one child destroyed another child's toy, sometimes accidentally and sometimes deliberately. Popular and rejected children were asked what they would have done if the toy had been theirs. In addition, mothers of these children were asked what they would have told their children to do had the toy been theirs.

Rejected children typically resorted to more aggressive solutions than did popular children, a result that could be anticipated based on research that we have already described. The novel finding was that mothers of rejected children advocated aggressive responding, whereas mothers of popular children more often proposed prosocial solutions. This result, and others like it (for example, Pettit, Dodge, and Brown, 1988), indicate that when parents habitually respond to conflicts or problems with aggression, their children will do the same; the long-term consequence is that their children become less popular.

The impact of parents extends beyond the specific interpersonal behaviors that they demonstrate for their children. Earlier in this chapter (pages 320–21), we described how some parents pave the way to popularity by actively managing their children's early peer interactions. In addition, as we discussed in Chapter 9, parental disciplinary practices have well-established consequences for children's behavior. When parents are inconsistent in their discipline—sometimes punishing a child harshly for a misdeed and sometimes ignoring the same act altogether—the usual result is that children behave in an antisocial manner, which often includes aggression. Such antisocial behavior makes children unpopular with their peers, starting the vicious cycle of aggression and rejection that we described earlier. In addition, inconsistent parental discipline is associated with poorer performance in school, which also contributes to rejection by peers (Dishion, 1990).

Obviously, the forces that contribute to popularity and rejection are complex. Figure 10-15 provides a summary of these relations. Antisocial

FIGURE 10-15

A model that summarizes the forces that contribute to peer rejection and popularity. The two immediate causes of popularity and rejection are social and scholastic talent, which are, in turn, influenced by biological factors and parents' behavior.

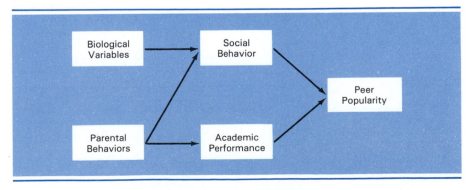

behavior can be linked to biological factors and to parental behaviors, including disciplinary practices and interactions with others. Parental behavior also helps to determine scholastic success. When parental discipline is fair, consistent, and explained to youngsters, they get better grades and are unlikely to behave antisocially. In turn, a child's social and scholastic skill are the chief determinants of popularity and rejection. Popular children are typically socially and scholastically talented, whereas rejected children are neither.

A lifetime of peer rejection need not be any child's destiny, however. A number of positive steps can be implemented. For example, training programs have been created that teach youngsters more effective social skills. By learning conventional and proven ways of interacting with peers, rejected children need not rely upon aggressive and other antisocial behaviors that their peers dislike (Mize and Ladd, 1990). Programs of this sort are encouraging. The sequence of aggression→rejection→school failure and criminality can be disrupted; socially awkward youngsters can become accepted by their peers and enjoy this companionship rather than experience the pain of rejection.

SUMMARY

1.   Interactions with peers can be traced to infancy. Between 6 and 12 months of age, infants begin to look at and to vocalize with others. Parallel play, in which infants play independently but in proximity to others, emerges between 12 and 15 months.

2.   Throughout the toddler and preschool years, interactions become more coordinated, reflecting expanding cognitive and linguistic skills. Cooperative play, which is organized around a theme and has distinct roles, becomes common. Make-believe play emerges during the preschool years, and apparently allows children to understand emotional topics.

3.   During childhood and adolescence, social rules govern interactions between peers. Both boys and girls now enjoy rough-and-tumble play, which resembles aggressive behavior but is friendly. Groups also become an influential force in children's and adolescents' interactions.

4.   Parents often regulate their children's interactions with peers directly, by organizing interactions, as well as by prohibiting some types of interactions. Parents also influence their children's peer interactions indirectly: The quality of the parent-child relationship is linked to the quality of the child's peer relationships, in that children with secure parental attachments tend to interact more successfully with peers.

5.   Cooperation is more common in some cultures than in others, and becomes more frequent as children grow. The degree of cooperation is influenced by the presence of rewards for cooperation as well as by the presence of cooperative peers or models.

6.   Harry Stack Sullivan proposed a general developmental framework for friendships: During the preschool years, children's social relationships are primarily with adults; in the early elementary school years, peers become playmates and companions, but the relationships are often short lived; beginning in the middle elementary school years, children begin to form chumships, which are intimate and reciprocal relationships with peers.

7. Precursors of friendship can be seen in the first few years of life, where toddlers and preschoolers will interact selectively and preferentially with their peers. Beginning at approximately 8 years of age, children begin to distinguish friends from acquaintances and form higher expectations for their friends. Friendships are particularly important during adolescence, and are characterized by a greater emphasis on self-disclosure, loyalty, and a willingness to share.

8. Children most often form friendships with peers who are similar in age, sex, and race. Friends also have similar but not identical abilities and interests, which allows friends to complement one another. Friends are valuable resources that can ease the stresses in children's lives, such as the stress associated with entering a new school.

9. In the Robbers Cave experiment, a role structure consisting of leaders and followers rapidly formed within each group. Competition between the two groups fostered hostility and stereotypes, and these stereotypes were eliminated only by imposing common goals that required the groups to collaborate.

10. For monkeys and people alike, groups are characterized by a dominance hierarchy, in which individuals differ systematically in the amount of social power that they exert over others. Physical dominance is important in preschoolers' hierarchies, but for older children, dominance is often determined by features that are important to the group's function, such as academic talent. Children's and adolescents' behaviors are more strongly influenced by groups in domains where standards are subjective (for example, in tastes in clothes or music) than in domains where more widely accepted standards of appropriate behavior exist.

11. Popularity of individuals can be measured by observing children's interactions or by asking children to nominate or rate their peers according to whether they like them or not. These procedures typically distinguish the categories of popular, rejected, controversial, neglected, and average children.

12. Popular children tend to be attractive, intelligent, and socially skilled. Rejected children are more heterogeneous. Some are withdrawn; others, who are more deviant, are aggressive and have behavior problems. Children who are rejected by their peers are more likely to drop out of school and to become involved in criminal activity.

13. Rejection may be related to biological variables, such as temperament, but most of the evidence links popularity and rejection to parental factors. Children who become rejected may learn ineffective interpersonal skills from their parents. In addition, these youngsters may be disciplined inconsistently, and this may foster antisocial behaviors such as aggression.

Moral Understanding And Behavior

The very young child's behavior is controlled to a large extent by outside influences: the expectations of others, parental rewards and punishments, and peer pressures—to name only a few. But as a child grows older, he or she begins to behave "appropriately" without immediate, direct pressure from outside sources. The child continues to obey rules that were previously enforced by the parents. The child may decide, even when alone, to ignore immediate rewards in favor of long-range goals. He or she may "do the right thing" when faced with a moral dilemma.

In this chapter we discuss four closely related developments: self-control, moral reasoning, prosocial behavior, and aggression. Some of the following examples foretell the issues that will emerge as we consider how most children come to behave in ways that their culture considers to be moral:

▶ Newborns cry when they are hungry and the usual result is that they are promptly fed. Such immediate gratification of wants doesn't last long. By the time infants can crawl, parents begin to forbid certain behaviors. Within a short time, parents even expect their babies to avoid these behaviors themselves. The development of such self-control has long been a topic discussed by philosophers, theologians, and social critics. As we shall see in the first part of this chapter, psychologists, too, have made important contributions in recent years to an understanding of the development of self-control.

▶ During their early years, most children develop a set of values or principles regarding correct, appropriate, or good behavior. Until recently using the word *morality* has been almost a taboo among psychologists because of its historical associations with religion and philosophy. But during the past few decades, theory and research in the area of moral development have grown enormously. We will examine some of these findings in the second part of this chapter.

▶ Consider the following hypothetical experiment: Mother Teresa and Adolf Hitler are placed side-by-side as 6-month-olds. Do you believe that as a result of observation you could then predict which baby would emerge as one of the great samaritans and which one would become one of the great villains? Probably not. What factors, then, are responsible for the development of behaviors that help other humans? What causes aggression and other antisocial behaviors to emerge? Answers to these questions come in the last two sections of this chapter, dealing with prosocial and aggressive behavior, respectively. ◀

SELF-CONTROL

In *Walden Two* (1948), B. F. Skinner's novel describing a utopia built on the principles of behaviorism, each preschool child is given a lollipop every morning. The lollipop is not just a treat; it plays an important role in teaching self-control. Each lollipop is dipped in powdered sugar so that a single touch of the tongue can be detected. Each child is allowed to eat his or her lollipop in the afternoon but only if the child can keep from licking it at all in the meantime. In this situation, the child who takes the small immediate pleasure of licking will have to forfeit a larger but delayed reward, the whole lollipop.

The child's problem is to learn **delay of gratification**, a form of self-control involved whenever a child or an adult postpones an immediate reward for the sake of a more valued outcome that will come only with patience and effort. A college student who gives up a weekend movie today in order to study so that next week she can enjoy a movie *and* an A on her exam is displaying the delay of gratification. So is the teenager who waits for a sale so that he can buy more (or better) clothes with the same money.

Delay of gratification is but one of many forms of self-control. It occurs whenever a person rises above the immediate pressures of a situation or avoids giving in to an immediate impulse. Let's look at how a child gradually achieves self-control as he or she develops.

Developmental Change

In an influential analysis, Kopp (1982, 1987) has identified a series of phases in the mastery of self-control. In the first, typically beginning at approximately 12 months of age, infants become aware that people impose demands on them, to which they must react accordingly. Youngsters learn that they are *not* entirely free to behave as they wish; instead, others set limits on what they can do. These limits often reflect concern for the infant's safety ("Don't touch!—It's hot."), but also they emerge as part of parent's early socialization efforts (for example, when parents discourage their children from grabbing toys away from playmates).

Beginning at about 24 months of age, toddlers are capable of this control in the absence of their parents. That is, they have internalized some of the controls imposed by others and are now capable of self-control. At this age, children may inhibit their wish to grab an attractive toy from a playmate because they remember a prior parental admonishment.

The last phase begins at about 3 years of age, and continues for many years. Now, according to Kopp (1987), children are capable of self-regulation, which "involves flexible and adaptive control processes that can meet quickly changing situational demands" (p. 38). That is, children can devise effective plans for regulating their own behavior. To return to the example of a playmate's attractive toy, children might tell themselves that they really don't want to play with the toy, or they might suggest an alternative activity that removes the temptation to grab the attractive toy.

Kopp and her colleagues have demonstrated the earliest phases of self-control in experiments in which children are shown a tempting object, then told not to touch it. For example, in a study by Vaughn, Kopp, and Krakow (1984), the experimenter entered the room with a decorated package and said, "Look what I have found! It's a present and it's for you. I wonder what it could be?" (p. 993) Then the experimenter asked the child not to touch the object for a few minutes while the experimenter and the child's mother completed some work. The gift was placed near the child, who was given toys to play with. Before touching the object, the 18-month-olds waited about 30 seconds, compared to just over 1 minute for 24-

Delay of gratification A type of self-control in which a person favors a more valuable future outcome over a less valuable but immediate outcome.

FIGURE 11-1
By 2 years of age, children are sometimes capable of controlling their behavior in a parent's absence.

month-olds and nearly 2 minutes for 30-month-olds. Similarly, age trends were found on other similar tasks in which an unusually shaped telephone and desirable food were the tempting objects. Clearly, self-control emerges rapidly during the toddler years, just as Kopp's analysis (1982, 1987) suggests.

Of course, the 2½-year-olds' mastery of self-control in these experiments is only impressive in comparison with the younger children. In absolute terms, these youngsters have much to learn about regulating impulsive behavior. In fact, such control is achieved only gradually, throughout the elementary school years. For example, in a study by Rotenberg and Meyer (1990), after children had completed a task, they were offered the choice of a relatively small reward immediately or a much larger reward if they waited one day. (Previous testing had confirmed the value of these rewards for these children.) Only about one-third of the 6- to 8-year-olds opted to wait for the larger reward, as did about half of the 9- to 11-year-olds. By 12 to 15 years of age, nearly everyone waited a day to obtain the larger reward.

Thus, self-control is first evident in toddlers, but its mastery is very gradual. And, at any age, there is enormous variation in children's self-control. In the study by Vaughn and colleagues (1984) described previously, correlations between self-control on the three tasks ranged from 0.29 to 0.47. These moderate correlations indicate that children who resisted the temptation to touch the gift, for example, also tended to resist the temptation to touch the unusually shaped telephone. Why are some children better able than others to exert self-control? What factors determine if children can resist impulses? Answers to these questions are described in the next section of this chapter.

Factors Determining Self-Control

PARENTAL AND CULTURAL INFLUENCES. There is a county in Nova Scotia, Canada, where conflicting subcultures have lived side by side for generations (Bandura and Walters, 1963). In the community of Lavallée, children are expected to control immediate impulses and work toward distant goals. Educational and vocational achievement is stressed. In this community parents spend large amounts of time with their children and transmit the adult patterns of their subculture with great efficiency. The children of Lavallée are unlikely to give in to the temptation to take an immediate small pleasure when it means forfeiting something worthwhile in the future.

In the same Nova Scotian county lives another group of people whose community is strikingly lacking in cohesion: fighting, drunkenness, theft, and other antisocial acts occur frequently. Adults in this subculture have a philosophy of life that emphasizes escaping from life's problems as rapidly as possible. Their children are exposed to models exhibiting an overwhelming preference for immediate gratification.

But what would happen if a child from this subculture was adopted by parents in Lavallée and a child from Lavallée was adopted by parents from the community that emphasizes immediate gratification? Would the behavior of either of these children be influenced by the new models with whom they would have contact?

Bandura and Mischel (1965) set up a laboratory experiment to find an answer to this question, and they demonstrated the importance of modeling in the transmission of delay-of-gratification behavior. In the first part of the study, fourth-grade and fifth-grade children were given a delay-of-gratification test in which they were to make a series of choices between a small immediate reward and a larger delayed reward. For instance, they were asked to choose between a small candy bar that would be given to them immediately or a larger one that would require a week of waiting. Children who displayed strong preferences for immediate reward or delayed reward were identified and then assigned to a modeling or a control condition.

In the modeling condition children observed an actual adult model make a series of choices between a less valuable item, which could be obtained immediately, and a more valuable item, which required delay. The model consistently chose the immediate reward item in the presence of children who had demonstrated a preference for the larger delayed reward. The model observed by children who preferred smaller immediate rewards always selected the delayed reward item. In both cases, the model also briefly summarized a philosophy about the behavior he was displaying. For example, when the choice was between a plastic chess set to be given immediately and a more expensive wooden set to be given in two weeks, the model commented, "Chess figures are chess figures. I can get much use out of the plastic ones right away" (p. 701).

In a control condition in which no model was present, children were simply shown the series of paired objects. All children were then given a delay-of-reward test in the model's absence. To assess the stability of any changes in behavior, they also were given another test one month later.

The results of the experiment were clear: Children exposed to a model who delayed gratification shifted their own preferences so that on a posttest about 50 percent of all their choices were for the larger outcomes that required waiting. Even after a month's time these effects were still present. In complementary fashion, most of the children exposed to models who showed little self-control were easily swayed by the impulsive model and abandoned their own self-control.

From the results, we might well expect that a child from the impulsive subculture in Nova Scotia would be influenced by the self-restraint in the behavior of the citizens of Lavallée, and that the behavior of a child from Lavallée would be influenced toward less self-restraint through observation of impulsive models in the other subculture.

Correlational studies provide converging evidence that parents influence their children's self-control. Several investigators report that self-control is lower in children whose parents are very strict with them. For example, Feldman and Wentzel (1990) found a correlation of -0.38 between use of authoritarian and punitive discipline by mothers and a teacher's ratings of the sixth-graders' restraint in the classroom. One interpretation of this relation is that authoritarian mothers "overcontrol" their children: They constantly direct them to do one thing but not another. With constant overcontrol, children have neither the opportunity nor the incentive to internalize control. Consistent with this viewpoint, Silverman and Ragusa (1990) reported a correlation of 0.43 between parental encouragement of independence and toddlers' ability to resist touching a tempting object.

COGNITIVE FACTORS. Although Skinner's *Walden Two* community would certainly offer children a number of adult models of self-control, more direct efforts to teach delay of gratification are also prescribed. Here is the way Frazier, the storyteller of *Walden Two*, puts it:

> First of all, the children are urged to examine their own behavior while looking at the lollipops. This helps them to recognize the need for self-control. Then the lollipops are concealed and the children are asked to notice any gain in happiness or any reduction in tension. Then a strong distraction is arranged—say, an interesting game. Later the children are reminded of the candy and encouraged to examine their reaction. The value of the distraction is generally obvious. . . .When the experiment is repeated a day or so later, the children all run with the lollipops to their lockers . . . a sufficient indication of the success of our training. (Skinner, 1948, p. 108)

In this example, delaying gratification first involves the initial decision to wait and then an effort to maintain resolve and bridge the waiting time. Walter Mischel, who did much of the pioneering experimental work in this area, has identified some of the skills that children develop to regulate their behavior while waiting for future rewards. A groundbreaking experiment by Mischel and Ebbesen (1970) tested two views of what children should do to delay their gratification. Although distraction was used in

Walden Two, Freud (1969) suggested that delay of gratification could be maintained by creating mental images of the desired object, thereby producing substitute satisfactions to ease the frustration of delay. That is, viewing rewards should serve as a vivid reminder that the reward is worth waiting for, and should also increase the child's trust that he or she would actually receive the reward. This prediction obviously contradicts the principle of distraction described in *Walden Two*.

To test these hypotheses, Mischel and Ebbesen (1970) set up the following situation: Preschool children first were asked which of two foods (cookies or pretzels) they preferred. Each youngster was then told he or she would wait alone in a room until the experimenter returned, when the preferred food would be provided. The child could call the experimenter back to the room at any time by a prearranged signal; but in this case only the nonpreferred food would be provided. The experimenter then left, leaving on the table both foods, the preferred food only, the nonpreferred food only, or neither food. He returned in fifteen minutes, or earlier if signaled to do so by the child.

The length of time children in the different food conditions waited was the dependent measure of the study. Figure 11-2 shows the results: Children who were exposed to neither of the foods delayed significantly more than those exposed to both or one of the foods. The children in this group were able to sit alone for an average of over eleven minutes—and 75 percent of them had to be interrupted at the 15-minute mark.

Observations of all the children's behavior through a one-way mirror provided a clue to how the waiting time was bridged. Elaborate distraction techniques were designed spontaneously: Some children sang, talked to

FIGURE 11-2

Average amount of time children were able to wait for the delayed but preferred food in Mischel and Ebbesen's (1970) experiment. Notice that children were able to wait longest when no foods were present in the room. They were least able to wait when both foods were present. Which food (preferred or nonpreferred) was present did not seem to matter.

(Adapted from Mischel and Ebbesen, 1970.)

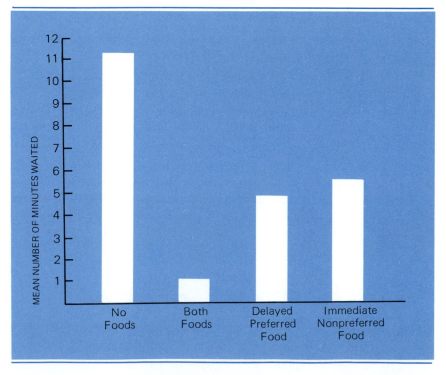

themselves, and invented games. Among those children who successfully waited when food was present, many avoided looking at it by covering their eyes with their hands or resting their heads on their arms.

Apparently any activity that converted the situation into a less frustrating experience could increase the children's ability to delay gratification, so Mischel and his associates began to experiment directly with various techniques. These later studies revealed that the ability to delay gratification is helped by clear plans or blueprints for action (Mischel, Shoda, and Rodriguez, 1989). Children who have a concrete way to handle the situation are far better able to resist temptations and to continue working in the situation. These plans can include (1) reminders to avoid looking at the tempting object, (2) reminders of the prohibition against touching a tempting object, and (3) activities designed to divert one's attention from the tempting object. Thinking about an absent reward in a way that is concrete and arousing (for example, thinking about eating the pretzels or cookies for which one is waiting) robs the child of self-control almost as thoroughly as looking at the real thing. However, self-control improves if children pretend that the real object in front of them is only a picture.

Overall, then, it is how the child thinks about the desired object or outcome that seems to make all the difference. Even among preschool children, self-control can be gained through plans that provide appropriate self-instruction.

Consequences of Self-Control

Considered by itself, a child's preference for a small candy bar immediately instead of a larger candy bar later is not a major developmental phenomenon. Remember, however, that children's ability to resist temptation is moderately consistent across tasks. Consequently, we might expect that children who want their candy immediately would also prefer immediate gratification in more significant intellectual and social situations. They might do their homework hurriedly to have the immediate satisfaction of finishing a boring task rather than taking more time and receiving the delayed gratification of a better grade. In the social realm, children may not resist the temptation to deviate from group rules, and, consequently they may alienate their peers.

Longitudinal research has established that children's performance on laboratory measures of self-control does predict their subsequent behavior in school and with peers. Funder, Block, and Block (1983) measured 4-year-olds' resistance to temptation, then examined the children's behavior at 7 and 11 years of age. Among boys, the ability to delay gratification at age 4 was associated with the ability to control impulses (in school at age 11) and the ability to pay attention, concentrate, and behave dependably. For girls, the ability to resist impulses at age 4 was not particularly related to later impulse control but was related to social competence. That is, 4-year-old girls who resisted temptation were judged in later years by teachers to be more socially resourceful and competent than other girls. The girls at age 4 who were unable to resist temptation appeared to have problems later. According to Funder and his associates,

FIGURE 11-3
Many children are able to delay their gratification, as, for example, doing a careful, though time-consuming, job on homework in order to get the delayed reward of a good grade.

they "tended to go to pieces under stress, to be victimized by other children, and to be easily offended, sulky, and whiny" (1983, p. 1212).

Similar widespread developmental consequences of self-control were reported by Shoda, Mischel, and Peake (1990). These investigators tracked down nearly 200 15- to 18-year-olds who had participated in delay-of-gratification experiments as 4-year-olds. In the original experiments, children had been told that they would receive a large prize if they waited for the experimenter to return. Or they could ring a bell to signal the experimenter to return, whereupon they would receive a much smaller prize.

Shoda and colleagues found that the length of time that 4-year-olds waited was related to a host of characteristics some 11 to 14 years later. Shown in Table 11-1 are some of the significant correlations between 4-year-olds' ability to delay gratification and adolescents' coping skills, their personality characteristics, and their SAT scores. In general, 4-year-olds who waited the longest before calling the experimenter were, as 15- to 18-year-olds, still better able to exert self-control, were more attentive and planful, and had higher SAT scores. Clearly, the ability to delay gratification at age 4 predicts an impressive array of traits more than 10 years later.

TABLE 11-1
Correlations between Amount of Time that Preschoolers' Delayed Gratification and Measures of Coping, Personality, and Achievement during Adolescence.

Measure	r
Coping	
How likely is your child to exhibit self-control in frustrating situations?	0.58
How likely is your child to yield to temptation?	−0.50
When trying to concentrate, how distractible is your son or daughter?	−0.41
How capable is your child of exhibiting self-control when frustrated?	0.40
Personality	
Is planful, thinks ahead	0.36
Is attentive and able to concentrate	0.39
Uses and responds to reason	0.43
Tends to go to pieces under stress, becomes rattled and disorganized	-0.34
SAT scores	
Verbal scale	0.42
Quantitative scale	0.57

Source: From Y. Shoda, W. Mischel, and P. K. Peake, "Predicting adolescent cognitive and self-regulatory competencies from preschool delay of gratification: Identifying diagnostic conditions," in Developmental Psychology, 26, 1990, *pp. 978–986, tables 2–4. Copyright 1990 by the American Psychological Association. Reprinted by permission.*

We have seen that children gradually acquire the ability to control and regulate their own behavior, and that some individuals do so more effectively than others. The self-regulation occurs, in part, because many cultures want children to control impulsive behaviors that are not considered appropriate. Another part of this socialization into the cultural group involves distinguishing "right" from "wrong." Such moral reasoning has been studied extensively by developmental psychologists and is our next topic.

MORAL REASONING

The traditional view of morality, favored in nineteenth-century Europe, presumed that values of the kind we call "moral" were provided by God. Then Freud suggested that the reverse is true: The newborn, he argued, is naturally without concern for the welfare of others. Moral values, if they are present at all, must be cultivated after birth. Psychoanalytic theory offers a view of moral development rooted in the emergence of the superego. The superego—a part of each individual's personality—is said to develop as the child "takes in" parental values, at about the fourth or fifth year of life.

The implications of Freud's theory are straightforward. The child will either develop moral values like those of the parents or, if identification does not occur and the youngster has an inadequate superego, few moral values or none at all. In either case, though, the critical period is presumed to be the first few years of life.

An extensive review of the available evidence does not support this view of moral development (Hoffman, 1988). This does not mean that parents are not important models in the moral sphere, for they certainly are. But it is simply not plausible that early identification with parents is *solely* responsible for all our moral attitudes and actions in adulthood. Young children lack the cognitive skills needed to classify parental examples of moral behavior or infer their motivations, and furthermore, parents rarely express morally relevant feelings (for example, guilt or self-criticism) in their children's presence. The importance of Freud's work was that it redirected our attention toward the social origins of moral values.

Kohlberg's Approach

Piaget was the first to suggest the possibility of a sequence of stages of moral growth, roughly paralleling his general theory of cognitive development. Another cognitive theorist, Lawrence Kohlberg, has explored the development of moral values within a cognitive stage theory framework. He has been concerned primarily with the development of moral judgments. The child, says Kohlberg, must be viewed as a "moral philosopher."

But what is the child's philosophy? To answer this question, Kohlberg analyzed free responses to hypothetical moral dilemmas such as the following:

> In Europe, a woman was near death from cancer. One drug might save her, a form of radium that a druggist in the same town had recently discovered. The druggist was charging $2,000, ten times what the drug cost him to make. The sick woman's husband, Heinz, went to everyone he knew to borrow the money, but he could only get together about half of what it cost. He told the druggist that his wife was dying and asked him to sell it cheaper or let him pay later. But the druggist said, "No." The husband got desperate and broke into the man's store to steal the drug for his wife. Should the husband have done that? Why? (Kohlberg, 1969, p. 379)

A child's response to dilemmas such as this one is usually based on one or more general aspects of the problem, such as the motives or intentions of the people involved. After eliciting responses to a large number of dilemmas from many children, Kohlberg was able to distinguish three levels of moral thinking: **preconventional, conventional,** and **post-conventional.** Within each of these three levels, Kohlberg (1981, 1984) suggests, are two discernible stages, producing the full complement of six stages, as shown in Table 11-2.

Concrete examples of the type of moral judgments made in response to the dilemma described in the story of Heinz and his dying wife are

Preconventional level
The first of Kohlberg's levels, in which moral judgments are based upon their physical consequences, deference to superior power, and satisfying one's own needs.

Conventional level The second of Kohlberg's levels, in which moral judgments are characterized by conformity to the existing social order and by the desire to maintain that order.

Postconventional level
The third and most advanced of Kohlberg's levels, in which moral judgments are guided by universal moral principles.

TABLE 11-2
Kohlberg's Six Stages of Moral Development

Preconventional Level

Stage 1
Punishment and obedience orientation. The physical consequences of an action determine whether it is good or bad. Avoiding punishment and bowing to superior power are valued positively.

Stage 2
Instrumental relativist orientation. Right action consists of behavior that satisfies one's own needs. Human relations are viewed in marketplace terms. Reciprocity occurs, but is seen in a pragmatic way, i.e., "you scratch my back and I'll scratch yours."

Conventional Level

Stage 3
Interpersonal concordance (good boy–nice girl) orientation. Good behaviors are those that please or are approved by others. There is much emphasis on conformity and being "nice."

Stage 4
Orientation toward authority ("law and order"). Focus is on authority or rules. It is right to do one's duty, show respect for authority, and maintain the social order.

Postconventional Level

Stage 5
Social-contract orientation. This stage has a utilitarian, legalistic tone. Correct behavior is defined in terms of standards agreed upon by society. Awareness of the relativism of personal values and the need for consensus is important.

Stage 6
Universal ethical principle orientation. Morality is defined as a decision of conscience. Ethical principles are self-chosen, based on abstract concepts (e.g., the Golden Rule) rather than concrete rules (e.g., the Ten Commandments).

---

shown in Table 11-3. The stages are not differentiated by what decision is made, but by the reasoning that underlies the decision.

According to Kohlberg, the preconventional child is often well behaved and sensitive to labels such as good and bad. But the labels of good or bad are interpreted simply in terms of their physical consequences (punishment, reward, exchange of favors) or in terms of the power of those who make the rules. There is, then, no real standard of morality at the preconventional level. The conventional level is characterized by conformity to the existing social order and an implicit desire to maintain that order. Most American adults, according to Kohlberg, operate at the level of conventional morality. Finally, the postconventional level is said to be governed by moral principles that are universal, and therefore valid independent of the authority of the groups who support them.

Kohlberg reports that moral development may be either fast or slow, but that it does not skip stages. Evidence consistent with this claim comes from a major longitudinal study by Colby, Kohlberg, Gibbs, and Lieberman (1983) conducted over a period of 20 years. As children and adolescents,

TABLE 11-3
Moral Reasoning at Various Stages in Response to Heinz's Dilemma

Stage 1
Action is motivated by avoidance of punishment and "conscience" is irrational fear of punishment.
Pro—If you let your wife die, you will get in trouble. You'll be blamed for not spending the money to save her and there'll be an investigation of you and the druggist for your wife's death.
Con—You shouldn't steal the drug because you'll be caught and sent to jail if you do. If you do get away, your conscience would bother you thinking how the police would catch up with you at any minute.

Stage 2
Action motivated by desire for reward or benefit. Possible guilt reactions are ignored and punishment viewed in a pragmatic manner. (Differentiates own fear, pleasure, or pain from punishment-consequences.)
Pro—If you do happen to get caught you could give the drug back and you wouldn't get much of a sentence. It wouldn't bother you much to serve a little jail term, if you have your wife when you get out.
Con—You may not get much of a jail term if you steal the drug, but your wife will probably die before you get out so it won't do you much good. If your wife dies, you shouldn't blame yourself; it wasn't your fault she has cancer.

Stage 3
Action motivated by anticipation of disapproval of others, actual or imagined hypothetical (e.g., guilt). (Differentiation of disapproval from punishment, fear, and pain.)
Pro—No one will think you're bad if you steal the drug but your family will think you're an inhuman husband if you don't. If you let your wife die, you'll never be able to look anybody in the face again.
Con—It isn't just the druggist who will think you're a criminal, everyone else will too. After you steal it, you'll feel bad thinking how you've brought dishonor on your family and yourself; you won't be able to face anyone again.

Stage 4
Action motivated by anticipation of dishonor, i.e., institutionalized blame for failure of duty, and by guilt over concrete harm done to others. (Differentiates formal dishonor from informal disapproval. Differentiates guilt for bad consequences from disapproval.)
Pro—If you have any sense of honor, you won't let your wife die because you're afraid to do the only thing that will save her. You'll always feel guilty that you caused her death if you don't do your duty to her.
Con—You're desperate and you may not know you're doing wrong when you steal the drug. But you'll know you did wrong after you're punished and sent to jail. You'll always feel guilt for your dishonesty and lawbreaking.

Stage 5
Concern about maintaining respect of equals and of the community (assuming their respect is based on reason rather than emotions). Concern about own self-respect, i.e., to avoid judging self as irrational, inconsistent, nonpurposive. (Discriminates between institutionalized blame and community disrespect or self-disrespect.)
Pro—You'd lose other people's respect, not gain it, if you don't steal. If you let your wife die, it would be out of fear, not out of reasoning it out. So you'd just lose self-respect and probably the respect of others too.
Con—You would lose your standing and respect in the community and violate the law. You'd lose respect for yourself if you're carried away by emotion and forget the long-range point of view.

Stage 6
Concern about self-condemnation for violating one's own principles. (Differentiates between self-respect for general achieving rationality and self-respect for maintaining moral principles.)
Pro—If you don't steal the drug and let your wife die, you'd always condemn yourself for it afterward. You wouldn't be blamed and you would have lived up to the outside rule of the law but you wouldn't have lived up to your own standards of conscience.
Con—If you stole the drug, you wouldn't be blamed by other people but you'd condemn yourself because you wouldn't have lived up to your own conscience and standards of honesty.

Source: Rest, Unpublished doctoral dissertation, University of Chicago, 1969.

and later as adults, subjects were tested with moral dilemmas like the one about the druggist described earlier. According to the theory, older individuals should have more advanced moral reasoning; in fact, the correlation between age and moral reasoning score was 0.78.

Two other aspects of the results of this research provide even stronger evidence for Kohlberg's "stage" theory, which says that as a person's moral reasoning develops, it will progress through stages—that is, individuals should not "skip" stages as their reasoning develops. It is consistent with this claim that in no instance during this research did individuals skip stages. Another property of stage theory has to do with the direction of change. Individuals may either advance in their level of moral reasoning or stay at a particular level, but they should not regress (move to a lower stage). In longitudinal studies (for example, Walker and Taylor, 1991), it is common for individuals to progress from one stage of moral reasoning to a more advanced stage, and when they do not progress, they usually remain at the same level. Only a small percentage of individuals—about 5 percent in the Colby et al. (1983) sample—revert to a less advanced stage.

Another source of evidence for Kohlberg's theory is the relation between moral reasoning scores and moral action. The logic here is that individuals with more advanced moral reasoning would be compelled to moral action in situations where individuals with less mature reasoning might not act. Consider a situation in which a person must decide to help another. For children in the preconventional level of moral reasoning, action would be determined by the likelihood that they would be rewarded for helping (or punished for not helping), or by the possibility that the person might return the favor in the future. These children would be unlikely to help in situations where there was little chance of reward, punishment, or help in return. Individuals in the conventional level know that helping is "good" behavior that is socially valued; these people would be more likely to help others in the absence of reward, punishment, or help in return.

A good deal of evidence supports this link between moral reasoning and moral action. For example, aggressive boys tend to have lower moral reasoning scores than do nonaggressive boys (Bear, 1989). Altruism is also related to moral reasoning: Individuals with higher moral reasoning scores are more likely to help than individuals with lower scores (Eisenberg, 1988). In one study, Gibbs and his colleagues (1986) asked high school teachers to rate students' moral courage. Teachers judged if pupils would defend their principles, even in difficult situations, or if they would act only when it was popular or convenient. Teachers' ratings of moral courage were significantly related to students' moral reasoning scores, but were unrelated to variables such as the students' IQ, empathy, and locus of control.

KOHLBERG'S CRITICS. Kohlberg's conclusions have not gone unchallenged, and in fact his theory and the research on which it is based have been the subject of serious criticism on numerous logical and empirical grounds (Schrader, 1990). We consider two interrelated examples, dealing with Kohlberg's claims that moral development is universal in its course and invariant in its sequence of development.

The most distinctive and controversial element in Kohlberg's theory is his claim that there are universal, absolute standards of right and wrong and that he has demonstrated their existence through scientific research. Kohlberg's claim to have discovered universally true moral principles, as seen in the substance of postconventional morality, is a radical departure from Piagetian and related cognitive-developmental theory.

Research indicates that the sequence of Kohlberg's stages *is* found in many cultures, thereby supporting Kohlberg's claim for the universality of the stages of moral reasoning. However, the highest level of moral reasoning varies among Western, industrialized, and traditional societies. Higher levels of reasoning are more common in cultures in which children are granted more autonomy and are less shielded by parents and others (Eisenberg, Hertz-Lazarowitz, and Fuchs, 1990). This variation among cultures is not consistent with the claim of universal sequence.

Also inconsistent with the claim that the sequence is universal is the fact that Stages 5 and 6 are not found in many cultures; and in the cultures in which they are found, they are rare (Walker and Taylor, 1991). The absence of Stages 5 and 6 in most cultures should not be surprising; postconventional moral reasoning as Kohlberg has defined it depends on a specific philosophical commitment. For example, in explaining Stage 6 moral reasoning Kohlberg states: "First of all, recognition of the moral duty to save a human life whenever possible must be assumed" (1971, p. 208). Kohlberg also defines Stage 6 partly in terms of accepting "the assumption that all other actors' claims [in a moral conflict] are also governed by the Golden Rule and accommodated accordingly" (1973, p. 643). Logical considerations alone simply do not give rise to these particular assumptions; rather, they reflect Kohlberg's preferences (as well as his culture) for justice as the cornerstone of morality. As we see in the Close-Up, some theorists have proposed alternatives to justice as the basis for moral reasoning.

Moral Rules

The moral problems studied by Kohlberg, Gilligan, and their colleagues are called dilemmas because they are deliberately constructed to balance alternative courses of action in terms of right and wrong. These moral problems *do* typify many of the situations that people encounter in their lives. At the same time, for many situations, cultures have well-defined rules that dictate morally right and wrong actions. According to Darley and Shultz (1990), "A rule is a moral one if adherence to it is experienced as obligatory, it applies to all people regardless of their attitude toward it, and if its force is impersonal and external . . ." (p. 529). This definition can be used to distinguish **moral rules** from **social conventions,** which are defined as standards of behaviors that have been agreed to by a cultural group, but which are not really obligatory. For example, rules against murder and theft are moral, but rules concerning dress, manners, and the like are social conventions.

By 3 years of age, most children distinguish moral rules from social conventions. They judge hurting other people or taking their possessions to be more serious transgressions than eating ice cream with one's fingers or not paying attention to a story (Smetana and Braeges, 1990).

When a moral transgression occurs, questions of blame and responsibility arise. Piaget (1932) pioneered research in this area more than a

Moral rule A rule that people are obligated to follow regardless of their attitude toward it; examples would include rules against thievery and murder.

Social convention A standard of behavior agreed upon by a cultural group, but one that is not obligatory, as a moral rule would be.

CLOSE-UP

Care, Responsibility, and Moral Reasoning

Carol Gilligan (1982, 1985) has proposed that moral reasoning—particularly for women—is also based on a greater understanding of care and responsibility in interpersonal relationships. She writes:

> The moral imperative that emerges repeatedly in interviews with women is an injunction to care, a responsibility to discern and alleviate the "real and recognizable trouble" of this world. For men, the moral imperative appears rather as an injunction to respect the rights of others and thus to protect from interference the rights to life and self-fulfillment. (1982, p. 100)

In interviews with women facing a real-life moral dilemma—whether to abort a pregnancy—Gilligan identified three developmental stages in reasoning, each characterized by a greater understanding of caring and responsibility. In the first stage, individuals are concerned with the self and their own needs. This gives way in a second stage to caring for others and particularly to a concern for dependent individuals. However, defining "care" only in terms of others creates tension, because the individual is excluding herself or himself. Hence, in the final stage, caring for others and for oneself become linked in a concern for caring in all human relationships and in denouncing exploitation and violence between people.

Thus, like Kohlberg, Gilligan believes that thinking about moral issues becomes progressively more sophisticated as individuals develop. And, also like Kohlberg, Gilligan has identified a number of distinct stages in the developmental sequence. But unlike Kohlberg, Gilligan believes these stages reflect progressively greater insights into caring, rather than into justice.

Research stimulated by Gilligan's views has revealed that many people do emphasize care and responsibility as they wrestle with moral problems. For example, in a study by Garrod, Beal, and Shin (1990), moral dilemmas were presented to 6- to 10-year-olds. In one problem, a dog decided to nap in an ox's stall. When the ox returned, eager for dinner, the dog awoke angrily and snapped at the ox when he tried to eat his hay. When asked to solve the problem, some children adopted a justice-oriented viewpoint: They argued that the stall belonged to the ox and, therefore, that the dog should leave. Many children, however, provided care-oriented responses. Typical is a 6-year-old boy's reply:

> I would get the dog a nice bale of hay and then I would open it up and then I would make a nice bed and then I'd let the dog sleep on it . . . That way the dog could take a nap and then the ox can eat, and they'd both be happy. (Garrod et al., 1990, p. 22)

However, in this study, as in others (Walker, 1989), boys and girls did not differ in their frequency of justice- and care-oriented solutions.

Thus, the primary contribution of Gilligan's work may be in recognizing the multiple ways in which both females and males grapple with moral issues. As Kohlberg claimed, justice is an important factor. However, as Gilligan has argued, it is not the sole factor; caring and responsibility for others are also important considerations.

half-century ago. He presented stories in which a child's actions caused damage. In one story, a young child accidentally causes much damage:

> A little boy who is called John is in his room. He is called to dinner. He goes into the dining room. But behind the door there was a chair, and on the chair there was a tray with 15 cups on it. John couldn't have known that there was all of this behind the door. He goes in, the door knocks against the tray, "bang" go the 15 cups, and they all get broken! (Piaget, 1932, p. 122)

In a second story, a child's deliberate misbehavior results in a small amount of damage:

> Once there was a little boy named Henry. One day when his mother was out, he tried to get some jam out of the cupboard. He climbed up on a chair and stretched out his arm. But the jam was too high up, and he couldn't reach it and have any. But while he was trying to get it he knocked over a cup. The cup fell down and broke. (Piaget, 1932, p. 122)

Following presentation of both stories, Piaget asked children to decide which of the two children was naughtier. Prior to age 7, children typically selected John, indicating a belief that the outcome of an action is the primary factor that determines guilt. By age 9, children consistently selected Henry as the naughtier of the two boys, reflecting a developmental shift to the belief that it is a person's intention that determines the morality of behavior, not the outcome of the actions.

FIGURE 11-4

By 6 years of age, children realize that people should not be blamed when their behavior accidentally causes harm.

Subsequent work has lowered the age of this transition by a few years: Modern research suggests that by 6 or 7 years of age, children view intentional acts as more worthy of blame than accidents. At this age, children can also distinguish unintentional but foreseeable behavior from accidental behavior. A child who is helping to set the table and drops the plates because he tried to carry too many is seen as blameworthy—"He should have known better"—that is, even though his intentions were to help, he should have had the foresight to realize that his actions could result in harm (Darley and Shultz, 1990).

Thus, children understand many fundamental moral rules of their culture at an early age and are capable of progressively greater insights into moral issues as they develop. If this more sophisticated moral understanding leads to moral behavior, we would expect children to become capable of more prosocial behavior as they develop. Let's explore the factors governing children's prosocial behavior in more depth.

PROSOCIAL BEHAVIOR

Most parents, most teachers, and most religions try to teach children to act in cooperative, helping, or giving ways—at least some of the time and in some situations. Such behavior is usually thought to be in the greater interest of others and society. Developmental psychologists use the term **prosocial behavior** to refer to any of these behaviors that benefit another person or persons, regardless of its underlying motivation.

Altruism, in contrast, tends to describe actions that are motivated by ideals of responsibility toward others or society, rather than actions motivated by an effort to avoid punishment or to serve selfish or personal needs. Distinguishing altruism from other prosocial behavior is often easier in theory than it is in practice: When a prosocial behavior is both altruistic and motivated by other needs is not entirely clear in many situations (Eisenberg, 1988). For this reason, the discussion here focuses on various types of altruistic or prosocial behavior (for example, helping and sharing) with a minimum number of assumptions about possible underlying motivations. We begin by examining the development of prosocial behavior, then look at the many factors responsible for prosocial behavior.

Development of Prosocial Behavior

Prosocial behavior A behavior that benefits other people, regardless of the motivation for the behavior.

Altruism Behavior that benefits others and that is motivated by a concern for others.

Rudimentary acts of helping and caring, as well as signs of emotional distress when others are hurt or uncomfortable, have been noted in toddlers as young as 18 months. Obviously, these youngsters are limited in their ability to understand others' experiences and in their ability to provide help. However, during the preschool and elementary school years, children's ability to behave prosocially expands rapidly. Some of the first insights into these development changes came from Piaget (1932): He suggested that the motives which cause children to behave prosocially follow a developmental trend that parallels cognitive development. Piaget believed that the preoperational child's egocentrism makes sharing and other forms of prosocial behavior unlikely. During the concrete operational period, children begin to appreciate the views and feelings of peers, thereby making them more likely to share with them and to help them.

In one experiment designed to demonstrate this progression, Bar-Tal and his associates had pairs of 4- to 8-year-olds play a game, giving the winner seven pieces of candy as a prize, while the loser received none (Bar-Tal, Raviv, and Leiser, 1980). The question was the following: How much pressure would be required to cause the winner to share with the loser? It was answered by using a cleverly arranged set of events following the game.

Shortly after the candy was given to the winning child, the experimenter left the room for three minutes, so that the winner and loser were alone. When the experimenter returned she noted whether the winner had shared any candy with the loser. Children who shared under these circumstances were assumed to do so for altruistic reasons. If the winning child did not share, the experimenter went on to the second condition. The following story was read to the children:

> A child was invited to a birthday party and there received a bag filled with candy. On the way home the child met his/her friend who asked about the bag. The child said that he/she had received some candy and decided to share it with the friend. Both of them sat down and ate the candy. It is very nice to share candies with a friend. Good children share candy with other children who do not have any. (Bar-Tal et al., 1980, p. 519)

After the story, the experimenter again left the room for three minutes and returned. Children who shared after hearing the story were assumed to have been motivated by the "norm of sharing"—sharing in situations in which it is generally considered a good thing to do.

If the winner did not share after hearing the story, the experimenter went on to the next condition, in which she told the children that their teacher had promised to give an important role in an upcoming school play to one of the children who shared. The children were again left alone for three minutes. Winners who now shared were assumed to do so on their own initiative in the hope of receiving a specific external reward, the role in the play. If the winner still had not shared, the experimenter now told the winning child to do so and went to the corner of the room for two minutes. Children who now shared were assumed to be motivated by compliance to authority. Finally, if the winners still had not shared, the experimenter again told the winner to do so, promising a "big prize" for compliance. This caused every winner who had not yet shared to now share with the loser.

The results of this experiment were quite clear. Only 7 percent of the 4- and 5-year-olds shared without promise of external reward, but 23 percent of the 6- and 7-year-olds and 38 percent of the 8- and 9-year-olds did so. Complementing this pattern, fully 24 percent of the 4- and 5-year-olds did not share until the last condition (when they were specifically told to share and also offered a prize), whereas only 4 percent of the 6- and 7-year-olds and 1 percent of the 8- and 9-year-olds waited until the

FIGURE 11-5
Helping another person by talking with them is a form of prosocial behavior that develops late in childhood.

very end before sharing. Therefore, the findings indicate that as children grow older, their reasons for sharing become more altruistic and less dependent upon the motivation to comply with authority or to receive an external reward.

When young children intend to behave altruistically, they are sometimes limited in their knowledge of what they can do to help. During the childhood years, youngsters acquire an ever-larger number of strategies that they can use to help others, and the preferred strategies become more adultlike.

This pattern is illustrated in a study by Strayer and Schroeder (1989). Videotapes of emotionally evocative vignettes were shown to 5- to 13-year-olds. For example, in one story, a boy and girl argue. Later, the boy lies to a parent about what had happened. The parent believes the boy's story and wrongfully punishes the girl. Subjects in the experiment were asked if and how they would help the girl. A common tactic was to offer to act as a mediator to try to set the record straight. However, younger children also frequently suggested aggressive means to help the girl, such as kicking or hitting the boy. The 12- and 13-year-olds rarely used this approach; instead, they proposed verbal strategies, such as talking to the girl to help her to feel better.

Thus, the intent to act prosocially increases with age, as do children's resources in being able to help or to share. Of course, not all children react similarly to the needs of others, either in toddlerhood or at later ages. Some children are eager to help but others attach greater priority to looking out for their own interests. And, the tendency to behave prosocially is influenced by the setting: Children who readily act prosocially in one situation may be reluctant to do so in others. Let's look at some of the factors that influence children's prosocial behavior.

Skills Underlying Prosocial Behavior

Today, developmental psychologists recognize that prosocial behavior is often the product of a number of cognitive-social skills, including perspective-taking, empathy, and moral reasoning.

PERSPECTIVE-TAKING. In Chapter 6, we encountered Piaget's concept of egocentrism, which refers to a preoperational youngster's inability to see things from another's point of view. Egocentrism can sometimes limit children's ability to share or help because they do not realize the need for such prosocial behavior. For example, young children might not aid an elderly adult carrying several packages because they cannot envision how much this is a burden to the older person. In contrast, older children, who can take the perspective of others—and see how tiring this would be to an elderly adult—would be more inclined to help.

Perspective-taking skill is consistently related to prosocial behavior. That is, those children who better understand the thoughts and feelings of other people are more willing to share and help others (Underwood and Moore, 1982). This link between perspective-taking and prosocial behavior is nicely illustrated in a study by Hudson, Forman, and Brion-Meisels (1982). They began by testing 7-year-olds' role-taking ability and then classifying the children as high or low in role-taking skill based on the test. Later, each child was given the job of teaching two younger children how to make paper caterpillars using scissors, glue, and crayons. The younger children could not do very well at this task on their own, so the 7-year-olds were in fact being tested in terms of how much help they would give.

The differences in the amount and quality of help offered by the two groups of role takers, depicted in Figure 11-6, were quite striking. The

FIGURE 11-6
This graph shows some of the many ways in which children with high role-taking skills were more responsive tutors to younger children than were children with low role-taking skills.
(Data from Hudson, Forman, and Brion-Meisels, 1982.)

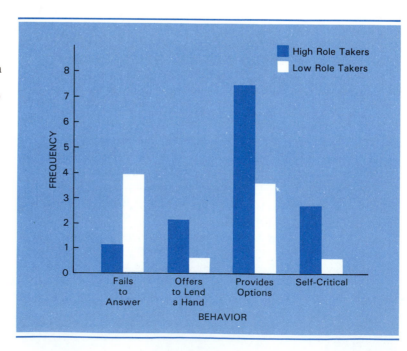

high-skilled role takers not only answered questions willingly, but went out of their way to give helpful demonstrations, and to make numerous supportive comments. Low-skilled role takers either failed or refused to answer questions, or gave answers that were unhelpful or inadequate. Similar results have been obtained with older children and adults (Eisenberg, 1988).

EMPATHY. Closely related to role-taking ability is the idea of **empathy.** Specifically, role-taking ability is the ability to be aware of another person's feelings; empathy is the ability to experience them yourself. Thus, empathy takes role-taking ability one step further by introducing an emotional or affective component: Not only must the child understand how another person is feeling, the child must experience those same emotions.

The hypothesized link between empathy and prosocial behavior is straightforward. Children who deeply feel another person's fear, disappointment, sorrow, or loneliness should be more inclined to help that person than a child who does not feel these emotions. Consistent with this hypothesis, in a comprehensive review, Eisenberg and Miller (1987) concluded that empathy is positively related to prosocial behavior. For example, in one study (Lennon, Eisenberg, and Carroll, 1986), $4\frac{1}{2}$-year-olds viewed a videotape in which preschoolers fell on a playground, then cried for help. While children watched the tape, the experimenter surreptitiously recorded their facial and gestural reactions. After viewing the tape, children were allowed to help make a game for the children injured in the videotape. The correlation between degree of emotional responding to the tape and time spent helping was 0.44. In other words, $4\frac{1}{2}$-year-olds who empathized with the injured children (as assessed by their facial expressions and other bodily signals) were the ones who offered the most help to the injured children (by working the longest on the game).

MORAL REASONING. Prosocial behavior and altruism also is associated with children's emerging ideas about moral reasoning and fairness. Earlier in this chapter we saw that potential rewards and punishments influence young children's moral reasoning whereas a concern for moral principles marks adolescents' and adults' moral decision making. This work leads us to expect greater prosocial behavior as children develop because such behavior acquires the force of a moral imperative—children feel that they *should* behave prosocially. Younger children, in contrast, lack this sense of obligation to behave prosocially; their prosocial behavior is more determined by the chances of being rewarded for behaving prosocially or punished for behaving antisocially.

Greater understanding of fairness also is a force in some aspects of children's prosocial behavior (Damon, 1980). Preschool children often give little thought to fairness: Asked to divide rewards among a group of children, preschoolers typically want to keep all the rewards for themselves. Or they may allocate the rewards to a group of children to which they belong. A girl, for example, might say that only the girls should receive the reward. Older preschoolers and kindergarten children believe that rewards should be divided equally among all members in a class,

Empathy Experiencing the feelings or emotions of another person.

regardless of their effort or need. Finally, beginning in the early elementary school years, there is growing belief that the fair distribution of rewards involves decisions about a number of factors, such as each child's efforts and needs, and the nature of the work leading to the reward.

In short, as children's cognitive skills mature during the preschool and elementary school years, they begin to realize the complexities involved in deciding what is fair and what is just. More mature ideas of fairness and justice should be linked to greater prosocial behavior, and the evidence indicates that they usually are (Eisenberg and Shell, 1986).

Socialization of Prosocial Behavior

Prosocial behavior becomes more common as youngsters grow, but at all ages individual children differ markedly in their tendencies to behave prosocially. What are the roots of prosocial behavior? What experiences seem to foster altruism? Among the keys are parental discipline, modeling, and praise.

PARENTAL DISCIPLINE. Parents whose favored disciplinary strategy is reasoning tend to have children who commonly behave prosocially (Hoffman, 1988). This disciplinary approach often emphasizes the consequences of the child's misbehavior to others and the moral unacceptability of such behavior. Thus, discipline through reasoning stresses many of the components underlying prosocial behavior: perspective-taking, empathic responding, and moral reasoning.

MODELING. Behavioral examples represent an effective way to elicit and teach sharing and other prosocial behaviors. Laboratory studies make it clear that children will imitate the altruistic behaviors of their peers (Wilson, Piazza, and Nagle, 1990).

FIGURE 11-7
Sharing is often learned by watching others share.

Of course, parents are the models to whom children are most continuously exposed, so it should come as no surprise that they exert a powerful influence on sharing, as well as on cooperation and helpfulness. For example, parents who report frequent feelings of warmth and concern for others (for example, "I often feel concerned for those less fortunate than I") tend to have children who experience stronger feelings of empathy (Eisenberg et al., 1991). And the more responsive and helpful a mother is, the more likely are her children to imitate her by being cooperative, helpful, sharing, and less critical toward one another (Bryant and Crockenberg, 1980).

PRAISE. Perhaps the most obvious way to elicit sharing and other altruistic behavior from children is to reward them directly for acts of generosity. Fischer (1963) found that 4-year-old children became more likely to share marbles with unknown peers if such beneficence was directly rewarded with bubble gum.

Most parents, however, do not customarily reward their children materially for prosocial acts. They are more inclined to praise them verbally with phrases such as "I'm proud of you for sharing your candy with your sister" (Grusec, 1991). Recent work indicates that **dispositional praise** seems particularly effective in promoting altruism. This sort of praise involves remarks in which the child's prosocial behavior is attributed to the child's underlying altruistic nature. The previous example would illustrate dispositional praise if the parent added, "This tells me that you're really a helpful person."

Praise of this sort apparently fosters prosocial behavior by changing a child's self-concept. By repeatedly experiencing dispositional praise, children come to internalize the view that they are nice (friendly, helpful, and the like). Consequently, when they encounter a situation in which prosocial behavior is appropriate, their self-concept prompts them to act prosocially (Mills and Grusec, 1989).

Situational Factors

Kind children may disappoint us by being cruel and children who are usually stingy sometimes surprise us by their generosity. Examples like these remind us that the context has a powerful influence on whether children will act prosocially. Let's look at three contextual factors known to influence altruism.

FEELINGS OF RESPONSIBILITY. Adults are less likely to help another when there are other bystanders than when they are alone with the person in need. This has been explained as the **diffusion of responsibility** effect. When other bystanders are present, the responsibility experienced by any one of them is presumed to be diffused: "She could help, so I don't have to." Because they feel less responsible in this setting, adults are not as likely to help (Latané and Nida, 1981).

Does diffusion of responsibility also occur with children? A study by Peterson (1983) indicates that it does. The children in her study, 6- to 11-year-olds, were shown how to play a game involving wheels, cranks,

Dispositional praise Praise that attributes a behavior to some underlying trait of a person.

Diffusion of responsibility A feeling that one is less responsible for a person in distress because a large number of other potentially responsible people are also present.

handles, and other complex parts. After children had played the game for a bit, they were moved to a waiting room and told that another child (the "victim-to-be") was now playing the game. At this point, half the children in each age group were led to believe that a third child (the "other bystander") was in a room next to the game and waiting rooms; the remaining children heard no mention of the "other bystander." Then the "emergency" occurred: A young child's voice (actually prerecorded) came from the game room, crying:

> "Oh, my finger!" "Oh, rats, it really hurts (sob)." "Oh, my hand is hurt, I can't get it out." "I can't get it out, I wish someone would help me." Between verbal cues, labored breathing and a struggle with the machine could be heard. (Peterson, 1983, pp. 875–876)

At all ages, more children helped when they thought they were the only bystander than when they thought another child could help. Overall, of the children who believed that only they alone could help, approximately 60 percent helped, compared to about 20 percent of the children who believed that a third child, the "other bystander," was present. Like adults, children are much more inclined to act prosocially when they feel the burden of responsibility than when they feel the responsibility is shared with others.

MOOD AND EMOTIONAL STATE.   A child's willingness to share is influenced by his or her immediate emotional state. Children who are asked to think happy thoughts share more than those not given this positive set, whereas those asked to think sad thoughts tend to share a bit less than uninstructed children in a control group also invited to share (Moore, Underwood, and Rosenhan, 1973). Similarly, the feeling or experience of being successful seems to produce a "warm glow of success" in children that makes them more generous. Conversely, failure and its associated feelings decrease generosity in young and old alike (Isen, Horn, and Rosenhan, 1973).

COST OF PROSOCIAL BEHAVIOR.   Disasters are often accompanied by gripping stories of people who help save would-be victims, usually at great risk to themselves. These actions are definitely the exception rather than the rule: In general, people act prosocially more often when this behavior incurs few "costs" to themselves. For example, in one study (Eisenberg and Shell, 1986), $4\frac{1}{2}$-year-olds who had received stickers as rewards were asked if they wanted to donate some of their stickers to poor children whose parents could not afford to buy them any Christmas presents. Children who had received 10 identical, unattractive stickers donated more than did children who had received 10 different, attractive stickers. Later, some of the $4\frac{1}{2}$-year-olds were told that they could help make a game for hospitalized children or could play with some toys. Other $4\frac{1}{2}$-year-olds were simply asked if they wished to help make the games— playing with toys was not an alternative. Children spent nearly twice as much time helping to make the game when playing with the toys was not an available alternative. Thus, preschoolers both helped and shared more when the cost was minimal—in the one case, the stickers were unattractive, and, in the other case, making the game for other children did not entail the sacrifice of not playing with toys.

Interestingly, for those children who participated in the high-cost conditions (attractive stickers and toys available for play), the level of moral reasoning was correlated positively with both helping and sharing. When the costs of prosocial behavior were high, children with the most advanced moral reasoning were those who helped and shared the most.

Our discussion of prosocial behavior has revealed that cognitive-social skills, parental behavior, and situational factors all play a role in determining when children will act prosocially. This complex pattern of causation is also apparent as we turn to the other side of the coin and consider what is often thought of as the most serious form of antisocial behavior, aggression.

AGGRESSION

At some time or another virtually everyone aggresses—acts in a way that brings, or might bring, discomfort to someone else. We know that the type of aggression a person displays and the ability of a person to control such aggression change in important ways with age and experience. The roots of these patterns and changes have long been of interest to developmental psychologists.

We need to say something here about the difference between assertiveness and aggressiveness. In some contexts (for example, in business and politics) the words are used synonymously. We hear praise for an "aggressive business person" or an "aggressive program of affirmative action." Psychologists and other behavioral scientists, however, see an important difference between the ideas underlying the two terms. Assertive behaviors are goal-directed actions to further the legitimate interests of individuals or the groups they represent, while respecting the rights of other persons. In contrast, aggressive behavior, which may be physical or verbal, is intended to harm, damage, or injure, and is carried out without regard for the rights of others.

Change and Stability in Aggressive Behavior

By the time youngsters are old enough to play with one another, aggression can be seen in these interactions. When 1- and 2-year-olds play, conflicts frequently arise—often over contested playthings—and aggression is a common strategy for resolving the conflicts. In one study (Cummings, Iannotti, and Zahn-Waxler, 1989), 2-year-olds who were playing together were aggressive about 5 percent of the time. Common aggressive behaviors included hitting, kicking, pushing, or biting the other child, or trying to grab a toy.

As Figure 11-8 shows, this sort of physical aggression declines over the preschool years. However, this decrease is offset by an increase in

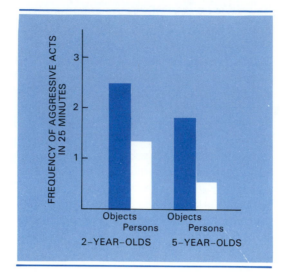

FIGURE 11-8
Physical aggression becomes less frequent during the preschool years.
(Data from Cummings, Iannotti, and Zahn-Waxler, 1989.)

verbal aggression and other nonphysical forms of aggression in which the sole intent is to hurt another person (Eisenberg, 1988).

Although the typical form of aggression changes with development, individual children's tendencies to behave aggressively are moderately stable, especially among boys. Cummings, Iannotti, and Zahn-Waxler (1989), for example, found that the correlation between overall physical aggression at two years of age and physical aggression at five years of age was 0.59 for boys and 0.36 for girls. And, for boys, the correlation between physical aggression at 2 years of age and verbal aggression at 5 years of age was 0.40. Clearly, aggressive toddlers tend to remain aggressive over the preschool years.

Particularly convincing evidence for the stability and the severity of childhood aggression comes from two longitudinal studies. Kupersmidt and Coie (1990) measured aggressiveness in a group of 11-year-olds by having children list the names of classmates who frequently started fights. Seven years later, more than half of the aggressive children had police records, compared with less than 10 percent of the nonaggressive children. In the second study, conducted by Stattin and Magnusson (1989) in Sweden, teachers rated the aggressive behavior of more than 1,000 10-year-olds. These ratings accurately predicted subsequent criminal activity, a relation that is shown in Figure 11-9. Boys who were in the least aggressive group had committed relatively few criminal offenses of any sort. In contrast, two-thirds of the boys in the most aggressive group had committed offenses and nearly half had committed major offenses such as assault, theft, or robbery. Overall, women committed far fewer offenses, but teachers' ratings of aggressive behavior still predicted which girls were more likely to have criminal records.

Findings like these should make it clear that children's aggression is not simply a case of playful pushing and shoving that most children outgrow. On the contrary, the small minority of children who are highly

FIGURE 11-9
Children who were rated more aggressive by their teachers were, as adolescents and young adults, more likely to have criminal records. This is true for both major and minor offenses.
(Data from Stattin and Magnusson, 1989.)

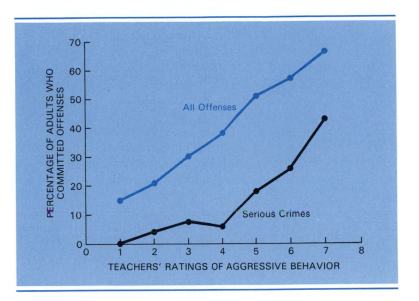

aggressive develop into young adults who create havoc in modern societies. What causes children to behave aggressively? Let's look at some of the roots of aggressive behavior.

Sources of Aggressive Behavior

FRUSTRATION. One view of how aggression is elicited is the famous frustration-aggression hypothesis, first spelled out by John Dollard and his associates at Yale University in 1939. These theorists argued that frustration, defined as any blocking of goal-directed activity, naturally leads to aggression. According to the original statement, aggression was said to always be a consequence of frustration, and frustration was said to always lead to some form of aggression. Such a statement is too strong. In many cases most people, even if severely frustrated, will refrain from showing any direct acts of aggression: Speeding drivers will typically not assault, or even raise their voices to, the police officer who has stopped them. Consequently, although frustration may play some role in children's aggression (Berkowitz, 1989), other factors need to be considered, too.

IMPACT OF PARENTS. Early family experiences are a prime training ground for learning patterns of aggression (Widom, 1989). The pioneering work in this area was conducted by Gerald Patterson (1982, 1984), whose approach is unique because his data and conclusions derive almost entirely from careful, systematic observations of aggressive children in their home environments. One fact that comes through clearly in this work is that parents and siblings play an enormous role in cultivating the behavior of aggressive children, and in ways that are subtle as well as obvious. Many parents and older siblings, for example, punish aggressive behavior. Although the immediate effect may be to suppress aggression, it also serves as a model and illustrates vividly that punishment "works" as a means of controlling others. A parent who hits a child for aggression is saying, in effect, "You were right. The best way to get people to do what you want, or to stop them from doing what you don't want, is to hit them hard enough."

Not surprisingly, harsh physical punishment is associated with aggression. Dodge and his colleagues (1990) studied children who had experienced physical punishment so harsh that bruises resulted or that the child received medical treatment. These children were rated twice as aggressive—by both teachers and peers—as children who had not experienced such harsh punishment.

But strong or aggressive parental responses are not essential in the making of an aggressive child. Even low-key anger responses and unfair accusations by parents may pave the way for later aggressiveness. Finally, a vicious circle appears to develop in the families of many aggressive children. Compared with families with nonaggressive children, both aggressive children and their parents are more likely to respond to neutral behavior with aggression. Furthermore, once an aggressive exchange has begun, both parents and children are likely to escalate the exchange, rather than break it off. And once a child has been labeled aggressive by parents and others, that child is more likely to be accused of aggression and to be singled out for punishment, even when the child has been behaving entirely appropriately on the occasion in question (Patterson, 1984).

This work emphasizes the point that hitting a child for aggression does not usually inhibit aggression for very long, because aggression is often a natural response to being the target of aggression, regardless of the other person's motives. It is best to respond to young children's aggression by ignoring it, while at the same time reinforcing and encouraging various forms of nonaggressive social behavior.

THE INFLUENCE OF TELEVISION AND MOVIES. Most children today are regular television watchers by the age of 3. By the time they are 15 they will have spent more time watching television than going to school. In fact, throughout childhood they will have spent more time watching television than in any other activity but sleep (Liebert and Sprafkin, 1988).

What do they see when watching all this television? The answer varies somewhat from child to child, but in the main the commercial entertainment shown on contemporary American television is of the "action-adventure" genre. This means that most of what they see contains a heavy dose of modeled aggression. Heroes and "good-guys" on these shows almost invariably end up in a fist-, knife-, or gunfight with the "bad guys." The "good guys" always win, of course, and are typically rewarded with praise, admiration, and sometimes more tangible rewards (such as a vacation in the sun). Thus, on television, aggression in the service of society is rewarded.

What are the effects of watching all these rewarded aggressive models for so long? This has not been an easy question to answer. Studies done in the 1960s by Bandura and his colleagues (Bandura and Walters, 1963) presented preschool children with aggressive modeling scenes on specially created television programs and demonstrated that children could

FIGURE 11-10
Television presents many examples of aggressive behavior.

learn new ways of behaving aggressively, which they demonstrated by assaulting a plastic "Bobo doll." But critics were quick to point out the limitations of these early "studies of TV violence" and questioned whether observing violence in more realistic settings would produce aggression (Klapper, 1968).

Numerous studies followed, most aimed at further mapping out and quantifying the relation between TV violence and children's aggressive behavior. One such study, for example, showed that an eleven-day "diet" of aggressive cartoons led preschoolers to become more aggressive toward their peers (Steuer, Applefield, and Smith, 1971). Other investigators took a correlational tack, and related violence observed on commercial television programs (measured by questionnaires and diaries kept by young viewers) to various measures of aggressive behavior. Most of the studies pointed to a modest but consistent link between viewing of TV violence and aggression (Wood, Wong, and Chachere, 1991).

One of the most methodologically sophisticated studies of TV violence and aggression ever done was reported by Huesmann, Eron, and their colleagues (1986; Huesmann, Lagarspetz, and Eron, 1984). These investigators followed almost 1,000 elementary school boys and girls in both the United States and Finland for three years. Such an in-depth, cross-cultural study permitted an examination of both TV violence viewing and other factors that may be contributors to childhood aggression over time. It also provided an opportunity to consider the interaction among these factors. The results clearly supported the conclusion of earlier laboratory studies and studies of commercial TV programs. The extent of TV violence viewing predicted future levels of aggression for boys and girls in both cultures. In addition, the large sample size and the volume of detailed information available about the children and their families permitted Huesmann and his colleagues to identify some of the boundary conditions and moderating variables that increase and minimize the TV violence-aggression link.

One major finding from this study is that TV violence viewing and aggressive behavior are bidirectional in their effects. That is, watching TV violence stimulates a child to be more aggressive, while a child's becoming more aggressive stimulates additional TV violence viewing. Equally important is the demonstration that aggression is almost always multiply determined. In both Finland and the United States, children who were most aggressive watched a lot of violent TV, believed that such shows portrayed life as it is, and identified strongly with the aggressive heroes in those shows. At the same time, these aggressive children also tended to have frequent aggressive fantasies, to have mothers who were quite aggressive themselves, to come from poorer than average homes, to do poorly in school, and to be unpopular with their peers.

What all this suggests, of course, is that TV violence is not the sole cause of aggression in children. Rather, it is an important contributing factor in a highly complex process in which parents and peers also contribute. As we have already seen, similarly complex patterns have been found when we try to understand any facet of children's social behavior.

COGNITIVE-SOCIAL PROCESSES. It should come as no surprise that aggression, like prosocial behavior, appears to have an important cognitive component. Kenneth Dodge and his collaborators were the first to chart this territory. In an early experiment, Dodge (1980) compared boys who had been judged by their teachers as aggressive or nonaggressive when they reacted to a situation in which their half-completed puzzle was dropped by another child. The other child made one of three statements: (1) he had dropped the puzzle deliberately, (2) he dropped the puzzle by accident, or (3) he made an ambiguous statement regarding the incident. Both aggressive and nonaggressive boys were most aggressive when the other child's intent was hostile and least aggressive when the other child had dropped the puzzle accidentally. However, the aggressive and nonaggressive boys differed in their response to the ambiguous statement. When the motives of the child who had dropped the puzzle were ambiguous, aggressive boys typically assumed he had had a hostile intent, whereas nonaggressive boys did not assume hostility.

At least some of this inappropriate responding occurs because these children are less skilled at interpreting behaviors and, unable to determine other children's intentions, often respond aggressively by default. For example, Dodge, Bates, and Pettit (1990) presented brief stories to children. In the stories, a negative event (for example, having one's building block knocked down by a peer) was accompanied by hostile, benign, or neutral intentions. Children were asked to explain why the child in the story had caused the negative event. Regardless of the actual intent, aggressive children were more prone to attribute the child's act to hostile, aggressive motives.

FIGURE 11-11
The model proposed by
Dodge and his colleagues
(1986) of the steps
involved in interpreting
and responding to a
social stimulus.

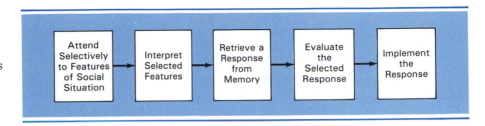

From findings like these, Dodge and his collaborators (Dodge, Pettit, McClaskey, and Brown, 1986) have formulated an information-processing model of aggressive children's thinking. In their model, responding to a social stimulus (such as having one's toys taken) involves several steps, which are summarized in Figure 11-11. First, children selectively attend to certain features of the social stimulus but not others in the manner described on pages 210–11 of Chapter 7. Second, children try to interpret the features that they have processed; that is, they try to give meaning to the social stimulus. Third, a behavioral response that is associated with this interpretation is retrieved from memory. Fourth, children evaluate this response to determine if it is appropriate. Finally, the child proceeds with the behavior if it has been deemed appropriate.

Dodge has shown that aggressive children's processing is biased and restricted in many of these steps. For example, aggressive children are less likely to attend to features that would signal nonhostile motives. A surprised, chagrined look that suggests that a negative event was an accident is often not processed by aggressive children. And, as we have already seen, when the features of a social situation do not lead to an obvious interpretation, aggressive youngsters *assume* the intent to be hostile.

If aggressive children are unskilled at interpreting and responding to others' actions, would training these skills lead to improved social behavior? The answer seems to be yes (Dodge and Crick, 1990). One approach is to teach aggressive children that aggression is painful and does not solve problems, that intentions can be understood by attention to relevant cues, and that there are more effective, prosocial ways to solve interpersonal disputes. This approach, which we first encountered in the Close-Up in Chapter 1, leads to reduced aggressive behavior and more positive interactions with peers.

We have seen that the vicious cycle of aggression can begin early. Once youngsters are labeled aggressive, environmental factors may lead them quite unwittingly along an aggressive path. The punishments that parents and teachers dole out may increase the child's hostility and serve as further evidence that aggression "works." The child may then choose aggressive companions who further encourage aggressive behavior.

This cycle can be avoided. Parents and teachers can deal with misbehavior with reasoning instead of physical punishment. And, children prone to aggressive responding can be taught other, equally effective but more prosocial ways to deal with problems that arise with peers.

SUMMARY

1. Self-control emerges in three phases. At about 1 year of age, infants become aware that parents impose constraints on their behavior. Beginning at 2 years of age, toddlers can exert self-control in the absence of a parent. At 3 years of age, youngsters become more flexible in the regulation of their behavior, a skill that continues to improve during childhood and adolescence.

2. Children's self-control is influenced by models. Delay of gratification is more likely when children observe models behaving in this manner. Cognitive skills are also important. Children can delay gratification longer using strategies that allow them to regulate their behavior during the delay.

3. Delay of gratification during the preschool years is related to later behavior. Preschool children who delay gratification longer are, as older children and adolescents, better able to pay attention, more planful, more socially resourceful, and more successful academically.

4. Freud believed that most people during childhood develop a superego—that part of personality that guides morality, by identifying with the parents or other authority figures. However, research does not support the claim that identification with parents early in life is a key event in the development of morality.

5. Kohlberg's approach to the development of morality is an elaborated version of the cognitive-developmental viewpoint. He concludes that moral development proceeds in a universal, invariant sequence through three levels—preconventional, conventional, and postconventional. Critics have argued that Kohlberg's theory places too much emphasis on justice; Gilligan's approach emphasizes *caring* as the basis for moral reasoning.

6. By the end of the preschool years, children distinguish moral rules from social conventions. Also, in judging blame, children distinguish intentional, unintentional but foreseeable, and accidental behaviors.

7. Altruism and prosocial behavior refer to helping and sharing, especially in circumstances and in ways that appear to be self-sacrificing rather than self-serving. Prosocial behavior becomes more common with development. Prosocial behavior requires appropriate cognitive-social skills. Among these are perspective-taking, empathy, and moral reasoning.

8. Prosocial behavior is influenced by parents' disciplinary practices and by observing models who behave prosocially. Also, children are more inclined to behave prosocially when they are made to feel responsible, when they are in a good mood, and when the costs of such behavior are less.

9. Aggression is action designed to hurt others, and must be discriminated from assertiveness, the socially acceptable expression of one's rights and feelings. Physical aggression can be seen in 1-year-olds, but becomes less frequent during the preschool years. Verbal aggressiveness becomes more common during this same period.

10. Frustration sometimes leads to aggression, but not always. Parental aggressive behavior is an important influence, often producing a vicious cycle in which both parent and child become more aggressive over time. Exposure to TV violence leads to increased aggressive attitudes, impulses, and behavior, primarily in children who are aggressive to begin with. Aggressive children often are biased in their interpretation and response to peers' behaviors.

C·H·A·P·T·E·R 12

The Development of Sex Differences and Gender Identity

Of all the ways in which individuals are categorized, probably none is as influential as gender. Immediately after birth, family and well-wishers ask about the sex of a newborn child. Why should a child's sex be of such overwhelming importance? The reason is that the labels "female" and "male" do not refer simply to biological sex; they function as social categories that carry broad implications for development. Widely held assumptions, standards, and values are associated with the terms boy, girl, woman, and man. An individual is perceived and treated differently according to his or her sex, or gender.

Because gender has such a central place in human interaction, it has been the subject of much research—and even more speculation. Today's heightened interest in this subject is partly due to concern about the negative impact of classification according to a person's sex. There is special concern about how women and girls might be adversely affected by sex-role classification. Some examples will illustrate the pervasive impact of gender on development.

▶   Joe and Debbie were elated: Debbie had just given birth to a fifth child, a daughter named Trudy, who would join her four brothers at home. When mother and daughter were discharged from the hospital, 3-day-old Trudy wore a pink gown trimmed with lace. The boys were eager to see their new sister and each wanted to hold her. Joe cautioned them to be especially gentle with her.

▶   At the bank, Vonnie recognized Sharon, a friend from college that she hadn't seen in several weeks. Vonnie introduced Sharon to her 4-year-old daughter: "This is Sharon, a friend of mine who is a doctor at the clinic downtown." On the way home, Vonnie's daughter frowned and asked, "Mama, Sharon's not really a doctor, is she?" Vonnie replied, "Why yes, and she happens to be a very good one." Vonnie's daughter wasn't convinced: "I think you're wrong. She's really a nurse; only men can be doctors."

▶   Throughout elementary school, Darlene had always been the top student in her class, getting straight As. As Darlene moved into junior and senior high school, she took the hardest courses that the school had to offer. Darlene noticed, with considerable pride, that she continued to get the highest grade in her math classes. She also realized that, as each year went by, more and more of her classmates were boys, and that they did as well or better than she on the standardized tests of math achievement that the school administered every spring.   ◀

In this chapter, we will examine the impact of gender on human development. We begin by considering cultural stereotypes concerning males and females. Next, we will examine actual psychological differences between boys and girls. In the third section, we focus on sex typing, how children come to differentiate male and female and learn to identify with one sex or the other. Finally, we discuss recent changes in sex roles and their impact on development.

STEREOTYPES: HOW WE VIEW FEMALES AND MALES

Sex, or gender, stereotypes are the widespread, relatively stable beliefs and images that are held about the sexes. They are abstractions or generalizations that may or may not be true. All societies hold stereotypes about males and females, but people often are unaware that they hold such beliefs. To demonstrate, imagine the following scenes: a physician and a nurse caring for a child, a person chopping wood, a child setting the table for dinner. Chances are that you pictured a male physician and a female nurse in the first scene; a large, muscular man in the second scene; and a girl in the third scene. Such images would be consistent with gender stereotypes that adults in the United States and Canada hold for occupations and activities.

Components of Stereotypes

Gender stereotypes consist of several components: physical characteristics, social roles, interests, sexuality, and psychological characteristics (Kite and Deaux, 1987). The nature of these components of gender ster-

TABLE 12-1
Stereotypes Associated with Males and Females

Characteristics of Males	Characteristics of Females
independent	emotional
aggressive	grateful
not excitable in minor crisis	home-oriented
skilled in business	strong conscience
mechanical aptitude	kind
outspoken	cries easily
acts as leader	creative
self-confident	understanding
takes a stand	considerate
ambitious	devotes self to others
not easily influenced	needs approval
dominant	gentle
active	aware of others' feelings
knows the ways of the world	excitable in a major crisis
loud	expresses tender feelings
interested in sex	enjoys art and music
makes decisions easily	doesn't hide emotions
doesn't give up easily	tactful
stands up under pressure	feelings hurt
not timid	helpful to others
good at sports	neat
likes math and science	religious
competitive	likes children
adventurous	warm to others
sees self running show	need for security
outgoing	
feels superior	
forward	

Source: From T. L. Ruble, "Sex stereotypes: Issues of changes in the 1970s," in Sex Roles, *9, 1983, 397–402, table 1. Reprinted with permission.*

Instrumental
Psychological
characteristics that
describe a person who
acts on and influences
the world.

Expressive Psychological
characteristics that
describe a person who
is focused on emotions
and interpersonal
relationships.

eotypes have been revealed in research by presenting social-psychological
or personality characteristics to subjects and then asking the subjects to
indicate how typical each one is of males and females. Illustrative results
are shown in Table 12–1. Males are more often seen as rational, active,
independent, competitive, and aggressive. This cluster of traits is referred
to as **instrumental**, reflecting a characterization of individuals who are
acting on the world and influencing it. In contrast, females are more often
described as emotional, passive, dependent, sensitive, and gentle. This
cluster of feminine traits is labeled **expressive**, denoting an emphasis on
interpersonal relationships and emotional functioning.

Traditional stereotypes have changed somewhat in the last few decades. Most notable is a change in the perception of women's social roles.
During the 1970s and the 1980s, attitudes became more favorable toward
the participation of women in the work force and in family decision
making (Thornton, Alwin, and Camburn, 1983). Once seen as maladjusted
and less feminine than homemakers, today's career-oriented women are
viewed as psychologically adjusted and satisfied (Yogev, 1983). Such change
is important, because stereotypes operate in complex ways that powerfully
influence the development of sex roles and gender identity.

How Stereotypes Work

Stereotypes set up expectations that, based on their gender, individuals
will appear, act, and feel in particular ways. These expectations, in turn,
affect how we perceive and treat others. The nature of sex-biased perceptions has been revealed by research in which an infant wears gender-
neutral clothing and is described as a boy to some subjects and as a girl
to others. Typically, perceptions of the infant vary depending on whether
the child has been labeled a girl or a boy. When labeled as a girl, adults
perceive the infant to be less aggressive, quieter, less angry, and more

FIGURE 12-1

Sex stereotypes shape our perception of young children. Lacking unambiguous
cues as to the sex of the toddler shown here, most people would infer that the
toddler surrounded by masculine-stereotyped toys is a boy whereas the toddler
surrounded by feminine-stereotyped toys is a girl. The toddler surrounded by
feminine-stereotyped toys would also be perceived to be quieter and more
readily frightened, although in reality, girls are neither.

afraid than when the infant is labeled a boy. And, as early as the preschool years, children respond in the same gender-specific way to infants who are said to be boys or girls (Stern and Karraker, 1989).

It is clear that stereotypes are not simply neutral descriptions of the sexes; instead, they act as differential prescriptions, norms, or standards for males and females. Socialization is generally aimed at developing members of society to fit these standards. However, before we examine these socialization practices, we need to address the important question of how the sexes actually differ.

SEX DIFFERENCES: FACT AND FICTION

We all recognize that the sexes differ in interesting ways. Primary sex differences in the reproductive system are obvious, as are secondary sex characteristics such as voice pitch, beard growth, and breast development. Males are typically larger and stronger than females throughout most of the life span. They display more developed muscles, whereas females have a greater proportion of fat tissue than males. As infants, boys are more active than girls and this difference increases during childhood (Eaton and Enns, 1986). Females have a lower mortality rate from the moment of conception, they are less susceptible to many diseases and dysfunctions, and they are less vulnerable to stress (Zaslow and Hayes, 1986).

The picture is less clear when intellectual and psychosocial attributes are examined. In 1974 Eleanor Maccoby and Carol Jacklin wrote an extremely influential book in which they summarized results from approximately 1,500 research studies relevant to sex differences, mostly in young children. They concluded that gender differences had been established in only four areas—verbal ability, mathematical ability, spatial ability, and aggression. They also suggested that the findings were too ambiguous or inadequate to draw conclusions about many behaviors. Other presumed sex differences were labeled "cultural myths" because, according to Maccoby and Jacklin, evidence derived from their research did not support them. These cultural myths included the beliefs that girls are more social and suggestible than boys, have lower self-esteem, are less analytical in thinking, and lack achievement motivation.

Maccoby and Jacklin's conclusions did not go unquestioned. Maccoby and Jacklin had included some weak studies and had defined behaviors in ways in which other researchers might not (Block, 1976). Other writers questioned their findings about specific behaviors. Through this debate more research was stimulated, some involving new statistical techniques that allow finer analyses of sex differences (Eagly, 1983). It now appears that gender differences may be somewhat more extensive than Maccoby and Jacklin had suggested—but, as we will see, the issue is not easily settled. Summarized in Table 12-2 are some recent findings; we first consider results concerning intellectual development, then those dealing with social behavior.

TABLE 12-2
Comparisons of Female and Male Performance

Verbal Ability	From childhood through adulthood females display higher skills.
Mathematics	No childhood differences; or females do better in computation. From adolescence on, males do better overall.
Spatial Ability	From childhood on, males do better on some tasks, not others.
Activity Level	From preschool age to young adulthood, males are more active, especially in the presence of others and in restricted settings.
Aggression	Males are more aggressive from the preschool years. Differences are greater early in life.
Anxiety	Females may be more anxious from childhood on, although the data on this issue are mostly self-reports.
Helping	Differences in altruism often not found. Females are more empathic on self-reports but not other measures. Behavior may depend heavily on the situation.
Impulsivity	Young females show more delay of gratification and less risk taking, fewer temper tantrums, less disruptive behavior. Studies of adults lacking.
Motive to Achieve	Few overall differences. Some females may be more motivated by the presence of others; males by challenging, competitive situations.
Social Influence	Females are more responsive to social influence, perhaps especially under group pressure.
Social Orientation	Females gaze and smile more at others; women are better than men at interpreting nonverbal communication. Female friendships are intimate, supportive; male friendships are more oriented to the group.

Source: Based primarily on Becker (1986); Block (1983); Deaux (1985); Eagly and Carli (1981); Eagly and Crowley (1986); Eaton and Enns (1986); Eisenberg and Lennon (1983); Hall and Halberstadt (1986); Hyde (1981, 1984); Hyde and Linn (1988); Hyde, Fennema, and Lamon (1990); Kimball (1989); Maccoby and Jacklin (1974, 1980); Ruble (1988); and Wylie (1979).

Intellectual Abilities

Based on a long fascination with intellectual ability, researchers continue to investigate gender differences in verbal, mathematical, and spatial abilities.

VERBAL ABILITY. Females have typically been given the edge in verbal ability (Maccoby and Jacklin, 1974). In a recent review, Hyde and Linn

(1988) found that females had greater verbal ability in 75 percent of the 165 studies that they analyzed. The difference was usually quite small, but was larger for general measures of verbal ability, for the ability to solve anagrams, and in the quality of speech production. This same pattern of sex differences was found for children, adolescents, and adults. Further evidence for the sex difference in verbal ability is the finding that more boys than girls have reading and other language-related problems, such as stuttering (Halpern, 1986).

MATHEMATICS. A complex pattern of sex differences exists for mathematics. Let's start with performance on standardized tests of math achievement. These tests emphasize computational skills during the elementary school years and the middle school years, and girls usually have higher scores than boys at this time. Problem solving and application of math concepts become the focus in high school and college; here, boys' scores are most often higher than girls' scores. Understanding of math concepts is assessed at all ages, with the usual outcome being that males and females do not differ. Thus, initially girls excel in math computation but later boys and men excel in math problem solving (Hyde, Fennema, and Lamon, 1990).

By high school, boys have taken more math courses than girls. However, this alone cannot account for the sex difference. When math background is taken into account, the sex difference becomes smaller but does not disappear (Kimball, 1989).

Paradoxically, a different pattern emerges for grades in math courses. Often no differences are detected in boys' and girls' grades, but when a difference is found, it invariably favors girls. This is even true for courses in high school and college—precisely the time when men are getting higher scores on math achievement tests (Kimball, 1989).

Why do girls get better grades in math courses but lower scores on math achievement tests? One idea is that, on the one hand,

> girls are motivated to do well and are confident when dealing with familiar material but are less confident and sometimes debilitated when dealing with novel material. Thus they do better on classroom math exams that cover relatively more familiar material, but they do less well on standardized tests that are more likely to contain novel material and are a more unusual testing situation. On the other hand, boys are motivated to do well and are more confident when dealing with novel or challenging material or situations but are less motivated to perform well when faced with familiar material. Thus they do better on standardized tests, which offer more of a challenge, but do less well on classroom exams, which appear to be less of a challenge and perhaps not worth the effort. (Kimball, 1989, p. 206)

Consistent with this idea, girls often perform as well as boys on standardized tests that are based largely on classroom learning. Also, among boys and girls of equal math skill, girls are less confident of their future success in math (Kimball, 1989).

Thus, because of the attitudes of parents and teachers and since there are relatively few women mathematicians to serve as role models, talented girls and women are unsure of their ability to succeed in math. The consequence may be that girls achieve lower scores on challenging math achievement tests and shy away from enrolling in advanced math courses. Also, math is stereotyped as a masculine pursuit, and, in females, better performance in math is associated with masculine personality traits (Signorella and Jamison, 1986). This stereotype, along with different math experiences, attitudes, and expectations, seem to be at least partly responsible for sex differences in math problem solving (Kimball, 1989).

SPATIAL ABILITY. In Chapter 8, we noted that spatial ability is a major component of most hierarchical theories of intelligence. Spatial ability encompasses several related skills, illustrated in Figure 12-2, including mental rotation, spatial perception, and spatial visualization. As was the case for mathematics, a unique pattern of sex differences is associated with each of these specific areas (Linn and Peterson, 1985). Mental-

FIGURE 12-2

In mental-rotation tasks, labeled (a), the aim is to find the response that is a rotated version of the standard. Spatial-perception tasks, labeled (b), require a person to determine horizontal or vertical orientation; here, the aim is to find the tilted bottle with the horizontal water line. Spatial-visualization tasks, labeled (c), typically involve patterns embedded in elaborate arrays; here, the person must find the simple shape in the more complex shape. Sex differences are large for mental rotation tasks and relatively small for spatial-perception tasks. Sex differences typically are not found for spatial-visualization tasks.
(From M. C. Linn and A. C. Petersen, "Emergence and characterization of sex differences in spatial ability: A meta-analysis," in Child Development, 56, 1985, 1479–1498. ©The Society for Research in Child Development, Inc.)

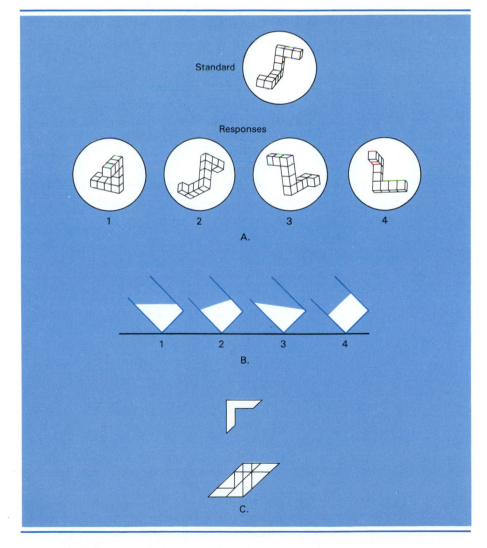

rotation tasks, problems involving mental rotation in two dimensions, are mastered during middle childhood. From this point on, boys solve problems more rapidly than do girls. In like manner, boys' greater skill on three-dimensional mental-rotation problems (like those shown in Figure 12-2) is evident from the time these problems are mastered in adolescence. For spatial-perception problems, sex differences have been established only for adults, although the trend is for boys' performance to surpass that of girls. Finally, on spatial-visualization problems, males and females perform comparably.

One suggestion is that a recessive gene on the X chromosome facilitates spatial ability. In this type of inheritance, which we first encountered on pages 38–39, males would have an advantage because they would inherit high ability when their mothers transmit the recessive gene on the X chromosome. Females would inherit high ability only when *both* parents pass on a recessive gene on the X chromosome. Some investigators report findings consistent with this genetic model, but others have not (Boles, 1980). Part of the inconsistency could stem from the fact that the genetic model may only influence some aspects of spatial ability, such as the speed of mental-rotation processes (Thomas and Kail, 1991).

Other speculation about the causes of sex differences in spatial ability focuses on differential brain functioning. In Chapter 4 we mentioned that, for most adults, the right hemisphere of the cortex of the brain is specialized for the processing of spatial information and the left hemisphere for the processing of verbal information. In adult males the right cerebral cortex seems to be more specialized than in adult females, which suggests that the right hemisphere in males can process spatial-visual information more efficiently.

The degree of specialization of the brain may be related to the timing of puberty: Both females and males who experience late maturation have sometimes been found to perform better on tests of spatial ability than those who mature earlier (Newcombe and Bandura, 1983). Since boys typically mature two years later than girls, this might help account for the gender difference. But how? Waber (1977) proposed that brain specialization in childhood ceases around the time of puberty. Late maturers thus have more time for specialization, which results in the ability to perform more skillful processing of spatial information. Several studies have found supporting evidence for this proposal, but others have not (Newcombe and Dubas, 1987; Newcombe, Dubas, and Baenninger, 1989).

Yet another explanation of the sex difference in spatial ability is rooted on the possibility of different experiences. Many activities may foster the development of spatial skill. Examples would include estimating the trajectory of an object such as a baseball or a twirling baton as they move through space, or using two-dimensional plans to assemble an object such as a scale model. These activities are linked to greater spatial skill, and boys do participate in these activities more often, which could give rise to their greater spatial abilities (Baenninger and Newcombe, 1989).

These several explanations of sex differences in spatial ability are not mutually exclusive. All these processes could contribute to the ability, with some being more influential in particular aspects of spatial skill than others.

Social Behavior

As Table 12-2 shows, many social behaviors have been examined for sex differences. We will look at a few in detail.

HELPING. According to sexual stereotypes, females are more altruistic than males. Females are viewed as more empathic and sympathetic; these characteristics, in turn, are related to altruistic behaviors (Eisenberg and Miller, 1987). Moreover, the female social role calls for women to be nurturant and caring toward others (Gilligan, 1982).

Despite the prevalence of these stereotypes, research indicates that whether males or females are more altruistic depends upon situational factors (Zarbatany, Hartmann, Gelfand, and Vinciguerra, 1985). In one review of studies that focused on brief encounters with needy others (Eagly and Crowley, 1986), males were actually more helpful than females. Overall, men helped more than women to the extent that (1) women perceived the situation to be dangerous, (2) someone was likely to witness the helping activity, and (3) men saw themselves as competent and comfortable in the situation. When helping in close, long-term relationships is the focus, females may be more helpful, consistent with the stereotype in which nurturant behaviors are considered to be feminine.

SOCIAL INFLUENCE. Experiments on social influence examine the effects of others' directions, persuasive messages, and persuasive behaviors. It is widely held that females are more dependent than males and thus are more open to social influence. Does research support this view? Very young girls are more likely than young boys to comply with the directions of adults (Maccoby and Jacklin, 1974). Girls and women are also influenced more than their male counterparts by persuasive messages and the behavior of others in a variety of situations, perhaps especially when they are under group pressure (Becker, 1986). The size of the difference depends on how influence is measured. And in some settings male researchers are more likely to find female conformity than are female researchers (Eagly and Carli, 1981).

One hypothesis put forth to explain sex differences in social influence is that females are socialized to be dependent and passive. Females may also strive to maintain group harmony—and thus seem to buckle under to group pressure (Miller, Danaher, and Forbes, 1986). Sex differences in status may also play a role (Eagly and Chrvala, 1986). Individuals who occupy high-status roles are believed to have the right to influence others. Because males typically hold higher positions in work and marriage, they more often have the power to influence. According to this interpretation, when females are in roles associated with power—for example, when they are managers—they become the influencers. In fact, some evidence supports this view.

AGGRESSIVE BEHAVIOR. Perhaps the most firmly established difference between the sexes is the greater aggressiveness found in males. This pattern, found in most cultures, may appear as early as the preschool years and continues into adulthood (Eagly and Steffen, 1986; Maccoby and

FIGURE 12-3
Many experiments have found that females are more prone to social influence than are males. However, these results may simply reflect the fact that males are more often in powerful positions in which they can wield influence. When females are placed in these positions, they are quite capable of exerting their influence.

Jacklin, 1974). Interestingly, sex differences tend to be larger in preschool children than in older children, adolescents, and adults. In adults, sex differences are more pronounced for aggression that produces physical harm than for aggression that produces psychological or social harm.

The display of aggression also depends on situational factors. Males are surely not aggressive in all situations, and females can be aggressive (Figure 12-4). For example, when confronted with male partners who became increasingly aggressive, women's levels of aggression escalated in turn, wiping out the initial sex difference (Taylor and Epstein, as cited

FIGURE 12-4
Although males are often more aggressive than females, females are certainly capable of displaying aggression and do so in a variety of situations.

by Frodi, Macaulay, and Thome, 1977). Aggression in females is inhibited by the belief that aggression harms others, is dangerous to the self, and causes guilt and anxiety. In contrast, aggression is more acceptable in males and many male social roles actively incorporate aggression (for example, the roles of soldier or football player). The high status of male roles also permits some types of aggression (Eagly and Steffen, 1986).

Aggression is also partly determined by biological variables (Maccoby and Jacklin, 1974, 1980). As we have already seen, sex differences in human aggression are not only widespread, but evident a few years after birth. It is unlikely that socialization accounts for early aggression, because parents do not appear to shape aggression differentially in their very young children. In addition, similar sex differences are found in nonhuman species, and male sex hormones have been associated with such aggression (Huston, 1983).

Hormones may regulate aggression and other behaviors in two ways (Parke and Slaby, 1983). First, the presence or absence of certain hormones during sensitive periods of prenatal growth may permanently organize parts of the biological systems that control the behaviors. This organizing influence of hormones on aggression has been established in nonhuman species. The presence of male hormones at sensitive times in developing females can lead to unusually high levels of aggression in later life, and the presence of female hormones at sensitive times in developing males can reduce later urges to fight in these males (Tieger, 1980).

Hormones may also regulate aggression at any one time depending on the hormone levels in the bloodstream. Evidence exists for an association between levels of the male hormone, testosterone, and fighting in rodents and primates. Also, injections of testosterone in female primates have resulted in increased aggression (Joslyn, 1973). In humans, levels of testosterone and related hormones are positively related to aggression in adolescents and to criminal behavior (Parke and Slaby, 1983; Susman et al., 1987). Nevertheless, the testosterone-aggression link is not always found, which suggests that other factors are involved. And causation is difficult to prove because, rather than causing aggression, increased hormonal levels might be triggered by aggression. Finally, the relationship between the variables might be indirect; for example, testosterone is related to muscularity and strength, which could affect the occurrence of aggression.

How Important Are Sex Differences?

The many analyses of sex differences in intellectual abilities and in social behaviors hardly present a clear picture. What conclusions can we reach about the importance of gender differences? There is no easy answer to this question, because it is difficult to judge the impact of any differences between the sexes. Nevertheless, it is helpful to review the following points:

1. *Differences do exist in several intellectual and social domains.* Some differences appear during childhood; some are apparent in adolescence; some begin at or persist into adulthood. However, the more exten-

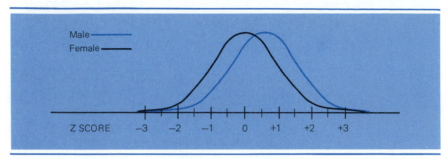

FIGURE 12-5

This graph shows the approximate average difference between males and females for spatial ability and aggression. Notice that the distributions for females and males overlap considerably. This means that a large percentage of females surpass the performance of the average male.

sive the research, the more complex the results. There is *no* domain in which one sex surpasses the other without qualification. Instead, intellectual and social skills consist of numerous components, each with a unique profile of sex differences. Sex differences can vary depending upon past experience, social class, attitudes, and specific situations. And, sex differences may wax and wane with the sociopolitical and economic spirit of the times, making them particularly difficult to track down.

2. *Differences between the sexes have broad social implications that may prejudice researchers to report some findings but not others.* In fact, both male and female investigators may be more likely to report results favorable to their own sex (Deaux, 1985). Experiments in which no sex differences are found may go unreported, which would lead us to overestimate the extent of sex differences.

3. *When gender differences are found, they are quite small.* As shown in Figure 12-5, small differences in group averages mean that the sexes overlap substantially. Many females are more aggressive than males; many males are more susceptible to social influence than females. At the same time, sex differences are not unimportant. Even with small average differences like those shown in Figure 12-5, inequality exists at the ends of the distributions. Thus, for example, relatively few females reach the high level of performance in mathematics that is necessary for engineering or physics, which in turn limits the career choices and successes of women.

4. *The laboratory setting, although certainly helpful in describing sex-related behaviors, gives an incomplete picture.* Indeed, the absence or smallness of gender differences reported in laboratory studies is often viewed suspiciously by those who observe people in everyday life. This is partly because the sexes vary in ways not emphasized by laboratory research: in occupations, interests, and activities, to name a few. Were we to observe males and females as they go about their everyday lives, a more extensive set of sex differences might emerge. This shortcoming does not discount the value of existing laboratory work; it simply reminds us that the research enterprise requires continuous expansion and improvement.

5. The factors responsible for most sex differences are still subject to debate and investigation. Heredity, experience, and their interaction are involved in a combination that probably varies with the domain and that may change over the course of development. Here we need to remember the models of gene-environment interactions that were described on pages 45–49 of Chapter 2. To illustrate, children of parents who are spatially talented may inherit their parents' talent. Their parents, because of their spatial talent, may provide experiences that foster their children's spatial ability. And, as their spatial skill grows, children may elect to participate in activities that further improve their spatial skill.

SEX TYPING

According to the old saying, "Boys will be boys and girls will be girls . . ." But how, in fact, do boys become boys and girls become girls, when it comes to sex-role socialization? That is, how do children acquire their culture's views of the behaviors, attitudes, and attributes that are appropriate for their own sex as well as those that are appropriate for members of the other sex? Sex typing involves two related aims. First, children acquire **gender identity,** which refers to the awareness of one's self as a female or male. Second, children also learn **gender roles,** the behaviors expected of females and males.

Historically, Freud's psychoanalytic theory provided the first insights into sex typing. In the 1905 edition of *Three Essays on the Theory of Sexuality*, Freud argued that from approximately 3 to 6 years of age, children experience a conflict that plays a central role in gender development. The male child, desirous of his mother, fears castration at the hands of his father. The child resolves this **Oedipal conflict** by identifying with his father, thereby vicariously possessing his mother. This identification results in the young boy becoming like his father in ways that are relevant to his gender.

Freud faced a dilemma in accounting for female development. He believed that girls formed a sexual attachment to their fathers, but he also assumed that, like boys, girls became attached to the mother very early in life. How was Freud to explain a daughter's attachment to her father? Freud dealt with this dilemma by proposing **penis envy;** he said:

> They notice the penis of a brother or playmate, strikingly visible and of large proportions, at once recognize it as the superior counterpart of their own small and inconspicuous organ [the clitoris], and from that time forward fall a victim to envy for the penis. (Freud, 1925, in Stewart, 1976, pp. 49.)

According to Freud, the girl holds her mother responsible for her physical shortcomings, and maternal attachment weakens. One more critical step occurs: In some unknown way the wish for a penis is substituted by the wish for a child. This leads to identifying the father as a love object and to feeling jealousy toward the mother. The child now must deal with this **Electra conflict,** which she does by internalizing her mother's behavior, including the female gender identity and role.

Gender identity Children's awareness that they are female or male.

Gender roles Behavior that a culture expects of females and males.

Oedipal conflict In Freud's theory, the turmoil caused by a young boy's desire for his mother, which causes him to fear castration by his father.

Penis envy In Freud's theory, a young girl's feelings of envy for the male sex organ; this prompts her to identify with her father.

Electra conflict In Freud's theory, the turmoil caused by a young girl's identifying with her father as a love object and feeling jealous of her mother.

One important side effect of Freud's explanations relates to the growth of the superego. According to psychoanalytic theory the superego is born when the Oedipal or Electra conflict is resolved. Freud believed this process to be powerful and dramatic in boys because it is motivated by the fear of castration. Because the castration complex is lacking in girls, motivation to resolve the conflict is weaker and this results in a relatively weaker superego in women.

What is the impact of Freud's work today? Many developmentalists reject the idea of penis envy. There is also no evidence that one sex is morally superior to the other (Garrod, Beal, and Shin, 1990). And most theorists cast gender development within a network that is much broader than parental influence. These points cast serious doubt on many of Freud's claims. His view has largely been replaced by the three different perspectives on sex typing that we consider in the next several pages: the biological approach, the social learning perspective, and the cognitive view.

Biological Influences

Theorists who believe that biology is important in sex typing do not claim a direct and rigid path from biology to gender-related behavior. Instead, their position is that biological factors may cause cultures to assign some roles more often to females and others more often to males (Bardwick, 1979).

If this argument is true, there should be some consistency worldwide in the roles assigned to males and females. A review of hundreds of anthropological descriptions by D'Andrade (1966) pointed to many common patterns in the division of labor. Male activities involve action that is strenuous, cooperative, and which may require travel. Female activities are physically easier, more solitary, and less mobile. Moreover, D'Andrade reported that males were found to be more sexually active, more deferred to, more dominant and aggressive, less nurturant, less responsible, and less emotionally expressive than females. It is possible, of course, that the data—collected by anthropologists of different peoples in strange cultures—are biased by the investigators' stereotypes. But the hypothesis that biological sex differences underlie at least some gender differences in behavior is not unreasonable.

Biological influences on gender identity have also been examined in studies of clinical populations. Various things can go wrong during prenatal growth that expose the developing organism to unusual levels of hormones. Sometimes the sex organs develop abnormally, with the result that an individual's apparent sex—based on his or her genitals—is not the same as the sex dictated by the sex chromosomes. This condition, known as **hermaphroditism,** is sometimes identified and treated early. In other instances, it goes undiscovered and children are reared according to their apparent sex. What happens to these children? Do prenatal hormones determine sex typing or are the rearing environments the primary influence?

Hermaphroditism A term used to describe an infant whose sexual anatomy is improperly differentiated, so that the infant's sex is ambiguous or actually differs from that associated with the sex chromosomes.

Perhaps the first evidence that could be used to answer these questions came from an extensive study by Money and Ehrhardt (1972) of 25 hermaphroditic girls. These girls had been born with masculinized external organs: The clitoris was enlarged or penislike and an "empty" scrotum was obvious. The malformations were due to an inherited genetic disorder in some cases; in other cases, the mother had taken hormones to prevent miscarriages. In both conditions, the girls had been exposed prenatally to male hormones when their sex organs were developing.

The malformations were corrected through surgery and these children were then reared as girls. Money and Ehrhardt (1972) found that, compared with a control group, the affected girls were generally tomboys of high energy who preferred athletic and masculine activities, male playmates, and slacks instead of dresses. They placed less value on marriage and were more interested in careers than in infants. However, they did not oppose wearing dresses, nor did they engage in fighting. Childhood sexuality and romantic fantasies also did not differ from those of the girls in the control group. When these girls were young adults, they had no problems in careers, in relationships, or in behaving heterosexually (Money and Matthews, 1982).

Another clinical population, being studied in the Dominican Republic, consists of males who, due to an inherited genetic condition, are born with female-appearing genitals and are reared as girls (Imperato-McGinley, Peterson, Gautier, and Sturla, 1979). Despite the genital "error," the child is exposed to testosterone before and after birth. Somewhere between 7 and 12 years of age, most begin to realize that they differ from other girls. At puberty, muscle mass increases, the genitals become masculine (though not completely normal), and the capacity for sexual relations approaches normality. Male-gender identity then evolves gradually from no longer feeling like girls, to feeling like men, to the conscious awareness that they are men. These men are sexually interested in women and live with or are married to women. They work as farmers, woodsmen, and other occupations typical of men in the villages where they live.

What should we make of these studies of fascinating cases? Evidence for biological factors comes from the masculine-oriented behavior of the girls studied by Money and his colleagues, who argue that the prenatal exposure to male hormones is responsible for this more masculine behavior. Also pointing to a role for biology is the apparent ease with which the children in the Dominican Republic group can shuck years of upbringing as girls and swiftly adopt their biologically appropriate sex roles as men.

However, each of these projects also signals the importance of socialization. The girls studied by Money clearly identified themselves as females and even their masculine-oriented behaviors were well within the acceptable range of female behaviors. And, the boys in the Dominican Republic lived relatively normal lives as "girls" despite actually being males. These facts indicate that whatever the contribution of biology, socialization by parents, peers, and others has considerable influence. We examine this in more detail in the next section.

Social Learning Theory

According to social learning theorists like Albert Bandura (1977, 1986) and Walter Mischel (1970), learning processes determine children's adoption of gender-related behaviors. Both believe the same learning principles involved in the socialization of other behaviors can be applied to sex-role development. And typical of this view, the process is seen as a cumulative one, even though the early years may be more important.

The social learning view emphasizes reinforcement and punishment in the acquisition of sex roles. Parents and other people are thought to apply gender labels to babies and deliberately or inadvertently shape appropriate gender roles in children. The social learning view also assigns great weight to observational learning. Opportunities for such learning are seen in children's exposure to models—to parents, other adults, peers, and characters in literature and on television.

Let's start our study of the social learning approach by looking at how adults' treatment of boys and girls shapes sex typing. Parents *do* treat sons and daughters differently but not as extensively as was once thought. The folk wisdom is that parents teach girls to be submissive, emotional, and neat; to play with dolls; and to prefer reading to mathematics. Boys are taught to be independent, aggressive, and achievement-oriented; to play with trucks and hammers; and to excel in mathematics. In fact, along a number of these dimensions, parents treat sons and daughters similarly. In an extensive analysis of 172 studies involving 27,836 children, Lytton

FIGURE 12-6
Sex-role learning is reinforced and encouraged both directly and in subtle ways.

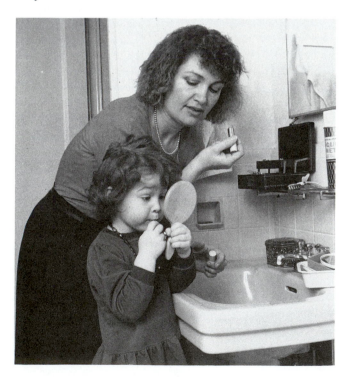

and Romney (1991) showed that parents interact equally with sons and daughters, are equally warm to both, and encourage both sons and daughters to achieve and to be independent. The primary exception is in sex-typed activities, where parents respond differently to sons and daughters. Activities such as playing with dolls, dressing up, or helping an adult are encouraged more often in daughters than in sons; rough-and-tumble play, or playing with blocks is encouraged more in sons than in daughters.

Parents also assign sons and daughters different household chores. Daughters tend to be assigned stereotypically female chores such as washing dishes or house cleaning, whereas sons are assigned stereotypically male chores such as taking out the garbage or mowing the lawn. When women are employed outside of the home, both sons and daughters end up doing more stereotypically female chores (McHale, Bartko, Crouter, and Perry-Jenkins, 1990).

Interesting perspectives on the extent of parental influence on sex typing come from the Family Lifestyles Project, a study tracing the lives of more than 200 families who have their roots in the countercultures of the 1960s and 1970s (Weisner and Wilson-Mitchell, 1990). Included in the study are families living in communes and other group-living settings, families in which couples are not married, and a comparison group of more traditional middle-class families. The most revealing outcomes involve "avant garde" families. Adults in these families are highly committed to sex-egalitarian values, including a lack of emphasis on the sex typing of their children. Domestic, child-care, and financial tasks are shared by men and women in these families. Despite these differences in parental attitudes and behaviors, children from avant garde families cannot be distinguished from the comparison sample in terms of their preferences for sex-typed toys and activities nor in their preference for same-sex friends. However, girls from avant garde families had decidedly nonstereotypic views of occupations generally and of their own occupational goals in particular.

Why should youngsters in avant garde families resemble other children instead of their parents? Maybe this reflects the impact of biology on sex typing. Perhaps children in the avant garde families were responding to stereotypes that they encountered beyond their own family. Regardless, the message here is that parental influence on sex typing is limited; parents are but one of many players in the game of sex typing of children.

Fathers may be more influential than mothers in the socialization of gender. More than mothers, they view boys and girls as different and are more likely to treat them differently. Some investigators report that fathers are more prone to encourage gender-related play, to initiate physical closeness with daughters, punish sons more, and accept dependence in daughters (Snow, Jacklin, and Maccoby, 1983). Fathers' actions may reflect their own experiences and gender identities, which tend to be more rigid among males than among females. The more flexible maternal style may reflect the more flexible socialization of girls. And the maternal role may incorporate sensitivity to the individual needs of children, needs that are more important to mothers than society's stereotypes.

After parents, teachers may be the most influential adults in the lives of many children. The direct influence of teachers on sex typing seems quite complex. With very young children, whose behavior can be difficult to interpret, nursery school teachers may use gender as the basis for responding. For example, in one study teachers responded more often to girls who used gentle touches and talk and to boys who cried and whined (Fagot, Hagan, Leinbach, and Kronsberg, 1985). For teachers of elementary school and older students, appropriate classroom behavior is a priority. Consequently, they tend to favor behaviors that are considered feminine—being task oriented, nondisruptive, and perhaps dependent (Minuchin and Shapiro, 1983). Not surprisingly, teachers have more negative interactions with boys: They scold them more, and disapprove of their disruptive behaviors. At the same time, boys get more overall attention in classrooms, more positive feedback for their schoolwork, and are viewed as being more capable intellectually (Block, 1983).

Thus, both at home and at school, adults often treat girls and boys differently. By their encouraging words or critical looks, adults can influence boys' and girls' development to proceed along distinct paths.

In addition to direct tutelage of children, adults influence sex-role development by serving as models of the behaviors, attitudes, and aspirations that a culture associates with mature males and females. Television is one potent source of adult models of sex-typed behavior, a topic that we explore in detail in the Close-Up.

Originally, social learning theorists predicted children would be more inclined to imitate adults of the same sex. However, extensive research has demonstrated that when shown adult models engaged in sex-typed behaviors, children attend to and learn from models of both sexes (Ruble, 1988). The lesson here is that learning sex roles by observation involves more than just simple imitation. What is learned from gender models, and what is imitated, depend to a very great extent upon many cognitive variables. For example, imitation of a same-sex model is more likely in older children, who already have established a gender identity. Cognitive factors are so important that they form the basis of new theories, which we will examine in the next section.

FIGURE 12-7
Teachers direct more attention—both positive and negative—to the boys in their classes.

CLOSE-UP

Television and Gender Roles

Children spend more of their waking hours watching television than they spend in any other single activity, including time in school and time spent in family activities. Television has, to a certain extent, replaced parents and books as sources of information about one's culture. As one writer put it,

> Our children are born into homes in which, for the first time in human history, a centralized commercial institution rather than parents, church, or school, tells most of the stories. The world of television shows and tells us about life—people, places, striving, power, and fate. It presents both the good and bad, the happy and sad, and lets us know who is successful and who a failure. (Signorielli, 1990).

The "stories" told on television have impact: As we saw in Chapter 11, watching televised violence contributes to aggressive behavior in children.

Sex roles represent another domain in which television is a powerful socializer. Television presents graphic images of men and women, boys and girls, images that influence young viewers. In trying to understand the impact of television, we first need to consider how females and males are depicted on television. Here the evidence is straightforward and has not changed substantially since the 1950s. The depiction of women on television does not accurately reflect women's roles and behaviors in American society. Most television women are not employed but are, instead, depicted in romantic, marital, or family roles. When television women are employed outside of the home, they hold a limited number of stereotyped positions, such as secretary or nurse. Women on television tend to be emotional, passive, and weak, in contrast to men who are rational, active, and strong (Liebert and Sprafkin, 1988).

Of course, not all women are shown in stereotyped roles (for example, *Murphy Brown*) but

women in strictly professional roles are clearly the exception. And even when television women are employed outside of the home, this aspect of their character may not be emphasized. For example, Claire Huxtable on *Cosby* is an attorney but her roles as wife and mother are emphasized in the program (Signorielli, 1990).

Television commercials continue this pattern. Women are generally depicted in sex-typed roles and most ads portray the home as a woman's proper place. Women are rarely heard in the voiceover, the authoritative audio description that often accompanies the video image. Men's voices are almost always used, even when the ad is targeted exclusively at women (Signorielli, 1990).

What is the impact of this stereotypic depiction on young viewers? Investigators usually find that television is an important source of children's knowledge of occupations and that their sex-typed beliefs about occupations reflect what they have seen on television. Other forms of sex-role stereotypes are also influenced by television viewing. In one study (Kimball, 1986), after television was introduced in a Canadian town that had not had television previously, girls' perceptions of interpersonal relationships, for example, became much more stereotyped than they had been previously.

The message for adults generally and parents specifically is clear. Television's portrayal of women's lives is highly selective. Few women are shown employed outside of the home, for example, when in fact a majority of U. S. women are employed in this way. In effect, television misleads children by depicting women and men in consistent, stereotypic roles and by not acknowledging the great diversity of attitudes, roles, and behaviors associated with women and men. If television is to be our cultural story-teller, then children deserve to hear the stories told accurately and not distorted as they are now.

Cognitive-Developmental Theories

Based on Piaget's formulations, cognitive-developmental theory was set forth by Lawrence Kohlberg (1966; Kohlberg and Ullian, 1974). Sex typing is seen as the result of cognitive growth. The main focus is on the construction of the concept of gender. Kohlberg stressed that children gradually develop a basic understanding that they are either female or male. Gender then serves to organize many perceptions, attitudes, values, and behaviors. Full understanding of gender is said to develop gradually in three steps.

First, children recognize that they are either boys or girls, and label themselves accordingly. Such self-recognition is presumed to be based on overt physical differences between the sexes, such as size and strength. Next, children come to recognize **gender stability;** that is, that gender does not change over time, and that boys invariably become men and girls invariably become women. Finally, children understand **gender consistency,** that maleness and femaleness do not change over situations or according to personal wishes. The achievement of stability and consistency together provide **gender constancy**, and with it the completion of a basic gender identity. The entire process is said to occur by 6 or 7 years of age.

It is at this time that gender identity is thought to become a powerful organizer of children's social perceptions and actions (Kohlberg and Ullian, 1974). Based on what they already know about femaleness and maleness, children actively seek to shape their behavior to fit gender stereotypes. Why would they do this? It seems that they are motivated by the need for self-consistency and self-esteem. Children who identify themselves as females, for example, are interested in and value females and the activities and attributes of females. Thus, children become active self-socializers.

In recent years, other cognitive theories have been described. Martin

Gender stability The understanding that gender remains constant throughout development.

Gender consistency The understanding that gender is constant across situations and does not change according to personal wishes.

Gender constancy The mastery of gender stability and gender consistency.

FIGURE 12-8
Once basic gender identity has been established, the child actively seeks to shape his or her behavior to match sex identity.

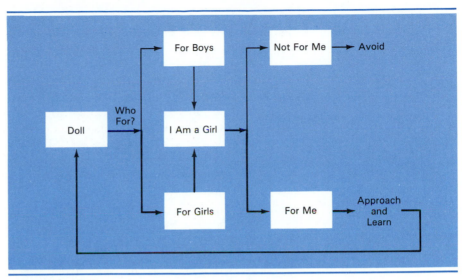

FIGURE 12-9

Martin and Halverson's schematic model of sex typing. Children first decide if a toy, occupation, or activity is for boys or girls. If the stimulus is sex-role appropriate, they will tend to "approach" it to learn more about it; if the stimulus is not sex-role appropriate, they will try to avoid it and learn nothing about it.

(From C. L. Martin and C. F. Halverson, "A schematic processing model of sex typing and stereotyping in children," in Child Development, *52, 1981, 1119–1134, fig. 1. ©The Society for Research in Child Development, Inc.)*

Gender schemes
Networks of associations concerning sex stereotypes.

In-group–out-group scheme A scheme used to distinguish female behaviors, activities, and objects from male behaviors, activities, and objects.

Own-sex scheme A scheme with detailed information about behaviors, activities, and objects appropriate to one's own gender.

and Halverson (1981, 1987; Martin, 1991) and Bem (1981, 1984) propose that sex typing derives, at least in part, from children's processing information from the environment on the basis of **gender schemes.** Schemes are cognitive constructs—networks of associations—that influence perception, regulate behavior, and provide a basis for interpreting information.

Martin and Halverson propose that sex stereotypes are the basis for two schemes involved in sex typing (see Figure 12-9). One scheme is an **in-group–out-group scheme** which consists of all the general information used to categorize behaviors, activities, and objects as female or male. This scheme guides behavior by informing the child about what is appropriate for his or her sex. For example, if a girl is presented with a doll, she will decide that dolls are for girls, and since she is a girl, dolls are for her. She will avoid a truck as a thing not for her. The second, more specific schema is an **own-sex scheme,** which consists of information about the behavior, activities, and objects that characterize one's own gender. This scheme contains detailed plans of action required to conduct sex-appropriate behaviors. Having selected the doll, a girl will learn how to interact with the doll. These actions then become part of her own-sex scheme. As children grow older, their own-sex scheme is elaborated.

Martin and Halverson's theory makes the important prediction that schemes can limit children's learning and recall of information (Bradbard, Martin, Endsley, and Halverson, 1986). Girls will learn the details of housekeeping but not of auto repair; boys will do just the opposite. Thus, because only gender-specific information can be incorporated, gender schemes can restrict children's competence.

Martin and Halverson (1983) point out that stereotypes are almost self-perpetuating, because information consistent with a particular stereotype is remembered and inconsistent information is distorted to make it conform to the stereotype. When children are shown pictures of males and females performing sex-consistent or sex-inconsistent activities (a boy playing with trains, a girl sawing wood), their memory for sex-consistent activities is better than that for sex-inconsistent activities (Levy, 1989). Moreover, children's memory for sex-inconsistent activities is distorted, so that the the sex of the individual in the sex-inconsistent activity is made to conform to gender stereotypes.

The schemes that are central to Halverson and Martin's theory have been combined with elements of social learning in a theory developed by Sandra Bem (1981, 1984). She emphasizes that society not only teaches gender schemes but also teaches that gender is relevant to virtually all aspects of functioning. Society thus makes the gender schemes extremely important. Children select characteristics and activities that apply to their own sex, their self-concepts become sex typed, and they learn to evaluate themselves in terms of gender schemes.

These cognitive-developmental theories have led to a number of insights into the acquisition of gender identity and sex roles. Let's take a glimpse at some of this work.

UNDERSTANDING OF GENDER IDENTITY. As we saw in Chapter 2, the newborn has no knowledge of itself as separate and distinct from others, much less an understanding of itself as male or female. But by 15 to 18 months of age, some babies respond differentially to pictures of males and females (Lewis and Brooks-Gunn, 1979). Thus, the social category of gender begins to be constructed remarkably early in life.

The preschool years represent a period of rapid growth in the understanding of gender. Some of the typical shortcomings in preschoolers' thinking about gender is revealed in this conversation between Johnny, a 4½-year-old who understands that gender is stable and Jimmy, a 4-year-old who does not:

> JOHNNY: I'm going to be an airplane builder when I grow up.
> JIMMY: When I grow up, I'll be a mommy.
> JOHNNY: No, you can't be a mommy, you have to be a daddy.
> JIMMY: No, I'm going to be a mommy.
> JOHNNY: No, you're not a girl; you can't be a mommy.
> (Kohlberg and Ullian, 1974, p. 211).

Martin and Little (1990) have traced the development of the different components of gender understanding. Most of the 3- and 4-year-olds in their experiment knew gender labels. They could accurately associate pictures of boys and girls with the labels "boy" and "girl." At this age, most children were also aware of their own group; shown a picture of themselves along with pictures of a boy and a girl, they would select the same-sex picture as the one most like them. Gender stability developed later: The question, "When you grow up, will you be a mommy or a daddy?" was not answered correctly by a majority of children until at least 4 years of age.

Children who learn gender labels earlier tend to be more sex-typed later in life. Fagot and Leinbach (1989) found that children who knew gender labels at 27 months of age discriminated male and female sex roles more extensively as 4-year-olds than did children who as 27-month-olds did not know gender labels.

KNOWLEDGE OF GENDER STEREOTYPES. Within the first few years of life children begin to learn what is for girls and what is for boys. By 3 years of age, they select sewing and playing with dolls as activities for girls but climbing trees and playing with trucks as activities for boys. By 4 or 5 years of age, stereotypic views of occupations are held; children believe that females become teachers and secretaries and that males become doctors and carpenters. By age 7, children have quite sophisticated knowledge of gender-appropriate clothing, interests, and activities (Ruble, 1988).

Understanding of gender-related psychosocial attributes develops somewhat more slowly than other stereotypes, probably because psychosocial attributes are more abstract than stereotypes about appearances or behaviors. Research in this area typically involves describing a trait, then asking children to decide whether the trait is more characteristic of a woman or of a man. For example, a person might be described as "emotional—one who cries when both good and bad things happen." The child is then asked if the described person is a woman or a man. Typically, a few 5-year-olds answer questions like these in a stereotyped way; by age 8 years, most children do. Furthermore, a similar pattern of development is found for children living in the United States, England, and Ireland (Best et al., 1977). Thus, by middle childhood, both boys and girls describe males as aggressive, unemotional, and strong; females are submissive, emotional, and weak.

This gradual increase in children's awareness of gender-related stereotypes is accompanied by important changes in children's understanding of stereotypes per se. Older children and adolescents become more flexible about stereotypes, viewing them as similar to social conventions, such as rules of etiquette or appropriate classroom behavior. Gender-stereotypic rules come to be seen as more flexible than certain social conventions, moral rules, and natural laws. In other words, it is easier and less serious to break a gender-related rule (for example, for a girl to have a crew cut) than to violate other social or moral conventions (for example, hitting another child). Furthermore, adherence to gender stereotypes is seen as more a matter of personal choice (Smetana, 1986). Thus, although children become more familiar with gender stereotypes concerning occupations, interests, and traits, they also come to see at the same time these stereotypes as general guidelines for behavior that are not necessarily binding upon boys and girls (Signorella, Bigler, and Liben, in press).

According to this line of reasoning, older children should be more willing than younger children to ignore stereotypes when judging other children. Martin (1989) has shown this to be true. In her experiment, 4- and 8-year-olds listened to descriptions of hypothetical children that included the hypothetical child's sex and age, the sex of the child's best friend, and the child's favorite activity. Some of the hypothetical children had same-sex friends and sex-role appropriate interests. Others had other-sex friends and sex-role inappropriate interests: "Tommy is a 5-year-old boy whose best friend is a girl. Tommy likes to iron with an ironing board." Children were asked how much the hypothetical child would like to play with masculine and feminine toys. The key result was that 4-year-olds based their judgments solely on the hypothetical child's sex: The hypothetical boys would like masculine toys, the hypothetical girls, the feminine ones. In contrast, the 8-year-olds also considered the hypothetical child's stated interests. They believed, for example, that a boy whose interests were not stereotypic would be more interested in feminine toys.

SEX-TYPED PREFERENCES AND BEHAVIORS. By as early as 18 months of age, some children begin to prefer toys that are considered sex appropriate (O'Brien and Huston, 1985). Boys prefer blocks, trucks, and carpentry tools; girls prefer tea sets and "dress-up" clothes. This preference, demonstrated in actual play or picture choice, is firmly established by 3 years of age. It is displayed in the home, at preschool, and in the laboratory.

Undoubtedly, one of the most distinguishing characteristics of children's behavior is a preference to affiliate with and like same-sex peers.

FIGURE 12-10
Even very young children tend to play with sex-typed toys.

FIGURE 12-11
Beginning early in childhood most youngsters prefer to interact with peers of their own sex.

This preference emerges quite early. LaFreniere, Strayer, and Gauthier (1984) observed children who attended a day-care center in Montreal. By 27 months of age children began to prefer same-sex interaction. The preference to associate with children of one's own sex increased with age, so that 6-year-olds chose same-sex play partners 70 percent of the time. During childhood, this preference continues to increase, along with a dislike of the other sex (Hayden-Thomas, Rubin, and Hymel, 1987). A peak is reached in preadolescence; then, due at least in part to romantic and sexual attraction, the tide begins to turn (Hartup, 1983). However, even in adulthood, time spent at work and at leisure is, quite commonly, segregated by sex.

Eleanor Maccoby (1990) recently summarized research on children's preferences for playmates. Her conclusions were that the preference for same-sex playmates is (a) widespread, appearing in all cultures in which children choose playmates, (b) evident even in the absence of adult pressure, (c) resistant to change, and (d) evident in gender-neutral play as well as in sex-typed play.

Maccoby (1988, 1990) believes that the choice of same-sex play companions can be traced to two factors. First, boys prefer rough-and-tumble play specifically, and they generally are more concerned with competition and dominance in their interactions with one another. Girls' play is less competitive and not as rough, and Maccoby argues that boys' style of play may be aversive to girls. A second factor is that when girls and boys play together, girls do not readily influence boys. Girls' interactions with one another are typically **enabling**—that is, their actions and remarks tend to

Enabling An interactive style common among girls in which one's actions and remarks support other people and help to continue the interaction.

support others and to sustain the interaction. Conversely, boys' interactions are often **constricting**—one partner tries to emerge as the victor by threatening or contradicting the other, by exaggerating, and so on. When these styles are brought together, girls find their enabling style to be ineffective with boys. The same subtle overtures that work with other girls—polite but persistent suggestions, for example—have no impact on boys.

Regardless of the exact cause, segregation of boys and girls is already evident when children's knowledge of gender is extremely limited. As a consequence, when Mary prefers to play with Susan instead of Jack, this is probably because of their styles of play not because Mary understands that she and Susan are and always will be girls. However, this early segregation of playmates by style of play surely helps to solidify a youngster's emergent sense of membership in a particular gender group.

SEX DIFFERENCES IN SEX TYPING. An overall theme that emerges from studies of sex-role acquisition is that males become more strongly sextyped than females. Boys' preferences for masculine toys show up earlier and male occupational aspirations are more traditional. Girls' preferences for feminine activities and interests at first increase but then appear to decline during childhood and, perhaps, adolescence. In fact, girls show increased preference for things considered masculine, whereas boys continue to prefer masculine things (Signorella, Bigler, and Liben, in press).

This pattern can be interpreted in different ways. Perhaps some qualities—such as high activity and intellectual stimulation—are more inherent in masculine pursuits and these qualities become increasingly attractive to females. Or perhaps both sexes realize early that society places greater value on maleness. Girls express greater sex-role dissatisfaction than boys and their dissatisfaction grows with age (Burns and Homel, 1986). And males are permitted less deviation from the sex-role norm than females: People are more inclined to give a football to a girl than a doll to a boy, because "tomboys" are more acceptable than "sissies."

What this all amounts to is that male behaviors and roles may actually be more restricted than those of females, but society places higher value on what is male. Both sexes become sex typed, but females have more latitude in sex roles than males, due to the combined influence of biological, social, and cognitive factors. However, these factors must also be considered in the context of changing social and cultural attitudes towards women, which is the focus of the last section of this chapter.

SEX ROLES IN TRANSITION

Constricting An interactive style common among boys in which one person tries to dominate the other with, for example, threats or exaggeration.

We hear much today about important changes in sex roles. One of the most obvious is the continued movement of women into paid employment outside the home. More than half of the women in the United States are in the work force, and the percentage continues to increase. Women's occupations still remain limited by stereotyping, lack of early training, or attitudes that keep women from entering certain fields. However, the number of females in medicine, law, and engineering has increased during

FIGURE 12-12
Recent advocacy for changes in sex roles focuses on increased opportunity for females—whether to practice law, to work in coal mines, or to have paper routes.

the last decade. And prejudice against women's occupational competence seems to be lessening, especially when women have high professional status. Pressure also exists for change in other gender-related behaviors and in the values placed on femininity and masculinity.

Until recently, masculinity and femininity had been seen as opposite poles on one dimension of behavior. Individuals possessing many of the attributes at the male pole were considered highly masculine; individuals possessing many of the attributes at the female pole were considered highly feminine. Newer conceptualizations view masculinity and femininity according to the two independent dimensions of instrumentality and expressiveness (Bem, 1974, 1984). In this new framework, masculine individuals are rated high on instrumentality/low on expressiveness, feminine individuals are low on instrumentality/high on expressiveness, androgynous persons are high on both dimensions, and undifferentiated people are low on both dimensions.

Androgyny is of great interest to both psychological theorists and to feminists. The term, which originated from the Greek *andro* (male) and *gyn* (female) captures the idea that androgynous individuals display both instrumental and expressive behaviors. They may be passive in some situations and aggressive in others; cold in one instance and warm in another; dependent in one relationship and independent in another. Bem (1984) and others have argued that the ability to react with such a broad range of behaviors is psychologically healthier than being restricted to

Androgyny A sex-role orientation in which an individual may display instrumental or expressive behaviors, depending upon the situation.

FIGURE 12-13

Masculinity and femininity were once viewed as opposite ends of a common dimension. Now, however, masculinity, femininity, and androgyny are defined by the two dimensions of instrumentality and expressiveness.

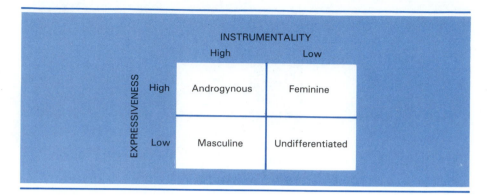

instrumental or expressive behaviors. In fact, androgyny has been related to high self-esteem and less social conformity in females and to college students' feeling comfortable when participating in other-sex activities (Bem and Lenney, 1976; Brehony and Geller, 1981).

Still, the picture is not as clear as it might seem. Because androgyny encompasses both feminine and masculine attributes and behaviors, researchers have asked whether one or the other of these dimensions is actually responsible for the adaptive, healthy characteristics of androgynous persons. As it turns out, the masculine dimension accounts for many of these healthy characteristics (for example, see Welch, Garrard, and Huston, 1986). Femininity in both sexes is related to sensitivity and caring. But the masculine dimension relates to the kind of achievement and competence that are so highly valued in industrialized societies.

The fact that some masculine behaviors and activities are so highly valued is also reflected in the ways in which changes are occurring in sex roles. When we speak of transcending sex roles, we frequently mean that women should be given the opportunity to be more like men. However, the traditional masculine role has serious disadvantages, as described by one concerned male:

> It is not just the traditional female role which has disadvantages. Sociologists remind us that, according to statistics, men have a higher criminal record, more stress and illness due to strenuous work, higher suicide rates, and, as a rule, die at an earlier age than women. In school it is the boys who have the greater adaption problems. Men who are divorced and living alone have greater difficulties managing than do divorced women. The interpretation is that the social pressures on the man to assert himself, to fight his way in life, to be aggressive, and not to show any feelings create contact difficulties and adaption difficulties. Sociologists consider that one should not speak of "the problems of woman's role in society" but of "the sex-role problem," in order to emphasize that the problem also concerns the traditional male role. (Palme, 1972, p. 241)

Thus it can be argued that a balance of expressiveness and instrumentality is most adaptive across life's many tasks. More balanced views have been achieved, at least on a short-term basis, by modifying children's stereotypes and sex-typed behavior. In one study (Bigler and Liben, 1990), 6- to 11-year-olds in an experimental condition were taught how to decide if a person can perform a particular job or occupation. They were told that the person's sex is not relevant; instead, they needed to decide if the person would like to do at least some of the activities that are part of the job, and to decide if the person has some of the skills necessary for the job. For example, to be a construction worker, a person should like to build things and should know how to drive heavy machinery. When tested later on a measure of attitudes about household activities and occupations, these children had significantly more nonstereotyped responses than children who had not been taught the links among occupations, interests, and skills.

In another study, Katz and Walsh (1991) found that modeling could be used to modify children's gender-stereotyped behavior. Children who saw a same-sex model rewarded for engaging in nontraditional behaviors (for example, reading comic books associated with the other sex, or pretending to make a television commercial advertising a toy for the other sex) were more likely to engage in these nontraditional behaviors themselves. Interestingly, 7-year-old children were more influenced when the model was a 9-year-old child than an adult; however, for 10-year-olds, an adult model was more effective than a 12-year-old model.

These interventions make it clear that more balanced attitudes and behaviors are possible. Balance can occur only if sex roles are relatively flexible. However, resistance to the adoption of flexible gender roles is strong. Social change is stressful because the fabric of social life comes undone, often with few or no alternative frameworks to replace the old ways. And sex roles are strongly tied to identity, so that change can be threatening to the concept of the self.

Perhaps the most extreme concern is that a loosening of sex roles will foster changes in sexual behavior itself. It is highly unlikely that allowing greater overlap between the sexes with regard to occupation and social behavior will bring about such consequences. Money and Ehrhardt (1972) have made the distinction between **procreative imperatives**—those tied to impregnation, menstruation, gestation—and the many options for behavior that are peripheral to these functions. They note that children develop a secure sex identity when there are clear cultural signals about procreative imperatives, no matter what the signals concerning peripheral options happen to be.

Bem (1981) argues that the distinction between the sexes is subtly woven into perception, behavior, and values to an unwarranted degree:

> In elementary schools, for example, boys and girls line up separately or alternately; they learn songs in which the fingers are "ladies" and thumbs are "men"; they see boy and girl paper doll silhouettes alternately placed on the days of the month in order to learn about the calendar. (p. 363)

Procreative imperatives
Behaviors associated with impregnation, menstruation, and gestation, in which males and females invariably have well-defined and specific roles.

According to Bem, such experiences overemphasize gender. Gender schemes come to include not only aspects directly related to sex (reproductive function, sexual attractiveness, and the like), but an enormous number of elements not central to sex. Bem suggests that we think seriously about limiting the scope of gender schemes to aspects relevant to sexual functioning. Gender schemes would then cease to have the overwhelming power to organize and thereby control so many individual interests, activities, aspirations, and behaviors.

SUMMARY

1.   Categorization according to gender has a powerful influence on development throughout the life span. Male and female categories function as social categories that have broad implications for many aspects of individuals' lives.

2.   Gender stereotypes are widely held beliefs about characteristics, roles, and activities of females and males. Females are viewed as expressive; males, as instrumental. Such generalized views set up expectations and standards based on gender for others' and one's own behavior.

3.   There are several agreed-upon physical sex differences but less agreement exists on the psychological differences between the sexes. Best established are differences in verbal, mathematical, and spatial abilities, and in social influence and aggression. Gender differences depend on both biological and environmental factors. The differences tend to be relatively small, indicating that distributions of males and females overlap a great deal.

4.   Sex typing includes the development of gender identity (awareness of one's self as a boy or girl) and the development of sex roles (the learning of the behaviors and attitudes associated with gender). The first theory of sex typing was Freud's; it stressed the resolution of the Oedipal and Electra conflicts as catalysts for sex typing. This theory is not widely accepted today.

5.   According to biological views of sex typing, biological factors cause some social roles to be assigned routinely to males, and other roles to females. Research with clinical populations indicates that hormones may influence sex typing, but this research also implicates environmental factors.

6.   Social learning theory emphasizes operant and observational learning in sex typing. Parents treat sons and daughters differently in sex-typed activities and household chores but otherwise treat them in a fairly similar manner. Teachers give boys more attention but favor feminine behaviors. Children learn by watching female and male models, but whether they imitate these models depends upon cognitive factors.

7.   Cognitive-developmental theory hypothesizes that after children acquire a constant gender identity, they attempt to match their behavior to this identity. Other cognitive theories emphasize that children acquire gender schemes—networks of associations—and use these schemes in processing information. By about 18 months of age children are already constructing gender as a social category, and by 2 to 3 years of age they label themselves as boys or girls. By 4 or 5 years of age they have recognized gender stability—that is, they realize that gender does not change over time.

8. Gender stereotyping of activities and occupations is well established in preschool children, but stereotyping of social-psychological attributes lags behind. Knowledge of stereotypes generally increases throughout childhood, but uncritical acceptance of them declines, particularly among girls.

9. Both girls and boys prefer to play with same-sex peers, a tendency that is clear long before gender stability is established. This segregation by gender can be linked to girls' aversion to the rough-and-tumble play that is popular among boys, and to girls' inability to influence boys.

10. Sex roles are changing, as is obvious by the increased number of women in paid employment and in occupations previously considered masculine. Masculinity and femininity had at one time been conceived as one dimension of behavior with two opposite poles; they are now viewed as representing two dimensions, instrumentality and expressiveness. Although high value is placed on masculinity, the masculine sex role is related to negative outcomes as well. In the final analysis, limiting gender schemes and sex roles to behaviors that are connected to reproduction could increase individual freedom for all human beings.

P·A·R·T F·O·U·R

Perspectives from Child Development

In 1991, Magic Johnson stunned sports fans across North America when he announced that he was retiring from professional basketball because he had tested positive for HIV, the virus that causes AIDS. Throughout a professional career that had started when he was 20 years old, Johnson had evidently engaged in unprotected sex with many partners, a behavior that eventually led him to contract the virus. For much of Johnson's career, the factors that place

a person at risk for becoming infected with HIV had been known. And advertisements like this one, prepared by the Centers for Disease Control, have urged sexually active persons to use condoms to protect themselves, a precaution that Johnson apparently did not take consistently. Part of the tragedy of AIDS, then, is that people contract the disease because they ignore precautions and repeatedly behave in ways that are no less deadly than driving the wrong direction on an interstate highway or jumping from the top of a tall building.

In this final unit of the book, entitled "Perspectives from Child Development," we use the knowledge of child development gathered from the first 12 chapters of the book to probe two issues that can be seen in the AIDS tragedy: First, people often behave in ways that are dysfunctional—that do them more harm than good. In Chapter 13, "Developmental Psychopathology," we will look at some examples of behavioral disorders. Second, the romantic and sexual feelings that begin to emerge in early adolescence remain salient throughout much of the rest of adolescence and adulthood. Sexuality and romance, like identity and vocational choice, are challenges that children face as they make the transition to adulthood, a topic that we explore in Chapter 14, "Adolescence."

C·H·A·P·T·E·R 13

Behavioral Problems: Development Gone Awry

We have come far in describing and discussing the basic processes of development. With few exceptions—notably mental retardation and genetic disorders—our focus has been on normal processes that lead to typical behaviors and attitudes. This chapter is devoted to a fuller discussion of childhood and adolescent behavioral problems.

The range of disorders that may affect children is illustrated by some examples.

▶   Like most children, Douglas had been toilet-trained successfully a few months before his third birthday. During the day, he always went to the bathroom when necessary; at night, he still wore training pants but most mornings they were dry. When Douglas was in kindergarten, his best friend moved away and he found himself without close friends. Soon afterward, Douglas began wetting his bed during the night.

▶   At first glance, Max seemed to be a typical 8-year-old boy, bursting at the seams with energy. The problem was that Max had difficulty channeling his energy in one direction. He might start one task but soon abandon it for something different. When asked to do something boring or repetitive, he rapidly lost interest. In school, he would often answer questions without raising his hand or leave the room without first getting permission.

▶   Charlene looks like a typical teenager. What makes her unusual is that she is convinced that she is a dog and that she is growing fur all over her body. Once she insisted that she be taken to a veterinarian so that she could have a distemper shot. Another time, she chased a cat in the backyard.   ◀

Today, behavior difficulties like these receive enormous attention. This was not always so. Not until the middle 1800s were efforts made to classify and understand childhood and adolescent behavioral disorders (Rie, 1971). Mental retardation was studied most extensively; also noted were hyperactivity, aggression, and psychosis, as well as "masturbatory insanity." Heredity and biological causes were emphasized; psychological causes, if mentioned at all, were seen as acting directly on the nervous system by irritating the brain and exhausting the nerves. Young people who displayed behavioral problems were often considered possessed, wicked, insubordinate, and incorrigible.

The 1900s brought notable positive changes. The problems of youth were distinguished from adult behavioral disorders, and more serious attention was given to psychological and social causes. Today the study of behavioral problems has entered a new phase in which increased knowledge of normal development is being used to explain the development of disordered behaviors.

In this chapter, we begin by examining some connections between normal and unusual development. Next we sample some of the problems that may arise. Finally, we look at approaches to treating behavioral disorders.

SETTING THE STAGE: DEFINITIONS, PREVALENCE, AND CAUSES

Disordered behaviors, whether displayed by the young or the old, attract attention because they are often strange or disruptive. People react to them with curiosity, confusion, fear, anger, or embarrassment. Society is motivated to understand and treat behavioral dysfunctions partly in response to these negative reactions, but also out of concern for the individuals themselves.

The study and treatment of behavioral disorders have historically been left to clinical psychologists, researchers specializing in abnormal psychology, psychiatrists, and social workers. These professionals have grappled with identifying and describing behavioral problems and have searched for causes and workable treatments. Developmental psychologists, more interested in normal growth, have only recently begun to apply their knowledge to understanding behavioral disorders. Nevertheless, a developmental perspective is tied to major questions about problem behaviors. One of these questions concerns the definition and identification of problem behaviors; another concerns their prevalence; still another concerns causation.

What Is Problem Behavior?

There is no simple way to define disordered functioning. However, all behavioral disorders are "abnormal" in that they are unfavorable deviations from average or standard behaviors. ("Abnormal" means *away* from the norm.) Obviously, then, standards must exist against which to judge behaviors. These standards derive from what happens in normal development.

Development may deviate from the normal in many ways. The rate of growth of skills and knowledge may be retarded. Three-year-olds typically speak in short sentences; most 10-year-olds still prefer same-sex to other-sex friendships; most 19-year-olds use formal operational thinking to some extent. Not meeting these basic growth norms can signal that something is wrong, that is, that something is abnormal. Behaviors can also be disturbed in degree; that is, they may occur too frequently or infrequently, be too intense or too weak, endure over too long or too short a period of time. For example, it is not unusual for a child to exhibit fear, but the child may be judged to have a problem if he or she is fearful in many situations, has extremely intense reactions, and does not grow out of the fears. Finally, behaviors may emerge in odd forms, such as is seen in stuttering (Garber, 1984).

Prevalence and Continuity of Behavioral Problems

Concern about behavioral disorders is reflected in two fundamental questions frequently asked of mental health professionals: How many young people show behavioral disturbances? How likely is it that problem behaviors continue in later life?

Both questions are of enormous importance; they have implications for all youth and their families and thus for social policy regarding treatment and behavioral research. But they are not easy questions to answer.

One way to study prevalence is to survey cases that arise in clinics, hospitals, schools, and in the offices of various professional workers. This method is not without its weaknesses. Disorders are defined differently by various workers, and they may be based on differential expectations according to the socioeconomic class and sex of the children being surveyed. In addition, many cases go unreported altogether.

Another way to evaluate prevalence is to survey all children in a geographic area or a representative sample of the area. Although this procedure, known as an **epidemiological study,** also suffers from the just-described weaknesses, it does provide a rough estimate of what might be considered normal childhood problems that are judged tolerable or temporary.

Some general conclusions can be drawn from the different investigations (for example, see Jenkins, Owen, and Hart, 1984). First, severe disorders are relatively infrequent. For instance, mental retardation occurs in about 3 percent of the overall population, whereas infantile autism occurs in less than 1 percent of the population. Second, the prevalence of less severe problems in the general population is quite high. For example, 5 to 10 percent of all school-age children are diagnosed as hyperactive. Mothers typically report high frequencies of behavioral disturbances in their children. In one study, mothers of a representative sample of all 6- to 12-year-olds in Buffalo, New York, reported that 49 percent of their youngsters were overactive, 48 percent lost their tempers twice weekly, 28 percent experienced nightmares, and 10 percent wet their beds (Lapouse and Monk, 1958). Third, age is associated with prevalence; overall, problems tend to decline in school-age children and to increase somewhat in adolescence. However the prevalence of specific disorders often varies with age. Some disorders appear more frequently in young children than in older children (for example, bed-wetting); others appear more frequently in adolescents than in young children (for example, depression).

Research has also provided detailed information about the likelihood of dysfunctions in the young persisting into the later years. Severe disorders, such as mental retardation and autism, often persist into adulthood, with or without treatment. Antisocial behaviors (aggression, truancy, vandalism) also show relatively high continuity (for example, Eron and Huesmann,1990), and some individuals diagnosed as hyperactive in childhood have educational, work, and social problems as adults. Nevertheless, a good deal of instability also has been noted. Many adolescents who commit acts of aggression and theft become well-adjusted adults. And children judged to be shy, withdrawn, or inhibited are typically no more likely to display maladapted behavior in later life than are children judged normal (Kohlberg, LaCrosse, and Ricks, 1972).

Epidemiological study A survey of a sample of children, adults, or both in order to determine the prevalence of a disorder.

The fact that many childhood disorders persist—in some form—into adolescence and beyond makes it imperative that we understand the causes of behavioral disorders. As we shall see in the next section, most childhood disorders have been linked to a multitude of causes.

The Causes of Behavioral Disorders

Individuals interested in behavioral disorders are, in some sense, all developmentalists, because they seek the roots, or origins, of the behavior. Both normal and abnormal behaviors arise from interactions among a common set of variables: genetic disposition, bodily structure and function, cognition, and socioemotional factors.

Consider, for example, the well-established fact that boys exhibit more behavioral deviance than girls in many disorders, including learning difficulties, hyperactivity, bed-wetting, and antisocial behavior (Wicks-Nelson and Israel, 1991). Why should this be so? Explanations for this sex difference rest on broad developmental hypotheses, which fall into two general types: those that focus on the biological endowment of the sexes, and those that focus on social variables. The lack of genes on the Y chromosome is suspect because it is clearly related to dysfunctions such as color blindness and hemophilia; perhaps it is also related to behavioral problems through subtle biochemical pathways. Certain male vulnerabilities are well recognized: Males appear to suffer more from major diseases, malnutrition, and poverty. These facts all suggest some biological basis for the sex differences in behavioral disturbance.

But we also know that boys and girls are socialized differently. This may produce more antisocial behavior in males. Male deviance may be reported more frequently. Mothers tend to believe that difficulties with girls are temporary (Shepherd, Oppenheim, and Mitchell, 1966), and parents and teachers are less tolerant of male hyperactivity, lack of persistence, distractibility, and disruption (Serbin and O'Leary, 1975). Perhaps adult tolerance is lower for males because adults have generally experienced greater difficulty in handling males. In effect, then, biological endowment may interact with socialization and social expectation to create a vicious cycle for the male child.

Most major developmental theories have been used to explain behavioral dysfunctions. Psychoanalytic theory played a central role in offering hypotheses, but social-learning and cognitive theories are now more influential. Not surprisingly, various biological influences have also been hypothesized. And, many modern theories combine elements of biological, cognitive, and social-learning views. But despite the wealth of hypotheses, the causes of many behavioral disorders are still not clear.

Of course, the behavioral disorders that affect children and adolescents are extremely diverse in severity, type, and course of development. The disorders that we examine in the next few sections of this chapter reflect this diversity and illustrate how theories of development help us to understand abnormal behavior.

PROBLEMS IN ELIMINATION AND EATING HABITS

The development of appropriate control over the basic physiological functions of elimination and eating is a socialization goal in all societies (Liebert and Fischel, 1990). Children's physical health may be directly influenced by the habits they form. Just as important, the development of proper habits is related to psychosocial growth, particularly with regard to the child-parent relationship. When socialization proceeds smoothly both child and parents feel satisfaction and a sense of competence. In the face of difficulties, interpersonal conflict and other negative consequences can occur. In some cases the handling of these tasks may set the stage for the child's future style of interaction with parents and even with others. Lack of control of elimination can also result in poor peer relationships and ostracism in school (Parker and Whitehead, 1982).

It is common for children to have some problems in acquiring elimination and eating behaviors. Although the difficulties may be solved by parents themselves, professional assistance is often sought when developmental or cultural norms are not being met (Routh, Schroeder, and Koocher, 1983).

Toilet Training

The concern of parents about toilet training is reflected in a survey showing that of 22 categories of possible preschool problems, parents rated difficulties in toilet training as second in importance (Mesibov, Schroeder, and Wesson, 1977).

Attitudes toward toilet training have changed markedly over the years (Walker, 1978). Early and strict training was once advocated. Children who trained easily were considered intellectually superior, and their parents were viewed as exceptional. More permissive attitudes eventually prevailed, and many parents simply believed that no effort was necessary—or sufficient—to train the child. The more reasonable middle-of-the-road approach recognizes that toilet training and control of elimination depend upon maturation, but that they are also aided by parental encouragement of the practices accepted by society.

ENURESIS. The decision that a child suffers from **enuresis,** the failure to control urination consistently, depends very much on normative data about bladder control. In the United States about 50 percent of 2-year-olds achieve daytime bladder control; this figure rises to 85 percent for 3-year-olds and 90 percent for 4-year-olds. Night control is achieved more slowly; one investigator reported that it is established by 67 percent of 3-year-olds, 75 percent of 4-year-olds, 80 percent of 5-year-olds, and 90 percent of $8\frac{1}{2}$-year-olds (Erickson, 1987). Figure 13-1 shows this comparison. Nocturnal enuresis, or nighttime bed-wetting, the most frequent clinical complaint regarding elimination, is rarely considered a problem before 3 years of age, may not be reported until school age, and decreases markedly by adolescence.

Organic factors such as chronic disease, structural abnormalities, or a bladder with limited capacity play a role in no more than 10 percent of the cases. In the remaining cases, control of urination is physically possible but the child does not do so consistently. In the psychodynamic view, the child's lack of control stems from emotional factors. Toilet training is seen as a struggle between children and their parents. Bed-wetting is said to be a symptom of this conflict (Liebert and Fischel, 1990). Re-

Enuresis The failure to control urination appropriately, which occurs more commonly during the night than during the day.

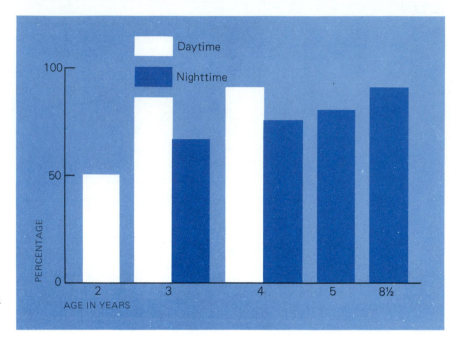

FIGURE 13-1

The percentage of children at various ages achieving daytime and nighttime bladder control. Control during the day is achieved much earlier than control at night.

search has not provided much support for this specific mechanism, but it has revealed that stressful life events can trigger the onset of enuresis. For example, the birth of a sibling can lead to enuresis, as can parental separation or divorce (Jarvelin, Moilanen, Vikevainen-Tervonen, and Huttunen, 1990).

Modern explanations of enuresis also emphasize the role of learning. In a toilet-trained child, a full bladder is a distinct stimulus to which the child has been conditioned to respond appropriately: The child inhibits urination until an appropriate time by regulating the muscles that retain urine in the bladder. Enuresis occurs when children either fail to recognize the distinctive bodily symptom of a full bladder, or do not associate this stimulus with the required muscular control.

ENCOPRESIS. Inappropriate defecation, typically when the child is awake, is a much rarer problem known as **encopresis.** Estimates of the frequency of this disorder range from 1 to 8 percent. Although most studies of encopresis have simply been case reports, several organic conditions are known to result in the disorder, including allergies to food, infections of the large intestine, and abnormalities of the intestinal tract. Encopresis is frequently associated with constipation, which, in turn, may be caused by diet, reaction to stress, and the like. Defecation occurs alternately with constipation or the seeping out of fecal material. A much smaller number of children suffer from diarrhea, seemingly as a reaction to stressful situations (Doleys, 1989).

As with enuresis, emotional disturbance has been suggested as a cause. Some cases of encopresis can be traced to coercive toilet-training practices. In these instances, toilet training is successful initially, but bowel control deteriorates over time, apparently reflecting rebellion against the harshness of the training (Anthony, 1957).

Encopresis Inappropriate defecation.

Learning, too, plays an important role. Some children either fail to recognize the bodily cues that signal the need to defecate or they recognize the cues but do not regulate the muscles correctly. More common is another form of learning. Some children find defecation very painful or frightening, and their response to the bodily cues to defecate is to retain feces in the bowel. This material becomes impacted, and ultimately the bowel overflows and fecal matter leaks around the impacted matter (Wicks-Nelson and Israel, 1991). Thus, in some cases, children have not learned to respond to the bodily cues; in other cases, they have learned to respond by inhibiting defecation.

Eating Habits

Many eating and feeding difficulties are reported in the young, including overeating, undereating, selective eating, bizarre habits, annoying mealtime behavior, and delays in self-feeding (Wicks-Nelson and Israel, 1991). Some of these problems actually threaten the health of the child; most cause psychological or social difficulties. Our discussion focuses on two eating problems currently under extensive investigation: obesity and anorexia nervosa.

OBESITY. Obesity is defined in terms of excessive body weight (when an individual is 15 to 20 percent overweight) or excessive body fat. An estimated 20 to 30 percent of the U.S. population is obese. Great concern is expressed about obesity: Weight loss programs, diet pills, and diet books

FIGURE 13-2
Feeding and eating problems are common with young children, and may cause them and their parents much distress.

FIGURE 13-3
Obesity can have adverse physical and psychological effects.

form a major industry in the 1990s. The trim body that is put forth as ideal is undoubtedly extreme and unrealistic, but overweight can have negative consequences. And although obesity increases with age, being overweight in youth is associated with being overweight in adulthood. Of particular concern is evidence that childhood obesity has become more prevalent in recent years (Dietz, 1988).

Childhood obesity may contribute to medical problems, such as later cardiovascular disease. Also, obese children are often viewed unfavorably by their peers and by adults. In fact, a panel of the United States National Institutes of Health concluded that psychological suffering may be the greatest single burden associated with obesity (NIH, 1985). Although some studies indicate no differences in psychological adjustment between obese and normal-weight children, others show that obese children have poorer self-concepts and more psychological problems (Wadden, Foster, Brownell, and Finley, 1984). In studying obese children enrolled in a weight loss program, Israel and Shapiro (1985) requested the parents of the children to rate their offspring on a variety of problems. Compared with children in the general population, the ratings were higher for obese children of both sexes. But the ratings for the obese children were not as high as the ratings of children with problem behaviors being seen in psychological clinics (Figure 13-4). We must be cautious in interpreting these results because the behavioral problems reported in overweight children could cause the obesity, or these problems could be the result of being overweight. However, it seems likely that the negative way in which obesity is viewed influences development and that some psychological difficulty is probable.

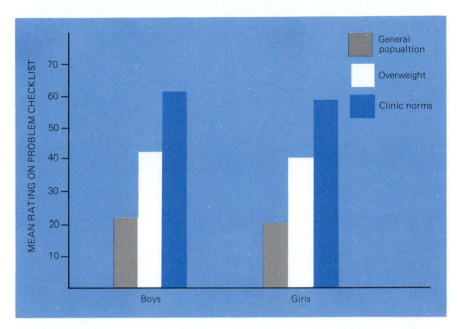

FIGURE 13-4

Average behavioral problem scores for children in the general population, for overweight children enrolled in a weight-loss program, and for children seen in psychological clinics. Notice that overweight boys and girls experience more problems than children from the general population, but fewer problems than children attending psychological clinics.

(Adapted from A. C. Israel and L. S. Shapiro, "Behavior problems of obese children enrolling in a weight reduction program," in Journal of Pediatric Psychology, 10, *1985, 449–460.)*

What causes obesity? Despite the ease with which many of us might answer this question, obesity is not completely understood. There are many biological theories concerning body weight. **Set point theory** suggests that each person has a point at which body weight is set and maintained, and that the hypothalamus plays a central role in this process. Obese individuals are presumed to have a high set point. **Fat cell theory** focuses on the importance of fat tissue in determining body weight. It is assumed that increases in the number of fat cells or in their size can result in obesity, and that obese persons have a larger number of fat cells than normal weight or thin people. Dieting is thought to reduce the size of the cells but not the number, so that dieting goes only so far in reducing obesity. Another biological proposal suggests that obese persons, due to the lack of an enzyme, use less energy in cellular functioning, which results in fewer calories being expended and more fat storage (Keesey and Powley, 1986).

Psychosocial factors certainly contribute to the development of obesity. Weight gain is directly due to excessive calorie intake along with inadequate calorie expenditure, which suggests that it may result from certain eating or activity patterns. In fact, some obese children eat more rapidly than nonobese children, which may reflect less self-control (Israel, Stolmaker, and Prince, 1984).

Set point theory A theory of body-weight control in which each person has a specific weight that is preset and maintained.

Fat cell theory A theory that links obesity to the number and size of fat cells.

Also important are the cues that signal children to start and to stop eating. For infants, internal cues are primary—Infants want to eat when they are hungry and they stop eating when they feel full. By the end of the preschool years, however, external cues for eating are well established. Children may now want to eat at 6 P.M. not because they feel hungry but because they are accustomed to eating at this time. And, they may continue eating despite feeling full because parents urge them to "clean their plates." Obese children may be more sensitive to external cues than to internal ones, which could lead them to overeat (Birch, 1991).

Common sense would seem to indicate that obesity and activity levels should be linked, but research is inconsistent in this regard. For example, Klesges and his colleagues (1990) actually found that overweight children were somewhat *more* active than their normal-weight counterparts. Other investigators (Sunnegardh et al., 1986) have found that obese children are less active. Why should the relation between obesity and physical activity be so difficult to discern? One possibility is that only extreme levels of inactivity lead to obesity; within the normal levels of children's activity, there might be no relation to obesity. Another factor is that physical activity actually accounts for a relatively small percentage of the calories consumed: For children, basal metabolic rate and growth consume most of the body's energy, which means that variation in activity level affects only a relatively small percentage of the number of calories consumed daily (Holliday, 1986).

Clearly, the popular idea that obesity simply reflects overeating is inadequate. Eating patterns do contribute to obesity, but usually in conjunction with other psychosocial and biological factors.

ANOREXIA NERVOSA AND BULIMIA. A persistent refusal to eat that seems motivated by fear of excessive body weight describes a disorder known as **anorexia nervosa**. Unlike obesity, which often begins quite early in life, this condition typically begins either with the onset of adolescence or during the transition from adolescence to young adulthood. Anorexia is rare in males but may affect between 5 and 10 percent of adolescent females (Attie, Brooks-Gunn, and Petersen, 1990).

The characteristic change from normal body size to skeleton-like proportions is quite dramatic in many cases. The seriousness of this disorder is reflected in the following description:

> . . . she looked like a walking skeleton, with her legs sticking out like broomsticks, every rib showing, her shoulder blades standing up like little wings. Her mother mentioned, "When I put my arms around her I feel nothing but bones, like a frightened little bird." Alma's arms and legs were covered with soft hair, her complexion had a yellowish tint, and her dry hair hung down in strings. Most striking was the face—hollow like that of a shriveled-up old woman with a wasting disease, Alma insisted that she looked fine and that there was nothing wrong with her being so skinny. "I enjoy having this disease and I want it." (Bruch, 1979, pp. 2–3)

Anorexia nervosa A disorder in which individuals refuse to eat for fear of gaining weight; most commonly found in adolescent females.

The typical profile of the anorexic adolescent is that of a well-behaved, conscientious, somewhat introverted, and perfectionistic individual who

FIGURE 13-5
Adolescent girls suffering from anorexia believe that they are overweight despite being grossly underweight.

Amenorrhea The absence or suppression of the menstrual cycle, a frequent byproduct of anorexia.

Bulimia An eating disorder characterized by binge eating, an unreasonable concern about not being able to stop eating voluntarily, self-induced vomiting and purging, and depressed mood.

is usually a good student. The families of anorexics are typically of middle or upper social classes; they are often affluent and well educated (Attie et al., 1990). **Amenorrhea,** the absence or suppression of menstruation, frequently occurs in anorexic females, as do biological disturbances such as low blood pressure and chemical imbalances. As in the case just described, anorexic adolescents have a distorted body image: They insist they are overweight even when they are painfully thin.

A related disorder is **bulimia,** in which individuals eat in uncontrolled binges and then deliberately vomit or use laxatives to expel the food. Anorexics and bulimics share some of the same concerns about being obese, but bulimics usually maintain normal body weight while experiencing bouts of bingeing or vomiting. The exact relation between anorexia and bulimia is still debated. Bulimia is more often accompanied by depression than is anorexia (Hinz and Williamson, 1987). Also, many investigators find that bulimic individuals were more anxious prior to the onset of the disorder, and that they came from families in which there was greater conflict. Nevertheless, because the overall pattern of symptoms is similar, one common approach is to consider two subtypes of anorexic individuals: dieters, who continually limit their intake of food, and bulimics, who alternate between binge eating and vomiting or purging (Attie et al., 1990).

What are the causes of such strange eating behavior? Because anorexia has such dramatic effects on the body, it is not surprising that biological causes have been sought. The hypothalamus plays a central role in eating, which has led to the hypothesis that anorexia reflects a malfunctioning hypothalamus (Russell, 1985). The evidence for this hypothesis is inconsistent, and, in any case, there is the question of the direction of causality. Starvation or psychological stress could cause the hypothalamus to malfunction, rather than the other way around.

Various psychological explanations have been suggested. The psychodynamic model focuses on disturbed sexuality, guilt, aggression, or the mother-child relationship. According to the family systems approach, interaction and communication within the families of anorexics are distorted. One result is that at adolescence the child is unable to achieve the individual identity necessary at this time of life, and so begins to rebel by a refusal to eat (Attie et al., 1990).

Results reported by Stern and his colleagues (1989) are consistent with the view that family interactions differ in families of anorexic females. Anorexic females and their parents each completed questionnaires designed to assess the family environment. Compared with families without anorexic females, families with anorexic women were rated as less concerned about and committed to other family members. Also, the expression of feelings was encouraged less in families of anorexics. Apparently, adolescent females are at risk when they perceive that their families are not committed to them and they cannot express their feelings openly.

Cultural factors contribute to anorexia as well. Pubescent females growing up in the United States and Canada learn their culture's view of the idealized female body, which encourages a thin figure. This ideal is particularly salient at the onset of puberty, when the typical adolescent girl will experience a "fat spurt" in which she adds about 25 pounds of body weight in the form of fat. These physical changes produce changes in a teenage girl's body image. Pubescent girls who perceive themselves to be overweight are usually dissatisfied with the image of their body and begin to diet. This phenomenon is pronounced in girls whose mothers are preoccupied with their own weight. In contrast, mothers who are less concerned about achieving the ideal thin body tend to have daughters who are much less prone to anorexia (Attie et al., 1990).

Some combination of biological, family, and cultural factors explains most cases of anorexia. Our growing understanding of the causes of anorexia is important for it provides the clues to its prevention and treatment, which is essential for this disorder: Left untreated, 10 to 15 percent of anorexics die (Wicks-Nelson and Israel, 1991).

EMOTIONAL DISORDERS: FEARS AND DEPRESSION

The study of emotional disorders in children has focused on fears, anxiety, worry, and depression. Our discussion is limited to childhood fears and to depression.

Fears and Phobias

Anyone observing children—or looking back on his or her own childhood—knows that fearful situations are encountered almost daily. The

FIGURE 13-6

As children get older, fewer events are frightening to them. *(Reprinted with permission from N. J. King et al., "Fears of children and adolescents: A cross-sectional Australian study using the Revised-Fear Survey Schedule for Children," in Journal of Child Psychology and Psychiatry and Allied Disciplines, 30, 1989, 775–784. Copyright 1989, Pergamon Press Ltd.)*

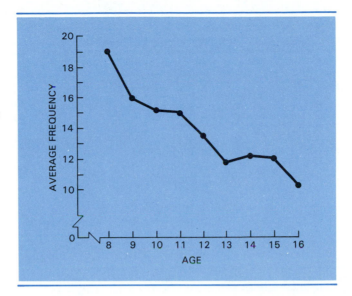

Moro reflex, in which the newborn throws back its head and extends its arms outward in response to sudden noise or loss of support, is often considered to be an innate fear reaction. Other fearlike behaviors are exhibited during the first year. Infants placed on the visual cliff at about 6 months of age appear frightened of the apparent depth, and fear of strangers occurs by about 7 months of age.

In a classic study, Jersild and Holmes (1935) disclosed a number of fears common in infancy and early childhood, including fears of noise, strange objects, imaginary creatures, the dark, animals, being alone, dreams, and threats of harm from fire, traffic, and the like. Among the most comprehensive of modern studies of children's fears was conducted by King and his colleagues (1989) in Australia. More than 3,000 Australian 8- to 16-year-olds completed the Revised Fear Schedule for Children. This questionnaire includes 80 potentially fear-provoking events, such as "snakes," "death or dead people," "falling from high places," "being hit by a car or truck." Subjects respond by indicating the degree of fear elicited by each event. As shown in Figure 13-6, specific fears become less frequent as children develop. The 8-year-olds reported nearly 20 events that frightened them "a lot" compared to about 10 events for 16-year-olds. Nevertheless, the most common fears were similar at each age, as shown in Table 13-1: Nuclear war, being hit by a car, and not being able to breathe provoke fear in most children and adolescents.

Different types of fears can be identified on the basis of developmental patterns (Rutter and Garmezy, 1983). The first group is characteristic of infancy; it includes fear of noises, of falling, and of strange persons and objects. These fears peak before the age of 2 and decrease rapidly during the preschool years. Another group of fears arises during the preschool years, only to decrease during middle childhood. It includes fear of animals, the dark, and imaginary creatures. A third group shows a less consistent age trend. It includes specific fears, such as fears of snakes and storms, that often arise in childhood and remain relatively common in

TABLE 13-1
Percentage of Children Reporting Fears According to Age

8- to 10-year-olds		11- to 13-year-olds		14- to 16-year-olds	
Item description	Percent Endorsement	Item description	Percent Endorsement	Item description	Percent Endorsement
Nuclear war	68	Nuclear war	80	Nuclear war	69
Being hit by a car	72	Not being able to breathe	62	Not being able to breathe	55
Not being able to breathe	68	Being hit by a car or truck	62	Bombing attacks—being invaded	53
Bombing attacks—being invaded	65	Bombing attacks—being invaded	62	Being hit by a car or truck	50
Earthquakes	62	Earthquakes	51	Fire—getting burned	48

Source: Adapted and reprinted with permission from N. J. King et al., "Fears of children and adolescents: A cross-sectional Australian study using the Revised-Fear Survey Schedule for Children." Journal of Child Psychology and Psychiatry, 30, 1989, 775–784. Copyright 1989, Pergamon Press Ltd.

adulthood. Also included are more generalized fears that may be associated with a timid and anxious temperament, such as fear of meeting strangers. Finally, some unusual fears tend to appear in late childhood and adolescence, or even in adulthood. These include fears of closed spaces, **claustrophobia,** and open spaces, **agoraphobia.**

FIGURE 13-7
The threat of nuclear disasters is frightening to children and adolescents.

Claustrophobia Fear of enclosed places.

Agoraphobia Fear of open spaces.

The first three groups of fears are considered to be normal aspects of development (Rutter and Garmezy, 1983). However, these fears can become abnormal if they become excessive and incapacitating. The fears in the fourth group are considered abnormal; they occur infrequently and may persist even with treatment.

Of course, individual children vary a great deal in the fears they exhibit and in the intensity with which they display fearfulness. In addition, a gender difference appears from about the time children enter school. From that time onward females exhibit more specific fears and more phobias—that is, severe and unrealistic fears of specific events, people, and circumstances. During middle childhood girls also display more general fearfulness. The explanation for these gender differences remains uncertain, although differential expectations for the sexes probably is at least partly involved (Wicks-Nelson and Israel, 1991).

EXCESSIVE FEARS. Although fears are common and can be useful in signaling potentially dangerous situations, in excess they create considerable discomfort and social drawbacks.

Why are some people too fearful? Perhaps some biological factor predisposes individuals toward excessive fears. Parents and professionals describe some children as generally timid, cautious, and inhibited (Kagan, Reznick, and Snidman, 1990). This temperamental tendency, which shows some stability over time, is associated with a specific pattern of heart functioning when children are confronted with unfamiliar events. Nevertheless, some form of learning is usually involved in the development of phobias. Watson and Rayner conditioned fear in the young child, Albert, by pairing a neutral stimulus with noise that already elicited fear. Such classical conditioning may play a role in creating apparently irrational phobias. Children also learn fears by observing that others react in a similar fashion (Wicks-Nelson and Israel, 1991).

For a specific application of these psychological explanations we turn to school phobia, which has been studied extensively.

SCHOOL PHOBIA. The term **school phobia** seems simple enough to define: It should refer to an irrational, strong fear of the school situation that would lead to resistance to going to or remaining in school. In fact, although the avoidance of school is very much a part of the disorder, the motivation for avoidance is complicated.

To begin, we must distinguish school phobic children from truants, both of whom refuse to attend school (Galloway, 1983). Truant children tend to be intermittently absent, wander from their homes, get into trouble by lying and stealing, and experience inconsistent home discipline. Phobic children display a fear of school; they worry about academic performance, suffer nausea and abdominal pain, and worry about their parents. They remain mostly at home when they are not in school, sometimes for long periods of time.

Fear of leaving the parent has been given as much weight, if not more, than fear of school itself as a cause of school phobia. In many cases, school phobic children and their mothers have developed a mutually

School phobia Fear of going to school, which is often linked to fear of separation from parents.

dependent relationship in which separation is difficult or disturbing. School merely represents an occasion that demands separation. Observation in nursery schools of mothers and their school-phobic offspring has shown that the mother contributes at least as much as the child to the separation problem.

> During the first days a typical child would remain close to mother and then begin to oscillate toward and away from the attractions of the play area. As the child began to look less at mother and move away from her, she would take a seat closer to the child and occasionally use a pretext of wiping his nose or checking his toilet needs for intruding into the child's activity. Separation was as difficult for mother as for the child. (Hetherington and Martin, 1972, p. 59)

Such separation anxiety on the part of both parent and child is viewed as fulfilling basic needs. The child may fear being left alone in the world, and may worry about the death of the parent. The parent, in turn, may be overprotective and overindulgent.

Social learning theorists also acknowledge that fear of losing the mother may be involved in many cases of school phobia. However, they are less likely to focus on psychic conflict. School sometimes becomes a conditioned stimulus for fear by being paired with fear-eliciting state-

FIGURE 13-8
Many youngsters who are afraid to go to school are simply reluctant to leave their parents.

ments such as "One of these days when you come home from school, I won't be here." Staying at home reduces fear, and is therefore reinforced. Social learning theorists also take into account that the school situation may elicit specific and quite understandable fear reactions. Many children express fear of academic failure and of particular teachers. In the child's view, avoidance of school would be profitable in those situations. Moreover, reinforcers such as toys, television, and attention in the home may strengthen the child's desire to remain there (Wicks-Nelson and Israel, 1991).

It appears that various factors are involved in different cases of school phobias. The child who has strong dependency habits that are encouraged by the parent, who is unhappy in school, and who receives reinforcement for staying at home would seem to be the most vulnerable in developing this disorder.

Depressive Disorders and Feelings

Depression is characterized by mood disturbances (feelings of sadness, being "blue," irritability), bodily disturbances (sleeplessness, poor appetite, slowed or agitated movements), and certain thoughts (guilt, low self-esteem, self-reproach). About 5 to 10 percent of preadolescent boys and girls suffer from moderate to severe depression. With the onset of adolescence, reports of depressed feelings increase and so does the diagnosis of a depressive disorder, with prevalence of the disorder becoming greater in girls than in boys. Suicides and attempted suicides also increase; at least some of these cases are associated with depression (Kazdin, 1990).

We need to be cautious in interpreting rates of depression in children;

FIGURE 13-9
Depressed children and adolescents have little energy and enthusiasm.

the current figures may actually underestimate the true incidence because depression in the young is particularly difficult to assess. The most common assessment techniques are self-reports and clinical interviews. Assessment requires the individual to describe how she or he feels and to connect these feelings with personal meanings (Rutter and Garmezy, 1983). Young children who are depressed may not articulate their feelings accurately, and, consequently, will not be diagnosed accurately. Fortunately, research confirms that specific nonverbal reactions, such as a lack of smiling, frowning, and slowness in response, are associated with depression in children. Judgments of these reactions may prove helpful in identifying depression in very young children (Kazdin, Sherick, Esveldt-Dawson, and Rancurello, 1985).

CAUSES OF DEPRESSION. Why do some young people find so little pleasure in what is supposed to be a joyful time of life? A common theme in psychological theories is that depressed individuals suffered early separation or loss, or otherwise experienced a poor parent-child relationship. In fact, early parental rejection and loss has been associated with depression in children and adolescents (Lefkowitz and Tesiny, 1984). Bowlby (1980) proposed that the child who experiences an insecure attachment to the parent, a lack of love, or a parental death may interpret a later loss in terms of personal inability, which, in turn, leads to depression.

Explanations of depression in terms of learning processes also involve the effects of loss and separation (Lewinsohn, 1974). Here the child is viewed as suffering from a lack of a primary source of reinforcement, which then leads to depression. The first step toward depression is a life change that produces a drop in positive reinforcement. Many of the life

FIGURE 13-10

Depression in children and adolescents is often triggered by the loss of a loved one.

events that can trigger depression deprive the person of important sources of reinforcement. Loss of a friend's companionship or loss of a valued position in a school would result in a sizable decrease in the frequency of positive reinforcement that a child experienced, and as a result the child would feel sad. For example, if a child's friends were to move away, the child would lose a major source of positive reinforcement, leading the child to feel morose.

How does sadness develop into full-fledged depression? Feeling sad and listless, the child is less likely to be social, thereby depriving himself or herself further of opportunities to be positively reinforced. This additional lowering of positive reinforcements should increase the feelings of depression. These feelings are then compounded because, after an initial sympathetic response, other children may avoid the depressed child because interactions are so unrewarding for them. The child may complain about life problems to solicit attention and support, but this too becomes irritating and annoying for others when heard again and again. Other children, normally a source of help, are consequently alienated by the depressed child.

Thus, the gist of the learning approach to depression is that a serious loss in positive reinforcement can rapidly degenerate into a vicious circle in which the depressed person's behavior is progressively less likely to be rewarded.

According to one cognitive view (Beck, 1967), depression results from the way individuals interpret life events. Errors in thinking about the world distort even mildly adverse events into thoughts of self-blame and failure. Depressed individuals overgeneralize: after being rebuffed by a classmate, a child may believe that she will never find another friend. Depressed children sometimes make conclusions about themselves that are based on only part of the evidence, a phenomenon known as *selective abstraction*. A child who forgot one line in a school play may conclude that he ruined the production, when, in reality he was a star.

These errors in the way depressed people think about themselves and their actions form a larger pattern that is known as **learned helplessness** (Seligman and Peterson, 1986). Depressed children often believe that they have little control of their own destinies. They blame themselves for bad outcomes but do not take credit for good outcomes, attributing them to luck. When depressed children do poorly on exams, they feel it is because they are stupid; when they do well, it is because the exam was too easy, or because they made lots of lucky guesses, or because no smart students were in the class.

Learned helplessness often begins with a situation in which people actually are helpless—they cannot control the situation. For example, a child may do poorly on a test because a family emergency interfered with studying. Or a child may perform poorly in a school play because the teacher did not plan enough rehearsals. However, instead of remaining tied to a particular helpless situation, these feelings of helplessness are generalized by the child. Depressed children feel they are at the mercy of external events, with no ability to control outcomes that are important to them.

Learned helplessness A sense of lack of control over one's environment that is learned from experiences in which one's behavior was ineffective; characteristic of depressed persons.

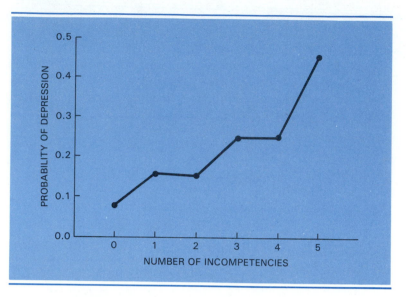

FIGURE 13-11
Children are more likely to be depressed if they perceive themselves to be incompetent in many domains.
(From D. A. Cole, "Preliminary support for a competency-based model of depression in children," in Journal of Abnormal Psychology, 100, 1991, 181–190.)

Yet another approach emphasizes the role of children's feelings of competence in staving off depression. Academics, social acceptance, athletic skill, personal conduct, and physical appearance are all domains that are important to at least some children. Children who are competent in at least one domain are unlikely to be depressed: In the process of comparing themselves with their peers, there is one domain in which they stand out, which creates positive self-esteem. However, when children perceive themselves to be incompetent, feelings of depression often follow, particularly if they are incompetent in more than one domain (see Figure 13-11). That is, if children's experiences lead them to believe that they are not attractive, not accepted, not academically talented, and the like, they will not form positive self-concepts, and they will therefore be at risk for depression (Cole, 1991).

Many of these approaches are not contradictory; rather the approaches complement one another. In the final analysis, we might anticipate that different explanations will be required for subsets of depression—for example, for children versus adolescents, and for transitory versus chronic symptoms. It is also likely that interactions among learning histories, current life events, and perhaps biological predispositions will ultimately explain the negative feelings and thoughts that are central in depression.

HYPERACTIVITY

Attention deficit disorder
A disorder commonly known as hyperactivity in which children are overactive, inattentive, and impulsive.

Unlike the emotional disorders just discussed, **attention deficit disorder**—commonly known as hyperactivity—seems to be directed at others. This may be quite unintentional, because hyperactive children lack control of their behavior in many situations and, indeed, often appear to be driven by some unknown force.

CLOSE-UP

A Day in the Life of a Depressed Child

Most of our knowledge of depressed children and adolescents is based on interviews or questionnaires that are administered once or twice in a clinic or in some research setting. A recent study by Larson and his colleagues (1990) provides a much more informative glimpse of the daily lives of depressed children and adolescents. These investigators had 10- to 15-year-olds wear an electronic pager daily; the pagers were set to signal seven times each day at unpredictable intervals. When signaled, the subjects completed a brief questionnaire that assessed the subjects' present situation and their internal state at the moment. Overall, depressed subjects reported more feelings of unhappiness, anger, and irritation whereas nondepressed subjects reported feeling happy, friendly, and cheerful. Depressed subjects' moods also varied more than those of nondepressed subjects; depressed children and adolescents might be relatively happy and full of energy on one occasion but angry or bored or drowsy on another.

As you can see in Figure 13-12, depressed and nondepressed subjects also differed in how friendly they thought others were toward them. Depressed children and adolescents consistently rated other people as less friendly to them; this was true for other family members, friends, and classmates. Finally, depressed children and adolescents were much more likely to report that they wanted to be alone. For example, when they were with family members, for 40 percent of that time depressed subjects wished that they were alone. Nondepressed subjects wished that they were alone only 20 percent of the time that they spent with their family members. Clearly, depressed children and adolescents do not experience much happiness in their daily lives and interactions with others, and, often, they would simply prefer to be left alone.

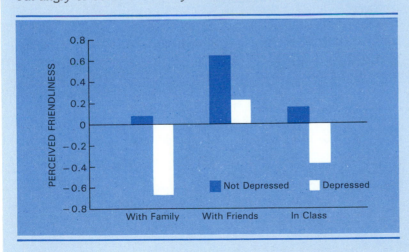

FIGURE 13-12
Compared with nondepressed children, depressed children perceive family members, friends, and classmates to be less friendly.
(From R. W. Larson et al., "Ecology of depression in late childhood and early adolescence: A profile of daily states and activities," in Journal of Abnormal Psychology, *99, 1990, 92–102. Copyright 1990 by the American Psychological Association. Reprinted by permission.)*

FIGURE 13-13
Hyperactive children often are overactive, inattentive, and impulsive, which
usually leads to low school achievement.

First described in 1845 by a German physician, Henrich Hoffmann
(Cantwell, 1975), hyperactivity was not really studied until the late 1950s.
At that time concern was growing for children with learning and behavioral problems, both of which are frequently displayed by hyperactive
children (Safer and Allen, 1976). Then, in the late 1960s, drug treatment
for the disorder began, further increasing interest and concern. Today
hyperactivity is one of the most commonly recognized childhood problems; it occurs in 3 to 20 percent of all elementary school children, with
a sex ratio of three or more boys with the disorder to every girl (Wicks-
Nelson and Israel, 1991).

Hyperactive children are active beyond what is typical for their age,
especially in structured situations that require motor control. One investigative team described such children in this way:

> Hyperactive children seem to be constantly searching for something inter-
> esting. In an office they often act as though they are "turning over rocks"
> to see what interesting things may lie below. Unfortunately, this applies to
> dismantling the dictaphone, turning over the ashtray, and uprooting the
> rubber plant. (Klein and Gittelman-Klein, 1975, p. 53)

In the classroom hyperactive children leave their seats frequently and fidget restlessly. Parents of such children report that their children always seemed unusually energetic, fidgety, and unable to keep their hands still. This overactivity often begins early in childhood and is a serious problem when the child begins school.

Another major feature is deficiency in attention. Hyperactive children skip from activity to activity; they rarely watch an entire television program or complete a school assignment. Teachers complain that they do not pay attention to directions and cannot concentrate. Attention deficits are so widely noted that they are now considered central in hyperactivity (Douglas, 1983). The problem may be distractibility—that is, an inability to ignore disruptions from the environment. Distraction is likely when an activity is boring or difficult and the distracters are new or interesting. However, the more basic problem appears to be a difficulty is sustaining attention.

Laboratory experiments confirm these conclusions. In one study (Schachar and Logan, 1990), children performed a simple response-time task in which they were to press one button when they saw the letter X and a second button when they saw the letter O. Hyperactive children responded just as rapidly as control subjects of the same age. However, the picture changed when the task was made more complicated by requiring children to press a third button whenever they heard a tone, which was presented intermittently. At this point, hyperactive children responded more slowly to both the letters and to the tone. Clearly, managing attention is a problem for hyperactive children.

The third major sign of hyperactivity is impulsivity which, simply put, is acting without thinking. The child may run across a street without looking for oncoming traffic, or jump into a swimming pool without being able to swim. Impulsivity in the classroom includes such behaviors as interrupting others' speech, calling out, or clowning (Routh, 1980). In the laboratory it is displayed by children who respond when they need not. For example, if the child is asked to respond to a particular stimulus—to a blue X—the hyperactive child would commonly respond to either a blue T or to a white X (Kupietz, 1990). Apparently, hyperactive children sometimes act impulsively because they are less able to inhibit responses.

Two other problem areas—conduct disturbance and academic deficits—are so common that they are best considered byproducts of hyperactivity. Misconduct is noted in perhaps as many as 70 percent of the cases. Parents and teachers complain of aggression, quarreling, disobedience, temper tantrums, negativism, bullying, bossiness, and low frustration tolerance. It is not surprising, then, that these children are not liked by their peers and are rejected (Barkley, 1990).

Hyperactive children perform poorly on tests of reading, spelling, arithmetic, and other academic subjects, and they are often said to be learning disabled. By the time they reach adolescence, many hyperactive children will have repeated a grade in school. The causal role of hyperactivity in poor academic performance remains unclear. One hypothesis is that some neurological impairment causes both hyperactivity and poor academic performance. Another possibility is that hyperactivity interferes with attention so that learning is inadequate, or that impulsivity interferes with learning. There is growing evidence that the child's failure to inhibit responding is more strongly associated with poor task performance and poor academic achievement than is high activity level (Edelbrock, Costello, and Kessler, 1984).

The concept of hyperactivity as a syndrome is based on the belief that overactivity, attention deficits, and impulsivity frequently occur together. Several studies show, however, that these behaviors are not consistently related to one another. This means that children who are overactive are not necessarily impulsive (Barkley, 1991). Moreover, children may appear hyperactive in many situations or be hyperactive in one situation but not another (Luk, 1985). Perhaps the best interpretation of these results is that children who are labeled hyperactive may well be a mixed group: some overactive, some inattentive, some impulsive, and some a combination of these behaviors (Barkley, 1981).

The Causes of Hyperactivity

Hyperactivity has long been associated with the idea that there is some kind of minor abnormality in the child's central nervous system. The search for biological causes has taken many paths. There is tentative evidence that heredity may play a role: Identical twins are more often both diagnosed as hyperactive than are fraternal twins (Goodman and Stevenson, 1989). Some investigators have discovered reduced blood flow and reduced EEG activity in the frontal lobes of hyperactive children; others have reported abnormalities in neurotransmitters, the chemicals that carry nerve impulses between neurons (Wicks-Nelson and Israel, 1991).

These signs are not uniquely associated with hyperactivity; they also appear in children with other kinds of disorders. Furthermore, not all hyperactive children show the same pattern of deficits for the various measures of functioning in the central nervous system. Nevertheless, a biological cause for at least some cases of hyperactivity is likely.

Another suspected cause of hyperactivity has been the diet of some children. Many parents suspect that simple sugar can cause behavior disturbances. Although a few studies have shown a correlation between sugar intake and behavioral hyperactivity, most experimental studies have found no causal connection (Roshon and Hagen, 1989).

The diet hypothesis that has received the most attention is Feingold's (1975) claim that foods containing artificial dyes and flavors, certain preservatives, and naturally occurring salicylates (for example, apricots, tomatoes, and cucumbers) cause hyperactivity. Feingold claimed that 25 to 50 percent of hyperactive learning-disabled children could benefit from a special diet that eliminated these substances (Harley and Mathews, 1980). His proposition received a great deal of media coverage and was adopted by many parents. Research evidence indicates that allergies may be a factor in hyperactivity for a minority of children, particularly preschoolers (Weiss, 1982). For these youngsters, allergic responses to foods or food dyes may trigger an imbalance in the autonomic nervous system (discussed on pages 104–5), which leads to difficulties in regulating attention and behavior (Marshall, 1989). However, we should emphasize that a changed diet (be it Feingold's or another's) is not a cure for hyperactivity because only a minority of hyperactive children have allergies to food or other substances.

Learning may not cause hyperactivity, but behaviors relevant to hyperactivity may be shaped and maintained by the environment. For example, learning to remain in one's seat in school and to attend to relevant tasks can be modified by numerous behavioral procedures. Also, a chaotic home environment may interfere with the child's efforts to pay attention and to inhibit responses. Perhaps some cases of hyperactivity can be attributed to a predisposition for the disorder that is made worse by certain environmental circumstances (Wicks-Nelson and Israel, 1991).

Whatever the causes of hyperactivity, problems associated with the disorder decrease somewhat as children mature. By adulthood, many children diagnosed as hyperactive will function quite well. Many, however, continue to describe themselves as restless and impulsive. And, a minority suffer from more serious disorders, such as criminal behavior or alcoholism. Research has not yet revealed why hyperactivity is limited primarily to childhood and adolescence for some individuals but is the precursor of greater pathology for others in later life.

CONDUCT DISORDERS

In Chapter 11 we mentioned that some children, usually boys, respond aggressively to many social stimuli. This behavior sometimes is a manifestation of a conduct disorder, which is the most common of all behavioral disorders affecting children and adolescents. In many clinics, more than half of the children and adolescents are being treated for conduct disorders; epidemiological studies estimate that about 5 percent of children and adolescents suffer conduct disorders, with boys outnumbering girls by at least a 4 to 1 ratio (Baum, 1989).

Symptoms commonly associated with conduct disorders are illustrated in the following case study:

> Doug is an eight-year-old white male who was brought in for treatment by his mother because of his unmanageable behavior at home. Her specific concern was with Doug's aggressive behavior, especially aggression toward his 18-month-old brother. When Doug is angry he chokes and hits his younger brother and constantly makes verbal threats of physical aggression. . . . Apart from his aggression in the home, Doug has played with matches and set fires over the last three years. These episodes have included igniting fireworks in the kitchen of his home, setting fires in trash dumpsters in the neighborhood, and starting a fire in his bedroom, which the local fire department had to extinguish. (Kazdin, 1985, pp. 3–4).

Such symptoms of conduct disorder seem to appear in two clusters (Quay, 1986). One cluster, often called the undersocialized aggressive syndrome, refers to children who fight, have temper tantrums, and are disobedient, impertinent, uncooperative, and destructive. Another cluster of symptoms, more often seen in adolescents, is the socialized aggressive syndrome. These youths often associate with peers who have bad reputations. They may join gangs, steal, and, finally, often become truant from school and absent from home.

The behaviors that define these clusters of conduct disorders are fairly stable over time. As we saw earlier (pp. 369–71), aggressive youngsters typically grow up to be aggressive adolescents and adults and are often involved in illegal activities. Other research indicates that children with conduct disorders are frequently overactive and difficult to control as preschoolers (Martin and Hoffman, 1990). Antisocial or noncompliant behavior is particularly likely to be stable over time when the first antisocial behavior occurs at a young age, is frequent, appears in more than one setting (for example, at home *and* at school), and consists of several distinct forms of antisocial behavior (Loeber, 1982, 1990). Thus, a 7-year-old boy who lies and steals frequently at home and at school is at much greater risk than a 10-year-old boy who occasionally lies while at home.

Links with Other Behavioral Disorders

The aggressive and antisocial behaviors that typify conduct disorders often bring children and adolescents into conflict with the law. Hence, many conduct-disordered children are juvenile delinquents. Delinquency, however, is a *legal* term, referring to youths who have engaged in illegal acts; it must be distinguished from the behavioral disorders that may produce delinquency, including conduct disorders.

Two behavioral disorders that we have already discussed in this chapter are related to conduct disorders. First, many boys with conduct disorders also have the attentional problems or impulsivity that are characteristic of attention-deficit-disorder. It is possible to identify youths who have the symptoms of attention-deficit disorder without conduct disorder as well as conduct-disordered youths who do not have attention-deficit disorder. However, many children and adolescents meet the criteria for both disorders. Stewart and colleagues (1981) found that three-fourths of the children who met the criteria for the undersocialized aggressive syndrome were also hyperactive, while two-thirds of the children diagnosed as hyperactive also met the criteria for the undersocialized aggressive syndrome: Clearly there is substantial overlap between these disorders.

A more complex relation exists between conduct disorders and depression. Recall from pages 429–30 that depression is difficult to diagnose in young children because they cannot easily articulate the feelings of sadness, guilt, or low self-worth that mark depression in older children, adolescents, and adults. Some theorists have proposed that depression in children may be masked and expressed as other maladjustments such as complaints about bodily ailments, poor performance in school, or antisocial behavior (Malmquist, 1977). A number of investigations have revealed that diagnosis for conduct disorders and depression is fairly common. Puig-Antioch (1982), for example, found that one-third of the boys referred to a depression clinic also met the criteria for conduct disorders.

The overlap between conduct disorders and depression is not as great as it is between conduct disorders and attention-deficit-disorder. Additional research is needed to help us identify those conduct-disordered children and adolescents who are also at risk for depression.

Causes of Conduct Disorders

Biological, psychological, and parental factors all play a role in conduct disorders. Twin studies suggest that heredity is involved but we know relatively little about the exact mechanism that is involved. Temperament is one possibility: Temperaments are inherited, and temperamentally difficult youngsters are more likely to become antisocial adolescents and adults (Baum, 1989).

Psychological factors are also important. Compared to samples of normal children, conduct-disordered children are usually less responsive to social reinforcement, less empathic, and less sophisticated in their understanding of and response to their peers' behavior (Baum, 1989). The causal nature of some of these effects is difficult to discern. For example, does antisocial behavior cause a decrease in empathy or does lower empathy lead to more antisocial behavior? We can say, however, that poor understanding of and inappropriate responding to social stimuli is a cause of aggressive behavior. Recall, from Chapter 11, that training youths in the proper interpretation of their peers' behavior results in less frequent aggressive responses.

Parental influences have also been observed. Parental psychopathology has been linked to the onset of conduct disorders in children. Specific influences that foster conduct disorders are maternal depression and anxiety as well as paternal antisocial behavior. The means by which these adult psychopathologies give rise to conduct disorders in youngsters is not clear. Some of the effects may be direct: Children who see depressed or antisocial behaviors daily may simply imitate these parental behaviors. Or, the effects may be indirect: The parents' psychopathology may interfere with their efforts to rear their children effectively (Baum, 1989).

Of course, not all conduct-disordered children have parents who suffer psychopathologies. Many conduct-disordered children have parents whose behavior is not disordered but whose parental style is authoritarian (see pages 292–94). Strict discipline in conjunction with parental rejection can be an important ingredient in the development of conduct disorders.

These biological, psychological, and parental influences usually work together to produce conduct disorders. For example, a difficult temperament plus authoritarian parenting would immediately place a child at risk for conduct disorders. Add some unpleasant experiences with peers—perhaps brought about because of the individual's difficult temperament—and the child is inching further along the developmental pathway that leads to conduct disorders.

INFANTILE AUTISM
AND CHILDHOOD SCHIZOPHRENIA

Although all the disorders we have discussed can seriously affect development, none affect children quite as seriously as **infantile autism** and **childhood schizophrenia.** Both disorders involve severe distortions in basic psychological processes. Infantile autism and childhood schizophrenia had once been referred to as **psychoses** and **schizophrenia**—terms also applied to severe disturbances of thinking, emotion, and social interaction in adults. It had been assumed that both infantile autism and childhood schizophrenia were like the adult schizophrenic processes, although with somewhat different symptoms than those found in adults. Childhood schizophrenia is still viewed in this light, but autism is now seen as a pervasive developmental disorder unrelated to schizophrenia. Autistic children may display some of the same behaviors as schizophrenic children, but many symptoms do not overlap, and the two groups differ in other ways as well.

Infantile Autism

In 1943, Leo Kanner described 11 severely disturbed children whose behavioral patterns, he claimed, could be differentiated from those of other seriously disturbed children. He later (1944) coined a new label for the syndrome—early infantile autism—and noted that it included about 10 percent of all severely disturbed children, and affected more boys than girls.

On the basis of case studies Kanner described many characteristics of autistic children that have stood the test of time. He noted an inability to relate to people from almost the beginning of life. Parents described their children to Kanner as "self-sufficient," "happiest when left alone," and "like in a shell," (1973, p. 33). Kanner referred to this extreme aloneness as autism, absorption in the self or one's own mental activity. He pointed to several other features. Often, the children displayed unusual speech patterns, were delayed in speech, or developed virtually no speech. They were obsessed by maintaining a sameness in their environment. For example, one child was upset by changes in routine and in the placement of furniture. Finally, Kanner noted that the children were strongly attracted to inanimate objects and repetitive action.

Although autism is associated with all degrees of intellectual ability, about 75 percent of the children show some impairment in general intelligence (Rutter and Garmezy, 1983). Many of them engage in behaviors that suggest deficits in sensory-motor processing. For example, they fail to respond to sounds, flap their hands and arms, show a bizarre preoccupation with moving objects, whirl, and rock (see Table 13-2)

Language, too, is delayed in autistic children, and may be absent altogether. Half of the autistic children in one study were without speech at 5 years of age, and 75 percent of those with speech displayed unusual language (Rutter, 1978). **Echolalia**—the echoing back of the speech of others—and pronoun reversals—referring to the self as "you" or "he" or

Infantile autism A serious disorder in which, from very early in life, children seem unable to relate to others.

Childhood schizophrenia A version of schizophrenia that is rare prior to 6 years of age, but is more common in childhood and adolescence.

Psychoses Severe disorders in which gross distortions in the rate, timing, and sequence of many basic psychological processes are present.

Schizophrenia A serious disorder in which the primary symptoms are hallucinations, delusions, and disordered thought.

Echolalia Abnormal repetition of the speech of others, commonly found in infantile autism.

TABLE 13-2
Percentages of Autistic Children with Disturbances
of Sensory-Motor Processing

Disturbance	Percentage
Ignored or failed to respond to sounds	71
Excessively watched the motion of own hands or fingers	71
Stared into space as if seeing something that was not there	64
Preoccupied with things that spin	57
Preoccupied with minor visual details	57
Preoccupied with the feel of things	53
Let objects fall out of hands as if they did not exist	53
Preoccupied with scratching surfaces and listening to the sound	50
Agitated at being taken to new places	48
Agitated by loud noises	42
Flapped arms or hands in repetitive way	76
Whirled around without apparent reason	59
Rocked head or body	51
Ran or walked on toes	40

Source: From E. M. Ornitz, "Neurophysiologic studies," in M. Rutter and E. Schopler, Eds., Autism: A Reappraisal of Concepts and Treatment. *New York: Plenum Press, 1978, table 1. Reprinted with permission of Plenum Press and the author.*

"she"—are common patterns. Autistic children do relatively poorly on tasks that need verbal abstraction, even when no actual speech is required. They also have particular difficulty with the meanings and social context of language (Tager-Flusberg, 1981).

How are we to link these many and varied symptoms? Kanner proposed that the basic defect in autism is a profound disturbance in socioemotional functioning, which leads to language impairment and other deficits. There is much evidence that abnormal social interaction begins early in life and endures into adulthood, but the accepted view today is that some cognitive dysfunction underlies abnormal social and emotional behavior (Howlin and Yule, 1990). Specifically, autistic children are unable to attribute—either to themselves or to others—distinct mental states. In their performance on laboratory tasks and in their spontaneous speech, autistic youngsters reveal virtually no understanding of the psychological states represented by terms like "believe," "guess," "know," "pretend," "think," or "understand" (Leslie, 1992; Tager-Flusberg, 1992). Lacking the understanding of and the language to describe their and others' mental states, it is not surprising that autistic children have difficulty relating to others.

The prognosis for infantile autism is disheartening. Kanner (1973) reported that of 96 autistic children, only 11 were maintaining themselves when they were in their second and third decades of life. In a later comparison, Lotter (1974) indicated that in three independent investigations conducted in England and the United States, approximately two-thirds of the disturbed children were judged as having poor or very poor status several years after initial contact. That is, most children were severely handicapped and were unable to lead independent existences.

These findings have been confirmed in more recent research (Wicks-Nelson and Israel, 1991). Why are some children able to emerge from autism and lead normal lives? Kanner pointed to only two facts: All 11 children who could support themselves had been able to speak before the age of 5 years, and none had been committed to a state institution. This same profile has been identified by others: speech capacity, IQ, and the original severity of the disorder predict outcome (Rutter, 1985). Children with at least some speech, relatively high IQ scores, and relatively mild symptoms have the best chance to lead normal lives as adults.

WHAT CAUSES AUTISM? Kanner described the parents of his autistic sample as upper class, highly intelligent, professionally accomplished, and preoccupied with scientific, literary, and artistic abstractions. He later said that the children had been exposed to mechanical, cold attention with regard to their material needs (Kanner, 1949). In much the same vein, Bettelheim (1967a, 1967b) hypothesized that normal development depends on the child's acting successfully in the environment to fulfill needs and on communicating with others. If all goes well, the child continues to act in the world and develops a sense of the self. If parents are unresponsive during the first few years of life, the child perceives the environment as threatening and destructive and withdraws into an autistic "empty fortress."

As fascinating as these psychological theories are, they are not really accepted today. Although many parents of autistic children are highly intelligent and fall into the upper social classes, the entire spectrum of intelligence levels and social classes is represented (Tsai, Stewart, Faust, and Shook, 1982). These parents display no tendency toward thought disorders, schizophrenia, obsession, deviant personality, or lack of empathy. When they occasionally appear different from the parents of normal children, it is likely that the difference stems from having an autistic child rather than from having innate difficulties themselves. This is not to say that the family environment plays no role in shaping or maintaining autistic behavior, but the family environment does not seem to explain the severity and bizarre quality of autism (Wicks-Nelson and Israel, 1991).

Evidence for biological causes of autism is accumulating. Hereditary factors are suggested by twin studies. Most investigators have found that if one fraternal twin is autistic, the other is not. However, among identical twins, the odds are much greater that both twins will be autistic. In one study, 9 of 10 identical twin pairs were both autistic as were all three children in a set of identical triplets (Steffenburg et al., 1989). Family studies also provide some evidence for genetic influence (Folstein and Rutter, 1988). Although only about 2 percent of the siblings of autistic children display the condition, this figure is 50 times the expectation for the general population.

Autistic children are more likely to suffer adverse prenatal and perinatal complications. Abnormalities have been found in EEG recordings as well as in the biochemistry of the nervous system of autistic children.

And it is not unusual for autistic children to have seizures and to develop epilepsy on reaching adolescence. But efforts to find a pattern of brain dysfunctioning that is specific to autism have not been successful. All the evidence taken together points to the likelihood that autism may result from nervous system damage that occurs from conception to the first few years of life (Hagamen, 1980). The environment may play a role by interacting with biological factors to produce the condition or to maintain it in some way (Wicks-Nelson and Israel, 1991).

Childhood Schizophrenia

Of all the professionals associated with the study of childhood schizophrenia, Lauretta Bender stands out most as a pioneer. Working at New York City's Bellevue hospital for many years, she described, treated, and followed the development of a group of severely disturbed children. Bender believed that her patients suffered from schizophrenia that manifested itself in different ways depending on the developmental status of the children. Bender (1972) noted disturbances in every aspect of nervous system functioning: vegetative, motor, perceptual, intellectual, emotional, and social. Sleeping and eating were disturbed, as well as growth patterns and the timing of puberty. The children's movements were awkward, and they displayed intellectual retardation, language problems, distorted thinking, and disturbed social relationships. Bender viewed the primary psychological problem as a difficulty in identifying one's self and thus a difficulty in relating to the rest of the world.

Schizophrenia is extremely rare before the age of 6 years, becomes more common in childhood, and is much more prevalent during adolescence. Among children, twice as many boys as girls suffer from childhood schizophrenia. By adolescence, however, schizophrenia is equally common in boys and girls. Childhood schizophrenia is also linked to social class: Children from lower class homes more often suffer from schizophrenia (Wicks-Nelson and Israel, 1991).

The primary symptoms associated with childhood schizophrenia are hallucinations, delusions, and disordered thought. **Hallucinations** are perceptual experiences that occur in the absence of stimuli. Schizophrenic children will report seeing or, more commonly, hearing stimuli that are not present. For example, one schizophrenic child reported that a kitchen light said to do things and said "to shut up" (Russell, Bott, and Sammons, 1989).

Also common in childhood schizophrenia are **delusions,** which are beliefs that are contrary to reality. Delusions often focus on themes of persecution—children may believe that a parent wants to kill them (Russell et al., 1989).

Finally, a schizophrenic child's thought is often disordered and disconnected, making it incoherent. The following example is from an interview with a 7-year-old boy living in Los Angeles:

Hallucinations
Perceptual experiences in the absence of stimuli.

Delusions Beliefs that have no basis in reality.

> I used to have a Mexican dream. I was watching TV in the family room. I disappeared outside of this world and then I was in a closet. Sounds like a vacuum dream. It's a Mexican dream. When I was close to that dream earth

> I was turning upside down. I don't like to turn upside down. Sometimes I
> have Mexican dreams and vacuum dreams. It's real hard to scream in dreams.
> (Russell et al., 1989, p. 404)

Although the individual sentences in this interview make sense, they seem
to jump from one bizarre topic to another.

Of course, not all schizophrenic children will show all three symptoms. Auditory hallucinations appear to be the most common; several
investigators have found that more than three-fourths of the child schiz-
ophrenics reported these symptoms. Delusions are reported by approximately half of the children with schizophrenia. Estimates of disordered
thought are more variable, ranging from 40 to 100 percent. These differences may well stem from differing definitions of disordered thought
(Wicks-Nelson and Israel, 1991).

CAUSES OF CHILDHOOD SCHIZOPHRENIA. Evidence exists for biological
causes of childhood schizophrenia. Both twin studies and family studies
indicate an hereditary component to schizophrenia. Also, abnormalities
in the nervous system have been inferred from abnormalities in posture,
gait, motor coordination, muscle tone, and sensory functioning, and in
EEG recordings, as well as from reports of convulsions (Cantor, 1988).

These biological factors do not *cause* schizophrenia. Instead, they
place children at risk for the disorder. The other necessary ingredient
seems to be extreme stress (Asarnow, Goldstein, and Ben-Meir, 1988).
According to this view, schizophrenia is more common in lower-class
children because coping with poverty is too stressful for children who
are hereditarily predisposed to schizophrenia. Along the same lines, schizophrenia may be triggered by the stress generated from a parent who
suffers serious psychopathology or who is overly critical and hostile.

Children who have inherited a tendency to schizophrenia may never
develop the symptoms if their lives are free from stress. This fact emphasizes the need to identify children who may be at risk for schizophrenia
and to provide a buffer for them from extreme stress during their
development.

TREATMENT

So far in this chapter we have focused on descriptions and causes of
several behavioral disorders. We now look at various efforts to treat behavioral disorders in the young. In the United States, vigorous intervention
efforts began in the 1930s, largely inspired by the writings of Freud. A
number of clinics opened at that time to provide treatment based on
traditional psychoanalytic and counseling therapy. Then, in the 1950s,
came an explosion of new therapeutic techniques, due in part to Hans J.
Eysenck's (1952) and E. E. Levitt's (1957) reports of the failure of the then-
current approaches to treatment. Whereas the traditional approaches had
emphasized relatively lengthy "talking" techniques, the new methods
focused on behavioral techniques, the use of medication, and the partic-

ipation of the child's family and school in treatment (McDermott and Char, 1984).

Along with changes in treatment methods came sensitivity to certain issues concerning the treatment of the young. Let's begin by examining some of these.

Working with Child and Adolescent Clients

The professional care of the young frequently involves practitioners from several disciplines: psychologists, teachers in regular and special classrooms; psychiatrists, other physicians, nurses; social workers; and representatives of the legal system. It is usual for a psychologist working with young clients to have contact with other professionals.

Treating young people is fundamentally different from treating adults. The young have relatively little control over whether or not they participate in treatment or who they will see. Children, and to a lesser extent adolescents, enter treatment at the suggestion or coercion of adults. Professionals must therefore be especially sensitive to the child's perspective and motivation.

Dealing with youthful clients typically demands working closely with parents, who vary greatly in their sensitivities and capacities to bring about productive change. For the most part, it is safe to assume that parents have their children's welfare at heart. Nevertheless, parental needs and judgments can work against youthful clients. Take the case of authoritarian parents who bring their son to a clinic for conduct problems. It is questionable that the child will be genuinely helped by being encouraged to bring his behavior into line with the parents' excessive expectations for obedience. In this case, the therapist's primary task might be to modify parental expectations because the child's behavior is not disturbed by most standards. There are obvious ethical considerations in a situation like this. In fact, balancing the interests of young clients and their parents can be the most challenging part of treating youth.

Developmental Guidelines for Treatment

All treatment efforts are based on the assumption that human beings are capable of change. However, the child's ability to change is influenced by developmental processes. Treatment should be planned according to what is known about these processes. Based on research in child development, it is helpful to look at three aspects of the child: the child as stimulus, the child as processor, and the child as agent (Kendall, Lerner, and Craighead, 1984).

THE CHILD AS STIMULUS. First consideration is given to the well-established fact that socialization is reciprocal, that children influence parents (and other agents of socialization) and are influenced by them. The child influences parents and receives feedback as a result of these influences on the parents, and feedback may further influence development. Children with difficult temperaments may influence their caretakers in ways such that they are treated, in turn, in certain ways, which then increase the risk of behavioral dysfunctions (Thomas and Chess, 1976). So it is necessary to evaluate the stimulus quality of the child, the reactions of the caretakers, the feedback to the child, and the resulting effects on the child. Moreover, interventions should focus not on the child or parents, but on the interactions between them.

THE CHILD AS PROCESSOR. Individuals undergo developmental change that makes it more or less likely that a specific therapy technique will be successful. Children are all too often seen as alike when, in fact, their abilities grow immensely in a period of just a few years. Developmental data offer guidelines for evaluating children and for selecting intervention techniques that might best fit the child's developmental status.

One example concerns the use of self-instruction techniques to achieve greater self-control. These techniques assume that some children can benefit from being trained to guide their own behavior by verbal self-directions or instructions (Kendall and Braswell, 1982). The children are taught self-directions and how to use them. For example, impulsive children are taught steps for problem solving, and are encouraged to say the steps to themselves at the appropriate moments. Developmental status influences the success of this treatment: Children under 6 years of age do not readily respond.

THE CHILD AS AGENT. Children generally benefit by being able to meet the demands of the social environments in which they find themselves; that is, by attaining a "good fit" within that environment. Of course, good matches do not always occur, so it is helpful for children to be able to change situations as well as to modify themselves. By having this flexibility, children become their own agents for change.

If flexibility is to be a goal of intervention, what guidelines for therapy might be productive? Certainly it would be important to assess the child's ability in sizing up situations, in judging his or her own characteristics, and in evaluating the match between the two. Assessments must also be made of the child's ability to select situations in which a good fit is easily achieved. When selection is impossible and the fit is not good (when a child is assigned to a teacher with whom conflict is inevitable), assessment must be made of the child's ability to modify the situation or himself or herself. These assessments would guide further intervention goals, but in one way or another efforts would be made to enhance the child's self-regulation.

Suppose, for example, a 10-year-old girl was performing poorly in mathematics and believed that she could do little to improve this situation. In other words, she felt powerless. How could this child be helped? A child who does poorly in mathematics and who also perceives herself as ineffective in bringing about change will often withdraw from the situation. Withdrawal results in missed opportunities for practice and improvement. By increasing the child's belief in herself as having the power to effect change, the possibility for the child's improvement in mathematics can follow. Flexibility for change in cases like this one rests on the therapist's modifying the child's beliefs about herself (Bandura and Schunk, 1981).

An Overview of Approaches to Treatment

The ways in which behavior disorders are evaluated and treated depend in part on the age of the client and the nature of the disorder. The theoretical assumptions of therapists also determine what happens to children and adolescents once they enter treatment.

For many years, treatment for children was derived almost exclusively from Freud's theory. In this view, behavioral problems are symptoms of underlying conflicts among instinctual demands (id), conscious thoughtful regulation (ego), and self-evaluative thoughts (superego). The conflict is said to be unconscious, and treatment is designed to bring it into consciousness, resulting in a resolution of the conflict and relief of the symptoms. Therapy focuses on "working through" the conflict, perhaps through the patient's free associations or through the interpretation of dreams.

Although psychoanalytic approaches are sometimes used today with children, they have largely been replaced by other forms of therapy that seem to be more effective. Let's examine three.

DRUG THERAPY. Many of the disorders that we have discussed in this chapter have biological bases. Examples would include hyperactivity and schizophrenia. In some of these cases, drugs can be prescribed that alleviate or sometimes eliminate the symptoms associated with the disorder.

Drug therapy has its shortcomings, however. Some children simply do not respond to drug treatment. Other children may experience undesirable side effects when taking medication. And, even when drugs are successful in reducing abnormal behaviors, "normal" behaviors do not spontaneously appear in their place. For all of these reasons, drug therapy is often used in conjunction with some psychologically oriented treatment such as family therapy or behavior modification.

FAMILY THERAPY. All family therapy approaches view the family as a critical component of therapeutic change. The interaction of the family is seen as the problem, not simply the child or adolescent who displays the disturbed behavior. That is, the family is considered to be a complex unit that may instigate and maintain the child's disordered behavior. The family therapy approach identifies the entire family as the focus of treatment. Treatment aims to uncover and modify maladaptive family structures and interactions. Specific techniques are quite varied and may have family members and the child consult with different therapists.

BEHAVIOR MODIFICATION. Of all of the innovative treatment approaches that have appeared, perhaps none is as popular today as behavior modification. Within this model, maladaptive behaviors are considered learned ways of dealing with the world that are in themselves the problems. That is, rather than relying on tests of personality or of adjustment to assess difficulties, behavior modification relies more on direct observation and assessment of the actual behavior of each youngster. The child's behaviors are not viewed as symptoms of underlying conflicts. Rather, the behaviors themselves are the direct focus of therapy.

FIGURE 13-14
Although family therapy comes in various forms, all of them consider the
family critical for therapeutic change.

Behavior modification is characterized by a very specific, detailed, and systematic plan for intervention, generally with an eye to altering particular consequences for behaving in certain ways. When a manipulation is tried, an immediate effort is made to determine whether the desired changes are occurring. If not, a different manipulation is introduced, and then it is evaluated. Repeated assessment, based on regular direct evaluation, is typical of this approach.

A recent addition to behavior modification is an increased attention to mental processes such as thinking and imagining. Cognition is considered to influence which environmental events are attended to, how the events are interpreted, and how the events might affect behavior. By focusing on children's interpretations of reinforcement and by providing children with rules that help them to regulate their own behavior, behavior modification has become even more useful in treating children and adolescents.

Some Examples of Treatments

Let us now look at a few specific examples of treatment of very different kinds of childhood behavioral problems.

ENURESIS. History records treatments for enuresis before the dawn of Christianity. One old remedy was to place a shaved hare's scrotum in wine for the child to drink (Ollendick and Hersen, 1983). Today's treatments are linked to the view that enuretic children have not learned to awaken before bed-wetting occurs. Presumably this is because internal stimulation (bladder tension) does not arouse them from sleep. Many years ago Mowrer and Mowrer (1938) related the problem to classical conditioning. They reasoned that the desired response could be produced by pairing the ringing of a fairly loud bell (a UCS, or unconditioned stimulus, which would inevitably awaken the child) with bladder stimulation (the CS, or conditioned stimulus). Waking up—an unconditioned response (UCR) to the bell—should then become a conditioned response to the bladder tension alone, permitting the child to reach the toilet in time.

Using the behavioral techniques just described, the Mowrers attempted to treat enuretic youngsters. The children slept on a specially prepared pad made of two pieces of bronze screening separated by a heavy layer of cotton. When urination occurred it would seep through the fabric, close an electrical circuit, and cause the bell to ring. After repeated pairings, bladder tension alone would be expected to waken the child. Thirty children were treated by the Mowrers in this way, for a maximum period of two months, and bed-wetting was successfully eliminated in every case. The bell and pad apparatus devised by the Mowrers has been successfully used ever since. Approximately 75 percent of the children who use the bell and pad apparatus respond to treatment, typically in 5 to 12 weeks. Relapses are common but most children respond to retraining (Doleys, 1989).

An alternate method, dry-bed training, is also used. Based more on operant conditioning, this method incorporates several procedures (Azrin, Sneed, and Foxx, 1974). The urine alarm is placed in the parents' bedroom to awaken them in the event of the child's wetting. The first step is an intensive night of training. Therapists come into the home and explain the procedures. Before going to bed the child practices appropriate toileting behaviors, and then he or she is awakened each hour, praised for dryness, and given liquids. Wetting episodes are followed by the child's changing the bed and nightclothes and by practicing appropriate toileting. On subsequent nights parents direct these same procedures, as well as positively reinforcing the child on the day following any night when bed-wetting did not occur. After seven consecutive dry nights the alarm is removed, but cleanliness training and toileting practice are provided if morning bed inspection reveals a wet bed.

This method can help a great majority of children, typically in about 7 to 8 weeks of training. As with the bell and pad approach, relapses are common, but they can be treated with additional training (Kaplan, Breit, Gauthier, and Busner, 1989).

HYPERACTIVITY. Behavior modification and medication are the most common treatments for hyperactivity. The use of medication to alleviate hyperactivity is based on the assumption that some nervous system dysfunction underlies the condition. Stimulant drugs such as Ritalin, Dexedrine, and Cylert are most commonly used. On the surface, stimulant drugs would seem to be inappropriate for hyperactive children. As it turns out, they generally have a paradoxical effect in that they calm behavior and focus attention.

Stimulants provide at least short-term help to many children. When hyperactive children receive drug treatment, common consequences are reduced impulsivity, increased sustained attention, and increased goal-directed behavior. Stimulants apparently increase attention and decrease impulsivity, which in turn improve learning, perception, and motor ability. However, there is little evidence that stimulants improve children's academic performance (Wicks-Nelson and Israel, 1991).

Research points to other shortcomings of medication use as well. A large percentage, perhaps 35 percent, of hyperactive children do not respond to stimulant medication. Negative side effects, such as short-term anorexia, nausea, insomnia, and headaches, sometimes occur. Also of concern is the impact of the repeated use of medication on children's sense of their ability to control their own behavior. The potential problem is illustrated in the following interview with an 11-year-old girl:

> Interviewer: This is an "imagination" question. Let's say you stopped taking Ritalin altogether.
> Child: Oh wow, I'd stay home from school!
> Interviewer: How come?
> Child: Because I know what would be happening if I didn't. I wouldn't get my work done at all.
> Interviewer: How about your friends?
> Child: Nobody would like me then, if I didn't take it. (Whalen, 1989, p. 158).

Clearly, this child believes that the medication regulates her behavior and that, without it, she would be less able to cope.

Because of the shortcomings associated with medication, behavioral approaches are also popular in the treatment of hyperactivity. Various kinds of behavior modification strategies are used, but positive reinforcement by teachers and parents is the predominant approach. Families are trained in observation and management techniques aimed at reducing aggression, irritability, and noncompliance in the home. Parents are also trained to encourage attention and goal-directed behavior (Anastopoulos, DuPaul, and Barkley, 1991). A cognitive component is sometimes included as well. Children are taught rules that they should recite to themselves to help direct their attention toward goals. For example, children are told to remind themselves to stop and read instructions before starting assignments (Kendall, 1987).

The growing trend is for comprehensive treatment programs that combine all of these methods of treatment. No single approach seems to address all of the problems associated with hyperactivity, but combined various approaches can be very effective (Whalen and Henker, 1991).

INFANTILE AUTISM. Although autism is extremely difficult to treat, some success has been achieved with highly structured learning procedures. Particularly notable in this area is the work of O. Ivar Lovaas and

FIGURE 13-15
The use of positive reinforcement—food and praise—is helpful in the shaping of appropriate behavior in autistic children.

his associates (Lovaas and Smith, 1988). These researchers found that self-destructive action is reduced by isolating the children, echolalic speech is decreased by nonattention, and normal speech is gradually shaped by food rewards for imitation of the experimenter's (or therapist's) verbalizations (see Figure 13-15). Realizing that social reinforcement is the cornerstone for building and modifying behavior in the natural environment and that autistic children appear unresponsive to such reinforcement, Lovaas and his associates try to establish the importance of social rewards by pairing them with tangible ones. For example, when food reinforcement is presented for a particular act, it is paired with the word "good." Later, praise alone may become a reinforcer.

The use of highly structured behavioral tasks is embedded in TEACCH, a statewide program that began as a research project at the University of North Carolina (Schopler, Mesibov, and Barker, 1982). (TEACCH stands for Treatment and Education of Autistic and related Communications Handicapped Children.) TEACCH operates five regional centers and 35 classrooms located in the public schools. The program encourages and organizes cooperative efforts among parents, teachers, and therapists.

At the regional centers children receive individualized assessment that provides a basis for treatment. Classroom teaching is tailored to meet the child's needs. Teachers also instruct parents on home teaching programs. Parents are given training as cotherapists for their children, as well as counseling. Help is given to strengthen family adjustment and community support.

The effectiveness of TEACCH is evaluated in various ways. For example, autistic children who received highly structured operant conditioning sessions were compared with those who received nondirective and psychoanalytic play therapy. The structured approach was more effective in bringing about changes in attention, affect, language, and bizarre behavior. Parental teaching skills have also been evaluated by rating mother-child interaction before treatment and two months later. Improvement was noted on all measures including organization of material, teaching pace, language use, behavior control, and the atmosphere of enjoyment. When asked to evaluate TEACCH, parents rated it as extremely helpful in improving their children's behavior and in increasing their own understanding and feelings of competence. Thus, although autism continues to have negative consequences of varying degrees on youth and their families, TEACCH helps reduce the consequences (Schopler, 1987).

A recurring theme in this book is that children's development can only be understood by considering the combined impact of biological, cognitive, and social variables. In this chapter, we've seen that this theme extends to developmental psychopathology as well: Biology, cognition, and social forces are key players in abnormal behaviors. And, in the last few pages, each of these has been shown to be an important factor in contributing to treatment as well.

SUMMARY

1.   Behavioral disorders of the young are receiving much attention today, but only in this century have they been extensively studied. Developmental psychologists have recently joined this effort, and the concept of development is important in defining behavioral disorders.

2.   All behavioral dysfunctions are abnormal or atypical in that they are deviations from normal development. Deviation may be apparent in the rate of growth or in the frequency, intensity, duration, quality, or underlying processes of behaviors. Boys are at greater risk for behavioral dysfunction than girls. However, the causes of most behavioral disorders are still to be clarified.

3.   Children commonly have some difficulties surrounding habits of elimination and eating, which can affect their health and social relationships. Enuresis and encopresis (inappropriate bladder and bowel elimination) are defined in terms of developmental norms. Both disorders are explained in terms of the child's failure to associate appropriate muscular control with a distinctive stimulus.

4.   The obese child probably suffers from social adversity, although psychological maladjustment is not inevitable. Obese children appear to eat faster than non-obese children, and a lack of self-control may be involved in eating patterns. Among the several biological theories are those that focus on a set point of body weight, the importance of fat cells, and cell metabolism. The learning of poor eating habits is also widely recognized as a possible cause of obesity.

5.   Anorexia nervosa is seen primarily in adolescent girls and is characterized by a refusal to eat, by excessive thinness, disturbed body image,

amenorrhea and other medical disturbances, and perhaps by bizarre eating habits. The anorexic girl is often well behaved, conscientious, somewhat introverted, and perfectionistic. The psychodynamic view focuses on disturbed sexuality, guilt, aggression, or the mother-child relationship. Family theories hypothesize that disturbances in family relationships underlie anorexia. Social-learning theory emphasizes fear of being overweight and poor family relationships.

6. Excessive fears and depression are among the emotional disturbances found in children and adolescents. Parental and self-reports reveal many specific fears that change in content with age and often disappear spontaneously. Phobias are excessive and unrealistic fears that require treatment. In school phobia, worries about school, an excessively dependent parent-child relationship, and reinforcement of a refusal to go to school are viewed as likely causes.

7. Mood and bodily disturbances and depressive thoughts are the hallmarks of depression, which is difficult to assess in the young. Depressed children and adolescents often see the world as unfriendly to them and they prefer to be left alone. Explanations of depression emphasize the loss of loved ones, the absence of positive reinforcement, learned helplessness, and feelings of incompetence.

8. About 5 to 10 percent of elementary school children are diagnosed as hyperactive. Overactivity, impulsiveness, and attention deficits are the primary manifestations of this disorder. Many hyperactive children also exhibit disturbances in conduct and academic deficiencies. Nervous system dysfunctions have long been suspected as a cause of hyperactivity, and some support exists for this proposition. Diet may also play a role, and learning may help to maintain behaviors associated with hyperactivity.

9. Children and adolescents with conduct disorders often fight and are disobedient, uncooperative, and destructive; some join gangs, steal, and are truant. Youth with conduct disorders often also have symptoms of attention-deficit-disorder and, less frequently, symptoms of depression. Temperament, understanding of peers' behavior, parental psychopathology, and authoritarian parenting have all been linked to the onset of conduct disorders.

10. Infantile autism is characterized by social isolation, language disturbance, a desire for sameness in the environment, and stereotypic, bizarre behaviors. Childhood schizophrenia is characterized by disturbances in speech, motor functioning, posture, and personality; in addition, there is a loss of contact with reality. Biological causes seem central in both these disorders.

11. The treatment of behavioral disorders found in children and adolescents is approached in various ways, but it always requires special sensitivities. Interventions can be enhanced or limited by developmental status and processes. Drug therapy attempts to correct the biological basis of a disorder; family therapy assumes that the family is a critical component of both the child's behavioral disorder and its treatment; behavior modification views the opportunity for new learning by the child as central to therapy.

C·H·A·P·T·E·R 14

Adolescence:
The Passage
to Adulthood

Through much of this book, we've spoken of adolescence as if it were a destination, the endpoint of childhood. At the beginning of the twentieth century, this would have been close to the truth: The onset of puberty roughly coincided with the end of schooling for most adolescents, who then entered the labor force and shortly began their own families. Today, however, we know that adolescence in industrialized countries is simply another phase in the life span, a time of gradual transition from childhood to adulthood. Most individuals continue their education and gradually gain the autonomy that characterizes adults.

In this last chapter, the spotlight is on some of the unique characteristics of this passage from the world of children to the world of adults. Let's start by looking at some of the issues that we'll examine in this, the final chapter of the book:

▶   The rebellious teenager is a major figure in modern American folklore. From James Dean's role in the film *Rebel without a Cause*, through the counterculture of the 1960s and the punk rockers of more recent years, there is a view that youth, in their quest for an identity, become increasingly combative with parents and society in general. What is identity? Is acquiring it necessarily as stormy as folklore suggests? We answer these questions in the first part of the chapter.

▶   You've probably seen the television commercials . . . while a familiar jingle plays in the background, a perky teenage girl behind the register takes your order and asks if you're going to eat in or carry out. With her boundless energy for work, she seems to personify the ethic that labor is virtuous and rewarding. This seems too good to be true. Is it? We'll examine this and other questions about adolescents' work and career choices in the second part of the chapter.

▶   Compared with previous generations, today's adolescents are exposed to more sexuality in the media and are more experienced sexually. But these same adolescents are astonishingly ignorant about sexual matters in some respects: Many adolescents believe that if a girl really doesn't want to have a baby, she won't get pregnant, even though she has unprotected sexual intercourse. What do teenagers understand about conception and contraception? What do they need to learn? These and other questions provide the focus for the third part of this chapter, which concerns romance, sexuality, and family life.   ◀

IDENTITY

If asked "Who are you?" or "Will you tell us about yourself?" most of us would be able to provide descriptions of ourselves. We would surely identify our sex, probably our age, and perhaps some physical characteristics, such as height and eye color. We would describe our relationships, the kind of work we do, our beliefs and expectations, and our social and psychological characteristics. One way or the other we would have little difficulty in answering the question, because we long ago began to acquire a sense of self—that is, an **identity** or self-concept.

Identity formation has long interested philosophers, but Erik Erikson has been foremost among psychologists in focusing on it. According to Erikson, identity is characterized by the "actually attained but forever to-be-revised sense of the reality of the self within social reality" (1968, p. 211). It is a subjective sense of coherence and continuity of self. A lifelong process, identity formation begins in childhood and is considered a vital step during adolescence.

We can identify the precursors of identity in preschoolers. Four-year-olds tend to distinguish themselves from others according to their curly hair, the bike they own, or the games they play. Activities are especially important for preschoolers. By the time children are 8 or 9 years of age, they distinguish the physical self from the mental self. Now one is different from others not just because one looks different, but because one has distinct feelings and thoughts. The basic nature of the self becomes more internal—more psychological. Thus, during childhood the sense of self shifts: At first based on concrete physical attributes, material possessions, and activities, identity later begins to reflect more abstract social characteristics, thoughts, and emotions (Harter, 1983).

One account of this transformation is offered by Robert Selman (1986). In his view, the young child initially is unaware of psychological experience as separate from physical action and attributes. Desires, preferences, and choices are based on physical functioning. "Doing" is the core of personal experience. By about age 6, children understand that inner experience is not the same as outer experience, but they believe that inner and outer experience are consistent. By approximately age 8, children realize that inner experience may not be consistent with external action. This is a significant change. Children now can consciously determine when and to what extent inner experience will match outer behavior. They are able consciously to deceive or put on façades. More important, they come to a fuller appreciation of the private, subjective part of the self.

With the arrival of adolescence, identity formation becomes central (Marcia, 1991). In describing themselves, adolescents increasingly use abstract psychological and social terms. Perhaps even more striking, adolescents come to have a new respect for their ability to monitor, manipulate, and judge their thinking and actions (Harter, 1983). They now can think about the process of thought itself. Self-reflection and self-awareness may become acute, with rejection of previous concepts about the self and a search for a new identity that integrates elements from the past and the present.

One particularly influential view of adolescent identity formation is Erik Erikson's, which is the focus of the next section.

Erikson's View

Identity A coherent sense of self; self-concept.

Following in Freud's footsteps, Erikson has fashioned his own psychoanalytic views of human development. Like Freud, he assumes there are stages of development, several of which coincide with Freudian ones.

However, Erikson places much greater emphasis on the role of the ego, or rational part of the personality; whereas Freud concentrated largely on the nonrational, instinctual components of the personality, the id. In addition, Erikson viewed the growing individual within the larger social setting of the family and the cultural heritage rather than in the more restricted triangle of the mother-child-father.

A distinct feature of Erikson's theory is that he views development as consisting of a series of crises or challenges for individuals. Each crisis is an expected part of growth; biological and social forces simply converge to provide particular challenges at different phases in development. For example, the challenge of infancy is the establishment of trust. Newborns are seen as coming into the world having left the warmth and regularity of the uterus. Yet they are not defenseless. Parents generally respond to their infant's bodily needs, and the handling of the child largely determines the formation of attitudes of trust or mistrust. If a consistent and regular satisfaction of needs is received, the child comes to trust the environment and, in doing so, becomes open to new experiences.

Erikson's recognition that humans continue to develop throughout the entire life span resulted in a developmental scheme involving eight stages extending from infancy to old age. The stages and the challenges associated with them are shown in Table 14-1.

According to Erikson, the crisis of adolescence is identity versus role confusion. The basis of the crisis lies not only in societal demands regarding impending adulthood, but also in the physical changes taking place in the individual's body. Previous trust in one's physical being and bodily functions can be reestablished only by a reevaluation of the self. Adolescents seek to discover who they will become.

How does the adolescent achieve this vital identity? Erikson suggests that our culture allows a psychosocial moratorium during which the rapidly developing child has the opportunity to become integrated into society. A certain amount of experimentation is expected. The adolescent may indeed "try on" various commitments and identities, much as one tries on new clothes before selecting the best fit. This "trying on" is manifested in many ways: a seemingly endless examination with others of the self, of vocations, and of ideologies; a rich fantasy life involving the taking on of a variety of roles; and the identification with particular

TABLE 14-1
Erik Erikson's Stages of Life

Chronological Age	Stage
Infancy	Basic trust vs. mistrust
1½–3 years (approximately)	Autonomy vs. shame, doubt
3–5½ years (approximately)	Initiative vs. guilt
5½–12 years (approximately)	Industry vs. inferiority
Adolescence	Identity vs. role confusion
Young adulthood	Intimacy vs. isolation
Adulthood	Generativity vs. stagnation
Maturity	Ego integrity vs. despair

FIGURE 14-1
According to Erikson, the primary challenge of adolescence is to develop an
identity, which includes a commitment to a particular political ideology.

individuals, frequently involving hero worship. Choosing a vocation is
particularly important. And "falling in love" can be a means to arrive at
a definition of self by seeing oneself reflected in and gradually clarified
through another (Erikson, 1963).

According to Erikson (1968), the young adult faces the crisis of trying
to establish intimate, sharing relationships with others that involve personal commitment. Although these relationships include friendships of
various sorts, establishing a special sexual bond is paramount. Such intimacy goes beyond an obsessive reduction of sexual tensions to mutual
sexual experiences that regulate the differences between the sexes and between individuals. True intimacy means that one is willing to be at least
partly defined by one's mate. Erikson notes that intimacy is not possible
until the psychosocial conflict of the adolescent stage is resolved—that
is, until a sense of identity is achieved. Only when a person is secure in
the self can he or she risk fusion with another. Failure to develop intimacy
results in what Erikson labels isolation, which is characterized by settling
for stereotyped interpersonal relations.

RESOLVING THE IDENTITY CRISIS. Adolescents try to resolve the identity crisis in many different ways. Marcia (1980, 1991) has helped to

distinguish four different identity statuses. These have been revealed in semistructured interviews about occupations, ideology (politics and religion), and interpersonal relations. The interviews are scored according to two criteria: (1) the degree to which individuals have actually confronted the identity crisis by exploring alternatives, and (2) the degree of commitment to a specific ideological position or viewpoint. Using these criteria, adolescents can be classified into four major statuses:

1. *Identity achievement*: Individuals in this category have experienced the crisis, explored alternatives, and now are secure in their commitment to a particular occupation and ideology.

2. *Moratorium*: For individuals in this status, crises are ongoing; individuals are still struggling with alternatives and searching for suitable ideologies and occupations.

3. *Foreclosure*: These individuals have stated ideologies and occupations; however, they achieved these commitments without extensive search and exploration, relying instead upon the advice of parents or other adults.

4. *Diffusion*: Unlike the other three statuses, individuals in this status have neither faced the crisis nor made commitments. Instead, they seem to be lacking in direction.

Because Erikson views identity formation as a developmental task, age changes in status would be anticipated. In fact, as you can see in Figure 14-2, between 12 to 24 years of age the percentage of individuals

FIGURE 14-2

The percentage of individuals at various ages who are in the four identity statuses described by Marcia (1980, 1991). Notice that the achievement status becomes more common among older adolescents, whereas diffusion and foreclosure become less common.

(*Adapted from P. W. Meilman, "Cross-sectional age changes in ego identity status during adolescence," in* Developmental Psychology, *15, 1979, pp. 230–231.*)

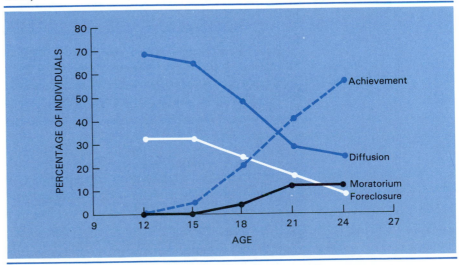

CLOSE-UP

Ethnic Identity

By the mid-1990s, approximately one-third of the 15- to 25-year-olds in the United States will be members of minority groups. These individuals face a special challenge in the development of identity, namely, forming an ethnic identity. The components of ethnic self-concept include identification with the group, a feeling of belonging to the group, and an awareness of the group's culture, including its language, values, and history (Phinney, 1990).

One view of ethnic development (Phinney, 1990) includes three phases that correspond to Marcia's identity statuses. In the initial phase, corresponding to Marcia's diffusion and foreclosure statuses, ethnic identification has not been examined, perhaps because of lack of interest or perhaps because one simply adopts others' views of ethnicity. A Mexican-American adolescent boy in this phase commented: "My past is back there; I have no reason to worry about it. I'm American now." (Phinney, 1989, p. 44). The second phase, corresponding to the moratorium status, involves exploring the meaning of ethnicity and seeking the meaning of ethnic identity for oneself. An Asian-

American adolescent boy reported, "There are a lot of non-Japanese people around me and it gets pretty confusing to try and decide who I am." (Phinney, 1989, p. 44). In the final phase, an individual achieves a well-defined sense of ethnic identity, illustrated in this remark by a black female: "I used to think being light was prettier, but now I think there are pretty dark-skinned girls and pretty light-skinned girls. I don't want to be white now. I'm happy being black." (Phinney, 1989, p. 44).

Research shows that ethnic identification is generally associated with more positive psychological and social functioning. Phinney (1989), for example, studied black, Mexican-American, and Asian-American high school students who were in the three phases of ethnic identity development. In all three ethnic groups, adolescents who had achieved an ethnic identity (that is, they were in the last phase) were more positive about themselves and reported more satisfying interactions with peers and with family.

A central issue concerning ethnic identity is whether identification with one's ethnic group comes

in the achievement status increases, whereas the percentage in foreclosure and moratorium statuses decreases (Meilman, 1979). And studies with late adolescents have shown that during the college years those who initially experience identity diffusion gradually move toward more advanced levels of identity status (Adams and Fitch, 1982). However, no identity status is inherently stable. Individuals who are in the identity achievement and foreclosure statuses sometimes shift to the more unstable statuses of moratorium and diffusion. This, of course, fits with the idea that identity, at least for some people, is continually reworked as new circumstances are met. Dissolution and reconstitution may indeed be crucial in adolescence, but they occur throughout life.

MULTIDIMENSIONAL VIEWS OF SELF-CONCEPT. For Erikson and theorists like him, self-concept is a global construct that provides a coherent at the expense of identification with the majority culture. One view is that ethnic identity represents a continuum, anchored at one end with strong ties to one's culture, and, at the other end, with ties to mainstream culture (Andujo, 1988). Another view is that ties to minority and majority cultures are independent (Phinney, 1990). Identification with either culture may be strong or weak, resulting in the four prototypic types of ethnic orientation depicted in Table 14-2.

Research actually supports both models. In some situations, individuals readily maintain strong ties to both ethnic and mainstream cultures. Many Chinese-Americans, for example, embrace both Chinese and American culture. In other contexts, identification with two cultures is problematic. Among Israelis living in the United States, identi-fication as an American comes at the expense of identification as an Israeli (Phinney, 1990).

These results should *not* be viewed as con-tradictory. A contextual perspective on develop-ment highlights the fact that there is no single, common minority experience. Racial and ethnic groups in Canada and the United States represent a diverse assortment of peoples; the experiences of growing up as an Irish-, black, Mexican-, or Asian-American differ and we should not expect the process of identification to be the same in all groups. Even within groups, the processes may vary, for example, changing over successive gen-erations. Understanding identification in different ethnic groups is a task of enormous proportions, but the result will enrich our images of human development.

TABLE 14-2
Ethnic Orientation, Based on Identification with One's Own Ethnic Group and the Majority Group

Identification with Majority Group	Identification with Ethnic Group	
	Strong	Weak
Strong	Bicultural	Assimilated
Weak	Separated	Marginal

Source: Adapted from J. S. Phinney, "Ethnic identity in adolescents and adults," in Psychological Bulletin, 108, 1990, p. 502. Copyright 1990 by the American Psychological Association. Adapted by permission.

structure to one's identity. Other theorists have proposed that self-concept consists of many components, each tied to a particular aspect of oneself. Marsh and Shavelson (1985), for example, proposed that what others have called self-concept really embodies academic self-concept, social self-concept, and physical self-concept. That is, they propose that individuals have identities in each of these areas. And, members of minority groups develop an ethnic self-concept as well, a topic that we examine in detail in the Close-Up.

Self-concepts tend to become more differentiated throughout the teenage years. In early adolescence, different self-concepts are usually related. A 13-year-old who believes that she is smart will tend to believe that she is also socially skilled and that she is attractive. Later in adoles-cence, a person's self-concepts are often more varied (Marsh, 1989).

Recognition of specific self-concepts does not eliminate the need for a global or general self-concept such as that described by Erikson. The problem can be resolved in much the same way that a similar problem was resolved for intelligence (see pages 239–40). Adolescents may well have specific self-concepts in many domains, but these are organized in a hierarchy. One's general self-concept is the sum of its constituent self-concepts (for example, academic, social, and physical), and these constituent self-concepts may, in turn, be broken down into even more specific self-concepts. For example, Marsh and Shavelson (1985) distinguish self-concepts that concern physical appearance and physical ability. Which self-concept is particularly salient to an adolescent will usually be determined by the context or situation.

The Storm of Adolescence: Fact or Fiction?

Because adolescence involves a search for individual identity, and an implicit breaking away from the childhood notion of simply being a part of the family, many theorists have viewed it as a stormy time.

G. Stanley Hall, the founder of child study in the United States, was among the first psychologists to investigate and speculate about adolescence in this way. He was particularly influential in popularizing the storm and stress view. Hall's ideas, presented in *Adolescence* (1904, 1905), depended heavily on evolutionary theory. Hall viewed development as occurring in stages that parallel the development of the human species. He speculated that from infancy to adolescence the child reflects human history—from its apelike ancestry through primitive cave dwelling, hunting, and fishing. Hall believed that adolescence represents the most recent stage of human development. And he also noted that enormous storm and stress occurred because of the conflict between impulses such as sensitivity versus cruelty, selfishness versus altruism, and radicalism versus conservatism.

FIGURE 14-3

It is popular to view adolescence as a time of storm and stress, but, appearances notwithstanding, most adolescents love and respect their parents, and turn to them for advice.

Hall's idea of storm and stress was also integral to psychoanalytic theories, in which upheaval was seen as a necessary and even positive aspect of adolescent development (A. Freud, 1972). The storm and stress idea of adolescence is still followed by many contemporary theorists (Steinberg, 1990) and by the general public as well. One self-help book advises adolescents: "You may feel full of energy or lie around and sleep a lot. Your moods may shift quickly, uncontrollably, surprising you." (Bell, 1987, p. 5).

Despite its popularity, the idea of adolescent storm and stress receives little support from research (Steinberg, 1990). The vast majority of adolescents report that they feel warmly toward their parents; they admire and love them, and they turn to them for advice. Most adolescents adopt many of their parents' values. And most adolescents feel that they, in turn, are loved and appreciated by their parents. At the same time, there is more petty arguing over mundane issues during the adolescent years. A teen does less with his or her parents and is less inclined to express affection to them. However, these seem to be byproducts of the adolescent's emerging independence and a shift toward a more egalitarian parent-child relationship. Nothing in these findings even hints that the tempestuous adolescent is the norm.

If the evidence provides so little support for storm and stress, why has the idea remained so popular? Several factors have contributed (Bandura, 1964):

1. *Overinterpretation of adolescent nonconformity and fads.* Faddish group behavior does occur, but adults behave in this way as well. In this respect, adolescents are not all that different.

2. *Mass-media sensationalism.* The adolescent of the media is portrayed as passing through a semidelinquent or neurotic phase, because that character seems so much more fascinating than the run-of-the-mill, relatively undisturbed adolescent.

3. *Overgeneralization from deviant youth.* Descriptions of adolescents often come from mental health professionals who actually come into contact with a biased sample of adolescents—those who truly are disturbed.

4. *Overemphasis on biological determinants of sexual behavior.* This view paints the adolescent as in the throes of sudden erotic conflict, rather than under the more moderate influence of social learning variables that largely govern human sexuality.

Society's expectation that adolescents are rebellious, wild, and unpredictable may well increase the chance of just such outcomes. Although adolescence might not be completely problem free in any event, for some individuals, the cultural commitment to the storm and stress hypothesis becomes a self-fulfilling prophecy.

THE WORLD OF WORK

Few aspects of our lives are as important to us as our work careers. Beginning with early childhood, children are asked what they want to be when they grow up. Until recently, most people chose an occupation somewhere between childhood and adolescence and then pursued that occupation for their entire working lives. And until recently, almost all men but only a minority of women had occupations outside the home. Today women are almost as likely as men to have some kind of career. And most youth first experience the world of work with part-time employment during school.

Part-Time Work

Most high school students in the United States hold part-time jobs while attending school. About 75 percent of high school seniors work part time, for an average of about 20 hours per week. This phenomenon is relatively recent, dating from the 1970s. And, it is much more characteristic of youth in the United States than in other industrialized countries. In contrast, in Canada, about 40 percent of high school students are employed; in Japan fewer than 10 percent are employed (Reubens, Harrison, and Rupp, 1981).

Most adolescents with jobs are from middle-class homes (although teens from lower-class homes work longer hours). Adolescents typically find employment as restaurant workers, as cashiers or salespeople in retail

FIGURE 14-4
Many adolescents work part-time in the fast-food industry, where the work is often repetitive and stressful.

stores, as clerical help, or as unskilled laborers (Mortimer, 1991). Employers clearly distinguish "boy" jobs and "girl" jobs. Nearly all busboys, gardeners, manual laborers, and newspaper carriers are boys; whereas, most food-counter workers, maids, and baby sitters are girls. Boys usually work longer hours than girls and boys' average pay is better than girls' (Greenberger and Steinberg, 1983).

Many adults applaud this upward trend in adolescent employment. They claim that adolescent workers learn self-discipline, feel useful, and gain self-confidence. In addition, adolescent youths may learn many specific skills that will transfer to later employment, such as being prompt and working well with others (Snedeker, 1982).

This rosy picture of adolescent employment does not square with the evidence. Research indicates that extensive employment during the school year—defined as working more than 15 or 20 hours weekly—is harmful to many facets of adolescent development. One of the most elaborate studies of the effects of adolescent employment was reported by Steinberg and Dornbusch (1991). These investigators studied nearly 4,000 sophomores, juniors, and seniors attending high schools in California and Wisconsin. Their results, shown in Figure 14-5, revealed harmful effects of employment on school performance as well as on psychological and behavioral functioning. As the number of hours of work increases, students spend less time on homework; they cut more classes and their grades drop. Also, more time spent working is associated with increased drug use and increased psychological distress, with symptoms such as anxiety, depression, or fatigue. These findings held equally for white, African-American, Asian-American, and Hispanic students.

Why is employment so detrimental to youth? The impact on school performance may simply reflect that most adolescents cannot cope with the combined demands of school and extensive employment. Balancing these responsibilities may simply require greater discipline, foresight, and maturity than the average youth has. Psychological and behavioral dysfunction may stem from the fact that many teenagers are employed in jobs that are repetitive and boring, but are sometimes highly stressful, a topic that we examine in the Close-Up.

Another supposed advantage of adolescent employment is that it teaches youth "the value of a dollar." Here, too, the myth is often at odds with reality. Adolescents spend the vast majority of their money on themselves for clothes, food, cosmetics, and entertainment (Bachman, 1983). As Figure 14-6 shows, relatively little income is deferred for future education or to help pay for family living expenses. Rather than being a benefit, the typical adolescent work experience is potentially quite misleading:

> . . . the "reality" faced by the typical high school student with substantial part-time earning is just not very realistic. In the absence of payment for rent, utilities, groceries, and the many other necessities routinely provided by parents, the typical student is likely to find that most or all of his/her earnings are available for discretionary spending. . . . It seems likely that some will experience . . ."premature affluence"—affluence because $200 or more per month represents a lot of "spending money" for a high school

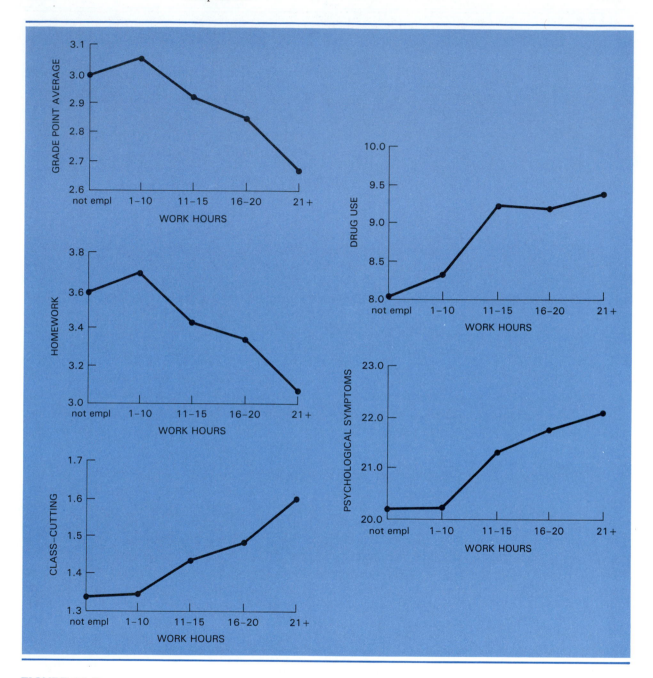

FIGURE 14-5

These graphs show the impact of amount of part-time work per week on school
performance and behavior. In each case, the influence is negative.
(Reprinted from L. Steinberg and S. M. Dornbusch, "Negative correlates of
part-time employment during adolescence: Replication and elaboration," in
Developmental Psychology, 27, 1991, pp. 304–313. Copyright 1991 by the
American Psychological Association. Reprinted by permission.)

CLOSE-UP

The Burger Blues

Today more adolescents in the United States work in fast-food restaurants than in any other employment setting. Although these youthful workers often radiate enthusiasm in television commercials, the reality of work in the fast-food industry is quite different. Relatively few teenage employees work more than a few months; instead, most quit because of low pay coupled with much job pressure.

"I quit because I didn't like the way the managers treated us," says a 17-year-old who was a cashier at an Atlanta McDonald's last summer. "The managers," she says, "are real snotty. They yell at the workers in front of customers and call you stupid. At the end of August, fifteen of us quit because of one manager. Otherwise, most of us would have kept working after school. . . ."

Low pay is a constant irritant. A 16-year-old who quit an Atlanta Wendy's last fall says he was "doing more work than I was getting paid for" at $2.65 an hour. "Sometimes I'd have to work 12 hours a day. Other times there weren't enough of us for lunch-time crowds. One month we went through five assistant managers. When I get another job it won't be in fast foods."

A counter employee in Texas complained: "Management puts tremendous mental strain on the employees. We have all learned how to successfully steal enough money . . . to make working here with all the bull and pressure worthwhile." (Montgomery, 1979, p. 1).

These remarks typify the experiences of many adolescents who work part time. Employment does not increase self-esteem in these youthful employees nor does it make them feel useful. Instead, they believe that employers take advantage of them.

Adolescents' feelings may well reflect unrealistic expectations; teenagers may naively believe that they should have greater independence in the workplace and that employers should have more concern for them. In any case, it seems obvious that the common experience benefits neither employees nor employers in the long run: Youth may become cynical about work and employers face a constant turnover of dissatisfied workers.

FIGURE 14-6
Adolescents spend most of their money on themselves, for clothes, entertainment and the like; relatively little is saved for education or to help pay family expenses.
(*Adapted from J. Bachman, "Premature affluence: Do high school students earn too much?," in* Economic Outlook USA, *Summer, pp. 64–67.*)

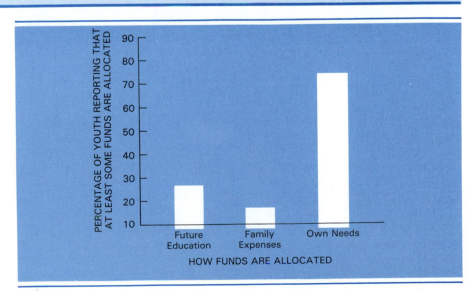

student, and premature because many of these individuals will not be able to sustain that level of discretionary spending once they take on the burden of paying for their own necessities. (Bachman, 1983, p. 65)

As awareness of the potential pitfalls of adolescent employment has grown, some communities have responded with legislation that limits the employment of youths. In 1986, Pinellas County in Florida limited adolescents to 30 hours of work each week during the school year. Although this is a valuable first step, a glance at the results in Figure 14-5 indicates that 30 hours are far too many for most youths. A better limit would be 10-15 hours: For most of the measures in Figure 14-5, students who worked 1 to 10 hours per week resembled students who did not work.

Vocational Choice

Ideally, each of us should have the opportunity to follow a vocation that suits our talents, interests, and personality. It is not a simple matter for an adult to assess himself or herself adequately, to be aware of the wide range of vocations, to prepare for a vocation, and then to make a realistic "best" job choice. For the adolescent, these tasks are even more difficult.

Donald Super (1976) proposed that an adolescent's self-concept plays a central role in career choice. During middle adolescence—14 to 18 years of age—adolescents form ideas about work that fit their emerging self-concepts. In this process, which Super calls **crystallization**, youths begin to narrow career possibilities, based on their perception of their own abilities and values. A teenager who is outgoing and friendly may decide that he or she wants a career that involves working with people. An adolescent who enjoys art may decide that he or she would like to be a professional photographer. These early decisions are tentative; youths "try on" potential vocations and try to imagine what the chosen careers would be like.

Crystallization is followed, from about 18 to 21 years of age, by a period of **specification**. A youth narrows his or her career options further, begins to seek information about particular careers, and obtains specific training for the chosen line of work. These processes represent a continuation of the activities that were begun during the crystallization phase; the chief difference is a clearer focus on potential careers. The 16-year-old who had decided to work with people might, as a 20-year-old, elect to become a nurse, teacher, or psychologist.

Implementation begins in the early twenties, when a person completes his or her education and actually starts a chosen career at an entry-level position. In their mid- or late twenties, many individuals enter a period of **stabilization** in which they settle into a specific career. In the mid-thirties, many people enter the last of Super's phases, **consolidation**, during which individuals attempt to advance their careers and achieve higher-status positions.

Like many other stage theories that we have encountered in this book, the ages associated with Super's theory are only rough guidelines. More important is the emphasis on the gradual manner in which adoles-

Crystallization The first of Super's phases of vocational development, typically occurring from about 14 to 18 years of age, in which youths begin to identify career possibilities and experiment with different career choices.

Specification The second of Super's phases of vocational development, typically occurring from about 18 to 21 years of age, during which youths further narrow career possibilities and begin training for specific careers.

Implementation The third of Super's phases of vocational development, typically occurring in the early twenties, when adults complete career training and start a career.

Stabilization The fourth of Super's phases of vocational development, typically occurring in the mid- or late twenties, when adults become established in a career.

Consolidation The fifth and last of Super's phases of vocational development, typically beginning in the mid-thirties, when individuals try to advance themselves in their line of work and achieve greater status.

FIGURE 14-7
Many teenagers experiment with different vocational identities to determine how they "feel."

cents come to match their own skills and interests with the characteristics of different careers. The theory also emphasizes the role of accurate information—about the student's self-concept and the characteristics of different jobs—in deciding upon a career that will be satisfying.

Super's theory specifies the types of career-related decisions that individuals make at different phases of adolescence and young adulthood. A theory by John Holland (1985) helps to explain why individuals find particular careers satisfying. In his **personality type theory**, Holland argues that people find their jobs most satisfying when the distinguishing characteristics of their jobs fit their personalities. A person is usually unhappy with his or her work when it does not mesh well with the individual's personality.

Holland believes that six prototypic personalities are important when people select occupations:

1. *Realistic.* These individuals like to solve practical problems and often prefer work requiring physical labor and motor coordination instead of social skills. Careers involving these characteristics would include farming, truck driving, and construction work.

2. *Investigative.* These individuals are thinkers, not doers; they enjoy grappling with abstract concepts and sometimes prefer avoiding interpersonal relations. Careers in math and science would interest these people.

Personality type theory
A view, proposed by John Holland, that work is most often satisfying when the distinguishing characteristics of a job match the worker's personality.

FIGURE 14-8
According to Holland's personality type theory of vocational choice, individuals with the prototypic enterprising personality are attracted to positions of power and status.

3. *Social*. These individuals are often verbally skilled and very fluent with language; they value interpersonal relations. They are often attracted to the "people" professions, such as teaching, counseling, and social work.

4. *Conventional*. These people prefer structured work environments and prefer to work under the direction of others. Jobs as bank tellers, file clerks, or secretaries interest these individuals.

5. *Enterprising*. Individuals in this category like to supervise and direct others, and they are attracted to positions of power and status. They are best suited for careers in sales, politics, and management.

6. *Artistic*. These individuals enjoy unstructured tasks and have a strong need to express themselves. Individuals with this orientation enjoy careers as writers, artists, musicians, and actors.

Most adolescents don't match these personality groupings exactly; instead, their orientation will represent some combination of the six prototypes. By completing any of several well-known measures of vocational interest, such as the Strong-Brown Vocational Interest Inventory or the Self-Directed Search, adolescents can learn more about the fit of their interests and preferences to different vocations.

Of course, an individual's likes and dislikes are far from the only factors that determine vocational choice. Much broader social influences are also at work. Let's examine some.

SOCIETY'S NEEDS AND REWARDS. Society sets the limits within which any young person can realistically choose a vocation. Today there is considerably less opportunity for agricultural and unskilled workers because our society has become highly technical. Many recent Ph.D.'s are also having trouble finding positions because society's needs in certain areas have shrunk, or because too many people have prepared for positions in these areas. In contrast, an increasing need is anticipated for social service workers. Although young people may try to direct themselves toward areas in which they think the best job opportunities exist, this strategy is limited because employment opportunities can be projected accurately and completely for only a few years.

Aside from changing demands, other social determinants come into play. The amount of reward given by society—in terms of financial return, prestige, or freedom—determines which adolescents will enter certain vocations. In one study (Hesketh, Elmslie, and Kaldor, 1990) in which high school students judged the atttractiveness of different occupations, prestige—as represented by greater pay, status and power—was ranked nearly as important as the interests represented by the work. Prestige was equally important to boys and girls.

SOCIAL CLASS AND ATTITUDES. Vocational aspirations of adolescents have always been clearly related to their socioeconomic backgrounds, with youths from the higher classes selecting the more prestigious vocations (Conger and Petersea, 1984). This pattern is demonstrated by the results of a classic study in which adolescents from a small midwestern city listed their preferred future occupations. Of those categorized in the higher social strata, 77 percent chose business and professional vocations, whereas only 7 percent of those in the lower social strata chose these vocations (Hollingshead, 1949). Many of these adolescents were also undecided about their futures.

These social-class differences in vocational preference can be linked to a number of factors. Some concern information: Middle-class youths often have a better idea of what is required in more prestigious occupations, in part because their families will often include parents and siblings who have these types of careers. Other factors concern attitudes: Adolescents from middle-class homes are encouraged to be independent and achievement oriented. This makes them more inclined to achieve in school, which is a prerequisite for many business and professional occupations. In addition, middle-class youths are attracted to professional occupations because they allow them to continue to achieve and to demonstrate their achievement through status and wealth. Finally, the greater income of middle-class families opens career doors that may be closed to adolescents from less affluent homes. More money is available to middle-class youths for the necessary education or enrichment experiences needed to pursue professional occupations.

SEX DIFFERENCES. There are sex differences in vocational selection. In fact, selection of a career itself is considered far more important for males than for females. Occupational choice not only potentially defines the social status of the male and his family, but is also considered part of his identity as a male and as a person. For many adolescent girls, choosing occupations means merely picking jobs that will serve as stop-gaps until they settle down to homemaking. The high percentage of women in the work force contradicts this notion—but many working women still do not view their occupations as central to their identities, despite the influence of the women's movement. For other women, occupational choice is very important. And in contrast to earlier times, many women today no longer prefer traditionally female occupations (Clemson, 1981).

Females also get less family support than males in financing professional educations. In a study of 183 families, 80 percent indicated they would give the career goals of their sons priority over the career goals of their daughters if finances were tight (Peterson, Rollins, Thomas, and Heaps, 1982).

Unemployed Adolescents

Media reports sometimes suggest that unemployment is rampant among adolescents. In fact, only about 5 percent of adolescents in the United States are out of school and unemployed, but looking for work. Of these, the vast majority—approximately 90 percent—find work within 6 months or less. What *is* cause for concern is that unemployment is not evenly distributed among different racial and ethnic groups. For example, approximately one-third of black adolescents are unemployed. Compared with peers who are still in school or who are employed, unemployed youths usually experience greater feelings of anxiety, helplessness, and anger (Kieselbach, 1991).

For many adolescents, unemployment is a result of leaving school ill-prepared for the world of work. Many adolescents take vocational training in high school, but research suggests that this coursework is beneficial only to high school graduates. Employers are simply reluctant to consider individuals who have not graduated from high school, even if they have had training that might be relevant to a job (Hamilton, 1991).

FIGURE 14-9

Unemployment particularly affects minority youths, who often leave school poorly trained and unable to find satisfactory work.

Addressing the problem of adolescent unemployment will require the cooperation of schools, government, and industry. Internships and apprenticeships, in which adolescents' work is monitored and supervised by teachers, would help to bridge the gap between school and work. At the same time, instruction in academic skills needs to continue, but in a way that links these skills to performance at the workplace. More counseling and guidance should be available to students who leave school before graduating. Too often, youths look for work on their own, ignorant of opportunities that may be available and of the skills that may be required (W. T. Grant Foundation Commission, 1988).

ROMANCE, SEX, AND FAMILY LIFE

Marriage, parenting, and family life are the most important aspects of most adults' lives. As they entered their senior years, the men in Terman's study of gifted men (Chapter 8) said a happy family life was the most important goal they had set for themselves. And in a survey of the quality of American life, adults rated marriage as the most important life domain, even ahead of health and income (Doherty and Jacobson, 1982). There is little doubt that adolescent dating plays a fundamental role in the formation and maintenance of these intimate relationships. So we begin our discussion with these first romantic encounters with members of the opposite sex.

Dating

The scene is a familiar one in adolescence: It's Thursday night and a teenager does not yet have a date for the dance on Saturday. With each passing minute, our teen becomes more anxious, hoping that the phone will ring, and, at the same time, wondering if she (or he) should take the initiative and call someone.

This somewhat peculiar ritual has been a part of the American adolescent experience for much of the twentieth century. Beginning in early adolescence, boys and girls begin to express romantic interest in members of the opposite sex. Dating can take many forms, but often begins with group dates in which several boys and several girls go out and spend most of their time together as a group. Casual dating involving two or three couples is also common, as are serious relationships with steady girlfriends or boyfriends.

In the United States, girls usually begin to date at 13 or 14 years of age. Boys are about one year older when they start to date, a difference that reflects girls' more rapid physical development. An implication of the age difference is that most girls' early dating is with older boys. By age 16, most teenagers have begun to date and nearly half will have one or more dates per week.

These ages are, of course, approximate and are strongly influenced by school and community standards with regard to when dating should begin and how frequently teens should date (Simmons and Blyth, 1987).

FIGURE 14-10
Dating in adolescence can take many forms, including a group date in which several boys and girls go out and spend time together as a group.

Earlier-maturing girls date earlier than later-maturing girls, and white girls begin dating earlier than black girls (Phinney, Jensen, Olsen, and Cundick, 1990).

Dating serves many functions. It provides adolescents with recreation, entertainment, social participation; it is a means of seeking status; it may provide sexual gratification; it can lead to courtship and mate selection; it socializes boys and girls regarding their culture's standards for heterosexual interaction; and it is a means for achieving independence from adult norms (for example, when adolescents cross social-class lines).

From dating, boys learn to become more sensitive and more caring. That is, girls apparently play an important role in teaching boys to become more expressive of their emotions and feelings. This finding is not surprising based on our earlier discussion of same-sex friendships (pages 327–28). You may recall that girls are much more expressive with their same-sex friends than boys are. So, in dating, girls are simply taking social and emotional skills that they have developed with their girl friends and applying them to heterosexual relationships. For most boys, expression of intimacy has not been a part of their friendships, so they have much to learn (Buhrmester and Furman, 1987).

The impact of dating on girls is more complicated. On the one hand, girls who date early and intensively tend to be less mature socially than their peers; on the other hand, adolescent girls who do not date at all feel insecure, are overly dependent upon their parents, and are less skilled socially (Douvan and Adelson, 1966). And, regardless of age, compared with group activities with boys, serious dating seems to have negative effects on girls, perhaps because of the pressure to become involved sexually (Simmons and Blyth, 1987).

This last result reminds us that sexuality is an integral component of dating and intimate relationships. The first expressions of romantic and sexual interests usually take place at parties and involve experimentation with kissing, hugging, and light petting. Let's turn now to a discussion of adolescent sexual behavior.

Awakening of Sexual Interests

Sexual interest awakens about the time of puberty for both sexes, but the form it takes is quite different for boys than it is for girls. For boys, adolescent sexuality begins between ages 13 and 16 with erotic dreams, often accompanied by the release of semen during sleep. During the day, the adolescent boy may find himself suddenly displaying an erection and fantasizing about sexual activities. For girls, adolescence is more likely to bring romantic fantasies. Thus, in early adolescence, a boy's interest in girls is erotic, but a girl's interest in boys is romantic. By later adolescence, boys too begin to experience romantic feelings. And for both sexes, the feeling of being in love is often the motivation and justification for sexual activities (Katchadourian, 1991).

SEXUAL BEHAVIOR. For adolescents growing up in Canada and the United States, sexual behavior has changed markedly since the mid-1960s. Sex before marriage has become much more common. In 1971, 46 percent of 19-year-old unmarried women in the United States had experienced sexual intercourse. This figure rose to 60 percent in 1976, 69 percent in 1979, and settled back to 62 percent in 1982. And, ever-younger teenagers are sexually experienced. In 1971, 14 percent of American 15-year-old girls had experienced sexual intercourse. This figure peaked at 23 percent in 1979 and then fell back to 18 percent in 1982. Figure 14-12 shows the current information on the percentage of black, Hispanic, and white boys

FIGURE 14-11
Sexual interests first become evident in adolescence.

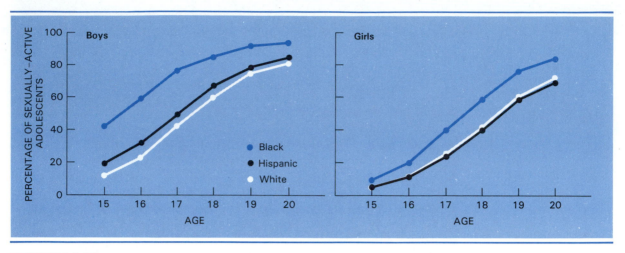

FIGURE 14-12

These graphs depict developmental change in the percentage of boys and girls who have experienced sexual intercourse. At each age, more boys than girls are sexually experienced, and blacks are more experienced than Hispanic or white adolescents.
(Adapted from National Research Council, Risking the future: Adolescent sexuality, pregnancy, and childbearing, *Vol. 1. Washington, D. C.: National Academy Press, 1987, table 2-6.)*

Restrictive culture A culture in which adolescent sexual behavior is prohibited; this prohibition is enforced by rigid segregation of the sexes throughout adolescence.

Semirestrictive culture A culture in which adolescent sexual behavior is formally forbidden, but in which adolescents and adults alike ignore this prohibition with little fear of reproof.

Permissive culture A culture in which sexual behavior is viewed as a routine part of normal behavioral development.

and girls at different ages who are sexually active. For all races, boys and older adolescents are more active. Black youths tend to be more sexually active than Hispanic and white youths (National Research Council, 1987).

These changes are a source of great concern to many, who fear that they portend the demise of American and Canadian culture. The changes need to be kept in perspective, however. More than adolescent sexual behavior has changed. During the past 25 years, people of all ages have become more tolerant of and open-minded toward many behaviors that were once considered taboo. In addition, increased sexual activity is not synonymous with more casual sex or promiscuity. For most adolescents, sex occurs in the context of feelings of love for one's partner, and sexually active adolescents expect loyalty from their partners (Sorensen, 1973).

The sexual behavior of adolescents in the United States and Canada also needs to be considered from the perspective of sexual attitudes worldwide. In a classic work published in 1951, *Patterns of Sexual Behavior,* Clellan Ford and Frank Beach described the sexual activity of adolescents in more than 200 cultures. They believed that cultures could be classified as **restrictive, semirestrictive,** or **permissive** with regard to adolescent sexual activities. In restrictive cultures, sex before marriage is absolutely forbidden and regulated by physically separating boys and girls throughout adolescence. At the other extreme, in permissive cultures, sexual activity is a regular and accepted part of behavioral development in childhood and adolescence. For example, one culture in India believes

that girls will not mature without benefit of sexual intercourse. Early sex play among boys and girls characteristically involves many forms of mutual

> masturbation and usually ends in attempted copulation. By the time they are 11- or 12-years-old, most girls regularly engage in full intercourse. (Ford and Beach, 1951, p. 190)

Semirestrictive cultures are in between these extremes and typically have formal cultural standards against adolescent sexual behavior. However, these standards are usually ignored, without penalty, by both adults and adolescents. By these definitions, the United States has evolved from a restrictive to semirestrictive culture, but it certainly remains conservative in its sexual attitudes compared with many cultures worldwide.

Of course, even with today's semirestrictive views of sexual behavior, not all adolescents are sexually active. For example, among Hispanic 18-year-olds, 67 percent of boys and 40 percent of girls have experienced sexual intercourse; a substantial minority of boys and most girls have not. What factors help to determine teenagers' sexual behaviors? As we have already seen (see Figure 14-12), older adolescents and black adolescents are more likely to have experienced sexual intercourse. In addition, girls who mature early become sexually experienced at a younger age (Bingham, Miller, and Adams, 1990).

Parents' and friends' attitudes are also important. Treboux and Busch-Rossnagel (1990) studied 361 high school students' sexual attitudes and behaviors as well as their beliefs about their parents' and friends' approval or disapproval of sexual behavior. Students completed questionnaires about their own behavior and about their attitudes toward the propriety of various sexual behaviors. In other questionnaires, students were asked how friends and parents would react if they knew that the student was engaging in different sexual behaviors (for example, kissing, petting, intercourse). These investigators found that positive attitudes toward sex by parents and friends was associated with students' positive attitudes, which, in turn, were associated with more frequent and more intense sexual behavior. In other words, when parents and friends approved of sex, students had more open attitudes and were more likely to be sexually active.

This result highlights a phenomenon that we mentioned in Chapter 10 when discussing the impact of peers on adolescents' behavior (pages 335–36). When standards for appropriate behavior are fuzzy, as they are for adolescent sexual behavior, youths are often influenced by their peers' attitudes.

CONTRACEPTION. Although adolescents' sexual behavior may not be a cause for grave concern, adolescent pregnancies are—approximately one in ten American adolescents will become pregnant before marriage (Zelnick, Kantner, and Ford, 1981). Most of these pregnancies are not planned and occur because the partners failed to use birth control. Throughout adolescence, only a minority of sexually active teenagers use birth control. Contraceptives are more often used when individuals plan, in advance, to have sex and are more often used by older adolescents (National Research Council, 1987).

Why do adolescents use birth control so infrequently, when the con-

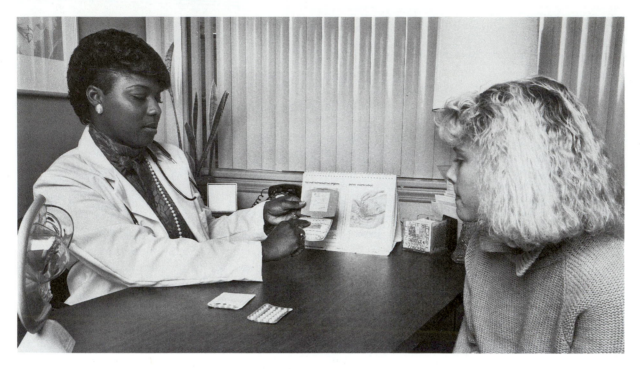

FIGURE 14-13
Sexually-active adolescents typically do not use contraceptives, in part because obtaining them is often awkward or embarrassing for adolescents.

sequences of not doing so are so momentous? Ignorance is surely part of the answer. Many adolescents are seriously ill-informed about the facts of conception: In one nationwide survey of teenagers, one-third agreed with the statement that "If a girl truly doesn't want to have a baby, she won't get pregnant even though she may have sex without taking any birth control precautions" (Sorensen, 1973). For those who do understand conception, access to contraceptives can be a problem. Teens may not know where to obtain contraceptives or may find it awkward to do so.

Psychological factors also come into play. Some adolescents discount the risk involved and assume that only others become pregnant. And some teenagers do not use birth control because, in so doing, they would be admitting that their sexual behavior was planned rather than spontaneous. That is, when adolescents are ambivalent or anxious about having sex, if they buy condoms hours or days before, they cannot then rationalize their sexual behavior as simply giving in to temptation during the heat of passion (Gerrard, 1987).

Clearly, if society is willing to tolerate adolescent sexual behavior, then there is an obligation to educate adolescents about appropriate methods of contraception and to make these means available to adolescent boys and girls. And, as the data in Figure 14-12 remind us, sex education programs during high school are not early enough; information is needed earlier in adolescence.

AIDS. Teenagers represent no more than 1 percent of the cases of AIDS in the United States. However, this figure is growing, and, more importantly, approximately one-fourth of all AIDS cases involve 20- to 29-year-olds, most of whom were probably infected during adolescence. Many factors converge to make adolescents a high-risk group for contracting AIDS. The actions most likely to lead to infection—unprotected sex and the use of intravenous drugs—are both much too common in adolescence. In addition, adolescence is often a time of sexual experimentation involving multiple partners, which further increases the risk of contracting AIDS (Rotheram-Borus and Koopman, 1991). Finally, adolescents often naively feel invulnerable to risk—"it couldn't happen to me." In one study (Moore and Rosenthal, 1991) nearly 30 percent of sexually active 17- to 20-year-olds engaged in sexual practices that placed them at great risk for AIDS, such as vaginal or anal intercourse without condoms; yet this age group judged themselves to be not at risk.

In the face of such widespread ignorance or denial of the reality of AIDS, programs are needed to teach adolescents about the disease and how to avoid contracting it. Such programs are particularly useful for adolescents who, too frequently, rely upon peers for their information about health and sexuality (Boyer and Hein, 1991).

FIGURE 14-14

Many adolescents do not understand the dangers of AIDS and the behaviors that place them at risk. Posters like this are one part of an effort to educate adolescents about AIDS.

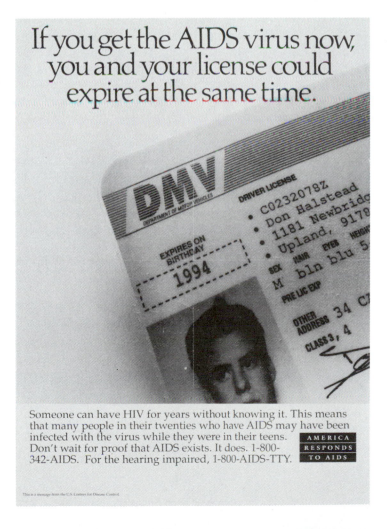

Marriage and Family

Earlier in the text we discussed family influences on the child. Here we view the family from the vantage point of adulthood. Although adult life styles appear more variable now than they did in the past, most individuals still experience the "traditional" nuclear or extended family. In fact, over 90 percent of all adults marry at some time in their lives, and most do so by age 25. Further, the great majority of these people have children, usually two, as opposed to the three or four raised by previous generations.

In our culture we say that we marry for love; indeed, being in love appears to be a strong motivating force for marrying. But many other factors are involved in the selection of a spouse. As unromantic as it may be, proximity plays a role: We marry those who live nearby. In general, *homogamy* (the mating of like with like) is the rule with regard to age, social class, family background, religion, values, and perhaps even personality. Families undoubtedly encourage homogamy, feeling more comfortable with such potential family members and perhaps believing that "like with like" stands a better chance of survival. Finally, readiness for marriage is important. Such a feeling may be based on the age the individual thinks society prescribes for marriage; or it may be based on economic, educational, and occupational circumstances, and on psychological needs.

Historically, women have had less power over marital selection than men (Troll, 1985). One reason for this is that women in our culture do not usually initiate direct contact with men. Women also outnumber men, which means that women have fewer options than men in choosing a spouse. Finally, according to cultural stereotypes, the age range when people are considered "ideal candidates" for marriage is shorter for women than for men.

STAGES OF PARENTING. Throughout early and middle adulthood the parental role usually dominates much of the activity and efforts of adults. Alpert and Richardson (1980), who explored parenting as a major task of adulthood, describe five stages. The first stage is the period before becoming parents. For couples today, this is a time of decision making. Young adults today are much more likely than those in previous generations to plan on combining parenting and occupational/career roles. It appears, however, that the decision to have children is often made without a clear notion of what being a parent involves or how much effort it takes.

The next stage, for those who do choose to be parents, is pregnancy. Pregnancy can be a time of stress for couples. The third stage is childbirth and the postpartum period. Some women experience a degree of depression shortly after childbirth. New fathers may often show signs of depression as they experience loss of attention from their wives and difficulty in developing father/husband roles for themselves. What all this suggests is that having a new baby requires considerable adaptation by both parents (Osofsky and Osofsky, 1984), even though couples may indeed experience great joy in their newborns.

FIGURE 14-15
Many parents experience stress when their children are adolescents and start to demand more independence.

Next come the early and middle years of parenting, which begin when infancy ends and extend until the child reaches adolescence. Often this is a period of financial stress and anxiety.

Parenting adolescents is the fifth stage. Parents experience stress to the degree that their adolescent children are experiencing stormy periods of transition. At this time there is what has been called an "interlocking of developmental tasks" for middle-aged parents and their adolescent children (Aldous, 1978). The offspring may show uncertainty about leaving home, and their quest for independence may cause friction. And during these years, anywhere from the late thirties to the middle fifties, couples are often heavily involved in occupational and civic responsibilities, which may also burden the marital relationship. Both parents must deal with the beginning signs of biological aging. At the same time, middle-aged women and men are often in the role of adult children to their own aging parents. They may feel overburdened by the demands made on them by both the older and the younger generations (Brody, 1985).

As children become truly independent adults, many parents experience a deep sense of satisfaction, often accompanied by relief. Occasionally, though, mothers experience depression in the form of the "empty nest syndrome" as their children leave home after many years of dependence (Troll, 1985).

MARITAL SATISFACTION. Do adults like their marital experiences? The divorce rate in the United States certainly would lead us to answer a resounding no to this question. But the majority of divorced people remarry; one study estimated that 80 percent remarry and that 40 percent of all marriages are remarriages (Ihinger-Talman and Pasley, 1987). If Americans are disappointed in marriage, they apparently have not given up trying to find happiness in this type of relationship. Moreover, married people report being happier than divorced, widowed, or single people throughout their lives, and they also enjoy better physical and mental health than any of the other groups (Vernbrugge, 1979).

But the success and benefits of marriage depend on many factors. For example, early marriage is a hindrance to later development for most young people. Marrying in one's teens appears to lead to having more children, achieving less educationally and occupationally, and being more likely to divorce (Otto, 1979). Elder and Rockwell (1976) found that women who married under age 19 tended to experience "relative deprivation" throughout their lives, including inadequate material resources and an overwhelming child-care burden. Those who married after 22 tended to advance in social class, and this was true regardless of whether they had gone to college or ended their educations with high school. According to Hogan (1978), there is a typical sequence for young men: First finish school, then get a job, and then get married. Those who follow this sequence are more likely to have successful marriages and are less likely to divorce than those who follow another sequence (for example, marrying before finishing school or getting a job).

Marital satisfaction also fluctuates over time. Several studies show a modest relation between the family cycle and satisfaction. The example

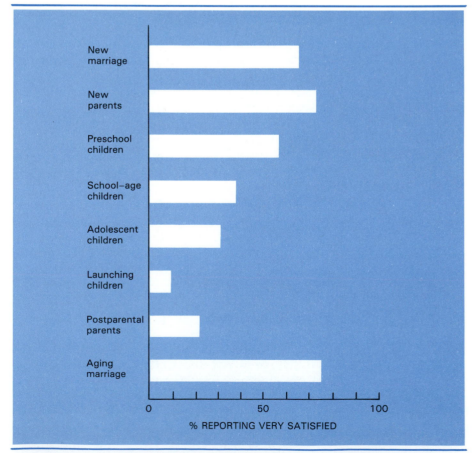

FIGURE 14-16
Percentage of adults who report that they are very satisfied at each stage of marriage. According to the graph, many of the years associated with child rearing are the least satisfying.
(From B. C. Rollins and H. Feldman, "Marital satisfaction over the family life cycle," in Journal of Marriage and the Family, 32, 1970, pp. 20–28. Copyrighted 1970 by the National Council on Family Relations, 3989 Central Ave. N.E., Suite #550, Minneapolis, MN 55421. Reprinted by permission.)

shown in Figure 14-16 indicates that the high satisfaction of the beginning years of marriage decreases as offspring grow older, and reaches the lowest point as the children approach adulthood and move out. As a couple is once again without children in the home, satisfaction gradually increases into the retirement years.

When adolescents and young adults leave home to begin work and, often, begin their own families, the cycle of development that we have examined throughout this book begins anew. The tale of human development that we have narrated to you does not end but is repeated, with countless variations that give the tale its mystery and its splendor. We hope that this book has increased your appreciation and understanding of this marvel. Thanks for reading.

SUMMARY

1. A focal point of adolescence is achieving an identity, which is a coherent sense of self. The roots of identity are found in childhood, when youngsters gradually begin to distinguish themselves from others in terms of psychological characteristics. Erikson views identity as one of many challenges facing individuals throughout the life span. He believed that adolescents enjoy a moratorium during which they can "try on" various identities before selecting the one that fits them best.

2. Marcia proposed that, at any particular time, an adolescent may have any of four identity statuses: achievement, moratorium, foreclosure, or diffusion. These differ in the degree to which adolescents have confronted the identity crisis and in their degree of commitment to particular views.

3. Other views emphasize more specific components of self-concept (such as academic, social, and physical self-concepts), which are organized to form a self-concept hierarchy. For some individuals, achieving an ethnic self-concept is an important task of adolescence, one that may involve the same identity status as global self-concept. Acquiring an ethnic self-concept may come at the expense of identification with the majority culture, but this depends upon the cultural context.

4. There is controversy about whether adolescents in search of identity invariably experience stormy periods. Adolescence clearly entails breaking away from some of the family ties of childhood and establishing closer involvement with the attitudes, values, and goals of peers. However, on most measures, adolescents resemble their parents and remain affectionate toward and respectful of them.

5. Most adolescents first experience the world of work as part-time employees. Although popular wisdom attributes many benefits to such part-time work, research generally demonstrates harmful effects: School performance suffers and behavioral problems increase if adolescents engage in much part-time work.

6. The first important occupational decisions are made during adolescence. According to Super, adolescents and adults go through five phases of vocational development: crystallization, specification, implementation, stabilization, and consolidation. In Holland's personality type theory, people enjoy their jobs when their personalities fit the salient characteristics of their work. His prototypic personalities include six categories: realistic, investigative, social, conventional, enterprising, and artistic. Vocational choices are also shaped by such factors as society's needs and rewards, and the individual's social class, attitudes, and gender.

7. Unemployment is common among minority youths and often occurs because they leave school inadequately prepared for employment. Additional job-related and academic training as well as job counseling are needed to enhance the employment prospects of these adolescents.

8. A happy family existence is for many the most important goal in life. Dating provides the first romantic exposure to members of the opposite sex and provides recreation, enhanced status, and sexual gratification. Girls begin to date at a younger age than boys, and the impact of dating seems to be greater on girls than on boys.

9. Adolescents in North America have become more sexually active in the past 25 years, but they still believe that sex should be accompanied by feelings of love. Modern attitudes in Canada and the United States toward sex would be classified as semirestrictive, in contrast to restrictive (in which adolescent sex is absolutely forbidden) or permissive (in which adolescent sex is encouraged). Sexual activity is more common among older and black adolescents and among teens whose parents and friends are open-minded toward sex.

10. Today, teenage pregnancies are too common and adolescent cases of AIDS are increasing. In both instances, ignorance of the relevant risks and an unwillingness to take appropriate precautions are at fault.

11. Most individuals choose to marry and have children. Marital happiness depends on many factors, but timing seems to be especially important: Marriage at a young age often imposes a lifelong burden.

12. Parenting is a central aspect of family life, and appears to go through five stages: (1) the decision to become parents, (2) pregnancy, (3) childbirth and the immediately ensuing period, (4) parenting during the early and middle years of childhood, and (5) the parenting of adolescents. Thereafter, some parents must adjust to the "empty nest" of the postparental years.

Glossary

abstract mappings A mental relation between concepts; an ability achieved in the second level of Fischer's abstract tier.

abstract tier The final stage of development in Fischer's theory, corresponding to Piaget's period of formal operational thought.

abstraction principle In Gelman's theory, the realization that objects need not be similar or related in order to be counted.

accommodation Piaget's term for the act of improving one's cognitive model of the world by adjusting it to external reality.

active gene-environment relation A component of Scarr and McCartney's (1983) model of heredity and environment in which people seek environments that fit their genotype.

adaptation A function in Piaget's theory that denotes the adjustments occuring between stimuli that are perceived and the mental structures used to interpret these stimuli.

adoption study An approach to reveal genetic factors in which relations are examined among adopted children, their biological parents, and their adoptive parents.

afterbirth The placental membranes, which are discharged after the fetus has emerged from the uterus.

agoraphobia Fear of open spaces.

allele A member of a gene pair.

altruism Behavior that benefits others and is motivated by a concern for others.

amniocentesis A method of prenatal diagnosis in which a needle is injected into the amnionic sac to obtain a sample of amnionic fluid containing fetal cells, which are then examined for evidence of abnormalities.

amnion A thin membrane that forms a sac around the embryo.

androgyny A sex-role orientation in an individual who may display instrumental or expressive behaviors, depending upon the situation.

animism Attributing lifelike properties to inanimate objects.

anorexia nervosa A disorder in which individuals refuse to eat for fear of gaining weight; adolescent females are primarily affected.

amenorrhea The absence or suppression of the menstrual cycle, a frequent byproduct of anorexia nervosa.

anoxia A lack of oxygen at birth, caused when the umbilical cord fails to provide oxygen before the newborn begins to use his or her lungs.

arborization The growth of dendrites that resembles the branching of a tree.

artificial insemination A medical procedure used to fertilize an ovum by inserting sperm cells into the uterus.

assimilation Piaget's term for the interpretation of reality in terms of one's internal model of the world that has been constructed from previous knowledge.

attachment The affectionate, reciprocal relationship that is formed between one individual and another, especially between a child and his or her primary caregivers.

attention The selection of information to be processed.

485

attention deficit disorder A disorder, commonly known as hyperactivity, in which children are overactive, inattentive, and impulsive.

authoritarian A style of parenting in which parents exert considerable control over their children but are relatively uninvolved with them.

authoritative A style of parenting in which parents are fairly controlling of their children but also respond to their needs.

automatization A state achieved after much practice in which a task can be performed without processing resources.

autonomic nervous system A division of the peripheral nervous system consisting of neurons that are linked to smooth muscles, such as those in the stomach and intestines.

autosomes All the chromosomes in human cells except the sex chromosomes.

avoidant attachment A type of insecure attachment in which, after separation from the mother, infants avoid her.

axon The part of the neuron that transmits information.

babbling Infant speech, common from 4 to 12 months of age, that consists of alternating vowel and consonant sounds.

basal metabolic rate The rate at which energy is consumed to support basic bodily functions.

binocular cues Cues to depth perception that involve the comparison of the visual images in both eyes.

birth center A medical clinic in which doctors, nurses, and other staff members encourage natural childbirth.

birthing room A room where a pregnant woman will stay for labor and delivery in which there is a homelike atmosphere in order to help the woman feel more relaxed.

breech position An abnormal birth position, in which the infant's buttocks emerge first instead of the head.

bulimia An eating disorder characterized by binge eating, concern about not being able to stop eating voluntarily, self-induced vomiting and purging, and depression.

Caesarean section The surgical removal of the fetus through the uterine and abdominal walls.

canalization A genetic predisposition for the development of certain characteristics thought to be adaptive for a species.

cardinality principle In Gelman's theory, the understanding that the final number name denotes the number of objects counted in a series of objects.

case study The systematic description of the behavior of a single individual.

cell body The part of the neuron (nerve cell) containing life-supporting structures.

cerebral hemispheres The largest and most recently evolved part of the brain, responsible for those functions

(such as personality) that distinguish humans from other animals.

childhood schizophrenia A version of schizophrenia that is rare prior to 6 years of age, but is more common in later childhood and adolescence.

chorion The outer embryonic membrane that is associated with the formation of the placenta.

chorionic villus sampling (CVS) A method of prenatal diagnosis in which a tube is inserted into the uterus to obtain a sample of embryonic tissue.

chromosome A threadlike structure in the cell nucleus that contains the genetic code in the form of DNA (deoxyribonucleic acid) molecules.

chronological age Age since birth.

chumship The last of Sullivan's phases of friendship, during which children form intimate and reciprocal relationships with peers.

classical conditioning A form of learning in which, through paired presentation with an unconditioned stimulus, a neutral stimulus elicits the response associated with that unconditioned stimulus.

claustrophobia Fear of enclosed places.

cognitive-developmental theory A theory, proposed by Jean Piaget, in which development consists of four stages, each with a characteristic type of thinking.

cognitive map A mental configuration of an environment that includes landmarks and routes.

cohort A group of people of the same age.

concrete operational period The third of Piaget's four stages of intellectual development, corresponding approximately to the years 7 to 11.

conditioned response (CR) A response to a conditioned stimulus that is acquired through the pairing of that stimulus with an unconditioned stimulus.

conditioned stimulus (CS) A stimulus that, when paired with an unconditioned stimulus, comes to elicit a conditioned response.

cones Receptors in the retina of the eye that are sensitive to color.

consanguinity study A way to determine the genetic bases of a trait by examining people who differ in how closely they are related to one another.

consolidation The fifth and last of Super's phases of vocational development, typically beginning in the mid-thirties, when individuals try to advance themselves in their line of work and achieve greater status.

constricting An interactive style common among boys in which one person tries to dominate the other with, for example, threats or exaggeration.

contents Piaget's term for the outward, observable manifestations of the intellect.

contingency An expectation that, given presentation of

a conditioned stimulus, the unconditioned stimulus will follow.

continuum of caretaking casualty The relation between the quality of the caregiving environment and the quality of the child's development.

continuum of reproductive casualty The relation between degree of pregnancy and birth complications and degree of adverse developmental outcomes.

controversial children Youngsters who are liked by many classmates and also disliked by many classmates.

conventional level The second of Kohlberg's levels, in which moral judgments are characterized by conformity to the existing social order and the desire to maintain that order.

convergent thinking A type of thinking in which people start with established information and arrive at an answer that is known to be correct.

cooing Vowel-like sounds made by infants, typically starting at about 3 months of age.

cooperative play A form of play common during the preschool years in which play revolves around a common theme and in which children have specified roles.

corpus callosum A bundle of nerve fibers that links the left and right cerebral hemispheres.

correlation coefficient A measure of the degree and direction of the relation between two variables.

cortisol A hormone secreted during times of stress.

counterconditioning Conditioning in which an aversive response to a stimulus is eliminated by pairing the aversive stimulus with pleasant stimuli.

counterimitation A form of observational learning in which the consequences to a model's actions indicate a behavior that should not be done.

critical period A very short span of time in the life of an organism during which it may be especially sensitive to specific influence.

cross-sectional study A study of groups of different individuals of various ages at a specific point in time to determine developmental changes.

cross-sequential design A combination of cross-sectional and longitudinal studies in which several different age groups are followed longitudinally.

crystallization The first of Super's phases of vocational development, typically occurring from about 14 to 18 years of age, in which youth begin to identify career possibilities and experiment with different career choices.

culture The full set of specific attitudes, behaviors, and products that characterize an identifiable group of people.

deferred imitation The repetition of actions some time after the original actions have been performed by some other person.

delay of gratification A type of self-control in which a person favors a more valuable future outcome over a less valuable but immediate outcome.

delusions Beliefs that have no basis in reality.

dendrite A treelike structure that extends from the cell body of a neuron (nerve cell) and that receives information.

dependent variable A measurable aspect of the subject's behavior that may change as the independent variable is altered.

developmental psychology The branch of psychology that studies how people change throughout the life span.

developmental quotient A measure of an infant's performance on an intelligence test.

dichotic listening A task used to assess brain organization in which different information is presented to the left and right ears.

differentiation The progressive refinement of motor development, usually in reference to infants or young children.

diffusion of responsibility A feeling that one is less responsible for a person in distress because a large number of other, potentially responsible people are present at the time of the distress.

dispositional praise Praise that attributes a behavior to some underlying trait of a person.

divergent thinking A type of thinking in which, instead of seeking a predetermined correct answer, people consider many alternatives or explore new possibilities.

DNA (deoxyribonucleic acid) Strands of phosphate and sugar in chromosomes that carry genetic information from generation to generation.

dominance hierarchy An ordering within a group from the most socially powerful individual to the least.

dominant gene A gene that will display itself in an offspring when it is paired with a dissimilar gene form for a particular characteristic.

Down syndrome A chromosomal aberration in which there is an extra twenty-first chromosome, resulting in moderate to severe mental retardation.

echolalia Abnormal repetition of the speech of others, commonly found in infantile autism.

ecological theory An approach that focuses on the need to study development in the contexts or settings in which it naturally occurs.

ego The practical, rational component of personality in Freud's theory.

egocentric frame of reference A framework, typical until about one year of age, in which objects are located in space by their position relative to the infant's body.

egocentrism A characteristic of preoperational thought in which children believe that others see the world, literally and figuratively, as they do.

elaboration A memory strategy in which information to

be remembered is linked by a mental image or a vivid sentence.

Electra conflict In Freud's theory, the turmoil caused by a young girl's feelings of love and sexual attraction toward her father, coupled with feelings of jealousy toward her mother.

electroencephalogram A record of the electrical activity of the brain, obtained from electrodes placed on the scalp.

embryo In prenatal development, the name assigned to the developing organism from about the second to the eighth week after conception.

empathy Experiencing the feelings or emotions of another person.

enabling An interactive style common among girls in which one's actions and remarks support the other person and help to continue the interaction.

encopresis Inappropriate defecation.

enculturation The processes by which children acquire the rules and habits of their culture.

enuresis The failure to control urination appropriately, which is more common during sleep than during wakefulness.

enzymes Protein substances that play a critical role in the body's biochemistry.

epidemiological study A survey of a sample of people in order to determine the prevalence of a disorder.

epistemology Branch of philosophy that deals with the origin and nature of knowledge.

equivalence A logical statement in which the conclusion can follow only when the stated premise is true.

erythroblastosis A disorder in which the offspring's red blood cells are destroyed by antibodies produced in the mother's system in reaction to the foreign protein (Rh factor) that is threatening her system.

eugenics The attempt to improve the genetic characteristics of a species.

evocative gene-environment relation A component of Scarr and McCartney's (1983) model of heredity and environment in which each genotype evokes a unique response from the environment.

expressive Psychological characteristics that describe a person who is focused on emotions and interpersonal relationships.

extended family A household that includes not only parents and their children but also other relatives, such as grandparents, aunts, uncles, and cousins.

extinction The gradual diminution of a conditioned response, resulting in the eventual elimination of the response.

factor analysis A statistical technique used to identify clusters of abilities or skills.

fast mapping The processes whereby young children rapidly associate new words with the correct referents.

fat cell theory A theory that links obesity to the number and size of fat cells.

fetal alcohol syndrome The pattern of congenital malformation of the fetus due to daily consumption of three or more alcoholic drinks by the mother during pregnancy.

fetus In prenatal development, the name assigned to the developing organism from about the eighth week after conception until birth.

field experiment An experiment that includes independent and dependent variables and that is conducted in the setting where the behavior occurs naturally.

filter Removing irrelevant information so that only relevant information is processed.

fissures Grooves in the hemispheres of the brain that are used to identify specific regions in the brain.

formal operational period The fourth of Piaget's four stages of intellectual development, beginning at approximately 11 years of age and extending through adulthood.

fricatives Consonants that involve hissing sounds, because air from the lungs is forced through narrow openings made by the lips, teeth, or tongue.

frontal lobe The part of the brain that controls personality and goal-directed behavior.

functions Piaget's term for the two basic processes—organization and adaptation—that direct cognitive development throughout the life span.

gender consistency The understanding that gender is constant across situations and does not change according to personal wishes.

gender constancy The mastery of gender stability and gender consistency.

gender identity Children's awareness that they are female or male.

gender roles Behavior that a culture expects of females and males.

gender schemes Networks of associations concerning sex stereotypes.

gender stability The understanding that gender remains constant throughout development.

gene The functional unit of a chromosome that acts as a blueprint for development.

genotype The entire genetic endowment of an individual.

grammar The rules that specify how the words in a language can be arranged to form phrases and sentences.

grammatical morphemes Words such as prepositions and articles that are not essential to the meaning of a sentence but make it grammatically correct.

habituation Diminished responding that occurs after repeated presentation of the same stimulus.

hallucinations Perceptual experiences in the absence of stimuli.

hermaphroditism A term used to describe an infant whose sexual anatomy is improperly differentiated, so that the infant's sex is ambiguous or actually differs from that associated with the sex chromosomes.

heterozygous A term used to describe gene pairs whose alleles are different.

heuristics Rules of thumb that can help to solve problems.

hierarchic integration The combination of individual actions into more complex and sophisticated patterns of behavior.

hierarchical theory of intelligence A theory of intelligence in which general ability can be differentiated into more specific skills.

homozygous A term used to describe gene pairs whose alleles are the same.

hypothesis A prediction derived from a theory.

hypothetical-deductive reasoning Reasoning that starts with a fact or premise and leads to conclusions.

id An aspect of personality described by Freud that is a reservoir of primitive instincts and that presses for immediate gratification of bodily needs and wants.

identity A coherent sense of self; self-concept.

implementation The third of Super's phases of vocational development, typically occurring in the early twenties, when adults complete career training and start a career.

implication A logical statement in which if the premise is true, then a specific conclusion follows.

independent variable A condition in an experimental situation created by the experimenter, or a manipulation of the subject by the experimenter.

indifferent-uninvolved A parenting style in which parents are emotionally uninvolved with their children and invest relatively little time or attention in them.

inductive reasoning Reasoning that involves determining facts from different experiences.

indulgent-permissive A parenting style in which warm, caring parents place few demands on their children.

infantile autism A serious disorder in which, from very early in life, children seem unable to relate to others.

inflection A suffix that changes the sense of a word (for example, makes it plural) without changing its basic meaning.

information processing An approach to cognitive development that emphasizes the similarities between human thinking and the processes of a modern computer.

in-group—out-group scheme A scheme used to distinguish female behaviors, activities, and objects from male behaviors, activities, and objects.

insecure attachment A relation between infant and mother in which, after separation from the mother, the infant does not respond positively to the mother.

instrumental Psychological characteristics that describe a person who acts on and influences the world.

intellectual realism A common error during the preoperational period in which children, when told the nature of a disguised object, claim that the object has its normal appearance.

intelligence quotient (IQ) Traditionally, the ratio of an individual's mental age to his or her chronological age, multiplied by 100.

intonation A pattern of rising or falling pitch in speech that often indicates whether the utterance is a statement, question, or command.

in vitro fertilization A medical technique in which ova and sperm are mixed in a petri dish to create a zygote, which is then inserted into the woman's uterus.

kinetic cues Cues to depth perception that are derived from the movement of objects.

Kleinfelter's syndrome A chromosomal aberration found exclusively in males that is associated with atypical sexual development and below normal intelligence.

labor The process by which the fetus is expelled from its mother's uterus, occurring within a few hours to a few weeks after lightening.

lamaze program A program in which women are taught techniques that help them to relax throughout labor and delivery so that use of drugs can be minimized.

landmarks Salient, distinctive objects in an environment.

latchkey A word used to refer to children who care for themselves after school.

learned helplessness A sense of lack of control over one's environment that is learned from experiences in which one's behavior was ineffective; characteristic of depressed persons.

lexical development The child's acquisition of the meaning of words.

lightening The beginning of the biological preparation for birth in which the head of the fetus turns down, relieving the pressure against the mother's diaphragm.

linear perspective A cue to depth perception in which distant objects take up less space in the visual field.

lobes Areas of the brain typically set apart by fissures.

longitudinal study The process of observing or testing individuals at different points in their lives, noting stability and change in their behavior and characteristics over time.

malnutrition The lack of sufficient nourishment to support growth properly.

maturation The changes that take place more or less inevitably in all normal members of a species as long as they are provided with an environment suitable to the species.

maturational theory The view that most psychological changes reflect maturation.

means-end analysis An heuristic in which the action

that is taken is one that reduces the difference between the current situation and the goal.

meiosis The specialized cell division of the reproductive cells that occurs during cell maturation, resulting in the ova and sperm having half of the number of chromosomes as the other cells of the body.

menarche The beginning of menstruation, typically occurring at approximately 13 years of age.

mental age (MA) On intelligence tests, a measure of a person's performance corresponding to the chronological age of those whose performance the person equals.

mental operation Mental actions that are the psychological analogs of arithmetic operations and that emerge during the concrete operational period.

mental representation The child's internal, symbolic depiction of the world.

mental retardation Intellectual functioning that is significantly below average, existing concurrently with deficits in adaptive behavior.

microcephaly An excessively small head, caused by many disorders such as CMV.

mitosis Typical cell division in which chromosomes in each cell duplicate before the cell divides into two identical daughter cells.

mnemonics Strategies that are used to aid memory.

moral rule A rule that people are obligated to follow regardless of their attitude toward it; examples would include the rule against robbery.

motherese Speech from adults to infants that is slower and higher pitched than normal speech.

motor cortex A part of the brain that plays a key role in regulating muscle movements.

mutual exclusion A rule used by young children which says that a new word cannot denote an object whose name is already known, but, instead, that it must denote a novel object.

myelin A fatty sheath that surrounds axons in the brain and spinal cord, resulting in faster transmission of information.

negative punishment Any stimulus that, when removed, decreases the likelihood of a response.

negative reinforcement Any consequence that, when ended, makes the preceding response more likely.

neglected children Youngsters who are neither liked nor disliked by their classmates.

neural plate A group of embryonic cells that folds to form the neural tube.

neuron A cell in the body that can transmit information and that is the basic unit of the nervous system.

neurotransmitters Chemicals that are released by one neuron into a synapse, carrying the neural signal to an adjacent neuron.

Oedipal conflict In Freud's theory, the turmoil caused by a young boy's desire for his mother, which in turn causes him to fear castration by his father.

olfaction The sense of smell.

one-to-one principle In Gelman's theory, the idea that each object to be counted must have just one number name.

operant Any behavior of an organism.

optokinetic nystagmus A reflexive sideways movement of the eye in response to movement.

order irrelevance A principle in Gelman's theory that states that objects can be counted in any order.

organization A function in Piaget's theory denoting the fact that, at any age, schemes are always linked to form a cohesive mental structure.

ovum The egg cell produced in the ovaries that combines with sperm to produce the zygote.

own-sex schema A scheme with detailed information about behaviors, activities, and objects appropriate to one's own gender.

parallel play A form of interaction common in infancy in which two or more youngsters play independently but near each other, while maintaining eye contact with each other.

parasympathetic The component of the autonomic nervous system that controls ordinary body functions.

passive correlation A study in which investigators examine associations that exist naturally between variables.

passive gene-environment relation A component of Scarr and McCartney's (1983) model of heredity and environment in which parents pass on genes to their offspring and provide an environment that reflects their own genotype.

penis envy In Freud's theory, the feelings of envy that a young girl has toward her father because she does not have a penis as he does.

perception The selection, organization, and modification by the brain of specific input from the different sense organs.

peripheral nervous system The part of the nervous system that runs toward and away from the brain and spinal cord.

permissive culture One in which sexual behavior is viewed as a routine part of normal behavioral development.

personality type theory A view, proposed by John Holland, that work is most often satisfying when the distinguishing characteristics of a job match the worker's personality.

phenomenism An error, common among preoperational children, that involves claiming that an object is what it appears to be.

phenotype The outward manifestation of one's genetic makeup.

phonemes Distinctive speech sounds that can be grouped together to form words.

phonology The study of people's perception and production of speech sounds.

pictorial cues Cues to depth perception provided by stimuli.

placenta A structure that develops in the uterus following conception and through which nutrients and wastes are exchanged between mother and fetus.

polygene inheritance Inheritance of a characteristic that is influenced by many genes.

popular children Youngsters who are liked by most of their classmates.

positive punishment A stimulus, such as electric shock, that when presented reduces the likelihood of the preceding response.

positive reinforcement Any consequence that, when presented, makes the preceding response more likely.

positron emission tomography (PET-scan) A medical technique used to evaluate brain activity in which the presence of a radioactive form of glucose in different areas of the brain is recorded.

postconventional level The third and most advanced of Kohlberg's levels, in which moral judgments are guided by universal moral principles.

preconventional level The first of Kohlberg's levels, in which moral judgments are made depending upon the physical consequences that would result, a deference to superior power, and the satisfaction of one's own needs.

preoperational period The second of Piaget's four stages of intellectual development, corresponding approximately with the years 2 to 7.

preparedness The idea that members of a species are genetically influenced to learn certain responses more readily than other responses.

primary circular reaction A chance event involving direct sensory stimulation that infants find pleasing, which in turn leads them to try to repeat the event.

processing resources Mental energy that is needed to perform cognitive tasks and that is limited in supply.

procreative imperatives Behaviors associated with impregnation, menstruation, and gestation, and in which males and females invariably have well-defined and specific roles.

prosocial behavior A behavior that benefits other people, regardless of the motivation for the behavior.

psychoanalytic theory A theory proposed by Freud in which development is explained in terms of the interplay between components of personality.

psychoses Severe disorders in which gross distortions in the rate, timing, and sequence of many basic psychological processes are present.

puberty The point in development, usually in early adolescence, when body characteristics typifying adulthood (for example, pubic hair) emerge.

punisher Any consequence of a behavior that weakens the behavior.

random assignment When subjects have an equal chance of being assigned to any of the conditions in an experiment.

reaction range The broadest possible expression of a genotype.

recessive gene A gene that will display itself only when paired with the same type of allele.

reciprocal influence The view that socialization involves the interplay of parental influences on children as well as the children's influences on parents.

reflex An unlearned and automatic response that is triggered by a specific stimulus.

regulator genes Genes that control the structural genes, turning them "on" or "off" as necessary to meet the body's needs.

rehearsal A memory strategy in which stimuli are named repeatedly.

reinforcer Any consequence to a behavior that strengthens the behavior.

rejected children Youngsters who are disliked by most of their classmates.

reliability The consistency with which a person will receive the same score on successive administrations of a test.

remarried families Families in which at least one of the adults has been married previously and has children from that marriage.

representational tier The second stage of development according to Fischer, including both the preoperational and concrete operational periods of Piaget's theory.

representative sample A group of individuals that accurately and proportionately displays the characteristics of some larger population of interest.

resistant group A type of insecure attachment in which, after separation from the mother, the infant desires interactions with the mother but also appears angry at the mother.

response cost A form of negative punishment in which a possession is taken from the child.

restrictive culture A culture in which adolescent sexual behavior is prohibited; this prohibition is enforced by a rigid segregation of the sexes throughout adolescence.

Rh factor A protein found in the blood that can cause erythroblastosis in the infant when the father and the infant have the factor but the mother does not.

rough-and-tumble play A form of play common among school-age children that involves chasing, wrestling, or mock fighting, but not true aggression.

routes Sequences of actions that link landmarks.

scheme For Piaget, the mental structure underlying a sequence of behaviors.

schizophrenia A serious disorder in which the primary symptoms are hallucinations, delusions, and disordered thought.

school phobia Fear of going to school, which is often linked to fear of separation from the parents.

scientific method An approach to understanding nature that emphasizes careful observation, the construction of hypotheses, and the evaluation of the hypotheses according to empirical evidence.

scripts A part of knowledge describing events that occur in a particular order.

search Scanning an environment to find a specific stimulus.

secondary circular reaction A chance event involving indirect sensory input that is pleasing to an infant, who then tries to repeat the event.

secure attachment A relation between infant and mother in which, after separation from the mother, the infant maintains proximity to the mother and seeks interactions with her.

semirestrictive culture A culture in which adolescent sexual behavior is forbidden formally, but in which adolescents and adults alike ignore this prohibition with little fear of reproof.

sensation Stimulation of the sensory receptors by physical energy from the internal and external environment.

sensorimotor period The first of Piaget's four stages of intellectual development, corresponding to infancy.

sensorimotor tier The first stage of cognitive development in Fischer's theory, corresponding to the sensorimotor stage in Piagetian theory.

sensory cortex A part of the brain that receives input from the senses, for example from the sense of touch, which can sense both heat and cold.

separation of variables A formal operational scheme used to identify causal relations between events.

set point theory A theory that states that each person has a specific body weight that is preset and maintained.

sex chromosomes The two chromosomes, X and Y, that determine an individual's sex.

shaping The application of conditioning processes to achieve social goals.

short-term storage space In Case's theory, a temporary, working memory of limited capacity.

simultaneous processing A type of mental activity assessed on the K-ABC intelligence test in which different information must be integrated simultaneously.

skeletal age A measure of physical growth based on the maturity of the bones.

social cognitive view An approach to socialization that emphasizes the roles of children's interpretation of events and children's social goals.

social convention A standard of behavior agreed upon by a cultural group, but one that is not obligatory, as a moral rule would be.

social learning theory A view of development that emphasizes the role of observation, reward, and punishment.

social referencing Searching another's face or behavior for information about ambiguous environmental events.

socioeconomic status (SES) A measure of social class, reflecting occupation, income, and education.

somatic nervous system A division of the peripheral nervous system consisting of neurons that are linked to skeletal muscles.

somatosensory cortex An area of tissue at the junction of the frontal and parietal lobes that is central to sensory and motor functioning.

specification The second of Super's phases of vocational development, typically occurring from about 18 to 21 years of age, during which youths further narrow their career possibilities and begin training for specific careers.

speech center A large area in the brain responsible for understanding and producing language.

sperm The male reproductive cell.

stabilization The fourth of Super's phases of vocational development, typically occurring in the mid- or late twenties, when adults become established in a career.

stable-order principle In Gelman's theory, the requirement that number names be used in the same order.

standardized test A test in which the apparatus, procedure, and scoring have been fixed so that exactly the same test is given at different times and places.

stop consonants Consonant sounds produced by briefly stopping the flow of air from the lungs.

structural genes Genes that are involved in the production of protein.

structures Organized schemes that provide the distinguishing characteristics of thought for each of Piaget's four periods of cognitive development.

successive processing A type of mental activity assessed on the K-ABC intelligence test in which information is integrated sequentially.

superego The moral component of personality, according to Freud.

sympathetic component The component of the autonomic nervous system that functions during stressful situations.

synapses The gap between adjacent neurons; information is transmitted across it by neurotransmitters.

syntax The aspect of language that concerns how words are combined into phrases and sentences.

systems of abstract systems Coordination between sets of abstract concepts, usually not achieved until the final level of cognitive development, according to Fischer.

temperament Personality-like characteristics of infants, such as emotionality and activity level.

teratology The study of malformations and other deviations from normal prenatal development.

tertiary circular reaction The most advanced form of a circular reaction in which infants systematically vary their actions in an apparent effort to understand more about the properties of objects.

texture gradient A cue to depth perception conveyed by the fact that texture is perceived as more dense in distant objects.

theories A framework used to organize known facts and to derive testable hypotheses.

tier A stage of cognitive development in Fischer's theory that encompasses several cognitive levels.

time-out A form of negative punishment in which children are isolated so that they cannot receive positive reinforcement.

trial-and-error One heuristic in which approaches are tried in a haphazard order until the solution is found.

triarchic theory A theory of intelligence proposed by Robert Sternberg that includes contextual, experiential, and componential subtheories.

Turner's syndrome A chromosome aberration found in females who lack a second X chromosome, it is associated with mild mental retardation, a failure to develop secondary sex characteristics, and short stature.

twin study A way to reveal genetic factors by comparing identical twins with fraternal twins.

ultrasound A method of prenatal diagnosis in which sound waves are passed through a pregnant woman's abdomen and the reflected waves are used to generate a video image of the fetus.

umbilical cord The ''lifeline'' between the placenta and the fetus composed of arteries and veins that serves as a transport system in the womb between the developing child and his or her mother.

unconditioned response (UR) A reflexive response to a stimulus.

unconditioned stimulus (US) A stimulus that reflexively elicits an unconditioned response.

validity The degree to which a test actually measures what it purports to measure.

verbal ability A specific component in hierarchical theories of intelligence that refers to a person's vocabulary and general skill in understanding and using words.

visual acuity The ability of individuals to detect both small stimuli and small details of large visual patterns.

way-finding Movement in large environments in which the destination cannot be seen at the start.

zygote The cell mass that is the result of the union of an ovum and a sperm.

References

Abramovitch, R., Corter, C., Pepler, D. J., & Stanhope, L. (1986). Sibling and peer interaction: A final follow-up and a comparison. *Child Development, 57*, 217–229.

Abravenal, E. (1991). Does immediate imitation influence long-term memory for observed actions? *Journal of Experimental Child Psychology, 51*, 235–244.

Abravanel, E., & Sigafoos, A. D. (1984). Exploring the presence of imitation during early infancy. *Child Development, 55*, 381–392.

Acredolo, L. P. (1978). Development of spatial orientation in infancy. *Developmental Psychology, 14*, 224–234.

Acredolo, L. P. (1979). Laboratory versus home: The effect of environment on the 9-month-old infant's choice of spatial reference system. *Developmental Psychology, 15*, 666–667.

Acredolo, L., & Goodwyn, S. (1988). Symbolic gesturing in normal infants. *Child Development, 59*, 450–466.

Adams, G. R., & Fitch, S. A. (1982). Ego state and identity status development: A cross-sequential analysis. *Journal of Personality and Social Psychology, 43*, 574–583.

Adams, J. A. (1984). Learning of movement sequences. *Psychological Bulletin, 96*, 3–28.

Adams, K., & Markham, R. (1991). Recognition of affective facial expressions by children and adolescents with and without mental retardation. *American Journal on Mental Retardation, 96*, 21–28.

Adams, R. J. (1982). Obstetrical medication and the human newborn: The influence of alphaprodine on visual behavior. *Developmental Medicine and Child Neurology, 31*, 650–656.

Adams, R. J. (1989). Newborns' discrimination among mid- and long-wavelength stimuli. *Journal of Experimental Child Psychology, 47*, 130–141.

Ainsworth, M. D. S. (1967). *Infancy in Uganda*. Baltimore, Md.: Johns Hopkins University Press.

Ainsworth, M. D. S. (1977). Infant development and mother-infant interaction among Ganda and American families. In P. H. Leiderman, S. R. Tulkin, and A. Rosenfeld (Eds.), *Culture and infancy: Variations in the human experience.* New York: Academic Press.

Ainsworth, M. D. S. (1982). Attachment: Retrospect and prospect. In C. M. Parkes and J. Stevenson-Hinde (Eds.), *The place of attachment in human behavior.* New York: Basic Books.

Ainsworth, M. D. S., & Bell, S. M. (1974). Mother-infant interaction and the development of competence. In K. Connolly and J. Bruner (Eds.), *The growth of competence.* London: Academic Press.

Ainsworth, M. D. S., & Wittig, B. A. (1969). Attach-

494

ment and exploratory behavior of one-year-olds in a strange situation. In B. M. Foss (Ed.), *Determinants of infant behavior*. London: Methuen.

Alberman, E. (1982). The epidemiology of congenital defects: A pragmatic approach. In M. Adinolfi, P. Benson, F. Giannelli, and M. Seller (Eds.), *Clinics in developmental medicine, No. 83. Pediatric research: A genetic approach*. Philadelphia: J. B. Lippincott.

Albert, R. S. (1975). Toward a behavioral definition of genius. *American Psychologist, 30*, 140–151.

Aldous, J. (1978). *Family careers: Developmental change in families*. New York: Wiley.

Alford, B. B., & Bogle, M. L. (1982). *Nutrition during the life cycle*. Englewood Cliffs, N.J.: Prentice Hall.

Allen, G. L., Kirasic, K. C., Siegel, A. W., & Herman, J. F. (1979). Developmental issues in cognitive mapping: The selection and utilization of environmental landmarks. *Child Development, 50*, 1062–1070.

Allen, M. C., & Alexander, G. R. (1990). Gross motor milestones in preterm infants: Correction for degree of maturity. *Journal of Pediatrics, 116*, 955–959.

Alley, T. R. (1983). Growth-produced changes in body shape and size as determinants of perceived age and adult caregiving. *Child Development, 54*, 241–248.

Alpert, J. L., & Richardson, M. S. (1980). Parenting. In L. Poon (Ed.), *Aging in the 1980s*. Washington, D.C.: American Psychological Association.

Amato, P. R., & Keith, B. (1991). Parental divorce and the well-being of children: A meta-analysis. *Psychological Bulletin, 110*, 26–46.

Ames, G. J., & Murray, F. B. (1982). When two wrongs make a right: Promoting cognitive change by social conflict. *Developmental Psychology, 18*, 894–897.

Ames, L. B. (1967). Predictive value of infant behavior examination. In J. Hellmuth (Ed.), *Exceptional infant*. New York: Brunner/Mazel.

Anastasi, A. (1958). Heredity, environment, and the question of "How?" *Psychological Review, 65*, 197–208.

Anastasi, A. (1968). *Psychological testing*. New York: Macmillan.

Anastasi, A. (1982). *Psychological testing* (5th ed.). New York: Macmillan.

Anastopoulos, A. D., DuPaul, G. J., & Barkley, R. A. (1991). Stimulant medication and parent training therapies for attention deficit-hyperactivity disorder. *Journal of Learning Disabilities, 24*, 210–218.

Anders, T. F., Carskadon, M. A., & Dement, W. C. (1980). Sleep and sleepiness in children and adolescents. In I. Litt (Ed.), *Pediatric clinics of North America*, Vol. 27, No. 1. Philadelphia, Pa.: W. B. Saunders.

Anderson, K. E., Lytton, H., & Romney, D. M. (1986). Mothers' interactions with normal and conduct-disordered boys: Who affects whom? *Developmental Psychology, 22*, 604–609.

Andujo, E. (1988). Ethnic identity of transethnically adopted Hispanic adolescents. *Social Work, 33*, 531–535.

Anooshian, L. J., & Siegel, A. W. (1985). From cognitive to procedural mapping. In C. J. Brainerd and M. Pressley (Eds.), *Basic processes in memory development*. New York: Springer-Verlag.

Anooshian, L. J., & Young, D. (1981). Developmental changes in cognitive maps of a familiar neighborhood. *Child Development, 52*, 341–348.

Anthony, E. J. (1957). An experimental approach to the psychopathology of childhood: Encopresis. *British Journal of Medical Psychology, 30*, 146–175.

Antonarakis, S. E., & the Down Syndrome Collaborative Group. (1991). Parental origin of the extra chromosome in trisomy 21 as indicated by analysis of DNA polymorphisms. *New England Journal of Medicine, 324*, 872–876.

Arlin, P. K. (1975). Cognitive development in adulthood: A fifth stage? *Developmental Psychology, 11*, 602–606.

Aronson, E., & Rosenbloom, S. (1971). Space perception in early infancy: Perception within a common auditory-visual space. *Science, 172*, 1161–1163.

Arterberry, M., Yonas, A., & Bensen, A. S. (1989). Self-produced locomotion and the development of responsiveness to linear perspective and texture gradients. *Developmental Psychology, 25*, 976–982.

Asarnow, J. R., Goldstein, M. J., & Ben-Meir, S. (1988). Paternal communication deviance in childhood onset schizophrenia spectrum and depressive disorders. *Journal of Child Psychology and Psychiatry, 29*, 825–838.

Ashcraft, M. H. (1982). The development of mental arithmetic: A chronometric approach. *Developmental Review, 2*, 212–236.

Ashmead, D. H., & McCarty, M. E. (1991). Postural sway of human infants while standing in light and dark. *Child Development, 62,* 1276–1287.

Aslin, R. N. (1987). Visual and auditory discrimination in infancy. In J. D. Osofsky (Ed.), *Handbook of infant development* (2nd ed.). New York: Wiley.

Aslin, R. N., Pisoni, D. B., & Jusczyk, P. (1983). Auditory development and speech perception in infancy. In M. M. Haith and J. J. Campos (Eds.), *Handbook of child psychology,* Vol. 3. New York: Wiley.

Astbury, J., Orgill, A. A., Bajuk, B., & Yu, V. Y. H. (1990). Neurodevelopmental outcome, growth and health of extremely low-birthweight survivors: How soon can we tell? *Developmental Medicine and Child Neurology, 32,* 582–589.

Attie, I., Brooks-Gunn, J., & Petersen, A. C. (1990). A developmental perspective on eating disorders and eating problems. In M. Lewis and S. M. Miller, (Eds.), *Handbook of Developmental Psychopathology.* New York: Plenum.

Au, T. K., & Glusman, M. (1990). The principle of mutual exclusivity in word learning: To honor or not to honor? *Child Development, 61,* 1474–1490.

Azrin, N. H., Sneed, T. J., & Foxx, R. M. (1974). Dry Bed Training: Rapid elimination of childhood enuresis. *Behaviour Research and Therapy, 12,* 147–156.

Bachman, J. (1983). Premature affluence: Do high school students earn too much? *Economic Outlook USA,* Summer, 64–67.

Baenninger, M. A., & Newcombe, N. (1989). The role of experience in spatial test performance: A meta-analysis. *Sex Roles, 20,* 327–344.

Bahrick, L. E. (1988). Intermodal learning in infancy: Learning on the basis of two kinds of invariant relations in audible and visible events. *Child Development, 59,* 197–209.

Baillargeon, R. (1987). Object permanance in $3\frac{1}{2}$- and $4\frac{1}{2}$-month-old infants. *Developmental Psychology, 23,* 655–664.

Balla, D., & Zigler, E. (1979). Personality development in retarded persons. In N. R. Ellis (Ed.), *Handbook of mental deficiency.* Hillsdale, N.J.: Lawrence Erlbaum.

Bancroft, J., Axworthy, D., & Ratcliffe, S. (1982). The personality and psycho-sexual development of boys with 47XXY chromosome constitution. *Journal of Child Psychology and Psychiatry, 23,* 169–180.

Bandura, A. (1964). The stormy decade: Fact or fiction? *Psychology in the Schools, 1,* 224–231.

Bandura, A. (1977). *Social learning theory.* Englewood Cliffs, N.J.: Prentice Hall.

Bandura, A. (1986). *Social foundations of thought and action: A social-cognitive theory.* Englewood Cliffs, N.J.: Prentice Hall.

Bandura, A., & Mischel, W. (1965). Modification of self-imposed delay of reward through exposure to live and symbolic models. *Journal of Personality and Social Psychology, 2,* 698–705.

Bandura, A., & Schunk. D. H. (1981). Cultivating competence, self-efficacy, and intrinsic interest through proximal self-motivation. *Journal of Personality and Social Psychology, 41,* 586–598.

Bandura, A., & Walters, R. H. (1959). *Adolescent aggression.* New York: Ronald Press.

Bandura, A., & Walters, R. H. (1963). *Social learning and personality development.* New York: Holt, Rinehart & Winston.

Banks, M. S., & Dannemiller, J. L. (1987). Infant visual psychophysics. In P. Salapatek and L. Cohen (Eds.). *Handbook of infant perception,* Vol. 1. Orlando, Fla.: Academic Press.

Barber, B. L., & Eccles, J. S. (1992). Long-term influence of divorce and single parenting on adolescent family- and work-related values, behaviors, and aspirations. *Psychological Bulletin, 111,* 108–126.

Barden, R. C., Ford, M. E., Jensen, A. G., Rogers-Salyer, M., & Salyer, K. E. (1989). Effects of craniofacial deformity in infancy on the quality of mother-infant interactions. *Child Development, 60,* 819–824.

Bardwick, J. M. (1979). *In transition.* New York: Holt, Rinehart & Winston.

Barenboim, C. (1977). Developmental changes in the interpersonal cognitive system from middle childhood to adolescence. *Child Development, 48,* 1467–1474.

Barglow, P., Vaughn, B. E., & Molitor, N. (1987). Effects of maternal absence due to employment on the quality of infant-mother attachment in a low-risk sample. *Child Development, 58,* 945–954.

Barkley, R. A. (1981). Hyperactivity. In E. J. Mash and L. G. Terdal (Eds.), *Behavioral assessment of childhood disorders.* New York: Guilford Press.

Barkley, R. A. (1990). Attention deficit disorders: History, definition, and diagnosis. In M. Lewis and S. M. Miller, (Eds.), *Handbook of developmental psychopathology.* New York: Plenum.

Barr, H. M., Streissguth, A. P., Darby, B. L., & Sampson, P. D. (1990). Prenatal exposure to alcohol, caffeine, tobacco, and aspirin: Effects on fine and gross motor performance in 4-year-old children. *Developmental Psychology, 26,* 339–348.

Barrera, M. E., Rosenbaum, P. L., & Cunningham, C. E. (1987). Corrected and uncorrected Bayley scores: Longitudinal developmental patterns in low and high birth weight preterm infants. *Infant Behavior and Development, 10,* 337–346.

Barron, F., & Harrington, D. M. (1981). Creativity, intelligence, and personality. *Annual Review of Psychology, 32,* 439–476.

Bar-Tal, D., Raviv, A., & Leiser, T. (1980). The development of altruistic behavior: Empirical evidence. *Developmental Psychology, 16,* 516–524.

Barton, M. E., & Tomasello, M. (1991). Joint attention and conversation in mother-infant-sibling triads. *Child Development, 62,* 517–529.

Bates, E., Benigni, L., Bretherton, I., Camaioni, L., & Volterra, L. (1979). Cognition and communication from nine to thirteen months: Correlational findings. In E. Bates (Ed.), *The emergence of symbols: Cognition and communication in infancy.* New York: Academic Press.

Bates, J. E. (1987). Temperament in infancy. In J. D. Osofsky (Ed.), *Handbook of infant development* (2nd ed.). New York: Wiley.

Baum, C. (1989). Conduct disorders. In T. H. Ollendick and M. Hersen (Eds.), *Handbook of child psychopathology,* (2nd ed.). New York: Plenum.

Baumrind, D. (1975). *Early socialization and the discipline controversy.* Morristown, N.J.: General Learning Press.

Baumrind, D. (1991). Parenting styles and adolescent development. In R. M. Lerner, A. C. Petersen, and J. Brooks-Gunn (Eds.), *Encyclopedia of adolescence.* New York: Garland.

Baydar, N., & Brooks-Gunn, J. (1991). Effects of maternal employment and child-care arrangements on preschoolers' cognitive and behavioral outcomes: Evidence from the children of the National Longitudinal Survey of Youth. *Developmental Psychology, 27,* 932–945.

Bayley, N. (1970). Development of mental abilities. In P. H. Mussen (Ed.), *Carmichael's manual of child psychology.* New York: Wiley.

Beal, C. R., & Belgrad, S. L. (1990). The development of message evaluation skills in young children. *Child Development, 61,* 705–712.

Bear, G. G. (1989). Sociomoral reasoning and antisocial behaviors among normal sixth graders. *Merrill-Palmer Quarterly, 35,* 181–196.

Beck, A. T. (1967). *Depression: Clinical, experimental, and theoretical aspects.* New York: Harper & Row.

Becker, B. J. (1986). Influence again: An examination of reviews and studies of gender differences in social influence. In J. S. Hyde and M. C. Linn (Eds.), *The psychology of gender differences. Advances through meta-analysis.* Baltimore, Md.: Johns Hopkins University Press.

Beilin, H. (1965). Learning and operational convergence in logical thought development. *Journal of Experimental Child Psychology, 2,* 317–339.

Bell, R. (1987). *Changing bodies, changing lives: A book for teens on sex and relationships* (Rev. ed.). New York: Vintage Books.

Bellinger, D., Leviton, A., Waternaux, C., Needleman, H., & Rabinowitz, M. (1987). Longitudinal analyses of prenatal and postnatal lead exposure and early cognitive development. *New England Journal of Medicine, 316,* 1037–1043.

Belmont, J. M., & Mitchell, D. W. (1987). The general strategies hypothesis as applied to cognitive theory in mental retardation. *Intelligence, 11,* 91–105.

Belsky, J. (1980). Child maltreatment: An ecological integration. *American Psychologist, 35,* 320–335.

Belsky, J., Fish, M., & Isabella, R. (1991). Continuity and discontinuity in infant negative and positive emotionality: Family antecedents and attachment consequences. *Developmental Psychology, 27,* 421–431.

Belsky, J., & Rovine, M. (1990). Q-sort security and first-year nonmaternal care. In K. McCartney (Ed.), *Child care and maternal employment: A social ecology approach.* San Francisco: Jossey-Bass.

Belsky, J., Steinberg, L., & Draper, P. (1991). Childhood experience, interpersonal development, and reproductive strategy: An evolutionary theory of socialization. *Child Development, 62,* 647–670.

Bem, S. L. (1974). The measurement of psychological androgyny. *Journal of Consulting and Clinical Psychology, 42,* 155–162.

Bem, S. L. (1981). Gender schema theory: a cognitive account of sex typing. *Psychological Review, 88,* 354–364.

Bem, S. L. (1984). Androgyny and gender schema theory: A conceptual and empirical integration. In T. B. Sonderegger (Ed.), *Nebraska Symposium on Motivation, 1984: Psychology and gender.* Lincoln, Neb.: University of Nebraska Press.

Bem, S. L. & Lenney, E. (1976). Sex typing and the avoidance of cross-sex behavior. *Journal of Personality and Social Psychology, 33,* 48–54.

Bender, L. (1972). Childhood schizophrenia. In S. I. Harrison and J. F. McDermott (Eds.), *Childhood psychopathology.* New York: International Universities Press.

Berko, J. (1958). The child's learning of English morphology. *Word, 14,* 150–177.

Berko Gleason, J. (1989). *The development of language.* Columbus, Ohio: Merrill.

Berkowitz, L. (1989). Frustration-aggression hypothesis: Examination and reformulation. *Psychological Bulletin, 106,* 59–73.

Berndt, T. J. (1981). Relations between social cognition, nonsocial cognition, and social behavior: The case of friendship. In J. H. Flavell and L. D. Ross (Eds.), *Social cognitive development: Frontiers and possible futures.* Cambridge: Cambridge University Press.

Berndt, T. J. (1982). The features and effects of friendship in early adolescence. *Child Development, 53,* 1447–1460.

Berndt, T. J. (1988). The nature and significance of children's friendships. In R. Vasta (Ed.), *Annals of child development,* Vol. 5. Greenwich, Conn.: JAI Press.

Berndt, T. J., Hawkins, J. A., & Hoyle, S. G. (1986). Changes in friendship during a school year: Effects on children's and adolescents' impressions of friendship and sharing with friends. *Child Development, 57,* 1284–1297.

Berndt, T. J., & Hoyle, S. G. (1985). Stability and change in childhood and adolescent friendships. *Developmental Psychology, 21,* 1007–1015.

Berndt, T. J., & Keefe, K. (1991). How friends influence adolescents' adjustment to school. Presented at the biennial meeting of the Society for Research in Child Development, Seattle, Wash.

Berndt, T. J., & Perry, T. B. (1986). Children's perceptions of friendships as supportive relationships. *Developmental Psychology, 22,* 640–648.

Berndt, T. J., & Perry, T. B. (1990). Distinctive features and effects of early adolescent friendships. In R. Montemayor, G. R. Adams, and T. P. Gulotta (Eds.), *From childhood to adolescence: A transitional period.* Newbury Park, Calif.: Sage.

Best, D. L., Williams, J. E., Cloud, J. M., Davis, S. W., Robertson, L. S., Edwards, J. R., Giles, H., & Fowles, J. (1977). Development of sex-trait stereotypes among young children in the United States, England, and Ireland. *Child Development, 48,* 1375–1384.

Bettelheim, B. (1967a). *The empty fortress.* New York: The Free Press.

Bettelheim, B. (1967b, February 12). Where self begins. *New York Times.*

Bialystok, E. (1988). Levels of bilingualism and levels of linguistic awareness. *Developmental Psychology, 24,* 560–567.

Bigler, R. S., & Liben L. S. (1990). The role of attitudes and interventions in gender-schematic processing. *Child Development, 61,* 1440–1452.

Bingham, C. R., Miller, B. C., & Adams, G. R. (1990). Correlates of age at first sexual intercourse in a national sample of young women. *Journal of Adolescent Research, 5,* 18–33.

Birch, L. L. (1991). Obesity and eating disorders: A developmental perspective. *Bulletin of the Psychonomic Society, 29,* 265–272.

Bjorklund, D. F., & Harnishfeger, K. K. (1990). The resources construct in cognitive development: Diverse sources of evidence and a theory of inefficient inhibition. *Developmental Review, 10,* 48–71.

Black, B. (1989). Interactive pretense: Social and symbolic skills in preschool play groups. *Merrill Palmer Quarterly, 35,* 379–397.

Blass, E. M., Fillion, T. J., Rochat, P., Hoffmeyer, L. B., & Metzger, M. A. (1989). Sensorimotor and motivational determinants of hand-mouth coordination in 1–3-day-old human infants. *Developmental Psychology, 25,* 963–975.

Blass, E. M., Ganchrow, J. R., & Steiner, J. E. (1984). Classical conditioning in newborn humans 2–48 hours of age. *Infant Behavior and Development, 7,* 223–235.

Block, E. M., & Kessell, F. S. (1980). Determinants of the acquisition order of grammatical morphemes: A re-analysis and re-interpretation. *Journal of Child Language, 7,* 181–188.

Block, J. (1971). *Lives through time.* Berkeley, Calif.: Bancroft Books.

Block, J. (1976). Debatable conclusions about sex differences. *Contemporary Psychology, 21,* 517–522.

Block, J. H. (1983). Differential premises arising from differential socialization of the sexes: Some conjectures. *Child Development, 54,* 1335–1354.

Bloom, L. M. (1973). *One word at a time: The use of single word utterances before syntax.* The Hague: Mouton.

Bloom, L. M., Lifter, K., & Hafitz, J. (1980). Semantics of verbs and the development of verb inflections in child language. *Language, 56*, 386–412.

Bohannon, J. N., MacWhinney, B., & Snow, C. (1990). No negative evidence revisited: Beyond learnability or who has to prove what to whom. *Developmental Psychology, 26*, 221–226.

Bohannon, J. N., & Stanowicz, L. (1988). The issue of negative evidence: Adult responses to children's language errors. *Developmental Psychology, 24*, 684–689.

Boles, D. B. (1980). X-linkage of spatial ability: A critical review. *Child Development, 51*, 625–635.

Bornstein, M. H. (1981). Psychological studies of color perception in human infants: Habituation, discrimination and categorization, recognition, and conceptualization. *Advances in Infancy Research, 1*, 1–40.

Bornstein, M. H. (1989). Information processing (habituation) in infancy and stability in cognitive development. *Human Development, 32*, 129–136.

Bouchard, T. J. (1983). Do environmental similarities explain the similarity in intelligence of identical twins reared apart? *Intelligence, 7*, 175–184.

Bower, T. G. R. (1974). *Development in infancy*. San Francisco: W. H. Freeman.

Bower, T. G. R. (1977). *The perceptual world of the child*. Cambridge, Mass.: Harvard University Press.

Bowerman, M. (1976). Semantic factors in the acquisition of rules for word use and sentence construction. In D. M. Morehead and A. E. Morehead (Eds.), *Normal and deficient child language*. Baltimore, Md.: University Park Press.

Bowerman, M. (1982). Reorganizational processes in lexical and syntactic development. In E. Wanner and L. R. Gleitman (Eds.), *Language acquisition: The state of the art*. Cambridge: Cambridge University Press.

Bowlby, J. (1969). *Attachment and loss*, Vol. 1. New York: Basic Books.

Bowlby, J.(1980). *Attachment and loss*, Vol. 3. New York: Basic Books.

Boyer, C. B., & Hein, K. (1991). AIDS and HIV infection in adolescents: The role of education and antibody testing. In R. M. Lerner, A. C. Petersen, and J. Brooks-Gunn (Eds.), *Encyclopedia of adolescence*, Vol. 1. New York: Garland.

Bradbard, M. R., Martin, C. L., Endsley, R. C., & Halverson, C. F. (1986). Influence of sex stereotypes on children's exploration and memory: A competence versus performance distinction. *Developmental Psychology, 22*, 481–486.

Bradley, R. H., Caldwell, B. M., & Rock, S. L. (1988). Home environment and school performance: A ten-year follow-up and examination of three models of environmental action. *Child Development, 59*, 852–867.

Bradley, R. H., Caldwell, B. M., Rock, S. L., Casey, P. M., & Nelson, J. (1987). The early development of low-birthweight infants: Relationship to health, family status, family context, family processes, and parenting. *International Journal of Behavioral Development, 10*, 301–318.

Bradley, R. H., Caldwell, B. M., Rock, S. L., Ramey, C. T., Barnard, K. E., Gray, C., Hammond, M. A., Mitchell, S., Gottfried, A. W., Siegel, L., & Johnson, D. L. (1989). Home environment and cognitive development in the first 3 years of life: A collaborative study involving six sites and three ethnic groups in North America. *Developmental Psychology, 25*, 217–235.

Brady, J. E., Newcomb, A. F., & Hartup, W. W. (1983). Context and companion's behavior as determinants of cooperation and competition in school-age children. *Journal of Experimental Child Psychology, 36*, 396–412.

Braine, M. D. S. (1963). The ontogeny of English phrase structure: The first phrase. *Language, 39*, 1–13.

Braine, M. D. S. (1976). Children's first word combinations. *Monographs of the Society for Research in Child Development, 41*, Serial No. 164.

Brainerd, C. J. (1977). Cognitive development and cognitive learning: An interpretative review. *Psychological Bulletin, 84*, 919–939.

Braungart, J. M., Plomin, R., DeFries, J. C., & Fulker, D. W. (1992). Genetic influence on tester-rated infant temperament as assessed by Bayley's Infant Behavior Record: Nonadoptive and adoptive siblings and twins. *Developmental Psychology, 28*, 40–47.

Brazelton, T. B. (1970). Effect of prenatal drugs on the behavior of the neonate. *American Journal of Psychiatry, 126*, 1261–1266.

Brazelton, T. B. (1973). Neonatal behavioral assessment scale. *Clinics in developmental medicine*, No. 50. London: Spastics International Medical Publications in association with William Heinemann Medical Ltd.

Brazelton, T. B., Nugent, J. K., & Lester, B. M. (1987). Neonatal behavioral assessment scale. In J. D.

Osofsky (Ed.), *Handbook of infant development* (2nd ed). New York: Wiley.

Brehony, K. A., & Geller, E. S. (1981). Relationships between psychological androgyny, social conformity, and perceived locus of control. *Psychology of Women Quarterly, 6*, 204–217.

Bretherton, I. (1989). Pretense: The form and function of make-believe play. *Developmental Review, 9*, 383–401.

Bridges, L. J., Connell, J. P., & Belsky, J. (1988). Similarities and differences in infant-mother and infant-father interaction in the strange situation: A component process analysis. *Developmental Psychology, 24*, 92–100.

Brody, E. M. (1985). Parent care as normative family stress. The Donald P. Kent Memorial Lecture, presented at the 37th annual meeting of the Gerontological Society of America, San Antonio, Tex.

Brodzinsky, D. M., & Rightmyer, J. (1980). Individual differences in children's humor development. In P. McGhee and A. Chapman (Eds.), *Children's humour*. Chichester, Eng.: Wiley.

Broman, S. H., Nichols, P. L., & Kennedy, W. A. (1975). *Preschool IQ: Prenatal and early developmental correlates*. Hillsdale, N.J.: Lawrence Erlbaum.

Bronfenbrenner, U. (1979). *The ecology of human development*. Cambridge, Mass.: Harvard University Press.

Bronfenbrenner, U. (1989). Ecological systems theory. In R. Vasta (Ed.), *Annals of child development*, Vol. 6. Greenwich, Conn.: JAI Press.

Bronson, G. W. (1991). Infant differences in rate of visual encoding. *Child Development, 62*, 44–54.

Brooks-Gunn, J., & Warren, M. P. (1988). The psychological significance of secondary sexual characteristics in nine- to eleven-year-old girls. *Child Development, 59*, 1061–1069.

Brown, A. L., & Smiley, S. S. (1978). The development of strategies for studying texts. *Child Development, 49*, 1076–1088.

Brown, R. (1965). *Social psychology*. New York: The Free Press.

Brown, R. (1973). *A first language: The early stages*. Cambridge, Mass.: Harvard University Press.

Browne, A., & Finkelhor, D. (1986). Impact of child sexual abuse: A review of the research. *Psychological Bulletin, 99*, 66–77.

Bruch, H. (1979). *The golden cage: The enigma of anorexia nervosa*. New York: Vintage Books.

Bryant, B. K., & Crockenberg, S. B. (1980). Correlates and dimensions of prosocial behavior: A study of female siblings with their mothers. *Child Development, 51*, 529–554.

Bryant, P. (1974). *Perception and understanding in young children: An experimental approach*. London: Methuen.

Buelke-Sam, J. (1986). Postnatal functional assessment following central nervous system stimulant exposure: Amphetamine and caffeine. In E. P. Riley and C. V. Vorhees (Eds.), *Handbook of behavioral teratology*. New York: Plenum.

Buhrmester, D. (1990). Intimacy of friendship, interpersonal competence, and adjustment during preadolescence and adolescence. *Child Development, 61*, 1101–1111.

Buhrmester, D., & Furman, W. (1987). The development of companionship and intimacy. *Child Development, 58*, 1101–1113.

Buhrmester, D., & Furman, W. (1990). Perceptions of sibling relationships during middle childhood and adolescence. *Child Development, 61*, 1387–1398.

Buhrmester, D., Goldfarb, J., & Cantrell, D. (1992). Self-presentation when sharing with friends and nonfriends. *Journal of Early Adolescence, 12*, 61–79.

Burchard, J. D., & Barrera, F. (1972). An analysis of timeout and response cost in a programmed environment. *Journal of Applied Behavior Analysis, 5*, 271–282.

Burgess, R. L., & Richardson, R. A. (1984). Coercive interpersonal contingencies as determinants of child abuse: Implication for treatment and prevention. In R. F. Dangel and R. A. Polster (Eds.), *Behavioral parent training*. New York: Guilford Press.

Burns, A., & Humel, R. (1986). Sex role satisfaction among Australian children: Some sex, age, and cultural groups comparisons. *Psychology of Women Quarterly, 10*, 285–296.

Buss, A. H., & Plomin, R. (1975). *A temperamental theory of personality development*. New York: Wiley-Interscience.

Buss, A. H., & Plomin, R. (1984). *Temperament: Early developing personality traits*. Hillsdale, N.J.: Lawrence Erlbaum.

Butler, K. M. et al. (1991). Deoxyinosine in children with symptomatic human immunodeficiency virus infection. *New England Journal of Medicine, 324*, 137–144.

Butterworth, G., & Castillo, M. (1976). Coordination of auditory and visual space in newborn infants. *Perception, 5*, 155–161.

Butterworth, G., & Hopkins, B. (1988). Hand-mouth coordination in the new-born baby. *British Journal of Developmental Psychology, 6*, 303–314.

Caldwell, B. (1964). The effects of infant care. In M. Hoffman and L. Hoffman (Eds.), *Review of child development research*, Vol. 1. New York: Russell Sage Foundation.

Caldwell, B., & Bradley, R. (1984). *Home Observation for Measurement of the Environment*. Little Rock, Ark.: University of Arkansas.

Caldwell, B. M., & Richmond, J. B. (1962). The impact of theories of child development. *Children, 9*, 73–78.

Campos, J. J., Barrett, K. C., Lamb, M. E., Goldsmith, H. H., & Stenberg, C. (1983). Socioemotional development. In P. H. Mussen (Ed.), *Handbook of child development*, Vol. 2. New York: Wiley.

Campos, J. J., Langer, A., & Krowitz, A. (1970). Cardiac response on the visual cliff in prelocomotor human infants. *Science, 170*, 196–197.

Canfield, R. L., & Haith, M. M. (1991). Young infants' visual expectations for symmetric and asymmetric stimulus sequences. *Developmental Psychology, 27*, 198–208.

Cantor, S. (1988). *Childhood schizophrenia*. New York: Guilford Press.

Cantwell, D. P. (1975). *The hyperactive child*. New York: Spectrum.

Capelli, C. A., Nakagawa, N., & Madden, C. M. (1990). How children understand sarcasm: The role of context and intonation. *Child Development, 61*, 1824–1841.

Capute, A. J., Accardo, P. J., Vining, E. P. G., Rubenstein, J. E., & Harryman, S. (1978). *Primitive reflex profile*. Baltimore, Md.: University Park Press.

Carey, S. (1978). The child as a word learner. In M. Halle, J. Bresnan, and G. Miller (Eds.), *Linguistic theory and psychological reality*. Cambridge, Mass.: MIT Press.

Carmichael, L. (1970). Onset and early development of behavior. In P. H. Mussen (Ed.), *Carmichael's manual of child psychology* (3rd ed.). New York: Wiley.

Case, R. (1985). *Intellectual development: Birth to adulthood*. Orlando, Fla.: Academic Press.

Case, R. (1986). The new stage theories in intellectual development: Why we need them; what they assert. In M. Perlmutter (Ed.), *Minnesota symposium on child psychology*, Vol. 19. Hillsdale, N.J.: Lawrence Erlbaum.

Case, R., & Sowder, J. T. (1990). The development of computational estimation: A neo-Piagetian analysis. *Cognition and Instruction, 7*, 79–104.

Caspe, W. B. (1991). Introduction. *Journal of Pediatrics, Supplement, 119*, 53.

Cattell, R. B. (1965). *The scientific analysis of personality*. Baltimore, Md.: Penguin.

Cazden, C. B. (1968). The acquisition of noun with verb inflections. *Child Development, 39*, 433–448.

Chase-Lansdale, P. L., & Hetherington, E. M. (1990). The impact of divorce on life-span development: Short and long term effects. In P. B. Baltes, D. L. Featherman, and R. M. Lerner, (Eds). *Life-span development and behavior*, Vol. 10. Hillsdale, N.J.: Lawrence Erlbaum.

Chase-Lansdale, P. L., & Owen, M. T. (1987). Maternal employment in a family context: Effects on infant-mother and infant-father attachments. *Child Development, 58*, 1505–1512.

Chassin, L., Presson, C. C., Sherman, S. J., Montello, D., & McGrew J. (1986). Changes in peer and parent influence during adolescence: Longitudinal versus cross-sectional perspectives on smoking initiation. *Developmental Psychology, 22*, 327–334.

Cherlin, A. J., Furstenberg, F. F., Chase-Lansdale, P. L., Kiernan, K. E., Robins, P. K., Morrison, D. R., & Teitler, J. O. (1991). Longitudinal studies of effects of divorce on children in Great Britain and the United States. *Science, 252*, 1386–1389.

Chess S. (1974). The influence of defect on development in children with congenital rubella. *Merrill-Palmer Quarterly, 20*, 255–274.

Chess, S., & Thomas, A. (1986). *Temperament in clinical practice*. New York: Guilford Press.

Chi, M. T. H. (1978). Knowledge structures and memory development. In R. Siegler (Ed.), *Children's thinking: What develops?* Hillsdale, N.J.: Lawrence Erlbaum.

Chisholm, J. S. (1983). *Navajo infancy: An ethological study of child development*. New York: Aldine.

Chomsky, N. (1959). Review of B. F. Skinner's "Verbal Behavior." *Language, 35*, 26–129.

Chomsky, N. (1982). *Lectures on government and binding*. New York: Foris.

Chugani, H. T., & Phelps, M. E. (1986). Maturational changes in cerebral function in infants determined by 18FDG positron emission tomography. *Science, 231*, 840–843.

Clark, H. H., & Clark, E. V. (1977). *Psychology and language.* New York: Harcourt Brace Jovanovich.

Clark, J. E., Whitall, J., & Phillips, S. J. (1988). Human interlimb coordination: The first 6 months of independent walking. *Developmental Psychobiology, 21,* 445–456.

Clarke, A. M., & Clarke, A. D. (1989). The later cognitive effects of early intervention. *Intelligence, 13,* 289–297.

Clarke-Stewart, K. A. (1978). And daddy makes three: The father's impact on mother and young child. *Child Development, 49,* 466–478.

Clarke-Stewart, K. A. (1989). Infant day care: Maligned or malignant? *American Psychologist, 44,* 266–273.

Clarke-Stewart, K. A., & Fein, G. G. (1983). Early childhood programs. In P. H. Mussen (Ed.), *Handbook of child psychology,* Vol. 2. New York: Wiley.

Cleary, T. A., Humphreys, L. G., Kendrick, S. A., & Wesman, A. (1975). Educational uses of tests with disadvantaged students. *American Psychologist, 30,* 15–41.

Clemson, E. (1981). Disadvantaged youth: A study of sex differences in occupational stereotypes and vocational aspirations. *Youth and Society, 13,* 39–56.

Clifton, R., Perris, E., & Bullinger, A. (1991). Infants' perception of auditory space. *Developmental Psychology, 27,* 187–197.

Cohen, R., & Schuepfer, T. (1980). The representation of landmarks and routes. *Child Development, 51,* 1065–1071.

Cohen, R., & Weatherford, D. L. (1980). Effect of route travelled on the distance estimates of children and adults. *Journal of Experimental Child Psychology, 29,* 403–412.

Coie, J. D., Dodge, K. A., & Coppotelli, H. (1982). Dimensions and types of social status: A cross-age perspective. *Developmental Psychology, 18,* 557–570.

Colby, A., Kohlberg, L., Gibbs, J., & Lieberman, M. (1983). A longitudinal study of moral judgment. *Monographs of the Society for Research in Child Development, 48* (Serial No. 200).

Cole, D. A. (1991). Preliminary support for a competency-based model of depression in children. *Journal of Abnormal Psychology, 100,* 181–190.

Collis, G. M. (1977). Visual co-orientation and maternal speech. In H. R. Schaffer (Ed.), *Studies in mother-infant interaction.* London: Academic Press.

Conger, J. J., & Petersen, A. C. (1984). *Adolescence and youth: Psychological development in a changing world.* New York: Harper & Row.

Connolly, K., & Dalgeish, M. (1989). The emergence of a tool-using skill in infancy. *Developmental Psychology, 25,* 894–912.

Cooper, R. P., & Aslin, R. N. (1990). Preference for infant-directed speech in the first month after birth. *Child Development, 61,* 1584–1595.

Cornell, E. H., Heth, C. D., & Broda, L. S. (1989). Children's wayfinding: Response to instructions to use environmental landmarks. *Developmental Psychology, 25,* 755–764.

Cornwell, K. S., Harris, L. J., & Fitzgerald, H. E. (1991). Task effects in the development of hand preference in 9-, 13-, and 20-month-old infant girls. *Developmental Neuropsychology, 7,* 19–34.

Cousins, J. H., Siegel, A. W., & Maxwell, S. E. (1983). Way finding and cognitive mapping in large scale environments: A test of a developmental model. *Journal of Experimental Child Psychology, 35,* 1–20.

Craton, L. G., & Yonas, A. (1988). Infants' sensitivity to boundary flow information for depth at an edge. *Child Development, 59,* 1522–1529.

Crawley, S. B., Rogers, P. P., Friedman, S., Iacobbo, M., Criticos, A., Richardson, L., & Thompson, M. (1978). Changes in structure of mother-infant play. *Developmental Psychology, 14,* 30–36.

Crnic, K. A., Ragozin, A. S., Greenberg, M. T., Robinson, N. M., & Basham, R. B. (1983). Social interaction and developmental competence of preterm and full-term infants during the first year of life. *Child Development, 54,* 1199–1210.

Crockenberg, S., & Litman, C. (1991). Effects of maternal employment on maternal and two-year-old child behavior. *Child Development, 62,* 930–953.

Crook, C. (1987). Taste and olfaction. In P. Salapatek and L. Cohen (Eds.). *Handbook of infant perception,* Vol. 1. Orlando, Fla.: Academic Press.

Crouter, A. C., Perry-Jenkins, M., Huston, T. L., & McHale, S. M. (1987). Processes underlying father involvement in dual-earner and single-earner families. *Developmental Psychology, 23,* 431–440.

Culp, R. E., Appelbaum, M. I., Osofsky, J. D., & Levy, J. A. (1988). Adolescent and older mothers: comparison between prenatal maternal variables and newborn interaction measures. *Infant Behavior and Development, 11,* 353–362.

Cummings, E. M., Iannotti, R. J., & Zahn-Waxler, C.

(1989). Aggression between peers in early childhood: Individual continuity and developmental change. *Child Development, 60,* 887–895.

Curtis, L. E., & Strauss, M. S. (1983). Infant numerosity abilities: Discrimination and relative numerosity. Paper presented at the biennial meeting of the Society for Research in Child Development, Detroit, Mich.

Curtiss, S. (1977). *Genie: A psycholinguistic study of a modern day "wild child."* New York: Academic Press.

Cytryn, L., & Lourie, R. S. (1980). Mental retardation. In H. I. Kaplan, A. M. Freedman, and B. J. Sadock (Eds.), *Comprehensive textbook of psychiatry,* III, Vol. 3. Baltimore, Md.: Williams & Wilkins.

Damon, W. (1980). Patterns of change in children's social reasoning: A two-year longitudinal study. *Child Development, 51,* 1010–1017.

Damon, W. (1983). *Social and personality development: Infancy through adolescence.* New York: W. W. Norton.

D'Andrade, R. G. (1966). Sex differences and cultural institutions. In E. E. Maccoby (Ed.), *The development of sex differences.* Stanford, Calif.: Stanford University Press.

Dannemiller, J. L., & Stephens, B. R. (1988). A critical test of infant pattern preference models. *Child Development, 59,* 210–216.

Danner, F. W., & Day, M. C. (1977). Eliciting formal operations. *Child Development, 48,* 1600–1606.

Dansky, J. L. (1980). Make-believe: A mediator of the relationship between play and associative fluency. *Child Development, 51,* 576–579.

Darley, J. M., & Shultz, T. R. (1990). Moral rules: Their content and acquisition. *Annual Review of Psychology, 41,* 525–556.

Davidson, K. M., Richards, D. S., Schatz, D. A., & Fisher, D. A. (1991). Successful in utero treatment of fetal goiter and hypothyroidism. *New England Journal of Medicine, 324,* 543–546.

Davis, D. D., & Templer, D. I. (1988). Neurobehavioral functioning in children exposed to narcotics in utero. *Addictive Behaviors, 13,* 275–283.

Deaux, K. (1985). Sex and gender. *Annual Review of Psychology, 36,* 49–81.

DeCasper, A. J., & Sigafoos, A. D. (1983). The intrauterine heartbeat: A potent reinforcer for newborns. *Infant Behavior and Development, 6,* 19–25.

DeLoache, J. S. (1984). Oh where, oh where: Memory-based searching by very young children. In C.

Sophian (Ed.), *Origins of cognitive skills.* Hillsdale, N.J.: Lawrence Erlbaum.

DeLoache, J. S. (1987). Rapid change in the symbolic functioning of very young children. *Science, 238,* 1556–1557.

DeLoache, J. S. (1989). Young children's understanding of the correspondence between a scale model and a larger space. *Cognitive Development, 4,* 121–139.

DeLoache, J. S. (1991). Symbolic functioning in very young children: Understanding of pictures and models. *Child Development, 62,* 736–752.

Demchak, M. (1990). Response prompting and fading methods: A review. *American Journal on Mental Retardation, 94,* 603–615.

Dennis, W. (1966). Goodenough scores, art experience, and modernization. *Journal of Social Psychology, 68,* 211–228.

Dennis, W., & Dennis, M. G. (1940). The effects of cradling practices upon the onset of walking in Hopi children. *Journal of Genetic Psychology, 56,* 77–86.

deVilliers, J. G., & deVilliers, P. A. (1985). The acquisition of English. In D. I. Slobin (Ed.), *The cross-linguistic study of language acquisition.* Hillsdale, N.J.: Lawrence Erlbaum.

Diamond, A. (1991). Frontal lobe involvement in cognitive changes during the first year of life. In K. R. Gibson and A. C. Peterson (Eds.), *Brain maturation and cognitive development: Comparative and crosscultural perspectives.* New York: Aldine De Gruyter.

Dietz, W. H. (1988). Metabolic aspects of dieting. In N. A. Krasnegor, G. D. Grave, and N. Kretchmer (Eds.), *Childhood obesity: A biobehavioral perspective.* Caldwell, N.J.: Telford Press.

Dion, K. K. (1974). Children's physical attractiveness and sex as determinants of adult punitiveness. *Developmental Psychology, 10,* 772–778.

Dion, K. K., & Stein, S. (1978). Physical attractiveness and interpersonal influence. *Journal of Experimental Social Psychology, 14,* 97–108.

Dishion, T. J. (1990). The family ecology of boys' peer relations in middle childhood. *Child Development, 61,* 874–892.

Dix, T., Ruble, D. N., & Zambarano, R. J. (1989). Mothers' implicit theories of discipline: Child effects, parent effects, and the attribution process. *Child Development, 60,* 1373–1391.

Dodge, K. A. (1980). Social cognition and children's aggressive behavior. *Child Development, 51,* 162–170.

Dodge, K. A., Bates, J. E., & Pettit, G. S. (1990). Mechanisms in the cycle of violence. *Science, 250,* 1678–1683.

Dodge, K. A., & Crick, N. R. (1990). Social information-processing bases of aggressive behavior in children. *Personality and Social Psychology Bulletin, 16,* 8–22.

Dodge, K. A., Pettit, G. S., McClaskey, C. L., & Brown, M. M. (1986). Social competence in children. *Monographs of the Society for Research in Child Development, 51,* Serial No. 213.

Doherty, W. J., & Jacobson, N. S. (1982). Marriage and the family. In B. Wolman (Ed.), *Handbook of developmental psychology.* Englewood Cliffs, N.J.: Prentice Hall.

Doleys, D. M. (1989). Enuresis and encopresis. In T. H. Ollendick and M. Hersen (Eds.), *Handbook of child psychopathology* (2nd ed.). New York: Plenum.

Dornbusch, S. M., Ritter, P. L., Leiderman, P H., Roberts, D. F., & Fraleigh, M. J. (1987). The relation of parenting style to adolescent school performance. *Child Development, 58,* 1244–1257.

Douglas, V. I.(1983). Attentional and cognitive problems. In M. Rutter (Ed.), *Developmental neuropsychiatry.* New York: Guilford Press.

Douvan, E., & Adelson, J. (1966). *The adolescent experience.* New York: Wiley.

Downey, J., Elkin, E. J., Ehrhardt, A. A., Meyer-Bahlburg, H. F. L., Bell, J. J., & Morishima, A. (1991). Cognitive ability and everyday functioning in women with Turner syndrome. *Journal of Learning Disabilities, 24,* 32–39.

Dreyer, P. H. (1982). Sexuality during adolescence. In B. B. Wolman (Ed.), *Handbook of developmental psychology.* Englewood Cliffs, N.J.: Prentice Hall.

Drum, P. A. (1985). Retention of text information by grade, ability, and study. *Discourse Processes, 8,* 21–52.

Dubois, S., Doughtery, C., Duquette, M., Hanley, J. A., & Moutquin, J. (1991). Twin pregnancy: the impact of the Higgins Nutrition Intervention Program on maternal and neonatal outcomes. *American Journal of Clinical Nutrition, 53,* 1397–1403.

Duck, S. (1983). *Friends, for life: The psychology of close relationships.* New York: St. Martin's Press.

Dunn, J., and Kendrick, C. (1981). Social behavior of young siblings in the family context: Differences between same-sex and different-sex dyads. *Child Development, 52,* 1265–1273.

Eagly, A. H. (1983). Gender and social influence. *American Psychologist, 38,* 971–981.

Eagly, A. H., & Carli, L. L. (1981). Sex of researchers and sex-typed communications as determinants of sex differences in influenceability: A meta-analysis of social influence studies. *Psychological Bulletin, 90,* 1–20.

Eagley, A. H., & Chrvala, C. (1986). Sex differences in conformity: Status and gender role interpretations. *Psychology of Women Quarterly, 10,* 203–220.

Eagly, A. H., & Crowley, M. (1986). Gender and helping behavior: A meta-analytic review of the social psychological literature. *Psychological Bulletin, 100,* 283–308.

Eagly, A. H., & Steffen, V. J. (1986). Gender stereotypes, occupational roles, and beliefs about part-time employment. *Psychology of Women Quarterly, 10,* 252–262.

East, P. L., & Rook, K. S. (1992). Compensatory patterns of support among children's peer relationships: A test using school friends, nonschool friends, and siblings. *Developmental Psychology, 28,* 163–172.

Eaton, W. O., Chipperfield, J. G., & Singbeil, C. E. (1989). Birth order and activity level in children. *Developmental Psychology, 25,* 668–672.

Eaton, W. O., & Enns, L. R. (1986). Sex differences in human motor activity level. *Psychological Bulletin, 100,* 19–28.

Eckerman, C. O., Davis, C. C., & Didow, S. M. (1989). Toddlers' emerging ways of achieving social co-ordinations with a peer. *Child Development, 60,* 440–453.

Eckert, H. M. (1987). *Motor development* (3rd ed.). Indianapolis, Ind.: Benchmark Press.

Edelbrock, C., Costello, A. J., & Kessler, M. D. (1984). Empirical corroboration of attention deficit disorder. *Journal of the American Academy of Child Psychiatry, 23,* 285–290.

Eels, K. (1953). Some implications for school practice of the Chicago studies of cultural bias in intelligence tests. *Harvard Educational Review, 23,* 284–297.

Eichorn, D. H. (1963). Biological correlates of behavior. In H. W. Stevenson (Ed.), *Child psychology.* Chicago: University of Chicago Press.

Eisenberg, N. (1988). The development of prosocial and aggressive behavior. In M. H. Bornstein and M. E. Lamb (Eds.), *Developmental psychology: An advanced textbook* (2nd ed.). Hillsdale, N.J.: Lawrence Erlbaum.

Eisenberg, N., Fabes, R. A., Schaller, M., Carlo, G., & Miller, P. A. (1991). The relations of parental characteristics and practices to children's vicarious emotional responding. *Child Development, 62*, 1393–1408.

Eisenberg, N., Hertz-Lazarowitz, R., & Fuchs, I. (1990). Prosocial moral judgment in Israeli kibbutz and city children: A longitudinal study. *Merrill-Palmer Quarterly, 36*, 273–285.

Eisenberg, N., & Lennon, R. (1983). Sex differences in empathy and related capacities. *Psychological Bulletin, 94*, 100–131.

Eisenberg, N., & Miller, P. A. (1987). The relation of empathy to prosocial and related behaviors. *Psychological Bulletin, 101*, 91–119.

Eisenberg, N., & Shell, R. (1986). Prosocial moral judgment and behavior in children: The mediating role of cost. *Personality and Social Psychology Bulletin, 12*, 426–433.

Elder, G. H., & Rockwell, R. C. (1976). Marital timing in women's life patterns. *Journal of Family History, 1*, 34–53.

Engen, T., Lipsitt, L. P., & Kaye, H. (1963). Olfactory responses and adaptation in the human neonate. *Journal of Comparative and Physiological Psychology, 56*, 73–77.

Enns, J. T. (1990). Relations between components of visual attention. In J. T. Enns (Ed.), *The development of attention*. Amsterdam: North Holland.

Erickson, M. T. (1987). *Behavior disorders of children and adolescents*. Englewood Cliffs, N.J.: Prentice Hall.

Erikson, E. H. (1963). *Childhood and society*. New York: W. W. Norton.

Erikson, E. H. (1968). *Identity: Youth and crisis*. New York: W. W. Norton.

Eron, L. D., & Huesmann, L. (1990). The stability of aggressive behavior—even unto the third generation. In M. Lewis and S. M. Miller (Eds.), *Handbook of developmental psychopathology*. New York: Plenum.

Ervin, S. (1964). Imitation and structural change in children's language. In E. H. Lenneberg (Ed.), *New directions in the study of language*. Cambridge, Mass.: MIT Press.

Ervin-Tripp, S. (1970). Discourse agreement: How children answer questions. In J. R. Hayes (Ed.), *Cognition and the development of language*. New York: Wiley.

Eysenck, H. J. (1952). The effects of psychotherapy: An evaluation. *Journal of Consulting Psychology, 16*, 319–324.

Fagot, B. I., Hagan, R., Leinbach, M. D., & Kronsberg, S. (1985). Differential reactions to assertive and communicative acts of toddler boys and girls. *Child Development, 56*, 1499–1505.

Fagot, B. I., & Kavanagh, K. (1990). The prediction of antisocial behavior from avoidant attachment classifications. *Child Development, 61*, 864–873.

Fagot, B. I., & Leinbach, M. D. (1989). The young child's gender schema: Environmental input, internal organization. *Child Development, 60*, 663–672.

Falbo, T., & Polit, D. F. (1986). Quantitative review of the only child literature: Research evidence and theory development. *Psychological Bulletin, 100*, 176–189.

Fantz, R. L. (1969). Studying visual perception and the effects of visual exposure in early infancy. In D. Gelfand (Ed.), *Social learning in childhood*. Belmont, Calif.: Brooks/Cole.

Farrar, M. J. (1992). Negative evidence and grammatical morpheme acquisition. *Developmental Psychology, 28*, 90–98.

Farrar, M. J., & Goodman, G. S. (1992). Developmental changes in event memory. *Child Development, 63*, 173–187.

Feingold, B. F. (1975). *Why your child is hyperactive*. New York: Random House.

Feldman, S. S., & Wentzel, K. R. (1990). The relationship between parental styles, sons' self-restraint, and peer relations in early adolescence. *Journal of Early Adolescence, 10*, 439–454.

Fenton, N. (1928). The only child. *Journal of Genetic Psychology, 35*, 546–556.

Ferreira, A. J. (1969). *Prenatal environment*. Springfield, Ill.: Charles C Thomas.

Field, T. M., & Widmayer, S. M. (1982). Motherhood. In B. J. Wolman (Ed.), *Handbook of developmental psychology*. Englewood Cliffs, N.J.: Prentice Hall.

Field, T., Woodson, R., Greenberg, R., & Cohen, D. (1982). Discrimination and initiation of facial expressions by neonates. *Science, 218*, 179–181.

Fischer, K. W. (1980). A theory of cognitive development: The control and construction of hierarchies of skills. *Psychological Review, 87*, 477–531.

Fischer, K. W. (1983). Developmental levels as periods of discontinuity. In K. W. Fischer (Ed.),

Levels and transitions in children's development. San Francisco: Jossey-Bass.

Fischer, K. W., & Pipp, S. L. (1984). Processes of cognitive development: Optimal level and skill acquisition. In R. J. Sternberg (Ed.), *Mechanisms of cognitive development*. New York: W. H. Freeman.

Fischer, W. F. (1963). Sharing in preschool children as a function of amount and type of reinforcement. *Genetic Psychology Monographs, 68*, 215–245.

Fitzgerald, H. E., & Brackbill, Y. (1976). Classical conditioning in infancy: Development and constraints. *Psychological Bulletin, 83*, 353–376.

Flavell, J. H. (1963). *The developmental psychology of Jean Piaget*. New York: D. Van Nostrand.

Flavell, J. H. (1985). *Cognitive development*. (2nd ed.). Englewood Cliffs, N.J.: Prentice Hall.

Flavell, J. H., Beach, D. R., & Chinsky, J. M. (1966). Spontaneous verbal rehearsal in a memory task as a function of age. *Child Development, 37*, 283–299.

Flavell, J. H., Everett, B. A., Croft, K., & Flavell, E. R. (1981). Young children's knowledge about visual perception: Further evidence for the Level 1–Level 2 distinction. *Developmental Psychology, 17*, 99–103.

Flavell, J. H., Flavell, E. R., Green, F. L., & Wilcox, S. A. (1981). The development of three spatial perspective-taking rules. *Child Development, 52*, 356–358.

Flavell, J. H., Green, F. L., & Flavell, E. R. (1986). Development of knowledge about the appearance-reality distinction. *Monographs of the Society for Research in Child Development, 51*, Serial No. 212.

Flavell, J. H., Green, F. L., & Flavell, E. R. (1989). Young children's ability to differentiate appearance-reality and level 2 perspectives in the tactile modality. *Child Development, 60*, 201–213.

Folstein, S. E., & Rutter, M. L. (1988). Autism: Familial aggregation and genetic implications. *Journal of Autism and Developmental Disorders, 18*, 3–30.

Fontana, V. (1973). *Somewhere a child is crying: Maltreatment-causes and prevention*. New York: Macmillan.

Ford, C., & Beach, F. (1951). *Patterns of sexual behavior*. New York: Harper & Row.

Forssman, H. (1967). Epilepsy in an XYY man. *Lancet, 1*, 1389.

Fox, N. A., Kimmerly, N. L., & Schaffer, W. D. (1991). Attachment to mother/attachment to father: A meta-analysis. *Child Development, 62*, 210–225.

Francis, P. L., Self, P. A., & Horowitz, F. D. (1987). The behavioral assessment of the neonate: An overview. In J. D. Osofsky (Ed.), *Handbook of infant development* (2nd ed.). New York: Wiley.

Frankenburg, W. K., & Dobbs, J. B. (1967). The Denver Developmental Screening Test. *Journal of Pediatrics, 71*, 181–191.

French, D. C. (1988). Heterogeneity of peer-rejected boys: Aggressive and nonaggressive subtypes. *Child Development, 59*, 976–985.

French, D. C. (1990). Heterogeneity of peer-rejected girls. *Child Development, 61*, 2028–2031.

Freud, A. (1972). Adolescence. In J. F. Rosenblith, W. Alinsmith, and J. P. Williams, (Eds.), *The cause of behavior* (pp. 317–323). Boston: Allyn and Bacon.

Freud, S. (1969). *An outline of psycho-analysis*. New York: W. W. Norton.

Frey, K. A., Stenchever, M. A., & Warren, M. P. (1989). Helping the infertile couple. *Patient Care, 23*, 22–32.

Fried, P. A., & Watkinson, B. (1990). 36- and 48-month neurobehavioral follow-up of children prenatally exposed to marijuana, cigarettes, and alcohol. *Journal of Developmental and Behavioral Pediatrics, 11*, 49–58.

Friedman, L. J. (1983). Understanding stepfamilies (Review of E. Wald's *The Remarried Family*). *Contemporary Psychology, 28*, 279.

Friedman, R. M., Sandler, J., Hernandez, M., & Wolfe, D. A. (1981). Child abuse. In E. J. Mash and L. G. Terdal (Eds.), *Behavioral assessment of childhood disorders*. New York: Guilford Press.

Friedrich, L. K., & Stein, A. H. (1973). Aggressive and prosocial television programs and the natural behavior of preschool children. *Monographs of the Society for Research in Child Development, 38*, 1–64.

Frodi, A., Macaulay, J., & Thome, P. R. (1977). Are women always less aggressive than men? A review of the experimental literature. *Psychological Bulletin, 84*, 634–660.

Fulker, D. W., DeFries, J. C., & Plomin, R. (1988). Genetic influence on general mental ability increases between infancy and middle childhood. *Nature, 336*, 767–769.

Funder, D. C., Block, J. H., & Block, J. (1983). Delay of gratification: Some longitudinal personality correlates. *Journal of Personality and Social Psychology, 44,* 1198–1213.

Furman, L. N., & Walden, T. A. (1990). Effect of script knowledge on preschool children's communicative interactions. *Developmental Psychology, 26,* 227–233.

Furman, W., & Buhrmester, D. (1992). Age and sex differences in perceptions of networks of personal relationships. *Child Development, 63,* 103–115.

Furrow, D., Nelson, K., & Benedict, H. (1979). Mothers' speech to children and syntactic development: Some simple relationships. *Journal of Child Language, 6,* 423–442.

Galambos, N. L., & Maggs, J. L. (1991). Out-of-school care of young adolescents and self-reported behavior. *Developmental Psychology, 27,* 644–655.

Galloway, D. (1983). Research note: Truants and other absentees. *Journal of Psychology and Psychiatry, 24,* 607–611.

Gandour, M. J. (1989). Activity level as a dimension of temperament in toddlers: Its relevance for the organismic specificity hypothesis. *Child Development, 60,* 1092–1098.

Garber, J. (1984). Classification of childhood psychopathology: A developmental perspective. *Child Development, 55,* 30–48.

Gardner, H. (1983). *Frames of mind: The theory of multiple intelligences.* New York: Basic Books.

Gardner, R. A., & Gardner, B. T. (1969). Teaching sign language to a chimpanzee. *Science, 165,* 664–672.

Garrod, A., Beal, C., & Shin, P. (1990). The development of moral orientation in elementary school children. *Sex Roles, 22,* 13–27.

Garvey, C., & Berninger, G. (1981). Timing and turn taking in children's conversations. *Discourse Processes, 4,* 27–59.

Garvey, C., & Hogan, R. (1973). Social speech and social interaction: Egocentrism revisited. *Child Development, 44,* 562–568.

Gelman, R. (1969). Conservation acquisition: A problem of learning to attend to relevant attributes. *Journal of Experimental Child Psychology, 7,* 167–187.

Gelman, R. (1982). Basic numerical abilities. In R. J. Sternberg (Ed.), *Advances in the psychology of human intelligence,* Vol. 1. Hillsdale, N.J.: Lawrence Erlbaum.

Gelman, R., & Gallistel, C. R. (1978). *The child's understanding of number.* Cambridge, Mass.: Harvard University Press.

Gelman, R., & Meck, E. (1986). The notion of principle: The case of counting. In J. Hiebert (Ed.), *Conceptual and procedural knowledge: The case of mathematics.* Hillsdale, N.J.: Lawrence Erlbaum.

Gerrard, M. (1987). Sex, guilt, and contraceptive use revisited: The 1980s. *Journal of Personality and Social Psychology, 52,* 975–980.

Gesell, A. (1940). The stability of mental-growth careers. *39th Yearbook of the National Society for the Study of Education,* Part II, 149–159.

Gesell, A. (1956). *Youth: The years from ten to sixteen.* New York: Harper.

Getzels, J. W., & Jackson, P. W. (1975). The meaning of "giftedness"—an examination of an expanding concept. In W. B. Barbe and J. S. Renzulli (Eds.), *Psychology and education of the gifted.* New York: Halsted Press.

Gewirtz, J. L. (1972). Attachment, dependence, and a distinction in terms of stimulus control. In J. L. Gewirtz (Ed.), *Attachment and dependency.* Washington, D.C.: V. H. Winston.

Gewirtz, J. (1991). Social influence on child and parent via stimulation and operant-learning mechanisms. In M. Lewis and S. Feinman (Eds.), *Social influences and socialization in infancy.* New York: Plenum.

Ghim, H. (1990). Evidence for perceptual organization in infants: Perception of subjective contours by young infants. *Infant Behavior and Development, 13,* 221–248.

Gibbs, J. C., Clark, P. M., Joseph, J. A., Green, J. L., Goodrick, T. S., & Makowski, D. (1986). Relations between moral judgment, moral courage, and field independence. *Child Development, 57,* 185–193.

Gibson, E. J., & Walk, R. D. (1960). The "visual cliff." *Scientific American, 202,* 64–71.

Gibson, E. J., & Walker, A. S. (1984). Development of knowledge of visual-tactual affordance of substance. *Child Development, 55,* 453–460.

Gil, D. G. (1979). Unraveling child abuse. In R. Bourne and E. H. Newberger (Eds.), *Critical perspectives on child abuse.* Lexington, Mass.: Lexington Books, Heath.

Gilligan, C. (1982). *In a different voice: Psychological theory and women's development.* Cambridge, Mass.: Harvard University Press.

Gilligan, C. (1985). Remapping development. Presented at the biennial meeting of the Society for Research in Child Development, Toronto, Ont.

Ginsburg, H. (1977). *Children's arithmetic: The learning process.* New York: D. Van Nostrand.

Godwin, L. J., & Moran, J. D. (1990). Psychometric characteristics of an instrument for measuring creative potential in preschool children. *Psychology in the Schools, 27,* 204–409.

Golinkoff, R. M., Hirsh-Pasek, K., Bailey, L. M., & Wenger, N. R. (1992). Young children and adults use lexical principles to learn new nouns. *Developmental Psychology, 28,* 99–108.

Goodman, G. S., & Aman, C. (1990). Children's use of anatomically detailed dolls to recount an event. *Child Development, 61,* 1859–1871.

Goodman, G. S., Rudy, L., Bottoms, B. L., & Aman, C. (1990). Children's concerns and memory: Ecological issues in the study of children's eyewitness testimony. In R. Fivush and J. Hudson (Eds.), *What young children remember and know.* New York: Cambridge University Press.

Goodman, R., & Stevenson, J. (1989). A twin study of hyperactivity-II. The aetiological role of genes, family relationships and perinatal adversity. *Journal of Child Psychology and Psychiatry, 30,* 691–709.

Goosens, F. A., & van IJzendoorn, M. H. (1990). Quality of infants' attachments to professional caregivers: relation to infant-parent attachment and day-care characteristics. *Child Development, 61,* 832–837.

Gottfried, A. E., Gottfried, A. W., & Bathurst, K. (1988). Maternal employment, family environment, and children's development: Infancy through the school years. In A. E. Gottfried and A. W. Gottfried (Eds.), *Maternal employment and children's development: Longitudinal research.* New York: Plenum.

Gottlieb, L. N., & Mendelson, M. J. (1990). Parental support and firstborn girls' adaptation to the birth of a sibling. *Journal of Applied Developmental Psychology, 11,* 29–48.

Gottman, J. M. (1986). The world of coordinated play: Same- and cross-sex friendships in children. In J. M. Gottman and Jeffrey G. Parker (Eds.), *Conversations of friends.* New York: Cambridge University Press.

Gould, S. J. (1981). *The mismeasure of man.* New York: W. W. Norton.

Greenberger, E., & Steinberg, L. (1983). Sex differences in early work experience: Harbinger of things to come? *Social Forces, 62,* 467–486.

Greenfield, P. M., & Smith, J. H. (1976). *The structure of communication in early language development.* New York: Academic Press.

Grieser, D. L., & Kuhl, P. K. (1988). Maternal speech to infants in a tonal language: Support for universal prosodic features in motherese. *Developmental Psychology, 24,* 14–20.

Grieser, D., & Kuhl, P. K. (1989). Categorization of speech by infants: Support for speech-sound prototypes. *Developmental Psychology, 25,* 577–588.

Grimm, H. (1975). Analysis of short-term dialogues in 5–7 year olds: Encoding of intentions and modifications of speech acts as a function of negative feedback. Paper presented at the Third International Child Language Symposium, London.

Grinder, R. E. (1967). *A history of genetic psychology.* New York: Wiley.

Groen, G. J., & Resnick, L. B. (1977). Can preschool children invent addition algorithms? *Journal of Educational Psychology, 69,* 645–652.

Grossman, H. J. (Ed.). (1983). *Classification in mental retardation.* Washington, D.C.: American Association on Mental Deficiency.

Gruen, G. E., & Vore, D. A. (1972). Development of conservation in normal and retarded children. *Developmental Psychology, 6,* 146–157.

Grusec, J. E. (1991). Socializing concern for others in the home. *Developmental Psychology, 27,* 338–342.

Grych, J. H., & Fincham, F. D. (1990). Marital conflict and children's adjustment: A cognitive-contextual framework. *Psychological Bulletin, 108,* 267–290.

Guerra, N. G., & Slaby, R. G. (1990). Cognitive mediators of aggression in adolescent offenders: 2. Intervention. *Developmental Psychology, 26,* 269–277.

Guilford, J. P. (1957). Creative abilities in the arts. *Psychological Review, 64,* 110–118.

Guilford, J. P. (1966). Intelligence: 1965 model. *American Psychologist, 64,* 20–26.

Gunnar, M. R., Managelsdorf, S., Larson, M., & Hertsgaard, L. (1989). Attachment, temperament, and adrenocortical activity in infancy: A study of psychoendocrine regulation. *Developmental Psychology, 25,* 355–363.

Gutierrez, J., & Sameroff, A. (1990). Determinants of complexity in Mexican-American and Anglo-American mothers' conceptions of child development. *Child Development, 90,* 384–394.

Hagamen, M. B. (1980). Autism and childhood schizophrenia. In J. E. Bemporad (Ed.), *Child development in normality and psychopathology*. New York: Brunner/Mazel.

Hagen, J. W. (1972). Strategies for remembering. In S. Farnham-Diggory (Ed.), *Information processing in children*. New York: Academic Press.

Hagen, J. W., & Hale, G. W. (1973). The development of attention in children. In A. D. Pick (Ed.), *Minnesota symposia on child psychology*, Vol. 7. Minneapolis-St. Paul, Minn.: University of Minnesota Press.

Hahn, W. (1987). Cerebral lateralization of function: From infancy through childhood. *Psychological Bulletin, 101*, 376–392.

Hakuta, K. (1987). Degree of bilingualism and cognitive ability in mainland Puerto Rican children. *Child Development, 58*, 1372–1388.

Hakuta, K., & Garcia, E. F. (1989). Bilingualism and education. *American Psychologist, 44*, 374–379.

Hale, S. (1990). A global developmental trend in cognitive processing speed. *Child Development, 61*, 653–663.

Hall, G. S. (1904). *Adolescence, I*. New York: Appleton.

Hall, G. S. (1905). *Adolescence, II*. New York: Appleton.

Hall, J. A., & Halberstadt, A. G. (1986). Smiling and gazing. In J. S. Hyde and M. C. Linn (Eds.), *The psychology of sex differences. Advances through meta-analysis*. Baltimore, Md.: Johns Hopkins University Press.

Hallinan, M. T., & Teixeira, R. A. (1987). Students' interracial friendships: Individual characteristics, structural effects, and racial differences. *American Journal of Education, 95*, 563–583.

Halpern, D. F. (1986). *Sex differences in cognitive abilities*. Hillsdale, N.J.: Lawrence Erlbaum.

Halpern, J. J. & Luria, Z. (1989). Labels of giftedness and gender-typicality: Effects on adults' judgments of children's traits. *Psychology in the Schools, 26*, 301–310.

Hamerton, J. L. (1982). Population cytogenetics: A perspective. In M. Adinolfi, P. Benson, F. Giannelli, and M. Seller (Eds.), *Clinics in developmental medicine, No. 83: Pediatric research: A genetic approach*. Philadelphia: J. B. Lippincott.

Hamilton, S. F. (1991). Vocational training. In R. M. Lerner, A. C. Petersen, and J. Brooks-Gunn (Eds.), *Encyclopedia of adolescence*, Vol. 2. New York: Garland.

Hamstra-Bletz, L., & Blote, A. W. (1990). Development of handwriting in primary school: A longitudinal study. *Perceptual and Motor Skills, 70*, 759–770.

Hardyck, C., & Petrinovich, L. F. (1977). Left-handedness. *Psychological Bulletin, 84*, 385–404.

Haring, N. G., & Bricker, D. (1976). Overview of comprehensive services for the severely/profoundly handicapped. In N. G. Haring and L. J. Brown (Eds.), *Teaching the severely handicapped*. New York: Grune & Stratton.

Harley, J. P., & Matthews, C. G. (1980). Food additives and hyperactivity in children: Experimental investigations. In R. M. Knights and D. J. Bakker (Eds.), *Treatment of hyperactive and learning disordered children*. Baltimore, Md.: University Park Press.

Harrington, D. M., Block, J., & Block, J. H. (1983). Predicting creativity in preadolescence from divergent thinking in early childhood. *Journal of Personality and Social Psychology, 45*, 609–623.

Harris, L. J. (1983). Laterality of function in the infant: Historical and contemporary trends in theory and research. In. G. Young, S. J. Segalowitz, C. M. Corter, and S. E. Trehub (Eds.), *Manual specialization and the developing brain*. New York: Academic Press.

Harrison, M. R., & Adzick, N. S. (1991). The fetus as a patient: Surgical considerations. *Annals of Surgery, 213*, 279–291.

Harter, S. (1983). Developmental perspectives on the self-system. In P. H. Mussen (Ed.), *Handbook of child psychology*, Vol. 4. New York: Wiley.

Hartup, W. (1983). Peer relations. In P. H. Mussen (Ed.), *Handbook of child psychology*, Vol. 4. New York: Wiley.

Hartup, W. W. (1992). Peer relations in early and middle childhood. In V. B. Van Hasselt and M. Hersen (Eds.), *Handbook of social development: A lifespan perspective*. New York: Plenum.

Hartup, W. W. (in press). Friendships and their developmental significance. In H. McGurk (Ed.), *Contemporary issues in childhood social development*. London: Routledge.

Hartup, W. W., & Moore, S. G. (1990). Early peer relations: Developmental significance and prognostic implications. *Early Childhood Research Quarterly, 5*, 1–17.

Haskett, M. E., & Kistner, J. A. (1991). Social interactions and peer perceptions of young physically abused children. *Child Development, 62*, 979–990.

Hayden-Thomson, L., Rubin, K. H., & Hymel, S. (1987). Sex preferences in sociometric choices. *Developmental Psychology, 23*, 558–562.

Hazen, N. L., Lockman, J. J., & Pick, H. L. (1978). The development of children's representations of large-scale environments. *Child Development, 49*, 623–636.

Hecox, K. (1975). Electrophysiological correlates of human auditory development. In L. B. Cohen and P. Salapatek (Eds.), *Infant perception: From sensation to cognition*, Vol. 2. New York: Academic Press.

Helson, R., & Crutchfield, R. S. (1970). Mathematicians: The creative researcher and the average Ph.D. *Journal of Consulting and Clinical Psychology, 34*, 250–257.

Herman, J. F., Cachuela, G. M., & Heins, J. A. (1987). Children's and adults' long-term memory for spatial locations over an extended time period. *Developmental Psychology, 23*, 509–513.

Herman, J. F., Roth, S. F., & Norton, L. M. (1984). Time and distance in spatial cognition development. *International Journal of Behavioral Development, 7*, 35–51.

Hesketh, B., Elmslie, S., & Kaldor, W. (1990). Career compromise: An alternative account to Gottfredson's theory. *Journal of Counseling Psychology, 37*, 49–56.

Hetherington, E. M. (1989). Coping with family transitions: Winners, losers and survivors. *Child Development, 60*, 1–14.

Hetherington, E. M., & Martin, B. (1972). Family interaction and psychopathology in children. In H. C. Quay and J. S. Werry, (Eds.), *Psychopathological disorders of childhood*. New York: Wiley.

Hickey, T. L., & Peduzzi, J. D. (1987). Structure and development of the visual system. In P. Salapatek and L. Cohen (Eds.), *Handbook of infant perception*, Vol. 1. Orlando, Fla.: Academic Press.

Hinz, L. D., & Williamson, D. A. (1987). Bulimia and depression: A review of the affective variant hypothesis. *Psychological Bulletin, 102*, 150–158.

Hirshberg, L. M., & Svejda, M. (1990). When infants look to their parents: I. Infants' social referencing of mothers compared to fathers. *Child Development, 61*, 1175–1186.

Hiscock, C. K., Hiscock, M., Benjamins, D., & Hillman, S. (1989). Motor asymmetries in hemiplegic children: Implications for the normal and pathological development of handedness. *Developmental Neuropsychology, 5*, 169–186.

Ho, H., Glahn, T. J., & Ho, J. (1988). The fragile-X syndrome. *Developmental Medicine and Child Neurology, 30*, 257–261.

Hodapp, R. M. (1990). One road or many? Issues in the similar-sequence hypothesis. In R. M. Hodapp, J. A. Burack, and E. Zigler (Eds.), *Issues in the developmental approach to mental retardation*. Cambridge: Cambridge University Press.

Hodapp, R. M., Burack, J. A., & Zigler, E. (1990). The developmental perspective in the field of mental retardation. In R. M. Hodapp, J. A. Burack, and E. Zigler (Eds.), *Issues in the developmental approach to mental retardation*. Cambridge: Cambridge University Press.

Hodapp, R. M., & Mueller, E. (1982). Early social development. In B. B. Wolman (Ed.), *Handbook of developmental psychology*. Englewood Cliffs, N.J.: Prentice Hall.

Hoff-Ginsberg, E. (1991). Mother-child conversation in different social classes and communicative settings. *Child Development, 62*, 782–796.

Hoff-Ginsberg, E., & Shatz, M. (1982). Linguistic input and the child's acquisition of language. *Psychological Bulletin, 92*, 3–26.

Hoffman, L. W. (1989). Effects of maternal employment in the two-parent family. *American Psychologist, 44*, 283–292.

Hoffman, M. L. (1988). Moral development. In M. H. Bornstein and M. E. Lamb (Eds.), *Developmental psychology: An advanced textbook* (2nd ed.). Hillsdale, N.J.: Lawrence Erlbaum.

Hogan, D. P. (1978). The variable order of events in the life course. *American Sociological Review, 43*, 573–586.

Holland, J. L. (1985). *Making vocational choices: A theory of vocational personalities and work environments* (2nd ed.). Engelwood Cliffs, N.J.: Prentice Hall.

Holliday, M. A. (1986). Body composition and energy needs during growth. In F. Falkner and J. M. Tanner (Eds.), *Human growth: A comprehensive treatise, Vol. 2: Postnatal Growth, Neurobiology* (2nd ed.). New York: Plenum.

Hollinger, C. S., & Jones, R. L. (1970). Community attitudes toward slow learners and mental retardates: What's in a name? *Mental Retardation, 8*, 19–23.

Hollingshead, A. B. (1949). *Elmstown's youth*. New York: Wiley.

Holmes, D. L., Nagy, J. N., Slaymaker, F., Sosnowski, R., Prinz, S. M., & Pasternak, J. F. (1982). Early influences of prematurity, illness, and prolonged hospitalization on infant behavior. *Developmental Psychology, 18,* 744–750.

Honzik, M. P., MacFarland, J. W., & Allen, L. (1948). The stability of mental test performance between 2 and 18 years. *Journal of Experimental Education, 17,* 309–324.

Horn, J. M. (1983). The Texas Adoption Project: Adopted children and their intellectual resemblance to biological and adoptive parents. *Child Development, 54,* 268–275.

Hoving, K. L., Hamm, N., & Galvin, P. (1969). Social influence as a function of stimulus ambiguity at three age levels. *Developmental Psychology, 1,* 631–636.

Howes, C. (1983). Patterns of friendship. *Child Development, 54,* 1041–1053.

Howes, C. (1988). Peer interaction of young children. *Monographs of the Society for Research in Child Development, 53,* serial No. 217.

Howes, C., Unger, O., & Seidner, L. B. (1989). Social pretend play in toddlers: Parallels with social play and with solitary pretend. *Child Development, 60,* 77–84.

Howlin, P., & Yule, W. (1990). Taxonomy of major disorders in childhood. In M. Lewis and S. M. Miller (Eds.), *Handbook of Developmental Psychopathology.* New York: Plenum.

Hronsky, S. L., & Emory, E. K. (1987). Neurobehavioral effects of caffeine on the neonate. *Infant Behavior and Development, 10,* 61–80.

Hudson, J. A. (1990). Constructive processing in children's event memory. *Developmental Psychology, 26,* 180–187.

Hudson, L. M., Forman, E. A., & Brion-Meisels, S. (1982). Role-taking as a predictor of prosocial behavior in cross-age tutors. *Child Development, 53,* 1320–1329.

Huesmann, L. R., & Eron, L. D. (Eds.). (1986). *Television and the aggressive child: A cross-national comparison.* Hillsdale, N.J.: Lawrence Erlbaum.

Huesmann, L. R., Lagarspetz, K., & Eron, L. (1984). Invervening variables in the TV violence-aggression relation: Evidence from two countries. *Developmental Psychology, 20,* 746–775.

Humphreys, L. G., & Davey, T. C. (1988). Continuity in intellectual growth from 12 months to 9 years. *Intelligence, 12,* 183–197.

Huston, A. C. (1983). Sex typing. In P. H. Mussen (Ed.), *Handbook of child psychology,* Vol. 4. New York: Wiley.

Hutchings, D. E., & Fifer, W. P. (1986). Neurobehavioral effects in human and animal offspring following prenatal exposure to methadone. In E. P. Riley and C. V. Vorhees (Eds.), *Handbook of behavioral teratology.* New York: Plenum.

Huttenlocher, J., Haight, W., Bryk, A., Seltzer, M., & Lyons, T. (1991). Early vocabulary growth: Relation to language input and gender. *Developmental Psychology, 27,* 236–248.

Huttenlocher, J., Smiley, P., & Charney, R. (1983). Emergence of action categories in the child: Evidence from verb meanings. *Psychological Review, 90,* 72–93.

Huttenlocher, P. R. (1990). Morphometric study of human cerebral cortex development. *Neuropsychologia, 28,* 517–527.

Hutto, C., Parks, W. P., Lai, S., Mastrucci, M. T., Mitchell, C., Munoz, J., Trapido, E., Master, I. M., & Scott, G. B. (1991). A hospital-based prospective study of perinatal infection with human immunodeficiency virus type 1. *Journal of Pediatrics, 118,* 347–353.

Hyde, J. S. (1981). How large are cognitive gender differences? *American Psychologist, 36,* 892–901.

Hyde, J. S. (1984). How large are gender differences in aggression? A developmental meta-analysis. *Developmental Psychology, 20,* 722–736.

Hyde, J. S., Fennema, E., & Lamon, S. J. (1990). Gender differences in mathematics performance: A meta-analysis. *Psychological Bulletin, 107,* 139–155.

Hyde, J. S., & Linn, M. C. (1988). Gender differences in verbal ability: A meta-analysis. *Psychological Bulletin, 104,* 53–69.

Hymel, S., Rubin, K. H., Rowden, L., & LeMare, L. (1990). Children's peer relationships: Longitudinal prediction of internalizing and externalizing problems from middle to late childhood. *Child Development, 61,* 2004–2021.

Ihinger-Tallman, M., & Pasley, K. (1987). Divorce and remarriage in the American family: A historical review. In R. Pasley and M. Ihinger-Tallman (Eds.), *Remarriage and stepparenting: Current research and theory.* New York: Guilford Press.

Ingram, D., Christensen, L., Veach, S., & Webster, B. (1980). The acquisition of word-initial fricatives and affricates in English by children between 2 and 6 years. In G. Yeni-Komshian, J. F. Kavanagh, and C. A. Ferguson (Eds.), *Child phonology,* Vol. 1. New York: Academic Press.

Imperato-McGinley, J., Peterson, R. E., Gautier, T., &

Sturla, E. (1979). Androgens and the evolution of male-gender identity among male pseudohermaphrodites with 5 betareductase deficiency. *The New England Journal of Medicine, 300*, 1233–1237.

Inhelder, B. (1968). *The diagnosing of reasoning in the mentally retarded.* New York: John Day.

Inhelder, B., & Piaget, J. (1958). *The growth of logical thinking from childhood to adolescence.* New York: Basic Books.

Isabella, R. A., & Belsky, J. (1991). Interactional synchrony and the origins of infant-mother attachment: A replication study. *Child Development, 62*, 373–384.

Israel, A. C., & Shapiro, L. G. (1985). Behavior problems of obese children in a weight reduction program. *Journal of Pediatric Psychology, 10*, 449–460.

Israel, A. C., Stolmaker, L. S., & Prince, B. (1984). The relationship between impulsivity and eating behavior in children. *Child and Family Behavior Therapy, 5*, 71–75.

Jackson, N. E. & Butterfield, E. C. (1986). A conception of giftedness designed to promote research. In R. J. Sternberg and J. E. Davidson (Eds.), *Conceptions of giftedness.* Cambridge: Cambridge University Press.

Jacobs, P. A., Brunton, M., & Melville, M. M. (1965). Aggressive behavior, mental subnormality and the XYY male. *Nature, 208*, 1351–1352.

Jacobson, J. L., Jacobson, S. W., & Humphrey, H. E. B. (1990). Effects of in utero exposure to polychlorinated biphenyls and related contaminants on cognitive functioning in young children. *Journal of Pediatrics, 116*, 38–45.

Jaeger, E., & Weinraub, M. (1990). Early nonmaternal care and infant attachment: In search of process. In K. McCartney (Ed.), *Child care and maternal employment: A social ecology approach.* San Francisco: Jossey-Bass.

Jagiello, G. (1982). Meiosis and the aetiology of chromosomal aberrations in man. In M. Adinolfi, P. Benson, F. Giannelli, and M. Seller (Eds.), *Clinics in developmental medicine, No. 83. Paediatric research: A genetic approach.* Philadelphia: J. B. Lippincott.

Jarvelin, M. R., Moilanen, I., Vikevainen-Tervonen, L., & Huttunen, N. P. (1990). Life changes and protective capacities in enuretic and non-enuretic children. *Journal of Child Psychology and Psychiatry and Allied Disciplines, 31*, 763–774.

Jenkins, S., Owen, C., & Hart, H. (1984). Continuities of common behaviour problems in preschool children. *Journal of Child Psychology and Psychiatry, 25*, 75–98.

Jensen, M. D., Benson, R. C., & Bobak, I. M. (1981). *Maternity care.* St. Louis, Mo.: C. V. Mosby.

Jensh, R. P. (1986). Effects of prenatal irradiation on postnatal psychophysiological development. In E. P. Riley and C. V. Vorhees (Eds.), *Handbook of behavioral teratology.* New York: Plenum.

Jersild, A. T., & Holmes, F. B. (1935). *Children's fears.* New York: Bureau of Publications, Teacher's College, Columbia University.

Johnson, J. S., & Newport, E. L. (1989). Critical period effects in second language learning: The influence of maturational state on the acquisition of English as a second language. *Cognitive Psychology, 21*, 60–99.

Jones, M. C. (1924). A laboratory study of fear: The case of Peter. *Pedagogical Seminary, 31*, 308–315.

Jones, M. C. (1965). Psychological correlates of somatic development. *Child Development, 36*, 899–911.

Jones, M. C., & Mussen, P. H. (1958). Self-conceptions, motivations, and interpersonal attitudes of early and late maturing girls. *Child Development, 29*, 491–501.

Joslyn, W. D. (1973). Androgen-induced social dominance in infant female rhesus monkeys. *Journal of Child Psychology and Psychiatry, 14*, 137–145.

Jusczyk, P. W. (1981). The processing of speech and nonspeech sounds by infants: Some implications. In R. N. Aslin, J. R. Alberts, and M. R. Peterson (Eds.), *Development of perception,* Vol. 1. New York: Academic Press.

Kagan, J. (1989). Commentary. *Human Development, 32*, 172–176.

Kagan, J., & Klein, R. E. (1973). Cross cultural perspectives on early development. *American Psychologist, 28*, 947–961.

Kagan, J., Reznick, J. S., & Snidman, N. (1990). The temperamental qualities of inhibition and lack of inhibition. In M. Lewis and S. M. Miller (Eds.), *Handbook of developmental psychopathology.* New York: Plenum.

Kail, R. (1990). *The development of memory in children* (3rd ed.). New York: W. H. Freeman.

Kail, R. (1991). Development of processing speed in childhood and adolescence. In H. W. Reese (Ed.),

Advances in child development and behavior, Vol. 23. New York: Academic Press.

Kail, R. (1992). Development of memory in children. In L. R. Squire (Ed.), *Encyclopedia of learning and memory.* New York: Macmillan.

Kail, R., & Bisanz, J. (1992). The information-processing perspective on cognitive development in childhood and adolescence. In R. J. Sternberg, and C. A. Berg (Eds.), *Intellectual development.* New York: Cambridge University Press.

Kail, R., & Park, Y. (1990). Impact of practice on speed of mental rotation. *Journal of Experimental Child Psychology, 49,* 227–244.

Kaitz, M., Meschulach-Sarfaty, O., Auerbach, J., & Eidelman, A. (1988). A reexamination of newborns' ability to imitate facial expressions. *Developmental Psychology, 24,* 3–7.

Kaltenbach, K., & Finnegan, L. P. (1987). Perinatal and developmental outcome of infants exposed to methadone in-utero. *Neurotoxicology and Teratology, 9,* 311–313.

Kandel, B. B. (1978). Homophily, selection, and socialization in adolescent friendships. *American Journal of Sociology, 84,* 427–436.

Kanner, L. (1944). Early infantile autism. *Journal of Pediatrics, 25,* 211–217.

Kanner, L. (1949). Problems of nosology and psychodynamics of early infantile autism. *American Journal of Orthopsychiatry, 19,* 416–426.

Kanner, L. (1973). *Childhood psychoses: Initial studies and new insights.* Washington, D.C.: V. H. Winston.

Kaplan, S. L., Breit, M., Gauthier, B., & Busner, J. (1989). A comparison of three nocturnal enuresis treatment methods. *Journal of the American Academy of Child and Adolescent Psychiatry, 28,* 282–286.

Karniol, R. (1989). The role of manual manipulative stages in the infant's acquisition of perceived control over objects. *Developmental Review, 9,* 205–233.

Karp, L. E. (1976). *Genetic engineering: Threat or promise?* Chicago: Nelson-Hall.

Katchadourian, H. (1990). Sexuality. In S. S. Feldman and G. R. Elliott (Eds.), *At the threshold: The developing adolescent.* Cambridge, Mass.: Harvard University Press.

Katz, P. A., & Walsh, P. V. (1991). Modification of children's gender-stereotyped behavior. *Child Development, 62,* 338–351.

Kaufman, A. S. (1979). *Intelligent testing with the WISC-R.* New York: Wiley.

Kaufman, A. S., & Kaufman, N. L. (1983a). *K-ABC administration and scoring manual.* Circle Pines, Minn.: American Guidance Service.

Kaufman, A. S., & Kaufman, N. L. (1983b). *K-ABC interpretive manual.* Circle Pines, Minn.: American Guidance Service.

Kaye, D. B. & Ruskin, E. M. (1990). The development of attentional control mechanisms. In J. T. Enns (Ed.), *The development of attention.* Amsterdam: North Holland.

Kazdin, A. E. (1985). *Treatment of antisocial behavior in children.* Homewood, Ill.: Dorsey.

Kazdin, A. E. (1990). Childhood depression. *Journal of Child Psychology and Psychiatry and Allied Disciplines, 31,* 121–160.

Kazdin, A. E., Sherick, R. B., Esveldt-Dawson, K., & Rancurello, M. D. (1985). Nonverbal behavior and childhood depression. *Journal of the American Academy of Child Psychiatry, 24,* 303–309.

Keane, S. P., Brown, K. P., & Crenshaw, T. M. (1990). Children's intention-cue detection as a function of maternal social behavior: Pathways to social rejection. *Developmental Psychology, 26,* 1004–1009.

Keesey, R. E., & Powley, T. L. (1986). The regulation of body weight. *Annual Review of Psychology, 37,* 109–133.

Kendall, P. C. (1987). Cognitive processes and procedures in behavior therapy. In G. T. Wilson, C. M. Franks, P. C. Kendall, and J. P. Foreyt (Eds.), *Review of behavior therapy: Theory and practice* (11th ed.). New York: Guilford Press.

Kendall, P. C., & Braswell, L. (1982). Cognitive-behavioral self-control therapy for children: A components analysis. *Journal of Consulting and Clinical Psychology, 50,* 672–689.

Kendall, P. C., Lerner, R. M., & Craighead, W. E. (1984). Human development and intervention in childhood psychopathology. *Child Development, 55,* 71–82.

Keogh, J., & Sugden, D. (1985). *Movement skill development.* New York: Macmillan.

Kessen W. (1965). *The child.* New York: Wiley.

Kieselbach, T. (1991). Unemployment. In R. M. Lerner, A. C. Petersen, and J. Brooks-Gunn (Eds.), *Encyclopedia of adolescence,* Vol. 2. New York: Garland.

Kimball, M. M. (1986). Television and sex-role attitudes. In T. M. Williams (Ed.), *The impact of television: A natural experiment in three communities.* New York: Academic Press.

Kimball, M. M. (1989). A new perspective on women's math achievement. *Psychological Bulletin, 105,* 198–214.

King, N. J., Iacuone, R., Schuster, S., Bays, K., Gullone, E., & Ollendick, T. H. (1989). Fears of children and adolescents: A cross-sectional Australian study using the Revised-Fear Survey Schedule for Children. *Journal of Child Psychology and Psychiatry and Allied Disciplines, 30,* 775–784.

Kinsbourne, M. (1989). Mechanisms and development of hemisphere specialization in children. In C. R. Reynolds and E. Fletcher-Janzen (Eds), *Handbook of clinical child neuropsychology.* New York: Plenum.

Kite, M. E., & Deaux, K. (1987). Gender belief systems: homosexuality and the implicit inversion theory. *Psychology of Women Quarterly, 11,* 83–96.

Klahr, D. (1985). Solving problems with ambiguous subgoal ordering: Preschoolers' performance. *Child Development, 56,* 940–952.

Klahr, D. (1989). Information-processing perspectives. In R. Vasta (Ed.), *Annals of child development,* Vol. 6. Greenwich, Conn.: JAI Press.

Klapper, J. T. (1968). The impact of viewing "aggression": Studies and problems of extrapolation. In O. N. Larsen (Ed.), *Violence and the mass media.* New York: Harper & Row.

Klein, D. F., & Gittelman-Klein, R. (1975). Problems in the diagnosis of minimal brain dysfunction and the hyperkinetic syndrome. In R. Gittelman-Klein (Ed.), *Recent advances in child psychopharmacology.* New York: Human Sciences Press.

Klein, N. K., Hack, M., & Breslau, N. (1989). Children who were very low birth weight: Developmental and academic achievement at nine years of age. *Journal of Developmental and Behavioral Pediatrics, 10,* 32–37.

Klesges, R. C., Eck, L. H., Hanson, C. L., Haddock, C. K., & Klesges, L. M. (1990). Effects of obesity, social interactions, and physical environment on physical activity in preschoolers. *Health Psychology, 9,* 435–449.

Knight, B. C., Baker, E. H., & Minder. C. C. (1990). Concurrent validity of the Stanford-Binet: Fourth Edition and Kaufman Assessment Battery for Children with learning disabled students. *Psychology in the Schools, 27,* 116–125.

Knobloch, H., & Pasamanick, B. (1974). *Gesell and Amatruda's developmental diagnosis.* New York: Harper & Row.

Kogan, N. (1983). Stylistic variation in childhood and adolescence: Creativity, metaphor, and cognitive style. In P. H. Mussen (Ed.), *Handbook of child psychology,* Vol. 3. New York: Wiley.

Kohlberg, L. (1966). A cognitive-developmental analysis of children's sex-role concepts and attitudes. In E. E. Maccoby (Ed.), *The development of sex differences.* Stanford, Calif.: Stanford University Press.

Kohlberg, L. (1969). Stage and sequence: The cognitive-developmental approach to socialization. In D. A. Goslin (Ed.), *Handbook of socialization theory and research.* New York: Rand McNally.

Kohlberg, L. (1971). From is to ought: How to commit the naturalistic fallacy and get away with it in the study of moral development. In T. Mischel, (Ed.), *Cognitive development and epistemology.* New York: Academic Press.

Kohlberg, L. (1973). The claim to moral adequacy of a highest stage of moral judgment. *Journal of Philosophy, 70,* 630–646.

Kohlberg, L. (1981). *Essays on moral development, Vol. 1. The philosophy of moral development.* San Francisco: Harper & Row.

Kohlberg, L. (1984). *Essays on moral development, Vol. 2, The psychology of moral development.* San Francisco: Harper & Row.

Kohlberg, L., LaCrosse, J., & Ricks, D. (1972). The predictability of adult mental health from childhood behavior. In B. Wolman (Ed.), *Manual of child psychopathology.* New York: McGraw-Hill.

Kohlberg, L., & Ullian, D. Z. (1974). Stages in the development of psychosexual concepts and attitudes. In R. C. Friedman, R. M. Richart, and R. L. Van Wiele (Eds.), *Sex differences in behavior.* New York: Wiley.

Kolata, G. B. (1978). Behavioral teratology: Birth defects of the mind. *Science, 202,* 732–734.

Kolata, G. (1990). *The baby doctors.* New York: Delacorte Press.

Konner, M. (1977). Evolution of human behavior development. In P. H. Leiderman, R. S. Tulkin, and A. Rosenfield (Eds.), *Culture and infancy: Variations in human experience.* New York: Academic Press.

Konner, M. (1982). Biological aspects of the mother-infant bond. In R. N. Emde and R. J. Harmon (Eds.), *Development of attachment and affiliative systems.* New York: Plenum.

Konner, M. (1991). Universals of behavioral development in relation to brain myelination. In K. R. Gibson and A. C. Peterson (Eds.), *Brain maturation and cognitive development: Comparative and crosscultural perspectives*. New York: Aldine De Gruyter.

Kopp, C. B. (1982). The antecedents of self-regulation. *Developmental Psychology, 18*, 199–214.

Kopp, C. B. (1987). The growth of self-regulation: Caregivers and children. In N. Eisenberg (Ed.), *Contemporary topics in developmental psychology*. New York: Wiley.

Kopp, C. B., & Krakow, J. B. (1983). The developmentalist and the study of biological risk: A view of the past with an eye toward the future. *Child Development, 54*, 1086–1108.

Kopp, C. B., & McCall, R. B. (1982). Predicting later mental performance for normal, at-risk, and handicapped infants. In P. B. Baltes and O. G. Brim (Eds.), *Life-span development and behavior*, Vol. 4. New York: Academic Press.

Kotelchuck, M., Zelazo, P., Kagan, J., & Spelke, E. (1975). Infant reaction to parental separations when left with familiar and unfamiliar adults. *Journal of Genetic Psychology, 126*, 255–262.

Krasinski, K. (1991). Retroviral therapy and clinical trials for HIV-infected children. *Journal of Pediatrics, Supplement, 119*, 563–568.

Kuczaj, S. A. (1981). More on children's failure to relate specific acquisitions. *Journal of Child Language, 8*, 485–487.

Kuhl, P. K., Williams, K. A., Lacerda, F., Stevens, K. N., & Lindblom, B. (1992). Linguistic experience alters phonetic perception in infants by 6 months of age. *Science, 255*, 606–608.

Kupersmidt, J. B., & Coie, J. D. (1990). Preadolescent peer status, aggression, and school adjustment as predictors of externalizing problems in adolescence. *Child Development, 61*, 1350–1362.

Kupietz, S. S. (1990). Sustained attention in normal and in reading-disabled youngsters with and without ADDH. *Journal of Abnormal Child Psychology, 18*, 357–372.

Labouvie, E. W., Bartsch, T. W., Nesselroade, J. R., & Baltes, P. B. (1974). On the internal and external validity of simple longitudinal designs. *Child Development, 45*, 282–290.

Labov, M., & Labov, T. (1978). The phonetics of cat and mama. *Language, 54*, 816–852.

Ladd, G. W. (1990). Having friends, keeping friends, making friends, and being liked by peers in the classroom: Predictors of children's early school adjustment. *Child Development, 61*, 1081–1100.

Ladd, G. W., & Golter, B. S. (1988). Parents' management of preschooler's peer relations: Is it related to children's social competence? *Developmental Psychology, 24*, 109–117.

Ladd, G. W., & Mize, J. A. (1983). A cognitive-social learning model of social-skill training. *Psychological Review, 90*, 127–157.

LaFreniere, P., Strayer, F. F., & Gauthier, R. (1984). The emergence of same-sex affiliative preferences among preschool peers: A developmental/ethnological perspective. *Child Development, 55*, 1958–1965.

La Greca, A. M. (1980). Can children remember to be creative? An interview study of children's thinking processes. *Child Development, 51*, 572–575.

Lamaze, F. (1970). *Painless childbirth*. Chicago: Henry Regnery.

Lamb, M. E. (1986). The changing role of fathers. In M. E. Lamb (Ed.), *The father's role: Applied perspectives*. New York: Wiley.

Lamborn, S. D., Mounts, N. S., Steinberg, L., & Dornbusch, S. M. (1991). Patterns of competence and adjustment among adolescents from authoritative, authoritarian, indulgent, and neglectful families. *Child Development, 62*, 1049–1065.

Landry, S. H., Chapieski, L., Fletcher, J. M., & Denson, S. (1988). Three-year outcomes for low birth weight infants: Differential effects of early medical complications. *Journal of Pediatric Psychology, 13*, 317–327.

Langlois, J. H., Ritter, J. M., Roggman, L. A., & Vaughn, L. S. (1991). Facial diversity and infant preferences for attractive faces. *Developmental Psychology, 27*, 79–84.

Langlois, J. H., Roggman, L. A., & Rieser-Danner, L. A. (1990). Infants' differential social responses to attractive and unattractive faces. *Developmental Psychology, 26*, 153–159.

Langlois, J. H., & Stephan, C. (1977). The effects of physical attractiveness and ethnicity on children's behavioral attributions and peer preferences. *Child Development, 48*, 1694–1698.

Lapouse, R., & Monk, M. (1958). An epidemiologic study of behavior characteristics in children. *American Journal of Public Health, 48*, 1134–1144.

Larson, R. W., Raffaelli, M., Richards, M. H., Ham, M., & Jewell, L. (1990). Ecology of depression in late childhood and early adolescence: A profile of daily states and activities. *Journal of Abnormal Psychology, 99,* 92–102.

Latané, B., & Nida, S. (1981). Ten years of research on group size and helping. *Psychological Bulletin, 89,* 308–324.

Laupa, M., & Turiel, E. (1986). Children's conceptions of adult and peer authority. *Child Development, 57,* 405–412.

Lefkowitz, M., & Tesiny, E. P. (1984). Rejection and depression: Prospective and contemporaneous analyses. *Developmental Psychology, 20,* 776–785.

Legerstee, M. (1991). The role of person and object in eliciting early imitation. *Journal of Experimental Child Psychology, 51,* 423–433.

LeMare, L. J., & Rubin, K. H. (1987). Perspective taking and peer interaction: Structural and developmental analyses. *Child Development, 58,* 306–315.

Lennon, R., Eisenberg, N., & Carroll, J. (1986). The relation between nonverbal indices of empathy and preschoolers' prosocial behavior. *Journal of Applied Developmental Psychology, 7,* 219–224.

Leonard, L. B. (1975). The role of nonlinguistic stimuli and semantic relations in children's acquisition of grammatical utterances. *Journal of Experimental Child Psychology, 19,* 346–367.

Lerner, J. V., & Hess, L. E. (1991). Maternal employment influences on adolescent development. In R. M. Lerner, A. C. Petersen, and J. Brooks-Gunn (Eds.), *Encyclopedia of adolescence.* New York: Garland.

Leslie, A. M. (1992). Pretense, autism, and the theory-of-mind module. *Current Directions in Psychological Science, 1,* 18–21.

Lesser, G., Fifer, G., & Clark, D. H. (1965). Mental abilities of children from different social-class and cultural groups. *Monographs of the Society for Research in Child Development, 30*(4, Whole No. 102).

Lester, B. M. (1975). Cardiac habituation of the orienting response to an auditory signal in infants of varying nutritional status. *Developmental Psychology, 11,* 432–442.

LeVine, R. A. (1974). Parental goals: A cross-cultural view. *Teachers College Record, 76,* 226–239.

LeVine, R. A. (1983). Fertility and child development: An anthropological approach. In E. A. Wagner (Ed.), *Child development and international development: Research-policy interfaces.* San Francisco: Jossey-Bass.

Levitt, E. E. (1957). The results of psychotherapy with children: An evaluation. *Journal of Consulting Psychology, 21,* 189–196.

Levy, G. D. (1989). Developmental and individual differences in preschoolers' recognition memories: The influences of gender schematization and verbal labeling of information. *Sex Roles, 21,* 305–324.

Lewinsohn, P. (1974). A behavioral approach to depression. In R. J. Friedman and M. M. Katz (Eds.), The *psychology of depression: Contemporary theory and research.* Washington, D.C.: V. H. Winston.

Lewis, M., Alessandri, S. M., & Sullivan, M. W. (1990). Violation of expectancy, loss of control, and anger expressions in young infants. *Developmental Psychology, 26,* 745–751.

Lewis, M., & Brooks-Gunn, J. (1979). *Social cognition and the acquisition of self.* New York: Plenum.

Lewis, M., Feiring, C., McGuffog, C., & Jaskir, J. (1984). Predicting psychopathology in six-year-olds from early social relations. *Child Development, 55,* 123–136.

Lewis, M., & Feiring, C. (1989). Infant, mother, and mother-infant interaction behavior and subsequent attachment. *Child Development, 60,* 831–837.

Lieberman, J. N. (1977). *Playfulness: Its relationship to imagination and creativity.* New York: Academic Press.

Liebert, R. M., Sprafkin, J. N., & Poulos, R. W. (1975). Selling co-operation to children. In W. S. Hale (Ed.), *Proceedings of the 20th Annual Conference of the Advertising Research Foundation* (pp. 54–57). New York: Advertising Research Foundation.

Liebert, R. M., & Fischel, J. E. (1990). The elimination disorders: Enuresis and encopresis. In M. Lewis and S. M. Miller (Eds.), *Handbook of developmental psychopathology.* New York: Plenum.

Liebert, R. M., & Sprafkin, J. (1988). *The early window: Effects of TV on children and youth.* New York: Pergamon.

Lin, C. C., & Fu, V. R. (1990). A comparison of child-rearing practices among Chinese, immigrant Chinese, and Caucasian-American parents. *Child Development, 61,* 429–433.

Linn, M. C., & Petersen, A. C. (1985). Emergence and characterization of sex differences in spatial ability: A meta-analysis. *Child Development, 56,* 1479–1498.

Lipsitt, L. P., Engen, T., & Kaye, H. (1963). Developmental changes in the olfactory threshold of the neonate. *Child Development, 34,* 371–376.

Lipsitt, L. P., & Levy, N. (1959). Electrotactual threshold in the neonate. *Child Development, 30,* 547–554.

Little, A. H., Lipsitt, L. P., & Rovee-Collier, C. (1984). Classical conditioning and retention of the infant's eyelid response: Effects of age and interstimulus interval. *Journal of Experimental Child Psychology, 37,* 512–524.

Lockman, J. J., & Pick, H. L. (1984). Problems of scale in spatial development. In C. Sophian (Ed.), *Origins of cognitive skills.* Hillsdale, N.J.: Lawrence Erlbaum.

Lodico, M. G., Ghatala, E. S., Levin, J. R., Pressley, M., & Bell, J. A. (1983). The effects of strategy-monitoring training on children's selection of memory strategies. *Journal of Experimental Child Psychology, 35,* 263–277.

Loeber, R. (1982). The stability of antisocial and delinquent child behavior: A review. *Child Development, 37,* 125–155.

Loeber, R. (1990). Development and risk factors of juvenile antisocial behavior and delinquency. *Clinical Psychology Review, 10,* 1–41.

Loehlin, J. C., & Nichols, R. C. (1976). *Heredity, environment and personality.* Austin, Tex.: University of Texas Press.

Lorber, R., Felton, D. K., & Reid, J. B. (1984). A social learning approach to the reduction of coercive processes in child abusive families: A molecular analysis. *Advances in behavior research and therapy, 6,* 29–45.

Lotter, V. (1974). Social adjustment and placement of autistic children in Middlesex: A follow-up study. *Journal of Autism and Childhood Schizophrenia, 4,* 11–32.

Lovaas, O. I., & Smith, T. (1988). Intensive behavioral treatment for young autistic children. In B. B. Lahey and A. E. Kazdin (Eds.), *Advances in clinical child psychology,* Vol. 2. New York: Plenum.

Lovko, A. M., & Ullman, D. G. (1989). Research on the adjustment of latchkey children: Role of background/demographic and latchkey situation variables. *Journal of Clinical Child Psychology, 18,* 16–24.

Lozoff, B. (1989). Nutrition and behavior. *American Psychologist, 44,* 231–236.

Lucurto, C. (1990). The malleability of IQ as judged from adoption studies. *Intelligence, 14,* 275–292.

Luk, S. (1985). Direct observation studies of hyperactive behaviors. *Journal of the American Academy of Child Psychiatry, 24,* 338–344.

Lytton, H., & Romney, D. M. (1991). Parents' differential socialization of boys and girls: A meta-analysis. *Psychological Bulletin, 109,* 267–296.

Maccoby, E. E. (1988). Gender as a social category. *Developmental Psychology, 24,* 755–765.

Maccoby, E. E. (1990). Gender and relationships: A developmental account. *American Psychologist, 45,* 513–520.

Maccoby, E. E., & Jacklin, C. N. (1974). *The psychology of sex differences.* Stanford, Calif.: Stanford University Press.

Maccoby, E. E., & Jacklin, C. N. (1980). Sex differences in aggression: A rejoinder and reprise. *Child Development, 51,* 964–980.

Maccoby, E. E., & Martin, J. A. (1983). Socialization in the context of the family: Parent-child interaction. In P. H. Mussen (Ed.), *Handbook of child psychology,* Vol. 4. New York: Wiley.

MacFarland, A. (1975). Olfaction in the development of social preferences in the human neonate. In M. A. Hofer (Ed.), *Parent-infant interaction.* Amsterdam: CIBA Foundation Symposium.

Macken, M. A., & Ferguson, C. A. (1983). Cognitive aspects of phonological development: Model, evidence, and issues. In K. E. Nelson (Ed.), *Children's language,* Vol. 4. Hillsdale, N.J.: Lawrence Erlbaum.

MacKinnon, C. E. (1989). An observational investigation of sibling interactions in married and divorced families. *Developmental Psychology, 25,* 36–44.

MacKinnon, D. W. (1968). Selecting students with creative potential. In P. Heist (Ed.), *The creative college student: An unmet challenge.* San Francico: Jossey-Bass.

Madison, L. S., Mosher, G. A., & George, C. H. (1986). Fragile-X syndrome: Diagnosis and research. *Journal of Pediatric Psychology, 11,* 91–102.

Makin, J. W., & Porter, R. H. (1989). Attractiveness of lactating females' breast odors to neonates. *Child Development, 60,* 803–810.

Malina, R. M. (1986). Growth of muscle tissue and muscle mass. In F. Falkner and J. M. Tanner (Eds.), *Human Growth: A Comprehensive Treatise, Vol. 2, Postnatal Growth, Neurobiology* (2nd ed.). New York: Plenum.

Malmquist, C. P. (1977). Childhood depression: A clinical and behavioral perspective. In J. G.

Schulterbrandt and A. Raskin (Eds.), *Depression in childhood: Diagnosis, treatment, and conceptual models*. New York: Raven Press.

Mangelsdorf, S., Gunnar, M., Kestenbaum, R., Lang, S., & Andreas, D. (1990). Infant proneness-to-distress temperament, maternal personality, and mother-infant attachment: Associations and goodness of fit. *Child Development, 61*, 820–831.

Maratsos, M. (1983). Some current issues in the study of the acquisition of grammar. In J. H. Flavell and E. M. Markman (Eds.), *Handbook of child psychology*, Vol. 3. New York: Wiley.

Marcia, J. E. (1980). Identity in adolescence. In J. Adelson (Ed.), *Handbook of adolescent psychology*. New York: Wiley.

Marcia, J. E. (1991). Identity and self-development. In R. M. Lerner, A. C. Petersen, and J. Brooks-Gunn (Eds.), *Encyclopedia of adolescence*, Vol. 1. New York: Garland.

Marini, Z., & Case, R. (1989). Parallels in the development of preschoolers' knowledge about their physical and social worlds. *Merrill-Palmer Quarterly, 35*, 63–87.

Markman, E. M., & Wachtel, G. F. (1988). Children's use of mutual exclusivity to constrain the meanings of words. *Cognitive Psychology, 20*, 121–157.

Markovits, H., & Vachon, R. (1989). Reasoning with contrary-to-fact propositions. *Journal of Experimental Child Psychology, 47*, 398–412.

Marsh, H. W. (1989). Age and sex effects in multiple dimensions of self-concept: Preadolescence to early adulthood. *Journal of Educational Psychology, 81*, 417–430.

Marsh, H. W., & Shavelson, R. (1985). Self-concept: Its multifaceted, hierarchical structure. *Educational Psychologist, 20*, 107–123.

Marshall, P. (1989). Attention deficit disorder and allergy: A neurochemical model of the relation between the illnesses. *Psychological Bulletin, 106*, 434–446.

Marshall, W. A., & Tanner, J. M. (1986). Puberty. In F. Falkner and J. M. Tanner (Eds.), *Human Growth: A Comprehensive Treatise, Vol. 2. Postnatal Growth, Neurobiology* (2nd ed.). New York: Plenum.

Martin, B., & Hoffman, J. A. (1990). Conduct disorders. In M. Lewis and S. M. Miller (Eds.), *Handbook of developmental psychopathology*. New York: Plenum.

Martin, C. L. (1989). Children's use of gender-related information in making social judgments. *Developmental Psychology, 25*, 80–88.

Martin, C. L. (1992). The role of cognition in understanding gender effects. In H. W. Reese (Ed.), *Advances in child development and behavior*, Vol. 23. San Diego, Calif.: Academic Press.

Martin, C. L., & Halverson, C. F., Jr. (1981). A schematic processing model of sex typing and stereotyping in children. *Child Development, 52*, 1119–1134.

Martin, C. L., & Halverson, C. F., Jr. (1983). The effects of sex-typing schemas on young children's memory. *Child Development, 54*, 563–574.

Martin, C. L., & Halverson, C. F. (1987). The roles of cognition in sex roles and sex typing. In D. B. Carter (Ed.), *Current conceptions of sex roles and sex typing: Theory and research*. New York: Praeger.

Martin, C. L., & Little, J. K. (1990). The relation of gender understanding to children's sex-typed preferences and gender stereotypes. *Child Development, 61*, 1427–1439.

Masangkay, Z. S., McCluskey, K. A., McIntyre, C. W., Sims-Knight, J., Vaughn, B. E., & Flavell, J. H. (1974). The early development of inferences about the visual percepts of others. *Child Development, 45*, 357–366.

Mash, E. J., Johnston, C., & Kovitz, K. (1983). A comparison of the mother-child interactions of physically abused and non-abused children during play and task situations. *Journal of Clinical Child Psychology, 12*, 337–346.

Matheny, A. P., Wilson, R. S., & Dolan, A. B. (1976). Relations between twins' similarity of appearance and behavioral similarity: Testing an assumption. *Behavior Genetics, 6*, 343–351.

Mathew, A., & Cook, M. L. (1990). The control of reaching movements by young infants. *Child Development, 61*, 1238–1257.

Maurer, D., & Adams, R. J. (1987). Emergence of the ability to discriminate a blue from gray at one month of age. *Journal of Experimental Child Psychology, 44*, 147–156.

McBride, S. (1990). Maternal moderators of child care: The role of maternal separation anxiety. In K. McCartney (Ed.), *Child care and maternal employment: A social ecology approach*. San Francisco: Jossey-Bass.

McCall, R. B. (1989). Commentary. *Human Development, 32*, 177–186.

McCall, R. B., Applebaum, M. I., & Hogarty, P. S. (1973). Developmental changes in mental performance. *Monographs of the Society for Research in Child Development, 38* (Whole No. 150).

McCall, R. B., Parke, R. D., & Kavanaugh, R. D. (1977). Imitation of live and televised models by children one to three years of age. *Monographs of the Society for Research in Child Development, 42* (Whole No. 173).

McCarthy, D. (1954). Language development in children. In L. Carmichael (Ed.), *Manual of child psychology*. New York: Wiley.

McCartney, K., Harris, M. J., & Bernieri, F. (1990). Growing up and growing apart: A developmental meta-analysis of twin studies. *Psychological Bulletin, 107,* 226–237.

McCartney, W. (1968). *Olfaction and odours.* New York: Springer-Verlag.

McCauley, E., Kay, T., Ito, J., & Treder, R. (1987). The Turner syndrome: Cognitive deficits, affective discrimination, and behavior problems. *Child Development, 58,* 464–473.

McClearn, G. E. (1970). Genetic influences on behavior and development. In P. H. Mussen (Ed.), *Carmichael's manual of child psychology* (3rd. ed.). New York: Wiley.

McClearn, G. E., Plomin, R., Gora-Maslak, G., & Crabbe, J. C. (1991). The gene chase in behavioral science. *Psychological Science, 2,* 222–229.

McCormick, C. M., & Maurer, D. M. (1988). Unimanual hand preferences in 6-month-olds: Consistency and relation to familial-handedness. *Infant Behavior and Development, 11,* 21–29.

McDermott, J. F., & Char, W. F. (1984). Stage-related models of psychotherapy with children. *Journal of the American Academy of Psychiatry, 23,* 537–543.

McGhee, P. E. (1976). Children's appreciation of humor: A test of the cognitive congruency principle. *Child Development, 47,* 420–426.

McGhee, P. E. (1979). *Humor: Its origin and development.* San Francisco: W. H. Freeman.

McGhee, P. E. (1983). Humor development: Toward a lifespan approach. In P. E. McGhee and J. H. Goldstein (Eds.), *Handbook of humor research.* New York: Springer-Verlag.

McGilly, K., & Siegler, R. S. (1990). Conditional reasoning, representation, and level of abstraction. *Developmental Psychology, 26,* 931–941.

McHale, S. M., Bartko, W. T., Crouter, A. C., & Perry-Jenkins, M. (1990). Children's housework and psychosocial functioning: The mediating effects of parents' sex-role behaviors and attitudes. *Child Development, 61,* 1413–1426.

McKusick, V. A. (1990). *Mendelian inheritance in man: Catalogs of autosomal dominant, autosomal recessive, and X-linked phenotypes.* Baltimore, Md.: Johns Hopkins University Press.

McLaren, J., & Bryson, S. E. (1987). Review of recent epidemiological studies of mental retardation: Prevalence, associated disorders, and etiology. *American Journal of Mental Retardation, 92,* 243–254.

McManus, I. C., Sik, G., Cole, D. R., Kloss, J., Mellon, A. F., & Wong, J. (1988). The development of handedness in children. *British Journal of Developmental Psychology, 6,* 257–273.

McNally, S., Eisenberg, N., & Harris, J. D. (1991). Consistency and change in maternal child-rearing practices and values: A longitudinal study. *Child Development, 62,* 190–198.

McNemar, Q. (1942). *The revision of the Stanford-Binet Scale: An analysis of the standardization data.* Boston: Houghton-Mifflin.

Mead, M. (1928). *Coming of age in Samoa.* New York: Morrow.

Meilman, P. W. (1979). Cross-sectional age changes in ego identity status during adolescence. *Developmental Psychology, 15,* 230–231.

Meltzoff, A. N., Kuhl, P. K., & Moore, M. K. (1991). Perception and the control of action in newborns and young infants: Toward a new synthesis. In M. J. Weiss and P. R. Zelazo (Eds.), *Newborn attention: Biological constraints and the influence of experience.* Norwood, N.J.: Albex.

Meltzoff, A. N., & Moore, M. K. (1977). Imitation of facial and manual gestures by human neonates. *Science, 198,* 75–78.

Meltzoff, A. N., & Moore, M. K. (1989). Imitation in newborn infants: Exploring the range of gestures imitated and the underlying mechanisms. *Developmental Psychology, 25,* 954–962.

Mercer, J. R. (1971). Sociocultural factors in labeling mental retardates. *The Peabody Journal of Education, 48,* 188–203.

Merighi, J., Edison, M., & Zigler, E. (1990). The role of motivational factors in the functioning of mentally retarded individuals. In R. M. Hodapp, J. A. Burack, and E. Zigler (Eds.), *Issues in the developmental approach to mental retardation.* Cambridge: Cambridge University Press.

Merriman, W. E., & Bowman, L. L. (1989). The mutual

exclusivity bias in children's word learning. *Monographs of the Society for Research in Child Development*, Serial No. 220.

Mervis, C. B., & Johnson, K. E. (1991). Acquisition of the plural morpheme: A case study. *Developmental Psychology, 27*, 222–235.

Mesibov, G. B., Schroeder, C. S., & Wesson, L. (1977). Parental concerns about their children. *Journal of Pediatric Psychology, 2*, 13–17.

Miller, P. M., Danaher, D. L., & Forbes, D. (1986). Sex-related strategies of coping with interpersonal conflict in children aged five to seven. *Developmental Psychology, 22*, 543–548.

Miller, R. W. (1974). Susceptibility of the fetus and child to chemical pollutants. *Science, 184*, 812–813.

Miller, S. A., & Brownell, C. A. (1975). Peers, persuasion, and Piaget: Dyadic interaction between conservers and nonconservers. *Child Development, 46*, 992–997.

Mills, R. S. L., & Grusec, J. E. (1989). Cognitive, affective, and behavioral consequences of praising altruism. *Merrill-Palmer Quarterly, 35*, 299–326.

Minuchin, P. P., & Shapiro, E. K. (1983). The school as a context for social development. In P. H. Mussen (Ed.), *Handbook of child psychology*, Vol. 4. New York: Wiley.

Mischel, W. (1970) Sex-typing and socialization. In P. H. Mussen (Ed.) *Carmichaels' manual of child psychology*, Vol. 2. New York: Wiley.

Mischel, W. (1979). On the interface of cognition and personality: Beyond the person-situation debate. *American Psychologist, 34*, 740–754.

Mischel, W., & Ebbesen, E. (1970). Attention in delay of gratification. *Journal of Personality and Social Psychology, 16*, 329–337.

Mischel, W., Shoda, Y., & Rodriguez, M. L. (1989). Delay of gratification in children. *Science, 244*, 933–938.

Mize, J., & Ladd, G. W. (1990). A cognitive social-learning approach to social skill training with low-status preschool children. *Developmental Psychology, 26*, 388–397.

Moffit, T. E., Caspi, A., Belsky, J., & Silva, P. A. (1992). Childhood experience and the onset of menarche: A test of a sociobiological model. *Child Development, 63*, 47–58.

Molfese, D. L., & Burger-Judisch, L. M. (1991). Dynamic temporal-spatial allocation of resources in the human brain: An alternative to the static view of hemisphere differences. In F. L. Ketterle (Ed.),

Cerebral Laterality: Theory and Research. The Toledo Symposium. Hillsdale, N.J.: Lawrence Erlbaum.

Money, J., & Ehrhardt, A. (1972). *Man and woman; boy and girl.* Baltimore, Md.: Johns Hopkins University Press.

Money, J., & Matthews, D. (1982). Prenatal exposure to virilizing progestins: An adult follow-up study of twelve women. *Archives of Sexual Behavior, 11*, 73–83.

Money, J., & Nurcombe, B. (1974). Ability tests and cultural heritage: The Draw-a-Person and Bender tests in aboriginal Australia. *Journal of Learning Disabilities, 7*, 297–303.

Montgomery, J. (1979, March 15). Low pay, bossy bosses kill kids' enthusiasm for food-service jobs. *Wall Street Journal*, p. 1 ff.

Montie, J. E., & Fagan, J. F. (1988). Racial differences in IQ: Item analyses of the Stanford-Binet at 3 years. *Intelligence, 12*, 315–332.

Moore, B. S., Underwood, B., & Rosenhan, D. L. (1973). Affect and altruism. *Developmental Psychology, 8*, 99–104.

Moore, M. L. (1983). *Realities in childbearing.* Philadelphia: W. B. Saunders.

Moore, S., & Rosenthal, D. A. (1991). Adolescent invulnerability and perceptions of AIDS risk. *Journal of Adolescent Research, 6*, 164–180.

Morgan, B., & Gibson, K. R. (1991). Nutritional and environmental interactions in brain development. In K. R. Gibson and A. C. Peterson (Eds.), *Brain maturation and cognitive development: Comparative and crosscultural perspectives.* New York: Aldine De Gruyter.

Morison, P., & Masten, A. S. (1991). Peer reputation in middle childhood as a predictor of adaptation in adolescence: A seven-year follow-up. *Child Development, 62*, 991–1007.

Morrongiello, B. A. (1988). Infants' localization of sounds along the horizontal axis: Estimates of minimum audible angle. *Developmental Psychology, 24*, 8–13.

Morrongiello, B. A., Fenwick, K. D., & Chance, G. (1990). Sound localization acuity in very young infants: An observer-based testing procedure. *Developmental Psychology, 26*, 75–84.

Morrongiello, B. A., & Trehub, S. E. (1987). Age related changes in auditory temporal perception. *Journal of Experimental Child Psychology, 44*, 413–426.

Mortimer, J. T. (1991). Employment. In R. M. Lerner,

A. C. Petersen, and J. Brooks-Gunn (Eds.), *Encyclopedia of adolescence*, Vol. 1. New York: Garland.

Mowrer, O. H., & Mowrer, W. M. (1938). Enuresis: A method for its study and treatment. *American Journal of Orthopsychiatry, 8*, 436–447.

Mundy, P., & Kasari, C. (1990). The similar-structure hypothesis and differential rate of development in mental retardation. In R. M. Hodapp, J. A. Burack, and E. Zigler (Eds.), *Issues in the developmental approach to mental retardation*. Cambridge: Cambridge University Press.

Muuss, R. E. (1972). Adolescent development and the secular trend. In D. Rogers (Ed.), *Issues in adolescent development*. New York: Appleton-Century-Crofts.

Naeye, R. L. (1990). Maternal body weight and pregnancy outcome. *American Journal of Clinical Nutrition, 52*, 273–279.

Naglieri, J. A., & Jensen, A. R. (1987). Comparison of Black-White differences on the WISC-R and the K-ABC: Spearman's hypothesis. *Intelligence, 11*, 21–43.

Nagoshi, C. T., & Johnson, R. C. (1987). Cognitive abilities profiles of Caucasian vs. Japanese subjects in the Hawaii Family Study of Cognition. *Personality and Individual Differences, 8*, 581–583.

National Institutes of Health Consensus Development Panel on the Health Implications of Obesity. (1985). Health implications of obesity: National Institutes of Health consensus development conference statement. *Annals of Internal Medicine, 103*, 1073–1077.

National Research Council. (1987). *Risking the future: Adolescent sexuality, pregnancy, and childbearing*, Vol. 1. Washington, D.C: National Academy Press.

Nelson K. (1973). Structure and strategy in learning to talk. *Monograph of the Society for Research in Child Development, 38*, No. 149.

Nelson, K. (1974). Concept, word, and sentence: Interrelations in acquisition and development. *Psychological Review, 81*, 267–285.

Nelson, K. (1975). The nominal shift in semantic-syntactic development. *Cognitive Psychology, 7*, 461–479.

Nelson, K. E. (1982). Experimental gambits in the service of language acquisition: From the Fiffin Project to Operation Input Swap. In S. A. Kuczaj (Ed.), *Language development*, Vol. 1. Hillsdale, N.J.: Lawrence Erlbaum.

Newcombe, N., & Bandura, M. (1983). Effect of age at puberty on spatial ability in girls: A question of mechanism. *Developmental Psychology, 19*, 215–224.

Newcombe, N., & Dubas, J. S. (1987). Individual differences in cognitive ability: Are they related to timing of puberty? In R. M. Lerner and T. T. Foch (Eds.), *Biological-psychosocial interactions in early adolescence: A life-span perspective*. Hillsdale, N.J.: Lawrence Erlbaum.

Newcombe, N., Dubas, J. S., & Baenninger, M. (1989). Associations of timing of puberty, spatial ability, and lateralization in adult women. *Child Development, 60*, 246–254.

Newcombe, N., & Zaslow, M. (1981). Do $2\frac{1}{2}$-year-olds hint? A study of directive forms in the speech of $2\frac{1}{2}$-year-old children to adults. *Discourse Processes, 4*, 239–252.

Newell, K. M., & Kennedy, J. A. (1978). Knowledge of results and children's motor learning. *Developmental Psychology, 14*, 531–536.

Newport, E. L., Gleitman, L. R., & Gleitman, H. (1977). Mother, I'd rather do it myself: Some effects and non-effects of maternal speech style. In C. E. Snow and C. A. Ferguson (Eds.), *Talking to children: Language input and acquisition*. Cambridge: Cambridge University Press.

O'Brien, M., & Huston, A. C. (1985). Development of sex-typed play behaviors in toddlers. *Developmental Psychology, 21*, 866–871.

Ollendick, T. H., & Hersen, M. (1983). A historical overview of child psychopathology. In T. H. Ollendick and M. Hersen (Eds.), *Handbook of child psychopathology*. New York: Plenum.

Oller, D. K. (1986). Metaphonology and infant vocalizations. In B. Lindblom and R. Zetterstrom (Eds.), *Precursors of early speech*. Basingstoke, Hampshire: Macmillan.

Oller, D. K., & Eilers, R. E. (1988). The role of audition in infant babbling. *Child Development, 59*, 441–449.

Orlick, T., Zhou, Q. Y., & Partington, J. (1990). Cooperation and conflict within Chinese and Canadian kindergarten settings. *Canadian Journal of Behavioural Science, 22*, 20–25.

Ornitz, E. M. (1978). Neurophysiologic studies. In M. Rutter and E. Schopler (Eds.), *Autism: A reappraisal of concepts and treatment*. New York: Plenum.

Ornstein, P. A., Naus, M. J., & Liberty, C. (1975). Rehearsal and organizational processes in children's memory. *Child Development, 46,* 818–830.

Osofsky, J. D., & Osofsky, H. J. (1984). Psychological and developmental perspectives on expectant and new parenthood. In R. D. Parke (Ed.), *Review of child development research,* Vol. 7. Chicago: University of Chicago Press.

Otto, L. B. (1979). Antecedents and consequences of marital timing. In W. R. Bun, R. Hill, F. I. Nye, and I. L. Reiss (Eds.), *Contemporary theories about the family,* Vol. 1. New York: The Free Press.

Oviatt, S. L. (1980). The emerging ability to comprehend language: An experimental approach. *Child Development, 51,* 97–106.

Oviatt, S. L. (1982). Inferring what words mean: Early development in infants' comprehension of common object names. *Child Development, 53,* 274–277.

Paikoff, R. L., Collins, W. A., & Laursen, B. (1988). Perceptions of efficacy and legitimacy of parental influence techniques by children and early adolescents. *Journal of Early Adolescence, 8,* 37–52.

Palme, O. (1972). The emancipation of man. In M. S. Mednick and S. S. Tangri (Eds.), New perspectives on women. *Journal of Social Issues, 28,* 237–246.

Park, K. A., & Waters, E. (1989). Security of attachment and preschool friendships. *Child Development, 60,* 1076–1081.

Parke, R. D., & Bahvnagri, N. P. (1989). Parents as managers of children's peer relationships. In D. Belle (Ed.), *Children's social networks and social supports.* New York: Wiley.

Parke, R. D., MacDonald, K. B., Beitel, A., & Bahavnagri, N. (1988). The role of the family in the development of peer relationships. In R. Dev. Peters and R. J. MacMahon (Eds.), *Social learning and systems approaches to marriage and the family.* New York: Brunner/Mazel.

Parke, R. D., & Slaby, R. G. (1983). The development of aggression. In P. H. Mussen (Ed.), *Handbook of child psychology,* Vol. 4. New York: Wiley.

Parke, R. D., & Suomi, S. J. (1981). Adult male-infant relationships: Human and nonhuman primate evidence. In K. Immelmann, G. W. Barlow, L. Petrinovich, and M. Main (Eds.), *Behavioral Development: The Bielefeld Interdisciplinary Project.* Cambridge: Cambridge University Press.

Parker, J. G., & Asher, S. R. (1987). Peer relations and later personal adjustment: Are low-accepted children at risk? *Psychological Bulletin, 102,* 357–389.

Parker, L., & Whitehead, W. (1982). Treatment of urinary and fecal incontinence in children. In D. C. Russo and J. W. Varni (Eds.), *Behavioral pediatrics.* New York: Plenum.

Parten, M. (1932). Social participation among preschool children. *Journal of Abnormal and Social Psychology, 27,* 243–269.

Patterson, G. R. (1982). *A social learning approach to family intervention, Vol. 3: Coercive family processes.* Eugene, Ore.: Castalia.

Patterson, G. R. (1984). Microsocial process: A view from the boundary. In J. C. Masters and K. Yarkin-Levin (Eds.), *Boundary areas in social and developmental psychology.* New York: Academic Press.

Pearce, J. M., & Hall, G. (1980). A model for Pavlovian learning: Variations in the effectiveness of conditioned but not of unconditioned stimuli. *Psychological Review, 87,* 532–552.

Pearson, J. L., Hunter, A. G., Ensminger, M. E., & Kellam, S. G. (1990). Black grandmothers in multigenerational households: Diversity in family structure and parenting involvement in the Woodlawn community. *Child Development, 61,* 434–442.

Pederson, D. R., Moran, G., Sitko, C., Campbell, K., Ghesquire, K., & Acton, H. (1990). Maternal sensitivity and the security of infant-mother attachment: A Q-sort study. *Child Development, 61,* 1974–1983.

Pellegrini, A. D. (1989). Categorizing children's rough-and-tumble play. *Play and Culture, 2,* 48–51.

Pellegrino, J. W., Hunt, E. B., & Yee, P. (1989). Assessment and modeling of information coordination abilities. In R. Kanfer, P. L. Ackerman, and R. Cudeck (Eds.), *Abilities, motivation, and methodology: The Minnesota symposium on learning and individual differences.* Hillsdale, N.J.: Lawrence Erlbaum.

Peoples-Sheps, M. D., Siegel, E., Suchindran, C. M., Origasa, H., Ware, A., & Barakat, A. (1991). Characteristics of maternal employment during pregnancy: Effects on low birth weight. *American Journal of Public Health, 81,* 1007–1012.

Pepler, D. J., & Ross, H. J. (1981). The effects of play on convergent and divergent problem solving. *Child Development, 52,* 1202–1210.

Peterson, G. W., Rollins, B. C., Thomas, D. L., & Heaps, L. K. (1982). Social placement of adolescents:

Sex-role influences on family decisions regarding the careers of youth. *Journal of Marriage and the Family, 44,* 647–658.

Peterson, L. (1983). Role of donor competence, donor age, and peer presence on helping in an emergency. *Developmental Psychology, 19,* 873–880.

Peterson, L. (1989). Latchkey children's preparation for self-care: Overestimated, under rehearsed and unsafe. *Journal of Clinical Child Psychology, 18,* 36–43.

Petitto, L. A., & Marentette, P. F. (1991). Babbling in the manual mode: Evidence for the ontogeny of language. *Science, 251,* 1493–1496.

Pettit, G. S., Dodge, K. A., & Brown, M. M. (1988). Early family experience, social problem solving patterns, and children's social competence. *Child Development, 59,* 107–120.

Phinney, J. (1989). Stage of ethnic identity in minority group adolescents. *Journal of Early Adolescence, 9,* 34–49.

Phinney, J. S. (1990). Ethnic identity in adolescents and adults. *Psychological Bulletin, 108,* 499–514.

Phinney, V. G., Jensen, L. C., Olsen, J. A., & Cundick, B. (1990). The relationship between early development and psychosexual behaviors in adolescent females. *Adolescence, 25,* 321–332.

Piaget, J. (1929). *The child's conception of the world.* New York: Harcourt, Brace.

Piaget, J. (1932). *The moral judgments of the child.* New York: The Free Press. (reprinted 1965)

Piaget, J. (1952). *The origins of intelligence in children.* New York: International Universities Press.

Piaget, J., & Inhelder, B. (1956). *The child's conception of space.* Boston: Routledge & Kegan Paul.

Piaget, J., & Inhelder, B. (1967). *The child's conception of space.* New York: W. W. Norton.

Piaget, J., & Inhelder, B. (1969). *The psychology of the child.* New York: Basic Books.

Pitkin R. M. (1991). Screening and detection of congenital malformation. *American Journal of Obstetrics and Gynecology, 164,* 1045–1048.

Plomin, R. (1984). Childhood temperament. In B. Lahey and A. Kazdin (Eds.), *Advances in clinical child psychology,* Vol. 6. New York: Plenum.

Plomin, R. (1990). *Nature and nurture.* Pacific Grove, Calif.: Brooks/Cole.

Plomin, R., DeFries, J. C., & McClearn, G. E. (1990). *Behavioral genetics: A primer* (2nd ed.). New York: W. H. Freeman.

Porter, F. L., Porges, S. W., & Marshall, R. E. (1988). Newborn pain cries and vagal tone: Parallel changes in response to circumcision. *Child Development, 59,* 495–505.

Poulson, C. L., Kymissis, E., Reeve, K. F., Andreatos, M., & Reeve, L. (1991). Generalized vocal imitation in infants. *Journal of Experimental Child Psychology, 51,* 267–279.

Pratt, M. W., McLaren, J., & Wickens, G. (1984). Rules as tools: Effective generalization of verbal self-regulative communication training by first graders. *Developmental Psychology, 20,* 893–902.

Pratt, M. W., Scribner, S., & Cole, M. (1977). Children as teachers: Developmental studies of instructional communication. *Child Development, 48,* 1475–1481.

Premack, D. (1976). *Intelligence in ape and man.* Hillsdale, N.J.: Lawrence Erlbaum.

Price, W. H., & Whatmore, P. B. (1967). Criminal behavior and the XYY male. *Nature, 213,* 815.

Puig-Antich, J. (1982). Major depression and conduct disorder in pre-puberty. *Journal of the American Academy of Child Psychiatry, 21,* 118–128.

Quay, H. C. (1986). Conduct disorders. In H. C. Quay and J. S. Werry (Eds.), *Psychopathological disorders of childhood* (3rd ed.). New York: John Wiley.

Radziszewska, B., & Rogoff, B. (1991). Children's guided participation in planning imaginary errands with skilled adult or peer partners. *Developmental Psychology, 27,* 381–389.

Ramey, C. T., & Ramey, S. L. (1990). Intensive educational intervention for children of poverty. *Intelligence, 14,* 1–9.

Ratcliffe, S. G., & Field, M. A. S. (1982). Emotional disorder in XYY children: Four case reports. *Journal of Child Psychology and Psychiatry, 23,* 401–406.

Reisman, J. E. (1987). Touch, motion, and proprioception. In P. Salapatek and L. Cohen (Eds.), *Handbook of infant perception,* Vol. 1. Orlando, Fla.: Academic Press.

Reissland, N. (1988). Neonatal imitation in the first hour of life: Observations in rural Nepal. *Developmental Psychology, 24,* 464–469.

Reubens, B., Harrison, J., & Kupp, K. (1981). *The youth labor force, 1945–1995: A cross-national analysis.* Totowa, N.J.: Allanheld, Osmun.

Rice, M. L., Huston, A. C., Truglio, R., & Wright, J. (1990). Words from "Sesame Street": Learning vocabulary while viewing. *Developmental Psychology, 26,* 421–428.

Richardson, G. A., Day, N. L., & Taylor, P. M. (1989). The effect of prenatal alcohol, marijuana, and tobacco exposure on neonatal behavior. *Infant Behavior and Development, 12,* 199–209.

Rie, H. E. (1971). Historical perspectives of concepts of child psychopathology. In H. E. Rie (Ed.), *Perspectives in child psychopathology.* New York: Aldine-Atherton.

Rieser, J., Yonas, A., & Wikner, K. (1976). Radial localization of odors by human newborns. *Child Development, 47,* 856–859.

Robinson, B. E., Rowland, B. H., & Coleman, M. (1986). *Latchkey kids: Unlocking doors for children and their families.* Lexington, Mass.: Lexington Books, Heath.

Robinson, M. N., & Robinson H. B. (1976). *The mentally retarded child.* New York: McGraw-Hill.

Rochat, P. (1989). The discriminating nature of infants' exploratory actions. *Developmental Psychology, 25,* 871–884.

Roche, A. F. (1986). Bone growth and maturation. In F. Falkner and J. M. Tanner (Eds.), *Human growth: A comprehensive treatise, Vol. 2: Postnatal Growth, Neurobiology* (2nd ed.). New York: Plenum.

Rodning, C., Beckwith, L., & Howard, J. (1989). Characteristics of attachment organization and play organization in prenatally drug-exposed toddlers. *Development and Psychopathology, 1,* 277–289.

Roe, K. V., McClure, A., & Roe, A. (1983). Infant Gesell scores vs. cognitive skills at age 12 years. *Journal of Genetic Psychology, 142,* 143–147.

Rogoff, B., Ellis, S., & Gardner, W. (1984). Adjustment of adult-child instruction according to child's age and task. *Developmental Psychology, 20,* 193–199.

Rollins, B. C., & Feldman, H. (1970). Marital satisfaction over the family life cycle. *Journal of Marriage and the Family, 32,* 20–28.

Rose, S. A. (1983). Differential rates of visual information processing in full-term and preterm infants. *Child Development, 54,* 1189–1198.

Rose, S. A., Feldman, J. F., Wallace, I. F., & Cohen, P. (1991). Language: A partial link between infant attention and later intelligence. *Developmental Psychology, 27,* 298–805.

Rose, S. A., & Orlian, E. K. (1991). Asymmetries in infant cross-modal transfer. *Child Development, 62,* 706–718.

Rose, S. A., & Ruff, H. A. (1987). Cross-modal abilities in human infants. In J. D. Osofsky (Ed.), *Handbook of infant development* (2nd ed.). New York: Wiley.

Rosenstein, D., & Oster, H. (1988). Differential facial responses to four basic tastes in newborns. *Child Development, 59,* 1555–1568.

Roshon, M. S., & Hagen, R. L. (1989). Sugar consumption, locomotion, task orientation, and learning in preschool children. *Journal of Abnormal Child Psychology, 17,* 349–357.

Rotenberg, K. J., & Mayer, E. V. (1990). Delay of gratification in native and white children: A cross-cultural comparison. *International Journal of Behavioral Development, 13,* 23–30.

Rotheram-Borus, M. J., & Koopman, C. (1991). AIDS and adolescents. In R. M. Lerner, A. C. Petersen, and J. Brooks-Gunn (Eds.), *Encyclopedia of adolescence,* Vol. 1. New York: Garland.

Routh, D. K. (1980). Developmental and social aspects of hyperactivity. In C. K. Whalen and B. Henker (Eds.), *Hyperactive children.* New York: Academic Press.

Routh, D. K., Schroeder, C. S., & Koocher, G. P. (1983). Psychology and primary health care for children. *American Psychologist, 38,* 95–98.

Rovee, C. K., Cohen, R. Y., & Shlapack, W. (1975). Life-span stability in olfactory sensitivity. *Developmental Psychology, 11,* 311–318.

Rovee-Collier, C. (1987). Learning and memory in infancy. In J. D. Osofsky (Ed.), *Handbook of infant development* (2nd ed.). New York: Wiley.

Rowell, T. E. (1966). Hierarchy in the organization of a captive baboon group. *Animal Behavior, 14,* 430–433.

Ruble, D. N. (1988). Sex-role development. In M. H. Bornstein and M. E. Lamb (Eds.), *Developmental psychology: An advanced textbook* (2nd. ed.). Hillsdale, N.J.: Lawrence Erlbaum.

Ruble, T. L. (1983). Sex stereotypes: Issues of changes in the 1970s. *Sex Roles, 9,* 397–402.

Rubin, K. H. (1982). Nonsocial play in preschoolers: Necessarily evil? *Child Development, 53,* 651–657.

Rubin, Z. (1980). *Children's friendships.* Cambridge, Mass.: Harvard University Press.

Rugh, R., & Shettles, L. B. (1971). *From conception to birth.* New York: Harper & Row.

Russell, A. T., Bott, L., & Sammons, C. (1989). The phenomenology of schizophrenia occurring in childhood. *Journal of the American Academy of Child and Adolescent Psychiatry, 28,* 399–407.

Russell, G. F. M. (1985). Anorexia and bulimia nervosa. In M. Rutter and L. Hersov (Eds.), *Child and adolescent psychiatry: Modern approaches.* Oxford: Blackwell Scientific.

Rutter, M. (1978). Diagnosis and definition. In M. Rutter and E. Schopler (Eds.), *Autism: A reappraisal of concepts and treatment.* New York: Plenum.

Rutter, M. (1985). Infantile autism and other pervasive developmental disorders. In M. Rutter and L. Hersov (Eds.), *Child and adolescent psychiatry.* Boston: Blackwell Scientific.

Rutter, M., & Garmezy, N. (1983). Developmental psychopathology. In P. H. Mussen (Ed.), *Handbook of child psychology*, Vol. 4. New York: Wiley.

Sachs, J. S., Brown, R., & Salerno, R. A. (1976). Adults' speech to children. In W. van Raffler Engel and Y. LeBrun (Eds.), *Baby talk and infant speech (Neurolinguistics 5).* Amsterdam: Swets & Zeitlinger.

Safer, D. J., & Allen, R. P. (1976). *Hyperactive children. Diagnosis and management.* Baltimore, Md.: University Park Press.

Saigal, S., Szatmari, P., Rosenbaum, P., Campbell, D., & King, S. (1991). Cognitive abilities and school performance of extremely low birth weight children and matched term control children at age 8 years: A regional study. *Journal of Pediatrics, 118,* 751–760.

Salapatek, P. (1975). Pattern perception in early infancy. In L. B. Cohen and P. Salapatek (Eds.). *Infant perception: From sensation to cognition,* Vol. 1. New York: Academic Press.

Sameroff, A. J., & Chandler, M. J. (1975). Reproductive risk and the continuum of caretaking casualty. In F. D. Horowitz (Ed.), *Review of child development research,* Vol. 4. Chicago: University of Chicago Press.

Sanders-Phillips, K., Strauss, M. E., & Gutberlet, R. L. (1988). The effect of obstetric medication on newborn infant feeding behavior. *Infant Behavior and Development, 11,* 251–263.

Sanjose, S., Roman, E., & Beral, V. (1991). Low birthweight and preterm delivery, Scotland, 1981–84: Effect of parents' occupation. *The Lancet, 338,* 428–431.

Santrock, J. W., & Warshak, R. A. (1986). Development of father custody, relationships, and legal/clinical considerations in father-custody families. In M. E. Lamb (Ed.), *The father's role: Applied perspectives.* New York: Wiley.

Sarnat, H. B. (1978). Olfactory reflexes in the newborn infant. *Journal of Pediatrics, 92,* 624–626.

Saudino, K. J., & Eaton, W. O. (1991). Infant temperament and genetics: An objective twin study of motor activity level. *Child Development, 62,* 1167–1174.

Savin-Williams, R. C., & Berndt, T. J. (1990). Friendship and peer relations. In S. S. Feldman and G. R. Elliott (Eds.), *At the threshold: The developing adolescent.* Cambridge, Mass.: Harvard University Press.

Saxby, L., & Bryden, M. P. (1984). Left-ear superiority in children for processing auditory emotional material. *Developmental Psychology, 20,* 72–80.

Saxe, G. B. (1988). The mathematics of child street vendors. *Child Development, 59,* 1415–1425.

Saxe, G. B., Guberman, S. R., & Gearhart, M. (1987). Social processes in early number development. *Monographs of the Society for Research in Child Development, 52,* Serial No. 216.

Scarr, S. (1992). Developmental theories for the 1990s: Development and individual differences. *Child Development, 63,* 1–19.

Scarr, S., & Kidd, K. K. (1983). Developmental behavior genetics. In M. M. Haith and J. J. Campos (Eds.), *Handbook of child psychology,* Vol 2. New York: Wiley.

Scarr, S., & McCartney, K. (1983). How people make their own environments: A theory of genotype environment effects. *Child Development, 54,* 424–435.

Scarr, S., & Weinberg, R. A. (1983). The Minnesota Adoption Studies: Genetic differences and malleability. *Child Development, 54,* 260–267.

Scarr-Salapatek, S. (1975). Genetics and the development of intelligence. In F. D. Horowitz (Ed.), *Review of child development research,* Vol. 4. Chicago: University of Chicago Press.

Schachar, R., & Logan, G. (1990). Are hyperactive children deficient in attentional capacity? *Journal of Abnormal Child Psychology, 18,* 493–513.

Schaffer, H. R., & Emerson, P. E. (1964). The development of social attachments in infancy. *Monographs of the Society for Research in Child Development, 29,* No. 3.

Scheinfeld, A. (1973). *Twins and supertwins.* Baltimore, Md.: Penguin.

Scher, M. S., Richardson, G. A., Coble, P. A., Day, N. L., & Stoffer, D. S. (1988). The effect of prenatal alcohol and marijuana exposure: disturbances in neonatal sleep cycling and arousal. *Journal of Pediatric Research, 24,* 101–105.

Schmidt, C. R., & Paris, S. G. (1984). The development of verbal communication skills in children. In H. W. Reese (Ed.), *Advances in child development and behavior*, Vol. 18. New York: Academic Press.

Schmitt, B., Seeger, J., Kreuz, W., Enenkel, S., & Jacobi, G. (1991). Central nervous system involvement of children with HIV infection. *Developmental Medicine and Child Neurology, 33,* 535–540.

Schopler, E. (1987). Specific and nonspecific factors in the effectiveness of a treatment system. *American Psychologist, 42,* 376–383.

Schopler, E., Mesibov, G., & Baker, A. (1982). Evaluation of treatment for autistic children and their families. *Journal of the American Academy of Child Psychiatry, 21,* 262–267.

Schrader, D. (Ed.), (1990). *The legacy of Lawrence Kohlberg.* San Francisco: Jossey-Bass.

Schwartz, R. G., & Leonard, L. B. (1982). Do children pick and choose? An examination of phonological selection and avoidance in early lexical acquisition. *Journal of Child Language, 9,* 319–336.

Sears, R. R. (1975). Your ancients revisited: A history of child development. In E. M. Hetherington (Ed.), *Review of child development research*, Vol. 5. Chicago: University of Chicago Press.

Sears, R. R., Maccoby, E. E., & Levin, H. (1957). *Patterns of child rearing.* Evanston, Ill.: Row Peterson.

Seashore, H., Wesman, A., & Doppelt, J. (1950). The standardization of the Wechsler Intelligence Scale for Children. *Journal of Consulting Psychology, 14,* 99–110.

Seligman, M. E. P., & Peterson, C. A. (1986). A learned helplessness perspective on childhood depression: Theory and research. In M. Rutter, C. E. Izard, and P. Read (Eds.), *Depression in childhood: Developmental perspectives.* New York: Guilford Press.

Selman, R. L. (1981). The child as a friendship philosopher: A case study in the growth of interpersonal understanding. In S. R. Asher and J. M. Gottman (Eds.), *The development of children's friendships.* Cambridge: Cambridge University Press.

Selman, R. L. (1986). The development of social-cognitive understanding: A guide to educational and clinical practice. In T. Lickona (Ed.), *Moral development and behavior: Theory, research, and social issues.* New York: Holt, Rinehart & Winston.

Serbin, L., & O'Leary, K. D. (1975, December). How nursery schools teach girls to shut up. *Psychology Today,* 57–58.

Shaffer, D. R. (1988). *Social and personality development.* Pacific Grove, Calif.: Brooks/Cole.

Shatz, M., & Gelman, R. (1977). Beyond syntax: The influence of conversational constraints on speech modifications. In C. E. Snow and C. A. Ferguson (Eds.), *Talking to children: Language input and acquisition.* Cambridge: Cambridge University Press.

Shaw, G. M., Croen, L. A., & Curry, C. J. (1991). Isolated oral cleft malformations: Associations with maternal and infant characteristics in a California population. *Teratology, 43,* 225–228.

Shepherd, M., Oppenheim. A. N., & Mitchell, S. (1966). Childhood behavior disorders and the child guidance clinic: An epidemiological study. *Journal of Psychology and Psychiatry, 7,* 39–52.

Shepp, B. E., Barrett, S. E., & Kolbet, L. L. (1987). The development of selective attention: Holistic perception versus resource allocation. *Journal of Experimental Child Psychology, 43,* 159–180.

Sheridan, M. K., Radlinski, S. S., & Kennedy, M. D. (1990). Developmental outcome in 49, XXXXY Klinefelter syndrome. *Developmental Medicine and Child Neurology, 32,* 528–546.

Sherif, M., Harvey, O. J., White, B. J., Hood, W. R., & Sherif, C. W. (1961). *Intergroup conflict and cooperation. The robbers cave experiment.* Norman, Okla.: University Book Exchange.

Sherman, J. A., & Bushell, D. (1975). Behavior modification as an educational technique. In F. D. Horowitz (Ed.), *Review of child development research*, Vol. 4. Chicago: University of Chicago Press.

Shirley, M. M. (1933). *The first two years: A study of twenty-five babies.* Institute of Child Welfare Monograph Series, No. 7. Minneapolis, Minn.: University of Minnesota Press.

Shoda, Y., Mischel, W., & Peake, P. K. (1990). Predicting adolescent cognitive and self-regulatory competencies from preschool delay of gratification: Identifying diagnostic conditions. *Developmental Psychology, 26,* 978–986.

Shore, C., O'Connell, B., & Bates, E. (1984). First sentences in language and symbolic play. *Developmental Psychology, 20,* 872–880.

Shuter-Dyson, R. (1982). Musical ability. In D. Deutsch (Ed.), *The psychology of music.* New York: Academic Press.

Siegal, M., & Barclay, M. S. (1985). Children's evaluations of fathers' socialization behavior. *Developmental Psychology, 21*, 1090–1096.

Siegel, A. W., Kirasic, K. C., & Kail, R. V. (1978). Stalking the elusive cognitive map: The development of children's representations of geographic space. In I. Altman and J. Wohlwill (Eds.), *Human behavior and environment: Advances in theory and research*, Vol. 3. New York: Plenum.

Siegel, A. W., & White, S. H. (1975). The development of spatial representations of large-scale environments. In H. W. Reese (Ed.), *Advances in child development and behavior*, Vol. 10. New York: Academic Press.

Siegel, O. (1982). Personality development in adolescence. In B. B. Wolman (Ed.), *Handbook of developmental psychology*. Englewood Cliffs, N.J.: Prentice Hall.

Siegler, R. S. (1976). Three aspects of cognitive development. *Cognitive Psychology, 8*, 481–520.

Siegler, R. S. (1981). Developmental sequences within and between concepts. *Monographs of the Society for Research in Child Development, 46*, Serial No. 189.

Siegler, R. S. (1987). The perils of averaging data over strategies: An example from children's addition. *Journal of Experimental Psychology: General, 116*, 250–264.

Siegler, R. S. (1988). Strategy choice procedures and the development of multiplication skill. *Journal of Experimental Psychology: General, 117*, 258–275.

Siegler, R. S., Liebert, D. E., & Liebert, R. M. (1973). Inhelder and Piaget's pendulum problem: Teaching preadolescents to act as scientists. *Developmental Psychology, 9*, 97–101.

Siegler, R. S., & Shrager, J. (1984). Strategy choices in addition: How do children know what to do? In C. Sophian (Ed.), *Origins of cognitive skills*. Hillsdale, N.J.: Lawrence Erlbaum.

Signorella, M.L., Bigler, R. S., & Liben, L. S. (in press). Developmental differences in children's gender schemata about others: A meta-analytic review. *Developmental Review*.

Signorella, M. L., & Jamison, W. (1986). Masculinity, femininity, androgyny, and cognitive performance: A meta-analysis. *Psychological Bulletin, 100*, 207–228.

Signorielli, N. (1990). Children, television, and gender roles. *Journal of Adolescent Health Care, 11*, 50–58.

Silverman, I. W., & Ragusa, D. M. (1990). Child and maternal correlates of impulse control in 24-month-old children. *Genetic, Social, and General Psychology Monographs, 116*, 435–473.

Silverman, I. W., & Rose, A. P. (1982). Compensation and conservation. *Psychological Bulletin, 91*, 80–101.

Simmons, R., & Blyth, D. (1987). *Moving into adolescence*. New York: Aldine de Gruyter.

Simons, R. L., Whitbeck, L. B., Conger, R. D, & Chyi-In, W. (1991). Intergenerational transmission of harsh parenting. *Developmental Psychology, 27*, 159–171.

Simpson, G. G., Pittendrigh, C. S., & Tiffany, L. H. (1957). *An introduction to biology*. New York: Harcourt Brace Jovanovich.

Singer, D. L., & Rummo, J. (1973). Ideational creativity and behavioral style in kindergarten-age children. *Developmental Psychology, 8*, 154–161.

Singer, J. B., & Flavell, J. H. (1981). Development of knowledge about communication: Evaluations of explicitly ambiguous messages. *Child Development, 52*, 1211–1215.

Skinner, B. F. (1948). *Walden two*. London: Macmillan.

Slaby, R. G., & Guerra, N. G. (1988). Cognitive mediators of aggression in adolescent offenders: 1. Assessment. *Developmental Psychology, 24*, 580–588.

Slater, A., Morison, V., & Rose, D. (1984). Habituation in the newborn. *Infant Behavior and Development, 7*, 183–200.

Slobin, D. I. (1970). Universals of grammatical development in children. In G. B. Flores d'Arcais and W. J. M. Levelt (Eds.), *Advances in psycholinguistics*. Amsterdam: North Holland.

Slobin, D. I. (1971). *Psycholinguistics*. Glenview, Ill.: Scott, Foresman.

Smetana, J. G. (1986). Preschool children's conceptions of sex-role transgressions. *Child Development, 57*, 862–871.

Smetana, J. G., & Braeges, J. L. (1990). The development of toddlers' moral and conventional judgments. *Merrill-Palmer Quarterly, 36*, 329–346.

Smoll, F. L., & Schutz, R. W. (1990). Quantifying gender differences in physical performance: A developmental perspective. *Developmental Psychology, 26*, 360–369.

Snedeker, B. (1982). *Hard knocks: Preparing youth*

for work. Baltimore, Md.: Johns Hopkins University Press.

Snow, M. E., Jacklin, C. N., & Maccoby, E. E. (1983). Sex-of-child differences in father-child interaction at one year of age. *Child Development, 54,* 227–232.

Sonnenschein, S. (1984). How feedback from a listener affects children's referential communication skills. *Developmental Psychology, 20,* 287–292.

Sonnenschein, S. (1988). The development of referential communication: Speaking to different listeners. *Child Development, 59,* 694–702.

Sorensen, R. (1973). *Adolescent sexuality in contemporary society.* New York: World Book.

Sparrow, S., Balla, D., & Cicchetti, D. (1984). *Vineland Adaptive Behavior Scales.* Circle Pines, Minn.: American Guidance Services.

Spearman, C. (1904). "General intelligence" objectively determined and measured. *American Journal of Psychology, 15,* 201–293.

Spears, W. C., & Hohle, R. H. (1967). Sensory and perceptual processes in infants. In Y. Brackbill (Ed.), *Infancy and early childhood. A handbook and guide to human development.* New York: The Free Press.

Spelke, E. (1979). Perceiving bimodally specified events in infancy. *Developmental Psychology, 15,* 626–636.

Spelke, E. S. (1987). The development of intermodal perception. In P. Salapatek and L. Cohen (Eds.). *Handbook of infant perception,* Vol. 2. Orlando, Fla.: Academic Press.

Spetner, N. B., & Olsho, L. W. (1990). Auditory frequency resolution in human infancy. *Child Development, 61,* 632–652.

Springer, K., & Keil, F. C. (1989). On the development of biologically specific beliefs: The case of inheritance. *Child Development, 60,* 637–648.

Springer, K., & Keil, F. C. (1991). Early differentiation of causal mechanisms appropriate to biological and nonbiological kinds. *Child Development, 62,* 767–781.

Sroufe, L. A., & Fleeson, J. (1986). Attachment and the construction of relationships. In W. W. Hartup and Z. Rubin (Eds.), *Relationships and development.* Hillsdale, N.J.: Lawrence Erlbaum.

Sroufe, L. A., Fox, N. E., & Pancake, V. R. (1983). Attachment and dependency in developmental perspective. *Child Development, 54,* 1615–1627.

Standley, K., Soule, D., & Copans, S. A. (1979). Dimensions of prenatal anxiety and their influence on pregnancy outcome. *American Journal of Obstetrics and Gynecology, 135,* 22–26.

Stangel, J. J. (1988). *The new fertility and conception: The essential guide for childless couples* (2nd ed.). New York: New American Library.

Stark, R. E. (1980). Stages of speech development in the first year of life. In G. Yeni-Komshian, J. F. Kavanagh, and C. A. Ferguson (Eds.), *Child phonology,* Vol. 1. New York: Academic Press.

Starko, A. J. (1988). Effects of the Revolving Door Identification Model on creative productivity and self-efficacy. *Gifted Child Quarterly, 32,* 291–297.

Stattin, H., & Magnusson, D. (1989). The role of early aggressive behavior in the frequency, seriousness, and types of later crime. *Journal of Consulting and Clinical Psychology, 57,* 710–718.

Stechler, G., & Halton, A. (1982). Prenatal influences on human development. In B. B. Wolman (Ed.), *Handbook of developmental psychology.* Englewood Cliffs, N.J.: Prentice Hall.

Steffenburg, S., Gillberg, C., Hellgren, L., Andersson, L., Gillberg, I. C., Jakobsson, G., & Bohman, M. (1989). A twin study of autism in Denmark, Finland, Iceland, Norway, and Sweden. *Journal of Child Psychology and Psychiatry, 30,* 405–416.

Stangor, C. & McMillan, D. (1992). Memory for expectancy-congruent and expectancy-incongruent information: A review of the social and social developmental literatures. *Psychological Bulletin, 111,* 42–61.

Steinberg, L. (1986). Latchkey children and susceptibility to peer pressure: An ecological analysis. *Developmental Psychology, 22,* 433–439.

Steinberg, L. (1990). Autonomy, conflict, and harmony in the family relationship. In S. S. Feldman and G. R. Elliott (Eds.), *At the threshold: The developing adolescent.* Cambridge, Mass.: Harvard University Press.

Steinberg, L., & Dornbusch, S. M. (1991). Negative correlates of part-time employment during adolescence: Replication and elaboration. *Developmental Psychology, 27,* 304–313.

Steiner, J. E. (1979). Human facial expressions in response to taste and smell stimulation. In H. Reese and L. Lipsitt (Eds.), *Advances in child development and behavior,* Vol. 13. New York: Academic Press.

Stephan, C. W., & Langlois, J. H. (1984). Baby beautiful: Adult attributions of infant competence as a function of infant attractiveness. *Child Development, 55,* 576–585.

Stern, C. (1973). *Principles of human genetics.* San Francisco: W. H. Freeman.

Stern, M., & Karraker, K. H. (1989). Sex stereotyping of infants: A review of gender labeling studies. *Sex Roles, 20,* 501–522.

Stern, S. L., Dixon, K. N., Jones, D., Lake, M., Nemzer, E., & Sansone, R. (1989). Family environment in anorexia nervosa and bulimia. *International Journal of Eating Disorders, 8,* 25–31.

Sternberg, R. J. (1977). *Intelligence, information processing, and analogical reasoning.* Hillsdale, N.J.: Lawrence Erlbaum.

Sternberg, R. J. (1985a). *Beyond IQ: A triarchic theory of human intelligence.* Cambridge: Cambridge University Press.

Sternberg, R. J. (1985b). Implicit theories of intelligence, creativity, and wisdom. *Journal of Personality and Social Psychology, 49,* 607–627.

Sternberg, R. J. & Davidson, J. E. (1986). Conceptions of giftedness: A map of the terrain. In R. J. Sternberg and J. E. Davidson (Eds.), *Conceptions of giftedness.* Cambridge: Cambridge University Press.

Steuer, F. B., Applefield, J. M., & Smith, R. (1971). Televised aggression and the interpersonal aggression of preschool children. *Journal of Experimental Child Psychology, 11,* 442–447.

Stevenson, H. W., & Lee, S. (1990). Contexts of achievement. *Monographs of the Society for Research in Child Development, 55,* Serial No. 221.

Stewart, M. A., Cumming, C., Singer, S., & DeBlois, C. S. (1981). The overlap between hyperactive and unsocialized aggressive children. *Journal of Child Psychology and Psychiatry, 22,* 35–45.

Stewart, R. S. (1976). Psychoanalysis and sex differences: Freud and beyond Freud. In P. C. Lee and R. S. Stewart (Eds.), *Sex differences: Cultural and developmental dimensions.* New York: Urz.

Stifter, C. A., & Fox, N. A. (1990). Infant reactivity: Physiological correlates of newborn and 5-month temperament. *Developmental Psychology, 26,* 582–588.

Stocker, C., Dunn, J., & Plomin R. (1989). Sibling relationships: Links with child temperament, maternal behavior, and family structure. *Child Development, 60,* 715–727.

Strauss, M. S., & Curtis, L. E. (1984). Development of numerical concepts in infancy. In C. Sophian (Ed.), *Origins of cognitive skills.* Hillsdale, N.J.: Lawrence Erlbaum.

Strayer, J., & Schroeder, M. (1989). Children's helping strategies: Influences of emotion, empathy, and age. In N. Eisenberg (Ed.), *New directions for child development: Empathy and related emotional responses,* Vol. 44. San Francisco: Jossey-Bass.

Strayer, F. F., & Strayer, J. (1976). An ethological study of dominance formation and maintenance in a group of human adolescents. *Child Development, 47,* 980–997.

Streissguth, A. P., Barr, H. M., Sampson, P. D., Darby, B. L., & Martin, D. C. (1989). IQ at age 4 in relation to maternal alcohol use and smoking during pregnancy. *Developmental Psychology, 25,* 3–11.

Streissguth, A. P., Treder, R. P., Barr, H. M., Shepard, T. H., Bleyer, W. A., Sampson, P. D., & Martin, D. C. (1987). Aspirin and acetaminophen use by pregnant women and subsequent child IQ and attention decrements. *Teratology, 35,* 211–219.

Stuart, M. J., Steven, M. B., Gross, J., Elrad, H., & Graeber, J. E. (1982). Effects of acetylsalicylic-acid ingestion on maternal and neonatal hemostasis. *New England Journal of Medicine, 307,* 909–912.

Sullivan, H. S. (1953). *The interpersonal theory of psychiatry.* New York: W. W. Norton.

Sundet, J. M., Tambs, K., Magnus, P., & Berg, K. (1988). On the question of secular trends in the heritability of intelligence test scores: A study of Norwegian twins. *Intelligence, 12,* 47–59.

Sunnegardh, J., Bratteby, L. E., Hagman, U., Samuelson, G., & Sjolin, S. (1986). Physical activity in relation to energy intake and body fat in 8- and 13-year-old children in Sweden. *Acta Paediatrica Scandinavia, 75,* 955–963.

Super, C. M. (1981). Cross-cultural research on infancy. In H. C. Triandis and A. Heron (Eds.), *Handbook of cross-cultural psychology,* Vol. 4, *Developmental Psychology.* Boston: Allyn and Bacon.

Super, C. M., Herrera, M. G., & Mora, J. O. (1990). Long-term effects of food supplementation and psychosocial intervention on the physical growth of Colombian infants at risk of malnutrition. *Child Development, 61,* 29–49.

Super, D. E. (1976). *Career education and the meanings of work.* Washington, D.C.: U.S. Office of Education.

Susman, E. J., Inoff-Germain, G., Nottelmann, E. G., Loriaux, D. L., Cutler, G. B., & Chrousos, A. W. (1987). Hormones, emotional dispositions, and aggressive attributes in young adolescents. *Child Development, 58,* 114–134.

Susser, M. (1991). Maternal weight gain, infant birth weight, and diet: Causal sequences. *American Journal of Clinical Nutrition, 53,* 1384–1396.

Switzky, H., Rotatori, A. F., Miller, T., & Freagon, S. (1979). The developmental model and its implications for assessment and instruction for the severely/profoundly handicapped. *Mental Retardation, 17,* 167–170.

Tager-Flusberg, H. (1981). On the nature of linguistic functioning in early infantile autism. *Journal of Autism and Developmental Disorders, 11,* 45–65.

Tager-Flusberg, H. (1992). Autistic children's talk about psychological states: Deficits in the early acquisition of a theory of mind. *Child Development, 63,* 161–172.

Tanner, J. M. (1970). Physical growth. In P. H. Mussen (Ed.), *Carmichael's manual of child psychology* (3rd ed.). New York: Wiley.

Tanner, J. M. (1978). *Foetus into man.* Cambridge, Mass.: Harvard University Press.

Taylor, M., & Gelman, S. A. (1988). Adjectives and nouns: Children's strategies for learning new words. *Child Development, 59,* 411–419.

Taylor, M., & Gelman, S. A. (1989). Incorporating new words into the lexicon: Preliminary evidence for language hierarchies in two-year-old children. *Child Development, 60,* 625–636.

Telford, C. W., & Sawrey, J. M. (1972). *The exceptional individual.* Englewood Cliffs, N.J.: Prentice Hall.

Teller, D. Y., & Bornstein, M. H. (1987). Infant color vision and color perception. In P. Salapatek and L. Cohen (Eds.), *Handbook of infant perception,* Vol. 1. Orlando, Fla.: Academic Press.

Tesser, A., Campbell, J., & Smith, M. (1984). Friendship choice and performance: Self-evaluation maintenance in children. *Journal of Personality and Social Psychology, 46,* 561–574.

Teti, D. M., & Ablard, K. E. (1989). Security of attachment and infant-sibling relationships: A laboratory study. *Child Development, 61,* 1519–1528.

Thelen, E., & Fisher, D. M. (1982). Newborn stepping: An explanation for a "disappearing" reflex. *Developmental Psychology, 18,* 760–775.

Thelen, E., & Fisher, D. M. (1983). From spontaneous to instrumental behavior: Kinematic analysis of movement changes during very early learning. *Child Development, 54,* 129–140.

Thelen, E., & Ulrich, B. D. (1991). Hidden skills. *Monographs of the Society for Research in Child Development, 56,* Serial No. 223.

Thelen, E., Ulrich, B. D., & Jensen, J. L. (1989). The developmental origins of locomotion. In M. H. Wollacott and A. Shumway-Cook (Eds.), *Development of posture and gait across the life span.* Columbia, S.C.: University of South Carolina Press.

Thomas, A., & Chess, S. (1976). Evolution of behavior disorders into adolescence. *American Journal of Psychiatry, 133,* 539–542.

Thomas, A., Chess, S., & Birch, H. G. (1970). The origin of personality. *Scientific American, 223,* 102–109.

Thomas, H., & Kail, R. (1991). Sex differences in the speed of mental rotation and the X-linked genetic hypothesis. *Intelligence, 15,* 17–32.

Thomas, J. R., & French, K. E. (1985). Gender differences across age in motor performance: A meta-analysis. *Psychological Bulletin, 98,* 260–282.

Thompson, G. G. (1952). *Child psychology.* Boston: Houghton Mifflin.

Thompson, L. A., Detterman, D. K., & Plomin, R. (1991). Associations between cognitive abilities and scholastic achievement: Genetic overlap but environmental differences. *Psychological Science, 2,* 158–165.

Thompson, W. R., & Grusec, J. E. (1970). Studies of early experience. In P. H. Mussen (Ed.), *Carmichael's manual of child psychology.* New York: Wiley.

Thorndike, E. L. (1898). Animal intelligence: An experimental study of the associative process in animals. *Psychological Review Monograph Supplement, 2,* 4, Whole No. 8.

Thorndike, E. L. (1905). *The elements of psychology.* New York: Seiler.

Thornton, A., Alwin, D. F., & Camburn, D. (1983). Causes and consequences of sex-role attitudes and attitude change. *American Sociological Review, 48,* 211–227.

Thurstone, L. L., & Thurstone, T. G. (1941). Factorial studies of intelligence. *Psychometric Monograph,* No. 2.

Tieger, T. (1980). On the biological basis of sex differences in aggression. *Child Development, 51,* 943–963.

Treboux, D., & Busch-Rossnagel, N. A. (1990). Social network influence on adolescent sexual attitudes and behaviors. *Journal of Adolescent Research, 5,* 175–189.

Trehub, S. E. (1976). The discrimination of foreign speech contrasts by infants and adults. *Child Development, 47,* 466–472.

Trehub, S. E., Schneider, B. A., Thorpe, L. A., & Judge, P. (1991). Observational measures of auditory sensitivity in early infancy. *Developmental Psychology, 27,* 40–49.

Tricket, P. K., Aber, J. L., Carlson, V., & Cicchetti, D. (1991). Relationship of socioeconomic status to the etiology and developmental sequelae of physical child abuse. *Developmental Psychology, 27,* 148–158.

Tricket, P. K., & Kuczynski, L. (1986). Children's misbehaviors and parental discipline strategies in abusive and nonabusive families. *Developmental Psychology, 22,* 115–123.

Troll, L. E. (1985). *Early and middle adulthood* (2nd ed.). Monterey, Calif.: Brooks/Cole.

Tsai, L., Stewart, M. A., Faust, M., & Shook, S. (1982). Social class distribution of fathers of children enrolled in the Iowa Autism Program. *Journal of Autism and Developmental Disorders, 12,* 211–221.

Turkheimer, E., & Gottesman, I. I. (1991). Individual diffences and the canalization of human behavior. *Developmental Psychology, 27,* 18–22.

Underwood, B., & Moore, B. (1982). Perspective taking and altruism. *Psychological Bulletin, 91,* 143–173.

Uniform Crime Reports for the United States. (1990). Washington, D.C.: U.S. Government Printing Office.

Updegraff, R. (1930). The visual perception of distance in young children and adults: A comparative study. *University of Iowa Studies of Child Welfare, 4,* No. 40.

Uttal, D. H., & Wellman, H. M. (1989). Young children's representation of spatial information acquired from maps. *Developmental Psychology, 25,* 128–138.

Vandell, D. L., & Corasanti, M. A. (1990). Child care and the family: Complex contributors to child development. In K. McCartney (Ed.), *Child care and maternal employment: A social ecology approach.* San Francisco: Jossey-Bass.

Vandell, D. L., Owen, M. T., Wilson, K. S., & Henderson, V. K. (1988). Social development in infant twins: Peer and mother-child relationships. *Child Development, 59,* 168–177.

Vandell, D. L., & Ramanan, J. (1991). Children of the National Longitudinal Survey of Youth: Choices in after-school care and child development. *Developmental Psychology, 27,* 637–643.

Vandell, D. L., Wilson, K. S., & Buchanan, N. R. (1980). Peer interaction in the first year of life: An examination of its structure, content, and sensitivity to toys. *Child Development, 51,* 481–488.

van der Meulen, J. H. P., Gooskens, R. H. J. M., Willemse, J., Denier van der Gon, J. J., & Gielen, C. C. A. M. (1990). Arm tracking performance with and without visual feedback in children and adults: Developmental changes. *Journal of Motor Behavior, 22,* 386–405.

van Giffen, K., & Haith, M. M. (1987). Infant visual response to Gestalt geometric forms. *Infant Behavior and Development, 7,* 335–346.

van IJzendoorn, M. H., & Kroonenberg, P. M. (1988). Cross-cultural patterns of attachment: A meta-analysis of the strange situation. *Child Development, 59,* 147–156.

van Loosbroek, E., & Smitsman, A. W. (1990). Visual perception of numerosity in infancy. *Developmental Psychology, 26,* 916–922.

Vasta, R. (1982). Physical child abuse: A dual-component analysis. *Developmental Review, 2,* 125–149.

Vaughn, B. E., Kopp, C. B., & Krakow, J. B. (1984). The emergence and consolidation of self-control from eighteen to thirty months of age: Normative trends and individual differences. *Child Development, 55,* 990–1004.

Vaughn, B. E., Lefever, G. B., Seifer, R., & Barglow, P. (1989). Attachment behavior, attachment security, and temperament during infancy. *Child Development, 60,* 728–737.

Vaughn, B. E., & Waters, E. (1990). Attachment behavior at home and in the laboratory: Q-sort observations and strange situation classifications of one-year-olds. *Child Development, 61,* 1965–1973.

Vernbrugge, L. M. (1979). Marital status and health. *Journal of Marriage and the Family, 41,* 267–285.

Vernon, P. E. (1965). Ability factors and environmental influences. *American Psychologist, 20,* 723–733.

Vernon, P. E. (1979). *Intelligence: Heredity and environment.* San Francisco: W. H. Freeman.

Vital and Health Statistics. (1972). *Infant Mortality Rates: Socioeconomic Factors*. Series 22, No. 14. Rockville, Md.: U.S. Department of Health, Education, and Welfare.

Vuchinich, S., Hetherington, E. M., Vuchinich, R. A., & Clingempeel, W. G. (1991). Parent-child interaction and gender differences in early adolescents' adaptation to stepfamilies. *Developmental Psychology, 27*, 627–636.

Waber, D. P. (1977). Sex differences in mental abilities, hemispheric lateralization, and rate of physical growth at adolescence. *Developmental Psychology, 13*, 29–38.

Wachs, T. D. (1983). The use and abuse of environment in behavior-genetic research. *Child Development, 54*, 396–407.

Wachs, T. D. (1987). Specificity of environmental action as manifest in environmental correlates of infant's mastery motivation. *Developmental Psychology, 23*, 782–790.

Wachs, T. D., & Gruen, G. E. (1982). *Early experience and human development*. New York: Plenum.

Wadden, T. A., Foster, G. D., Brownell, K. D., & Finley, E. (1984). Self-concept in obese and normal-weight children. *Journal of Consulting and Clinical Psychology, 52*, 1104–1105.

Wagner, S., Winner, E., Cicchetti, D., & Gardner, H. (1981). "Metaphorical" mapping in human infants. *Child Development, 52*, 728–731.

Wagner, D. A., & Stevenson, H. W. (Eds.). (1982). *Cultural perspectives on child development*. San Francisco: W. H. Freeman.

Wahler, R. G. (1969). Oppositional children: A quest for parental reinforcement control. *Journal of Applied Behavioral Analysis, 2*, 159–170.

Wald, E. (1981). *The remarried family: Challenge and promise*. New York: Family Service Association.

Walk, R. D., & Gibson, E. J. (1961). A comparative and analytical study of visual depth perception. *Psychological Monographs, 75*, 15, Whole No. 519.

Walker, C. E. (1978). Toilet training, enuresis, and encopresis. In P. R. Magrab (Ed.), *Psychological management of pediatric problems*. Baltimore, Md.: University Park Press.

Walker, L. J. (1989). A longitudinal study of moral reasoning. *Child Development, 60*, 157–166.

Walker, L. J., & Taylor, J. H. (1991). Stage transitions in moral reasoning: A longitudinal study of developmental processes. *Developmental Psychology, 27*, 330–337.

Warden, D. A. (1976). The influence of context on children's use of identifying expressions and references. *British Journal of Psychology, 67*, 101–112.

Watson, J. B. (1925). *Behaviorism*. New York: W. W. Norton.

Watson, J. B., & Raynor, R. (1920). Conditioned emotional responses. *Journal of Experimental Psychology, 3*, 1–14.

Weatherley, D. (1964). Self-perceived rate of physical maturation and personality in late adolescence. *Child Development, 35*, 1197–1210.

Weisner, T. S., & Wilson-Mitchell, J. E. (1990). Nonconventional family lifestyles and sex typing in six-year-olds. *Child Development, 61*, 1915–1933.

Weiss, B. (1982). Food additives and environmental chemicals as sources of childhood deficit disorder. *Journal of the American Academy of Child Psychiatry, 21*, 144–152.

Welch, R., Gerrard, M., & Huston, A. (1986). Gender-related personality attributes and reaction to success/failure: An examination of mediating variables. *Psychology of Women Quarterly, 10*, 221–233.

Wellman, H. M., Cross, D., & Bartsch, K. (1986). Infant search and object permanance: A meta-analysis of the A-not-B error. *Monographs of the Society for Research in Child Development, 51*, Serial No. 214.

Welsh, M. C., Pennington, B. F., & Groisser, D. B. (1991). A normative-developmental study of executive function: A window on prefrontal function in children. *Developmental Neuropsychology, 7*, 131–149.

Werker, J. F., & Lalonde, C. E. (1988). Cross-language speech perception: Initial capabilities and developmental change. *Developmental Psychology, 24*, 672–683.

Werner, E. E. (1980). Environmental interaction. In H. E. Rie and E. D. Rie (Eds.), *Handbook of minimal brain dysfunctions*. New York: Wiley.

Werner, H. (1948). *Comparative psychology of mental development*. Chicago: Follet.

West, J. R. (1986). *Alcohol and brain development*. London: Oxford University Press.

Westling, D. L., Floyd, J., & Carr, D. (1990). Effect of single setting versus multiple setting training on learning to shop in a department store. *American Journal on Mental Retardation, 94*, 612–624.

Whalen, C. K. (1989). Attention deficit and hyperactivity disorders. In T. H. Ollendick and M. Hersen (Eds.), *Handbook of child psychopathology.* New York: Plenum.

Whalen, C. K., & Henker, B. (1991). Therapies for hyperactive children: Comparisons, combinations, and compromises. *Journal of Consulting and Clinical Psychology, 59,* 126–137.

White, S. H. (1992). G. Stanley Hall: From philosophy to developmental psychology. *Developmental Psychology, 28,* 25–34.

Whitehurst, G. J. (1969). Discrimination learning as a function of reinforcement condition, task complexity, and chronological age. *Journal of Experimental Child Psychology, 7,* 314–325.

Whitehurst, G. J., Falco, F. L., Longigan, C. J., Fischel, J. E., DeBaryshe, B. D., Valdez-Menchaca, M. C., & Caulfield, M. (1988). Accelerating language development through picture book reading. *Developmental Psychology, 24,* 552–559.

Whitehurst, G. J., & Vasta, R. (1977). *Child behavior.* Boston: Houghton Mifflin.

Whiting, J. W. M., & Child, I. L. (1953). *Child training and personality: A cross-cultural study.* New Haven, Conn.: Yale University Press.

Whitting, J. E., & Richards, P. N. (1987). The stability of children's laterality prevalences and their relationship to measures of performance. *British Journal of Educational Psychology, 57,* 45–55.

Wicks-Nelson, R., & Israel, A. C. (1991). *Behavior disorders of childhood* (2nd ed.). Englewood Cliffs, N.J.: Prentice Hall.

Widom, C. S. (1989). Does violence beget violence? A critical examination of the literature. *Psychological Bulletin, 106,* 3–28.

Wilkinson, L. C., Wilkinson, A. C., Spinelli, F., & Chiang, C. P. (1984). Metalinguistic knowledge of pragmatic rules in school-age children. *Child Development, 55,* 2130–2140.

William T. Grant Foundation Commission on Work, Family and Citizenship. (1988). *The forgotten half: Non–college-bound youth in America.* New York: William T. Grant Foundation.

Wilson, C. C., Piazza, C. C., & Nagle, R. (1990). Investigation of the effect of consistent and inconsistent behavioral example upon children's donation behavior. *Journal of Genetic Psychology, 151,* 361–376.

Wilson, N. (1989). Child development in the context of the black extended family. *American Psychologist, 44,* 380–385.

Wilson, R. S. (1978). Synchronies in mental development: An epigenetic perspective. *Science, 202,* 939–948.

Wilson, R. S. (1983). The Louisville Twin Study: Developmental synchronies in behavior. *Child Development, 54,* 298–316.

Winer, G. A., Craig, R. K., & Weinbaum, E. (1992). Adults' failure on misleading weight-conservation tests: A developmental analysis. *Developmental Psychology, 28,* 109–120.

Wishart, J. G., & Bower, T. G. R. (1982). The development of spatial understanding in infancy. *Journal of Experimental Child Psychology, 33,* 363–385.

Witelson, S. F. (1987). Neurobiological aspects of language in children. *Child Development, 58,* 653–688.

Witkin, H. A., Mednick, S. A., Schulsinger, F., Bakkestrøm, E., Christiansen, K. O., Goodenough, D. R., Hirshhorn, K., Lundsteen, C., Owen, D. R., Philip, J., Rubin, D. B., & Stocking, M. (1976). Criminality in XYY and XXY men. *Science, 193,* 547–555.

Wolfe, D. A. (1985). Child-abusive parents: An empirical review and analysis. *Psychological Bulletin, 97,* 462–482.

Wolfe, D. A., Fairbank, J., Kelly, J. A., & Bradlyn, A. S. (1983). Child abusive parents' physiological responses to stressful and non-stressful behavior in children. *Behavioral Assessment, 5,* 363–371.

Wolff, P. H. (1969). The natural history of crying and other vocalizations in early infancy. In B. M. Foss (Ed.), *The determinants of human behavior.* London: Methuen.

Wood, W., Wong, F. Y., & Chachere, J. G. (1991). Effects of media violence on viewers' aggression in unconstrained social interaction. *Psychological Bulletin, 109,* 371–383.

Woody-Ramsey, J., & Miller, P. H. (1988). The facilitation of selective attention in preschoolers. *Child Development, 59,* 1497–1503.

Woollacott, M. H., Shumway-Cook, A., & Williams, H. (1989). The development of balance and locomotion in children. In M. H. Woollacott, & A. Shumway-Cook (Eds.), *Development of posture and gait across the life span.* Columbia, S.C.: University of South Carolina Press.

Wootten, J., Merkin, S., Hood, L., & Bloom, L. (1979). Wh-questions: Linguistic evidence to explain the sequence of acquisition. Presented at the biennial meeting of the Society for Research in Child Development, Denver, Colo.

Worobey, J., & Blajda, V. M. (1989). Temperament ratings at 2 weeks, 2 months, and 1 year: Differential stability of activity and emotionality. *Developmental Psychology, 25,* 257–263.

Worobey, J., & Lewis, M. (1989). Individual differences in the reactivity of young infants. *Developmental Psychology, 25,* 663–667.

Wylie, R. C. (1979). *The self-concept,* Vol. 2. Lincoln, Neb.: University of Nebraska Press.

Yazigi, R. A., Odem, R. R., & Polakoski, K. L. (1991). Demonstration of specific binding of cocaine to human spermatozoa. *Journal of the American Medical Association, 266,* 1956–1959.

Yogev, S. (1983). Judging the professional woman: Changing research, changing values. *Psychology of Women Quarterly, 7,* 219–234.

Yonas, A., & Owsley, C. (1987). Development of visual space perception. In P. Salapatek and L. Cohen (Eds.), *Handbook of infant perception,* Vol. 2. Orlando, Fla.: Academic Press.

Zarbatany, L., Hartmann, D. P., Gelfand, D. M., & Vinciguerra, P. (1985). Gender differences in altruistic reputation: Are they artifactual? *Developmental Psychology, 21,* 97–101.

Zaslow, M. J., & Hayes, C. D. (1986). Sex differences in children's responses to psychosocial stress: Toward a cross-context analysis. In M. E. Lamb, A. L. Brown, & B. Rogoff (Eds.), *Advances in developmental psychology,* Vol. 4. Hillsdale N.J.: Lawrence Erlbaum.

Zelazo, P. R., Weiss, M. J., Papageorgiou, A. N., & Laplante, D. P. (1989). Recovery and dishabituation of sound localization among normal-, moderate-, and high-risk newborns: Discriminant validity. *Infant Behavior and Devolopment, 12,* 321–340.

Zelazo, P. R., Zelazo, N., & Kolb, S. (1972). "Walking" in the newborn. *Science, 176,* 314–315.

Zelnick, M., Kantner, J., & Ford, K. (1981). *Sex and pregnancy in adolescence.* Beverly Hills, Calif: Sage.

Zigler, E., & Balla, D. (1972). Developmental cause of responsiveness to social reinforcement in normal children and institutionalized retarded children. *Developmental Psychology, 6,* 66–73.

Zigler, E., & Valentine, J. (Eds.). (1979). *Project Head Start: A Legacy of the War on Poverty.* New York: The Free Press.

Photo Credits

Name Index

Subject Index